The Longwood Reader

Fourth Edition

Edward A. Dornan

Orange Coast College

Charles W. Dawe

Late of Orange Coast College

Allyn and Bacon

Boston   London   Toronto   Sydney   Tokyo   Singapore

Vice President, Humanities: Joseph Opiela
Editorial Assistant: Mary Beth Varney
Executive Marketing Manager: Lisa Kimball
Production Administrator: Rowena Dores
Editorial-Production Service: Lauren Green Shafer
Cover Administrator: Linda Knowles
Composition Buyer: Linda Cox
Manufacturing Buyer: Suzanne Lareau
Designer: Pat Torelli
Electronic Composition: Modern Graphics

Library of Congress Cataloging-in-Publication Data

The Longwood reader / [edited by] Edward A. Dornan, Charles W. Dawe. -
- 4th ed.
    p.   cm.
  ISBN 0-205-30801-5
    1. College readers.   2. English language—Rhetoric.   I. Dornan,
Edward A.   II. Dawe, Charles W.
PE1417.L66   1999
808'.0427—dc21
                                                           99-27491
                                                              CIP

Copyright acknowledgments begin on page 739, which constitutes an extension of the copyright page.

Printed in the United States of America

10 9 8 7 6 5 4 3 2 1   RRDV   02 01 00 99

Contents

"The school seal has been pressed over a photograph of my mother at the age of thirty-seven. . . . She stares straight ahead as if she could see me and past me to her grandchildren and grandchildren's grandchildren."

"This must be why the hyena has such a snake of a neck—so it can delve deep into a dying animal and eat the best parts before thieves chase it away."

"The handcuffs are a tool of the trade and an emblem of it, as are the gun and the nightstick."

"Bellevue. The name conjures up images of an indoor war zone: the wounded and bleeding lining the halls, screaming for help while harried doctors in blood-stained smocks rush from stretcher to stretcher fighting a losing battle against exhaustion and the crushing number of injured."

"I don't know if I am alive, but if not, how do I know I am dead? My body is leaden, heavier than gravity. Gravity is done with me. No more sinking and rising or bobbing in currents."

"Negro girls in small Southern towns, whether poverty-stricken or just munching along on a few of life's necessities, were given as extensive and irrelevant preparation for adulthood as rich white girls shown in magazines. Admittedly the training was not the same."

"One after the other, a pair of wrestlers enter the ring. The two men join, twist, jerk, tug, bend, yank, and throw. Then they leave and are replaced by another pair. At last it is the main event. 'The Angel vs. The Masked Marvel.' "

"Sparring with men, I feel liberated from generations of fear, self-doubt, finger-waving and genteel restrictions: men aren't so tough. . . ."

"Kay Smith was the very model of a Severn, Md., housewife and working mother, so perfect that no one around her can believe she was once a hard-drinking, pill-popping criminal with a gun."

"Their silence is . . . telling. They lack a public identity. They remain profoundly alien. Persons apart."

"It is not a large wood—it contains scarcely any trees, and it is intersected, blast it, by a public footpath. Still it is the first property that I
have owned. . . ."

"The mythic horror movie, like the sick joke, has a dirty job to do. It
deliberately appeals to all that is worst in us. It is morbidity unchained,
our most base instincts let free, our nastiest fantasies realized . . . and
it all happens, fittingly enough, in the dark."

"In these stories, anything can happen, not because the world's a magical place rich with wonder—as in folktales of yore—but because our
world is so utterly terrifying."

"Imagine being told by your peers, the records you hear, the programs
you watch, the 'leaders' you see on TV, classmates, prospective employers—imagine being told by virtually everyone that in order to be your
true self you must be ignorant and poor, or at least seem so."

"While families nurture children by encouraging growth through the
assumption of responsibility and then by letting them rest in the bosom
of the family from the rigors of growing up, the mall as a structural
mother encourages passivity and consumption."

Contents

Thematic Table of Contents

Humans and Animals

Humans and Nature

Humor and Satire

Language

Politics and Government

Work

Politics and Government

Work

Pairs of Essays

Although the selections in *The Longwood Reader* are arranged by rhetorical patterns, we have included a Thematic Table of Contents grouping the selections under sixteen subject areas.

In addition, we offer the following suggestions for those who wish to assign pairs of essays. Such pairing may be useful for discussion of contrary and/or complementary views of similar subjects or situations, choices of style and presentation strategies, as well as different ways of using a particular rhetorical strategy.

Individual teachers will, of course, discover additional pairings equally valid and informative.

Preface to the Fourth Edition

This fourth edition of *The Longwood Reader* maintains the rhetorical arrangement of the first three editions but also includes several new features. We have added Chapter 12, "The Artful Essay," which presents five artfully written essays for close examination. In this new chapter, we have also included an unusual sequence of writing tasks for students who are ready to pursue essay writing from a purely personal perspective. Initially, we ask writers to complete several weeks of directed notebook entries. Then, we ask them to draw from their entries to write an essay that reflects on one aspect of their experience. To help students organize their own essays, we have included a student essay that embodies the characteristics of reflective essay writing. Our goals for Chapter 12 are quite simple: We hope to approximate the creative process many writers describe when working from notebook entries. We also hope that completing the writing sequence will awaken the young writer's curiosity about the possibilities of self-exploration through writing.

We have made several other significant changes in this edition. In Chapter 1, "The Reading Process," we provide a student example and guidelines for writing in-class responses to reading assignments. We emphasize the importance of understanding the assignment, developing a three-minute outline, and following common writing practices related to writing about reading.

In Chapter 2, "The Writing Process," we've integrated more information on editing and revising in a section titled "Ten Tips for Revising Sentences." Now writers will have more detailed examples showing how to polish their final drafts.

Throughout *The Longwood Reader,* we have revised our commentary on the student essays that serve in each chapter as illustrations of rhetorical methods of development. Instead of glossing these essays in detail, we now follow each selection with a series of questions aimed at revealing the writer's strategy. We have added this section, called "Reviewing with a Writer's Eye," because our experience tells us that such questions are more engaging than merely reading a comprehensive analysis. Moreover, this new format encourages group discussion of student essays much in the way that questions encourage discussion of professionally written essays.

Over one-third of the essays are new to this edition of *The Longwood Reader.* While selecting these new pieces, we were guided by the same principle that guided our selections for past editions: the assumption that good reading influences good writing.

By "good reading" we mean the activity that engages a reader's imagination when he or she picks up a text. We mean the ability to question an author's ideas, to subject an author's argument to skeptical scrutiny, to use a pencil to note disagreements and counterpoints in a text's margins. By good reading we also mean the ability to read with a "critical eye," that is, to read with the ability to see an author's strategies: the way paragraphs are shaped, the way sentences create rhythm and impact, and the way images create feeling. Every writing course must then also be a course in reading with a second sight that sees beneath a text's skin to examine its bones and vital organs. Unfortunately, reading like a writer, reading with a critical eye, does not come naturally; students must acquire the ability.

How?

They must gather information about the writing craft, and they must study the craft at work. As we perceive the process, student writers must go into "training" much like student actors, dancers, musicians, or painters must train. A vital part of this training is studying the works of those who have mastered the art of writing, writers like Maya Angelou, E. B. White, George Orwell, Maxine Hong Kingston, Gretel Ehrlich, and others represented in *The Longwood Reader.*

You will notice that Chapter 1 of *The Longwood Reader* prepares students to read with a critical eye. We explain the reader–writer contract: A reader must assume that a writer has created an understandable work; a writer must assume that a reader wants to understand the work. Together the reader and writer create meaning, relying on writing conventions to aid their effort. We explain the importance of reading to understand a writer's purpose, strategy, and style, a framework that establishes the pattern for the discussion questions that follow each essay. We also present five tips for the first reading of an essay. We illustrate the practice of reading with a pencil in hand with Williard Gaylin's "What You See Is the Real You" accompanied by student notes. We close the Introduction with five tips for rereading an essay.

Chapter 2, "The Writing Process," features a student essay, one we use throughout the chapter to illustrate key concepts. In this chapter we define the essay, place essay writing in the college classroom context, and then discuss the composing process. The discussion begins with ways to find subjects and follows with an explanation of prewriting techniques that help writers explore their subjects.

We then offer methods for sorting and grouping information in rough form by using clusters or informal outlines. Next we explain the thesis statement—how to find one and shape it to serve as an essay's guiding principle. We go on to explain and illustrate formal planning with a clear sense of a reader in mind (a step many students resist). We then discuss essay structure in detail—a discussion that concentrates on strategies for writing introductions, discussions, and conclusions. We also present guidelines for maintaining unity, coherence, developing content.

"Ten Tips for Revising Sentences" follows. These are practical tips, ones we believe will not overwhelm students writers with technical detail but still provide them with enough direction to polish their essays.

We conclude "The Writing Process" with a detailed discussion of peer review sessions. Here we cover peer review responsibilities, which includes explanation and illustrations of effective ways of giving and receiving advice. We also present guidelines for reading and discussing a fellow student's essay.

We arranged Chapters 3 through 11 according to traditional writing methods, beginning with description and ending with argumentation. We believe there is a slight risk in teaching rhetorical modes. When misunderstood, they may generate "cookie-cutter" prose, but we believe the benefit of mastering rhetorical modes outweighs the risk. When students understand these common development patterns, they can examine them at work in professional essays, thus sharpening their critical reading skills. By way of caution, however, throughout *The Longwood Reader* we discuss essays as having a dominant mode. We point out that during the composing process writers respond primarily to their material by selecting paragraph and essay patterns that best suit their subject and purpose instead of trying to fit their material into preselected patterns.

Each chapter that concentrates on a rhetorical mode begins with a detailed discussion that explains the writing method, offers strategies for using the method, and presents a sample of student work, several paragraphs in length, that illustrates the method at work in college writing. Here we wish to emphasize "detailed," for *The Longwood Reader* offers a thorough, though economical, discussion of each rhetorical mode and uses a variety of examples to illustrate major concepts. In Chapter 4, "Narration," for instance, you will find an explanation of narrative effect illustrated by a brief tale from Zen Buddhist lore. You will find advice on writing the opening, body, and climax of a narrative as well as a discussion of conflict, point of view, chronological and psychological time, and scene and summary. We use several examples to illustrate these concepts to help students understand them in the essays that comprise this chapter. In Chapter 5, "Examples," you will find a detailed discussion of specific, typical, and hypothetical examples as well as the practice of mixing different types of examples in an essay. The discussion is amply illustrated by eight paragraph examples. We continue this practice throughout the text.

Eight chapters have five essays each, while Chapter 11, "Persuasion and Argument," has six paired essays. Each essay is introduced with a brief biography of the author, brief comments to place the essay in context, and a prompt to initiate attentive reading. Each essay is followed by questions grouped under the headings Meaning and Purpose, Strategy, and Style. Two writing assignments follow the study questions, and each chapter closes with additional writing assignments, one designed to generate a response to a photograph, developed to challenge students with a wide range of essay topics from which to choose.

The Longwood Reader offers two important reference features. The Glossary defines rhetorical terms that appear throughout the text. When a term first appears, it is highlighted in bold type to signal its appearance in the Glossary. *The Longwood Reader* also offers a thematic table of contents for readers who wish to read several essays on a common subject and a list of paired readings for those who wish to read for similarities or differences in perspective and style.

We thank those colleagues from colleges and universities around the country who reviewed the fourth edition of *The Longwood Reader:* Kathleen Byrd, South Puget Sound Community College; Ragina Copeland, West Virginia University at Parkersburg; Patricia Creed, Temple College; Jacqueline Goffe-McNish, Dutchess Community College; Randy Oldaker, West Virginia University at Parkersburg; Andrea Porter, Mississippi State University.

Once again we thank those who advised us on previous editions: Kathleen L. Bell, University of Central Florida; Maggie Berdine, West Virginia University at Parkersburg; Michael Bobkoff, Westchester Community College; Judith M. Boschult, Phoenix College; Leigh Boyd, Temple Junior College; Patricia Creed, Temple Junior College; Shirley Curtis, Polk Community College; Charles Dodson, University of North Carolina—Wilmington; Jane Dugan, Cleveland State University; Janet Ever, County College of Morris; Judith Haberman, Phoenix College; Leslie Harris, Georgia State University; Elaine Sheridan Horne, Manchester Community College; Gloria Johnson, Broward Community College; Russell R. Larson, Eastern Michigan University; Peggy Jolly, University of Alabama—Birmingham; Robert A. Kelly, Macon College; Joseph LaBriola, Sinclair Community College; Russell R. Larson, Eastern Michigan University; Barry Maid, University of Arkansas—Little Rock; Thomas E. Martinez, Villanova University; Jerry McElveen, Richland College; Michael J. Meils,

El Paso Community College; Gratia Murphy, Youngstown State University; Ruth Peña, El Paso Community College; Rebecca Phillips, West Virginia University—Parkersburg; Beth Richards, University of Nebraska; Connie Rothwell, University of North Carolina—Charlotte; Gerald Schiffhorst, University of Central Florida; David E. Schwalm, Arizona State University; Carole M. Sherman, College of DuPage; Ann Spurlock, Mississippi State University; Laurence J. Starczyk, Kent State University; Jo Koster Tarvers, Rutgers University; Donna Tobin, Bucks County Community College; Eugene Wright, University of North Texas.

We also thank the professionals at Allyn and Bacon who guided previous editions through the production process: Alicia Reilly, Amy Capute, and Rowena Dores. And we continue to appreciate Kathy Daniel's and David Lynch's fine work on the final manuscript for the first edition.

For all four editions we owe a special debt of gratitude to our sponsoring editor Joe Opiela for his advice throughout the process. We also thank Editorial Assistant Mary Varney, Permissions Editor Laurie Frankenthaler, Production Administrator Rowena Dores, and Production Editor Lauren Shafer for their help in preparing the fourth edition manuscript for publication.

We also wish to acknowledge an immense debt to our colleagues Don Pierstorff and Mike Finnegan for their extensive contributions to *The Longwood Reader.* Finally, a special thank you is due John Finnegan for his ability to translate illegible handwriting into finished copy.

1

The Reading Process

There's a story from the 1960s that has become part of educational lore. Students were challenging campus authorities. A contingent of dissatisfied students began haggling with the faculty and administration over curriculum changes. Finally, months of negotiation ended in deadlock. Frustrated, the students called a rally. A representative from administration began to speak, offering the "official" view. Suddenly, a student leader leaped to the platform and grabbed the microphone. Veins pulsed in his neck; his face turned crimson; his eyes blazed with anger. Everyone became excited, ready for a fiery attack on the administration and faculty, but instead he shouted, "Words, Words, Words! I'm sick of words!" He dug into a bag and began tossing lecture notes, essay shreds, and pages torn from textbooks at the astonished crowd. "If words were feathers," he bellowed, "everyone on this campus would smother before anything changed." And then he stormed to the admissions office and promptly withdrew from his classes.

Or so the story goes.

A true story? Who knows for sure? It does, nevertheless, illustrate a common belief that words slow action. Indeed, taking direct action seems much easier than agonizing over a thoughtful, well-reasoned argument. But education relies primarily on words, written words—words *you* read and words *you* write. Reading and writing are sometimes slow, frustrating activities that at first glance may seem to oppose each other. On the contrary, though, reading and writing complement each other. The better reader you are, the better writer you can become.

Of course, you've been reading since grammar school. You might even spend some leisure time reading for pleasure, perhaps becoming engrossed in the psychological twists and turns of a popular thriller or enthralled by the intricate social weaving of a historical narrative. But you probably spend more time reading for information, gleaning facts from history, psychology, and science textbooks. While reading textbooks, you concentrate on a goal, which often has something to do with a midterm or final examination. In other words, you've learned efficient reading techniques. You've learned to approach a textbook as if it were a lake in which to trawl for facts and theories instead of bass or trout.

2

Certainly, reading in this way helps you to prepare for tests. It will also help after graduation when you face the heaps of memoranda, reports, and research that every profession generates. It won't, however, help you to become a better writer. For your writing to improve, you must learn to read like a writer. You can begin by learning to read with a "critical eye." The critical eye reveals a writer's purpose and strategies. It scrutinizes the way words work in sentences. The critical eye pierces a work's surface and reveals its bones and heart.

We offer the essays in this anthology as a means to help you to develop a critical eye. The essay is often described as a well-organized nonfiction composition in which the author concentrates on a single aspect of a subject. Usually, this kind of essay is written in formal English and designed to convey information. But essays as a group cover a much broader territory. They often rise to the level of artful prose and should be read with as much concentration as you would read a poem or short work of fiction. Artful essays are usually impressionistic or exploratory. They express personal feelings or attitudes based on a writer's experience and insights.

Because essays are so varied, these selections represent a great range, all the better, we believe, to help you sharpen your critical eye. They include works by such well-known essayists as George Orwell, Joan Didion, and E. B. White, as well as works by less-known, rising essayists, such as Gretel Ehrlich and Phyllis Rose. The essays are from varied sources: newspapers, magazines, academic and scientific journals, and nonfiction books. They cover many subjects: crime and violence, men and women, work and play, country and city life, even culture and customs. The collection embodies several styles, ranging from the newswriter's objective report to the poet's subjective expression. Some are serious. Some are playful. All are worth your attention.

To deepen your understanding of the essay, we have arranged *The Longwood Reader* by rhetorical patterns, that is, according to the dominant strategies writers use to organize the content of their essays. These are common strategies—description, narration, examples, comparison and contrast, cause and effect, process analysis, classification and division, definition, and persuasion and argument. Perhaps you already have a casual acquaintance with a few of these patterns. Good—but now you can get to know them intimately. *The Longwood Reader* examines them closely by beginning each chapter with a detailed explanation of a pattern and a student example of the pattern at work. As you study them, hold one idea in mind: You are reading like a writer; that is, reading to develop your writing skill—reading with a critical eye.

The Writer–Reader Contract

Pause for a moment. Imagine an essayist pushing back from a typewriter desk. The writer stretches and yawns before slipping a final manuscript into an envelope and sending it off for publication. You might think this is the critical moment—when the essay is completed and in the mail to the publisher.

But it isn't.

The critical moment comes when the work falls into a reader's hands—your hands. To begin reading an essay is the first act in a dynamic interaction—not between you and the writer, as you might guess—but between you and the essay itself.

This is not to deny that a relationship connects you and the writer. In fact, readers and writers are joined by an implicit agreement, a "contract." To meet the writer–reader contract, a writer agrees to create an understandable work; a reader agrees to try to understand the work.

Unfortunately, communicating in written language is often difficult. A writer cannot gaze over your shoulder and whisper into your ear to make understanding an essay any easier. Only the essay speaks to you. To fulfill the writer–reader contract, a writer employs principles known as "conventions" to help you understand the essay. Even if the essay is difficult, you must trust that the writer has kept the reader in mind during the writing. You must trust that the writer has seen the essay through *your* eyes. In other words, you must trust that the writer has used the conventions of essay writing to help you understand the work.

Generally, these conventions dictate that essays have a purpose, use clear strategies to achieve the purpose, and employ an appropriate style. Understanding these conventions will help you to decipher most nonfiction texts. Indeed, understanding the conventions will help to sharpen your critical eye.

Reading for Purpose

Writers know that readers expect a purpose to be at work behind a piece of writing. They tend to view purpose from two perspectives: the general purpose of the entire essay and the particular purpose of a paragraph or passage.

General Purpose

A general purpose gives an essay direction. It provides a destination. It keeps a reader on the track. Some writers, especially when the primary intent is to convey information, state a general purpose: "My purpose is to explain the ways in which human beings have decorated their bodies through the ages: by tattooing, by scarring, and by reshaping bone structure." Other writers, especially those writing personal narration and description, do not state a general purpose as directly, thus encouraging the reader to become more deeply involved in interpretation. You must then formulate the general purpose in your own way: "The writer narrates an early childhood experience to show how important imaginative play is." When an essay is rich enough to invite interpretation, much like a careful reading of an intricate poem or short story, then all that you have heard, tasted, touched, smelled, seen, and thought, all your knowledge of people, books, music, art, culture, and language—literally everything you have lived through—are the raw material at your disposal. Drawing on that rich resource, you apply your knowledge to interpret the essayist's general purpose.

Particular Purpose

The particular purpose refers to what a writer intends in a single paragraph or short passage that helps to develop the general purpose. Consider a short passage from Norman Mailer's *Fire on the Moon*, a work in which he concentrates on the U.S. space program. In this passage, astronauts Neil Armstrong and Buzz Aldrin have completed their historic moon walk on the Sea of Tranquility. The event takes place at the end of their first day on the moon.

> It was about three-thirty in the morning when the astronauts finally prepared for sleep. They pulled down the shades and Aldrin stretched out on the floor, his nose near the moon dust. Armstrong sat on the cover of the ascent engine, his back leaning against one of the walls, his legs supported in a strap he had tied around a vertical bar. In front of his face was the eyepiece of the telescope. The earth was in its field of view, and the earth "like a big blue eyeball" stared back at him. They could not sleep. Like the eye of a victim just murdered, the earth stared back at him.

One clear purpose is to describe the astronauts' preparations for sleep, but toward the end of the passage, Mailer compares the earth to a murder victim. Moreover, he suggests that Armstrong is haunted by the image of the earth "like the eye of a victim" staring at him. Is the comparison merely a dramatic flourish? We doubt it. The description will lead a sensitive reader to explore the deeper purpose in Mailer's comparison. Mailer does not spell out what the passage means. Instead, he invites the reader to interpret it. That puts the reader in an interesting spot, for just as Mailer has drawn on his knowledge and experience to create the image, readers must draw on theirs to interpret it, to find a meaning.

The meaning may vary from reader to reader, depending on each one's knowledge and experience. One reader might recall Edgar Allan Poe's macabre tale of murder, "The Tell-Tale Heart." In Poe's story the murder victim's eye—"a pale blue eye"— haunted the murderer, as the blue earth seems to haunt Armstrong. Does the image suggest, therefore, that the earth has been abandoned like a corpse by astronauts who seek other worlds?

Another reader might explore technological associations. The 1969 Apollo II flight was history's most advanced scientific achievement. But at what price? Aren't the human thirst for scientific achievement and the technology it generates sapping mother earth's natural resources? In a metaphorical sense, therefore, isn't technology killing the earth? And couldn't Mailer be using the moon landing to suggest that "ecological crime"? Who, then, are the perpetrators? Perhaps all humankind, represented by the astronaut who, Mailer suggests, feels accused by the "big blue eyeball" staring at him.

Not all essays invite a careful interpretation of purpose, but the many that do are rich in detail and express a personal vision.

Reading for Strategy

A *strategy* is composed of the various approaches, plans, or methods writers rely on to construct their essays. Any writer must develop a strategy to execute an essay's purpose.

Audience

A writer might first develop a sense of audience and a strategy for addressing them: To whom is the essay directed? How much do they know about the subject? How much time are they likely to spend with the essay? Will they want a straightforward treatment of the subject or an exploration through richly textured prose? Answering questions such as these will give a writer a sense of the audience, a feel for the person sitting at a desk or in an easy chair reading the essay.

Structure

Having acquired a sense of the audience, the writer might next develop a strategy for the essay's structure, knowing that readers want essays to have clear organization. Usually, writers choose a dominant rhetorical pattern to organize their work. Rhetorical patterns are not formulas. They don't offer a magic recipe for success in writing. Moreover, professional writers seldom stick to any one pattern, choosing instead to use several within a dominant structure. We suggest that you look at rhetorical patterns as tools to guide your writing and to provide effective ways to fulfill a reader's desire for structure.

To see how rhetorical patterns can work, imagine that you are a film critic and want to compare and contrast two movies. You pick thrillers and narrow your subject to plot structure. You decide to explain the similarities and differences in each director's way of hooking an audience, generating suspense, building to a climax, and constructing the resolution. Thorough knowledge of comparison-and-contrast patterns will help you to balance the similarities and differences in your analysis.

While composing your essay, however, you find yourself bringing the plot of a third movie into the discussion, one that represents still another structure. A warning light flashes in the back of your mind. You pause to think through what you're doing. Your knowledge of rhetorical patterns helps you to realize you're drifting into classification, which is a pattern different from comparison and contrast, perhaps one best avoided for this writing situation. You stop. You return to your original strategy or reconsider and in fact move to classification.

At still another stage, you drift into discussing the effects of thriller plots on an audience. It makes sense—an exciting plot does affect an audience, right? Of course it does. But you would be employing yet another rhetorical pattern, cause and effect. After some thought, though, you might decide to explore the effect on the audience, but you will do it in another section of your paper, and you will arrange it according to cause-and-effect technique.

Our point is quite simple: Knowledge of rhetorical patterns helps writers to organize their work. These aren't cookie-cutter patterns that writers press into the dough of their thought. They are effective strategies that writers use to organize their material and guide a reader through an essay. They also help writers to remain flexible, shifting smoothly from pattern to pattern according to the demands of the subject. The best way we know for you to build knowledge of rhetorical patterns is to examine how professional writers use them—that is, to read with a critical eye.

Reading for Style

People usually think of style as appearance. Imagine someone with a certain style walking across your campus. To what kinds of things are you referring when you speak of his or her "style"? Perhaps it's the black leather jacket and silver studs; the hair dyed black, swept into a peak, and shaved at the sides; the defiant swagger; even the throaty voice, rasping across the quad—all these details, and more, create the image, the "style" that this person generates.

Word Selection

Writing embodies many details that work together to generate a "style." To identify a writer's style, you might begin by examining word selection. Are the words abstract or concrete? Do the words lull you into inattention, like the speech of a politician trying to obscure past transgressions, or do they catch your attention, like pebbles pinging against a window? Are the words common, found in everyone's vocabulary? Or are they scholarly, obscure words used by specialists? Or does the writer mix common with scholarly language?

Sentence Structure

You might also study a writer's sentences. Notice how the writer builds sentences and varies their structure. We have no simple rules for this technique. Writers learn a feel for sentences, the way potters develop a feel for clay. They shape them. They vary their length. They alter their rhythm to increase or slow the pace of reading for emphasis.

Figures of Speech

Writers use sentences to create figures of speech, the bits and pieces of colorful language sparkling through the essay. A writer might use figurative language to compare two things that are essentially different but alike in some way. With a crisp simile, Flannery O'Connor compares a woman's determination to a truck: Mrs. Freeman's "forward expression was steady and driving like the advance of a heavy truck." In another memorable simile, Ralph Waldo Emerson offers a fresh way to see a child: "A sleeping child gives me the impression of a traveler in a very far country." With figurative language, writers not only help their readers to understand what is being said, but also add vigor to their prose.

Tone

Word choice, sentence variety, and figurative language combine to create another element of style: tone. Begin to think of tone as an expression of a writer's attitude, much as tone of voice may reflect a speaker's attitude. Imagine, for a moment, that you have given a speech. The next day you receive this note:

> That was an effective speech. You carefully covered the main points. We all thank you.

A straightforward compliment? We think so, don't you? But with a few word substitutions and additions and by altering emphasis, the tone changes dramatically:

> That was . . . *some* speech. You *lingered* on all the points—at least three times each. Thanks a lot.

The message no longer expresses appreciation. It now expresses snide criticism. In other words, the tone has changed.

Some kinds of writing are dominated by well-defined tones. News reporters seem to share a tone, an objective presentation of events—just the facts, please. Thriller and romance writers seem to favor a breathless, frenzied tone. Essayists, however, struggle to find the exact tone to fit the subject, audience, and attitude. The same writer may use one tone for one subject and another tone for another subject. The tone may be formal, informal, flippant, conversational, intimate, solemn, playful, or ironic. The tone may even reveal the writer's awe of the subject. Consider the opening lines from Richard Selzer's essay on skin:

> I sing of skin, layered fine as baklava, whose colors shame the dawn, at once the scabbard upon which is writ our only signature, and the instrument by which we are thrilled, protected, and kept constant in our natural place.

Selzer brings to his essay years of experience as a surgeon and medical school teacher. A reader with knowledge of Selzer's background might expect him to treat the skin in a matter-of-fact way, as merely a thin barrier that must be sliced through to reach the vital organs. But this is clearly not his attitude. He writes rhapsodically, "I sing of skin"; he makes a rich comparison, "layered fine as baklava"; and he claims its "colors shame the dawn." The sentence is a tribute to skin, and the tone expresses his sense of awe.

Style is difficult territory to explore, no doubt about it. If you devote time to reading for style, you will achieve a *feel* for it. Study a writer's words and you will learn to choose the right words. Study a writer's sentences and you will learn to shape your sentences. Study a writer's figurative language and you will soon be writing colorfully. Study a writer's tone and soon a voice will rise from your pages.

Five Tips for a First Reading

When reading to improve your writing, you cannot sweep through an essay and then set it aside. You should be prepared to read it several times. The first reading may be quick, designed to give you a view of the content, a sense of the purpose, and a feeling for the style. When you begin the first reading, we suggest that you keep five tips in mind.

1. *Know the Writer*

Whatever you learn about an author will help you to anticipate his or her biases. If the author is identified as a liberal politician and the subject is poverty, then you might anticipate an argument supporting government aid to the poor. If the author is an environmentalist and the subject is the greenhouse effect, then you might expect a plea to save the world's rain forests. Many periodicals and essay anthologies include information about an author, usually on the first page of the essay or in a section often titled "Notes on Contributors." In this collection, each essay is introduced by a headnote, which includes an author profile and brief comments on the essay. Read each profile with care; it will prepare you for your first reading of the essay.

2. *Consider the Place and Year of Publication*

Knowing where the essay was first published is necessary in establishing a writer's credentials. An essay titled "Bigfoot: Hoax or Hysteria?" would have more credibility if published in *Media, Culture, and Society* than it would if it were published in *The National Enquirer*. Why? *Media, Culture, and Society* is a highly respected periodical known for its analysis of the influence exerted by newspapers, television, and cinema on reader and viewer perceptions. In contrast, *The National Enquirer* is a popular tabloid known for its sensationalism. Knowing when an essay was first published will also give you clues about the social environment it was written in. Certainly, an essay on civil liberty written in the early 1960s is going to display different assumptions from those in one written in the late 1980s.

3. *Examine the Title*

Seems obvious, right? Well, you would be surprised at how many readers mistakenly believe that an essay begins with its first line. It doesn't. It begins with a title.

A title can help you to anticipate what is to follow. It might announce the writer's subject, suggest the dominant rhetorical pattern, or hint at the writer's attitude. The title "A Hanging" lets you know you won't be going to a tea party. It makes sense to anticipate an essay about an execution, which will not be a pretty experience. The title "Cyclone! Rising to the Fall" is a little more ambiguous. Does "cyclone" refer to the destructive natural phenomenon? Or does it mean a roller coaster? Or could "Cyclone" be the name of a bronco? Anyway, you probably expect a description of a thrilling, or even frightening, experience, so get a tight grip on the book. "I Want a Wife" seems like a straightforward title. But if you know that a woman wrote the essay, you might expect an ironic tone.

4. Take Quick Notes

Always read with a pencil in hand. Don't just chew on the eraser, though. Star key passages, underline startling images, bracket shifts in thought, and scribble notes in the margins. Roughly trace your reactions to the text, questions that come to mind, even disagreements with the writer. Ah yes, circle words you don't know so that you can refer to a dictionary for their meaning before the second reading.

Why go to all this trouble for a first reading? We don't suggest that you linger on any page for very long, but a first reading is like traveling in new territory. Much like markings on a map, markings on an essay will help your exploration during the return visit.

5. Record Your First Impressions

We urge you to record your first impressions after the first reading and before going on to a second reading. Write down what you think the writer was trying to achieve—the purpose. Identify the dominant strategies. Describe the audience. Jot down your thoughts on style. Record any impressions you have.

Now let's look at an essay, Willard Gaylin's "What You See Is the Real You," with notes that reflect the guidelines for a first reading.

Gaylin is a psychiatrist and psychoanalyst—that is, his profession concentrates on the mind and behavior. As well as teaching and lecturing at colleges and universities around the world, he has also written several books on psychiatry and the law. This 1977 essay, published in *The New York Times*, a highly respected newspaper, deals with an interesting question: Should people be judged primarily by their outward behavior rather than their inward potential?

What does this brief description add up to? Clearly, Gaylin seems to be an informed authority in psychiatry; therefore his observations on the mind and behavior should be respected (which doesn't mean that you have to agree with his position). The article was published in a newspaper known for its high standards, but it was published over twenty years ago, which suggests that it might be dated.

With the author's background in mind, read the essay and the handwritten observations based on the suggestions in "Five Tips for a First Reading." Remember, the observations were jotted down for the reader herself, not for an audience. Even though they are often elliptical, maybe even cryptic, they clearly represent a reader's encounter with a serious essay.

A bit of advice: Since book margins are seldom wide enough for extensive notes, place a sheet of paper along the side of the margin and jot down your notes on the paper. Indicate paragraphs by number in your notes to help you track your observations.

❦ Willard Gaylin ❦

What You See Is the Real You

It was, I believe, the distinguished Nebraska financier Father Edward J. Flanagan who professed to having "never met a bad boy." Having, myself, met a remarkable number of bad boys, it might seem that either our experiences were drastically different or we were using the word "bad" differently. I suspect neither is true, but rather that the Father was appraising the "inner man," while I, in fact, do not acknowledge the existence of inner people.

Since we psychoanalysts have unwittingly contributed to this confusion, let one, at least, attempt a small rectifying effort. Psychoanalytic data —which should be viewed as supplementary information—are, unfortunately, often viewed as alternative (and superior) explanation. This has led to the prevalent tendency to think of the "inner" man as the real man and the outer man as an illusion or pretender.

While psychoanalysis supplies us with an incredibly useful tool for ex-

15

Idea: motives are not moral or immoral — behavior is!

Analogy: points out that the underlying structure is less important than the outward appearance.

*

repeats key idea established above.

Writer: Cat's Cradle & Slaughter-house Five. Dark humor. Supports view: a person is what a person does. Example supporting idea that people are what they do, not what they think. Good people have bad thoughts.

plaining the motives and purposes underlying human behavior, most of this has little bearing on the moral nature of that behavior.

Like roentgenology, psychoanalysis is a fascinating, but relatively new, means of illuminating the person. But few of us are prepared to substitute an X-ray of Grandfather's head for the portrait that hangs in the parlor. The inside of the man represents another view, not a truer one. A man may not always be what he appears to be, but what he appears to be is always a significant part of what he is. A man is the sum total of *all* his behavior. To probe for unconscious determinants of behavior and then define *him* in their terms exclusively, ignoring his overt behavior altogether, is a greater distortion than ignoring the unconscious completely.

Kurt Vonnegut has said, "You are what you pretend to be," which is simply another way of saying, you are what we (all of us) perceive you to be, not what you think you are.

Consider for a moment the case of the ninety-year-old man on his deathbed (surely the Talmud must deal with this?) joyous and relieved over the success of his deception. For ninety years, he has shielded his evil nature from public observation. For ninety years he has affected courtesy, kindness, and generosity—suppressing all the malice he knew was within him while he calculatedly and artificially substituted grace and charity. All his life he had been fooling the world into believing he was a good man. This "evil" man will, I predict, be welcomed into the Kingdom of Heaven.

Contrasting example: bad person has good thoughts.

Similarly, I will not be told that 7
the young man who earns his pocket money by mugging old ladies is "really" a good boy. Even my generous and expansive definition of goodness will not accommodate that particular form of self-advancement.

It does not count that beneath the 8
rough exterior he has a heart—or, for that matter, an entire innards—of purest gold, locked away from human perception. You are for the most part what you seem to be, not what you would wish to be, nor, indeed, what you believe yourself to be.

*Echoes point of view.

Tone: ironic, sounds as if he is exhausted by hearing the same old tales. Spare me! a plea to stop.

Spare me, therefore, your good in- 9
tentions, your inner sensitivities, your unarticulated and unexpressed love. And spare me also those tedious psychohistories which—by exposing the goodness inside the bad man, and the evil in the good—invariably establish a vulgar and perverse egalitarianism, as if the arrangement of what is outside and what inside makes no moral difference.

Alludes to 1. Saint — Francis

Saint Francis may, in his uncon- 10
scious, indeed have been compensating for, and denying, destructive, unconscious Oedipal impulses identi-

2. Conqueror — Attilla

cal to those which <u>Attilla</u> projected and acted on. But the similarity of the unconscious constellations in the two men matters precious little, if it does not distinguish between them.

3. Nazi — Hitler only behavior can be judged.

I do not care to learn that <u>Hitler's</u> heart was in the right place. A knowledge of the unconscious life of the man may be an adjunct to understanding his behavior. It is *not* a substitute for his behavior in describing him.   11

Only behavior causes joy or suffering.

The inner man is a (fantasy.) If it helps you to identify with one, by all means, do so; preserve it, cherish it, embrace it, but do not present it to others for evaluation or consideration, for excuse or exculpation, or, for that matter, for punishment or disapproval.   12

Restates Key idea/central point.

Like any (fantasy,) it serves your purposes alone. It has no standing in the real world which we share with each other. Those character traits, those attitudes, that behavior—that strange and alien stuff <u>sticking</u> out all over you—that's the real you!   13

Echoes the title.

Final Notes —

Purpose: to show that people should be judged by what they do, not by what they think.

Strategy: argues the point, sets up opposites, Good vs bad; inner vs outer. Problem — no shades of grey between black and white.

Style: Tone is ironic at times and authoritative. He seems to be shaking a finger at the reader. Sexist use of Pronouns & "Man".

After the first reading, you should be familiar with the essay's content and purpose. You should have a sense of the writer's strategies and the tone. You also should have jotted down general impressions and responses to the essay. In other words, you've left your markings. Now you're ready to return to the territory.

Five Tips for Rereading

Before reading the essay, review your notes and reconsider the title: Did it accurately reflect the content or purpose of the essay? Did it embody the tone? If not, how does it function? Now you're ready to begin. Once again, you should read with pencil in hand, ready to explain or change your previous observations and make new ones. Remember, too, that you're attempting to read like a writer examining another writer's techniques—that is, you're reading with a critical eye.

1. Review the Beginning and End

The beginning and end are critical sections. The opening paragraphs usually will, directly or indirectly, establish the purpose of the essay. Sometimes the purpose will be immediately clear, as it is in Gaylin's "What You See Is the Real You." Clearly, his purpose is to argue that people should be judged by the sum total of their behavior, not by their "unconscious determinants." The end will often restate or dramatize the purpose. Gaylin's essay ends by restating the purpose, thus making his intent unmistakable.

2. Reread with the Purpose in Mind

The purpose can serve as a beacon that will guide you as you reread the essay. Knowing the purpose will clarify the strategies the writer uses to achieve that purpose. For example, two of Gaylin's examples become clear on a rereading: the X-ray of

Grandfather's head and the anecdote about a man who suppressed his "evil" nature and lived a virtuous life.

3. Examine the Style

You'll already have a sense of the style from the first reading. Now's the time to pin it down. Notice the selection of words. Pay close attention to the shapes and rhythms of sentences. Underline phrases that embody the tone. Gaylin has the tone of a highly educated but authoritative writer. He sometimes uses erudite vocabulary, which might be difficult for the average reader—"roentgenology," referring to the use of film in X-rays; "overt behavior," referring to action; and "exculpation," referring to having been declared innocent of a crime. He also makes several literate allusions, which demonstrate his wide knowledge and which he expects his reader to know—Father Edward J. Flanagan, founder of a home for wayward boys he called "Boys Town"; Kurt Vonnegut, the author of such satiric novels as *Cat's Cradle* and *Slaughterhouse Five*; the Talmud, the Jewish book of spiritual laws; Francis of Assisi, who renounced his wealth and founded the Franciscan religious order and was made a saint in 1228.

Sometimes his authoritative tone sounds exasperated—"I will not be told that the young man who earns his pocket money by mugging old ladies is 'really' a good boy." Other times he sounds ironic—"Even my generous and expansive definition of goodness will not accommodate *that particular form of self-advancement*," which is an ironic way to say "mugging." Always he sounds pompous, especially when he uses "man" and all its pronouns to refer to people in general.

4. Linger on Interesting Passages

Pause while rereading to examine passages that catch your attention. What's an interesting passage? That, of course, is a judgment call. Perhaps a passage will be an interestingly structured paragraph or a series of paragraphs. Later, you might want to use it as a model to emulate in your writing practice.

For example, in one interesting paragraph, Gaylin makes a point through metaphor; that is, he makes a brief comparison between dissimilar subjects.

> Like roentgenology, psychoanalysis is a fascinating, but relatively new, means of illuminating the person. *But few of us are prepared to substitute an X-ray of Grandfather's head for the portrait that hangs in the parlor.* The inside of the man represents another view, not a truer one. A man may not always be what he appears to be, but what he appears to be is a significant part of what he is. A man is the sum total of *all* his behavior. To probe for unconscious determinants of behavior and then define *him* in their terms exclusively, ignoring his overt behavior altogether, is a greater distortion than ignoring the unconscious completely.

The metaphor comparing an X-ray and a portrait to the concept of the inner and outer person makes the abstract discussion concrete, that is, something that the reader can visualize and that reflects Gaylin's point.

5. Record Your Closing Impressions

Your impressions may be related to purpose, strategy, and style. They may also include your associations with the essay: Does it bring to mind any experiences you've had? Do you associate it with something you've learned or something you've seen or heard about? Does it stir a specific meaning in you? And, perhaps most important, does it call to mind any ideas you might like to explore in writing?

The guidelines for a first reading and for rereading give you a procedure to follow when reading any essay or written work that deserves your attention. In *The Longwood Reader* we've also added questions on purpose, strategy, and style after each essay—all written to help you understand an author's methods. Your instructor might assign the questions and ask you to respond to them in writing. But if they are not assigned, we suggest that you review them on your own as an independent way to become a more critically minded reader.

In-Class Responses to Reading

Sometimes your instructor will ask you to write a brief in-class response to a reading assignment without the aid of your textbook. Usually, you will be given fifteen to twenty minutes to demonstrate your understanding of the assigned essay. If you've read the essay thoroughly and have taken notes, as we suggested earlier, then you should be able show that you have read the essay with care and understand the main elements. But writing a successful in-class response takes more than careful reading. You must not only be able to state your understanding of the essay; you must also do it under time pressure.

Understand the Assignment

Before beginning to write, you should have a clear understanding of what your instructor wants you to do. If you are asked to summarize an essay, then you state what the essay covers as objectively as you can. If you are asked to evaluate the essay, then you offer your opinions related to the essay. Do not offer your opinions when asked to summarize an essay and do not merely summarize an essay when the instructor has asked for your opinions.

Develop a Three-Minute Outline

Before you begin to write, scratch out a brief outline of your response. Even though you might have only fifteen minutes to write your response, you should allow yourself three minutes to jot down your thoughts in logical order. A scratch outline such as this will keep you from straying during the writing process.

Follow Common Writing Practices

In responding to writing, there are several practices you should follow, whether the assignment is to write in class or not:

1. In the first sentence, state the author, the title, and the author's purpose. Be sure to spell the author's name correctly and state the exact title.
2. After stating the author's full name in the opening sentence, use only the last name when referring to the author. Don't use Mr., Mrs., Dr., Ms., or any such designation with the last name.
3. Use specific references to the essay and attribute them to the author throughout your response. Try to use active verbs besides "says" when attributing something to an author, such as "argues," "claims," "maintains," "points out."
4. Use the historical present—that is, the present tense of verbs—throughout your response.
5. Close with a clincher, that is, a comment that echoes the opening.

What follows is a typical in-class assignment asking students to write a response to a reading assignment, in this case to Gaylin's essay.

In 100 to 125 words, state Willard Gaylin's main purpose in "What You See Is the Real You" and trace his line of thought. You have 20 minutes to write your response. This is a closed-book assignment.

Now read an in-class response to the assignment and the margin comments that point out common in-class writing practices.

Effective opening: identifies author and title, and responds directly to the assignment. Uses historical present throughout. After having stated full name above, uses author's last name throughout.

Willard Gaylin in "What You See Is the Real You" argues that what has become known as the "inner" person doesn't exist. He maintains that only the "outer" person exists. Gaylin says that people are the sum total of what they do, not of what they think or feel.

Gaylin holds psychoanalysis responsible for people thinking that the inner person is the real person. He points out that the deep reasons for what people do don't matter. It's their actual behavior that matters. To illustrate his point, Gaylin says that a person

Makes specific references to Gaylin's essay.

who has an "evil" nature but resists doing evil deeds by doing "good" deeds is a good person, not an evil one, because he did good in the world.

Gaylin uses an analogy to make his point clear. He says that judging people by their thoughts and feelings, instead of by their outer behavior, would be like hanging on the wall an X-ray instead of a photograph

Closes with clincher.

of a person. A person is not what you don't see; a person is what you do see.

Allow Yourself Time to Proofread

Even in a fifteen to twenty-minute in-class writing assignment, you should allow yourself time to proofread your response. Don't count on rewriting. Instead, scratch out unnecessary words, make additions in the margins or between lines, and correct any punctuation errors. Your instructor will not hold in-class writing to the same standard as out-of-class writing; nevertheless, you should be as precise and neat as time allows.

2

The Writing Process

The situation has changed. The writer–reader roles are reversed. You are no longer the reader. You are now the writer, in this case the essayist. The writer–reader contract still applies to the situation, but now you must meet the obligation you have to your reader, which is to compose an understandable work. You, in other words, will be using writing conventions to guide your reader, and your reader will rely on these conventions to decipher your essay. Bluntly, you, like every successful writer, must fulfill your half of the writer–reader contract: You must use what you have learned from reading with a critical eye.

Remember, essays are relatively brief nonfiction compositions. Essays concentrate on a single aspect of a topic. Effective essays always have a well-defined purpose, use clear strategies to achieve their purpose, and employ an appropriate style. Sometimes essays, especially in college writing, integrate research, but usually they tend to be personal, embodying a writer's voice and analyzing or interpreting a subject from a writer's personal perspective. Keep in mind, however, that even though an essay embodies a writer's perspective, it is not necessarily about the writer. Instead, essays gain their personal character from the individual writer's insights and values as manifested in the discussion.

Rhetorical Patterns

Although a writer might combine several rhetorical patterns in an essay (each discussed in a separate chapter in this text), one of nine common patterns will usually dominate the overall work, depending on the subject and the writer's approach.

1. *Description* captures the sense of an experience. Description renders what something looks like, its characteristics, the impressions it makes. (See Chapter 3.)
2. *Narration* relates events. Narration shows what happened, when and where it took place, who was involved, and why it happened. (See Chapter 4.)

3. *Examples* illustrate ideas. Examples offer typical cases and concrete instances to develop a point. (See Chapter 5.)
4. *Comparison and contrast* presents similarities and differences. Comparison relates how something is like something else. Contrast relates how something is different from something else. Combined, the pattern relates how two things are both alike and different. (See Chapter 6.)
5. *Cause and effect* identifies reasons and results. Cause and effect explores why something happened, what the consequences are, how something is related to something else. (See Chapter 7.)
6. *Process analysis* explains experience step by step. Process analysis shows how something happens, how it works, how it is made. (See Chapter 8.)
7. *Classification and division* establishes categories. Classification and division sorts things by their common components and characteristics. (See Chapter 9.)
8. *Definition* limits meaning. Definition explains what something is, what it means, how it is like and different from other members in its class. (See Chapter 10.)
9. *Persuasion and argument* convinces readers. Persuasion and argument attempts to move people to action or to convince them to change their opinions. (See Chapter 11.)

Writers use rhetorical patterns to help them make writing choices. Imagine, for a moment, that you have been assigned an essay on advertising. Once you decide on your essay's purpose, you will then decide which rhetorical pattern would best help to achieve the purpose; thus the pattern dominates the essay's development. For example, if your purpose is to relate consumer stories, you would choose narration. If your purpose is to reveal the subliminal messages in advertising images, you would choose description. If your purpose is to explain the similarities and differences between two advertising campaigns, you would choose comparison and contrast. Or if your purpose is to convince a reader that film directors should stop including "disguised" cigarette advertisements in movies, then you would choose argumentation. No matter which choice you make, your final essay will reflect the rhetorical conventions of the pattern you choose, thus helping the reader trace the development of the essay's central purpose.

College Essays

Once you decide on a dominant rhetorical pattern and are ready to write, you can employ another conventional essay strategy by structuring your essay in three main parts: an introduction, a discussion, and a conclusion. Often referred as the thesis-support essay or the college essay, it is the most commonly used essay structure in academic writing, which doesn't mean that it is the only effective essay structure you can use. It is, however, the one we emphasize in this chapter.

Part 1: Introduction

Introductions are composed of one or more paragraphs, all designed to introduce an essay's central purpose—or, as we like to call it, your promise to your reader. An introduction should arouse curiosity, provide appropriate background information, and clarify any questions the reader might need to have answered to understand the central purpose. An introduction should also display the thesis, which is a clear, limited statement of the essay's general purpose. Think of the thesis statement as a direct promise to a reader put into specific language. It is a promise that clearly sets the course for the rest of the essay.

Part 2: Discussion

Discussions fulfill the promise made in the thesis. An essay's discussion should be several paragraphs long, substantially longer than the introduction, all organized by topic sentences that identify subpoints of the thesis statement. The topic sentences should also *echo* the thesis to show the promise is being fulfilled and to rivet the reader's attention to the essay's central purpose.

Part 3: Conclusion

Conclusions bring an essay to a satisfactory close. At the very least, a conclusion should show that the promise made in the thesis statement has been fulfilled. One point to keep in mind: A conclusion should never apologize for covering the subject inadequately.

Typically, a college essay is between 500 and 1,500 words, but more appropriately, the length should be determined by the complexity of the subject and the amount of detailed discussion necessary to support the thesis.

Please don't get the wrong impression. Effective essays are not as mechanically contrived as our brief description might suggest, a fact that you can quickly substantiate by thumbing through several selections in this text. Our purpose here, before discussing the process involved in composing an essay, is to emphasize that writers employ a few common conventions to help them meet their part of the writer–reader contract. How well writers use those conventions depends on their skills.

A Student Essay for Study

Now, with this brief description in mind, study the following essay on one aspect of the topic *propaganda*. The student author, Lane Williams, has the following to say about his essay:

> For me composing an essay is a chaotic activity. Whenever I reread a final draft and it makes sense, I'm always surprised. The development of this essay was especially chaotic. I created it from my own ideas, class notes, and by looking at magazine and television advertisements.
>
> One major problem I had to overcome was to think about an essay in more complicated ways than I had been

taught in high school where I learned to write five-paragraph essays. For this project I had too much information to fit into a simple five-paragraph structure, so I needed to work very hard at organization. But once I had all my material gathered, the central purpose emerged and the actual writing process began to organize itself. What is my purpose? I wanted to explain some ways advertisers use propaganda devices to trick us into spending our money. Clearly my essay had to define some important terms, but overall I knew the rhetorical pattern would be dominated by examples.

Now study Williams's essay. After reading the essay through once, reread it along with the marginal notes, which point out some of the conventional strategies Williams uses.

Who's Come a Long Way, Consumers?

Title uses an allusion to suggest essay will deal with advertising.

First sentence introduces the general subject: propaganda.

To propagandize is to attempt to convince people of something by appealing to their emotion rather than to their reason. For good or evil, propaganda is everywhere in our lives. It helps shape our attitudes on thousands of subjects. Nowhere is propaganda more visible than in advertising. For example, why is investing in Fidelity Federal retirement account an investment in "the American way?" Or how can buying Betty Crocker cake mix confirm a sense of "motherhood"? Or how can a feeling of "freedom" be gained from smoking a Marlboro? Advertisers suggest there is a relationship between these products and the language they use to sell them. But in reality they are merely obvious attempts to trick consumers. Advertisers associate pleasing language with products to make consumers feel good about buying them. Such language is called glitter-

Briefly mentions glittering generality, one propaganda technique.

Key word, "trick."

ing generalities, or virtue words. They tug at a consumer's emotion rather than at his or her reason. Besides glittering generalities, advertisers use several other propaganda techniques to trick consumers into buying their products.

Thesis statement: Writer promises to explain propaganda techniques and show how they work.

Bandwagon is another technique advertisers use to trick consumers into buying their products. Through bandwagon, they urge people to buy a product because it is popular—that is, because everyone is doing it together. This call to "get on the bandwagon" appeals to the strong desire to join the crowd rather than be an outsider. An early 1990s television advertisement for Plymouth's mini van uses bandwagon to motivate car buyers. The advertisement features a group of people working out in a gym. A message over the loudspeaker announces, "There is a Plymouth mini van parked in the street." The message is clear: If you want to be part of the crowd, buy a mini van. An early magazine advertisement for Cuervo Gold tequila also makes use of bandwagon. The advertisement features sixteen young party people either sitting on the edge or standing in an empty swimming pool. They are clearly enjoying themselves, each holding a margarita and toasting the viewer outside the advertisement. Clearly, a Cuervo Gold party is fun. The message is that the consumer can join the party. How? Quite obviously, buy Cuervo Gold . . . and hop on the bandwagon.

Topic sentence presents one subpoint of thesis.

Bandwagon briefly defined.

Example 1

Example 2

This brief paragraph links bandwagon discussion with next subpoint, testimonial.

The Cuervo Gold tequila advertisement also features a prominent television personality—Dennis Miller. Miller stands in the group's center and also holds a Cuervo margarita. His presence adds prestige to the product, suggesting that if Cuervo Gold is good enough for a celebrity like Dennis Miller, it certainly is good enough for the

Brief definition of testimonial.

average consumer. The technique of using a celebrity to sell a product is called testimonial, another method advertisers use to entice consumers.

Opening sentence sets up a more detailed discussion of testimonial.

Testimonial is a commonly used advertising ploy. For years, celebrities from motion pictures, music, and sports have lent (more accurately, sold) the use of their names to pitch products: music performer Michael Jackson for soft drinks, basketball star

Presents a catalogue of celebrities.

Michael Jordan for athletic shoes, retired actress June Allyson for adult diapers, comedienne Martha Raye for denture cleaner, and, among advertising's more clever use of testimonial, former Jets quarterback Broadway Joe Namath's classic advertisement for pantyhose. What do these celebrities know about the products they have pitched? Probably very little, but advertisers bank on consumers being attracted to products because a celebrity claims to use it. The appeal is to emotion, not to reason.

This paragraph begins with a clear topic sentence and defines "Plain folks" with a brief comparison to testimonial.

Another device advertisers use to trick consumers is plain folks. In one way plain folks is like testimonial. Both involve someone standing up to praise a product, urging consumers to rely on his or her word, not on sound evidence, to make a product decision. But whereas testimonial features a respected celebrity, plain folks features someone "just like ourselves" to promote confidence in a product. Often plain folks takes the form of a dentist praising a toothpaste or a friendly neighbor recommending

Examples of "common folks" who praise products.

a brand of coffee or a Little League coach explaining that a detergent is powerful enough to remove grass stains. Of course what advertisers do not reveal is that these are all actors who are paid (just as celebrities are paid) to pitch the toothpaste, coffee, and detergent.

This opening sentence signals that the "plain folks" discussion will continue.

An advertisement for Solgar Vitamin Supplements features a potent use of the

An extended example

plain folks device. This advertisement features a young attractive working mother, who is obviously a single parent trying to make ends meet. In the middle of the advertisement, she stands behind her son, smiling with her arms wrapped around him in a protective embrace, and looks directly at the viewer. The son, about eight years old, is also smiling and holding on to his mother's arm. Both seem to be healthy and to care deeply for each other. Above the photograph is the phrase "First Things First," suggesting that loved ones come first. Below the photograph, the son is quoted as saying, "You're the most important thing to me, Mom. Please take care of yourself." Featured next to the comment is a bottle of Solgar Vitamins. Implicitly, the average working mother and son are testifying to the power of Solgar Vitamins to maintain their health and their loving relationship.

Effective transition into next paragraph.

Briefly defines transfer.

Example 1

Also at work in this Solgar advertisement and in most advertisements, for that matter, is another propaganda device called transfer. Through transfer advertisers attempt to lure consumers into buying their products by associating them with something consumers love, desire, or respect. No manufacturer uses transfer more effectively than Philip Morris, Inc. For over two decades Philip Morris has effectively transferred the desire for the rugged cowboy's outdoor life to smoking Marlboro cigarettes. Marlboro advertisements feature images of cowboys herding cattle or riding horses across open spaces. More recently, Marlboro has concentrated less on cowboys at work and more on equipment these Marlboro men use: worn boots, spurs, lariats, saddles—each item designed to remind the reader of a life spent on open prairies with snow capped mountains in the background. And, in case the consumer misses the point, Marlboro advertisements usually include the slogan, "Come to Marlboro Country." How can consumers reach "Marlboro Country"? By lighting up a Marlboro cigarette, of course, thus completing the transfer.

Opening sentence connects with previous discussion of transfer.

Philip Morris also makes effective use of transfer in its Virginia Slims magazine campaign. Each advertisement features a beautiful woman staring boldly into the camera. Clearly, she is in charge of her life, the embodiment of the 1990s image of an independent woman. In a box placed in the corner of these advertisements is a contrasting image, a photograph of a woman from an earlier historical period serving a man. An ironic slogan links the two images, "You've come a long way, baby" (ironic because "baby" echoes sexism). Without much analysis the advertiser's ploy here is clear. Philip Morris hopes to entice women into smoking Virginia Slims by transferring a desire for personal independence to its product.

Example 2 of transfer (echoes title)

Conclusion opens with a "question."

Emphasizes critical thinking.

Echoes title "A long way."

Ends with a provocative question.

Do these propaganda ploys work? Can advertisers actually trick unwary consumers into buying their products? When subjected to critical examination, propaganda seems to be obvious, perhaps even ludicrous . . . certainly too clumsy to allow any manufacturer to pick a consumer's pocket. But the power of propaganda is emotional. Advertisers use propaganda techniques to operate beneath the level of intellect where images and concepts are not subjected to critical analysis. They work through suggestion, association, image. They seduce and their seductions have taken advertisers "a long way." Why else would they use these propaganda tactics to trick consumers year after year and decade after decade?

Williams's essay is effectively executed. He has established a strong purpose and expressed it in a clear thesis statement, which serves as his promise to the reader. He develops an ample discussion section by arranging his information around subpoints of the thesis statement, thus fulfilling his promise. And his conclusion successfully brings the essay to a close. In other words, Williams has met his part of the writer–reader contract.

Let's now examine the process that Williams and other writers follow to create their essays. We don't want to give you the impression that experienced writers sit down and write a perfect first draft—they don't. They struggle with subjects, shuffle rough notes, doodle with outlines—all in an effort to shape their material effectively into finished form. Generally, a finished essay unfolds according to a writer's unique composing methods, that is, the phases of the composing process that begin with finding a subject and end with a final draft.

Find a Subject

"What should I write about?" is an all too familiar question that often signals that a writer is blocked. If you find yourself asking this question, you must immediately turn the question to your advantage. Instead of "What should I write about?" ask, "How can I find a subject to write about?" The rephrased question gives you direction. You can stop chewing the pencil eraser and go to work.

Here's how to start.

Self-Initiated Assignments

Begin by keeping this writing principle firmly in mind: You will write your best essays on subjects you know and care about. We urge you, therefore, to examine your own experience for subjects. Look at your interests, your work, your values, your leisure activities. Watch the news, a film, or a television show for ideas. Browse through a newspaper or magazine for subject possibilities. Any of these sources can give you plenty to write about.

You must pursue this search actively. Engage yourself in the process by picking up a pencil and going to work. Try one of the following strategies:

1. *Create idea lists.* Time management experts urge busy people to keep lists of commitments—action lists. Action lists begin as random collections of upcoming events, commitments, or tasks. Once the list is complete, the list maker evaluates the entries, ranks them, and establishes a work schedule. The list provides the person with some clarity and direction for his or her activities.

   An idea list, like an action list, helps to bring your activity into focus. In this case the activity is writing. You can use an idea list to compile possible writing topics. Begin by setting a minimum time limit—perhaps thirty, forty, or sixty minutes—and stick to it. Your goal is to develop a *spontaneous* series of brief entries that capture your ideas and responses to them.

2. *Use a journal.* If you have kept a journal at any time in your life, browse through it for ideas. There is always a good chance that if an entry engages your interest, you can develop it into a full essay that will engage a reader's interest.

3. *Record from memory.* If a recent class discussion or lecture stimulated your curiosity or stirred a strong opinion that you hold, record the details you recall. Either the discussion or lecture could inspire an essay.

4. *Browse through current reading material.* Glance through a newspaper or magazine until a subject catches your attention, perhaps merely a headline or an article title. Jot down your responses. A response to an article can make an effective essay, especially if the article ignites a strong value you hold.

5. *Consult with others.* Writers often find that discussing or brainstorming writing ideas with other people helps them to imagine their project. You might become part of a writing group that discusses writing ideas. You could also con-

sult a writing buddy—another student or a friend who is more experienced with writing than you are. You can also engage your instructor in a discussion to see whether an idea would work. Be sure to take notes or use a tape recorder. Don't risk letting good ideas slip away.

Instructor-Initiated Assignments

Often college writing is initiated by class assignments. At first you might think that an assignment makes the writing task simple, but it usually does not. In fact, an assigned task might be harder to complete than one that you generate yourself. It might create a sense of false security by leading you to skip the exploration process and plunge directly into the first draft.

As a way of defending yourself from this mistake, remember a second writing principle: An assignment is not a subject. You must create a subject from the assignment.

For example, consider Lane Williams's essay. He wrote it in response to the following assignment: "In four to five typed pages, discuss the role of propaganda in political or commercial communication." To an experienced writer this assignment is much too large to be addressed successfully in a single essay. It must be placed in a more limited focus, reduced to a manageable subject. So instead of plunging into a first draft without exploring the assignment, he used the assignment wisely. Williams says,

> The assignment was just too broad to cover in a five-page essay. I would have to write about propaganda in politics and advertising. I immediately knew it had to be narrowed to manageable size so I decided to explore the assignment by writing an idea list. I knew if I listed enough of my interests I would eventually find something that would give me more direction.

Williams's idea list took the form of phrases capturing the flow of his thought. He put down whatever came to mind. Later he would judge the entries to see how they related.

Politicians and lying . . .
Campaign propaganda in the presidential race . . .
Local council members and land developers . . .
Advertisements and the consumer . . .
Why do people vote for politicians?
Why do people buy certain products?
How do advertisements get attention?
What propaganda techniques are effective in ads?
How can we protect ourselves from propaganda?
    In political decisions?
    In the marketplace?
I'm the victim of propaganda.
    In voting?
    In buying products?
What do advertisements reveal about consumers?
What does propaganda use reveal about politicians?
Propaganda undermines the democratic process.
Master propagandists—political "spin doctors."

Writing the list helped Williams to place his subject in focus. Although no single entry represented a clear subject, he was able to combine several ideas to shape a general subject, the role of propaganda in advertising.

Use Prewriting Techniques to Explore a Subject

You, like all writers, must place your subject in focus and clarify your purpose, often a long and difficult process. The most effective way to start the process is by using prewriting techniques to discover what you know and do not know about the subject.

What is prewriting and how does it work?

Well, prewriting is easy to understand. But first, consider how some writers talk about the mind in relation to writing—a simplified view but one that will help you to understand the writing process.

When discussing how they compose their works, writers often talk of intuition and intellect. They associate intuition with creativity. The creative part of the mind generates ideas, events, and metaphors, the raw material that makes fresh, interesting writing. In contrast, they associate intellect with criticism. The critical part of the mind judges content, organization, and logic, the refined evaluation that makes accurate, coherent writing. Intuition fuels the creative process; intellect guides the critical process. Through the creative process, writers *invent* their material; through the critical process, they evaluate and organize it for readers.

Both creative and critical abilities are necessary to write successfully. The creative process, however, is less self-conscious than the critical process. As a consequence, prewriting activities use the creative process while restraining the more self-conscious critical process.

Freewriting

Freewriting, or brainstorming, is valuable during any phase of the writing process. Freewriting is a method of free association for generating ideas. Freewriting can help you to frame a subject more accurately, generate material, clarify a purpose, and even develop a thesis. But perhaps its most important use is to start the actual writing process.

Once you have a subject, no matter how tentative, set aside some time for a writing session (as we advised you to do when compiling a memory list). While freewriting, abandon the urge to criticize yourself. Instead let the creative process take over, especially if you have a little voice in your head that automatically judges your writing efforts.

To direct the process, write your subject at the top of the page. Then go at it. Write down everything that comes to mind. Associate one idea to another. Don't judge your ideas or shut them out. Often the unexpected will present itself, ideas connecting to ideas in ways you could have never planned. Don't be concerned with the technical aspects of writing—grammar, punctuation, sentence structure, or logic. Merely enter the creative flow of your own thought, excluding the critical process. Remember—this draft is for your eyes only, not for your reader's. It is a rough map of your thought process, a chart of your mental meanderings, not a paper to be graded. About his freewriting process, Lane Williams says,

> Freewriting helps me gain perspective on my subject. The process releases a great deal of information I have some-how stored in my memory. By free writing, that is, merely following the pattern of my thought, I gain access to that information. The hard part, of course, is sorting through all that I have written.

The examination of freewriting can be difficult. You will quickly discover that much of your freewriting will not help you to develop an effective essay, such as obvious observations, clichéd thinking, dead-end ideas, stalled musings, odd digressions, but other parts will be valuable—"hot" ideas that you can pursue. Evaluating the material in freewriting involves the intellect more directly; that is, now apply the critical eye to decide what material will help develop an effective paper and what will not.

While reading your prewritten draft, mark passages that seem to be hot leads for further exploration. Once you have the leads, you can use them to start another freewriting session to generate more new material.

Freewriting will also reveal what you do not know about a subject. This knowledge can direct your search to the library; to class notes; to discussions with relatives, friends, or teachers; or to any number of sources that will be helpful. All these activities will help to define a general purpose and generate material for your final essay.

Asking Questions

Frame questions about a subject, sometimes referred to as reporter's questions: Who? What? When? Where? Why? and sometimes How?

Of course, not every question will be appropriate for your particular subject, but using the ones that are can ignite an association chain that will help you to view your subject from different perspectives.

For example, the subject of rude behavior could be approached through the following questions:

What is rude behavior?
Who is rude?
Who is affected by rudeness?
Who can change rude behavior?
What causes rudeness?
What is my attitude toward rudeness?
When did I first become interested in rudeness?
Where have I seen rude behavior?
Why are people rude?
How can rude behavior be corrected?

Asking questions will get you started on most general assignments. Keep in mind, though, that you might have to tailor questions for more specialized assignments.

Sort and Group Your Material

The freewriting is complete. Now is the time to sort and group your ideas in a logical arrangement. Here, one of two common strategies will help—clustering and informal outlining.

Clustering

Clustering visually shows the relationships between ideas. Often freewriting appears to create a hodgepodge of unrelated material, but if you rearrange the material around the central purpose that emerges from the freewritten draft, then you can begin to see connections. In one sense, a cluster brings order to the creative chaos.

Begin a cluster in a simple fashion. Write what you have determined to be your essay's purpose in the center of the page. Draw a circle around the purpose. As you examine the prewritten draft, arrange major ideas around the central purpose in "orbits" connected by lines. Also circle the major ideas. As you discover (or develop) ideas related to the major ideas, create another orbiting system. All this is done in single words or brief phrases. Remember that you can always return to the prewritten draft to examine the full entry. Through this process, you are simply dividing and subdividing your roughly drafted material, becoming more specific as you isolate facts, opinions, examples, and specific details that could be used effectively to develop your purpose.

Here is a tip: Be prepared to create more than one cluster. Clustering, like freewriting, often generates even more material. We also suggest you develop your cluster on a large piece of drawing paper, or at least be prepared to tape several sheets of notebook paper together to accommodate all your material.

Lane Williams created a cluster from his prewritten material. Examine the part of it that is reproduced in Figure 2–1.

Informal Outlining

Another approach to sorting and grouping your material involves arranging the major ideas related to your purpose under broad headings in an informal outline, or "scratch" outline. The complexity of the outline depends on how you like to work. It might include only the broadest heading, or it might include broad headings followed by more specific points, even phrases that capture specific information.

You might create several drafts of a scratch outline, each becoming more specific. Gradually, drafts of scratch outlines might suggest your essay's final development pattern.

If you find yourself dissatisfied with your outlines, rather than spending a great deal of time rewriting them, photocopy them and then cut and paste the photocopies until you have one that satisfies you.

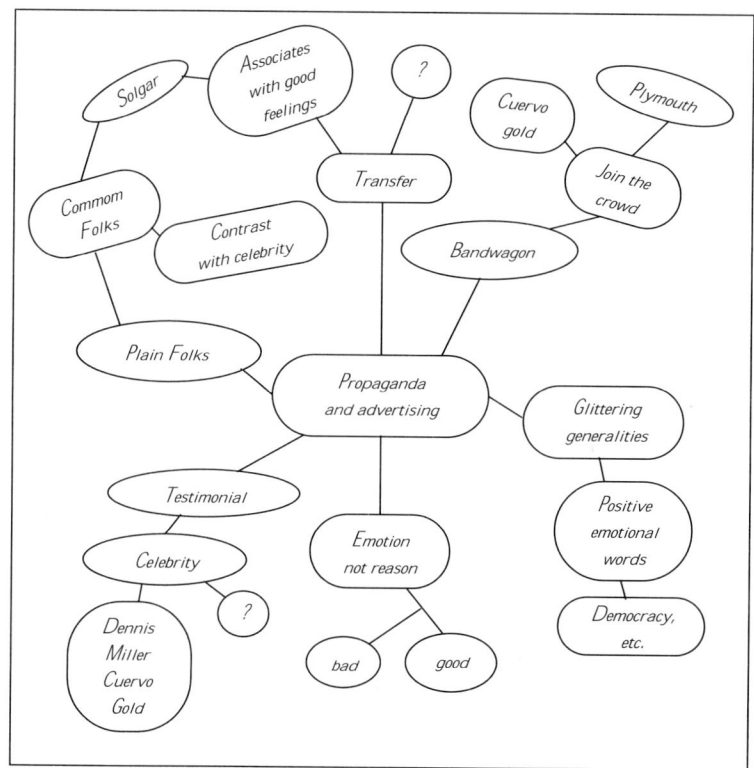

Figure 2–1

The example in Figure 2–2 shows part of the detailed scratch outline that Lane Williams developed from his cluster. About this outline Williams writes,

> I wasn't happy with just clustering. Eventually I have to develop a sense of my material as I imagine it will unfold in the essay. I'm not obsessed with detail or perfection at this stage of the writing process, but I do need to create a strong impression of how the development takes place. The cluster didn't give me the space to add the detail I wanted. For me,

Propaganda and advertising
  What is it: appeals to emotion
              rather than reason.
              Use for good and bad causes.

Methods:
  ① *Glittering Generalities:* Positive words to
  Develop   stir strong values.
  a list of   "Motherhood"
  G. G.   "Manhood"
              "American Way"

  ② *Bandwagon:* Invites consumers to
              join the crowd.
                Plymouth minivan – Health Club
                Cuervo Gold – Yuppie Crowd standing in an
                empty pool, drinking margaritas

                Link to Testimonial – Dennis Miller

  ③ *Testimonial:* Celebrities praise products
                Dennis Miller/Cuervo Gold – two methods
                working together.
                Develop extensive list of celebrities...
                include old Joe Namath ad for
                laughs.

Figure 2–2

an informal outline is a strong preliminary plan that helps me to see where I need to delete information or develop more information.

Develop a Thesis Statement

Always keep in mind that any essay you write unfolds through a process. Although throughout this discussion we describe the writing process as if it follows a predictable pattern, in actual practice you will find it does not always do so. An essay evolves, often changing its direction as you encounter new information and uncover new relationships in your material. Nevertheless, if there is a point at which an essay's final direction and shape become clear, it is at the point at which you form a clear thesis statement.

A thesis statement embodies your essay's central purpose. It is the statement that all the following paragraphs support, argue for, or illustrate. The thesis statement should be broad enough to serve as an umbrella for the discussion that follows it while at the same time it should limit the discussion to a manageable size. In other words, the thesis statement marks the territory of the essay.

Pause for a moment to consider how useful a clearly stated thesis statement is for writers and readers.

For writers, a thesis statement articulates the central purpose and keeps the essay unified. Once you have a clear thesis statement, you will find it easier to make decisions about what to include and exclude. If you have trouble developing your thesis statement, then you know that you must seek more information to flesh out your content.

For readers, a thesis statement tells where the essay is headed. A clearly phrased thesis statement helps them to put your discussion paragraphs in perspective. Imagine the burden you place on a reader if you develop several paragraphs but fail to provide the perspective to understand their purpose. A thesis statement provides that perspective.

Limit the Thesis

What are the characteristics of an effective thesis statement?

An effective thesis statement, usually expressed in a single sentence, limits the central purpose of your essay. If you were writing about crime, for example, and tried to develop the thesis statement "Crime is destroying the social fabric of America," you would soon discover the impossibility of your task. This thesis statement is much too broad for a three- or four-page essay. At best, you could develop only a few general—very general—observations, all unsupported by much specific detail. This thesis statement could be limited, however. Writers limit their thesis statements in two ways.

Limit the Subject.   As it now stands, the subject of the thesis statement is crime. But crime covers a large territory that includes murder, robbery, swindles, shoplifting, and so on. If the writer were to concentrate on one aspect of crime and modify the word *crime* to reflect that concentration, then the subject would be limited.

> *Violent* crime is destroying the social fabric of America.
> *Gang* crime is destroying the social fabric of America.
> Crime *against children* is destroying the social fabric of America.

Limit the Predicate.   These examples are still too broad, much too broad, for a brief essay, even though the subject is more narrow. Another way to limit a thesis is to limit the predicate part, in this example the part that reads "is destroying the social fabric of America."

The phrase "the social fabric of America" covers a great deal of territory, but if the writer were to write about his or her direct experience, the phrase might be narrowed to a city, town, or neighborhood.

> Violent crime is destroying the social fabric of my neighborhood.
> Gang crime is destroying the social fabric of my hometown.
> Crime against children is destroying the social fabric of our local elementary schools.

These statements are now manageable. A writer could develop them from personal observation, police reports, and newspaper articles.

State a Thesis Precisely

An effective thesis statement is always stated precisely and lends itself to development. Vague language and overly general assertions misguide readers. Use precise language, not fuzzy words, to phrase your thesis statement.

Not: The study of people in prisons is fascinating.

But: Psychological studies of imprisoned murderers reveal that the death penalty is no deterrent to killers.

The second example, phrased precisely in specific language, leaves no room for the reader to be confused about the purpose of this paper.

Finally, an effective thesis statement makes a promise to the reader to fulfill the essay's purpose, a promise the writer must keep or risk writing an unsuccessful essay.

For example, consider the following three thesis statements:

If a thug has the firepower, holding up a mom and pop grocery store is a simple process.

The promise: To explain the easy process of robbing the innocent.

Although there were over 450 arrests in my neighborhood last year, crime can be categorized into three groups.

The promise: To classify local crime.

Some people think the political buzz phrase "law and order" has something to do with putting criminals behind bars, but in reality it has a racist definition.

The promise: To redefine the political phrase "law and order."

Lane Williams developed his thesis statement in several phases. He says,

> By the time I had finished freewriting and grouping my material, I had a pretty clear idea of my general purpose. I wanted to expose how some advertisers misguide consumers. After I developed more material by reviewing class notes and finding some typical advertisements, I decided it was time to formulate a more specific purpose, that is, a thesis statement that would keep me on track.

I began with this statement: "The public needs to become aware of how advertisers deceive them." Sounds lame, doesn't it? At least that's what I thought. Just too vague. I rephrased it: "The public needs to know how advertisers use propaganda to deceive them." I didn't like this either. What was I, the public guardian? Mr. District Attorney? The statement made me feel pretentious. But when I had written the word "propaganda," my mind started firing. The assignment called for a discussion of propaganda so the word had to be in my thesis. Moreover, the word stirred up my anger. I hate to be tricked by people, and bottom line, that's what advertisers do—they trick people. So now I was on to my thesis, which finally became "Advertisers use propaganda devices to trick consumers into buying their products." I wasn't sure this statement would be phrased this way in my final draft, but I knew it would help me arrange my paper—and announce what to expect to the reader.

Develop a Formal Plan with a Reader in Mind

If you have not done so already, now is the time to imagine your reader. The reader you conceive in your imagination will influence choices you make about the content and vocabulary of your essay. If you were separately to report the events at an accident scene to a friend, your parents, a police officer, an insurance agent, or as a witness in court you would select different details and words for each occasion. In speech you make this adjustment quite easily. In writing you have to give this adjustment some thought. It is essential, therefore, that before you get too far into the writing process, you imagine who your reader will be so that you can determine how much he or she might already know about your subject, which will help you decide what to include and exclude.

For example, although Lane Williams was writing a paper for a critical thinking course, he decided his reader would be the "average consumer," one who did not know the meaning of propaganda and would not understand the way advertisers use it. This decision and the formulation of his thesis statement meant that he was ready to develop a more formal plan for his essay.

One method to plan your essay is to create a formal outline. Whereas an informal outline will help you to sort and group prewriting around ideas, a formal outline will help you to see the final arrangement of the material. A formal outline will include the thesis statement, the subpoints, and various levels of detail depending on the subject's complexity.

A formal outline can be written in topic or sentence form. The main items will be identified by Roman numerals, the first sublevel of items by capital letters, the second sublevel by Arabic numerals, the third sublevel by lowercase letters, the fourth sublevel by Arabic numerals enclosed in parentheses, and the fifth sublevel by lowercase letters enclosed in parentheses. All letters and numbers at the same level are indented to fall directly under one another.

```
I.   _____
  A. _____
  B. _____
     1. _____
     2. _____
        a. _____
        b. _____
           (1) _____
           (2) _____
               (a) _____
               (b) _____
II.  _____
```

You will rarely need all six levels, especially for college essays. But notice that each level is a division of the level above it. Therefore there must be two items at every level because, logically, a topic cannot be divided into one item. You cannot have an A without a B or a 1 without a 2, for example. Of course, there may be more than two items at any level.

Also keep in mind that all items at the same level must be expressed in parallel grammatical structure and the first word in each item must be capitalized. The following example is a formal topic outline for "Who's Come a Long Way, Consumers?"

Thesis: Advertisers use propaganda devices to trick consumers into buying their products.

I. Propaganda appeals to emotion not reason
   A. Glittering generalities
   B. Advertisers and propaganda

II. Bandwagon says join the crowd
   A. Plymouth minivan
   B. Cuervo Gold and bandwagon

III. Testimonial features celebrities
   A. Cuervo Gold and Dennis Miller
   B. All-star list
      1. Michael Jackson for soft drink
      2. Michael Jordan for shoes
      3. June Allyson for diapers
      4. Martha Raye for denture cleaner
      5. Joe Namath for pantyhose

IV. Plain folks features the common people
   A. Common folks list
      1. Dentist for toothpaste
      2. Neighbor for coffee
      3. Coach for detergent
   B. Solgar Vitamin Supplements

V. Transfer associates with good feelings
   A. Marlboro cigarettes and the outdoors
      1. Cowboys
      2. Western gear
   B. Virginia Slims and female independence
      1. Today's woman
      2. Yesterday's woman

VI. Advertising works

Developing a formal outline forces you to arrange your material for a reader. Throughout the process of constructing a formal outline, you will draw on the informal outline that you constructed earlier, your prewritten material, and any other material you collected. About his outlining process, Williams says,

> This is the first outline I have written. Before I finished I had my rough outline, prewriting, class notes, and the advertisements I planned to use as examples in a pile on my desk. I kept moving through the material, thinking how it should be arranged. I ended up with some surprises.
>
> For instance, I had planned to use glittering generalities as the topic for a discussion paragraph, but while outlining, I realized I didn't have enough material for a full discussion. As a result, I used it in the introduction.
>
> I decided to discuss transfer last because I thought my readers would be familiar with the Marlboro and Virginia Slims advertisements, and I also found them to be the most interesting.
>
> All in all, I discovered that writing a formal outline forced me to think through the actual essay before I started my first full draft. Looking back on the experience, I believe it saved me time overall.

Too often, beginning writers want to skip formal planning, yet it is an important part of the writing process, one that will force you to figure out the final arrangement of your material.

Develop Parts of the Essay

At this point in the writing process you should be aware of your reader and the conventions you will use to guide your reader. In other words, you are consciously trying to meet the writer–reader contract by seeing and shaping your material with a critical eye.

To start, reread the final draft of Lane Williams's essay (pp. 30–34). Study how the material from his formal plan was developed into a full essay. Clearly, his initial strategy was to arrange his material in a traditional fashion—that is, to structure his essay with a clear introduction, discussion, and conclusion.

Write the Introduction

In a thesis-support essay the introduction presents the thesis statement. Actually, the term "presents" is not dramatic enough. Let's say that the introduction "showcases" a thesis statement, because to showcase is to display in a way the reader cannot miss. Remember that your thesis statement is your promise to the reader. Don't let the reader miss the promise.

Also remember that the introduction is your chance to grab the reader's interest, but too often student writers waste their introductions. They offer sweeping generalizations. They write aimless, dull comments. They end the sequence with an ill-phrased thesis statement. You should make your introductions do much more. Professional writers tend to use one of six strategies to begin their essays:

1. Relate a dramatic anecdote.
2. Expose a commonly held belief.
3. Present surprising facts and statistics.
4. Use a provocative quotation or question.
5. Create a dramatic narrative example.
6. Define a key term.

Any of these is an effective strategy to begin your essay—if it fits your purpose. That's the key to writing an effective introduction: It must be grounded in the essay's purpose and lead to the thesis statement.

Often introductions are only a paragraph long and end with the thesis statement. But an introduction can be one, two, three, or any number of paragraphs in length. We suggest that it be no longer than a fifth of the length of your entire essay, a reasonable length that should be determined by the complexity of your purpose.

Whatever approach you choose for your introduction, re-member that it is an integral part of the essay. It should grow from your purpose, arouse a reader's interest, and showcase the thesis statement, usually by placing it in the closing sentences of the in-troduction.

Write the Discussion

The discussion develops and supports the thesis statement. Discussion paragraphs present the subpoints and supporting de-tail necessary to convince your reader that the thesis statement is reasonable. In other words, the discussion keeps the promise implied in the thesis.

To be effective, discussion paragraphs should follow three paragraph conventions: They should be unified, coherent, and well developed.

Keep Paragraphs Unified. Discussion paragraphs are uni-fied when the information they present is clearly related to the main idea in the paragraph, which some writers shape in the form of a topic sentence. For example, consider the following para-graph from Olivia Vlahos's *Human Beginnings*. Vlahos opens with a clearly stated topic sentence, "Nearly all living creatures manage some form of communication," and follows with a series of exam-ples, each clearly related to the topic sentence.

Topic sentence sets a direction.

Series of examples clearly relates to the main idea.

Nearly all living creatures manage some form of communication. The dance patterns of bees in their hive help to point the way to distant flower fields or announce successful foraging. Male stickleback fish regularly swim up-side-down to indicate outrage in a courtship contest. Male deer and lemurs mark territorial ownership by rubbing their own body secretions on

{ boundary stones or trees. Everyone
has seen a frightened dog put his tail
between his legs and run in panic. We,
too, use gestures, expressions, postures, and movement to give our
words point.

Keep in mind also that the main idea or topic sentence is one step in fulfilling your promise to the reader. It identifies one subpoint of the thesis and supports that subpoint. For example, Lane Williams begins this process in his first discussion paragraph. He clearly relates his opening topic sentence to his thesis statement, which maintains that advertisers use propaganda devices to trick consumers into buying their products.

Williams's topic sentence establishes the subpoint "bandwagon."	Bandwagon is another technique advertisers use to trick consumers into buying their products. Through bandwagon, they urge people to buy a product because it is popular—that is, because everyone is doing it together.
Brief definition of "bandwagon."	This call to "get on the bandwagon" appeals to the strong desire to join the crowd rather than be an outsider. An early 1990s television advertisement for Plymouth's mini van uses bandwagon to motivate car buyers. The advertisement features a group of people working out in a gym. A message over the loudspeaker announces, "There is a Plymouth mini van parked in the street." The message is clear: If you want to be part of the crowd, buy a mini van. An early 1990s magazine advertisement for Cuervo Gold tequila also makes use of bandwagon. The advertisement features sixteen young party people either sitting on the edge or standing in an empty swimming
Bandwagon example 1	
Bandwagon example 2	

> pool. They are clearly enjoying them-
> selves, each holding a margarita and
> toasting the viewer outside the adver-
> tisement. Clearly, a Cuervo Gold party
> is fun. The message is that the con-
> sumer can join the party. How? Quite
> <u>obviously, buy Cuervo Gold . . . and</u>
> <u>hop on the bandwagon.</u>

While this paragraph is unified because the entire discussion relates to its topic sentence, it also adds to the overall unity of the essay because the topic sentence refers back to the thesis statement.
Echoing the thesis statement in topic sentences is an effective
strategy to use throughout an essay. The technique reminds the
reader of your thesis and shows how the subpoints are connected.

Maintain Coherence. Guide your readers smoothly and
logically from one sentence to another. Don't let them stray from
the direction you establish in the paragraph's opening. If they
do stray, you risk losing their attention. When a paragraph
flows smoothly and logically, the paragraph is coherent; that is,
the main idea advances from sentence to sentence in a well
constructed verbal web.

You can create coherence in your paragraphs in three conventional ways:

1. By repeating and rephrasing key words and concepts;
2. By using pronouns to refer to key nouns in previous sentences; and
3. By using transitional expressions that guide your reader
   through a paragraph.

Poet and novelist Erica Jong repeats a key word to create
coherence in the following paragraph from "The Artist as
Housewife." The paragraph's main idea deals with a poet's problem of creating a personal voice in her work. Jong then associates
with *authenticity* in the second sentence. She then repeats or
rephrases the key word *authenticity* throughout the paragraph.

Writer maintains coherence by effectively repeating "key word."

The main problem of the poet is to raise a voice. We can suffer all kinds of kinks and flaws in a poet's work except lack of authenticity. Authenticity is a difficult thing to define, but roughly it has to do with our sense of the poet as a mensch, a human being, an author (with the accent on authority). Poets arrive at authenticity in very different ways. Each poet finds her own road by walking it—sometimes backward, sometimes at a trot. To achieve authenticity you have to know who you are and approximately why. You have to know yourself not only as defined by the roles you play but also as a creature with an inner life, a creature built around an inner darkness. Because women are always encouraged to see themselves as role players

Rephrase this "key idea." and helpers ("help-mate" as a synonym for "wife" is illuminating here), rather than as separate beings, they find it hard to grasp this authentic sense of self. They have too many easy cop-outs.

In the following paragraph, conservationist Cleveland Amory repeats a key noun—coyotes—and uses pronouns to refer back to it.

Coherence is created by the effective use of key nouns and their pronouns.

The coyote's only hope lies in his cleverness. And stories of coyotes outwitting hunters are legion. Coyotes will work in teams, alternately resting and running to escape dogs set upon them. They have even been known to jump on automobiles and flat cars to escape dogs. And they have also successfully resisted bombing. Lewis Nordyke reports that once when a favorite coyote haunt in Texas became a practice range for bombing, the coyotes left—temporarily. Soon they were back to investigate and found that the bombing kept people out. They decided to stay. Meanwhile, they learned the bombing schedule and avoided bombs.

Conscious and careful repetition of key words and ideas is a subtle way to keep a paragraph coherent. A more direct strategy is to use transitional words and phrases. In "Who's Come a Long Way, Consumers?" Lane Williams uses overt transitions effectively in one paragraph.

Williams uses overt transitions to create coherence.

A recent advertisement for Solgar Vitamin Supplements features a potent use of the plain folks device. This advertisement features a young attractive working mother, who is obviously a single parent trying to make ends meet. In the middle of the advertisement, she stands behind her son, smiling with her arms wrapped around him in a protective embrace, and looks directly at the viewer. The son, about eight years old, is also smiling and holding on to his mother's arm. Both seem to be healthy and to care deeply for each other. Above the photograph is the phrase "First Things First," suggesting that loved ones come first. Below the photograph, the son is quoted as saying, "You're the most important thing to me,

> Mom. Please take care of yourself."
> Featured next to the comment is a
> bottle of Solgar Vitamins. Implicitly,
> the average working mother and son
> are testifying to the power of Solgar
> Vitamins to maintain their health and
> their loving relationship.

No matter what strategy you use to create coherence, remember that the purpose is to direct the reader's attention as he or she reads from sentence to sentence.

Develop Paragraph Talk.   Beginning writers often ask the question, how long should a paragraph be? Paragraph length depends on several considerations: the complexity of material, the rhetorical method, and the length of preceding and following paragraphs. But most important, a paragraph should be developed enough to do justice to the main idea.

Well-developed paragraphs might contain examples, definitions, comparisons, causes, effects, facts, statistics—all presented in enough detail to make a paragraph several hundred words long, or a paragraph might serve as a transition between subpoints of a thesis statement and be only a sentence or two long. When a paragraph becomes exceptionally long, writers will often separate the material into two or more paragraphs to ease the reading process, even though the information amplifies the main idea in a single subpoint. For example, Williams breaks up several exceptionally long paragraphs in "Who's Come a Long Way, Consumers?" as the following example illustrates:

Topic sentence
introduces transfer.

> Also at work in this Solgar adver-
> tisement and in most advertisements, for
> that matter, is another propaganda device
> called transfer. Through transfer advertis-
> ers attempt to lure consumers into buying

First extended example of transfer.

their products by associating them with something consumers love, desire, or respect. No manufacturer uses transfer more effectively than Philip Morris, Inc. For over two decades Philip Morris has effectively transferred the desire for the rugged cowboy's outdoor life to smoking Marlboro cigarettes. Marlboro advertisements feature images of cowboys herding cattle or riding horses across open spaces. More recently, Marlboro has effectively transferred the desire for the rugged cowboy's outdoor life to smoking Marlboro cigarettes. Marlboro advertisements feature images of cowboys herding cattle or riding horses across open spaces. More recently, Marlboro has concentrated less on cowboys at work and more on equipment these Marlboro men use: worn boots, spurs, lariats, saddles—each item designed to remind the reader of a life spent on open prairies with snow-capped mountains in the background. And, in case the consumer misses the point, Marlboro advertisements usually include the slogan, "Come to Marlboro Country." How can consumers reach "Marlboro Country"? By lighting up a Marlboro cigarette, of course, thus completing the transfer.

Opening sentence continues the main idea from the previous paragraph.

Philip Morris also makes effective use of transfer in its Virginia Slims magazine campaign. Each advertisement features a beautiful woman staring boldly into the camera. Clearly, she is in charge of her life, the embodiment of the 1990s image of an independent woman. In a box placed in the corner of these advertisements is a contrasting image, a photograph of a woman from an earlier historical period serving a man. An ironic slogan links the two images, "You've come a long way, baby" (ironic because "baby" echoes sexism).

Second extended example of transfer.

> Without much analysis the advertiser's ploy here is clear. Philip Morris hopes to entice women into smoking Virginia Slims by transferring a desire for personal independence to its product.

In the opening sentence, Williams sets up the transition from one paragraph to another by referring to the previous discussion of Solgar Vitamin Supplements. He then develops the main paragraph idea with a brief definition of the transfer device. He follows with the analysis to two extended examples to show transfer at work in advertisements. But since the examples are long, he breaks the paragraph into parts, yet both parts amplify a single main idea—that is, advertisers use the transfer device to trick consumers. Williams is careful to begin the second paragraph with an opening statement that clearly shows the discussion of transfer is continuing, even though he has begun a new paragraph.

While composing an essay, you might discover that you need more information to develop an effective paragraph. You can take three actions: First, you can return to your freewriting draft for an idea. Second, you can actually develop more freewriting. Third, you can consult outside sources for more information. The process of inventing and acquiring material continues until the final draft is complete.

Write the Conclusion

Too often beginning writers treat their conclusions in a perfunctory manner—a couple of general statements about the subject and a rapid "That's all, folks" to close. Experienced writers, in contrast, use a different strategy based on the simple principle that readers remember best what they read last. They therefore treat their conclusions as a challenge, one that demands skill and concentration. Generally, writers use one of four common strategies to close their essays:

1. Review the subpoints and restate the essay's thesis statement.
2. Recommend a course of action.
3. Offer a prediction based on the discussion.
4. Present an appropriate quotation or anecdote that leads a reader to reflect about the subject.

Keep in mind that a conclusion must flow logically from the essay. If it does not, it will merely seem tacked on.

Create a Title

Titles are not afterthoughts, a phrase hastily typed at the top of the page before rushing to class. A title actually begins the essay. Titles should suggest the general subject and serve as an invitation to read the essay.

The best time to compose a title is after you have written your essay. Only then will you know the complete content. The title should be brief but interesting and may be taken directly from the essay. Often, however, it will echo a thought that runs through the essay. About his title, "Who's Come a Long Way, Consumers?" Lane Williams says,

> I usually have a hard time thinking of titles, but if I reread the essay or parts of it enough, a title will eventually come to mind . . . persistence, I guess, is my method.
>
> The title "Who's Come a Long Way, Consumers?" is my way of reworking the Virginia Slims slogan. I hope it is read ironically, since my essay's purpose is to make unaware consumers conscious of ploys advertisers use to get their hard-earned cash.

So how should you proceed in composing a title? Well, we can offer no clear guidelines because the process involves more intuition than logic. But once you have a title follow this rule: Never underline or place quotation marks around your own title. Use quotation marks or underlining for other people's titles, not yours.

Edit and Revise Your Sentences for Clarity

Once you have a well-structured essay in hand, you can begin the editing and revision process that will lead to the final draft. You might think each phase of the writing process refines the material for the final draft—and each does—but the final draft is the only part of the process your reader will see. We therefore suggest that you approach revision with care.

During the early phases of the composing process, we mentioned that you should imagine your reader. Now the reader becomes a major part of the process, as if he or she is sitting on your shoulder as you make revision decisions.

As you reread your essay with an eye toward revision, consider its style (see p. 9). Style, as you probably recall, has to do with word selection, sentence length and variety, and tone. For college papers, we suggest you employ a plain style that communicates your purpose clearly and directly. You should write in standard American English, which is taught in schools and used in mainstream magazines and newspapers. In most writing situations, standard English is appropriate.

Standard American English can be formal or informal. Informal writing is characterized by common expressions taken from spoken English and makes use of contractions such as "don't," "can't," "won't," and "could've," which are contractions of "do not," "cannot," "will not," and "could have." Formal written English seldom uses contractions and avoids other characteristics of informal writing, such as abbreviations and the personal point of view. About his style decision, Lane Williams says,

> I tried to conform to my instructor's view of English, which leans toward the formal. You may have noticed for instance that I avoided using some common abbreviations. I wrote out "television" and "advertisement" instead of using the more common "TV" and "ad." I also avoided using contractions, to create a more formal tone. I did, however, ad-

dress my reader as "you" now and then and used the personal pronouns "we" and "our" several times, decisions some instructors might discourage.

At this point in the writing process, you are ready to edit and revise your sentences to make them more readable. Unfortunately, no one has invented a clear procedure to follow in editing and revising prose. Some writers revise as they carefully work their way through a rough draft; others swoop through the first draft and then revise during a second or third draft. Each writer, it seems, devises his or her own approach.

Two preliminary steps in revision do seem to be adopted by all writers. First, they must learn what makes sentences effective. Second, they must pick up a pencil (or keyboard) and go to work on their sentences. Toward that end, we offer the following ten editing tips for refining sentences. We suggest that you study the ten tips with care before revising the sentences in your rough draft.

Ten Tips for Revising Sentences

1. Eliminate clutter.
2. Select specific and concrete words.
3. Make passive sentences active.
4. Rewrite trite expressions.
5. Place modifiers with care.
6. Correct faulty pronoun reference.
7. Eliminate inconsistencies.
8. Complete incomplete sentences.
9. Eliminate sexist language.
10. Revise for parallelism.

You should revise sentences with an eye for effectiveness—that is, for clarity, conciseness, diction, and style. Reread the essay slowly, preferably out loud. The ear often detects problems that the eye misses. As you read, make improvements directly on the page.

Ten Guidelines for Revision

1. Eliminate clutter.

Your goal is to write in a simple, clear style. Your words should be easily understood, and your sentences should move with some speed. You must therefore cut clutter from your sentences.

Cut empty phrases.

Often one or two words can replace a phrase.

              believes
Roland Barthes ~~is of the opinion~~ that culture can be

understood by reading the "signs" it generates.

       Diet   **usually**
~~It is usually the case that diet~~ books encourage the dieter's

fantasies about being slim.

Replace common empty phrases with shorter and clearer ways of saying the same thing.

Empty Phrase	Replacements
come to the realization	realize, see
of the opinion that	think, believe
in order to	to
present with	give
for the purpose of	for
in the nature of	like
concerning the matter of	about
prior to	before
subsequent to	after
during the course of	during
in the event that	if
in the amount of	for

regardless of the fact that	although
at this point in time	now
at that point in time	then
at any point in time	whenever
on the occasion of	when
in view of the fact that	as, since, because
for the reason that	because
make contact with	call
it is often the case that	often
the fact that	that
for the simple reason that	because
due to the fact that	because
on the occasion of	when, on
give consideration to	consider
make an adjustment	adjust
is of the opinion	believes
give encouragement to	encourage
make inquiry	ask
comes into conflict with	conflicts
give instruction to	instruct

Cut unnecessary there are *and* there is *constructions.*

The word *there* followed by a form of the plain verb *to be* is an expletive, a word used to fill out a sentence. Rewrite such sentences so that they are direct.

They disagreed for
~~There were~~ two reasons. ~~for the disagreement~~.

little
~~There is little~~ we can do for the rain forests.

Cut intensifiers.

Cut words such as *very, really, quite, totally, completely, definitely,* and *so.* When speaking, people use them with vocal emphasis.

The ~~really terrible~~ storm ripped across the bay and ~~totally~~

destroyed business buildings and homes when it hit shore. The

result was ~~very~~ disastrous: ~~So much~~ wreckage, ~~so many~~ helpless

people, ~~so many~~ lost dreams. The sight was ~~really~~ heart

breaking.

In writing, emphasis comes from using strong, specific words, not from vacant intensifiers.

Cut pretentious language.

Pretentious writing draws attention to itself. Pretentious vocabulary is unnecessarily complex, perhaps because the writer has thumbed through a thesaurus, replacing simple with difficult words. Always try to select simple, direct words.

The earthquake **killed** ~~struck with a malignant force that destroyed~~

~~the lives of~~ more than four thousand villagers.

Children ~~frolicking~~ **playing** with ~~their companions exhibit~~ **friends show** these fears.

~~Domesticated canines will contribute felicity to anyone's life.~~ **Dogs make good pets.**

Cut repetition and redundancy.

Repetition of key words is often necessary for parallel structure or for emphasis, but needless repetition leads to wordy sentences.

The Pacific ~~rattlesnake~~ **rattler** is California's most dangerous snake.

Redundancy unnecessarily conveys the same meaning twice, as in the phrases "visible to the eye" and "large in size."

By probing the ~~factual truth deeply~~ facts, researchers found the

solution.

Millions of ~~people who vote~~ voters support national health insurance.

Cut any of the following common redundancies from your writing:

advance forward	continue to go on
autobiography of her life	disappear from sight
basic fundamentals	factual truth
circle around	important essential
close proximity	refer back
combine together	repeat again
consensus of opinion	round in shape

2. Select specific and concrete words.

Definite, specific, and concrete language pulls the reader to the page. General, vague, and abstract language pushes the reader from the page. As an ad writer might phrase this thought: Vivid language gives an "up-close" feeling; vague language gives a "far-back" feeling.

Far Back
He was old when he gained success.

Up Close
He had turned gray and had seen his seventy-first birthday when he won the Nobel Prize.

Far Back
The police arrested him in an alley.

Up Close
Six police officers with drawn pistols captured him in an alley.

Far Back
At Bernard's the sales staff greets customers courteously.

Up Close
At Bernard's the sales staff greets customers with a smile.

Far Back
For me to write an essay takes patience.

Up Close
For me to write an essay takes hours of pacing and pencil chewing, at least a hundred pages covered with useless scribbling, and several pots of black coffee.

Revise slang.

Slang can be colorful vocabulary that arises from the experience of a group of people with common interests, such as teenagers, rock stars, jazz musicians, actors, baseball fans, street gangs, surfers, skateboarders, even truck drivers. However, in college writing, you should generally revise your sentences to eliminate slang because it is imprecise and can be confusing.

As a type, comedians are ~~bummed out~~ (depressed) one moment and ~~flying~~ (elated) the next.

The reviewers ~~ragged on~~ (criticized) Kaufmann's poetry collection for being sentimental.

Revise euphemisms.

A euphemism is a word or phrase substituted for another word that is harsh or blunt. The funeral industry substitutes "loved one" or "the deceased" for "corpse," "vault" for "coffin," and "final resting place" for "grave."

Although euphemisms might often be necessary for tactfulness, they more frequently distract us from the realities of experience. We have become accustomed to "low-income," "inner city," and "correctional facility" as substitutes for "poor," "slum" or "ghetto," and "jail."

If you find euphemistic phrasing when revising your sentences, rewrite the phrase in more specific language.

His money problems
~~The deterioration of his economic status~~ began when he ~~became~~

lost his job.
~~unemployed~~.

lying
Military officials seem to believe that ~~misrepresenting the facts~~

is acceptable. ~~behavior.~~

Replace weak verbs with strong verbs.

Use strong, accurate verbs. For example, consider something as simple as saying how a man "walked."

The man *walked* down the street.

If you wanted to tell how the man walked, you might write,

A man *walked quickly* down the street.

Or you might say he *walked rapidly*. But a strong, more accurate verb could do it better:

A man *scurried* down the street.
A man *strode* down the street.
A man *swaggered* down the street.

When revising, check to see whether you can replace weak with strong verbs. Remember to select verbs that fit what you're saying; don't pick them because they sound fancy. For instance, you wouldn't be helping your prose much if you wrote, "A drunk perambulated down the street"—unless you wanted to get a laugh. Instead of *perambulate*, you would probably write *staggered*.

You might say that finding active verbs is easy to do for description, but what about using them in expository or argumentative writing? Well, it can be done. Read the following passage from C. M. Bowra's *Classical Greece:*

> The Greeks won their war with a famous ruse that military men and statesmen often *try to repeat* in other ways. They *gave* Troy a gift—a wooden horse with Greeks hidden inside. While the Trojans *slept*, the Greeks *crept* out and *opened* the city's gates to the rest of their army. Masters at last, the Greek soldiers *saw* Helen reunited with Menelaus, and everyone *started* for home. But one among them, the ingenious Odysseus who had *devised* the wooden horse trick, *found* the route 10 years long.

Verbs and verb phrases such as *won, gave, try to repeat, slept, crept, opened, saw, started, devised,* and *found* make this passage active. Whenever you can, use strong verbs to generate life in any writing you do.

Rewrite hidden verbs disguised as nouns.

In the following sentences, *was led, search,* and *perform* are not the real verbs. *Solved, replace,* and *analyze* are the real verbs, but they are hidden because they are disguised as nouns.

I ~~was led to the solution of~~ solved Travanian's identity.

Since John Simmons quit the committee, we must ~~search for a~~ replace him. ~~replacement.~~

To understand The Deer Hunter we must ~~perform an analysis~~ **analyze** ~~of~~ its imagery.

Avoid overuse of to be *verbs.*

Revise sentences and passages that overuse forms of to be. Often they add clutter to your writing.

At sixty-three, Max Ernst ~~Max Ernst was sixty-three and~~ knew madness and death **lay** ~~were~~

before him.

The ~~sun was setting. The~~ **setting sun turned the** few clouds ~~that were~~ on the horizon ~~were~~ orange.

~~Hemingway's "The Killers" is a story that is dominated by the~~ **The** feeling of impending violence **dominates Hemingway's "The Killers."**

3. *Make passive sentences active.*

Voice is the quality in verbs that shows whether a subject is the actor or is acted upon. "The arroyos were flooded by rain" is a passive sentence because the subject, "arroyos," is acted upon. In contrast, "Rain flooded the arroyos" is an active sentence because the subject, "rain," is the actor. Active sentences are more concise, direct, and forceful than passive sentences.

The tornado left death and despair.
~~Death and despair was left by the tornado.~~

Nelson Mandela's speeches captured the
~~The~~ Western world's attention ~~was captured by Nelson~~

~~Mandela's speeches.~~

Generally you should eliminate passive sentences, but at times the passive voice might be necessary. Passive sentences are appropriate when the subject is ambiguous or when you wish to emphasize the receiver of an action.

The mysterious story was sent by e-mail.

The writer does not know who sent the story.

His self-esteem was damaged by years of severe criticism.

The writer wishes to emphasize the thing that received the action: "self-esteem."

4. Revise trite expressions.

Trite expressions are phrases that have become stale from overuse. They include clichés (He ran around the neighborhood *like a chicken without a head*), wedded adjectives and nouns (They made a *lifelong commitment*), and overused phrases (We all know that *the rich get richer and the poor get poorer*).

Often trite expressions appear in rough drafts, especially if the writing has been rushed.

He was guilty beyond ~~a shadow of~~ doubt.

The company was sinking in ~~a sea of red ink.~~ **debt.**

~~To make a long story short,~~ **In brief,** the widow married the banker.

The following is a list of common trite expressions. If they appear in your writing, revise them to make them more direct or fresh.

a crying shame	in the final analysis
a thinking person	in the nick of time
after all is said and done	last but not least
at this point in time	method in his madness

depths of despair	never a dull moment
drop in the bucket	none the worse for wear
face the music	pay the piper
flat as a pancake	quick as a flash
in this day and age	sadder but wiser

5. Place modifiers with care.

A writer can confuse a reader by misplacing a modifier. When revising your sentences, be sure to place modifiers so that a reader will be certain which words they modify.

Correct dangling modifiers.

A dangling modifier is a phrase or clause that is not clearly related to any word in a sentence. To correct a dangling modifier, revise the sentence to relate it clearly to a specific word.

As he ran
~~Running~~ through the meadow, his breathing made steamy

clouds.

writer must keep a
To complete a screenplay, a daily schedule. ~~must be kept.~~

the man spent   his
After six months in therapy, ~~the~~ psychiatrist pronounced him

cured.

I was
When a student at Reed, Ken Kesey was the student body's

favorite writer.

Place modifiers close to the words they modify.

When a modifier or modifying phrase is placed away from the word it modifies, the result will be confusing.

in Hollywood restaurants
Many beginning actors wait on tables to support themselves~~in~~
                                                      ^   ^
~~Hollywood restaurants~~.

Aging athletes who exercise (occasionally) will hurt themselves.
                          ^

Be particularly aware of where you place limiting modifiers, such as "only," "hardly," "just," "nearly," "almost," and "ever." These modifiers can function in many positions in a sentence, but they modify the expression that immediately follows them. As these limiting modifiers change position in a sentence, the meaning of the sentence also changes.

> I will go *only* if he asks me. [Otherwise I will not go.]
> *Only* I will go if he asks me. [The others will not go.]
> I will go if *only* he asks me. [Please ask!]
> I will go if he asks *only* me. [If he asks others, I will not go.]

Rewrite faulty split infinitives.

An infinitive consists of "to" plus the simple form of a verb: "to dance," "to moan," "to study," and so on. Usually, a split infinitive can be revised effectively by placing the modifier more accurately.

Faulty
His inability to clearly explain the issues cost him the election.

Faulty Revision
His inability to explain the issues clearly cost him the election.

Good Revision
His inability to explain the issues in clear language cost him the election.

6. *Correct faulty pronoun reference.*

Pronoun reference is the relationship between a pronoun and its antecedent—that is, the word to which it refers. If a pronoun's reference word is unclear, the sentence will confuse or misinform a reader. Revise sentences so that a pronoun refers clearly to one antecedent.

> After Duff had studied Shakespeare for a decade, he realized
>
> **Shakespeare**
> that ~~he~~ was a master psychologist.

Revise sentences that use "this," "that," or "it" to make a broad reference to an entire sentence rather than to a specific antecedent.

> **I was**
> While watching *Friday the 13th* on television, my cat howled
> ^
> **, which**
> and sprang onto my lap. ~~This~~ frightened me.
> ^

Revise sentences that use "it," "they," and "you" without specific antecedents. In conversation these pronouns are often used to make vague reference to people and situations in general. In writing, this practice should be avoided.

> **one reporter**
> During the "Six O'clock News," ~~it~~ gave a special report on
> ^
> intelligence testing.

> **School policy does not**
> ~~They do not~~ allow soliciting on campus.

> **police officers**
> In law enforcement, ~~you~~ must stay alert to a community's
> **they**   **they**
> changing values. If ~~you~~ do not, ~~then you~~ will fail.

Using "you" to refer to "you the reader" is perfectly appropriate in all but the most formal writing as long as the reference to the reader is clear.

> If you major in accounting, then you should find a job easily.

Revise sentences with pronouns ending in "-self" and "-selves," used in place of other personal pronouns.

The philosophy professor tried to convince Robin and ~~myself~~ me

that Albert Camus was fundamentally an optimist.

Pronouns ending in "-self" and "-selves" should refer to words within the sentence.

To stay calm, *I* talked to *myself.*

Nick Ufre and *Janet Lee* tricked *themselves.*

7. Eliminate inconsistencies in sentences.

Revise sentences that make faulty shifts. Often faulty shifts takes place in pronoun references.

If you stretch your muscles before a workout, ~~a runner~~ you will not

face injury.

Faulty shifts in verb tenses can confuse time sequences.

The dancer rehearsed for six months, but finally ~~masters~~ mastered the

movement and was ready to perform.

Faulty shifts in the mood of a verb can be confusing.

Study the causes of World War I, and then ~~you should~~ study

World War II.

A common inconsistency befalls a writer who shifts from active to passive voice, thus dropping from the sentence someone or something performing the action.

> In the game of curling, a player slides a heavy stone over ice
>
>   **a teammate sweeps**
> toward a target, and the ice in front of the stone ~~is swept~~ to
>   ^
>
> influence its path.

You should also revise sentences that have shifts between direct and indirect discourse. Direct discourse includes a direct quotation: Dr. Jones said, "Life, my friends, is boring." Indirect discourse rephrases a direct quotation and therefore does not require quotation marks: Dr. Jones had indicated that life is without interest.

Faulty shift
The judge said to pay the fine and "Never return to my court again."

Revised
The judge said to pay the fine and never return to his court again.

Revised
The judge said, "Pay the fine and never return to my court again."

8. Complete incomplete sentences.

Some sentences are incomplete because they lack words a reader needs to understand them. Often comparisons are not complete. Revise your comparisons to make them clear and logical.

> Dr. Casey treats students better, **than other professors do.**
>
>   **are**
> Mystery novels are easier to read than romance novels.
>   ^
>
>   **the wail of**
> The silence of the streets was more frightening than a siren.
>   ^

In some sentence constructions, writers omit words that are understood. This practice is correct.

Correct
Two people control the city government: one is the mayor; the other, the mayor's husband.

But if omitted words do not fit consistently into the structure, the omission is faulty and the sentence must be revised.

In the woods I feel the peace of nature; now, I feel the violence of the

city.

Humans have a strong belief in and desire for love.

9. Eliminate sexist language.

Changes are taking place in American English usage that reflect a growing awareness of sexism in U.S. society. These changes affect what some social critics describe as a masculine bias embedded in our language. One striking illustration of this bias appears among masculine and feminine word pairs. Generally, female forms are created from male forms:

actor	actress
heir	heiress
hero	heroine
host	hostess
prince	princess

Although you might have a difficult time eliminating words such as these, you can avoid other words and usages that might be construed as carrying a masculine bias.

You can choose to avoid singular, masculine pronouns (he,

him, his) to refer to both men and women when the sex of the antecedent is unknown or when the antecedent consists of both males and females. One way to eliminate sexist language in this situation is to make the subject plural.

> **Managers**   **their**   **s**
> ~~Each manager~~ must post ~~his~~ schedule.
>   ∧

You can also avoid the generic use of *man* to refer to both men and women—"*Man* dominates the natural world"—by substituting *humans* or *human beings*, terms that are generally considered inclusive and less offensive.

Using recent coinages will also help you to avoid sounding biased. For instance, you can replace *chairman*, which in the recent past was used to refer to both men and women, with *chairwoman* when a woman holds the position and *chairperson* for either sex or when the person's sex is unknown.

At this time there is no comprehensive set of rules for avoiding the use of language that seems to carry a masculine bias. However, you should become sensitive to the social issue. Whenever possible, you should avoid perpetuating a masculine bias in your own writing.

10. Revise for parallelism.

Maintain parallel structure by keeping similar ideas in the same grammatical form. In a pair or a series, you must make items parallel to avoid awkward shifts in construction. A noun must be matched with a noun, a verb with a verb, a phrase with a phrase, and a clause with a clause. Revise your sentences to make coordinate ideas parallel.

>   **Anne Sexton's**
> She loved reading Anne Tyler's novels and ~~the~~ poetry ⊙ ~~of Anne~~
>   ∧
> ~~Sexton.~~

His summer activities were ~~the dances~~ *dancing* at Hotspur's and sleeping until noon.

Words such as "by," "in," "to," "the," and "that" should usually be repeated when they apply to both elements in parallel construction.

By not developing their land and *by* ignoring tax-reporting

requirements, the family found itself bankrupt.

Revise sentences to make compared and contrasted ideas parallel.

Ms. Lauko would prefer ~~to work~~ *working* on her physics project to

playing chess.

Zen masters are materially poor, but they are rich *spiritually* ~~in spirit~~.

Revise correlative constructions to make them parallel. The ideas that are joined by correlative conjunctions, such as "either . . . or," "rather . . . than," and "not only . . . but also," should be parallel.

The law applies not only to people but also *to* corporations.

Cosmo is either dreaming about the future or ~~in a deep~~

~~examination of~~ *examining* the past.

Proofread and Prepare the Final Draft

Proofread your edited and revised draft with care. Proof-reading involves checking the punctuation and spelling, the "nitty gritty" details of writing. Once you have carefully proofread your essay, you're ready to prepare the copy you'll turn in.

Use Standard Manuscript Form

Following standard manuscript form is a courtesy to the reader. These standard guidelines, as set by the Modern Language Association, make a paper easy to read.

Materials.   For handwritten papers use 8 1/2-by-11-inch lined white paper with neat edges, not pages torn from a spiral notebook. Use black or blue ink—not green or red—and write on one side only. Skip every other line to make reading and correcting easier.

For typewritten or computer-printed papers use 8 1/2-by-11-inch white typing paper. Do not use onionskin because it is flimsy; do not use erasable bond because it smudges. Double-space between lines and use one side of the paper only.

Use a type style or font that is standard and easily readable—that is, not italic or cursive. For computer-printed manuscripts, use a letter-quality printer or a dot matrix printer in a letter-quality mode.

Unless otherwise directed, use a paper clip to hold the pages together. Many instructors do not like pages stapled together, and no instructor likes the upper left-hand corner to have been dog-eared to hold the pages in place.

Margins.   Leave margins of one inch on all sides of the paper to avoid a crowded appearance. On lined white paper, the vertical line indicates a proper left-hand margin. On most computers, justification of the right margin creates awkwardly spaced lines. Turn the right justification control off while formatting your paper on a computer.

Indention.   Indent the first line of every paragraph uniformly—one inch in a handwritten manuscript, five spaces in a typewritten one, one-half inch in a typeset one.

Paging.   Place the page number, in Arabic numerals (2, not II), without a period or parentheses, in the upper right-hand corner, one-half inch from the top of each page. You may omit the number on the first page, but if you choose to include it, center it at the bottom.

Identification.   Include your name, your instructor's name, the course title and number, the date, and any other information your instructor requests. Place that information on separate double-spaced lines, beginning in the upper left-hand corner of the first page. Place the line that your name is on, one inch from the top of the page. Also put your last name in the upper right-hand corner, with the page number: Bennett 3.

Title.   In handwritten papers on lined paper, place the title in the center of the first line and begin the first sentence two lines below it. In typed papers, double-space below the date and center your title on the page. Begin the first sentence two lines below it. Capitalize the first and last words, any word that follows a colon, and all other words except articles, conjunctions, and prepositions. Do not underline the title or place quotation marks around it. If the title of another work or a quotation is part of your title, however, underline or use quotation marks as appropriate.

Peer Review

Having other class members review your work can be helpful before completing a final draft. We all have blind spots, but when several sets of eyes examine our essays, the blind spots will usually be revealed.

Some writing instructors organize formal peer-review sessions; that is, they require their writers to submit early drafts of their essays for other class members to comment on. Often peer review such as this is done in established writers groups whose members work together throughout the semester. Other times, instructors reform writers groups every few weeks to give everyone in class a chance to work together. In either case, writing instructors usually set aside some class time for the groups to complete their reviews. For these peer review sessions, instructors will generally provide review guidelines based on the particular requirements of the assignment, thus establishing clear directions for the evaluation process.

If your instructor does not require formal peer review, you and other classmates might wish to form an informal writers group to help revise early essay drafts. Or you may wish to merely work with another class member to review each other's work. But whether you work in a formal or in an informal writing group or in pairs, the goal will be the same: to see your work through another reader's eyes, for often an essay that may be perfectly clear to you will be confusing to a reader who has intellectual and emotional distance from the material.

Peer Review Responsibilities

You have two responsibilities during the peer review process: to receive advice and to give advice in a collegial manner.

Receiving Advice. Writing isn't easy, and sometimes it's in the flawed piece of writing that writers place the most emotional energy. When someone criticizes it, then, quite naturally, the tendency is to become combative. The writer will defend each paragraph, each sentence, each word against what may be perceived as an attack. Of course, when writers look at responses to their work unemotionally, it is easy to see that reviewer comments are offered as suggestions for improvement, not challenges. So relax when receiving advice. Judge the observations by what you are trying to accomplish and how well your effort is executed.

Once your work has been reviewed, read all written responses with care. Although they may be brief, they may still be valuable. Moreover, you can follow up written responses to a draft by asking the reviewer questions to help clarify or amplify any written advice. Be sure to consider all oral responses and note the advice you feel will help improve your draft. If a group member asks you a question, answer, but don't feel that you have to justify the decisions you made during the writing process. Most importantly, don't become defensive. Always remember that your reviewers will be evaluating the effectiveness of a piece of writing, not your character.

While revising, should you incorporate suggestions? To do so is your decision. Sometimes the responses will conflict, often reflecting a reviewer's inexperience or misconceived information. Other times the responses will agree, giving you a clear direction for revision. Remember, only you can decide which responses are appropriate and which are inappropriate. The responsibility for a final draft is all yours, not your group's nor your partner's.

Giving Advice.   When reviewing another writer's work, keep in mind that your task is not to rewrite the draft but to respond as a reader and offer advice for improvement. It's up to the writer to write the next draft.

What kind of advice should you offer?

First, know the assignment. Each draft that you read will be written in response to a writing assignment. To respond intelligently, you must be familiar with the assignment. The chances are you will be writing an essay for the same assignment, but if not, then it's your job to know what the assignment calls for and keep the requirements in mind when reviewing a writer's early draft.

Second, apply your knowledge of writing strategies when giving advice. You will have studied essay strategies, both as we will present them in the following chapters and as your instructor will present them in class. These strategies will help you make accurate observations and give you a vocabulary to describe your observations in a way the writer will be able to understand.

Third, offer specific advice. Identify a draft's strengths and weaknesses as specifically as you can. Vague and general observations don't help a writer. For example, the following two responses represent the extremes. One is ineffective, and one is effective.

Ineffective Response

Good work. I like the way it reads, even though it isn't clear. Also good use of words. I like it. Keep it up.

Clearly, this is an ineffective response. Why? Perhaps the reviewer fears hurting the writer's feelings. Or perhaps he has not read the assignment the writer is responding to. Or perhaps he's just plain lazy. Who knows? Still this fact remains: The student offers only vague, "feel-good" responses that avoid giving specific advice to improve the writer's draft.

Effective Response

Discussion of paragraph 2 is particularly strong. Using a question as a topic sentence followed by an answer clearly sets the pattern that follows: "How many situation comedies currently run on television? Only three, but they are broadcast under 23 different titles." This paragraph opening is effective, but the three categories that follow overlap—you should fix them.

One problem though is unity. You seldom refer to your thesis in topic sentences. To fix it wouldn't take much. I suggest you add a key word to your thesis, such as "dysfunctional" and work it, or synonyms for it, into your topic sentences. For example, "The dysfunctional family lurks behind all the antics in *I Love Lucy*." Just a suggestion. Take it or leave it, but you still need to improve unity one way or another.

Another strong point is your use of active verbs: "shrieked," "maul," "cavort," and so on. They all add specific detail—good.

This reviewer's response is effective. She identifies strengths and weaknesses in specific language. Where she can, she gives advice to help the writer revise. She does all this specifically and clearly.

Fourth, don't be distracted by surface errors when giving advice. Do not spend your time correcting grammar, punctuation, and mechanics. Tell the writer that the errors exist, but remember it's the writer's job to proofread carefully and correct surface errors. Instead, concentrate on the larger elements.

Five General Questions to Guide Peer Review

To stay on track, use the following five questions to guide your review:

1. Does the draft reflect the concepts presented in the assignment?
2. What is the dominant purpose and is the organization logical?
3. At what points is the draft confusing?
4. Is the draft adequately developed? Does it need more information or examples?
5. What is the draft's main strength? Weakness?

The first step in the review process is usually done in writing, then the reviewer will discuss the written review with the writer.

Five Guidelines to Discuss a Review

Always respond sensitively. Most beginning writers have no experience submitting their work for peer review. They might misconstrue genuine advice for criticism. To avoid sounding critical, make objectively descriptive comments instead of subjectively evaluative comments. Keep in mind that your responsibility is to help other writers, not to criticize them for their mistakes. When discussing your responses with a writer, keep in mind the following guidelines.

1. A review session should be a dialogue not a debate.
2. Ask questions that might help you develop a clear understanding of the writer's goals.
3. Take notes while reading a draft and use them to discuss the draft's strengths and weaknesses. Emphasize the strengths, but remember the writer needs to know the weaknesses.
4. Make suggestions for improvement related to the writer's intent.
5. Close your response by summarizing ways the writer can improve the draft.

Remember, the emphasis is on improvement—both for the writer as a writer and for the reviewer as a reader.

3

Description

Capturing Sensory Details

The Method

To describe is to picture in words—the people we meet, the places we visit, the conversations we hear, the infinite number of things we encounter. Description, like narration, is often associated with imaginative literature: children's tales, short stories, and novels. In fiction, narrative events provide a story's bones; description adds flesh to the skeletal structure, helping a reader to imagine the narrative events: "The wind rattled the windows . . . a tall figure wearing a cape emerged from the darkness . . . a pasty white face . . . black hair plastered like a swimmer's cap to his head . . . red lips curled in a sneer . . . the air smelling of rotting meat. . . ." For a descriptive passage to be effective, fiction writers know they must involve their readers' senses to create a reaction to the words. This requirement also applies to essayists who use description as a dominant essay pattern. They, too, must involve a reader's senses—that is, make their readers see, hear, smell, feel, and taste.

To see descriptive detail at work, consider the following passage. Two simple events take place: a wild stallion trying to trample a cowhand and the cowhand trying to escape. But before reading the passage, read a few of the descriptive details the writer uses to appeal to the reader's senses:

Sight

the stallion rearing back on its hind legs
hooves pawing the air
mane whipping its neck

Sound

clubbing the ground
throaty whinny echoing

Smell

dust filling his nostrils

Taste

dust coating his lips and teeth

Touch

hand grabbing the fence post
palm raked with slivers

Motion

the stallion rearing back
hooves pawing the air
its mane whipping

Now read the passage to see how the writer uses these and other descriptive details to create a sensuous picture of the action.

> The stallion reared back on its hind legs, its hooves pawing the air, its mane whipping around its neck. The wrangler rolled toward the fence, gasping for breath, dust filling his nostrils and coating his lips and teeth. The stallion's hooves clubbed the ground, and again it reared up, a whinny erupting from deep in its throat, echoing over the ranch, as the wrangler grabbed the bottom fence post, his hand raked by slivers, and scrambled from the corral before the hooves flashing sunlight pummeled him.

In this brief passage the descriptive details, not the events themselves, create the experience. Creative writers know that they must activate the senses or risk the chance that readers will become bored and set the work aside. You can take a page from the creative writer's notebook: Make your readers see, hear, smell, taste, touch, and sense movement in your descriptive passages.

Often inexperienced writers believe that adjectives and adverbs make for sensuous writing, so they pile these descriptive words against their nouns and verbs, a practice that can make for slack prose.

> The <u>shiny red</u> Porsche drove <u>quickly</u> through the <u>wet</u>
> streets. Its <u>massive</u> engine echoed <u>loudly</u> from the <u>tall</u>
> buildings that formed <u>vertical</u> canyons along the <u>asphalt</u>
> streets. Then a <u>shrill</u> siren erupted as a <u>mud-smeared</u> pa-
> trol car sped <u>rapidly</u> after the <u>out-of-control</u> Porsche.

If you reread the wild stallion example, you'll see that the writer uses only one adjective—"bottom," modifying "fence post," which functions as a compound noun, as does "hind legs." The descriptive power in this passage is carried by concrete nouns, active verbs, and verb phrases. If you have written a descriptive passage with excessive adjectives and adverbs, you can always rewrite it by restructuring adjectives into phrases and by finding accurate verbs to eliminate adverbs. Rewriting this way will make your description more vigorous. For instance, read the rewritten version of the Porsche example:

> The Porsche, sunlight glinting from its <u>red</u> paint,
> raced through the streets <u>slick</u> from rain. The engine's
> roar echoed from skyscrapers that formed canyons along
> the Porsche's path. Then a siren erupted in a <u>shrill</u> blast
> as a patrol car smeared in mud raced after the Porsche
> fishtailing out of control.

Now there are only three adjectives, *red, slick,* and shrill. The passage reads more quickly, the verbs are more accurate, and the descriptive detail is easier to visualize—an effective revision.

When description enhances an explanation, then adjectives and adverbs work effectively. For example, read the following passage from John Steinbeck's The Log from the Sea of Cortez. Steinbeck is providing his readers information about sea life that he and his companions collected.

> The reef was generally exposed as the tide went down,
> and on its flat top the tide pools were beautiful. We collected

as widely and rapidly as possible, trying to take a cross section of the animals we saw. There were purple pendent gor-
gonians like lacy fans; a number of small spine-covered
puffer fish which bloat themselves when they are attacked,
erecting the spines; and many starfish, including some
purple and gold cushion stars. The club-spined sea urchins
were numerous in their rock niches. They seemed to move
about very little, for their niches always just fit them and
have the marks of constant occupation. We took a number
of slim green and brown starfish and the large slim five-
rayed starfish with plates bordering the ambulacral grooves.

But if the primary purpose is to describe, not to explain, then
reduce the adjectives and adverbs by recasting your sentences.

How much descriptive detail should you include? Enough to
picture the experience. Keep in mind, that in descriptive writing,
your task is to create an impression of an experience, not to meticulously recreate the experience in words.

Strategies

When reading with a critical eye, study the techniques writers
use to involve your senses. Remember that serious writers calculate each detail in a descriptive passage, shaping the words to
touch a circuit in your imagination.

Objective and Subjective Description

Descriptive writing is either objective or subjective. In objective description, writers concentrate on the subject rather than on
their personal reactions or feelings toward it. In objective description the purpose is to create a literal picture of the subject.

Many college assignments require objective description. For
instance, marine science reports often involve precise descriptions
of weather patterns or sea currents. A history project might call for
a detailed description of a battle. A psychology assignment might

require an objective description of a personality type. Newspaper reports are also written with objective distance from events, giving readers only the factual details. Of course, complete objectivity is impossible to achieve. After all, a writer must select the subject and the words to describe the subject. Nevertheless, in objective description, writers try to keep their personal reactions out of their work. For example, in the following paragraph from The Mountains of California, naturalist John Muir objectively presents a panoramic view of the Sierra Nevada mountain range:

> The north half of the range is mostly covered with floods of lava, and dotted with volcanoes and craters, some of them recent and perfect in form, others in various stages of decay. The south half is composed of granite nearly from base to summit, while a considerable number of peaks, in the middle of the range, are capped with metamorphic slates, among which are Mounts Dana and Gibbs to the east of Yosemite Valley. Mount Whitney, the culminating point of the range near its southern extremity, lifts its helmet-shaped crest to a height of nearly 14,700 feet. Mount Shasta, a colossal volcanic cone, raises to a height of 14,440 feet at the northern extremity, and forms a noble landmark for all the surrounding region within a radius of a hundred miles. Residual masses of volcanic rocks occur throughout most of the granite southern portions also, and a considerable number of the old volcanoes on the flanks, especially along the eastern base of the range near Mono Lake and southward. But it is only to the northward that the entire range, from base to summit, is covered in lava.

For the most part, Muir keeps his objective distance from his subject. He presents a detailed overview of the range, including significant peaks, their heights, and the materials that compose the Sierras. He does give the reader a peek at his feelings by using the words colossal and noble, but not to the extent that the passage becomes subjective.

In subjective description, writers emphasize their personal reactions to or feelings toward a subject to create an impressionistic picture. Their goal is to get their readers to share these reactions or feelings. Sometimes writers will appear to present their material objectively but then end the passage with a subjective response. Consider, for example, the following passage from Sue Hubbell's *A Country Year: Living the Questions:*

> I've been out in the back today checking beehives. When I leaned over one of them to direct a puff of smoke from my bee smoker into the entrance to quiet the bees, a copperhead came wriggling out from under the hive. He had been frightened from his protected spot by the smoke and the commotion I was making, and when he found himself in the open, he panicked and slithered for the nearest hole he could find which was the entrance to the next beehive. I don't know what went on inside, but he came out immediately, wearing a surprised look on his face. I hadn't known that a snake could look surprised, but this one did. Then, after pausing to study the matter more carefully, he glided off to the safety of the woods.

Hubbell not only presents the objective detail of the experience, she also offers her impression of the snake, one that stands in sharp contrast to objective facts—that is, snakes do not look surprised, but her snake does.

Peter Schjeldahl, in the opening paragraph of "Cyclone," writes at the extreme of subjective description. He creates as much descriptive detail about how he feels riding the Coney Island roller coaster as he does objective description of the actual experience.

> The Cyclone is art, sex, God, the greatest. It is the most fun you can have without risking bad ethics. I rode the Cyclone seven times one afternoon last summer, and I am here to tell everybody that it is fun for fun's sake, the pure abstract heart of the human capacity for getting a kick out of anything. Yes, it may be anguishing initially. (I promise to tell the truth.) Terrifying, even, the first time or two the train is hauled upward with groans and creaks and with you in it.

At the top then—where there is sudden strange quiet but for the fluttering of two tattered flags, and you have a poignantly brief view of Brooklyn, and of ships far out on the Atlantic— you may feel very lonely and that you have made a serious mistake, cursing yourself in the last gleam of the reflective consciousness you are about, abruptly, to leave up there between the flags like an abandoned thought-balloon. To keep yourself company by screaming may help, and no one is noticing: try it. After a couple of rides, panic abates, and after four or five, you aren't even frightened, exactly, but stimulated, blissed, sent. The squirt of adrenaline you will never cease to have at the top as the train lumbers, wobbling slightly, into the plunge, finally fuels just happy wonderment because you can't, and never will, believe what is going to happen.

Schjeldahl's paragraph is packed with highly charged language: The Cyclone is art, sex, God, the greatest . . . fun for fun's sake . . . anguishing . . . terrifying. He also mixes objective detail with his impressions: the train is hauled upward with groans and creaks . . . a sudden strange quiet but for the fluttering of two tattered flags . . . a brief view of Brooklyn and of ships far out on the Atlantic . . . the train lumbers, wobbling slightly, into the plunge. To write effective subjective description, writers carefully mix objective detail with their responses.

Dominant Impression

To create an effective description, you might think writers do nothing more than record all they perceive. They do much more. As a critical reader, keep in mind that descriptive writing is not a haphazard activity. With so much detail available for any description, writers must select descriptive details with care and shape them with precision to achieve a *dominant impression*.

In subjective description, selecting detail to create a dominant impression is even more critical than in objective description. Writers must not only select but also embellish descriptive details to create the impression they want. When describing a desert, a writer might want to show that the land is hostile: "the harsh sunlight reflecting from the bleached sand like needles plunging into the hiker's eyes." Describing a politician, a writer might want to show him to be untrustworthy: "his face heavily lined from years of calculating behind closed doors, his eyes skipping around the crowd like those of a criminal about to be exposed." Writers seldom directly state the dominant impression they wish to create; they suggest it.

Consider this passage from Gretel Ehrlich's "A Season of Portraits." Ehrlich, who is an essayist, a novelist, and a Wyoming rancher, describes the dry summer of 1988, when raging fires consumed much of Yellowstone National Park forests. In this passage she concentrates on the wind, suggesting that it is a wind from hell, savage and ghostly, perhaps even isolating her as souls are isolated in a mythical underworld.

> A breeze stiffens. Gusts are clocked at forty-five, sixty, eighty-five miles per hour. Rainless thunderclouds crack above, shaking pine pollen down. *La bufera infernale*—that's what Dante calls winds that lashed at sinners in hell. I decide to go out in the infernal storm. "This is hell," a herder moving his sheep across the mountain says, grinning, then clears his parched throat and rides away. Wind carries me back and forth, twisting, punching me down.
>
> I'm alone here for much of the summer, these hot winds my only dancing partner. The sheep and their herder vanish over the ridge. I close my eyes, and the planet is auditory only: tree branches twist into tubas and saxes, are caught by large hands that press down valves, and everywhere on this ranch I hear feral music—ghostly tunes made not by animals gone wild but by grasses, sagebrush, and fence wire singing.

Once writers decide on a dominant impression and select the appropriate details to suggest it, they must arrange the details in an effective order. Often a structure will become visible during the writing and revision, one that will be unique for that passage.

Ehrlich arranges the passage above in two parts: the world she sees and the world she hears, which are clearly separated when she writes, "I close my eyes." She continues by suggesting that the wind plays the branches of trees like musical instruments and creates ghostly music by rushing through grasses, sagebrush, fence wire. By shutting her eyes, and yours as a sensitive reader, she transforms the world into a mysterious place.

Arrangement of Details

Although you will find no strict formulas for arranging descriptive details, writers do, however, follow some general principles. In visual description, a writer will usually structure the details in the way that the eye would record them, that is, by spatial arrangement—from left to right, right to left, near to far, far to near, center outward. A writer might begin with a broad picture and narrow to the particulars, like a film opening with a panoramic view of a landscape or city and gradually moving into the scene, finally focusing on one specific image.

To describe a person, a writer might begin with a general descriptive statement: "She looked as if she had stepped from the pages of *Vogue*, a stylish woman," and then moved downward from head to toe, "Her hair was the color of straw and cropped short; her neck seemed carved from ivory. . . ." Or this writer might begin by describing an unusual physical feature and work from there: "Her nose didn't fit her stylish appearance: it was a bit long and bent slightly to the left, as if it had stopped a boxer's left cross. Otherwise, she was unflawed. . . ." As you read descriptive passages, keep in mind that writers have many ways in which to organize a description. Critical readers examine writers' varied ways of structuring descriptive details and applying the techniques.

Description in College Writing

Vivid description supplements all but the most scientifically objective papers, often bringing life to arguments, explanations, and narrations. For example, if you were to take a position against allowing cigarettes to be sold in public vending machines where underage teens can easily buy them, your essay's dominant purpose would be to argue a position, but you might supplement your argument with a vivid description of a lung cancer victim. Or if you wanted to explain the effects of proposed cutbacks in medical aid to the poor, your essay's dominant purpose would be cause and effect, but you might supplement the explanation with a dramatic description of the impact on one impoverished family. If you wanted to write a personal narrative of the events that led to a dramatic insight, you would no doubt use some description to bring alive the people and places in the story. Finally, you might find yourself relying on description to write college reports for such courses as marine biology and art history, in which descriptive accuracy will be an important part of the assignment.

Guidelines for Writing Description

1. Select a subject that lends itself to description and examine it closely to decide whether your description will be subjective or objective.
2. Establish the dominant purpose, whether it is a supporting passage in an explanation or argument essay or the dominant method of development in a descriptive report.
3. Develop an extended list of descriptive details, then select the appropriate details from the list and arrange them for effect.
4. Decide on an appropriate structure and then write your essay, using concrete language.
5. Revise your essay, making sure that the dominant purpose is clear.

A Student Essay Developed by Description

In her contemporary art history class, Clarita Tan wrote a descriptive report in response to the following class assignment:

This assignment will require you to do minor background research and to attend a current art exhibit at a local gallery or museum. Select a contemporary artist currently being exhibited as your subject. Then review representative works on display and describe the artist's method of working.

Now examine Tan's essay. First, read it through once, noting descriptive techniques that Tan uses. Then study it in detail by responding to the questions that follow.

Imaginatively Chaotic Art

    The Fine Arts Gallery is featuring George McNeil, a   1
figurative Abstract Expressionist who lived and worked
his entire life in New York City. The ten canvases, drawn
together from local collections, are stunning for their color
and imagery. It is hard to separate color and imagery in
McNeil's work. From pools of purple, orange, and yellow
emerge massive faces, airplanes, bodies, and cryptic
scrawls. The imagery magically emerges from the method
McNeil uses to compose his canvases. The result is that
the viewer's mind is pulled from the real world into an
imaginatively chaotic world.
    In the foyer the curator displayed a series of pho-   2
tographs showing McNeil at work. The first photograph
shows him walking into his studio to begin his day. A
muted gray light streams from a skylight and McNeil
stands in the doorway. At first glance he looks like a re-
tiree getting ready to putter in a garden. He wears heavy
work boots, tattered, oversized jeans that ride on his hip
bones, a chambray shirt open at the neck with a T-shirt
underneath, and a watch cap against the morning chill.
But unlike a gardener's work clothes stained with soil and
grass, McNeil's are splattered with paint. In fact, his
boots are so crusted with paint they look like art objects.
    Two of McNeil's physical features are dramatically   3
riveting: his massive hands, gnarled from arthritis, that
hang at the ends of long arms and his riveting eyes, set in

the eighty-five-year-old face, that sparkle mischievously as if they belong to a spirited ten year old possessed by a humorous demon.

The next three photographs capture the initial phase 4 of his painting method. Like other abstract expressionists, such as Jackson Pollock who is noted for his drip and splatter paintings, McNeil begins by stapling his canvas to a plywood sheet and laying it on the studio floor. The first photograph in this sequence shows him in action. McNeil leans over the canvas, dripping paint from a Styrofoam cup taken from a nearby table covered with other Styrofoam cups running over with paint. The next photograph shows him aggressively slashing the air with a brush as if it were a weapon, paint arcing toward the canvas. The third photograph shows him whipping the brush back, lashing downward, a mischievous grin on his face, his eyes twinkling.

The final phase of his method is captured in the fifth 5 photograph. The canvas is now raised upright on the plywood base, a practice that deviates from Pollock's and that of other Abstract Expressionists. Here McNeil stands with his back to the camera and faces the massive canvas. He is hunched forward with an upraised brush held like a symphony conductor's baton, and I think of composer Paul Dukas's "Sorcerer's Apprentice." Indeed McNeil is performing artistic sorcery, for he is creating images that suggest themselves from the splattered configurations on the canvas.

The images themselves are startling to view, often 6 suggesting the untainted imagination of a child who knows none of the technical restraints of someone who is "trained" to paint. Two images in two paintings affected me the most. "Kennedy Airport" (1989, 78 x 64 inches) is awash in color with patches of blues, reds, purples, yellows, whites, oranges, and blacks. McNeil has created the feeling that the viewer is looking down from the sky at a flat surface. Nothing is to scale—a huge head dominates the upper left-hand corner and a smaller head, its mouth agape, fills the lower right-hand corner. In between floats a mysterious cartoonish world—a woman in high heels and net hose, two tiny airplanes, and many spirals and circles. All is aswirl, as if the images have been whipped

into the sky by an infernal wind that has brought havoc
to the airport.

"Diablo Disco" (1986, 78 x 64 inches) is as dramatic   7
as "Kennedy Airport." It, too, is alive with clashing colors. The central figure is a lime green dancer, whose high-
heeled feet touch the canvas bottom and tilted head
touches the canvas top. The figure is an abstraction, the
lips and eyes smeared on with thick layers of blue, red,
and purple paint. The hair, a massive mop, shoots upward. It is painted in orange, red, and yellow that suggest
flames. In the center of the dancer's body McNeil has
painted what appears to be a small city. The dancer herself is surrounded by other dancing figures, all much
smaller, but all equally bizarre, perhaps even devilish.

Every canvas in the show is powerful, offering a   8
unique vision of contemporary life. But perhaps the most
important element in the show is the opening photographs
that reveal this artistic magician at work. Without an understanding of how his paintings evolve from colorful
splatters and pools into chaotic figures, I would have
merely been distracted by the question, "How does anyone
think of these images?" No doubt this question is the
wrong one to ask when responding to art.

Reviewing with a Writer's Eye

1. Review Tan's writing assignment (see p. 100). It is composed
    of two parts. After selecting a contemporary artist, Tan had
    to review representative works and describe the artist's work-
    ing method. Does Tan's essay meet the assignment require-
    ments? Which paragraphs address part 1 and which address
    part 2?

2. In paragraph 1, the introduction, Tan provides important back-
    ground information and creates an impression of what her essay
    will cover. She also implies a general impression of how she
    wishes her readers to see George McNeil's art. What is that im-
    pression?

3. Creating a dominant impression (see pp. 96–98) can be an effec-
    tive strategy in descriptive writing. In Tan's description of

George McNeil, what dominant impression is she trying to create? List four key sentences that help to create the impression.

4. The arrangement of detail is important in descriptive passages (see p. 98). How does Tan arrange detail in paragraphs 5 and 6? How does she arrange detail in paragraphs 7 and 8? Briefly explain why her approach is different in these two sets of paragraphs.

5. Tan meticulously describes McNeil in paragraphs 2 and 3. Why? Do you think that the detail is excessive? Should it be cut? In a few sentences, explain your observations.

Peer Review

You may be asked to write an essay about one of the readings that follow. Before you meet with your writing group, review this introduction. As you read your group papers, use these general principles of description to help guide your comments.

1. A description should involve a reader's senses of sight, sound, smell, touch, and taste as appropriate for the subject being described.

2. A description should have an appropriate balance between the objective and the subjective. Look for a writer's feelings about what is described as well as the details of the description.

3. Concrete details make a description come alive. A reader cannot feel an experience conveyed only with general statements.

4. Details should be presented within an overall structure, usually, but not necessarily, in some variation of a spatial arrangement.

5. Except for purely objective descriptions, the paper should communicate some dominant impression. Without a dominant impression, what is the purpose of the description?

Description

6. To be effective, descriptive writing must appeal to a reader's senses (see pp. 93–96). Tan mainly appeals to the sense of sight. List a few phrases that appeal to other senses as well.
7. Identify two allusions (see the Glossary) that Tan makes in "Imaginatively Chaotic Art." What purpose do they serve?
8. Is Tan's essay primarily objective, primarily subjective, or a mixture of objective and primarily subjective description (see pp. 93–96)? Find passages that support your conclusion.
9. Write a note to Clarita Tan that states your overall response to her essay and details its strengths and weaknesses.

Most of us share senses—sight, sound, smell, touch, taste—and we have feelings. Professional writers know that by evoking sensory experience and feelings in their readers' minds they will enrich the reading experience. Read the essays in the following section. See how the authors evoke the senses; analyze their selection of descriptive details; and examine how they shape descriptive passages to achieve a dominant impression. Take notes as you read, mark an interesting passage, underline a vivid phrase. When you write your own descriptive passages, apply the principles you've learned from reading as a writer. Don't be timid about using a professional writer's passage for a model. The techniques of effective description are universal—available for everyone to use. Professional writers are challenged by the demands of description; certainly you, while developing writing skills, should also feel challenged.

🐛 Maxine Hong Kingston 🐛

Maxine Hong Kingston was born and raised in a Chinese-American community in Stockton, California, where her parents ran a laundry. She grew up listening to stories about China from her parents and relatives, who were first-generation immigrants. She attended the University of California at Berkeley and has taught creative writing at the University of Hawaii. Her stories, essays, and poems have been published in Ms., The New Yorker, *and* American Heritage. The Woman Warrior: Memoirs of a Girlhood among Ghosts, *Kingston's award-winning autobiography, describes her memories and retells the stories she heard as a child. Her second book,* China Men, *winner of the National Book Award, traces the lives of three generations of Chinese men in America. Her novel* Tripmaster Monkey *is a fable of a young Chinese-American writer.*

Photographs of My Parents

In this selection from The Woman Warrior, *Kingston looks at much more than photographs. Her searching descriptions of mundane objects reveal some of the deep differences between the culture she grew up in and the China her parents left. In writing of both the familiarity and the strangeness in the photographs of her parents, she reaches into the past to better understand the present.*

Try to visualize as vividly as you can the differences between the Chinese and the Chinese-American photographs that Kingston describes. Consider how these differences contribute to the essay's central meaning.

Once in a long while, four times so far for me, my mother   1
brings out the metal tube that holds her medical diploma. On the
tube are gold circles crossed with seven red lines each—"joy"
ideographs in abstract. There are also little flowers that look like
gears for a gold machine. According to the scraps of labels with
Chinese and American addresses, stamps, and postmarks, the
family airmailed the can from Hong Kong in 1950. It got crushed

105

in the middle, and whoever tried to peel the labels off stopped because the red and gold paint came off too, leaving silver scratches
that rust. Somebody tried to pry the end off before discovering
that the tube pulls apart. When I open it, the smell of China flies
out, a thousand-year-old bat flying heavy-headed out of the
Chinese caverns where bats are as white as dust, a smell that
comes from long ago, far back in the brain. Crates from Canton,
Hong Kong, Singapore, and Taiwan have that smell too, only
stronger because they are more recently come from the Chinese.

Inside the can are three scrolls, one inside another. The   2
largest says that in the twenty-third year of the National
Republic, the To Keung School of Midwifery, where she has had
two years of instruction and Hospital Practice, awards its
Diploma to my mother, who has shown through oral and written examination her Proficiency in Midwifery, Pediatrics,
Gynecology, "Medecine," "Surgary," Therapeutics, Ophthalmology, Bacteriology, Dermatology, Nursing and Bandage. This document has eight stamps on it: one, the school's English and
Chinese names embossed together in a circle; one, as the Chinese
enumerate, a stork and a big baby in lavender ink; one, the
school's Chinese seal; one, an orangish paper stamp pasted in the
border design; one, the red seal of Dr. Wu Pak-liang, M.D., Lyon,
Berlin, president and "Ex-assistant étranger à la clinique chirugi-
cale et d'accouchement de l'université de Lyon"; one, the red seal
of Dean Woo Yin-kam, M.D.; one, my mother's seal, her chop
mark larger than the president's and the dean's; and one, the number 1279 on the back. Dean Woo's signature is followed by
"(Hackett)." I read in a history book that Hackett Medical College
for Women at Canton was founded in the nineteenth century by
European women doctors.

The school seal has been pressed over a photograph of my   3
mother at the age of thirty-seven. The diploma gives her age as
twenty-seven. She looks younger than I do, her eyebrows are
thicker, her lips fuller. Her naturally curly hair is parted on the
left, one wavy wisp tendrilling off to the right. She wears a
scholar's white gown, and she is not thinking about her appearance. She stares straight ahead as if she could see me and past me

to her grandchildren and grandchildren's grandchildren. She has spacy eyes, as all people recently from Asia have. Her eyes do not focus on the camera. My mother is not smiling; Chinese do not smile for photographs. Their faces command relatives in foreign lands—"Send money"—and posterity forever—"Put food in front of this picture." My mother does not understand Chinese-American snapshots. "What are you laughing at?" she asks.

The second scroll is a long narrow photograph of the graduating class with the school officials seated in front. I picked out my mother immediately. Her face is exactly her own, though forty years younger. She is so familiar, I can only tell whether or not she is pretty or happy or smart by comparing her to the other women. For this formal group picture she straightened her hair with oil to make a chinlength bob like the others'. On the other women, strangers, I can recognize a curled lip, a sidelong glance, pinched shoulders. My mother is not soft; the girl with the small nose and dimpled underlip is soft. My mother is not humorous, not like the girl at the end who lifts her mocking chin to pose like Girl Graduate. My mother does not have smiling eyes; the old woman teacher (Dean Woo?) in front crinkles happily, and the one faculty member in the western suit smiles westernly. Most of the graduates are girls whose faces have not yet formed; my mother's face will not change anymore, except to age. She is intelligent, alert, pretty. I can't tell if she's happy.

The graduates seem to have been looking elsewhere when they pinned the rose, zinnia, or chrysanthemum on their precise black dresses. One thin girl wears hers in the middle of her chest. A few have a flower over a left or right nipple. My mother put hers, a chrysanthemum, below her left breast. Chinese dresses at that time were dartless, cut as if women did not have breasts; these young doctors, unaccustomed to decorations, may have seen their chests as black expanses with no reference points for flowers. Perhaps they couldn't shorten that far gaze that lasts only a few years after a Chinese emigrates. In this picture too my mother's eyes are big with what they held—reaches of oceans beyond China, land beyond oceans. Most emigrants learn the barbarians' directness—how to gather themselves and stare rudely into talking faces as if trying to catch lies. In America my mother has eyes as strong as boulders, never once skittering off a face, but she has not learned to place decorations and phonograph needles, nor has she stopped seeing land on the other side of the oceans. Now her eyes include the relatives in China, as they once included my father smiling and smiling in his many western outfits, a different one for each photograph that he sent from America.

He and his friends took pictures of one another in bathing   6
suits at Coney Island beach, the salt wind from the Atlantic blowing their hair. He's the one in the middle with his arms about the necks of his buddies. They pose in the cockpit of a biplane, on a motorcycle, and on a lawn beside the "Keep Off the Grass" sign. They are always laughing. My father, white shirt sleeves rolled up, smiles in front of a wall of clean laundry. In the spring he wears a new straw hat, cocked at a Fred Astaire angle. He steps out, dancing down the stairs, one foot forward, one back, a hand in his pocket. He wrote to her about the American custom of stomping on straw hats come fall. "If you want to save your hat for next year," he said, "you have to put it away early, or else when you're riding the subway or walking along Fifth Avenue, any stranger can snatch it off your head and put his foot through it. That's the way they celebrate the change of seasons here." In the winter he wears a gray felt hat with his gray overcoat. He is sitting on a rock in Central Park. In one snapshot he is not smiling; someone took it when he was studying, blurred in the glare of the desk lamp.

There are no snapshots of my mother. In two small portraits,   7
however, there is a black thumbprint on her forehead, as if someone had inked in bangs, as if someone had marked her.

"Mother, did bangs come into fashion after you had the pic-   8
ture taken?" One time she said yes. Another time when I asked, "Why do you have fingerprints on your forehead?" she said, "Your First Uncle did that." I disliked the unsureness in her voice.

The last scroll has columns of Chinese words. The only   9
English is "Department of Health, Canton," imprinted on my mother's face, the same photograph as on the diploma. I keep looking to see whether she was afraid. Year after year my father

did not come home or send for her. Their two children had been dead for ten years. If he did not return soon, there would be no more children. ("They were three and two years old, a boy and a girl. They could talk already.") My father did send money regularly, though, and she had nobody to spend it on but herself. She bought good clothes and shoes. Then she decided to use the money for becoming a doctor. She did not leave for Canton immediately after the children died. In China there was time to complete feelings. As my father had done, my mother left the village by ship. There was a sea bird painted on the ship to protect it against shipwreck and winds. She was in luck. The following ship was boarded by river pirates, who kidnapped every passenger, even old ladies. "Sixty dollars for an old lady" was what the bandits used to say. "I sailed alone," she says, "to the capital of the entire province." She took a brown leather suitcase and a seabag stuffed with two quilts.

Meaning and Purpose

1. Have you ever looked through old photographs of your parents or grandparents? What feelings did you have when you looked at them? What questions did you ask? What do the photographs tell you about yourself?

2. What are the contrasts between Chinese and Chinese-American photographs and what do these contrasts suggest about the meaning of "Photographs of My Parents"?

3. In paragraph 3, Kingston writes that "the school seal has been pressed over a photograph of my mother"; in paragraph 7, Kingston describes a small portrait of her mother, "there is a black thumbprint on her forehead . . . as if someone had marked her"; and in paragraph 9, she reports that another photograph has the English words "Department of Health, Canton" printed over her face. How do these descriptive details work in the essay?

4. What does paragraph 6 reveal about Kingston's father?

5. Discuss the significance of flowers pinned awkwardly on the graduates' dresses.
6. In the first paragraph, what does the "thousand-year-old bat" signify?

Strategy

1. What is Kingston's general organizational strategy for description? Where are the three transition points at which Kingston moves from one section to another?
2. Identify some descriptions that involve the senses and some that evoke impressions or feelings. What kinds of figures of speech are they—metaphor, simile, personification, descriptive image?
3. Is this descriptive essay subjective or objective, and how do you know?
4. What impression does Kingston give of the metal tube in the first paragraph? How does her description prepare you for the rest of the essay?

Style

1. How would you describe the tone of the essay or the narrator's feelings about the contents of the metal tube?
2. Consider the metal tube to be a symbol for Kingston's mother. What qualities does it suggest about her?
3. Kingston uses some medical terms. Be sure you know their meanings: *ophthalmology, pediatrics, gynecology, dermatology, therapeutics* (paragraph 2).

Writing Tasks

1. Study Kingston's essay to see how she uses photographs to reveal bits and pieces of her parents' history. Then select pho-

tographs of two friends or relatives who have both similar and opposing character traits. Use the photographs to write a description that reveals their character traits without stating them directly.

2. Describe a significant possession of someone you know, and show how it characterizes the person.

❦ Joanna Greenfield ❦

Joanna Greenfield grew up in Connecticut. Throughout her childhood she dreamed of going to Africa to work with wild animals. After graduation from college, she traveled to Israel to work in a game reserve dedicated to biblical animals. "Hyena" is her first publication.

Hyena

Experienced though she was, Greenfield, a person who is wise in the ways of animal behavior, let her guard drop once and, as a result, suffered horribly. As you read this essay, notice how Greenfield moves from describing action to describing background information and then back to describing action.

---

1   The van slowed, then stopped, for a hyena in the road. It was a spotted hyena, the kind people think of when they hear the word "hyena"—a dirty, matted creature, dripping with blood. It must have made a good kill. The prey must have been large enough for the hyena to thrust its whole head in, up to the block-like shoulders.

2   This must be why the hyena has such a snake of a neck—so it can delve deep into a dying animal and eat the best parts before thieves chase it away. Hyenas always go first for the softest parts, like entrails, although they have jaws stronger than a lion's, and can eat bones.

3   This hyena's belly bulged over its legs, and it sat in the road, as if musing, making no attempt to clean off the blood. The slurs that human beings cast at the species fall as useless as gossip about Greek gods. The hyena sat there despite all our encouragement to it to move, and, long past the point when a lion would have slunk peevishly away, we had to slither over a ditch to pass by.

4   As we drove away, I saw other hyenas stretched flat on the savanna. They were all dipped in blood, but every stain was different.

One could see which animal had gnawed at a leg, cheek pressed to bloody flank, or which had held a piece to its chest and embraced it there as it chewed. The prey animal, a wildebeest or a zebra, like one of the human shadows of Hiroshima, was left only in negative, fragmented about the savanna in ghostly prints of blood.

The deathbed was almost clean. A crowd of vultures pounced on and squabbled over pieces of skin ripped free when the hyenas pulled off their parts, and a few insects had already stripped clots of blood from the soaked grass. Nothing else was left.

Spotted hyenas are the sharks of the savanna, superpredators and astounding recyclers of garbage. They hunt in large, giggling groups, running alongside their prey and eating chunks of its flesh until it slows down through loss of blood, or shock, or sheer hopelessness, and then the hyenas grab for the stomach and pull the animal to a halt with its own entrails or let it stumble into the loops and whorls of its own body. They eat the prey whole and cough back, like owls, the indigestible parts, such as hair and hooves.

Hyenas in the wild can roam dozens of miles a day. They leave their young in small dens and trot or lope across the savanna, head down or held high and rear tucked under, until they've found a hare or a pregnant gazelle or a nicely rotted piece of flesh. But when the herds begin to migrate the hyenas leave their dens to follow them, and, passing over hills, through rifts and acacia stands, and along dry riverbeds, they reach the open plains of the Serengeti, where wildebeest beyond count mill and groan in clouds of dust.

I once saw a family of hyenas playing on an elephant skull. They rolled on their backs, biting gently at each other's legs. Two cubs squeezed under and then out of the elephant's mandible. A female turned on her side, paws in the air, and broke off a piece of the skull as if eating a biscuit in bed. Hyenas almost never kill humans—only now and then taking a piece from the cheek of a sleeping man, and that probably because some villages used to put out their dead for hyenas, flies, and any vultures in the area. As the man jumps up—perhaps he is a messenger between villages or someone searching for a bride—the hyena instantly, peaceably, retreats.

I had never wanted to work anywhere except in Africa, but after I graduated from college a wildlife-reserve director from Israel told me that he needed someone to set up a breeding site for endangered animals and I decided to go. When I got there, I was told that the project had been postponed and was asked if I'd mind taking a job as a volunteer at another reserve, cleaning enclosures. The reserve was dedicated to Biblical animals, many of them predators from the Israeli wild—hyenas, wolves, foxes, and one unmated leopard—attackers of kibbutz livestock. It was something to do, with animals, so I trudged off every day in the hundred-and-fourteen-degree heat with half a sandwich and a water canteen. I was being groomed for the job I'd initially been offered, but for the moment I sifted maggots for the lizards and snakes, and cleaned the fox, cat, hyena, wolf, and leopard corrals.   9

As the days got hotter, my fellow-workers and I carried gallon jugs of water in our wheelbarrows, poured it over our heads, and drank the rest until our stomachs were too full for food. It became a steady rhythm: sift dung, pour, drink, sift. We worked in pairs among the larger animals for safety, but toward the end of the month I was allowed to feed a young hyena and clean his cage. Efa had been taken from his parents as a cub because his mother rejected him. Also, he was a cross between a North African and an Israeli striped hyena, and nobody wanted him to confuse the gene pool further by mating. He was a beautiful animal. A mane trickled down sloped shoulders like a froth of leftover baby hair; he looked strangely helpless, as if weighed down by the tangled strands, and his back rounded to a dispirited slump. Even though he had a hyena's posture, he was like a German shepherd, a little dirty, but graceful, and so strong he didn't seem to have any muscles. His stripes twisted a bit at the ends and shimmered over the coat like feathers at rest. With his bat face and massed shoulders, he would have been at home in the sky, poised in a great leap, or swooping for prey. But here he was given aged meat, and he often left even that to rot before he ate it.   10

He had been, they said, an adorable cub, crying "Maaaaaa!" to 11
Shlomi, the gentlest of the workers and the one who reared him,
and he followed Shlomi everywhere. Then he grew too big to run
loose, and he started biting at people, so they put him in a corral—a square of desert surrounded by an electrified fence with a
large water basin perched in the center.

Efa was bored and lonely. He flipped the basin over every day, 12
attacking it as if it were prey. When we fed him in the morning,
there was nowhere to put his water. He knocked over everything,
so we had no choice: we had to put him in a holding cage outside
his corral while we built a concrete pool that he couldn't move.
This was worse. Locked in a cage, he rebelled. He refused to eat,
and every box we gave him for shade was torn to pieces. After a
few days, I walked by and saw him standing defiant in the cage,
his shade box in splinters and his water overturned again.
"Maaaaaaaa! Mmaaaaa!" he croaked at me. I made a note to return
and water him when I'd finished with the others.

I stopped to talk to the leopard, who was in heat. This was my 13
first chance to get near her; when she was not hormonally sedated,
she lunged at passersby, swatting her claws through the chicken
wire.

"You're so beautiful." 14

She purred, and rubbed against the mesh. The men said you 15
could stroke her like a house cat when she was in these moods. I
wanted to touch her, a leopard from the oases of Israel's last
deserts, but I stayed away, in case she changed her mind, and
squatted out of reach to talk to her. I didn't want to force her to
defend herself.

It might have been the attention I gave the leopard, but Efa 16
was in a frenzy of "Mmmaaaaaaaaa"s when I returned to his cage.
He crouched like a baby, begging for something. I filled a water
tray and unlatched the door that opened into a corridor running
between the cage and the corral, then I closed it. If only I'd just
squirted the hose into the cage, but instead I unlatched the cage
door and bent over to put the dish down, talking to him. The
mind, I found, is strange. It shut off during the attack, while my

body continued to act, without thought or even sight. I don't remember him sinking his teeth into my arm, though I heard a little
grating noise as his teeth chewed into the bone.

Everything was black and slow and exploding in my stomach.   17
Vision returned gradually, like an ancient black-and-white television pulling dots and flashes to the center for a picture. I saw at a
remove the hyena inside my right arm, and my other arm banging
him on the head. My body, in the absence of a mind, had decided
that this was the best thing to do. And scream. Scream in a thin
angry hysteria that didn't sound like me. Where was everyone?
My mind was so calm and remote that I frightened myself, but my
stomach twisted. I hit harder, remembering the others he'd
nipped. He'd always let go.

Efa blinked and surged back, jerking me forward. I stumbled   18
out of my sandals into the sand, thinking, with fresh anxiety, I'll
burn my feet. I tried to kick him between the legs, but it was awkward, and he was pulling me down by the arm, down and back
into the cage. When I came back from Africa the first time, I took
a class in self-defense so I'd feel safer with all the soldiers, guerrilla
warriors, and policemen when I returned. I remembered the move
I'd vowed to use on any attacker: a stab and grab at the jugular, to
snap it inside the skin. But the hyena has callused skin on its
throat, thick and rough, like eczema. I lost hope and felt the slowness of this death to be the worst insult. Hyenas don't kill fast, and
I could end up in the sand watching my entrails get pulled
through a cut in my stomach and eaten like spaghetti, with tugs
and jerks. I started to get mad, an unfamiliar feeling creeping in to
add an acid burn to the chill of my stomach. Another removal
from myself. I never let myself get mad. I want peace. I tried to
pinch his nostrils so he'd let go of my arm to breathe, but he
shook his head, pulling me deeper into the cage.

I think it was then that he took out the first piece from my arm   19
and swallowed it without breathing, because a terror of movement
settled in me at that moment and lasted for months. He moved up
the arm, and all the time those black, blank eyes evaluated me,
like a shark's, calm and almost friendly. By this time, my right arm
was a mangled mess of flesh, pushed-out globs of fat, and flashes

of bone two inches long, but my slow TV mind, watching, saw it as whole, just trapped in the hyena's mouth, in a tug-of-war like the one I used to play with my dogs—only it was my arm now instead of a sock. It didn't hurt. It never did.

The hyena looked up at me with those indescribable eyes and surged back again, nearly pulling me onto his face. I remembered self-defense class and the first lesson: "Poke the cockroach in the eyes." All the women had squealed, except me. "Ooooh, I could never do that." Ha, I'd thought. Anyone who wants to kill me has no right to live. I'd poke him in the eyes. 20

I looked at those eyes with my fingers poised to jab. It was for my family and my friends that I stuck my finger in his eyes. I just wanted to stop watching myself get eaten, either be dead and at peace or be gone, but other lives were connected to mine. I'm not sure if I did more than touch them gently before he let go and whipped past me to cower against the door to the outside, the Negev desert. 21

Events like this teach you yourself. We all think we know what we would do, hero or coward, strong or weak. I expected strength, and the memory of my tin-whistle scream curdles my blood, but I am proud of the stupid thing I did next. He cowered and whimpered and essentially apologized, still with those blank, unmoving eyes, and I stood still for a second. My arm felt light and shrunken as if half of it were gone, but I didn't look. From the corridor, I had a choice of two doors: the one through which I'd entered, leading back to the desert, and the one opening onto the corral. I didn't think I could bend over him and unlatch the door to the desert. He'd just reach up and clamp onto my stomach. And I didn't want to open the door to the corral, or he'd drag me in and be able to attack the men if they ever came to help me. My body, still in control, made the good hand grab the bad elbow, and I beat him with my own arm, as if I had ripped it free to use as a club. "No!" I shouted. "No, no!" Lo lo lo, in Hebrew. I might even have said "Bad boy," but I hope not. It was the beating that damaged my hand permanently. I must have hit him hard enough to crush a ligament, because there is a lump on my hand to this day, 22

five years later, but he didn't even blink. He came around behind
me and grabbed my right leg, and again there was no pain—just
the feeling that he and I were playing tug-of-war with my body—
but I was afraid to pull too hard on the leg. He pulled the leg up,
stretching me out in a line from the door, where I clung with the
good hand to the mesh, like a dancer at the barre. It felt almost
good, as if the whole thing were nearer to being over. In three
moves I didn't feel, he took out most of the calf.

I opened the door to the desert and he ran out, with a quick   23
shove that staggered me. I couldn't move the right leg, just
crutched myself along on it into the Negev. He waited for me.
The cold in my stomach was stabbing my breath away. The hyena
and I were bonded now. Even if someone did come to help,
there was still something left to finish between us. I was
marked—his. I saw, in color, that he was going to knock me
over, and I thought, in black-and-white, No, don't, you'll hurt
my leg, I should keep it still.

A workman stood by a shed uphill, leaning on a tool in the   24
sand. He watched me walk toward the office, with the hyena
ahead and looking back at me. He was the only spectator I noticed, though I was told later, in the hospital, that some tourists,
there to see the animals, were screaming for help, and three—or
was it five?—soldiers had had their machine guns aimed at us
throughout the whole thing. Israeli soldiers carry their arms
everywhere when they're in uniform; but they must have been
afraid to shoot. I don't know. Stories get told afterward. I didn't
see anyone except the workman, looking on impassively, and the
leopard, pacing inside her fence, roaring a little, with the peace of
her heat gone as suddenly as it had appeared.

I am sure Efa crawled out to greet me with no intention to kill.   25
He had cried to me like an infant in distress, hunched over and
rounded. His ruff lay flat and soft and his tail hung down. He attacked me, I think, in a moment of thirst-induced delirium and
loneliness. If he had wanted to eat or to attack, he could have
taken my arm in a snap: one sharp jab and jerk, and the wrist
would have been gone before I even noticed. If he had wanted to

kill me, he could have leaped for my stomach as soon as he had pulled me down by the arm.

Cheetahs often catch hold of their prey's nose and run along-   26
side it. As the victim stumbles and falls, or staggers, or tries to run, the cheetah holds tight, closing mouth and nostrils in one stapled hold, or—with larger prey—biting into the throat to cut off air. Leopards like to leap down from trees for a quick crack of the back. Lions improvise. Each has its own specialty. Some leap up from behind, like a terrestrial leopard; some try a daring front leap, risking hooves and horns to bite into neck or face.

Hyenas are far more efficient. They catch hold of flesh, not   27
with small nips and throwing of weight but by smoothly and quickly transferring chunks of it from prey to throat. Food slips instantly from toothhold to stomach. Like human infants nursing, they seem to swallow without pausing for breath, as if food and air travelled in separate channels. They are the only predators adapted to eating bone. Their dung is white with it.

I heard a story of a young boy in Nairobi who was watching   28
over a herd of goats and fell asleep leaning on his stick. A hyena appeared and opened the boy's stomach with one quick rip. For the hyena it might have been play, this trying on of assault. But he won, as he was bound to do. I was told that someone took the boy to a doctor and he died a while later. He could have lived; we don't need all our intestines, and the hyena had probably left enough behind. But maybe they didn't have the right antibiotics or sterile dressings. I would have liked to ask him what he saw in the hyena's eyes.

In the ambulance, the driver chatted for a bit, then said, "Don't   29
close your eyes. If you feel faint, tell me and I'll stop right away."

To do what, watch me? I didn't tell him that I'd been ex-   30
hausted for months—I'd got parasites in Africa—and always shut my eyes when I had the chance. I closed them now, and he asked me questions with an anxiety that warmed my heart. I love to be taken care of. It was good to be strapped down and bandaged, all decisions out of my hands after the hard ones, the life-and-death ones. It was also, I learned, a good thing to have the wounds hid-

den. Once they were open to the air, my stomach clenched with pain that made life temporarily not worth living. The arm, I finally noticed, was curled up on itself, like paper shrivelling inward in a fire, but heavy instead of too light.

We arrived at the hospital with a screech and a yank and a   31
curse. The doors were stuck, but the driver pushed, and ran me in. Then he left with a wave of farewell. I waited and waited. A doctor came in and plowed my arm in search of a vein with blood, going deep under the muscle, to attach a saline drip. My nails were white, like things soaked in formaldehyde, and I was freezing. Bled white, I was. Nothing left to fill a test tube.

I asked the doctor to talk with the reserve's veterinarian before   32
he did anything. Hyena bites are violently infectious. The animals' mouths are full of bacteria from rotten meat. He shrugged. But when Shlomi told him to wait for the vet he did. The vet told him to clean the holes out and leave them open for now, because the infection could kill me.

"The infection will probably take the leg anyway," the doctor   33
told me. "The chances are fifty-fifty that we'll have to amputate."

I looked down once at the leg before they began cutting out   34
the dirtier shreds of flesh and paring the whole surface of the wound. The holes were impossibly wide, more than twice the size of the hyena's face. I know now that skin and muscle are stretched over bone like canvas over a canoe. One thinks of skin as irrevocably bonded to flesh, and all as one entity. But skin is attached to flesh only with the lightest of bonds, and, once it has been ripped, the body gives way naturally, pulling the flesh back to its scaffolding of bone. The invisible woman, I thought, as the chill took me; I can see right through my leg.

I couldn't see all of it because of my bad eyesight, and the leg   35
was still covered with blood-stuck sand, but it was strange the way the leg went down normally, then cut in to the bone, along the bone, and then out again to a normal ankle, except for a small gash on the side with fat poking out. I couldn't yet see the other hole. It was lower down, starting halfway past the one I could see, and continuing around the back of the leg to the other side, so al-

most the whole leg was girdled around. I still don't know how blood got to that stranded wall of flesh.

The doctor worked on the leg for an hour, clipping pieces of flesh out of the wounds with little scissor snips, as if my leg were a piece of cloth that he was carefully tailoring with dull tools. I asked for a larger dose of anesthetic, not because I felt any pain— I never felt any, really—but because I could feel the scissors scissoring away the flesh and I couldn't breathe. Between bouts of cutting, I kept joking, happy it was over, or might be over, and people crowded into the room to watch. No sterilization? Who cares? I was alive. They pumped saline into me so fast that my arm swelled and I had to go to the bathroom. For the first time, I realized how my life had changed. There is, after all, no simple dichotomy: intact and alive versus torn and dead. 36

I had expected the hyena bite in Africa, not in Israel. I had expected the price I paid for Africa to be high. The need that had driven me since I was eight years old had made me willing to risk anything, even death, to be in Africa watching animals. Anyone who works with animals expects to get hurt. You are a guest in their life—any intrusion is a threat to them. It is their separateness that makes them worthy of respect. 37

After the hospital, I went back to America for physical therapy and treatment of the parasites, which burned a path in my stomach for the next six months. Before I left, people from the reserve asked me to stand near Efa's cage. They wanted to know if his animosity was specific to me. He looked at me, again with those friendly blank eyes, and then rose up against the wire with a crash so loud that I thought he was breaking through. For one second, I saw his face coming toward me, mouth open, and I hopped back. They told me they were going to send him to a zoo where the keepers wouldn't have to go into the cage, but I heard later that a veterinarian came and put Efa to sleep. ("Forever asleep," the workers said.) Shlomi was there. 38

Back in America, too ill for school, I read about animals on my own. Then I went to graduate school, but I found the statistical 39 and analytical approach to animals too reductive. So I gave it up. But I couldn't not return to Africa. Five years after the hyena bite, I went back. Without a job, or any scientific purpose, I back-packed between Tanzania and Kenya, seeing the savanna in short bursts of safaris and hired cars and matatu buses.

I had almost died, eaten alive, and I was glad to be alive. The 40 scars had healed. Three long dents ran around the arm and the leg, blurred with spider tracks of canine punctures. The one war wound, the bump that grew where I hit the hyena, still hurt, but I was back in Africa.

Meaning and Purpose

1. In the introductory three paragraphs of this essay, Greenfield describes a hyena in such a way that we can later picture her personal experience with a hyena. What are three qualities of a hyena mentioned in these paragraphs that help you to better understand what later happens to Greenfield?
2. Greenfield had wanted to go to Africa but instead worked in Israel. Why did she work in Israel?
3. Obviously, the relationship between Efa and Shlomi differs greatly from the relationship between Efa and Greenfield. Why do you think this is so?
4. How did the first lesson that Greenfield learned in a self-defense class help her to deal with Efa?
5. How can you tell from reading this essay that Greenfield does not blame Efa for the attack?

Strategy

1. In paragraph 6, what point does Greenfield make about wild creatures in general when she writes, "Spotted hyenas are the sharks of the savanna"? What do hyenas and sharks have in common?

2. How does Greenfield describe Efa's attack? How can you tell that the attack was sudden?
3. What is the importance of the term *dichotomy* in paragraph 36? Suggest an appropriate synonym.
4. In paragraph 27, why are hyenas called "efficient"?
5. As Greenfield also notes in paragraph 27, hyenas eat the bones of the animals that they have killed. How does this information add to the tension of Greenfield's experience?

Style

1. This essay interweaves two descriptions. What are those two descriptions, and how does one support or add understanding to the other one?
2. What would you say is the best description of the people in the vicinity, as conveyed in paragraph 24, when Efa was attacking Greenfield?
3. As used critically, the term *tone* often refers to an author's attitude towards her topic. What, in your opinion, is the tone of this essay?
4. Why is this essay titled simply "Hyena"?
5. In paragraph 22, why does Greenfield shout, "Lo, lo, lo!" to Efa?

Writing Tasks

1. Each of us has been in a tight spot, though let us hope in not as tight a spot as Greenfield found herself. Write an essay describing an incident in your life that caused you harm or could have caused you harm. Be sure to relate the details of the incident.
2. Many of us have pets that have reacted angrily, often with good reason. Write an essay describing an incident in your pet's life when the pet reacted in some unexpected ways, being sure to describe the incident so that your reader will be able to imagine it, to "see it" mentally.

❦ Marcus Laffey ❦

Marcus Laffey is the pen name of a New York police officer who wishes to remain anonymous so he can keep his beat while pursuing a passion for writing. Blue Blood, *a work of nonfiction, will be published in 2001.*

Cop Diary

Because of numerous police movies and television shows, many people have stereotyped police officers. As you read this essay, try to keep your own stereotypes of police officers in mind as you consider Laffey's commentary on what a real police officer does and thinks.

Over the past year, more than a hundred people have worn my handcuffs. Not long ago, in a self-defense class, I wore them myself. There was a jolt of dissonance, like the perverse unfamiliarity at hearing your own voice on tape. Is this me? They were cold, and the metal edge pressed keenly against the bone if I moved, even when they were loose. The catch of the steel teeth as the cuffs tighten is austere and final, and never so much so as when it emanates from the small of your back. I thought, Hey, these things work. And then, Good thing. Because their intransigent grip means that, once they're on the correct pair of hands, no one should get hurt. Barring an unexpected kick or a bite, the story's over: no one's going to lose any teeth or blood, we're both going safely to jail, and at least one of us is going home tonight. 1

The handcuffs are a tool of the trade and an emblem of it, as are the gun and the nightstick. People—especially children whose eye level is at my equipment belt—stare at them, sometimes with a fearful look, but more often with fascination. Since I hold them from the other end, I regard them differently, just as surgeons don't feel uneasy, as I do, at the sight of a scalpel or a syringe. Police work can look ugly, especially when it's done well: you might see a man walking down the street, untroubled, untrou- 2

124

bling, when two or ten cops rush up to him, shouting over sirens and screeching tires, with their guns drawn. You haven't seen the old man rocking on a stoop three blocks away with one eye swollen shut. You haven't heard his story, his description of the man being handcuffed: coat, color, height, the tattoo on his wrist.

The transformation from citizen to prisoner is terrible to behold, regardless of its justice. Unlike my sister the teacher or my brother the lawyer, I take prisoners, and to exercise that authority is to invoke a profound social trust. Each time a surgeon undertakes the responsibility of cutting open a human being, it should be awesome and new, no matter how necessary the operation, no matter how routine. A police officer who takes away someone's freedom bears a burden of at least equal gravity. Let me tell you, it's a pleasure sometimes.

I walk a beat in a neighborhood of New York City that is a byword for slum. Even if the reality of places like the South Bronx, Brownsville, and Bed-Stuy no longer matches the reputation, and maybe never did, these bad neighborhoods are still bad. Children still walk through three different brands of crack vials in the building lobbies. People still shit in the stairwells. Gunshots in the night may have become less common in my precinct, but many people, young and old, can still distinguish that hard, sharp crack—like a broomstick snapped cleanly in half—from fireworks or a car backfiring.

The genuine surprise is how wholesome and ordinary this neighborhood sometimes seems, with its daily round of parents' getting kids ready for school, going to work, wondering if a car or a coat will make it through another winter. Life in the projects and the tenements can be just the way it is in suburbia, except that it takes place on busier streets and in smaller rooms. Sometimes it's better, in the way that city life, when it's good, is better than life anywhere else. In the summer, you can walk through the projects beneath shady aisles of sycamore and maple, past well-tended gardens and playgrounds teeming with children. There will be families having cookouts, old ladies reading Bibles on the benches, pensive pairs of men playing chess.

Once, I went to the roof of a project and saw a hawk perched on the rail. Always, you can see Manhattan in the near distance, its towers and spires studded with lights, stately and slapdash, like the crazy geometry of rock crystal. There are many days when I feel sorry for people who work indoors.

The other revelation when I became a cop was how much 6
people like cops. In safe neighborhoods, a cop is part of the scenery. I used to notice cops the way I noticed mailboxes, which is to say only when I needed one. But in bad neighborhoods I notice people noticing me, and especially certain classes of people— older people, young kids, single women, people dressed for work or church. They look at me with positive appreciation and relief. I am proof that tonight, on this walk home, no one's going to start with them. Sometimes they express that appreciation. The exceptions are groups of young guys on the street (older, if they're unemployed). Sometimes they're just hanging out, sometimes they're planning something more ambitious, and you're a sign that this wild night's not going to happen—not as they hoped, not here. Sometimes they express themselves, too.

When I'm working, I wear a Kevlar vest, and I carry a night- 7
stick, pepper spray, a radio, a flashlight, two sets of handcuffs, and a gun with two extra fifteen-round magazines. A thick, leather-bound memo book has been squeezed into my back pocket, and leather gloves, rubber gloves, department forms, and binoculars are stuffed in various other pockets. When you chase someone in this outfit, it's like running in a suit of armor while carrying a bag of groceries. But I'm safe, and it's only very rarely that I feel otherwise. All the people I've fought with were trying to get away.

I walk around on patrol, keeping an eye out and talking to 8
people, until a job comes up on the radio. The radio is constant and chaotic, a montage of stray details, awful and comic facts:

"Respond to a woman cornered by a large rodent in her living 9
room."

". . . supposed to be a one-year-old baby with its head split 10
open."

"The perp is a male Hispanic, white T-shirt, bluejeans, 11
possible mustache, repeat, possible mustache."

The appeal of patrol is its spontaneity and variety, its respon- 12
siveness to the rhythms of the street: there will be long lulls and
then sudden convulsions as pickup jobs and radio runs propel
you into a foot pursuit, a dispute, or a birth. When the action's
over, the world can seem slow and small, drearily confined. And
then you have to do the paperwork.

When you arrest someone, it's like a blind date. You spend a 13
few hours with a stranger, a few feet apart, saying "Tell me about
yourself." You ask, "How much do you weigh?" and "Are you a
gang member? Really! Which one?" And you hold hands, for a few
minutes, as you take prints—each fingertip individually, then four
fingers together, flat, and the thumb, flat, at the bottom of the
card. A lot of people try to help you by rolling the fingers themselves, which usually smudges the print; sometimes that's their intent. Crackheads often don't have usable prints: their fingers are
burned smooth from the red-hot glass pipe. Junkies, as they're
coming down, can go into a whole-body cramp, and have hands
as stiff as lobster claws. Perps collared for robbery or assault may
have bruised, swollen, or bloody fingers. You try to be gentle, and
you wear latex gloves.

When you print a perp, you're close to him, and because 14
you're close you're vulnerable. You take off the cuffs and put your
gun in a locker. Once, I was printing a guy as he found out he was
not getting a summons but, instead, going through the system. He
became enraged at the desk sergeant, screaming curses and
threats, and I wondered if he'd make a run at him or, worse, at me.
But I was holding his hands and could feel that they were as limp
and loose as if he lay in a hot bath—as if his body were indifferent
to the hatred in his voice. So I went on printing as he went on
shouting, each of us concentrating on the task at hand.

The paperwork involved in policing is famously wasteful or is 15
a necessary evil, sometimes both. Often, it reaches a nuanced
complexity that is itself somehow sublime, like a martial art. If, for
example, you arrested a man for hitting his girlfriend with a tire
iron and then found a crack vial in his pocket, the paperwork

would include a Domestic Incident Report (for follow-up visits by the domestic-violence officer); a 61, or complaint, which describes the offense, the perp, and the victim; and an aided card, which contains information on the victim and what medical attention she received. The 61 and the aided are assigned numbers from the Complaint Index and the Aided and Accident Index. The aided number goes on the 61, and both the complaint and the aided numbers go on the On-Line Booking Sheet. The O.L.B.S. provides more detailed information on the perp; it has to be hand-written, and then entered into the computer, which in turn generates an arrest number.

You would also have to type two vouchers—both of which   16
have serial numbers that must be entered on the 61 and on the O.L.B.S.—for the tire iron and the crack vial; affix a lead seal to the tire iron; and put the crack vial in a narcotics envelope in the presence of the desk officer, writing your name, your shield number, and the date across the seal. You also fill out a Request for Lab Exam (Controlled Substance and Marihuana) and attach it to the envelope. Next, you run a warrant check on the computer, take prints, and bring the perp up to the squad room to be debriefed by detectives, who ask if he knows of and is willing to tell about other crimes.

The prisoner is then searched again and delivered to Central   17
Booking, at Criminal Court. There he waits in a holding cell until he is arraigned before a judge. At C.B., you photograph the prisoner and have him examined by the Emergency Medical Service, interviewed by the Criminal Justice Agency for his bail application, and searched yet again. Only then is he in the system, and out of your hands. Next, you see an assistant district attorney and write up and swear to a document that is also called a complaint. The entire process, from the arrest to the signing of the complaint, usually takes around five hours—if nothing goes wrong.

There are arrests that cops hope and train for like athletes, and   18
in this felony Olympics, collars for homicides, pattern crimes, drugs by the kilo, and automatic weapons are considered gold medals. But the likelihood that things will go wrong with arrests

seems to escalate with their importance: a baroque legal system, combined with the vagaries of chance, provides an inexhaustible source of misadventure. You feel like a diver on the platform who has just noticed that all the judges are Russian.

There was my rapist, a match for a pattern of sexual assaults on elderly women. My partner and I responded to a report that a suspicious person was lurking in the stairwell of a project, one floor up from the latest attack. When the man saw us, he ran, shouting, "Help me! Get a video camera!" We wrestled with him for what seemed like ages; he was limber and strong and sweat-soaked, as slippery as a live fish, and was chewing on a rolled-up dollar bill filled with cocaine. He looked just like the police sketch, and also had distinctive green eyes, which victims had described. He had been staying on that floor with his girlfriend until he beat her up and she threw him out, on the same day as the last attack. He was the rapist, beyond a doubt. 19

At the precinct, he collapsed, and he told the paramedics he'd ingested three grams of cocaine. At the hospital, his heart rate was two hundred and twenty beats per minute, and he was made to drink an electrolyte solution and eat activated charcoal, which caused him to drool black. He was handcuffed to a cot in the E.R. while the midnight pageant of medical catastrophes was brought in. There was an E.D.P. (an emotionally disturbed person) who had bitten clean through his tongue, clipping into it a precise impression of his upper teeth. Another E.D.P., an enormous drunk picked up from the streets, was writhing and thrashing as a diminutive Filipina nurse tried to draw blood: "Now I prick you! Now I just prick you!" An old man threw up, and another prisoner-patient, handcuffed to the cot next to him, kindly handed him the closest receptacle he could find—a plastic pitcher half filled with urine, which splashed back as he vomited, and made him vomit more. 20

I'd worked almost twenty-four hours by the time we got back to the precinct, when a detective from Special Victims called to say that my perp had already been taken in for a lineup, a few days before, and had not been identified as the rapist. This meant that we had to let him go. I'd felt nothing toward 21 my suspect throughout our ordeal, even when I fought with him, although I believed he had done hideous, brutal things. But now, suddenly, I hated him, because he was no longer a magnificent and malignant catch—he was just some random ass-hole who had stolen an entire day of my life.

A few days later, I saw him on the street, and he said hello. I didn't. A few days after that, he beat up his girlfriend again, then disappeared. The rapes stopped. 22

* * *

Now, after a few years on the job, I have my own war stories. On weekends, I'll sit back, lift up my feet, and tell my girlfriend, "I took a bullet out of a lady's living room. It must have been shot from Jersey. It went through the glass, and stopped on the sill. It landed there like a sparrow." Or "I talked a runaway into coming home. She was fourteen years old. All I had to do was tell her I'd lock up her boyfriend's whole family if she didn't." At times, the point of the job seems to be to make it home with an intact skin and a good story. The stories are a benefit, like the dental plan. 23

And you need them, like your handcuffs or your vest, to con-trol events when you have to, and to cover your back. If you're a cop, you need a quick tongue, to tell the victim, the perp, the crowd, the sergeant, the D.A., the judge, and the jury what you're doing, what you did, and why. Are you ready to make a state-ment? No? Then you just did. You told me you weren't ready. "Police were unprepared to answer," says the lead in the morning paper. Or the gossip in the locker room, or the word on the street. 24

I also hear more than my share of stories. And so, aside from the odd Christmas party or fund-raiser, I don't hang out with cops from the precinct. My friends who are cops were friends of mine before I went on the job. And most of the people I see regularly have nothing at all to do with police work. The job has enough of me. For five days a week, I stay off the streets unless I'm working them. And when I'm not in uniform I'd just as soon not see blue.

But I also notice that when I'm out on weekends and there's another cop there—at a wedding or a cookout or a club—I'll of-ten spend most of the time talking with him. There are things 25 you've done and places you've been that no one else has had to do or see in quite the same way.

Meaning and Purpose

1. How does Laffey quickly establish that he is well qualified to write this essay?
2. How does Laffey quickly establish that he is not the stereotypical "brutal cop"?
3. Laffey says, in paragraph 3, that a police officer "who takes away someone's freedom bears a burden of at least equal gravity" to that of the surgeon who cuts open a human being, but Laffey adds, "Let me tell you, it's a pleasure sometimes." What can be pleasurable, according to this essay, about taking away someone's freedom?
4. What is Laffey describing in paragraph 7, when he says he sometimes feels like he is "running in a suit of armor while carrying a bag of groceries"?
5. What is Laffey describing, in paragraph 18, when he says that sometimes "You feel like a diver on the platform who has just noticed that all the judges are Russian"?

Strategy

1. In paragraphs 15 and 16, why does Laffey list and discuss all the forms that he must fill out? How does this strategy add to the complete picture of the working life of a cop?
2. In paragraph 13, why does Laffey describe arresting someone by saying that it's "like a blind date"?
3. What strategy does Laffey use in this essay to show that he believes police officers must do too much paperwork?
4. The last sentence of the essay, "The rapes stopped," hints that Laffey suspects something. What might he suspect? Why does he use an indirect strategy in this sentence?

Style

1. Laffey says, in paragraph 8, that his radio is "a montage of stray details." What does montage mean in that phrase? Suggest a synonym.
2. What does Laffey mean, in paragraph 13, when he says that someone is "collared" for a robbery? What does that term suggest to you?
3. In paragraph 18, Laffey says that we have "a baroque legal system." What does the term baroque mean? Suggest a synonym for how that word is used in this essay.
4. As is noted in paragraph 12, at some point after a period of excitement, a police officer can become "drearily confined." In one or two sentences, describe Laffey's idea of dreary confinement.
5. What does the word emblem mean as it is used to describe handcuffs in paragraph 2? In what two or three other ways can the term emblem be used in other contexts?

Writing Tasks

1. All of us have had calm days that were suddenly punctuated by a period of excitement. Write an essay that describes such a day in your life, starting with your description of the day's calm beginnings and then moving to your description of the day's period of excitement. If your choice of topic permits, end the essay by describing the calmness at the end of that day.
2. Sometimes we believe that we know a person fairly well, and then that person suddenly gets angry or sad or ecstatic, seemingly for no reason, surprising us until we understand what caused the unexpected mood change. Write a descriptive essay that relates an incident that happened to you or one of your friends and caused you or your friend to suddenly change from acting "normal" to behaving unpredictably. Be sure to describe what caused the change in the person.

❦ George Simpson ❦

Born in Virginia in 1950, George Simpson studied journalism at the University of North Carolina. He wrote for the Carolina Financial Times *in North Carolina and for the* News-Gazette *in Virginia before joining the staff at* Newsweek. *In 1978 he was appointed* Newsweek's *director of public affairs. For a series of articles about the football program at the University of North Carolina, he won the Sigma Delta Chi Best Feature Writing Award. He has contributed stories to* The New York Times, Sport, Glamour, *and other major publications.*

The War Room at Bellevue

In this essay, first published in New York *magazine in 1983, George Simpson uses objective description of events during one night at Bellevue Hospital to achieve immediacy. Arranging the emergency room scenes in strict (by-the-clock) chronological order creates the impression of a minute-by-minute account and contributes to the power of the description.*

Simpson describes the staff at the Bellevue trauma center speedily responding to emergencies with both efficiency and care. Notice how they maintain commonplace relationships among themselves even amid the chaos.

Bellevue. The name conjures up images of an indoor war zone: the wounded and bleeding lining the halls, screaming for help while harried doctors in blood-stained smocks rush from stretcher to stretcher, fighting a losing battle against exhaustion and the crushing number of injured. "What's worse," says a longtime Bellevue nurse, "is that we have this image of being a hospital only for . . . ." She pauses, then lowers her voice; "for crazy people." 1

Though neither battlefield nor Bedlam is a valid image, there is something extraordinary about the monstrous complex that spreads for five blocks along First Avenue in Manhattan. It is said best by the head nurse in Adult Emergency Service: "If you have 2

133

any chance for survival, you have it here." Survival—that is why they come. Why do injured cops drive by a half-dozen other hospitals to be treated at Bellevue? They've seen the Bellevue emergency team in action.

9:00 P.M. It is a Friday night in the Bellevue emergency room.   3
The after-work crush is over (those who've suffered through the day, only to come for help after the five-o'clock whistle has blown) and it is nearly silent except for the mutter of voices at the admitting desk, where administrative personnel discuss who will go for coffee. Across the spotless white-walled lobby, ten people sit quietly, passively, in pastel plastic chairs, waiting for word of relatives or to see doctors. In the past 24 hours, 300 people have come to the Bellevue Adult Emergency Service. Fewer than 10 percent were true emergencies. One man sleeps fitfully in the emergency ward while his heartbeat, respiration, and blood pressure are monitored by control consoles mounted over his bed. Each heartbeat trips a tiny bleep in the monitor, which attending nurses can hear across the ward. A half hour ago, doctors in the trauma room withdrew a six-inch stiletto blade from his back. When he is stabilized, the patient will be moved upstairs to the twelve-bed Surgical Intensive Care Unit.

9:05 P.M. An ambulance backs into the receiving bay, its red   4
and yellow lights flashing in and out of the lobby. A split second later, the glass doors burst open as a nurse and an attendant roll a mobile stretcher into the lobby. When the nurse screams, "Emergent!" the lobby explodes with activity as the way is cleared to the trauma room. Doctors appear from nowhere and transfer the bloodied body of a black man to the treatment table. Within seconds his clothes are stripped away, revealing a tiny stab wound in his left side. Three doctors and three nurses rush around the victim, each performing a task necessary to begin treatment. Intravenous needles are inserted into his arms and groin. A doctor draws blood for the lab, in case surgery is necessary. A nurse begins inserting a catheter into the victim's penis and continues to feed in tubing until the catheter reaches the bladder. Urine flows through the tube into a plastic bag. Doctors are glad not to see blood in the urine. Another nurse records pulse and blood pressure.

The victim is in good shape. He shivers slightly, although the trauma room is exceedingly warm. His face is bloodied, but shows no major lacerations. A third nurse, her elbow propped on the treatment table, asks the man a series of questions, trying to quickly outline his medical history. He answers abruptly. He is drunk. His left side is swabbed with yellow disinfectant and a doctor injects a local anesthetic. After a few seconds another doctor inserts his finger into the wound. It sinks in all the way to the knuckle. He begins to rotate his finger like a child trying to get a marble out of a milk bottle. The patient screams bloody murder and tries to struggle free.

Meanwhile in the lobby, a security guard is ejecting a derelict who has begun to drink from a bottle hidden in his coat pocket. "He's a regular, was in here just two days ago," says a nurse. "We checked him pretty close then, so he's probably okay now. Can you believe those were clean clothes we gave him?" The old man, blackened by filth, leaves quietly.

9:15 P.M. A young Hispanic man interrupts, saying his pregnant girl friend, sitting outside in his car, is bleeding heavily from her vagina. She is rushed into an examination room, treated behind closed doors, and rolled into the observation ward, where, much later in the night, a gynecologist will treat her in a special room—the same one used to examine rape victims. Nearby, behind curtains, the neurologist examines an old white woman to determine if her headaches are due to head injury. They are not.

9:45 P.M. The trauma room has been cleared and cleaned mercilessly. The examination rooms are three-quarters full—another overdose, two asthmatics, a young woman with abdominal pains. In the hallway, a derelict who has been sleeping it off urinates all over the stretcher. He sleeps on while attendants change his clothes. An ambulance—one of four that patrol Manhattan for Bellevue from 42nd Street to Houston, river to river—delivers a middle-aged white woman and two cops, the three of them soaking wet. The woman has escaped from the psychiatric floor of a nearby hospital and tried to drown herself in the East River. The cops fished her out. She lies on a stretcher shivering beneath white blankets. Her eyes stare at the ceiling. She speaks clearly when an administrative worker begins routine questioning. The cops are given hospital gowns and wait to receive tetanus shots and gamma globulin—a hedge against infection from the befouled river water. They will hang around the E.R. for another two hours, telling their story to as many as six other policemen who show up to hear it. The woman is rolled into an examination room, where a male nurse speaks gently: "They tell me you fell into the river." "No," says the woman, "I jumped. I have to commit suicide." "Why?" asks the nurse. "Because I'm insane and I can't help [it]. I have to die." The nurse gradually discovers the woman has a history of psychological problems. She is given dry bedclothes and placed under guard in the hallway. She lies on her side, staring at the wall.

The pace continues to increase. Several more overdose victims   9 arrive by ambulance. One, a young black woman, had done a striptease on the street just before passing out. A second black woman is semiconscious and spends the better part of her time at Bellevue alternately cursing it and pleading with the doctors. Attendants find a plastic bottle coated with methadone in the pocket of a Hispanic O.D. The treatment is routinely the same, and sooner or later involves vomiting. Just after doctors begin to treat the O.D., he vomits great quantities of wine and methadone in all directions. "Lovely business, huh?" laments one of the doctors. A young nurse confides that if there were other true emergencies, the overdose victims would be given lower priority. "You can't help thinking they did it to themselves," she says, "while the others are accident victims."

10:30 P.M. A policeman who twisted his knee struggling with   10 an "alleged perpetrator" is examined and released. By 10:30, the lobby is jammed with friends and relatives of patients in various stages of treatment and recovery. The attendant who also functions as a translator for Hispanic patients adds chairs to accommodate the overflow. The medical walk-in rate stays steady—between eight and ten patients waiting. A pair of derelicts, each with battered eyes, appear at the admitting desk. One has a dramatically swollen face laced with black stitches.

11:00 P.M. The husband of the attempted suicide arrives. He   11 thanks the police for saving his wife's life, then talks at length with doctors about her condition. She continues to stare into the void and does not react when her husband approaches her stretcher.

Meanwhile, patients arrive in the lobby at a steady pace. A young G.I. on leave has lower-back pains; a Hispanic man complains of pain in his side; occasionally parents hurry through the adult E.R. carrying children into the pediatric E.R. A white woman of about 50 marches into the lobby from the walk-in entrance. Dried blood covers her right eyebrow and upper lip. She begins to perform. "I was assaulted on 28th and Lexington, I was," she says grandly, "and I don't have to take it *anymore*. I was a bride 21 years ago, and, God, I was beautiful then." She has captured the attention of all present. "I was there when the boys came home—on Memorial Day—and I don't have to take this kind of treatment." 12

As midnight approaches, the nurses prepare for the shift change. They must brief the incoming staff and make sure all reports are up-to-date. One young brunet says, "Christ, I'm gonna go home and take a shower—I smell like vomit." 13

11:50 P.M. The triage nurse is questioning an old black-man about chest pains, and a Hispanic woman is having an asthma attack, when an ambulance, its sirens screaming full tilt, roars into the receiving bay. There is a split-second pause as everyone drops what he or she is doing and looks up. Then all hell breaks loose. Doctors and nurses are suddenly sprinting full-out toward the trauma room. The glass doors burst open and the occupied stretcher is literally run past me. Cops follow. It is as if a comet has whooshed by. In the trauma room it all becomes clear. A half-dozen doctors and nurses surround the lifeless form of a Hispanic man with a shotgun hole in his neck the size of your fist. Blood pours from a second gaping wound in his chest. A respirator is slammed over his face, making his chest rise and fall as if he were breathing. "No pulse," reports one doctor. A nurse jumps on a stool and, leaning over the man, begins to pump his chest with her palms. "No blood pressure," screams another nurse. The ambulance driver appears shaken. "I never thought I'd get here in time," he stutters. More doctors from the trauma team upstairs arrive. Wrappings from syringes and gauze pads fly through the air. The victim's eyes are open yet devoid of life. His body takes on a 14 yellow tinge. A male nurse winces at the gunshot wound. "This guy really pissed off somebody," he says. This is no ordinary shooting. It is an execution. IV's are jammed into the body in the groin and arms. One doctor has been plugging in an electrocardiograph and asks everyone to stop for a second so he can get a reading. "Forget it," shouts the doctor in charge. "No time." "Take it easy, Jimmy," someone yells at the head physician. It is apparent by now that the man is dead, but the doctors keep trying injections and finally they slit open the chest and reach inside almost up to their elbows. They feel the extent of the damage and suddenly it is all over. "I told 'em he was dead," says one nurse, withdrawing. "They didn't listen." The room is very still. The doctors are momentarily disgusted, then go on about their business. The room clears quickly. Finally there is only a male nurse and the still-warm body, now waxy-yellow, with huge ribs exposed on both sides of the chest and giant holes in both sides of the neck. The nurse speculates that this is yet another murder in a Hispanic political struggle that has brought many such victims to Bellevue. He marvels at the extent of the wounds and repeats, "This guy was really blown away."

Midnight. A hysterical woman is hustled through the lobby   15
into an examination room. It is the dead man's wife, and she is nearly delirious. "I know he's dead, I know he's dead," she screams over and over. Within moments the lobby is filled with anxious relatives of the victim, waiting for word on his condition. The police are everywhere asking questions, but most people say they saw nothing. One young woman says she heard six shots, two louder than the other four. At some point, word is passed that the man is, in fact, dead. Another woman breaks down in hysterics; everywhere young Hispanics are crying and comforting each other. Plainclothes detectives make a quick examination of the body, check on the time of pronouncement of death, and begin to ask questions, but the bereaved are too stunned to talk. The rest of the uninvolved people in the lobby stare dumbly, their injuries suddenly paling in light of a death.

12:30 A.M. A black man appears at the admission desk and   16
says he drank poison by mistake. He is told to have a seat. The ambulance brings in a young white woman, her head wrapped in

white gauze. She is wailing terribly. A girl friend stands over her, crying, and a boyfriend clutches the injured woman's hands, saying, "I'm here, don't worry, I'm here." The victim has fallen downstairs at a friend's house. Attendants park her stretcher against the wall to wait for an examination room to clear. There are eight examination rooms and only three doctors. Unless you are truly an emergency, you will wait. One doctor is stitching up the elbow of a drunk who's been punched out. The friends of the woman who fell down the stairs glance up at the doctors anxiously, wondering why their friend isn't being treated faster.

1:10 A.M. A car pulls into the bay and a young Hispanic asks if a shooting victim has been brought here. The security guard blurts out, "He's dead." The young man is stunned. He peels his tires leaving the bay. 17

1:20 A.M. The young woman of the stairs is getting stitches in a small gash over her left eye when the same ambulance driver who brought in the gunshot victim delivers a man who has been stabbed in the back on East 3rd Street. Once again the trauma room goes from 0 to 60 in five seconds. The patient is drunk, which helps him endure the pain of having the catheter inserted through his penis into his bladder. Still he yells, "That hurts like a bastard," then adds sheepishly, "Excuse me, ladies." But he is not prepared for what comes next. An X-ray reveals a collapsed right lung. After just a shot of local anesthetic, the doctor slices open his side and inserts a long plastic tube. Internal bleeding had kept the lung pressed down and prevented it from reinflating. The tube releases the pressure. The ambulance driver says the cops grabbed the guy who ran the eight-inch blade into the victim's back. "That's not the one," says the man. "They got the wrong guy." A nurse reports that there is not much of the victim's type blood available at the hospital. One of the doctors says that's okay, he won't need surgery. Meanwhile blood pours from the man's knife wound and the tube in his side. As the nurses work, they chat about personal matters, yet they respond immediately to orders from either doctor. "How ya doin'?" the doctor asks the patient. "Okay," he says. His blood spatters on the floor. 18

So it goes into the morning hours. A Valium overdose, a woman who fainted, a man who went through the windshield of 19 his car. More overdoses. More drunks with split eyebrows and chins. The doctors and nurses work without complaint. "This is nothing, about normal, I'd say," concludes the head nurse. "No big deal."

Meaning and Purpose

1. Have you ever been in a hospital emergency room? How would you describe the experience? Were you aware of the attitudes of the doctors and nurses? Of the people waiting with the patients? Do any of Simpson's descriptions compare with what you saw?
2. What do you believe to be Simpson's purpose in "The War Room at Bellevue"?
3. What impressions of the hospital and its staff grow from the description? What details give you that impression?
4. Although Simpson does not describe the city that surrounds the hospital, what impression of the city does he leave you with? Support your answer with details from the essay.
5. Why does Simpson capitalize "Bedlam" in paragraph 2? What are the denotation and connotation of the word?

Strategy

1. What is the structure of this descriptive essay?
2. Many internal workings of "The War Room at Bellevue" are constructed on a stimulus–response pattern—that is, an event takes place and people respond. You'll find a stimulus–response pattern in paragraph 4: It opens with the arrival of an ambulance; a patient is rolled into the lobby on a mobile stretcher; a nurse screams "Emergent!"; and the scene explodes with action. Find a stimulus–response pattern in other passages of the essay.
3. Often Simpson has to describe simultaneous events—that is, separate actions that take place at the same time. Find at least four overt transitions at the beginning of paragraphs that capture the sense of simultaneous action.

4. Simpson describes the Bellevue emergency room in the present tense. What is the effect of using this tense?
5. Comment on the spatial arrangement of some of the descriptions. Is it broad to narrow? Near to far? Center outward? Give examples.

Style

1. How would you describe the narrator of "The War Room at Bellevue"? Is the material presented objectively or subjectively?
2. What words and images help to create the sense of a battle in the first two paragraphs?
3. How does the tone of the final paragraph differ from the tone that Simpson creates through most of the essay?
4. Identify phrases that help to create the sense of sound in paragraph 3. Find words that create a dominant sense impression in one or two other paragraphs.

Writing Tasks

1. Describe a scene in which a great deal of action takes place—a sports event, a shopping mall, an intersection, a park, or a school yard. Keep your description objective, carefully selecting the details to create, without emotion or judgment, a dominant impression.
2. Compare the subjective description in "Once More to the Lake," which you'll find in Chapter 12, with the objective description in "The War Room at Bellevue." What words make the essays predominantly subjective or objective? What is the overall effectiveness of each strategy and its suitability to the subject? Could each essay be told from the other point of view?

❦ Gretel Ehrlich ❦

Journalist, poet, fiction writer, and documentary film maker, Gretel Ehrlich was born in California and studied at Bennington College, UCLA Film School, and the New School for Social Research. After a journey to Wyoming to make a documentary film, Ehrlich decided to live there, doing various kinds of ranch work including branding, sheep herding, and helping with the births of lambs and calves. Her many books include a collection of essays, The Solace of Open Spaces; Drinking Dry Clouds: Stories from Wyoming; Arctic Heat: A Poem Cycle *(with David Buckland); and* A Match to the Heart: One Woman's Story of Being Struck by Lightning, *in which the work below appears.*

Struck by Lightning

This essay, from a larger work, imitates an ancient mystical journal from death or near-death to rebirth. While describing all of the events that occur as a result of Ehrlich's being struck by lightning, the essay also stirs emotions far below the event's surface, entering the realm of thoughts of death and how it is possible to describe that which one has not yet endured.

As you read this essay, pay particular attention to how Ehrlich uses time as a device to bring the reader in and out of the experience, just as Ehrlich herself mentally traveled through those events. And note how she uses description to appeal to the image-making qualities of a reader's mind. You not only can mentally "see" many events in this essay, but you can also "feel" many of its parts.

Deep in an ocean. I am suspended motionless. The water is 1 gray. That's all there is, and before that? My arms are held out straight, cruciate, my head and legs hang limp. Nothing moves. Brown kelp lies flat in mud and fish are buried in liquid clouds of dust. There are no shadows or sounds. Should there be? I don't know if I am alive, but if not, how do I know I am dead? My body is leaden, heavier than gravity. Gravity is done with me. No more sinking and rising or bobbing in currents. There is a terrible feeling of oppression with no oppressor. I try to lodge my mind against some boundary, some reference point, but the continent of the body dissolves . . .

A single heartbeat stirs gray water. Blue trickles in, just a tiny stream. Then a long silence.   2

Another heartbeat. This one is louder, as if amplified. Sound   3
takes a shape: it is a snowplow moving grayness aside like a heavy snowdrift. I can't tell if I'm moving, but more blue water flows in. Seaweed begins to undulate, then a whole kelp forest rises from the ocean floor. A fish swims past and looks at me. Another heartbeat drives through dead water, and another, until I am surrounded by blue.

Sun shines above all this. There is no pattern to the way its   4
glint comes free and falls in long knives of light. My two beloved dogs appear. They flank me like tiny rockets, their fur pressed against my ribs. A leather harness holds us all together. The dogs climb toward light, pulling me upward at a slant from the sea.

I have been struck by lightning and I am alive.   5

Before electricity carved its blue path toward me, before the   6
negative charge shot down from cloud to ground, before "streamers" jumped the positive charge back up from ground to cloud, before air expanded and contracted producing loud pressure pulses I could not hear because I was already dead, I had been walking.

When I started out on foot that August afternoon, the thun-   7
derstorm was blowing in fast. On the face of the mountain, a mile ahead, hard westerly gusts and sudden updrafts collided, pulling black clouds apart. Yet the storm looked harmless. When a distant thunderclap scared the dogs, I called them to my side and rubbed their ears: "Don't worry, you're okay as long as you're with me."

I woke in a pool of blood, lying on my stomach some distance   8
from where I should have been, flung at an odd angle to one side of the dirt path. The whole sky had grown dark. Was it evening,

and if so, which one? How many minutes or hours had elapsed since I lost consciousness, and where were the dogs? I tried to call out to them but my voice didn't work. The muscles in my throat were paralyzed and I couldn't swallow. Were the dogs dead? Everything was terribly wrong: I had trouble seeing, talking, breathing, and I couldn't move my legs or right arm. Nothing remained in my memory—no sounds, flashes, smells, no warnings of any kind. Had I been shot in the back? Had I suffered a stroke or heart attack? These thoughts were dark pools in sand.

The sky was black. Was this a storm in the middle of the day or was it night with a storm traveling through? When thunder exploded over me, I knew I had been hit by lightning.   9

The pain in my chest intensified and every muscle in my body ached. I was quite sure I was dying. What was it one should do or think or know? I tried to recall the Buddhist instruction regarding dying—which position to lie in, which direction to face. Did the "Lion's position" taken by the Buddha mean lying on the left or the right? And which sutra to sing? Oh yes, the Heart Sutra . . . gaté, gaté, paragaté . . . form and formlessness. Paradox and cosmic jokes. Surviving after trying to die "properly" would be truly funny, but the chances of that seemed slim.   10

Other words drifted in: how the "gateless barrier" was the gate through which one passes to reach enlightenment. Yet if there was no gate, how did one pass through? Above me, high on the hill, was the gate on the ranch that lead nowhere, a gate I had mused about often. Now its presence made me smile. Even when I thought I had no aspirations for enlightenment, too much effort in that direction was being expended. How could I learn to slide, yet remain aware?   11

To be struck by lightning: what a way to get enlightened. That would be the joke if I survived. It seemed important to remember jokes. My thinking did not seem connected to the inert body that was in such terrible pain. Sweep the mind of weeds, I kept telling myself—that's what years of Buddhist practice had taught me. . . . But where were the dogs, the two precious ones I had watched being born and had raised in such intimacy and trust? I wanted them with me. I wanted them to save me again.   12

It started to rain. Every time a drop hit bare skin there was an   13 explosion of pain. Blood crusted my left eye. I touched my good hand to my heart, which was beating wildly, erratically. My chest was numb, as if it had been sprayed with novocaine. No feeling of peace filled me. Death was a bleakness, a grayness about which it was impossible to be curious or relieved. I loved those dogs and hoped they weren't badly hurt. If I didn't die soon, how many days would pass before we were found, and when would the scavengers come? The sky was dark, or was that the way life flew out of the body, in a long tube with no light at the end? I lay on the cold ground waiting. The mountain was purple, and sage stirred against my face. I knew I had to give up all this, then my own body and all my thinking. Once more I lifted my head to look for the dogs but, unable to see them, I twisted myself until I faced east and tried to let go of all desire.

When my eyes opened again I knew I wasn't dead. Images   14
from World War II movies filled my head: of wounded soldiers dragging themselves across a field, and if I could have laughed— that is, made my face work into a smile and get sounds to discharge from my throat—I would have. God, it would have been good to laugh. Instead, I considered my options: either lie there and wait for someone to find me—how many days or weeks would that take?—or somehow get back to the house. I calmly assessed what might be wrong with me—stroke, cerebral hemorrhage, gunshot wound—but it was bigger than I could understand. The instinct to survive does not rise from particulars; a deep but general misery rollercoasted me into action. I tried to propel myself on my elbows but my right arm didn't work. The wind had swung around and was blowing in from the east. It was still a dry storm with only sputtering rain, but when I raised myself up, lightning fingered the entire sky.

It is not true that lightning never strikes the same place twice.   15
I had entered a shower of sparks and furious brightness and, worried that I might be struck again, watched as lightning touched down all around me. Years before, in the high country, I'd been hit by lightning: an electrical charge had rolled down an open meadow during a fearsome thunderstorm, surged up the legs of

my horse, coursed through me, and bounced a big spark off the top of my head. To be struck again—and this time it was a direct hit—what did it mean?

The feeling had begun to come back into my legs and after many awkward attempts, I stood. To walk meant lifting each leg up by the thigh, moving it forward with my hands, setting it down. The earth felt like a peach that had split open in the middle; one side moved up while the other side moved down and my legs were out of rhythm. The ground rolled the way it does during an earthquake and the sky was tattered book pages waving in different directions. Was the ground liquifying under me, or had the molecular composition of my body deliquesced? I struggled to piece together fragments. Then it occurred to me that my brain was torn and that's where the blood had come from.   16

I walked. Sometimes my limbs held me, sometimes they didn't. I don't know how many times I fell but it didn't matter because I was making slow progress toward home.   17

Home—the ranch house—was about a quarter of a mile away. I don't remember much about getting there. My concentration went into making my legs work. The storm was strong. All the way across the basin, lightning lifted parts of mountains and sky into yellow refulgence and dropped them again, only to lift others. The inside of my eyelids turned gold and I could see the dark outlines of things through them. At the bottom of the hill I opened the door to my pickup and blew the horn with the idea that someone might hear me. No one came. My head had swollen to an indelicate shape. I tried to swallow—I was so thirsty—but the muscles in my throat were still paralyzed and I wondered when I would no longer be able to breathe.   18

Inside the house, sounds began to come out of me. I was doing crazy things, ripping my hiking boots off because the bottoms of my feet were burning, picking up the phone when I was finally able to scream. One of those times, someone happened to be on the line. I was screaming incoherently for help. My last conscious act was to dial 911.   19

Dark again. Pressing against sore ribs, my dogs pulled me out of the abyss, pulled and pulled. I smelled straw. My face was on   20 tatami. I opened my eyes, looked up, and saw neighbors. Had they come for my funeral? The phone rang and I heard someone give directions to the ambulance driver, who was lost. A "first responder," an EMT from town who has a reputation with the girls, leaned down and asked if he could "touch me" to see if there were any broken bones. What the hell, I thought. I was going to die anyway. Let him have his feel. But his touch was gentle and professional, and I was grateful.

I slipped back into unconsciousness and when I woke again two EMTs were listening to my heart. I asked them to look for my dogs but they wouldn't leave me. Someone else in the room went outside and found Sam and Yaki curled up on the porch, frightened but alive. Now I could rest. I felt the medics jabbing needles into the top of my hands, trying unsuccessfully to get IVs started, then strapping me onto a backboard and carrying me out the front door of the house, down steps, into lightning and rain, into what was now a full-blown storm. 21

The ambulance rocked and slid, slamming my bruised body against the metal rails of the gurney. Every muscle was in violent spasm and there was a place on my back near the heart that burned. I heard myself yell in pain. Finally the EMTs rolled up towels and blankets and wedged them against my arms, shoulders, hips, and knees so the jolting of the vehicle wouldn't dislodge me. The ambulance slid down into ditches, struggled out, bumped from one deep rut to another. I asked to be taken to the hospital in Cody, but they said they were afraid my heart might stop again. As it was, the local hospital was thirty-five miles away, ten of them dirt, and the trip took more than an hour. 22

Our arrival seemed a portent of disaster—and an occasion for comedy. I had been struck by lightning around five in the afternoon. It was now 9:00 P.M. Nothing at the hospital worked. Their one EKG machine was nonfunctional, and jokingly the nurses blamed it on me. "Honey, you've got too much electricity in your body," one of them told me. Needles were jammed into my hand—no one had gotten an IV going yet—and the doctor on call hadn't arrived, though half an hour had elapsed. The EMTs kept assuring me: "Don't worry, we won't leave you here." When an- 23

other nurse, who was filling out an admission form, asked me
how tall I was, I answered: "Too short to be struck by lightning."

> "Electrical injury often results in ventricular fibrillation and   24
> injury to the medullary centers of the brain. Immediately
> after electric shock patients are usually comatose, apneic,
> and in circulatory collapse. . . ."

When the doctor on call—the only doctor in town, waddled into   25
what they called the emergency room, my aura, he said, was yellow and gray—a soul in transition. I knew that he had gone to
medical school but had never completed a residency and had been
barred from ER or ICU work in the hospitals of Florida, where he
had lived previously. Yet I was lucky. Florida has many lightning
victims, and unlike the doctors I would see later, he at least recognized the symptoms of a lightning strike. The tally sheet read
this way: I had suffered a hit by lightning which caused ventricular fibrillation—cardiac arrest—though luckily my heart started
beating again. Violent contractions of muscles when one is hit often causes the body to fly through the air: I was flung far and hit
hard on my left side, which may have caused my heart to start
again, but along with that fortuitous side effect, I sustained a con-
cussion, broken ribs, a possible broken jaw, and lacerations above
the eye. The paralysis below my waist and up through the chest
and throat—called kerauno-paralysis—is common in lightning
strikes and almost always temporary, but my right arm continued
to be almost useless. Fernlike burns—arborescent erythema—
covered my entire body. These occur when the electrical charge
follows tracings of moisture on the skin—rain or sweat—thus the
spidery red lines.

> "Rapid institution of fluid and electrolyte therapy is essential   26
> with guidelines being the patient's urine output, hematocrit,
> osmolality, central venous pressure, and arterial blood
> gases. . . ."

The nurses loaded me onto a gurney. As they wheeled me down   27
the hall to my room, a front wheel fell off and I was slammed into

the wall. Once I was in bed, the deep muscle aches continued, as did the chest pains. Later, friends came to visit. Neither doctor nor nurse had cleaned the cuts on my head, so Laura, who had herded sheep and cowboyed on all the ranches where I had lived and whose wounds I had cleaned when my saddle horse dragged her across a high mountain pasture, wiped blood and dirt from my face, arms, and hands with a cool towel and spooned yogurt into my mouth.

I was the only patient in the hospital. During the night, sheet lightning inlaid the walls with cool gold. I felt like an ancient, mummified child who had been found on a rock ledge near our ranch: bound tightly, unable to move, my dead face tipped back-wards toward the moon.

In the morning, my regular doctor, Ben, called from Massachusetts, where he was vacationing, with this advice: "Get yourself out of that hospital and go somewhere else, anywhere." I was too weak to sign myself out, but Julie, the young woman who had a summer job on our ranch, retrieved me in the afternoon. She helped me get dressed in the cutoffs and torn T-shirt I had been wearing, but there were no shoes, so, barefoot, I staggered into Ben's office, where a physician's assistant kindly cleansed the gashes in my head. Then I was taken home.

Another thunderstorm slammed against the mountains as I limped up the path to the house. Sam and Yaki took one look at me and ran. These dogs lived with me, slept with me, understood every word I said, and I was too sick to find them, console them—even if they would have let me.

The next day my husband, who had just come down from the mountains where he worked in the summer, took me to an-other hospital. I passed out in the admissions office, was loaded onto a gurney, and taken for a CAT scan. No one bothered to find out why I had lost consciousness. Later, in the emergency unit, the doctor argued that I might not have been struck by lightning at all, as if I had imagined the incident. "Maybe a me-teor hit me," I said, a suggestion he pondered seriously. After a blood panel and a brief neurological exam, which I failed—I

couldn't follow his finger with my eyes or walk a straight line—
he promptly released me.

"Patients should be monitored electrocardiographically for   32
at least 24 hours for significant arrhythmias which often
have delayed onset. . . ."

It was difficult to know what was worse: being in a hospital   33
where nothing worked and nobody cared, or being alone on an
isolated ranch hundreds of miles from decent medical care.

In the morning I staggered into the kitchen. My husband,   34
from whom I had been separated for three months, had left at
4:00 A.M. to buy cattle in another part of the state and would
not be back for a month. Alone again, it was impossible to do
much for myself. In the past I'd been bucked off, stiff and sore
plenty of times but this felt different: I had no sense of equi-
librium. My head hurt, every muscle in my body ached as if I
had a triple dose of the flu, and my left eye was swollen shut
and turning black and blue. Something moved in the middle
of the kitchen floor. I was having difficulty seeing, but
then I did see: a rattlesnake lay coiled in front of the stove. I
reeled around and dove back into bed. Enough tests of character. I closed my eyes and half-slept. Later, when Julie came
to the house, she found the snake and cut off its head with
a shovel.

My only consolation was that the dogs came back. I had   35
chest pains and all day Sam lay with his head against my heart.
I cleaned a deep cut over Yaki's eye. It was half an inch deep
but already healing. I couldn't tell if the dogs were sick or well,
I was too miserable to know anything except that Death resided
in the room: not as a human figure but as a dark
fog rolling in, threatening to cover me; but the dogs stayed
close and while my promise to keep them safe during a thunderstorm had proven fraudulent, their promise to keep me alive
held good.

Meaning and Purpose

1. If you had read this essay's first paragraph only what would you have imagined the rest of the essay to be about? What evidence do you have for your answer?
2. In paragraph 14, "Images from World War II movies" filled the author's head. Why do you suppose she would be mentally seeing such images?
3. What evidence is there to show that the author is interested in non-Western thought?
4. Why are paragraphs 24, 26, and 32 in quotation marks?

Strategy

1. Paragraph 2 begins with "A single heartbeat stirs gray water." Paragraph 3 begins with "Another heartbeat." What is the author descriptively emphasizing by this strategy?
2. What is the main purpose of the dogs in this essay? What do they illustrate?
3. In paragraph 25, Erlich says that the first doctor she saw had a poor professional medical background. Yet she was fortunate that that doctor was the first to see her. Why?
4. Paragraph 27, Erlich describes equipment and activities at the hospital. What do those descriptions tell you about the conditions at the hospital? Where else in the essay is evidence to strengthen your answer to this question? What is that evidence?

Style

1. What is humorous about the first sentence in paragraph 12?
2. Reread paragraph 15 and then read the definition of "rhetorical question" in this book's glossary. Is the question in paragraph 15 a rhetorical question? Give a reason for your answer.
3. In paragraph 19, the author says "sounds began to come out of me." Why didn't she simply say, "I began to make sounds"?

4. Paragraph 22 has the phrase "ten of them dirt." To what does that phrase refer?

Writing Tasks

1. Write an essay that thoroughly describes someone whom you know well. In the first paragraph, of not fewer than 100 words, begin your description by detailing a characteristic of that person in such a way that you purposely mystify your essay's audience. For example, one student described her uncle, an automobile mechanic. Her first paragraph began, "No one in this neighborhood can hear a car being started on a cold morning without thinking about my uncle." Then she went on to describe three cars briefly: One was an oil-burning clunker belonging to the next-door neighbor; one was a brand-new model that had blue smoke puffing from it every time its driver shifted gears; and one was an eight-year-old sedan that belonged to the elderly couple who lived across the street. It ran beautifully. Naturally, the elderly couple entrusted their car to the girl's uncle. After she pointed out that fact, the student described her uncle's other characteristics, habits, and physical features. Follow this strategy in your essay.

2. A small incident in a life can have an effect for a long time. The incident can be a happy one, a sad one, a thoughtful one, a reflective one, a cheerful one—almost any kind, in other words. If a small incident has strongly affected you, then describe that incident. Be sure to use details. Remember that you are trying to reinvent the incident in the reader's mind. To do that, use abstract words or broad-meaning words, such as "large," "pretty," "big," "great," and "nice" sparingly. When you use such words excessively, readers can only guess at what you saw. Be sure, therefore, to use specific and concrete words to help readers see in their mind's eye what you saw.

❦ Responding to Photographs ❦
Description

Woman Brushing Her Hair

Before children speak, they see. A child looks and recognizes before it can form words. At an early age we learn to respond to visual experience and interpret it. A smiling or scowling face, a closed or open hand, an erect or slumped body—all are gestures that invite our interpretation.

As we move through life, our interpretations of visual experiences become more complex. A young man walking down the street might go unnoticed. But add spiked hair, a leather coat, and torn jeans held up by a chain belt. Put a safety pin through one earlobe and thread an earring in his pierced nose, and this visual experience catches our attention. We examine the details of the young man's attire and perhaps draw conclusions about his character, lifestyle, personal values, or musical taste.

Photographs, unlike spontaneous visual experience, arrange details for a viewer. They are not, as is often assumed, a realistic

153

record of an experience, but an arranged and reproduced moment of experience. Whenever we look at a photograph we are being guided by the hand that held the camera. And whenever we look at a photograph we are being invited to respond to the image—to interpret it.

At first glance, "Woman Brushing Her Hair" seems to be a snapshot that captures a spontaneous moment in this woman's day. But on closer examination, the image seems to be carefully arranged, the hand of the photographer reaching to pull a response from the viewer.

With description as a dominant method of development, complete one of the following writing tasks. Before beginning your essay, reread the beginning of this chapter to familiarize yourself with the conventions of effective descriptive writing.

1. Write a "fly-on-the-wall" description, one that strictly reports the arrangement and content of "Woman Brushing Her Hair." After studying the contents of the photograph, decide on how you wish to arrange your description. Through your essay, be sure to follow the arrangement consistently.

2. Use "Woman Brushing Her Hair" as the basis of an *objective* description that creates a dominant impression of this woman's life. Like any writer, or photographer for that matter, you must select details, gestures, objects, arrangements that help to generate the dominant impression you wish to create. Remember, your task is not to describe everything in the photo, but to use material from the photo for your purpose.

3. Use "Woman Brushing Her Hair" as the basis of a *subjective* description that creates a dominant impression of this woman's life. As in assignment 2, you must select material from the photo that leads readers to a single impression, but because you are approaching the photograph subjectively, you may color the details with your feelings.

4. Select a photograph that engages your interest. Title the photograph, and then using it as the basis of your description, complete one of the writing tasks just outlined. Be sure to include the photograph as part of your final draft.

🦚 Additional Writing Tasks 🦚

Description

1. Recall a spot that you visited when younger, not far from your home. It should be a place you remember well but not one that you visit constantly. Once you have selected the spot, draw upon your strength of recollection: Visualize yourself in this place, seeing the physical features, hearing the sounds, and smelling the odors and aromas. Jot down your memories. What details do you recall and in what order of importance? Record your memories just as the place was at that time in your life. How would you tell what you saw if you were describing the scene for a stranger? Which details would create images in this stranger's mind? Try to write this part of the description from a child's perspective.

   Once you have described the place as you recall it, write a description of how the place appears now, after years have passed. This part of the description should be done from an adult's perspective. Perhaps the place has not held up under time's pressure. Perhaps your view of it has changed. Perhaps you colored this place with romantic illusions.

   Once the second rough description is completed, begin the first draft. Develop a structure that shifts between past and present, revealing both the child's and the adult's attitude.

2. Select several photographs that represent milestones in your life. Describe them as if you were a reporter relating the events that are taking place in the photo. Keep your description objective but vivid. Or, if you wish, use several magazine ads as the basis for a description. Here, too, describe the events in the advertisement objectively, merely reporting the image you see on the page, not interpreting it.

3. Describe an animal that you have encountered, perhaps a wild animal such as a coyote, wolf, deer, bear, or whale. Begin with a description of the animal from folklore, which will probably require a visit to the library. Then follow with a description of the animal as you experienced it. Seek a connection between the two elements in this description.

4. Do something slightly out of the ordinary, and describe the experience. Perhaps you will climb a tree and sit among the branches. Maybe you will sit in a closed closet for half an hour. You might roller-skate, stand on your head, dance a waltz, lie on the grass and stare at the clouds—the possibilities are endless. Once you have had the experience, describe it in detail.

5. Select a physical event and describe it in detail: the fog rolling through the woods or city streets, a storm gathering in the distance and sweeping toward you, a cloudburst, wind roaring through the trees and rattling the windows, an earthquake. In your description, capture a sense of motion, sound, and smell, as well as visual detail.

6. Describe people at work in various settings:
    A supermarket
    A fast-food restaurant
    A newsstand
    A factory
    A car wash
    A pizza parlor
    In your description, create a dominant impression.

4

Narration

Relating Events

The Method

Once upon a time is the phrase that begins countless childhood narratives. *To narrate* is to tell a story. Our lives are full of stories, some exciting, some dull. These stories might be as brief as an anecdote—"A funny thing happened to me today while dissecting a frog in biology." They might seem as simple as a fairy tale, such as "Little Red Riding Hood," or as complex as a novel, such as James Joyce's *Ulysses.*

Narratives are so common in human experience that some psychologists have claimed that their patterns are etched on the human psyche, that people actually *need* stories. Absurd? Well it is difficult to imagine that some people might require stories in the same way as they require affection. One fact, though, is certain: Effective narratives embody a few known characteristics, and good writers keep this fact in mind when composing their stories.

The most common of these characteristics is the **narrative effect**, which you may conceive as the narrative purpose, or, as some writers call it, the "payoff." Readers want a payoff—a moral, an insight, a message, a point, or just good entertainment. Often the narrative effect will be subtle, nothing more than getting the reader to utter a soft "Aha!" Consider this narrative, a teaching tale from Zen Buddhist lore. At first glance, it might seem to lack a narrative effect.

> A man traveling across a field encountered a tiger. He fled, the tiger after him. Coming to a precipice, he caught hold of the root of a wild vine and swung himself down over the edge. The tiger sniffed at him from above. Trembling, the man looked down to where, far below, another tiger was waiting to eat him. Only the vine sustained him.
>
> Two mice, one white and one black, little by little started to gnaw away the vine. The man saw a luscious strawberry near him. Grasping the vine with one hand, he plucked the strawberry with the other. How sweet it tasted!

What is the payoff? This is a fair question that every reader has the right to ask. Clearly, the narrative effect the storyteller might wish to achieve is not spelled out; the story reveals no thesis. But it certainly has something to do with being involved in the present and, perhaps, not worrying about what can't be controlled. One student suggests that fear of the past (represented by the first tiger pacing above the traveler) or fear of the future (the second tiger pacing below the traveler) should not interfere with our enjoyment of the present (the strawberry). But what about the mice? They're a detail that needs to be considered in any interpretation. Soon they will gnaw through the vine, sending the man to his death. Perhaps the tale suggests that when death is imminent, life becomes inordinately sweet.

Why create a story to illustrate a point, you might ask, even one as brief as this Zen tale? Why not just hold up a finger, smile sagely, and directly state a purpose? "Do not let fear of the past or present interfere with your enjoyment of the moment" or "Enjoy life now, for death may be near." In other words, why all the mystery?

Not all narratives are packed with hidden meanings or intended to provoke emotional responses. Many are factual reports, such as news reports or police reports, which simply recount events as they unfold, but narrative essays often deal with subjects that go beyond the limits of a report. Like the treasures in many children's tales, the purpose in many narratives—especially works of imagination such as tales, short stories, and novels—is therefore buried. In this way, the narrative essay offers its readers the opportunity to experience anything the storyteller has experienced—love, anger, fear, hate, prejudice, outrage, confusion, hope, disappointment—all the emotional states that we encounter in life. The events, therefore, must be dramatized, not explained, thus recreating, rather than reporting, events: First you live through a string of related experiences, and then you get the meaning—well, maybe you get the meaning.

Strategies

Because of the nature of narrative essays, the relationship between you and the storyteller is complex. Storytellers will entice you to use your imagination to re-create the experience. You should join, not resist, a writer in this effort. If the effort fails, then you will not make the creative leap that allows a narrative essay to achieve its emotional effect. Even if the purpose behind a narrative essay seems murky after a first reading, trust that the writer who chooses narration as a dominant essay pattern will always keep an eye on the purpose, usually dramatizing rather than stating it.

Narrative Structure

Every storyteller knows that readers love narratives to be driven by conflict between opposing forces, such as two figures in the narrative pitted against each other in a battle of wills or a single figure in conflict with his or her own feelings. But just as important, they also know that readers crave order, a sense that the action has direction, movement. To meet this need, many narrative essays are divided into three parts:

1. The **orientation**. The beginning sentences in a short narrative or the opening paragraphs in a long narrative are designed to establish the situation, identify the key figures, and suggest the conflict. The narrative purpose may be suggested, but the outcome should not be revealed.
2. The **complication**. The narrative should move forward through a series of scenes that intensify the conflict and build to a climax. The climax is the narrative's point of highest drama and sets up the narrative effect, that is, the writer's purpose, which always lurks within the climactic moment.
3. The **resolution**. The issues in the narrative should be resolved before the story ends. The resolution may be brief, often suggesting rather than directly stating the effect the writer has tried to create. At times the resolution will be ambiguous, thus forcing readers to reinterpret the narrative events in light of the closing observation.

You will find that most effective narrative essays follow this loose pattern. You can usually count on a storyteller to establish a story's situation in the orientation by providing information that answers these questions: Who? What? Where? and When? They will suggest a **conflict** as well. Consider this opening from Martin Gansberg's "Thirty-Eight Who Saw Murder Didn't Call the Police."

> For more than half an hour thirty-eight respectable, law-abiding citizens in Queens watched a killer stalk and stab a woman in three separate attacks in Kew Gardens.
>
> Twice their chatter and the sudden glow of their bedroom lights interrupted him and frightened him off. Each time he returned, sought her out, and stabbed her again. Not one person telephoned the police during the assault; one witness called after the woman was dead.
>
> That was two weeks ago today.

Whom does the situation involve? A murder victim, the murderer, and, most important, the "thirty-eight respectable, law-abiding citizens" who didn't call the police. What does the situation involve? Crime in the streets. Where did it take place? An area in Queens, a New York City borough. When did it happen? Two weeks before the date of the newspaper narrative. And the conflict? Gansberg clearly suggests a conflict related to social obligation: the indifference of the thirty-eight bystanders who fail to meet their legal and moral responsibility.

Point of View

Also in the orientation section of narrative essays, writers establish the **point of view**—that is, they reveal who is telling the story. As generally used in narrative essays, point of view is easy to understand. Stories are told either by a participant in the events (first-person point of view) or by a nonparticipant (third-person point of view).

Most often readers associate stories with the first-person point of view, which seems to give narrative essays authenticity: "I swear this is true—I was there! I lived it!" Often the events have directly affected the first-person storyteller in some emotional or intellectual way. At other times, the storyteller acts as a spectator, reporting events that he or she saw others experience. In either case, first-person narratives usually are more subjective than third-person narratives. They embody the storyteller's attitudes throughout the essay, directly in overt statements or indirectly in style. Writers almost always establish the point of view in the first paragraph. Consider the opening paragraph in Flannery O'Connor's essay, "The King of Birds."

> When I was five, I had an experience that marked me for life. Pathé News sent a photographer from New York to Savannah to take a picture of a chicken of mine. This chicken, a buff Cochin Bantam, had the distinction of being able to walk either forward or backward. Her fame had spread through the press, and by the time she reached the attention of Pathé News, I suppose there was nowhere left for her to go—forward or backward. Shortly after that she died, as now seems fitting.

O'Connor's opening paragraph illustrates one more bit of advice we can give you in reading first-person narratives: watch for the storyteller's own perspective. Notice that O'Connor begins by relating the emotional effect of an event that took place when she was five, but the first and last sentences clearly indicate that she is writing from an adult's perspective, not a five-year-old's, thus adding complexity, perhaps even irony, to the tone.

A writer who uses the third-person point of view usually relates events as accurately, and sometimes objectively, as possible. As a nonparticipant, the third-person narrator develops the story from reports by others, much as a journalist collects information for a story. This approach doesn't mean that a third-person narration lacks power or drama. It merely means that the storyteller is not part of the action. Consider the opening paragraph in Maxine Hong Kingston's brief narrative "The Wild Man of the Green Swamp."

> For eight months in 1975, residents on the edge of Green Swamp, Florida, had been reporting to the police that

they had seen a Wild Man. When they stepped toward him, he made strange noises as in a foreign language and ran back into the saw grass. At first, authorities said the Wild Man was a mass hallucination. Maneating animals lived in the swamp, and a human being could hardly find a place to rest without sinking. Perhaps it was some kind of a bear the children had seen.

Kingston's point of view is clearly **objective,** even dispassionate. We don't want to leave you with the impression, though, that third-person narrations are always objective and dispassionate. Review the opening from Gansberg's "Thirty-Eight Who Saw Murder Didn't Call the Police," presented on page 162. Gansberg's attitude toward the "thirty-eight respectable, law-abiding citizens" who watched a killer stalk his victim is clearly **subjective** and very passionate.

Chronological and Psychological Time

Because narratives unfold in time, storytellers must arrange the events so that the connections between them are clear. As you begin to read a narrative, notice the writer's narrative arrangement: Are the events arranged according to **chronological time,** that is, in sequence as they happened, step by step? Or are they arranged according to **psychological time,** that is, the way in which events might be connected in memory, shifting back and forth in time while keeping a sense of forward movement?

The decision a writer makes about the arrangement of a narrative essay is often determined by the subject. A historical essay, such as a narrative about a battle, usually marches along in chronological time. But if the subject comes from personal experience, then the essay may be arranged in psychological time, beginning *in medias res* ("in the middle of things") with an event that comes near the end of the actual chronology. This opening event can be highly dramatic, designed to keep readers in suspense until the essay closes, when its purpose becomes clear.

Writers use *flashback* and *flashforward* to shift the narrative action from one time frame to another. Flashback skips to the past to dramatize a previous event that has some bearing on the present. Flashforward skips to the future to help create suspense by showing a consequence that might result from present events. Although writers use flashback and flashforward mainly in psychologically arranged narratives, they can also use them, but to a much lesser extent, in narratives dominated by chronological development to add depth and variety to the predictable, step-by-step arrangement of events.

Whichever arrangement the writer chooses, he or she is obliged to guide you through the story. While reading with a critical eye, you should therefore watch for transitions in time. They may be complete sentences designed to smooth your way from one event to another: "My social life began to crumble into pieces like a stale oatmeal cookie after we settled in Santa Fe." They may take the form of brief phrases: "Two weeks later," "Only one year ago," "Soon I was to learn." Or they may be single words that help a writer to cut through time: "Now, Then," "Before, Today." Identifying the transitional tactics will help you follow the most complex narrative.

Scene and Summary

While crafting a narrative essay, the storyteller has two methods to use in presenting the events: **scene** and **summary.** You'll recognize scene because it directly portrays an event on the page. Like a scene in film or drama, a narrative-essay scene is played before your eyes. Summary is a synopsis of an event. It relates the high points but leaves out much of the specific detail that a scene usually includes. Many narratives include both scene and summary, with summary serving as the glue that holds the scenes together. It might help if you think of scene and summary as showing and telling: scene shows, summary tells. Consider this scene from a student's narrative that shows the writer's battle with fear:

> I stood paralyzed on the dock, my hands clenched and my knees locked tight. Bobby was flailing at the water, try-

ing to pull himself to the overturned boat. He shouted for help, his voice rising to a shrill pitch and carrying beyond the boathouse and into the empty woods.

I wanted to plunge into the lake, but my body would not unlock, and the horrible, empty spot in my mind threatened me like a black pit I might fall into. It was the water and all it symbolized—darkness, suffocation, a murky death.

The narrator presents this dramatic moment as if it were taking place before your eyes. He is showing it to you. Now compare this scene to a summarized version:

When my brother Bobby overturned the rowboat and fell into the lake, I panicked. You see, I had almost drowned once in this very lake. The experience left me with the deep, irrational fear that if I ever swam in it again, I would be swallowed up. Although I knew he needed help, fear of the water paralyzed me.

Here the writer tells about the event. This summary lacks the immediacy of the scenic version, yet it, too, is effective.

Writers often, but not always, use dialogue in scenes, which helps to dramatize an event. Usually, dialogue will reflect the give-and-take that takes place between two speakers and is integrated with action. For example,

Raymond leaned forward, jabbing a finger into Chico's chest, "You will never see Ellen again," he said. "Never!"

"You are wrong," Chico said, "We are going to be married."

Raymond, his face frozen in an angry mask, stared at Chico, who was much smaller and looked frail. Then Raymond glanced around the crowded locker room where the rest of the team had stopped to watch. "If you live," Raymond said before storming out the door.

In summary, writers will sometimes add key snatches of dialogue to create authenticity while moving on to more dramatic scenes. Look at the example at the top of the following page.

When Raymond confronted Chico in the locker room, their teammates watched in dismay. They had never seen Raymond so angry when he told Chico that he would never see Ellen again. Chico remained calm and told Raymond that he was wrong and then revealed that he and Ellen were to be married. Raymond could not hide his anger and said, "If you live," before storming out the door.

Whether writers use scene, summary, or both depends on the effect they wish to create. Often narrative essayists present the dramatic moments in scenes and use summary to move from scene to scene, thus skipping through the less significant events.

Narration in College Writing

College writers sometimes work brief narrative passages into an essay with other dominant patterns. In such papers, narrative passages may be used to create an interesting opening or to illustrate a point. In either case the narrative must have a clear structural purpose to justify its use. More frequently, however, narratives based on personal experience are frequent assignments in college courses. In cultural anthropology or social psychology classes you might be assigned a narrative report that requires your own observations. In a history class you might be asked to write from imagination a narrative about a historical event from a historical figure's point of view. In an English class you might be assigned an informal narrative essay based on personal experience that brought some insight.

Guidelines for Narrative Writing

1. Select an experience that lends itself to narrative development, and identify the narrative effect that you wish to achieve.
2. Determine the point of view to use: first person for a narrative based on experience or third person for a narrative compiled from outside information.

3. In prewriting, limit the events in your narrative. Pick out the highlights, then enrich them with descriptive detail. Remember, not every event should be presented in a scene. By dramatizing the emotional peaks, you will sustain your reader's interest.

4. Compose your first draft.

Write an *orientation* that sets the situation, identifies the key figures, establishes the conflict, and arouses interest.

Structure the *complication* by arranging events in climactic order with the most dramatic and revealing event serving as the climax.

Create a *resolution* that reveals, directly or indirectly, the narrative effect, that is, the narrative purpose or "payoff."

5. Revise your first draft with an eye for scene and summary. If you use dialogue, examine it to see whether you should present it in scene or summary. Be sure that your narrative has a strong forward movement with enough descriptive detail to engage the reader's senses.

A Student Essay Developed by Narration

Richard McKnight wrote a narrative essay in response to the following freshman composition assignment.

In "A Hanging" [p. 652], George Orwell uses first-person narration to communicate ideas without stating them directly. His narrator might not know the meaning of the events himself, but the reader is able to interpret the meaning from the way Orwell presents them. Write a 750- to 1000-word narrative in which you make a point without explicitly stating it. Tell a story of an incident that illustrates your point, such as (1) how a social event, such as a stylish wedding, shows that people care too much about money and appearance; (2) how a charismatic speaker shows that people are easily persuaded to believe something; or (3) how a sports event shows that old age is not the end of active living.

It was clear that McKnight had to arrange the narration in a way that would lead his readers to the lesson, thus allowing them to draw their own conclusions from the experience.

Read McKnight's final draft, which follows. First, note the narrative techniques that he uses, then study it in detail by responding to the items in Reviewing with a Writer's Eye.

The Last Ride

I watched a gray-haired surfer sitting on the longest board I had ever seen, waiting for a wave in Candle Cove. He was 40 yards beyond the edge of a reef that seemed to rise and fall dangerously as the sea sucked to and from the shore. Connie stood nearby, a year-round lifeguard who patrolled the beaches in a jeep during winter. I wondered why a man his age was alone and riding such dangerous winter swells. 1

At Candle Cove a winter swell can sometimes rise to twelve feet. Twelve feet is not a remarkable height for waves at sandy beaches where they break slowly and leave plenty of room for surfers to maneuver. But at the Cove waves break quickly and crash over a reef crusted with razor-sharp barnacles. Surfers must race across a wave's face to clear the reef and reach the sandy beach. Only the best surfers will risk being swept over the rocks, even for a spectacular ride. But sometimes even the best do not make it safely to the beach. 2

Just two weeks earlier, a hot-shot from Hawaii paddled out in the heavy surf that a Mexican storm had kicked up. He sat on his board beyond the break and waited for the big swells to roll in. Suddenly, he swung his board's nose toward shore to catch the day's biggest wave. He seemed to do everything right: He quickly leaped to his feet, cut sharply left, moved to the board's nose to gain speed as he shot ahead of the curl—but not in time. The massive wave broke over his shoulder and tossed him into the roiling foam. The breaking wave's force snapped his board in half and swept him over the reef. He survived, but barely. Lifeguards raced him to an emergency ward where doctors hovered above his body for two hours with needles and thread. 3

Now the old man was in that kind of danger but with 4
one difference—he was well past his prime, much too old
to be riding in dangerous waters.

"Better call him in," I said. "He's going to get hurt." 5
"He won't come in," Connie said. 6
"You're in charge of the beach." 7
"Don't you know who he is?" she said. 8
I said I didn't. She asked if I had ever seen Slippery 9
When Wet. The film was made by an amateur photographer thirty years earlier, had become a surfing classic in
the late 1950s. I told her I had. She said that when he
was a young man, the old surfer had been featured in it.
She said he was shown riding long boards on waves over
twenty-five feet high at Sunset Beach in Hawaii and that
he was even shown riding shore break at this beach. I
vaguely remembered him, but there were many surfers in
the film agilely maneuvering their boards as they rode
waves.

"He's a living legend," Connie said. 10
"A living legend should know when to quit." 11
"If it's in your blood, you don't quit." 12
"Look," I said, "the living legend's going to need an 13
ambulance."

The old surfer was paddling to catch a wave, the 14
largest since I had been watching. His arms dug three,
four times into the water before the wave swept him up,
the reef rising dangerously close. He sprang to his feet,
arched his back, and turned the board left as he raced
down the wave's face. The wave broke behind him and
crashed over the reef. Taking short, choppy steps, he
inched his way to the board's nose to gain more speed and
crouched low, avoiding the curl as it cracked behind him.
Suddenly he was out of sight. The wave had tossed forward, and the curl folded over his crouching body.

"He's tanked," I said, looking at the white water as it 15
washed over the reef. "Better get him."

"Wait," she said. 16
"Now!" I said, but didn't know why. I wasn't a life- 17
guard or her boss.

She looked at me. "Show a little courage," she said. 18
"He is."

She was right. Still bent low on the front of the board, 19
the old surfer shot out of the curl, well ahead of the white

water. And then an image from the film came back to me:
A young man, over thirty years younger than this man,
riding waves at this same beach. He, too, was shot out of
the curl and cleared the reef on a massive wave, bigger
then this one, that was crashing behind him. In the film,
the beach was crowded with cheering spectators. They had
seen a ride beyond their belief, but that was when surfing
was new and still viewed as an astounding feat.

Now, this time as an old man with only two people   20
watching, he once again cleared the reef and guided his
board toward shore. In shallow water he stepped from the
board, and swung it up under his arm, striding toward the
sand where we stood. He walked passed us, nodding to
Connie, who smiled at him. He looked ancient, his skin
thick from years of sun, his hair gray and thin, his face
wrinkled, and his belly growing thick. Yet his blue eyes
were full of life, full of future rides. I knew that I, like
that crowd in the film, had seen something special, an astounding feat, not just for someone with gray hair and
wrinkled skin, but for anyone, young or old.

Reviewing with a Writer's Eye

1. Narrative structure (see pp. 160–161) gives direction and movement to story events. The structure is fueled by conflict that gains
   the most energy at the narrative climax. Usually, narrative structure follows a loose pattern: orientation, complication, and resolution. Identify the paragraphs that make up the orientation,
   complication, and resolution of Richard McKnight's "The Last
   Ride." At what point does the climax occur?
2. Writers arrange narrative events chronologically, as they happen in real time, step by step, or psychologically, as they might
   be connected in memory (see pp. 163–164). McKnight's narrative is primarily arranged chronologically, but at two points
   he does use flashback. Identify where he uses flashback, and
   explain why.
3. What conflict (see p. 161) drives McKnight's narrative? Explain.
4. McKnight employs first-person point of view (see pp. 161–163),

which he immediately establishes in the opening sentence. Rewrite the opening paragraph in third-person point of view. What technical problems did you have to solve? Is third-person as effective as first-person point of view?

5. In a passage composed of dialogue and description, paragraphs 4 through 18, McKnight mixes scene and summary (see pp. 164–166). What do you believe his purpose to be? In particular, what is his purpose in paragraph 9?

6. The narrator's perception of the old surfer changes as the events unfold. Describe that change. What role does memory play?

7. McKnight chooses to suggest, rather than explain, what he wants his readers to gain from "The Last Ride." Explain what you think is the narrative effect McKnight is trying create.

8. Imagine that you are reviewing "The Last Ride" as a peer reader. In a 150- to 200-word note, explain to McKnight your overall

---

Peer Review

You may be asked to write an essay about one of the readings that follow. Before you meet with your writing group, review this introduction. As you read the group papers, use these general principles of narration to help guide your comments.

1. The situation should be clear, that is, the who, what, when, and why of the story.

2. Some sort of conflict should be suggested early. If there is no conflict, the paper may be flat and uninteresting.

3. The point of view (who is telling the story) should be clear.

4. People in the narrative should be carefully distinguished from one another.

5. The time sequence should be clear. Readers must be guided carefully through any changes in chronological order.

6. The narrative should have a purpose. Readers want a pay-off.

response to the essay and what you believe to be its strengths and/or weaknesses.

What follows is a collection of narrative essays by professional writers. As you read them, keep in mind that you are reading as a writer who is learning the craft, not merely reading to gather information for a test.

❦ Maya Angelou ❦

Maya Angelou's talents and accomplishments span many fields. She has achieved distinctions as a dancer, actress, film director, poet, scriptwriter, and civil-rights activist. She is perhaps best known for delivering an original poem at President Clinton's 1993 inauguration. In 1995 Angelou starred in the film How to Make an American Quilt. *She was already well known for her Emmy Award–nomination performance in the television series* Roots. *As a writer she is best known for* I Know Why the Cage Bird Sings, *the first volume in her five-part autobiography. Born Marguerite Johnson in 1928, Angelou surmounted the hardships of her youth. By age sixteen she had been raped, had experienced the break-up of her family, and had become an unwed mother. So traumatized by her experiences, she spent five years as a child without uttering a word. Angelou went on to achieve fame for her art and social activism. She currently lives in North Carolina, where she holds a lifetime chair in American Studies at Wake Forest University.*

Finishing School

This story describes a brief time in Maya Angelou's childhood in Arkansas, where she was sent to work in a white woman's house to learn "mid-Victorian values" as a black woman was supposed to know them. In the story, taken from I Know Why the Caged Bird Sings, *the author mixes chronological and psychological narrative to relate her growing awareness of the subtleties in white domination.*

Notice, as you read, how Maya Angelou's attitudes toward her employer, Mrs. Cullinan, change. What specific events occasion those changes?

Recently a white woman from Texas, who would quickly describe herself as a liberal, asked me about my hometown. When I told her that in Stamps my grandmother had owned the only Negro general merchandise store since the turn of the century, she exclaimed, "Why, you were a debutante." Ridiculous and even

173

ludicrous. But Negro girls in small Southern towns, whether poverty-stricken or just munching along on a few of life's necessities, were given as extensive and irrelevant preparations for adulthood as rich white girls shown in magazines. Admittedly the training was not the same. While white girls learned to waltz and sit gracefully with a tea cup balanced on their knees, we were lagging behind, learning the mid-Victorian values with very little money to indulge them. . . .

We were required to embroider and I had trunkfuls of color-   2
ful dishtowels, pillowcases, runners and handkerchiefs to my credit. I mastered the art of crocheting and tatting, and there was a lifetime's supply of dainty doilies that would never be used in sacheted dresser drawers. It went without saying that all girls could iron and wash, but the finer touches around the home, like setting a table with real silver, baking roasts and cooking vegetables without meat, had to be learned elsewhere. Usually at the source of those habits. During my tenth year, a white woman's kitchen became my finishing school.

Mrs. Viola Cullinan was a plump woman who lived in a three-   3
bedroom house somewhere behind the post office. She was singularly unattractive until she smiled, and then the lines around her eyes and mouth which made her look perpetually dirty disappeared, and her face looked like the mask of an impish elf. She usually rested her smile until late afternoon when her women friends dropped in and Miss Glory, the cook, served them cold drinks on the closed-in porch.

The exactness of her house was inhuman. This glass went here   4
and only here. That cup had its place and it was an act of impudent rebellion to place it anywhere else. At twelve o'clock the table was set. At 12:15 Mrs. Cullinan sat down to dinner (whether her husband had arrived or not). At 12:16 Miss Glory brought out the food.

It took me a week to learn the difference between a salad   5
plate, a bread plate and a dessert plate.

Mrs. Cullinan kept up the tradition of her wealthy parents.   6
She was from Virginia. Miss Glory, who was a descendant of slaves that had worked for the Cullinans, told me her history. She had

married beneath her (according to Miss Glory). Her husband's family hadn't had their money very long and what they had "didn't 'mount to much."

As ugly as she was, I thought privately, she was lucky to get a husband above or beneath her station. But Miss Glory wouldn't let me say a thing against her mistress. She was very patient with me, however, over the housework. She explained the dishware, silver-ware and servants' bells. The large round bowl in which soup was served wasn't a soup bowl, it was a tureen. There were goblets, sherbet glasses, ice-cream glasses, wine glasses, green glass coffee cups with matching saucers, and water glasses. I had a glass to drink from, and it sat with Miss Glory's on a separate shelf from the others. Soup spoons, gravy boat, butter knives, salad forks and carving platter were additions to my vocabulary and in fact almost represented a new language. I was fascinated with the novelty, with the fluttering Mrs. Cullinan and her Alice-in-Wonderland house. 7

Her husband remains, in my memory, undefined. I lumped him with all the other white men that I had ever seen and tried not to see. 8

On our way home one evening, Miss Glory told me that Mrs. Cullinan couldn't have children. She said that she was too delicate-boned. It was hard to imagine bones at all under those layers of fat. Miss Glory went on to say that the doctor had taken out all her lady organs. I reasoned that a pig's organs included the lungs, heart, and liver, so if Mrs. Cullinan was walking around without those essentials, it explained why she drank alcohol out of unmarked bottles. She was keeping herself embalmed. 9

When I spoke to Bailey about it, he agreed that I was right, but he also informed me that Mr. Cullinan had two daughters by a colored lady and that I knew them very well. He added that the girls were the spitting image of their father. I was unable to re-member what he looked like, although I had just left him a few hours before, but I thought of the Coleman girls. They were very light-skinned and certainly didn't look very much like their mother (no one ever mentioned Mr. Coleman). 10

My pity for Mrs. Cullinan preceded me the next morning like the Cheshire cat's smile. Those girls, who could have been her 11 daughters, were beautiful. They didn't have to straighten their hair. Even when they were caught in the rain, their braids still hung down straight like tamed snakes. Their mouths were pouty little cupid's bows. Mrs. Cullinan didn't know what she missed. Or maybe she did. Poor Mrs. Cullinan.

For weeks after, I arrived early, left late and tried very hard   12
to make up for her barrenness. If she had her own children, she wouldn't have had to ask me to run a thousand errands from her back door to the back door of her friends. Poor old Mrs. Cullinan.

Then one evening Miss Glory told me to serve the ladies on   13
the porch. After I set the tray down and turned toward the kitchen, one of the women asked, "What's your name, girl?" It was the speckled-faced one. Mrs. Cullinan said, "She doesn't talk much. Her name's Margaret."

"Is she dumb?"   14

"No. As I understand it, she can talk when she wants to but   15
she's usually quiet as a little mouse. Aren't you, Margaret?"

I smiled at her. Poor thing. No organs and couldn't even pro-   16
nounce my name correctly.

"She's a sweet little thing, though."   17

"Well, that may be, but the name's too long. I'd never bother   18
myself. I'd call her Mary if I was you."

I fumed into the kitchen. That horrible woman would never   19
have the chance to call me Mary because if I was starving I'd never work for her. . . .

That evening I decided to write a poem on being white, fat,   20
old and without children. It was going to be a tragic ballad. I would have to watch her carefully to capture the essence of her loneliness and pain.

The very next day, she called me by the wrong name. Miss   21
Glory and I were washing up the lunch dishes when Mrs. Cullinan came to the doorway. "Mary?"

Miss Glory asked, "Who?"   22

Mrs. Cullinan, sagging a little, knew and I knew. "I want Mary   23
to go down to Mrs. Randall's and take her some soup. She's not been feeling well for a few days."

Miss Glory's face was a wonder to see. "You mean Margaret,   24
ma'am. Her name's Margaret."

"That's too long. She's Mary from now on. Heat that soup   25
from last night and put it in the china tureen and, Mary, I want
you to carry it carefully."

Every person I knew had a hellish horror of being "called out   26
of his name." It was a dangerous practice to call a Negro anything
that could be loosely construed as insulting because of the centuries of their having been called niggers, jigs, dinges, blackbirds,
crows, boots and spooks.

Miss Glory had a fleeting second of feeling sorry for me. Then   27
as she handed me the hot tureen she said, "Don't mind, don't pay
that no mind. Sticks and stones may break your bones, but words
. . . You know, I been working for her for twenty years."

She held the back door open for me. "Twenty years. I wasn't   28
much older than you. My name used to be Hallelujah. That's what
Ma named me, but my mistress give me 'Glory,' and it stuck. I
likes it better too."

I was in the little path that ran behind the houses when Miss   29
Glory shouted, "It's shorter too."

For a few seconds it was a tossup over whether I would laugh   30
(imagine being named Hallelujah) or cry (imagine letting some
white woman rename you for her convenience). My anger saved
me from either outburst. I had to quit the job, but the problem
was going to be how to do it. Momma wouldn't allow me to quit
for just any reason.

"She's a peach. That woman is a real peach." Mrs. Randall's   31
maid was talking as she took the soup from me, and I wondered
what her name used to be and what she answered to now.

For a week I looked into Mrs. Cullinan's face as she called me   32
Mary. She ignored my coming late and leaving early. Miss Glory
was a little annoyed because I had begun to leave egg yolk on the
dishes and wasn't putting much heart in polishing the silver. I
hoped that she would complain to our boss, but she didn't.

Then Bailey solved my dilemma. He had me describe the   33
contents of the cupboard and the particular plates she liked best.
Her favorite piece was a casserole shaped like a fish and the

green glass coffee cups. I kept his instructions in mind, so on the next day when Miss Glory was hanging out clothes and I had again been told to serve the old biddies on the porch, I dropped the empty serving tray. When I heard Mrs. Cullinan scream, "Mary!" I picked up the casserole and two of the green glass cups in readiness. As she rounded the kitchen door I let them fall on the tiled floor.

I could never absolutely describe to Bailey what happened   34
next, because each time I got to the part where she fell on the floor and screwed up her ugly face to cry, we burst out laughing. She actually wobbled around on the floor and picked up shards of the cups and cried, "Oh, Momma. Oh, dear Gawd. It's Momma's china from Virginia. Oh, Momma, I sorry."

Miss Glory came running in from the yard and the women   35
from the porch crowded around. Miss Glory was almost as broken up as her mistress. "You mean to say she broke our Virginia dishes? What we gone do?"

Mrs. Cullinan cried louder. "That clumsy nigger. Clumsy little   36
black nigger."

Old speckled-face leaned down and asked, "Who did it,   37
Viola? Was it Mary? Who did it?"

Everything was happening so fast, I can't remember whether   38
her action preceded her words, but I know that Mrs. Cullinan said, "Her name's Margaret, goddamn it, her name's Margaret." And she threw a wedge of broken plate at me. It could have been the hysteria which put her aim off, but the flying crockery caught Miss Glory right over her ear and she started screaming.

I left the front door wide open so all the neighbors could hear.   39

Mrs. Cullinan was right about one thing. My name wasn't   40
Mary.

Meaning and Purpose

1. The message you take from this selection will be influenced by your own experiences and attitudes. Think of an experience from

your life, a movie or television program, reading, or knowledge of others' experiences, which in some way parallels Marguerite's experience. In what ways was this experience similar to and different from Marguerite's?

2. How would you describe Marguerite's feelings about Mrs. Cullinan before Mrs. Cullinan calls her Mary and then afterward? What actions or events does Angelou use in her narrative to show those feelings?

3. Do you think Angelou's primary purpose is to give information or to evoke emotion? Examine your own response to this selection as you decide. What words and sentences convince you of your choice?

4. How would you describe Angelou's intended audience? Does she expect that audience to empathize with the young black girl? How do you know?

5. What does Angelou reveal about the significance of being "called out of [one's] name" (paragraph 26)?

6. Why do you think Angelou included the story about Hallelujah's name being changed to "Glory"?

Strategy

1. What is the payoff in this narrative essay, that is, the moral, point, or message?

2. The first two paragraphs in this selection serve as introduction to the narrative, which begins in the third paragraph. How does this introduction prepare you for the narrative?

3. In the last scene, how does Angelou's telling you that she has trouble remembering exactly what happened affect the credibility of the narrative? How does this admission help to establish point of view?

4. The entire narrative covers several weeks. List some of the transitional phrases that Angelou uses to help her readers follow the passage of time.

5. What significance does the last sentence have? How does it pull the essay together and conclude it?

Style

1. Several times, Angelou presents the thoughts of the young girl. In paragraph 16, after being called Margaret instead of Marguerite, the girl thinks, "Poor thing. No organs and couldn't even pronounce my name correctly." Find other examples of Marguerite's thoughts, and discuss what they tell us about her.

2. Irony describes our recognizing a reality that is different from the one that appears to us. It can be expressed in words that actually mean the opposite of what they say. Explain the irony in these items:

    a. "During my tenth year, a white woman's kitchen became my finishing school."

    b. The careful attention to lists of names Marguerite had to learn (soup spoons, gravy boat, butter knives, and so on).

    c. "I would have to watch her carefully to capture the essence of her loneliness and pain."

    d. Mrs. Cullinan's reaction to Marguerite's breaking the dishes. Can you find other ironies in the selection?

3. How does humor work in this essay? Find examples.

Writing Tasks

1. Consider whether you think Mrs. Cullinan has learned a lesson from Marguerite's actions at the end of the selection. Write a narrative essay about an event in which the payoff (moral, point) involves a subordinate or "weaker" person's taking revenge on an authority figure or "stronger" person. End your narrative so that the person in authority either learns a lesson or not, according to whether or not you think Mrs. Cullinan does.

2. Write an essay expressing your feelings about the way in which Marguerite deals with prejudice. Before writing, consider these questions and others of your own: What choices do you think Marguerite had? Was she naive to empathize with Mrs. Cullinan's lack of children? Is Mrs. Cullinan merely a product of her culture's attitudes toward blacks? What responsibility do you think she has for what happens in the final scene?

❦ Richard Selzer ❦

Richard Selzer is a surgeon who writes essays and stories, aimed at a general audience, about the practice of medicine. Born in New York state in 1928, he studied at Union College and Albany Medical School and later at Yale University. He subsequently taught writing at Yale and both taught and practiced surgery at the Yale University Medical School. His articles, for which he received the National Magazine Award *in 1975 and an* American Medical Writer's Award *in 1985, have appeared in* Harper's, Esquire, *and* Redbook. *He has published a book of short stories,* Rituals of Surgery, *and several collections of essays, including* Mortal Lessons: Notes on the Art of Surgery, *and* Raising the Dead: A Doctor's Encounter with His Own Mortality.

The Masked Marvel's Last Toehold

Told in the first person, this narrative reveals the anguish of a patient through the eyes of his doctor, Richard Selzer. Selzer finds himself treating a man he had seen fight in a wrestling match many years earlier, when he was a boy. The author's perspective changes as he moves from the present to the childhood memory and back again to the present. The essay is from Selzer's The Confessions of a Knife, *published in 1979.*

On the fifth floor of the hospital, in the west wing, I know that a man is sitting up in his bed, waiting for me. Elihu Koontz is seventy-five, and he is diabetic. It is two weeks since I amputated his left leg just below the knee. I walk down the corridor, but I do not go straight into his room. Instead, I pause in the doorway. He is not yet aware of my presence, but gazes down at the place in the bed where his leg used to be, and where now there is the collapsed leg of his pajamas. He is totally absorbed, like an athlete appraising the details of his body. What is he thinking? I wonder. Is he dreaming the outline of his toes? Does he see there his foot's incandescent ghost? Could he be angry? Feel that I have taken from him something for which he yearns now with all his heart? Has he

181

forgotten so soon the pain? It was a pain so great as to set him apart from all other men, in a red-hot place where he had no kith or kin. What of those black gorilla toes and the soupy mess that was his heel? I watch him from the doorway. It is a kind of spying, I know.

Save for a white fringe open at the front, Elihu Koontz is bald. 2
The hair has grown too long and is wilted. He wears it as one would wear a day-old laurel wreath. He is naked to the waist, so that I can see his breasts. They are the breasts of Buddha, inverted triangles from which the nipples swing, dark as garnets.

I have seen enough. I step into the room, and he sees that I am 3
there.

"How did the night go, Elihu?" 4

He looks at me for a long moment. "Shut the door," he says. 5

I do, and move to the side of the bed. He takes my left hand 6
in both of his, gazes at it, turns it over, then back, fondling, at last holding it up to his cheek. I do not withdraw from this loving. After a while he relinquishes my hand, and looks up at me.

"How is the pain?" I ask. 7

He does not answer, but continues to look at me in silence. I 8
know at once that he has made a decision.

"Ever hear of The Masked Marvel?" He says this in a low voice, 9
almost a whisper.

"What?" 10

"The Masked Marvel," he says. "You never heard of him?" 11

"No." 12

He clucks his tongue. He is exasperated. 13

All at once there is a recollection. It is dim, distant, but com- 14
ing near.

"Do you mean the wrestler?" 15

Eagerly, he nods, and the breasts bob. How gnomish he looks, 16
oval as the huge helpless egg of some outlandish lizard. He has very long arms, which, now and then, he unfurls to reach for things—a carafe of water, a get-well card. He gazes up at me, urging. He *wants* me to remember.

"Well, . . . yes," I say. I am straining backward in time. "I saw 17
him wrestle in Toronto long ago."

"Ha!" He smiles. "You saw *me*." And his index finger, held   18
rigid and upright, bounces in the air.

The man has said something shocking, unacceptable. It must   19
be challenged.

"You?" I am trying to smile.   20

Again that jab of the finger. "You saw *me*."   21

"No," I say. But even then, something about Elihu Koontz,   22
those prolonged arms, the shape of his head, the sudden agility
with which he leans from his bed to get a large brown envelope
from his nightstand, something is forcing me toward a memory.
He rummages through his papers, old newspaper clippings, photographs, and I remember . . .

It is almost forty years ago. I am ten years old. I have been sent   23
to Toronto to spend the summer with relatives. Uncle Max has
bought two tickets to the wrestling match. He is taking me that
night.

"He isn't allowed," says Aunt Sarah to me. Uncle Max has   24
angina.

"He gets too excited," she says.   25

"I wish you wouldn't go, Max," she says.   26

"You mind your own business," he says.   27

And we go. Out into the warm Canadian evening I am not   28
only abroad, I am abroad in the *evening!* I have never been taken
out in the evening. I am terribly excited. The trolleys, the lights,
the horns. It is a bazaar. At the Maple Leaf Gardens, we sit high
and near the center. The vast arena is dark except for the brilliance
of the ring at the bottom.

It begins.   29

The wrestlers circle. They grapple. They are all haunch and   30
paunch. I am shocked by their ugliness, but I do not show it.
Uncle Max is exhilarated. He leans forward, his eyes unblinking,
on his face a look of enormous happiness. One after the other,
a pair of wrestlers enter the ring. The two men join, twist, jerk,
tug, bend, yank, and throw. Then they leave and are replaced
by another pair. At last it is the main event. "The Angel vs. The
Masked Marvel."

On the cover of the program notes, there is a picture of The   31
Angel hanging from the limb of a tree, a noose of thick rope
around his neck. The Angel hangs just so for an hour every day, it
is explained, to strengthen his neck. The Masked Marvel's trade
mark is a black stocking cap with holes for the eyes and mouth.
He is never seen without it, states the program. No one knows
who The Masked Marvel really is!

"Good," says Uncle Max. "Now you'll see something." He is   32
fidgeting, waiting for them to appear. They come down separate
aisles, climb into the ring from opposite sides. I have never seen
anything like them. It is The Angel's neck that first captures the
eye. The shaved nape rises in twin columns to puff into the white
hood of a sloped and bosselated skull that is too small. As though
strangled by the sinews of that neck, the skull had long since with-
ered and shrunk. The thing about The Angel is the absence of any
mystery in his body. It is simply *there*. A monosyllabic announce-
ment. A grunt. One looks and knows everything at once, the fat
thighs, the gigantic buttocks, the great spine from which hang
knotted ropes and pale aprons of beef. And that prehistoric head.
He is all of a single hideous piece, The Angel is. No detachables.

The Masked Marvel seems dwarfish. His fingers dangle knee-   33
ward. His short legs are slightly bowed as if under the weight of
the cask they are forced to heft about. He has breasts that swing
when he moves! I have never seen such breasts on a man before.

There is a sudden ungraceful movement, and they close upon   34
one another. The Angel stoops and hugs The Marvel about the
waist, locking his hands behind The Marvel's back. Now he
straightens and lifts The Marvel as though he were uprooting a tree.
Thus he holds him, then stoops again, thrusts one hand through
The Marvel's crotch, and with the other grabs him by the neck. He
rears and . . . The Marvel is aloft! For a long moment, The Angel
stands as though deciding where to make the toss. Then throws.
Was that board or bone that splintered there? Again and again, The
Angel hurls himself upon the body of The Masked Marvel.

Now The Angel rises over the fallen Marvel, picks up one foot   35
in both of his hands, and twists the toes downward. It is far beyond the tensile strength of mere ligament, mere cartilage. The

Masked Marvel does not hide his agony, but pounds and slaps the floor with his hand, now and then reaching up toward The Angel in an attitude of supplication. I have never seen such suffering. And all the while his black mask rolls from side to side, the mouth pulled to a tight slit through which issues an endless hiss that I can hear from where I sit. All at once, I hear a shouting close by

"Break it off! Tear off a leg and throw it up here!"   36

It is Uncle Max. Even in the darkness I can see that he is gray.   37
A band of sweat stands upon his upper lip. He is on his feet now, panting, one fist pressed at his chest, the other raised warlike toward the ring. For the first time I begin to think that something terrible might happen here. Aunt Sarah was right.

"Sit down, Uncle Max," I say. "Take a pill, please."   38

He reaches for the pillbox, gropes, and swallows without tak-   39
ing his gaze from the wrestlers. I wait for him to sit down.

"That's not fair," I say, "twisting his toes like that."   40

"It's the toehold," he explains.   41

"But it's not *fair*," I say again. The whole of the evil is laid open   42
for me to perceive. I am trembling.

And now The Angel does something unspeakable. Holding   43
the foot of The Marvel at full twist with one hand, he bends and grasps the mask where it clings to the back of The Marvel's head. And he pulls. He is going to strip it off! Lay bare an ultimate carnal mystery! Suddenly it is beyond mere physical violence. Now I am on my feet, shouting into the Maple Leaf Gardens.

"Watch out," I scream. "Stop him. Please, somebody, stop   44
him."

Next to me, Uncle Max is chuckling.   45

Yet The Masked Marvel hears me, I know it. And rallies from   46
his bed of pain. Thrusting with his free heel, he strikes The Angel at the back of the knee. The Angel falls. The Masked Marvel is on top of him, pinning his shoulders to the mat. One! Two! Three! And it is over. Uncle Max is strangely still. I am gasping for breath. All this I remember as I stand at the bedside of Elihu Koontz.

Once again, I am in the operating room. It is two years since I   47
amputated the left leg of Elihu Koontz. Now it is his right leg

which is gangrenous. I have already scrubbed. I stand to one side wearing my gown and gloves. And . . . *I am masked.* Upon the table lies Elihu Koontz, pinned in a fierce white light. Spinal anesthesia has been administered. One of his arms is taped to a board placed at a right angle to his body. Into this arm, a needle has been placed. Fluid drips here from a bottle overhead. With his other hand, Elihu Koontz beats feebly at the side of the operating table. His head rolls from side to side. His mouth is pulled into weeping. It seems to me that I have never seen such misery.

An orderly stands at the foot of the table, holding Elihu   48
Koontz's leg aloft by the toes so that the intern can scrub the limb with antiseptic solutions. The intern paints the foot, ankle, leg, and thigh, both front and back, three times. From a corner of the room where I wait, I look down as from an amphitheater. Then I think of Uncle Max yelling, "Tear off a leg. Throw it up here." And I think that forty years later I am making the catch.

"It's not fair," I say aloud. But no one hears me. I step forward   49
to break The Masked Marvel's last toehold.

Meaning and Purpose

1. The last sentence in this essay includes the words of the title. How does that sentence help you to interpret the title? In what sense does the doctor "break The Masked Marvel's last toehold"?
2. What is Selzer's purpose in telling the story of The Masked Marvel? How do you interpret the meaning of the essay?
3. How does the surgeon describe the pain he believes Elihu Koontz experiences during the wrestling match and as a patient? How does the surgeon's awareness of pain help you to understand him (the surgeon)?
4. The boy and his uncle have different reactions to the evening of wrestling. Discuss how this contrast enriches the essay.
5. In the last three paragraphs the surgeon takes on the role of wrestler. What details tell you so, and how effective are they in unifying the essay?

Strategy

1. Selzer departs from strict chronological order in this narrative. What order does he put the events in, and how does it affect the story?
2. Each of the three sections gives us a piece of The Masked Marvel's story, making a natural connection among them. But Selzer has taken pains to further connect the sections by repeating details from section one in section two and details from section two in section three. Examine these parallels. How do they affect your reading of the essay?
3. How does Selzer use transitions to let you know when the time order changes? Are the transitions clear and effective?
4. Though the surgeon narrates the whole essay, his perspective, or point of view, changes in each section. What picture do you have of his character because of these three perspectives?

Style

1. What does dialogue do for the story? How effective do you think the story would be without dialogue?
2. Authors don't always tell of past events in the past tense. Look at the tense used in each section. How does Selzer's choice of tense influence your experience of the events in the narrative and your understanding of the chronology?
3. In paragraph 36, when Uncle Max yells, "Tear off a leg and throw it up here!" you already know Elihu Koontz has lost a leg to diabetes. How is this irony sustained in the final section?

Writing Tasks

1. Think of a person or event that impressed you as a child and has some significant connection to your later life. Write a narrative

about it, using the same tense to describe both the past and the present, but also clearly separating past from present.

2. Write a narrative, incorporating somewhere in the story the exact words of the title you give it. How can you make the title significant?

❦ Rene Denfeld ❦

Rene Denfeld, author of The New Victorians: A Young Woman's Challenge to the Old Feminist Order *(1995) and* Kill the Body, the Head Will Fall: A Closer Look at Women, Violence, and Aggression, *took up boxing at age twenty-six. She was the first woman to win the Tacoma Golden Gloves tournament. Denfeld sees aggression as a "human condition, not confined to one sex."*

The Lady of the Ring

In the following essay, which first appeared in the New York Times Magazine *on August 24, 1997, Denfeld speaks of what boxing has taught her. As you read the essay, look for the key words and phrases that help you to understand her point of view.*

I started boxing as a lark, a fantasy. I saw myself becoming 1 glistening, fit and tough—a woman fighter. I saw myself rising from the canvas and fighting back, delivering amazing combinations until my opponent fell among the ropes, vanquished.

My first week in the gym in a run-down neighborhood in 2 Portland, Ore., squashed my fantasy as I began to understand the long, difficult training regimen ahead of me. But I fell in love with the sport: the sound of the timer and the guys talking; the flying, hissing jump ropes; the punishment of the heavy bags, and, above all, the relationships between the fighters and our trainer, Jess Sandoval.

When I first went into the gym, Jess was in his 70's and in- 3 creasingly infirm. He had lost his own professional career when he shipped out during World War II, but taught the sport afterward. He was shy around me, his only female fighter. We were all drawn close to Jess, though, an uneasy group, grieving in advance for the frail, titular head of our family.

Most of the other fighters were Mexican immigrants like Jess. 4 Sometimes, when they were away for a while, Jess would make sad remarks about prison. Still, their lives were not the easy, cheap simplifications about laziness and crime that many Americans believe about immigrants and illegal aliens. The younger ones seemed touchingly self-conscious despite their macho baggy pants and careful gang attire. Alberto worked at McDonald's and attended school. Bob supported his family by working as a janitor, while his wife sewed satin trunks for the fighters—$25 a pair.

Immigration got Ernesto, Jess told us grimly. But one day   5
Ernesto was back. He snuck in, Jess said, triumphant. I still think about how hard it must be for these young men, who are torn between a love for their native country (he changed flags, they said contemptuously of one Mexican fighter who trains under a gringo coach) and a longing to be wanted and appreciated right here.

I understand. As a woman in a boxing gym, I had changed   6
flags, too. I'm sure Jess never imagined training a woman, and I'm sure the other fighters never imagined having to spar with one. Ernesto would hit me as he would a man—hard enough to bruise my ribs, water my eyes, cut my lips and make my nose bleed. He had to, you see: if he didn't hit back, I would beat him. This is the dilemma I forced on these men. Hitting a woman? They think that only a bully, a wife beater, does that. But the prospect of being beaten by a woman? Only a sissy, a punk. And yet we found a way to manage. There in that safe place, we had an unspoken truce.

Sparring with men, I felt liberated from generations of fear,   7
self-doubt, finger-waving and genteel restrictions: men aren't so tough, I found, once you get close enough. Perhaps women's fear has been misplaced, conferring a malignant power on those who neither deserve nor desire it.

In entering this world, I lost more than superficial fantasy and   8
gained more than physical self-confidence. My perceptions of the sexes have been altered, and this has affected nearly every aspect of my life. I feel differently when I walk down the street alone— stronger, less fearful. No longer do I assume that I am less capable of handling anger and conflict.

But the greatest challenge was to the male fighters. I imagined   9
their worries: What will she think of us when she realizes we are not as tough, as cold or as mean as women everywhere have been

led to believe? Will she breathe a sigh of relief, or laugh in contempt?

A boxing gym is only one of many places where the myth of 10 male superiority in strength and aggressiveness remains unquestioned. But it is also a place where the myth can begin to unravel. Just as I have always been strong, and never realized it, men have always been vulnerable and complicated.

Now the fighter of my dreams is replaced by myself, in honest 11 memory, leaning over the ropes at the Golden Gloves after having won the title. My opponent was already receding, like a vapor behind me, while the men from the gym cheered in the audience, But there was only me, and Jess, and I was kissing his face, in thanks.

Not long ago, Jess passed away. When I heard the news, I put 12 down the phone and cried, thinking, with surprise, I've lost my father. I had gone into a boxing gym to learn how to be tough. But I also found affection, sincerity and caring—and the deep bond between athlete and coach. Boxing has, in the end, left me softer.

Meaning and Purpose

1. The first paragraph says that Denfeld started boxing "as a lark." What does she mean by that phrase?
2. Who is "the head of our family" in this essay? Why was he called "the head of our family"?
3. In paragraph 6, Denfeld says, "I had changed flags." What do you infer from that sentence?
4. What problems do the male boxers think they face when it comes to hitting a woman?
5. According to this essay, what were the greatest challenges that the male boxers faced?

Strategy

1. How do you know from reading the essay that Denfeld succeeded as a boxer?

2. In the essay, Denfeld said that she started boxing as "a fantasy." In your opinion, when did she discover that her "fantasy" was a reality?
3. What myth is discussed in this essay? Why is it called a "myth"?
4. In this essay, who is Denfeld's "fighter of my dreams"?
5. In this essay, who replaced Denfeld's "fighter of my dreams"?

Style

1. Look up the word *dilemma* in a reliable college-level dictionary. Which of its definitions is the most appropriate for the way *dilemma* is used in this essay (paragraph 6)? Suggest a synonym.
2. In this essay, who says, "Will she breathe a sigh of relief, or laugh in contempt?" (paragraph 9)? What is the purpose of that question?
3. Why does Denfeld describe gang attire as "careful" (paragraph 4)?
4. When Denfeld speaks of "entering this world" (paragraph 8), what world is she entering?
5. How can you tell that Jess was in either the Navy or the Merchant Marine during World War II?

Writing Tasks

1. In a narrative essay, tell about a time when you entered what was, for you, strange territory. For example, it could have been a club, another town or city, or a neighborhood quite different from your own. Describe your feelings while you were in that territory, and describe your feelings about it now, focusing on what you learned from having been in that territory.
2. Our first impression of a person often differs greatly from our later impression of that same person, after we have come to know her or him better. In a personal narrative, discuss a person who impressed you in one way when you first met that person and in quite another way when you came to know that person. Be sure to include enough details in your essay so that your reader will understand what made you change your mind about that person.

❦ Art Harris ❦

Art Harris is an award-winning journalist based in Atlanta. After graduating from Duke University, he began his journalism career with the Atlanta Constitution. He later worked for the San Francisco Examiner before joining the staff of the Washington Post, the paper for which he has since covered the South. His articles have appeared in Reader's Digest, GQ, Esquire, and Rolling Stone. Harris covered the downfall of evangelical preacher Jimmy Swaggart for the Washington Post and wrote the well-known article about Swaggart's demise for Penthouse magazine. He has won two National Headliner Awards for outstanding feature writing. He is on the staff at CNN news as a contributing correspondent for their investigative unit.

Trapped in Another Life

This newspaper article, originally published in the Los Angeles Times on February 23, 1989, tells the story of a woman who led two distinctly separate lives: one as a drug-abusing prostitute with a criminal record and the other as a model wife and mother. Because of the remarkable turnaround in this woman's life, the story raises questions about justice and punishment.

Harris carefully outlines the causes that led the woman who is the subject of this essay to live two diametrically opposed lives. Pay particularly close attention to those causes.

JESSUP, MD. She stares out the window past twin 12-foot   1
fences topped with razor wire, watchtowers manned by armed
guards, steel electronic gates, past the stand of hardwoods, the
nearby men's prison and up the road.

It's dusting snow, cold, bleak. Just over the hill, a 10-minute   2
drive if she could just drive out of here, and she would be home
in her split-level house with a devoted but baffled brood: her husband, Ray, two teen-age sons.

Kay Smith was the very model of a Severn, Md., housewife and 3
working mother, so perfect that no one around here can believe she
was once a hard-drinking, pill-popping criminal with a gun.

Dark Secrets Come to Light

But for a decade, until her capture last spring, she was a fugi- 4
tive from a South Carolina mill town. She had been imprisoned
for a string of armed robberies until she walked away from work
release and disappeared. Her first husband was a convicted killer.

These were secrets Kay Smith buried deep as she recast her 5
life. Over the years, she had become a doting mom to her two
boys and foster daughters. She ferried her sons to school and
sports, took courses at Anne Arundel Community College. As a
real estate agent for Gary Hart Realty in Glen Burnie, she sold
house after house—$1 million in sales last year.

Who could have suspected that she really was an outlaw 6
named Pamela Rodgers?

Kay Smith wore subdued suits and slacks, a bare wisp of Max 7
Factor. In her home, she warned her sons about drinking. She
spurned even a glass of wine, and politely insisted that friends
take half-empty bottles home after parties.

"I can't imagine for the life of me how this woman could do 8
anything remotely resembling what happened," says Bill
Cashman, who coached her sons in track at Old Mill High. "She'd
ask me what I thought about her sons' grades, their sports performance, the people they hung around with. Her family was always
first."

Somehow, she managed to keep it together as she lived in fear 9
and hid her past, even from her husband. "I just wanted to get my
boys through school," she says, "then I was going to straighten it
all out."

But detectives disrupted her plan last May. And when they 10
came for her, she had run so long and hard, she barely knew the
woman, handcuffed and under arrest. All at once, she again was
Pamela Rodgers—the woman she thought she had left behind. In
three months, she was on her way back to prison in South Carolina.

Just before Christmas, a routine interstate swap allowed her to   11
serve out the rest of her 12-year sentence for armed robbery near
home. She found herself in this stark red-brick campus, the
Maryland Correctional Institute for Women.

"At least I don't have to carry that terrible secret any more,"   12
she says, wrapping a sweater about her to ward off the chill.
Suddenly she looks panicked. "Oh, God, I'm so sorry my sons
were cheated."

She wears a purple prison jumpsuit, works in the prison li-   13
brary, clips recipes and frets about her family. Figuring "someday
they'll want honest answers," she writes letters she never mails.

Based on her record of violent crime and escape, Kay Smith   14
was classified by Maryland prison officials as a security risk. So
she awaits the outcome of early release pleas—by her reckoning
she could be here until March, 1993, unless authorities grant an
unlikely pardon, premature parole or work release.

Family and friends have canvassed the community, collecting   15
at least 3,000 signatures petitioning South Carolina's Pardon and
Parole Board for leniency.

"I'm not saying she ought to get a medal, but she's paid her   16
debt to society," argues John Hassett, a former prosecutor, who
took her case for expenses only.

In South Carolina, former prosecutor Dick Harpootlian took   17
up her cause too, saying, "I take other cases for money. Kay's case
is among those I take because I believe in the folks."

But sniffs Jim Anders, the South Carolina prosecutor who put   18
Kay Smith back in jail: "Don't make me cry. If we cut slack for her,
we encourage people to escape."

Jean Gilbert, Kay Smith's mother, says of her daughter in a   19
telephone interview from Greenville, S.C.: "If people could just
understand what brought her to this point. She was just a woman
desperate to have her kids, who was terrorized by bad men."

Kay Smith was born Pamela Annette Gilbert on Oct. 1,   20
1951, the second of six children raised by a trucker and a
grocer's daughter in the Blue Ridge foothills of Greenville, S.C.
She remembers her father's belt, his guns, his whiskey, his
temper.

Her father declines to discuss the past, but other family mem-   21
bers confirm her memories; her mother recalls stepping in to take
"many of those licks."

"I watched him whip her . . . when she was just 15 months   22
old," says her grandmother, Mary Hinton, 83.

Kay says of her father: "He just didn't know how to show af-   23
fection. I can't remember ever hearing him say 'I love you.' "

When Kay was a 10th-grader, she dropped out and took a job   24
at a convenience store, where she met stock boy Danny Rodgers,
another doprout.

"I knew I didn't love Danny," Kay reflects. "I married him to   25
get out. I thought I could make it work."

She was 16.   26

Bouncing between Rodgers' modest family farm in Cullman,   27
Ala., and her hometown in Greenville, they moved into a dinky
Greenville trailer.

"First time I ever saw him slap her," Kay's mother says, "I   28
hit him back. He said, 'You hit me,' and I said, 'You hit my daughter.'
So he informed me, 'It's not your daughter any more; it's my wife.' "

They moved to Florida, where Danny found construction   29
work at Disney World, but preferred hanging out. Danny Jr. was
born Dec. 17, 1969, as Pam was learning fast about her mercurial
husband, who relished "playing with guns and knives, very nice
one day and the next day beating the heck out of you."

Six months later, out of work, he ran off with a neighbor's   30
wife, she says. So Pam headed home again, hired on the midnight
shift as a cotton mill weaver. Danny returned, but she refused to
make up.

Then, one night, when she was at work, he snatched the baby   31
and ran, a tactic he repeatedly used to keep her in line. And it
worked: She kept going back to him. "It was the only way to keep
my baby," she says. Another son, James, was born in September,
1972, but life was only getting worse.

Kay moved home to Greenville, and in 1973 won temporary   32
custody of the boys. Rodgers stalked her, she says, and one day
showed up and fired a pistol into the roof of her trailer. Days later,

he snatched the boys again. Only this time Pam couldn't find them.

"She had dreams he'd drowned them because he swore he'd   33
do it before he'd let her have them," her mother says. "She woke up at night screaming and fell into drugs and alcohol."

She boxed up their toys, reminders of her "failure," and   34
dumped them at Goodwill. She reported her husband to the police, but no one offered any hope.

She found a kind of solace at the Little Darling, a Greenville   35
bar that drew hustlers such as Arthur Broome Jr., a distant cousin.

She was 22.   36

Broome was 43, owned a tile company, but never seemed to   37
work. He promised to help track her boys, and she moved into his trailer—a place police say attracted the local criminal fringe. Broome, she says, had money, and drugs to kill her pain.

Life was going badly for her. During the 1974 Masters golf   38
tournament, she drove to Augusta, Ga., to hang out with a bar mate—a former hooker, she says. A man approached them at a local restaurant. They began flirting. Suddenly, she says, she was under arrest for possessing amphetamines and soliciting an undercover cop for prostitution. Police records suggest that case was never prosecuted.

Meanwhile, back home, Broome was teaching her how to use   39
a gun—and everything a country girl needed to know about stick-ups. Together they held up stores in the Greenville area.

"I didn't really care if I got caught," she says. "I thought if I got   40
in enough trouble, Danny would tell me where the boys were. I wasn't thinking straight."

On Sept. 14, 1974, they hit Paces Jewelers just before closing.   41
Pulling a pistol from a large black bag, she ordered customers to the floor and grabbed 18 watches and $400 in cash.

Because witnesses had caught her license plate numbers, po-   42
lice easily tracked her to Broome's trailer, where both were arrested. But she got out on bail, and, high on uppers, hit a liquor store alone. Later, she drove the rolling countryside for hours,

realizing she would never get her sons back now. She went home and gobbled pills to end it all, then raced to find her mother.

"She said, 'Mama, I took a handful of pills and I'm gonna   43
die,'" her mother recalls. "I called an ambulance, they pumped her stomach and took her to the state hospital."

Rodgers got the news at his California apartment, where he   44
had taken the boys. He phoned, invited his wife to join him and try again. Ignoring bail rules against leaving the state, her mother put her on a plane. "I had to do it to save her," she says.

But it didn't work out.   45

Danny began knocking her around, but for the first time, she   46
fought back. When she called the police for help, Danny told them his wife was a bail jumper from South Carolina.

Detectives flew her home, where she pleaded guilty in state   47
court to five armed robberies. In October, 1975, she drew a 12 1/2-year sentence. Broome got 25 years; Kay wound up in Columbia's women's prison.

Rodgers filed for divorce and won permanent custody of the   48
children, but in March, 1977, he shot a man in California, for which he was convicted of second-degree murder and sentenced to five years in prison. The boys, 6 and 8, were dispatched to live with his family in Alabama.

Pam, who was told Danny was in a hospital, was being a   49
model inmate. After 18 months, she made work release and labored in a printing plant. But she fell off the wagon on the job— using pills and whiskey, she says. And she feared further setbacks would let Danny keep her children forever. There was only one way out: Take a walk.

With six or so months left to serve, in January, 1978, she   50
hitched as far as Glen Burnie, Md., rented a room, took a job as a waitress in a Greek diner. To avoid confusion with a waitress named Pam, she became Kay Smith. Days later, just after midnight, a short, balding trucker plopped down, spied the sad-eyed brunette in a white apron and fell in love.

She was crying. A cook was screaming at her. The trucker   51
asked her name.

"Ray and Kay," Ray Smith joked. "Pretty neat. We ought to get   52
along fine. We got the same names."

He was gentle, optimistic. He told her he had two daughters   53
by a woman he never had married, that he was lonely on the road
and looking for a co-pilot. At quitting time, she threw down her
apron and climbed aboard his snorting '74 Peterbilt.

High in the cab, hauling steel and furniture over the next   54
three months, they became friends. Ray talked of a hardscrabble
life, raised by grandparents in the West Virginia hollows. She was
amazed. He had suffered, yet was so happy. Kay hedged about her
past.

After three months on the road, he proposed marriage at the   55
Truck Stop of America in Knoxville. Her dilemma was right out of
some country song: How could she let someone she loved marry
an outlaw with a fake name? She had forged a birth certificate,
gotten a Social Security card and a Maryland driver's license.
"There was no right answer," she says. "So I just decided to block
out the past."

On July 1, 1978, Ray's family and drinking buddies, about   56
500 in all, crowded into a Pasadena, Md., church, and went from
there to a dance hall. "I was happier than anyone could be," he
says. "I knew she loved me."

Kay was determined to change her life. That Christmas, gam-   57
bling on her former in-laws to keep her secret, she drove to
Alabama with Ray to see her boys.

Studying on the road, she passed a high school equivalency   58
exam, enrolled in Anne Arundel Community College, began driving on her own.

In 1980, the Smiths bought a three-bedroom house in Severn,   59
outfitting bedrooms for the boys. Life without them still drove her
into the bedroom with a bottle.

When Ray drew the line over her drinking, she found a ther-   60
apist in Baltimore, and her story tumbled out for the first time.
She looked inside, read Norman Vincent Peale, tried biofeedback
and stopped drinking.

She made friends, becoming close to neighbor Cathy Moore,   61
a divorced mother who once rescued her dog. When Moore's

daughter left to live with her father in Wyoming, Kay "reassured me," she says. "I wondered, 'How comes she's so smart about life?' "

On one visit to Alabama, she learned her former husband was in prison. But she knew there was nothing she could do to get her boys back without giving herself away. 62

And there was nothing she could do when Danny got out, re- married, reclaimed the boys and resettled in his new wife's home- town, Boise, Idaho. 63

But she stayed in touch, sent money, opened local charge ac- counts for the boys, saw them at Boise's Flying J truck stop on trips west. 64

Meanwhile, she hired a Baltimore attorney to square her past. But he reported there was no record, raising her hopes. Only later did she discover her name had been misspelled in the search. 65

She grew more concerned for her sons. They had told her that Danny had recruited them to steal from the Salvation Army to fur- nish his yard sales. Then, in January, 1985, James attempted sui- cide; young Dan got into a fight with his father. One night, James sneaked out for a ride with a teen-ager who wrapped his car around a telephone pole, killing the driver. 66

Rodgers threw in the towel. "Come get them," he told his for- mer wife. "They're yours." 67

She flew west the next day to claim them before he changed his mind. Back in Severn, the boys made friends quickly, reveled in their rooms, Reeboks and new jeans. When Ray wheeled in, they sat grinning at the kitchen table. For the first time, he saw Kay was happy. Curfews were set; grades improved. It was a "Leave It to Beaver" home, they liked to say. 68

She seized on real estate as a way to sock away money for college. 69

But she remained haunted by the past and present. In 1987, her former husband was charged again with murder for shooting a 21-year-old Boise man over a drug deal, chopping him into 13 pieces and dumping them into a reservoir. Now he was calling 70 collect from jail; he wanted to see the boys, afraid he might get the chair.

After Rodgers was convicted last March, an Idaho pre-sentencing investigator ran a routine computer check of his former wife, discovered she was a fugitive and alerted South Carolina.   71

But the investigator, puzzling over an unlisted Maryland phone number in the killer's wallet, dialed it. He reached James, who confirmed his mother's maiden name and her hometown without knowing what he had done.   72

Now police had the tip they had been after. The phone rang and when she answered, it was Danny. "I guess we're in the same boat," he said. "They know about you."   73

She was numb, near hysterics.   74

Without alarming the boys, she hinted she "might have to go away for a little while" and phoned her attorney, who suggested she find a criminal lawyer. She found Hassett.   75

Then, on May 10, 1988, a patrolman knocked on her door. After her arrest, with handcuffs on, she turned white, broke into tears. "It's been 10 1/2 years," she said. "Why now?"   76

Ray was loading in New Jersey when he got the word. The boys were in school. The next day, out on $25,000 bail, she told the boys the rest of the story, then sat down with Ray, alone.   77

"She told me everything," he says. "She was crying. She said, 'I hope this doesn't break us up. I love you so much.' "   78

Now the house feels empty. Danny, a well-mannered 6-footer who has briefly curtailed college to work in a hospital billing department, cheers on James, who takes his anger out on a punching bag and works to stay afloat at Old Mill. Most Saturdays, they visit their mother for an hour in a communal room at the prison.   79

With Ray on the road, working double time to pay the bills, friends like Pam McLane, an Old Mill senior, drop by to fix dinner, help clean up and remember Kay.   80

As for Kay herself, "there wasn't any freedom for the last 10 years, not for anyone with a conscience," she reflects on this bleak Maryland winter day. "You overcome depression, drinking and   81 negative forces, but you're not free. I was 21 when it happened. I made a terrible, terrible mistake. I feel horrible about it. . . ."

But, she adds, "I am not Pam Rodgers any more. I just don't   82
want my children destroyed. That's my sense of urgency. Why destroy a family when it's on the verge of changing the cycle?"

Meaning and Purpose

1.   Taking the entire article into consideration and paying close attention to the last section (paragraphs 79–82), what do you think Harris's purpose is in this article?
2.   How does the title relate to the story?
3.   Examine the statements by John Hassett in paragraph 16 and Jim Anders in paragraph 18. Which statement more closely agrees with your thinking about reformed criminals in general? About Kay Smith–Pamela Rodgers in particular? Has Harris led you to a specific view? If so, how?
4.   What does Harris mean by "a bare wisp of Max Factor" in paragraph 7?
5.   What is the emotional effect of describing Kay as both "the very model of a Severn, Md., housewife and working mother" and "a hard-drinking, pill-popping criminal with a gun" in the same paragraph (paragraph 3)?

Strategy

1.   How do the first three paragraphs pull the reader into Kay Smith's story?
2.   Harris summarizes Kay's life in paragraphs 4–19, then begins her story again at an earlier time and in more detail, starting with paragraph 20. Why does he choose this order of events? Why doesn't he begin the article with "Kay Smith was born Pamela Annette Gilbert on Oct. 1, 1951 . . ." (paragraph 20)?
3.   Does Harris use the scene or summary method to present the events of the story? Give examples to support your answer.

4. Harris alternates between present and past tense in this essay. What logic do you think he uses in choosing tenses?

Style

1. What is Harris's attitude toward Kay's situation? How does he establish this attitude in the tone of the essay?
2. What do words in paragraphs 53–56 such as "co-pilot," "snorting," and "hardscrabble" tell you about Harris's intended audience? This article originally appeared in a mass-circulation newspaper. Does that background explain his choice of words?
3. This essay is a news article, and most news writers try to claim objectivity in reporting. Does Harris care about objectivity? How do you know?

Writing Tasks

1. The Kay Smith–Pamela Rodgers article begins in the present and then goes back in time to retrace her history. Write a narrative beginning with a description of a present situation as Harris does. Then go back to record the events leading to that situation. At the end of your narrative, return to the present.
2. Write an essay in which you compare style and effectiveness of the opening situations in this chapter's first four selections. Ask yourself how well each author grabs readers, establishes a situation and a conflict, and begins to create a mood. If necessary, read the chapter introduction again for some elements of narrative openings.

❦ Richard Rodriguez ❦

Richard Rodriguez was born in San Francisco in 1944 to Mexican-American parents who spoke only Spanish at home. Rodriguez nonetheless mastered the English language and went on to study at Stanford, Columbia, and the University of California at Berkeley, where he earned a Ph.D. in English literature. He also received a Fulbright fellowship to study English literature in London. In spite of several offers for teaching positions, Rodriguez made writing and journalism his profession. His books include Hunger of Memory, Mexico's Children, Days of Obligation: An Argument with My Mexican Father, *and* Movements.

Los Pobres

In this autobiographical essay from The Hunger of Memory, *published in 1982, Rodriguez describes his first experience of working at hard labor. The summer after he graduates from Stanford University, he takes a construction job that leads him to a vital insight about his relationship to the Mexican immigrant community he "left behind" because of his education.*

Be aware as you read how closely Rodriguez examines himself, particularly how he examines himself in relation to others.

I went to college at Stanford, attracted partly by its academic   1
reputation, partly because it was the school rich people went to. I
found myself on a campus with golden children of western
America's upper middle class. Many were students both ambitious
for academic success and accustomed to leisured life in the sun. In
the afternoon, they lay spread out, sunbathing in front of the library, reading Swift or Engels or Beckett. Others went by in con-
vertibles, off to play tennis or ride horses or sail. Beach boys
dressed in tank-tops and shorts were my classmates in undergrad-
uate seminars. Tall tan girls wearing white strapless dresses sat directly in front of me in lecture rooms. I'd study them, their

physical confidence. I was still recognizably kin to the boy I had been. Less tortured perhaps. But still kin. At Stanford, it's true, I began to have something like a conventional sexual life. I don't think, however, that I really believed that the women I knew found me physically appealing. I continued to stay out of the sun. I didn't linger in mirrors. And I was the student at Stanford who remembered to notice the Mexican-American janitors and gardeners working on campus.

It was at Stanford, one day near the end of my senior year, that   2
a friend told me about a summer construction job he knew was available. I was quickly alert. Desire uncoiled within me. My friend said that he knew I had been looking for summer employment. He knew I needed some money. Almost apologetically he explained: It was something I probably wouldn't be interested in, but a friend of his, a contractor, needed someone for the summer to do menial jobs. There would be lots of shoveling and raking and sweeping. Nothing too hard. But nothing more interesting either. Still, the pay would be good. Did I want it? Or did I know someone who did?

I did. Yes, I said, surprised to hear myself say it.   3

In the weeks following, friends cautioned that I had no idea   4
how hard physical labor really is. ("You only *think* you know what it is like to shovel for eight hours straight.") Their objections seemed to me challenges. They resolved the issue. I became happy with my plan. I decided, however, not to tell my parents. I wouldn't tell my mother because I could guess her worried reaction. I would tell my father only after the summer was over, when I could announce that, after all, I did know what "real work" is like.

The day I met the contractor (a Princeton graduate, it turned   5
out), he asked me whether I had done any physical labor before. "In high school, during the summer," I lied. And although he seemed to regard me with skepticism, he decided to give me a try. Several days later, expectant, I arrived at my first construction site. I would take off my shirt to the sun. And at last grasp desired sensation. No longer afraid. At last become like a *bracero*. "We need those tree stumps out of here by tomorrow," the contractor said. I started to work.

I labored with excitement that first morning—and all the days   6
after. The work was harder than I could have expected. But it was
never as tedious as my friends had warned me it would be. There
was too much physical pleasure in the labor. Especially early in
the day, I would be most alert to the sensations of movement and
straining. Beginning around seven each morning (when the air
was still damp but the scent of weeds and dry earth anticipated
the heat of the sun), I would feel my body resist the first thrusts of
the shovel. My arms, tightened by sleep, would gradually loosen;
after only several minutes, sweat would gather in beads on my
forehead and then—a short while later—I would feel my chest
silky with sweat in the breeze. I would return to my work. A nervous spark of pain would fly up my arm and settle to burn like an
ember in the thick of my shoulder. An hour, two passed. Three.
My whole body would assume regular movements; my shoveling
would be described by identical, even movements. Even later in
the day, my enthusiasm for primitive sensation would survive the
heat and the dust and the insects pricking my back. I would strain
wildly for sensation as the day came to a close. At three-thirty,
quitting time, I would stand upright and slowly let my head fall
back, luxuriating in the feeling of tightness relieved.

Some of the men working nearby would watch me and laugh.   7
Two or three of the older men took the trouble to teach me the
right way to use a pick, the correct way to shovel. "You're doing it
wrong, too fucking hard," one man scolded. Then proceeded to
show me—what persons who work with their bodies all their lives
quickly learn—the most economical way to use one's body in
labor.

"Don't make your back do so much work," he instructed. I   8
stood impatiently listening, half listening, vaguely watching, then
noticed his work-thickened fingers clutching the shovel. I was annoyed. I wanted to tell him that I enjoyed shoveling the wrong
way. And I didn't want to learn the right way. I wasn't afraid of
back pain. I liked the way my body felt sore at the end of the day.

I was about to, but, as it turned out, I didn't say a thing.   9
Rather it was at that moment I realized that I was fooling myself if
I expected a few weeks of labor to gain me admission to the world

of the laborer. I would not learn in three months what my father had meant by "real work." I was not bound to this job; I could imagine its rapid conclusion. For me the sensations of exertion and fatigue could be savored. For my father or uncle, working at comparable jobs when they were my age, such sensations were to be feared. Fatigue took a different toll on their bodies—and minds.

It was, I know, a simple insight. But it was with this realiza- 10 tion that I took my first step that summer toward realizing something even more important about the "worker." In the company of carpenters, electricians, plumbers, and painters at lunch, I would often sit quietly, observant. I was not shy in such company. I felt easy, pleased by the knowledge that I was casually accepted, my presence taken for granted by men (exotics) who worked with their hands. Some days the younger men would talk and talk about sex, and they would howl at women who drove by in cars. Other days the talk at lunchtime was subdued; men gathered in separate groups. It depended on who was around. There were rough, good-natured workers. Others were quiet. The more I remember that summer, the more I realize that there was no single type of worker. I am embarrassed to say I had not expected such diversity. I certainly had not expected to meet, for example, a plumber who was an abstract painter in his off hours and admired the work of Mark Rothko. Nor did I expect to meet so many workers with college diplomas. (There were the ones who were not surprised that I intended to enter graduate school in the fall.) I suppose what I really want to say here is painfully obvious, but I must say it nevertheless: The men of that summer were middle-class Americans. They certainly didn't constitute an oppressed society. Carefully completing their work sheets; talking about the fortunes of local football teams; planning Las Vegas vacations; comparing the gas mileage of various makes of campers—they were not *los pobres* my mother had spoken about.

On two occasions, the contractor hired a group of Mexican 11 aliens. They were employed to cut down some trees and haul off debris. In all, there were six men of varying age. The youngest in his twenties, the oldest (his father?) perhaps sixty years old. They

came and they left in a single old truck. Anonymous men. They
were never introduced to the other men at the site. Immediately
upon their arrival, they would follow the contractor's directions,
start working—rarely resting—seemingly driven by a fatalistic
sense that work which had to be done was best done as quickly as
possible.

I watched them sometimes. Perhaps they watched me. The   12
only time I saw them pay me much notice was one day at
lunchtime when I was laughing with the other men. The Mexicans
sat apart when they ate, just as they worked by themselves. Quiet.
I rarely heard them say much to each other. All I could hear were
their voices calling out sharply to one another, giving directions.
Otherwise, when they stood briefly resting, they talked among
themselves in voices too hard to overhear.

The contractor knew enough Spanish, and the Mexicans—or   13
at least the oldest of them, their spokesman—seemed to know
enough English to communicate. But because I was around, the
contractor decided one day to make me his translator. (He assumed I could speak Spanish.) I did what I was told. Shyly I went
over to tell the Mexicans that the *patrón* wanted them to do something else before they left for the day. As I started to speak, I was
afraid with my old fear that I would be unable to pronounce
Spanish words. But it was a simple instruction I had to convey. I
could say it in phrases.

The dark sweating faces turned toward me as I spoke. They   14
stopped their work to hear me. Each nodded in response. I stood
there. I wanted to say something more. But what could I say in
Spanish, even if I could have pronounced the words right?
Perhaps I just wanted to engage them in small talk, to be assured
of their confidence, our familiarity. I thought for a moment to ask
them where in Mexico they were from. Something like that. And
maybe I wanted to tell them (a lie, if need be) that my parents
were from the same part of Mexico.

I stood there.   15

Their faces watched me. The eyes of the man directly in front 16
of me moved slowly over my shoulder, and I turned to follow his
glance toward *el patrón* some distance away. For a moment I felt

swept up by that glance into the Mexicans' company. But then I heard one of them returning to work. And then the others went back to work. I left them without saying anything more.

When they had finished, the contractor went over to pay them in cash. (He later told me that he paid them collectively— "for the job"—though he wouldn't tell me their wages. He said something quickly about the good rate of exchange "in their own country.") I can still hear the loudly confident voice he used with the Mexicans. It was the sound of the *gringo* I had heard as a very young boy. And I can still hear the quiet, indistinct sounds of the Mexican, the oldest, who replied. At hearing that voice I was sad for the Mexicans. Depressed by their vulnerability. Angry at myself. The adventure of the summer seemed suddenly ludicrous. I would not shorten the distance I felt from *los pobres* with a few weeks of physical labor. I would not become like them. They were different from me.   17

After that summer, a great deal—and not very much really— changed in my life. The curse of physical shame was broken by the sun; I was no longer ashamed of my body. No longer would I deny myself the pleasing sensations of my maleness. During those years when middle-class Black Americans began to assert with pride, "Black is beautiful," I was able to regard my complexion without shame. I am today darker than I ever was as a boy. I have taken up the middle-class sport of long-distance running. Nearly every day now I run ten or fifteen miles, barely clothed, my skin exposed to the California winter rain and wind or the summer sun of late afternoon. The torso, the soccer player's calves and thighs, the arms of the twenty-year-old I never was, I possess now in my thirties. I study the youthful parody shape in the mirror: the stomach lipped tight by muscle; the shoulders rounded by chin-ups; the arms veined strong. This man. A man. I meet him. He laughs to see me, what I have become.   18

The dandy. I wear double-breasted Italian suits and custom made English shoes. I resemble no one so much as my father—the man pictured in those honeymoon photos. At that point in life when he abandoned the dandy's posture, I assume it. At the point when my parents would not consider going on vacation, I register   19 at the Hotel Carlyle in New York and the Plaza Athénée in Paris. I am as taken by the symbols of leisure and wealth as they were. For my parents, however, those symbols became taunts, reminders of all they could not achieve in one lifetime. For me those same symbols are reassuring reminders of public success. I tempt vulgarity to be reassured. I am filled with the gaudy delight, the monstrous grace of the nouveau riche.

In recent years I have had occasion to lecture in ghetto high   20
schools. There I see students of remarkable style and physical grace. (One can see more dandies in such schools than one ever will find in middle-class high schools.) There is not the look of casual assurance I saw students at Stanford display. Ghetto girls mimic high-fashion models. Their dresses are of bold, forceful color; their figures elegant, long; the stance theatrical. Boys wear shirts that grip at their overdeveloped muscular bodies. (Against a powerless future, they engage images of strength.) Bad nutrition does not yet tell. Great disappointment, fatal to youth, awaits them still. For the moment, movements in school hallways are dancelike, a procession of postures in a sexual masque. Watching them, I feel a kind of envy. I wonder how different my adolescence would have been had I been free. . . . But no, it is my parents I see—their optimism during those years when they were entertained by Italian grand opera.

The registration clerk in London wonders if I have just been   21
to Switzerland. And the man who carries my luggage in New York guesses the Caribbean. My complexion becomes a mark of my leisure. Yet no one would regard my complexion the same way if I entered such hotels through the service entrance. That is only to say that my complexion assumes its significance from the context of my life. My skin, in itself, means nothing. I stress the point because I know there are people who would label me "disadvantaged" because of my color. They make the same mistake I made as a boy, when I thought a disadvantaged life was circumscribed by particular occupations. That summer I worked in the sun may have made me physically indistinguishable from the Mexicans working nearby. (My skin was actually darker because, unlike

them, I worked without wearing a shirt. By late August my hands were probably as tough as theirs.) But I was not one of *los pobres.* What made me different from them was an attitude of *mind,* my imagination of myself.

I do not blame my mother for warning me away from the sun when I was young. In a world where her brother had become an old man in his twenties because he was dark, my complexion was something to worry about. "Don't run in the sun," she warns me today. I run. In the end, my father was right—though perhaps he did not know how right or why—to say that I would never know what real work is. I will never know what he felt at his last factory job. If tomorrow I worked at some kind of factory, it would go differently for me. My long education would favor me. I could act as a public person—able to defend my interests, to unionize, to petition, to speak up—to challenge and demand. (I will never know what real work is.) I will never know what the Mexicans knew, gathering their shovels and ladders and saws.   22

Their silence stays with me now. The wages those Mexicans received for their labor were only a measure of their disadvantaged condition. Their silence is more telling. They lack a public identity. They remain profoundly alien. Persons apart. People lacking a union obviously, people without grounds. They depend upon the relative good will or fairness of their employers each day. For such people, lacking a better alternative, it is not such an unreasonable risk.   23

Their silence stays with me. I have taken these many words to describe its impact. Only: the quiet. Something uncanny about it. Its compliance. Vulnerability. Pathos. As I heard their truck rumbling away, I shuddered, my face mirrored with sweat. I had finally come face to face with *los pobres.*   24

Meaning and Purpose

1. What picture of Rodriguez do you get from the first paragraph? How does he see himself?

2. Why is Rodriguez surprised to hear himself say yes (paragraph 3) to the offer of a summer job at manual labor? What is his motive for taking the job? Why doesn't he tell his parents?

3. Rodriguez talks about many things in this essay: being a student at Stanford, physical labor, the Italian suits he wears, and ghetto high school students. What do you think his main point is, and where does he state it?

4. Paragraph 10 begins "It was, I know, a simple insight." What is the insight and what triggers it? How does this insight connect with his later statement, "But I was not one of *los pobres*"?

5. Is it significant that the Mexican workers were paid as a group rather than individually? Explain.

6. Rodriguez begins paragraphs 23 and 24 with the words "Their silence stays with me." What does the silence signify?

Strategy

1. Rodriguez's narrative begins with one summer while he is a student at Stanford, then jumps to the vague time frame of "After that summer" (paragraph 18), then to "In recent years" (paragraph 20). Why does he choose to arrange the events and skip to the periods that he does?

2. Point to examples of Rodriguez expanding and compressing details of his summer job. Why does he do so?

3. Does Rodriguez use summary or scene to tell his story? Give examples.

4. What is Rodriguez's point of view? Give evidence from the essay of how effective it is.

Style

1. Locate the words *los pobres, bracero, patrón,* and *gringo* in the text. Can you define them using only the context of the narrative?

2. Rodriguez occasionally uses sentence fragments purposely. Find at least three in the first two paragraphs and explain how they affect the tone of the introduction.

3. A good narrative re-creates life. Does "Los Pobres" do so? Explain.

Writing Tasks

1. At some time in your life you have undoubtedly been an "outsider." It might have been in another country or at a new school, in a new neighborhood, or on a new job. Write a narrative about that time. As Rodriguez does in "Los Pobres," blend the details of the situation with your thoughts and insights from a later perspective.

2. Choose an event to narrate, and write it in two ways. In one version, use the scene method to dramatize the event and make it immediate. In the other version, use summary to tell more than show. Which version is more effective?

❦ *Responding to Photographs* ❦
Narration

The Storyteller

Ancient cultures viewed storytellers as being touched with divine madness. These storytellers had tales that explained life's mysteries.

But times have changed

Astronauts have soared through space. The deepest rain forests and highest mountain peaks have been photographed. What mysteries need to be explained? What lessons need to be taught? What is the role of the storyteller in an age when movie and television production companies create visual stories by formula?

Is the photograph "The Storyteller" commenting on the role of storytellers today?

The Storyteller's outfit suggests that he indeed might be touched by divine madness. He wears ribbons, balloons, stream-

214

ers, a whimsical laurel around his head, and a banner that identifies him.

Displayed on a wall are hundreds of photographs, many of
African-American and Native-American leaders, perhaps each embodying a story of its own. Behind his head, slightly obscured, are
the words of Martin Luther King, "I have a dream."

This storyteller stands in the classroom, but where are the students who might be eager to hear a meaningful story? He is looking and pointing outside the photographic frame, but at what or
whom? From the viewer's perspective he is alone . . . or is he?

In a unified narrative respond to one of the following writing
tasks. Before you begin the first draft, review effective narrative
conventions described at the beginning of the chapter.

1. Create your own tale about the storyteller in this photograph.
    Begin by studying the photograph. Imagine how the storyteller
    feels in his attire. Imagine how he feels during his performance.
    Imagine what his life is like when he is not being a storyteller.
    What does he do? Where does he live? What do his friends think
    of his storytelling? Is he a fulfilled person? A happy person? A sad
    person?

    As you imagine the storyteller, list your observations. Once
    this exploratory phase of the assignment is complete, review
    your observations, and determine what dominant impression
    you wish to create.

    Finally, to start your first draft, you might begin this way:
    "Once upon a time an ordinary man who lived in our city de-
    cided to become a storyteller." Throughout your draft, integrate
    physical details from the photograph.

2. Imagine that the storyteller in the photograph is fully aware that
    ancient mysteries have been clarified scientifically. He is still
    compelled to tell tales, meaningful tales designed to give people
    insight into a society that some people see as growing more and
    more chaotic.

    For this task, tell how the storyteller became successful.
    Include in your narrative a summary of one tale that gave his lis-
    teners insight into contemporary life.

❦ Additional Writing Tasks ❦

Narration

1. All of us have had experiences that can be retold in narrative form. Often these experiences stay with us much longer than impersonal events that we have merely observed. For this writing task, select an incident from your early years that involves a simple action that you can recall clearly and vividly. The incident does not have to be exceptionally dramatic, but it should be interesting enough to move from the opening through the body to the climax—the major components of narrative. The incident may involve you alone or it may involve others as well. It must have enough action with connected events to be developed as a narration.

    Because this is to be an incident from your early years, you might begin by setting aside time to explore your past. Begin by spontaneously jotting down memories from your early past as a way to begin the selection procedure. Make a list by devoting no more than three or four sentences to each experience you recall. These three entries are from one student's memory list:

    > I remember walking home from school one June morning. Hot. Humid. A man with a Bible and wearing a black suit stopped me and asked, "Have you been saved, Sonny?" I was frightened.

    > When I was ten I visited my grandfather in the hospital. He was very ill, dying. I recalled all the wonderful and all the horrible fishing trips we took together.

    > Why was my dog shot? The killer was never found. I remember searching the faces of strangers for looks of guilt.

    Each writer, of course, will have his or her own memories: an automobile accident, a mystery, a sudden appearance, a victory, a defeat, a meeting with a famous person, and so on.

    Once you have compiled a list, select one of the memories, perhaps the one that stirs the most emotion in you when you re-

216

call it, and use it as the basis for your narration. Before starting your first draft, take at least an uninterrupted hour to compose a rough sketch of the incident, capturing the movement of events and the people. Then you will be prepared to start the first draft. Begin by arranging the material in dramatic order to serve as a loose outline.

2. Select an incident to narrate that you have not directly experienced yourself. The incident might come from what you have seen, heard, or read. Perhaps you will select an incident from a television show, film, short story, news article, or friend's experience. If you select a newspaper article as your source, you might want to retell it as though you had witnessed the incident. If you want to convey a friend's story, you might add observations of your own. If you select an incident from a film or short story, you might want to concentrate on an incident involving one character and rearrange the events to suit your purpose. Keep in mind, though, that your task is not to merely summarize the story line; your task is to select material for your own narrative.

5

Examples

Illustrating Ideas

The Method

Examples bring the vague and abstract down to earth. They clarify the historian's lectures. They make concrete the philosopher's abstractions. They electrify the politician's arguments. By using examples effectively, you will not only help your readers to understand your point, but also improve your chances of holding their attention because vivid, concrete examples can make your writing more interesting to read.

Examples are much used, even in everyday conversation. If someone claims that advertisers use fear of rejection to manipulate consumers, you might say, "Show me."

Examples such as these would follow: "What about those mouthwash commercials? One actually shows a salesman rejected because he has bad breath. And then after a quick rinse, Presto! he makes the sale, and the customer drives away smiling. And what about the commercial that shows a young female banker passed over for a promotion? A wiser, older colleague whispers in her ear. In the next scene she is scrubbing her head with the advertiser's shampoo, and the commercial closes with the smiling banker now managing her own department."

The speaker is using examples to clarify the general observation that advertisers use fear of rejection to manipulate consumers into buying their products. Writers use examples with the same intent—to illustrate a generalization, that is, to select one thing from many to represent the *whole*. In fact, the word *example* derives from the Latin *exemplum,* which refers to "one thing selected from the many." Examples used to represent ideas are essential to clear communication because they give readers something concrete to visualize. It might be difficult for a reader to understand what social critic Jack Solomon means by this statement.

> No matter how you look at it, in the scant space of some forty years, television has revolutionized our lives. First introduced as a novelty alternative to radio, television has rapidly evolved into the most profound invention of the age. Nothing is immune from its influence.

For the sake of clarity, Solomon immediately provides several examples to illustrate his idea for the reader:

> Politicians play for the cameras, and so do international terrorists. Physicians call news conferences, and judges host courtroom dramas. Television, through its hyping of the Olympic Games, has transformed sport into politics and politics into sport, treating everything from presidential elections to military conflicts as prime-time entertainment. What is not televised is hardly thought of at all in a world in which television creates reality as much as it records.

These examples add clarity to Solomon's statement. Without them the reader would have only a vague understanding of Solomon's point in this paragraph, which would amount to a slip in communication.

Strategies

Professional writers use three kinds of examples—specific, typical, and hypothetical—to support their ideas. They can be used in any combination and are often mixed within one paragraph.

Specific Examples

Specific examples capture an experience, event, incident, or fact. Banesh Hoffman, in "My Friend, Albert Einstein," uses a specific example (an **anecdote**) to support the general comment that the essence of Einstein's personality was simplicity.

> He was one of the greatest scientists the world has ever known, yet if I had to convey the essence of Albert Einstein in a single word, I would choose *simplicity*. Perhaps an anecdote will help. Once, caught in a downpour, he took off his hat and held it under his coat. Asked why, he explained,

with admirable logic, that the rain would damage the hat, but his hair would be none the worse for its wetting. This knack for going instinctively to the heart of the matter was the secret of his major scientific discoveries.

Hoffman selects this specific example with a clear purpose in mind. He wants to make concrete the generalization in the topic sentence. The example is vivid and interesting, capturing Einstein's essence.

Hoffman's specific example illustrating Einstein's simplicity is a short narrative, but writers often shape examples in other ways. Sometimes the writer will use several specific examples in one paragraph. A series of brief examples might function like verbal snapshots, freezing in time several events or experiences. In this paragraph, naturalist Jane van Lawick-Goodall uses seven short visual examples to illustrate social behavior among the chimpanzees she studied in Tanzania.

> While many details of their [the chimpanzees'] social behavior were hidden from me by the foliage, I did get occasional fascinating glimpses. I saw one female, newly arrived in a group, hurry up to a big male and hold her hand toward him. Almost regally he reached out, clasped her hand in his, drew it toward him, and kissed it with his lips. I saw two adult males embrace each other in greeting. I saw youngsters having wild games through treetops, chasing around after each other or jumping again and again, one after the other, from a branch to a springy bough below. I watched small infants dangling happily by themselves for minutes on end, patting at their toes with one hand, rotating gently from side to side. Once two tiny infants pulled on opposite ends of a twig in a gentle tug-of-war. Often during the heat of midday or after a long spell of feeding, I saw two or more adults grooming each other, carefully looking through the hair of their companions.

Sometimes writers will create a *list* or a *catalogue* of specific examples to illustrate their observations. In this paragraph from *The*

Distant Mirror, historian Barbara Tuchman catalogues how people in fourteenth-century England might imagine the distant places they had heard of but never seen.

> Faraway lands, however—India, Persia, and beyond—were seen through a gauze of fabulous fairy tales revealing an occasional nugget of reality: forests so high they touch the clouds, horned pygmies who move in herds and grow old in seven years, brahmins who kill themselves on funeral pyres, men with dogs' heads and six toes, "cyclopeans" with only one eye and one foot who move as fast as the wind, the "monoceros" which can be caught only when it sleeps in the lap of a virgin, Amazons whose tears are of silver, panthers who practice the caesarean operation with their own claws, trees whose leaves supply wool, snakes 300 feet long, snakes with precious stones for eyes, snakes who so love music that for prudence they stop up one ear with their tail.

Tuchman's and Goodall's paragraphs also illustrate another point: Examples can come from various sources. Tuchman finds her specific examples by researching historical documents; Goodall gets hers by observing chimpanzees in their natural habitat. Both writers use their examples for the same purpose, however: to illustrate a general observation.

Typical Examples

In contrast to specific examples, writers compose **typical examples** by generalizing from many experiences, events, incidents, or facts. Consider this paragraph from Jonathan Kozol's essay "The Human Cost of an Illiterate Society." Kozol uses a typical example to develop the point that illiterates, people who cannot read, lead a precarious existence, even when they are in the care of professionals who are trained to provide for their health. As you read Kozol's paragraph, keep in mind that this typical example represents the experience of many people, not that of one specific person.

Illiterates live, in more than literal ways, an uninsured existence. They cannot understand written details on a health insurance form. They cannot read the waivers that they sign preceding surgical procedures. Several women I have known in Boston have entered a slum hospital with the intention of obtaining a tubal ligation and have emerged a few days later after having been subjected to a hysterectomy. Unaware of their rights, incognizant of jargon, intimidated by the unfamiliar air of fear and atmosphere of ether that so many of us find oppressive in the confines even of the most attractive and expensive medical facilities, they have signed their names to documents they could not read and which nobody, in the hectic situation that prevails so often in those overcrowded hospitals that serve the urban poor, had even bothered to explain.

Kozol begins with a general statement that establishes the dangers illiterate patients face. He follows with two sentences of background: Illiterate patients cannot understand insurance forms or the legal documents that give away their rights during surgery. He then supports his general statement with an extended typical example, thus illustrating, even dramatizing, the result of being unable to read: Several illiterate Boston women signed papers permitting hysterectomies when they wanted tubal ligations.

Typical examples, as Kozol's illustrates, are composites of many experiences. They are not rooted in specific times but compiled after many observations over an extended period. In the next paragraph, cultural anthropologist Edward T. Hall uses typical examples developed after extended observation to illustrate how people react when their sense of space is violated:

People are very sensitive to any intrusion into their spatial bubble. If someone stands too close to you, your first instinct is to back up. If that's not possible, you lean away and pull yourself in, tensing your muscles. If an intruder doesn't respond to these body signals, you may then try to protect yourself, using a briefcase, umbrella, or raincoat. Women— especially when traveling alone—often plant their pocketbook in such a way that no one can get very close to them.

As a last resort, you may move to another spot and position yourself behind a desk or a chair that provides screening. Everyone tries to adjust the space around himself in a way that's comfortable for him; most often, he does this unconsciously.

Hypothetical Examples

Sometimes writers create **hypothetical examples** from their imagination. Hypothetical examples are similar to typical examples, usually composed from bits and pieces of experience or information. Often a writer will use a hypothetical example where something concrete is needed to tie down an abstraction and no *actual* example is available. In the opening paragraph of *The White Album*, essayist and novelist Joan Didion uses hypothetical examples to illustrate why stories are important in life.

> We tell ourselves stories in order to live. The princess is caged in the consulate. The man with the candy will lead the children into the sea. The naked woman on the ledge outside the window on the sixteenth floor is a victim of accidie, or the naked woman is an exhibitionist, and it would be "interesting" to know which. We tell ourselves that it makes some difference whether the naked woman is about to commit a mortal sin or is about to register a political protest or is about to be, the Aristophanic view, snatched back to the human condition by the fireman in priest's clothing just visible in the window behind her, the one smiling at the telephoto lens. We look for the sermon in the suicide, for the social or moral lesson in the murder of five. We interpret what we see, select the most workable of the multiple choices. We live entirely, especially if we are writers, by the imposition of a narrative line upon disparate images, by the "ideas" with which we have learned to freeze the shifting phantasmagoria which is our actual experience.

Didion has clearly drawn these brief examples from her imagination, yet they are effective because they make her observation more concrete. With these conjectures she hopes to stir her readers' interest by appealing to typical experiences they might have encountered in fairy tales and newspapers, the mysterious experiences for which many seek explanations.

Mixing Examples

When studying professional writing, you'll notice that writers use different strategies to develop their examples. You'll find specific, typical, and hypothetical examples mixed, and you'll notice that sometimes examples illustrating one point will be presented in several paragraphs. In this passage from *No House Calls*, Peter Gott, a practicing physician and medical columnist, develops his point in several paragraphs and mixes examples with explanation to reveal the scientific facts behind the commercial claims of mouthwash and disinfectant companies.

> With people's increasing knowledge about bacteria, it was inevitable that some companies would, with success, try to play upon the fear that we have all developed about "bacterial infection." For instance, Listerine and Lysol are currently being advertised to produce "clean breath" and a clean environment, respectively, as a result of their bacteria-killing properties. While it is true that these compounds do, in fact, kill bacteria, the consumer would do well to demand more precision in evaluating their claims.
>
> As an example, the mouth contains billions of harmless bacteria. Some forms of bad breath are caused by bacterial decomposition of food between teeth. Listerine—and many other mouthwashes—will kill millions of bacteria on contact, but only a tiny proportion of the *total*. Furthermore, as soon as the Listerine has been spit out, billions of bacteria are reintroduced into the mouth during breathing and eating. So while the consumer's mouth will feel "fresh," in fact the bacterial count rapidly rises to "pretreatment" levels; essentially, nothing has been accomplished.
>
> Lysol spray when applied to surfaces will kill some bacteria, but most of these are nonpathogens and would do us

no harm anyway. Bacteria that cause venereal disease die quickly outside the body and would be unlikely to reside on public toilet seats long enough for the spray to make any difference. The Lysol spray will scent the air, however, and that seems to be the important consideration. Somehow, if we don't see or smell the germs, we assume they're all gone. The room must be safe. The evil has been repelled. We can take a shower.

Peter Gott's passage establishes an important principle to keep in mind: Every writer, whether a professional writer or a student writer, must develop an eye for examples. The most effective way we know of developing that eye is to read critically, that is, read as a writer reads. Study how professional writers shape their examples. Study how their examples relate to their generalizations. And study the kinds of examples they develop.

Examples in College Writing

Examples are so effective in clarifying an idea that you will probably use them in every college essay you write. The vivid, specifically written example brings to life the most abstract concept. Without examples an expository essay will lack vigor. In fact, turning in an essay without effectively using examples might indicate to your reader that your understanding of the subject is deficient, especially if you write a string of unsubstantiated generalizations.

Guidelines for Writing Examples

1. Select a subject that can be developed through examples, and determine whether you have enough information to develop examples.
2. Decide on a dominant purpose of the essay. Then use the dominant purpose to focus your prewriting to generate as many examples as you can.

3. Review your prewritten material, compose a thesis, and then select appropriate examples from your prewriting to develop it.
4. Decide on appropriate structure and arrange the examples to create the strongest effect. Vary the examples in length and type while keeping in mind the purpose they serve.
5. Revise your essay, making sure that the examples are adequately developed for your purpose.

A Student Essay Developed by Examples

Daniela Taylor wrote a personal experience essay about common behavior in response to this freshman composition assignment:

> In an 800- to 1000-word essay, identify and discuss a common behavior that suggests changing social attitudes. Consider the following general subject areas as possibilities:
>
> | | |
> |---|---|
> | dress | speech |
> | manners | dating practices |
> | public displays | possessions |
> | a sport | games |
> | service | charity |
>
> Use examples as the dominant development mode, and base your discussion on personal experience and observation.

Taylor developed the examples from firsthand experience, a film she had seen on television, and a news article. She decided to concentrate on the general subject of manners, which she narrowed to a more specific subject: increasing discourtesy in public places.

Now examine Taylor's essay. Read it through once to see how she uses examples to develop her thought. Then study the entire essay in detail by responding to items in Reviewing with a Writer's Eye.

We Are Not Alone

Whatever happened to courtesy? I am referring to the [1] everyday, run-of-the-mill courtesies people used to show each other, which now seem to have gone the way of helping the aged across busy intersections and quiet libraries. For example, last week as I came out of a grocery store, I saw a woman moving her groceries from a shopping cart to her trunk. That task completed, she shoved her shopping cart directly behind the car parked next to her. What was she thinking? Did she know that the driver of the other car would hit it if he failed to see it? Did she realize he would have to return her cart if he did see it? Did she care? The woman's behavior momentarily angered me and puzzled me. Sadly, however, my experience shows that this woman's discourteous behavior is not an isolated event. It seems that basic courtesy is rapidly being replaced by basic discourtesy. Everywhere I spend time in public—at school, at work, at shopping malls, in parks, in theaters, at sports events, at movies, and even on the highway—discourteous behavior seems to be increasing.

Nowhere has public discourtesy become more common [2] than in traffic. I recall my early driving experience as being pleasurable. Other drivers would follow right-of-way guidelines, waiting their turn to make a left turn or cross through an intersection. Now this courteous attitude seems to be changing. Like me, you have probably experienced angry drivers in a rush, shouting and shaking their fists at you. Typically, these drivers may be well-mannered people, but they often go berserk behind the wheel of a car. Near campus lately, I have noticed something new taking place. After a left turn signal turns red, three, four, five, or even six drivers still rush through the intersection, delaying the cars that now have a green light. These drivers seem to share the same discourteous attitude, "I waited long enough for this left turn light to turn green, and now I'm going through even if it turns red again." Another recent trend is the spontaneous creation of illegal left turn lanes to the right of the legal left turn lane. Of course, dangerous drivers have always been on the road, but now others are compounding the danger because of their discourteous impatience. Sometimes dis-

courtesy even erupts into anger. A recent survey of
Southern California drivers, a place where commuters often spend two to three grueling hours a day in their cars,
revealed that nearly 60% of those surveyed admitted giving chase to other motorists who had offended them.
Usually these chases are abandoned as tempers cool, but
sometimes the offended driver overtakes the offender and
a battle of words, gestures, and even weapons ensues.

Last week I began to notice discourteous behavior that   3
seems to have recently developed. Rollerbladers apparently find a challenge in weaving in and out of pedestrians strolling on public walkways. They seem to lack
common courtesy, failing to keep in mind that a pedestrian walking at a much slower pace than their skating
pace cannot always predict their movements. Their discourteous behavior can turn a relaxing afternoon stroll
into a nerve-racking game of dodge the Rollerblader. The
increase of cellular phones has given rise to another kind
of public discourtesy. People no longer retreat to enclosed
public phone booths to make private phone calls. They can
now phone friends, loved ones, and business associates
while standing in a crowd. Often their voices rise well
above normal speaking range, thus disrupting the casual
conversations of people who share the public space.

A recent Home Box Office showing of director Barry   4
Levinson's *Good Morning, Vietnam*, a 1987 film about the
exploits of an Armed Forces Radio disc jockey in Saigon at
the height of the Vietnam war, reminded me of how our
culture freely and discourteously uses obscenity. Disc
jockey Adrian Cronauer (played by Robin Williams) is
teaching a group of Vietnamese how to use English in
everyday situations. Cronauer bypasses all the conventional socially acceptable phrases and gets right to the
nitty-gritty of American obscenity, teaching the
Vietnamese which obscenities to use for which occasions.
Political implications aside, I at first thought the scene
was hilarious, perhaps the films most memorable scene.
But then I realized that beneath the obscene words and
phrases, so incongruous and humorous in the mouths of
non-English speakers, lies the very attitude that disturbs
me, an attitude that seems to be saying, "I have a right to
be as discourteous as I want, Mister!"

Now, over a decade later, I find the "Cronauer" atti-   5
tude to be increasing. In almost any public setting people
appear to be determined to pepper their conversations
with common obscenities that used to be reserved for
locker-room conversations, scribbling on restroom walls,
or moments of great frustration and anger. Recently, for
example, a friend and I were standing in line to buy tickets for a popular movie. Several people behind us were
speaking loudly and punctuating their observations with
gutter language and uproarious laughter. The epithets in
their rambling conversation, delivered by both young men
and women, were directed toward actors, musical groups,
members of the opposite sex, teachers, and each other
when they disagreed. Behind me an older couple waited in
line with their two children. They were clearly embarrassed, their faces turning red and their expressions
pained, but the speakers seemed to be unaware of their
embarrassment. I think such public use of generally unacceptable language reveals an aggressive, disrespectful attitude—perhaps the most extreme form of public discourtesy. It implicitly suggests that these teens feel free
to say whatever they please without being sensitive to
common social constraints. Should freedom of speech include the right to be publicly discourteous by spouting
four-letter words no matter how uncomfortable it makes
others who share the public space?

Why is public discourtesy increasing? I guess that   6
more and more people are focusing on themselves and
forgetting that their behavior might affect others around
them. I know at times I have, and you probably have too.
Yet by merely remembering that we share public spaces
with others, we might help replace basic discourtesy with
basic courtesy.

Reviewing with a Writer's Eye

1. Develop a scratch outline (see pp. 42–44) of Daniela Taylor's
    "We Are Not Alone." First, state the thesis statement in your own
    words. Then restate each topic sentence in your own words and

identify the supporting examples for each topic sentence. How are paragraphs 4 and 5 related?

2. Taylor uses a variety of examples (see pp. 221–227). By paragraph, identify each type of example she uses. For instance, in the introductory paragraph, Taylor uses a specific example based on personal experience.

3. To guide her readers through the essay, Taylor uses overt transitions. Review paragraph 2, and identify the words and phrases that Taylor uses to keep readers on track.

4. Review Taylor's introduction and conclusion. How do they relate to each other?

5. Sometimes Taylor presents examples with very little comment, as she does in paragraph 3. Other times she responds to the examples, as she does in paragraphs 4 and 5. Review paragraphs 3, 4, and 5, and identify the examples and Taylor's responses to them. Why do you think she chooses to comment on some examples and not others?

6. Imagine that Taylor has asked you to read her essay to see whether the organization is effective and the examples are clearly distinguished. In response, write Taylor a note identifying any strengths and/or weaknesses you find in the organization and presentation of examples.

As you read the essays in the following section, you will see the variety of ways in which writers develop examples. Sometimes a writer will use a single extended example to develop a point. At other times a writer will combine short and extended examples, specific and typical examples, and will include personal observations and background information.

Sometimes examples will serve as the dominant development pattern, but like narration and description, examples also function in essays with other dominant patterns, such as comparison and contrast, cause and effect, classification, and argumentation. Always, however, writers use examples with one fundamental purpose in mind: *to make the general more specific and the abstract more concrete.*

Peer Review

You may be asked to write an essay about one of the readings that follow. Before you meet with your writing group, review this introduction. As you read the papers of your group, use these general principles of using examples to help guide your comments.

1. All examples should clearly relate to the general statements they illustrate.
2. The number of examples should be enough to validate the general statement but not so many that the reader feels overwhelmed and loses interest. There is no mathematical way to measure this balance, so rely on your own judgment as you read the paper.
3. The examples should be combined with explanations to guide the reader to the desired conclusion.

❦ Amy Tan ❦

Amy Tan was born in Oakland, California, in 1952, two and a half years after her parents emigrated to the United States from China. Her parents expected her to become a neurosurgeon, but instead she became a consultant to programs for disabled children and then a freelance writer. She visited China for the first time in 1987 and felt an instant cultural identity with her parents' homeland. Her first novel, The Joy Luck Club, spent several weeks on American bestseller lists and earned much critical acclaim. It sensitively explores the relationships between young Chinese-American women and their immigrant mothers. Her second novel, The Kitchen God's Wife, further explores this theme. Tan has also written two books for children, The Moon Lady and The Siamese Cat. Her latest novel is The Hundred Secret Senses.

Mother Tongue

In the following essay, first published in Threepenny Review, Tan describes how her use of English changes according to the needs of the circumstance and moment. During her exploration of language she also manages to paint an affectionate portrait of her mother and the relationship she has with her.

Tan uses example after example to demonstrate her points. Notice how specific those examples are, how they aptly illustrate her generalizations, and how they lend interest to what she says.

I am not a scholar of English or literature. I cannot give you much more than personal opinions on the English language and its variations in this country or others. 1

I am a writer. And by that definition, I am someone who has always loved language. I am fascinated by language in daily life. I spend a great deal of my time thinking about the power of language—the way it can evoke an emotion, a visual image, a complex idea, or a simple truth. Language is the tool of my trade. And I use them all—all the Englishes I grew up with. 2

Recently, I was made keenly aware of the different Englishes I 3
do use. I was giving a talk to a large group of people, the same talk
I had already given to half a dozen other groups. The nature of the
talk was about my writing, my life, and my book, *The Joy Luck
Club*. The talk was going along well enough, until I remembered
one major difference that made the whole tale sound wrong. My
mother was in the room. And it was perhaps the first time she had
heard me give a lengthy speech, using the kind of English I have
never used with her. I was saying things like, "The intersection of
memory upon imagination" and "There is an aspect of my fiction
that relates to thus-and-thus"—a speech filled with carefully
wrought grammatical phrases, burdened, it suddenly seemed to
me, with nominalized forms, past perfect tenses, conditional
phrases, all the forms of standard English that I had learned in
school and through books, the forms of English I did not use at
home with my mother.

Just last week, I was walking down the street with my 4
mother, and I again found myself conscious of the English I was
using, the English I do use with her. We were talking about the
price of new and used furniture and I heard myself saying this:
"Not waste money that way." My husband was with us as well,
and he didn't notice any switch in my English. And then I realized why. It's because over the twenty years we've been together
I've often used that same kind of English with him, and sometimes he even uses it with me. It has become our language of intimacy, a different sort of English that relates to family talk, the
language I grew up with.

So you'll have some idea of what this family talk I heard 5
sounds like, I'll quote what my mother said during a recent conversation which I videotaped and then transcribed. During this
conversation, my mother was talking about a political gangster in
Shanghai who had the same last name as her family's, Du, and
how the gangster in his early years wanted to be adopted by her
family, which was rich by comparison. Later, the gangster became
more powerful, far richer than my mother's family, and one day
showed up at my mother's wedding to pay his respects. Here's
what she said in part.

"Du Yusong having business like fruit stand. Like off the street   6
kind. He is Du like Du Zong—but not Tsung-ming Island people.
The local people call putong, the river east side, he belong to that
side local people. That man want to ask Du Zong father take him
in like become own family. Du Zong father wasn't look down on
him, but didn't take seriously, until that man big like become a
mafia. Now important person, very hard to inviting him. Chinese
way, came only to show respect, don't stay for dinner. Respect for
making big celebration, he shows up. Mean gives lots of respect.
Chinese custom. Chinese social life that way. If too important
won't have to stay too long. He come to my wedding. I didn't see,
I heard it. I gone to boy's side, they have YMCA dinner. Chinese
age I was nineteen."

You should know that my mother's expressive command of   7
English belies how much she actually understands. She reads the
Forbes report, listens to *Wall Street Week,* converses daily with her
stockbroker, reads all of Shirley MacLaine's books with ease—all
kinds of things I can't begin to understand. Yet some of my friends
tell me they understand 50 percent of what my mother says. Some
say they understand 80 to 90 percent. Some say they understand
none of it, as if she were speaking pure Chinese. But to me, my
mother's English is perfectly clear, perfectly natural. It's my mother
tongue. Her language, as I hear it, is vivid, direct, full of observation and imagery. That was the language that helped shape the way
I saw things, expressed things, made sense of the world.

Lately, I've been giving more thought to the kind of English   8
my mother speaks. Like others, I have described it to people as
"broken" or "fractured" English. But I wince when I say that. It has
always bothered me that I can think of no way to describe it other
than "broken," as if it were damaged and needed to be fixed, as if
it lacked a certain wholeness and soundness. I've heard other
terms used, "limited English," for example. But they seem just as
bad, as if everything is limited, including people's perceptions of
the limited English speaker.

I know this for a fact, because when I was growing up, my   9
mother's "limited" English limited *my* perception of her. I was

ashamed of her English. I believed that her English reflected the quality of what she had to say. That is, because she expressed them imperfectly her thoughts were imperfect. And I had plenty of empirical evidence to support me: the fact that people in department stores, at banks, and at restaurants did not take her seriously, did not give her good service, pretended not to understand her, or even acted as if they did not hear her.

My mother has long realized the limitations of her English as 10 well. When I was fifteen, she used to have me call people on the phone to pretend I was she. In this guise, I was forced to ask for information or even to complain and yell at people who had been rude to her. One time it was a call to her stockbroker in New York. She had cashed out her small portfolio and it just so happened we were going to go to New York the next week, our very first trip outside California. I had to get on the phone and say in an adolescent voice that was not very convincing, "This is Mrs. Tan."

And my mother was standing in the back whispering loudly, 11 "Why he don't send me check, already two weeks late. So mad he lie to me, losing me money."

And then I said in perfect English, "Yes, I'm getting rather 12 concerned. You had agreed to send the check two weeks ago, but it hasn't arrived."

Then she began to talk more loudly. "What he want, I come to 13 New York tell him front of his boss, you cheating me?" And I was trying to calm her down, make her be quiet, while telling the stockbroker, "I can't tolerate any more excuses. If I don't receive the check immediately, I am going to have to speak to your manager when I'm in New York next week." And sure enough, the following week there we were in front of this astonished stockbroker, and I was sitting there red-faced and quiet, and my mother, the real Mrs. Tan, was shouting at his boss in her impeccable broken English.

We used a similar routine just five days ago, for a situation 14 that was far less humorous. My mother had gone to the hospital for an appointment, to find out about a benign brain tumor a CAT scan had revealed a month ago. She said she had spoken very good English, her best English, no mistakes. Still, she said, the hospital did not apologize when they said they had lost the CAT scan and she had come for nothing. She said they did not seem to have any sympathy when she told them she was anxious to know the exact diagnosis, since her husband and son had both died of brain tumors. She said they would not give her any more information until the next time and she would have to make another appointment for that. So she said she would not leave until the doctor called her daughter. She wouldn't budge. And when the doctor finally called her daughter, me, who spoke in perfect English—lo and behold—we had assurances the CAT scan would be found, promises that a conference call on Monday would be held, and apologies for any suffering my mother had gone through for a most regrettable mistake.

I think my mother's English almost had an effect on limiting   15
my possibilities in life as well. Sociologists and linguists probably will tell you that a person's developing language skills are more influenced by peers. But I do think that the language spoken in the family, especially in immigrant families which are more insular, plays a large role in shaping the language of the child. And I believe that is affected my results on achievement tests, IQ tests, and the SAT. While my English skills were never judged as poor, compared to math, English could not be considered my strong suit. In grade school I did moderately well, getting perhaps B's, sometimes B-pluses, in English and scoring perhaps in the sixtieth or seventieth percentile on achievement tests. But those scores were not good enough to override the opinion that my true abilities lay in math and science, because in those areas I achieved A's and scored in the ninetieth percentile or higher.

This was understandable. Math is precise; there is only one   16
correct answer. Whereas, for me at least, the answers on English tests were always a judgment call, a matter of opinion and personal experience. Those tests were constructed around items like fill-in-the-blank sentence completion, such as, "Even though Tom was _____, Mary thought he was _____." And the correct answer always seemed to be the most bland combinations of thoughts, for example, "Even though Tom was shy, Mary thought he was charm-

ing," with the grammatical structure "even though" limiting the correct answer to some sort of semantic opposites, so you wouldn't get answers like, "Even though Tom was foolish, Mary thought he was ridiculous." Well, according to my mother, there were very few limitations as to what Tom could have been and what Mary might have thought of him. So I never did well on tests like that.

The same was true with word analogies, pairs of words in which you were supposed to find some sort of logical, semantic relationship—for example, "*Sunset* is to *nightfall* as _____ is to _____." And here you would be presented with a list of four possible pairs, one of which showed the same kind of relationship: *red* is to *stoplight, bus* is to *arrival, chills* is to *fever, yawn* is to *boring.* Well, I could never think that way. I knew what the tests were asking, but I could not block out of my mind the images already created by the first pair, "*sunset* is to *nightfall*"—and I would see a burst of colors against a darkening sky, the moon rising, the lowering of a curtain of stars. And all the other pairs of words—red, bus, stoplight, boring—just threw up a mass of confusing images, making it impossible for me to sort out something as logical as saying: "A sunset precedes nightfall" is the same as "a chill precedes a fever." The only way I would have gotten that answer right would have been to imagine an associative situation, for example, my being disobedient and staying out past sunset, catching a chill at night, which turns into feverish pneumonia as punishment, which indeed did happen to me.

I have been thinking about all this lately, about my mother's English, about achievement tests. Because lately I've been asked, as a writer, why there are not more Asian Americans represented in American literature. Why are there few Asian Americans enrolled in creative writing programs? Why do so many Chinese students go into engineering? Well, these are broad sociological questions I can't begin to answer. But I have noticed in surveys—in fact, just last week—that Asian students, as a whole, always do significantly better on math achievement tests than in English. And this makes me think that there are other Asian-American students whose English spoken in the home might also be described as "broken" or "limited." And perhaps they also have teachers who are steering them away from writing and into math and science, which is what happened to me.

Fortunately, I happen to be rebellious in nature and enjoy the 19 challenge of disproving assumptions made about me. I became an English major my first year in college, after being enrolled as premed. I started writing nonfiction as a freelancer the week after I was told by my former boss that writing was my worst skill and I should hone my talents toward account management.

But it wasn't until 1985 that I finally began to write fiction. 20 And at first I wrote using what I thought to be wittily crafted sentences, sentences that would finally prove I had mastery over the English language. Here's an example from the first draft of a story that later made its way into *The Joy Luck Club*, but without this line: "That was my mental quandary in its nascent state." A terrible line, which I can barely pronounce.

Fortunately, for reasons I won't get into today, I later decided 21 I should envision a reader for the stories I would write. And the reader I decided upon was my mother, because these were stories about mothers. So with this reader in mind—and in fact she did read my early drafts—I began to write stories using all the Englishes I grew up with: the English I spoke to my mother, which for lack of a better term might be described as "simple"; the English she used with me, which for lack of a better term might be described as "broken"; my translation of her Chinese, which could certainly be described as "watered down"; and what I imagined to be her translation of her Chinese if she could speak in perfect English, her internal language, and for that I sought to preserve the essence, but neither an English nor a Chinese structure. I wanted to capture what language ability tests can never reveal: her intent, her passion, her imagery, the rhythms of her speech and the nature of her thoughts.

Apart from what any critic had to say about my writing, I 22 knew I had succeeded where it counted when my mother finished reading my book and gave me her verdict: "So easy to read."

Meaning and Purpose

1. What is Tan's thesis? Where does she state it?
2. Tan asserts that her mother's lack of command of standard English " belies how much she actually understands" (paragraph 7). How is this so?
3. Explain how her mother's "limited" English limited Tan's perception of her.
4. Explain how her mother's lack of English skills nearly limited some of the author's life possibilities.

Strategy

1. Tan uses anecdotes to illustrate her points, yet this is not a narrative essay. Why?
2. How effectively do Tan's examples illustrate her points?
3. Why does Tan distinctly break her essay at the end of paragraph 7 and again at the end of paragraph 17?

Style

1. In paragraph 7, Tan says that some of her friends claim to understand little of her mother's speech, while some others claim to understand none of it. Translate the transcription of her mother's language in paragraph 6. Can it be accurately described as an "expressive command of English" (paragraph 7)?
2. How many "Englishes" does Tan speak?
3. Tan says she eliminated the line "That was my mental quandary in its nascent state" from her novel *The Joy Luck Club* and labels the line "terrible." Why?
4. If necessary, look up the following in a good dictionary: *wrought, nominalized* (paragraph 3); *transcribed* (5); *belies* (7); *empirical* (9); *guise* (10); *impeccable* (13); *benign* (14); *insular* (15); *semantic* (16); *quandary, nascent* (19).

Writing Tasks

1. Using Amy Tan's essay as a model, write an essay in which you examine the various Englishes you use. What do you talk about when you speak with friends of the same sex? Of the opposite sex? With both sexes? With your co-workers? With your parents? How does your language change? Make sure your examples are many and specific.

2. If you work in a job that has specialized jargon or if you play a sport or participate in any social activity that has its own slang, write an essay in which you categorize and explain that language.

❦ Brent Staples ❦

Brent Staples, born in 1951 in Chester, Pennsylvania, attended Widener University in his home town, where he received a B.A. in behavioral sciences. He then attended graduate school at the University of Chicago, earning a Ph.D. in psychology. He has been a writer and editor for the Chicago Sun-Times, *the* Chicago Reader, Chicago *magazine, and* Down Beat. *Since 1985 he has been on the editorial board of the* New York Times, *where he writes regularly on politics and culture. He has also been a regular contributor to the* New York Times Magazine, New York Woman, Ms., *and* Harper's. *He published* Parallel Time: A Memoir *in 1991.*

Black Men and Public Spaces

"Black Men and Public Spaces" appeared in a slightly different form in the September 1986 issue of Ms. *magazine. The current version of the essay subsequently appeared in the December 1987 issue of* Harper's. *The essay is a provocative account of the ironic power and the real pain connected to being a young, black man in our race-conscious society.*

As you read, pay close attention to the number and kinds of examples Staples uses to make his points vivid and alive.

My first victim was a woman—white, well dressed, probably in her late twenties. I came upon her late one evening on a deserted street in Hyde Park, a relatively affluent neighborhood in an otherwise mean, impoverished section of Chicago. As I swung onto the avenue behind her, there seemed to be a discreet, uninflammatory distance between us. Not so. She cast back a worried glance. To her, the youngish black man—a broad six feet two inches with a beard and billowing hair, both hands shoved into the pockets of a bulky military jacket—seemed menacingly close. After a few more quick glimpses, she picked up her pace and was soon running in earnest. Within seconds she disappeared into a cross street.

That was more than a decade ago. I was twenty-two years old, a graduate student newly arrived at the University of Chicago. It was in the echo of that terrified woman's footfalls that I first began to know the unwieldy inheritance I'd come into—the ability to alter public space in ugly ways. It was clear that she thought herself the quarry of a mugger, a rapist, or worse. Suffering a bout of insomnia, however, I was stalking sleep, not defenseless wayfarers. As a softy who is scarcely able to take a knife to a raw chicken— let alone hold one to a person's throat—I was surprised, embarrassed, and dismayed all at once. Her flight made me feel like an accomplice in tyranny. It also made it clear that I was indistinguishable from the muggers who occasionally seeped into the area from the surrounding ghetto. That first encounter, and those that followed, signified that a vast, unnerving gulf lay between nighttime pedestrians—particularly women—and me. And I soon gathered that being perceived as dangerous is a hazard in itself. I only needed to turn a corner into a dicey situation, or crowd some frightened, armed person in a foyer somewhere, or make an errant move after being pulled over by a policeman. Where fear and weapons meet—and they often do in urban America—there is always the possibility of death.   2

In that first year, my first away from my hometown, I was to become thoroughly familiar with the language of fear. At dark, shadowy intersections, I could cross in front of a car stopped at a traffic light and elicit the *thunk, thunk, thunk, thunk* of the driver— black, white, male, or female—hammering down the door locks. On less traveled streets after dark, I grew accustomed to but never comfortable with people crossing to the other side of the street rather than pass me. Then there were the standard unpleasantries with policemen, doormen, bouncers, cabdrivers, and others whose business it is to screen out troublesome individuals before there is any nastiness.   3

I moved to New York nearly two years ago and I have remained an avid night walker. In central Manhattan, the near-   4 constant crowd cover minimizes tense one-on-one street encounters. Elsewhere—in SoHo, for example, where sidewalks are narrow and tightly spaced buildings shut out the sky—things can get very taut indeed.

After dark, on the warrenlike streets of Brooklyn where I live, I often see women who fear the worst from me. They seem to have set their faces on neutral, and with their purse straps strung across their chests bandolier-style, they forge ahead as though bracing themselves against being tackled. I understand, of course, that the danger they perceive is not a hallucination. Women are particularly vulnerable to street violence, and young black males are drastically overrepresented among the perpetrators of that violence. Yet these truths are no solace against the kind of alienation that comes of being ever the suspect, a fearsome entity with whom pedestrians avoid making eye contact.

It is not altogether clear to me how I reached the ripe old age of twenty-two without being conscious of the lethality nighttime pedestrians attributed to me. Perhaps it was because in Chester, Pennsylvania, the small, angry industrial town where I came of age in the 1960s, I was scarcely noticeable against a backdrop of gang warfare, street knifings, and murders. I grew up one of the good boys, had perhaps a half-dozen fistfights. In retrospect, my shyness of combat has clear sources.

As a boy, I saw countless tough guys locked away; I have since buried several, too. They were babies, really—a teenage cousin, a brother of twenty-two, a childhood friend in his mid-twenties—all gone down in episodes of bravado played out in the streets. I came to doubt the virtues of intimidation early on. I chose, perhaps unconsciously, to remain a shadow—timid, but a survivor.

The fearsomeness mistakenly attributed to me in public places often has a perilous flavor. The most frightening of these confusions occurred in the late 1970s and early 1980s, when I worked as a journalist in Chicago. One day, rushing into the office of a magazine I was writing for with a deadline story in hand, I was mistaken for a burglar. The office manager called security and, with an ad hoc posse, pursued me through the labyrinthine halls, nearly to my editor's door. I had no way of proving who I was. I could only move briskly toward the company of someone who knew me.

Another time I was on assignment for a local paper and killing   9
time before an interview. I entered a jewelry store on the city's affluent Near North Side. The proprietor excused herself and returned with an enormous red Doberman pinscher straining at the
end of a leash. She stood, the dog extended toward me, silent to
my questions, her eyes bulging nearly out of her head. I took a
cursory look around, nodded, and bade her good night.

Relatively speaking, however, I never fared as badly as another   10
black male journalist. He went to nearby Waukegan, Illinois, a
couple of summers ago to work on a story about a murderer who
was born there. Mistaking the reporter for the killer, police officers
hauled him from his car at gunpoint and but for his press credentials would probably have tried to book him. Such episodes are not
uncommon. Black men trade tales like this all the time.

Over the years, I learned to smother the rage I felt at so often   11
being taken for a criminal. Not to do so would surely have led to
madness. I now take precautions to make myself less threatening.
I move about with care, particularly late in the evening. I give a
wide berth to nervous people on subway platforms during the wee
hours, particularly when I have exchanged business clothes for
jeans. If I happen to be entering a building behind some people
who appear skittish, I may walk by, letting them clear the lobby
before I return, so as not to seem to be following them. I have been
calm and extremely congenial on those rare occasions when I've
been pulled over by the police.

And on late-evening constitutionals I employ what has proved   12
to be an excellent tension-reducing measure: I whistle melodies
from Beethoven and Vivaldi and the more popular classical composers. Even steely New Yorkers hunching toward nighttime des-
tinations seem to relax, and occasionally they even join in the
tune. Virtually everybody seems to sense that a mugger wouldn't
be warbling bright, sunny selections from Vivaldi's Four Seasons.
It is my equivalent of the cowbell that hikers wear when they
know they are in bear country.

Meaning and Purpose

1. Staples claims that he has the power "to alter public space in ugly ways" (paragraph 2). How and from where did he derive that power?
2. In what ways has this "ability to alter public space" affected Staples?
3. Does Staples suggest any solutions for the profound problems he describes in the essay?
4. Does Staples speak only for himself when he says in paragraph 11 that he "learned to smother [his] rage"? Explain.

Strategy

1. Staples begins his essay with an anecdote (see the term *anecdote* in the Glossary). Comment on the effectiveness of this introduction.
2. What is the function of paragraph 2?
3. Staples's claim that he has the "ability to alter public space in ugly ways" is rather abstract and vague. How does he make the term fully understandable to the reader?

Style

1. Is there a discrepancy between the language that Staples uses and the subject he describes? If there is, describe the effect that discrepancy creates.
2. In the first paragraph, Staples calls a woman who walked in front of him his "victim." Why is that designation ironic (see *irony* in the Glossary)? Is any real victim described in the essay?
3. Explain the analogy Staples uses in the final sentence.
4. If necessary, look up the following in a dictionary: *affluent, mean, impoverished, discreet* (paragraph 1); *unwieldy, quarry, dicey, foyer* (2); *taut* (4); *warrenlike, bandolier, forge, solace* (5); *bravado*

(7); *ad hoc, labyrinthine* (8); *cursory* (9); *skittish* (11); *constitu-tionals, steely, warbling* (12).

Writing Tasks

1. Using Staples's essay as a model, write an essay that describes how you or someone else have altered public space—how you or someone else, in other words, have changed other people's be-havior or attitudes by merely being present. Make sure you use as many examples as you can to demonstrate your points.
2. Write an essay in which you argue for or against Staples's point of view. Whatever position you take, make sure your thesis is clear, and be sure to refer to Staples's points in your essay. Be sure, too, to use plenty of examples to illustrate the validity of your observations.

❦ Phyllis Rose ❦

*Phyllis Rose was born in 1926 in New Jersey and attended Connecticut College, Duke University, and the University of Wisconsin, where she earned her Ph.D. in English. She has been a professor of English at the University of Hawaii and a member of the board of several Hawaiian councils for the arts and humanities. She has published two works of biography—*Woman of Letters: A Life of Virginia Woolf *and* Parallel Lives: Five Victorian Marriages*—and a collection of essays,* Writing of Women. *She wrote the "Hers" column for* The New York Times *for ten weeks and has contributed to numerous national publications, including* The Atlantic, Vogue, *and* The Nation. *Her most recent publication is* The Year of Reading Proust: A Memoir in Real Time.

Tools of Torture

In this work, first published in The Atlantic *in 1986, Phyllis Rose takes an uncompromising look at the social and psychological sources of and rationalizations for torture. She uses specific examples from an exhibit in Paris of torture instruments to draw conclusions about the relation of pleasure to pain.*

Determine, as precisely as you can, the answers to these questions: Why are there so many torture devices? Why were they invented in the first place? What are the justifications for institutionalized torture? What is the relationship of pleasure to pain?

In a gallery off the rue Dauphine, near the *parfumerie* where I   1
get my massage, I happened upon an exhibit of medieval torture
instruments. It made me think that pain must be as great a challenge to the human imagination as pleasure. Otherwise there's no
accounting for the number of torture instruments. One would be
quite enough. The simple pincer, let's say, which rips out flesh. Or
the head crusher, which breaks first your tooth sockets, then your
skull. But in addition I saw tongs, thumbscrews, a rack, a ladder,

ropes and pulleys, a grill, a garrote, a Spanish horse, a Judas cradle, an iron maiden, a cage, a gag, a strappado, a stretching table,
a saw, a wheel, a twisting stork, an inquisitor's chair, a breast
breaker, and a scourge. You don't need complicated machinery to
cause incredible pain. If you want to saw your victim down the
middle, for example, all you need is a slightly bigger than usual
saw. If you hold the victim upside down so the blood stays in his
head, hold his legs apart, and start sawing at the groin, you can get
as far as the navel before he loses consciousness.

Even in the Middle Ages, before electricity, there were many   2
things you could do to torment a person. You could tie him up in
an iron belt that held the arms and legs up to the chest and left no
point of rest, so that all his muscles went into spasm within minutes and he was driven mad within hours. This was the twisting
stork, a benign-looking object. You could stretch him out backward over a thin piece of wood so that his whole body weight
rested on his spine, which pressed against the sharp wood. Then
you could stop up his nostrils and force water into his stomach
through his mouth. Then, if you wanted to finish him off, you and
your helper could jump on his stomach, causing internal hemorrhage. This torture was called the rack. If you wanted to burn
someone to death without hearing him scream, you could use a
tongue lock, a metal rod between the jaw and collarbone that prevented him from opening his mouth. You could put a person in a
chair with spikes on the seat and arms, tie him down against the
spikes, and beat him, so that every time he flinched from the beating he drove his own flesh deeper onto the spikes. This was the inquisitor's chair. If you wanted to make it worse, you could heat
the spikes. You could suspend a person over a pointed wooden
pyramid and whenever he started to fall asleep, you could drop
him onto the point. If you were Ippolito Marsili, the inventor of
this torture, known as the Judas cradle, you could tell yourself you
had invented something humane, a torture that worked without
burning flesh or breaking bones. For the torture here was supposed to be sleep deprivation.

The secret of torture, like the secret of French cuisine, is that   3
nothing is unthinkable. The human body is like a foodstuff, to be

grilled, pounded, filleted. Every opening exists to be stuffed, all flesh to be carved off the bone. You take an ordinary wheel, a heavy wooden wheel with spokes. You lay the victim on the ground with blocks of wood at strategic points under his shoulders, legs, and arms. You use the wheel to break every bone in his body. Next you tie his body onto the wheel. With all its bones broken, it will be pliable. However, the victim will not be dead. If you want to kill him, you hoist the wheel aloft on the end of a pole and leave him to starve. Who would have thought to do this with a man and a wheel? But, then, who would have thought to take the disgusting snail, force it to render its ooze, stuff it in its own shell with garlic butter, bake it, and eat it?

Not long ago I had a facial—only in part because I thought I [4] needed one. It was research into the nature and function of pleasure. In a dark booth at the back of the beauty salon, the aesthetician put me on a table and applied a series of ointments to my face, some cool, some warmed. After a while she put something into my hand, cold and metallic. "Don't be afraid, madame," she said. "It is an electrode. It will not hurt you. The other end is attached to two metal cylinders, which I roll over your face. They break down the electricity barrier on your skin and allow the moisturizers to penetrate deeply." I didn't believe this hocus-pocus. I didn't believe in the electricity barrier or in the ability of these rollers to break it down. But it all felt very good. The cold metal on my face was a pleasant change from the soft warmth of the aesthetician's fingers. Still, since Algeria it's hard to hear the word "electrode" without fear. So when she left me for a few minutes with a moist, refreshing cheesecloth over my face, I thought, What if the goal of her expertise had been pain, not moisture? What if the electrodes had been electrodes in the Algerian sense? What if the cheesecloth mask were dipped in acid?

In Paris, where the body is so pampered, torture seems par- [5] ticularly sinister, not because it's hard to understand but because—as the dark side of sensuality—it seems so easy. Beauty care is among the glories of Paris. *Soins esthétiques* include makeup, facials, massages (both relaxing and reducing), depilatations (partial and complete), manicures, pedicures, and tanning, in addition to the usual run of *soins* for the hair: cutting, brushing, setting, waving, styling, blowing, coloring, and streaking. In Paris the state of your skin, hair, and nerves is taken seriously, and there is little of the puritanical thinking that tries to persuade us that beauty comes from within. Nor do the French think, as Americans do, that beauty should be offhand and low-maintenance. Spending time and money on *soins esthétiques* is appropriate and necessary, not self-indulgent. Should that loving attention to the body turn malevolent, you have torture. You have the procedure—the aesthetic, as it were—of torture, the explanation for the rich diversity of torture instruments, but you do not have the cause.

Historically torture has been a tool of legal systems, used to get information needed for a trial or, more directly, to determine guilt or innocence. In the Middle Ages confession was considered the best of all proofs, and torture was the way to produce a confession. In other words, torture didn't come into existence to give vent to human sadism. It is not always private and perverse but sometimes social and institutional, vetted by the government and, of course, the Church. (There have been few bigger fans of torture than Christianity and Islam.) Righteousness, as much as viciousness, produces torture. There aren't squads of sadists beating down the doors to the torture chambers begging for jobs. Rather, as a recent book on torture by Edward Peters says, the institution of torture creates sadists: the weight of a culture, Peters suggests, is necessary to recruit torturers. You have to convince people that they are working for a great goal in order to get them to overcome their repugnance to the task of causing physical pain to another person. Usually the great goal is the preservation of society, and the victim is presented to the torturer as being in some way out to destroy it.

From another point of view, what's horrifying is how easily you can persuade someone that he is working for the common good. Perhaps the most appalling psychological experiment of modern times, by Stanley Milgram, showed that ordinary, decent people in New Haven, Connecticut, could be brought to the point of inflicting (as they thought) severe electric shocks on other people in obedience to an authority and in pursuit of a goal, the advancement of knowledge, of which they approved. Milgram used—some would say abused—the prestige of science and the university to make his point, but his point is chilling nonetheless. We can cluck over torture, but the evidence at least suggests that with intelligent handling most of us could be brought to do it ourselves.

In the Middle Ages, Milgram's experiment would have had no point. It would have shocked no one that people were capable of cruelty in the interest of something they believed in. That was as it should be. Only recently in the history of human thought has the avoidance of cruelty moved to the forefront of ethics. "Putting cruelty first," as Judith Shklar says in *Ordinary Vices*, is comparatively new. The belief that the "pursuit of happiness" is one of man's inalienable rights, the idea that "cruel and unusual punishment" is an evil in itself, the Benthamite notion that behavior should be guided by what will produce the greatest happiness for the greatest number—all these principles are only two centuries old. They were born with the eighteenth-century democratic revolutions. And in two hundred years they have not been universally accepted. Wherever people believe strongly in some cause, they will justify torture—not just the Nazis, but the French in Algeria.

Many people who wouldn't hurt a fly have annexed to fashion the imagery of torture—the thongs and spikes and metal studs—hence reducing it to the frivolous and transitory. Because torture has been in the mainstream and not on the margins of history, nothing could be healthier. For torture to be merely kinky would be a big advance. Exhibitions like the one I saw in Paris, which presented itself as educational, may be guilty of pandering to the tastes they deplore. Solemnity may be the wrong tone. If taking one's goals too seriously is the danger, the best discouragement of torture may be a radical hedonism that denies that any goal is worth the means, that refuses to allow the nobly abstract to seduce us from the sweetness of the concrete. Give people a good croissant and a good cup of coffee in the morning. Give them an occasional facial and a plate of escargots. Marie Antoinette picked a bad moment to say "Let them eat cake," but I've often thought she was on the right track.

All of which brings me back to Paris, for Paris exists in the 10 imagination of much of the world as the capital of pleasure—of fun, food, art, folly, seduction, gallantry, and beauty. Paris is civilization's reminder to itself that nothing leads you less wrong than your awareness of your own pleasure and a genial desire to spread it around. In that sense the myth of Paris constitutes a moral touchstone, standing for the selfish frivolity that helps keep priorities straight.

Meaning and Purpose

1. What is the thesis of the essay, and where is it explicitly stated?
2. Rose gives a long list of garish torture devices in the first paragraph. What do you think her purpose is in using examples in this way? Do you feel that they overwhelm and discourage the reader, or hook the reader?
3. In paragraph 3, the author says, "The secret of torture, like the secret of French cuisine, is that nothing is unthinkable." How is this statement both a compliment and a condemnation?
4. According to the author, what is the primary cause of human torture? What does this idea imply about social values and human nature? What examples does the author give to demonstrate that those social and psychological tendencies are still with us?
5. In the last two paragraphs the author argues that hedonistic, selfish frivolity is just the thing to keep our moral priorities straight. Why?

Strategy

1. The author says in the opening sentence of paragraph 2 that even before electricity many ways had been devised to torture a person. Why does the author bring in the idea of electricity?

2. Can you point out one specific and one typical example in the essay? How effective is each?
3. Reread paragraphs 7, 8, and 9. Describe the focus of each paragraph and the logic of moving from one to the other.
4. In informative (some might say academic) essays like this one, writers use examples "to make the general more specific and the abstract more concrete" (page 223). What effect overall does Rose accomplish with her graphic examples of torture? Read as a writer, and assess how her examples affect tone and the reader's senses.

Style

1. Two French expressions go untranslated: *parfumerie* (paragraph 1) and *soins esthétiques* (paragraph 5). Presumably, the author thinks that their meanings should be evident from the context. Are they? What effect is created by leaving the words in the original French?
2. In the final paragraph, Rose generalizes when she uses Paris as *the* example of a place of pleasure, a "moral touchstone." How does this general paragraph, following as it does many paragraphs of specific and even graphic examples and facts, serve to close the essay?
3. Explain how the expression "puritanical thinking" is used in paragraph 5.
4. If necessary, check a dictionary for the meaning of these words: *benign* (paragraph 2); *aesthetician* (4); *malevolent* (5); *vetted* (6); *inalienable* (8); *transitory* (9); *touchstone* (10).

Writing Tasks

1. In "Tools of Torture," Rose uses an event in her life to generate a thesis. Can you think of an event or incident in your life that you can expand into an essay? Make the essay informative, develop-

ing your thesis with specific, concrete examples; you may have to do some research.

2. In a few paragraphs, write about a typical example of something—that is, a composite. You might write about a typical day at the beach, a typical American traveler overseas, a typical pet, a typical birthday, and so on.

❦ Neil Postman ❦

Since the 1960s, Neil Postman has written widely on education, often examining how language relates to education and calling for radical reform in the field. His books include Crazy Talk, Stupid Talk: How We Defeat Ourselves by the Way We Talk and What to Do about It, Teaching as a Conserving Activity, The Disappearance of Childhood, *and* Amusing Ourselves to Death: Public Discourses in the Age of Show Business. *He is also coauthor of several books on educational reform, including* Linguistics: A Revolution in Teaching, Teaching as a Subversive Activity, *and* The End of Education: Redefining the Value of Schools. *His most current publication is* Marshall McLuhan: The Medium and the Messenger. *Postman was born in 1931 and has been a professor of media ecology at New York University. His articles have appeared in major periodicals, including* The Atlantic *and* The Nation.

Future Shlock

In "Future Shlock," from his 1980 book Conscientious Objections: Stirring up Trouble about Language, Technology and Education *(1988), Postman uses a string of examples—from politics, religion, film, and literature—to illustrate the dangers of eroding intelligence in a society hooked on entertainment. He mentions in particular the danger of television, which presents everything, from news reports to religion, as entertainment.*

Keep Postman's contention that "We will become . . . a people amused into stupidity" in mind while you read the essay and his claim that such serious subjects as news broadcasting, politics, and religion have been reduced in this country to mere entertainment.

Human intelligence is among the most fragile things in na- 1
ture. It doesn't take much to distract it, suppress it, or even an-
nihilate it. In this century, we have had some lethal examples
of how easily and quickly intelligence can be defeated by any

one of its several nemeses: ignorance, superstition, moral fervor, cruelty, cowardice, neglect. In the late 1920s, for example, Germany was, by any measure, the most literate, cultured nation in the world. Its legendary seats of learning attracted scholars from every corner. Its philosophers, social critics, and scientists were of the first rank; its humane traditions an inspiration to less favored nations. But by the mid-1930s—that is, in less than ten years—this cathedral of human reason had been transformed into a cesspool of barbaric irrationality. Many of the most intelligent products of German culture were forced to flee—for example, Einstein, Freud, Karl Jaspers, Thomas Mann, and Stefan Zweig. Even worse, those who remained were either forced to submit their minds to the sovereignty of primitive superstition, or—worse still—willingly did so: Konrad Lorenz, Werner Heisenberg, Martin Heidegger, Gerhardt Hauptmann. On May 10, 1933, a huge bonfire was kindled in Berlin and the books of Marcel Proust, André Gide, Emile Zola, Jack London, Upton Sinclair, and a hundred others were committed to the flames, amid shouts of idiot delight. By 1936, Joseph Paul Goebbels, Germany's Minister of Propaganda, was issuing a proclamation which began with the following words: "Because this year has not brought an improvement in art criticism, I forbid once and for all the continuance of art criticism in its past form, effective as of today." By 1936, there was no one left in Germany who had the brains or courage to object.

Exactly why the Germans banished intelligence is a vast and largely unanswered question. I have never been persuaded that the desperate economic depression that afflicted Germany in the 1920s adequately explains what happened. To quote Aristotle: Men do not become tyrants in order to keep warm. Neither do they become stupid—at least not that stupid. But the matter need not trouble us here. I offer the German case only as the most striking example of the fragility of human intelligence. My focus here is the United States in our own time, and I wish to worry you about the rapid erosion of our own intelligence. If you are confident that such a thing cannot happen, your confidence is misplaced, I believe, but it is understandable.

After all, the United States is one of the few countries in the world founded by intellectuals—men of wide learning, of extraordinary rhetorical powers, of deep faith in reason. And although we have had our moods of anti-intellectualism, few people have been more generous in support of intelligence and learning than Americans. It was the United States that initiated the experiment in mass education that is, even today, the envy of the world. It was America's churches that laid the foundation of our admirable system of higher education; it was the Land-Grant Act of 1862 that made possible our great state universities; and it is to America that scholars and writers have fled when freedom of the intellect became impossible in their own nations. This is why the great historian of American civilization Henry Steele Commager called America "the Empire of Reason." But Commager was referring to the United States of the eighteenth and nineteenth centuries. What term he would use for America today, I cannot say. Yet he has observed, as others have, a change, a precipitous decline in our valuation of intelligence, in our uses of language, in the disciplines of logic and reason, in our capacity to attend to complexity. Perhaps he would agree with me that the Empire of Reason is, in fact, gone, and that the most apt term for America today is the Empire of Shlock.

In any case, this is what I wish to call to your notice: the frightening displacement of serious, intelligent public discourse in American culture by the imagery and triviality of what may be called show business. I do not see the decline of intelligent discourse in America leading to the barbarisms that flourished in Germany, of course. No scholars, I believe, will ever need to flee America. There will be no bonfires to burn books. And I cannot imagine any proclamations forbidding once and for all art criticism, or any other kind of criticism. But this is not a cause for complacency, let alone celebration. A culture does not have to force scholars to flee to render them impotent. A culture does not have to burn books to assure that they will not be read. And a culture does not need a Minister of Propaganda issuing proclamations to silence criticism. There are other ways to achieve stupidity, and it appears that, as in so many other things, there is a distinctly American way.

To explain what I am getting at, I find it helpful to refer to two   5
films, which taken together embody the main lines of my argument. The first film is of recent vintage and is called *The Gods Must
Be Crazy.* It is about a tribal people who live in the Kalahari Desert
plains of southern Africa, and what happens to their culture when
it is invaded by an empty Coca-Cola bottle tossed from the window of a small plane passing overhead. The bottle lands in the
middle of the village and is construed by these gentle people to be
a gift from the gods, for they not only have never seen a bottle before but have never seen glass either. The people are almost immediately charmed by the gift, and not only because of its novelty.
The bottle, it turns out, has multiple uses, chief among them the
intriguing music it makes when one blows into it.

But gradually a change takes place in the tribe. The bottle be-   6
comes an irresistible preoccupation. Looking at it, holding it,
thinking of things to do with it displace other activities once
thought essential. But more than this, the Coke bottle is the only
thing these people have ever seen of which there is only one of its
kind. And so those who do not have it try to get it from the one
who does. And the one who does refuses to give it up. Jealousy,
greed, and even violence enter the scene, and come very close to
destroying the harmony that has characterized their culture for a
thousand years. The people begin to love their bottle more than
they love themselves, and are saved only when the leader of the
tribe, convinced that the gods must be crazy, returns the bottle to
the gods by throwing it off the top of a mountain.

The film is great fun and it is also wise, mainly because it is   7
about a subject as relevant to people in Chicago or Los Angeles or
New York as it is to those of the Kalahari Desert. It raises two
questions of extreme importance to our situation: How does a culture change when new technologies are introduced to it? And is it
always desirable for a culture to accommodate itself to the demands of new technologies? The leader of the Kalahari tribe is
forced to confront these questions in a way that Americans have
refused to do. And because his vision is not obstructed by a belief
in what Americans call "technological progress," he is able with

minimal discomfort to decide that the songs of the Coke bottle are not so alluring that they are worth admitting envy, egotism, and greed to a serene culture.

The second film relevant to my argument was made in 1967. 8 It is Mel Brooks's first film, *The Producers*. *The Producers* is a rather raucous comedy that has at its center a painful joke: An unscrupulous theatrical producer has figured out that it is relatively easy to turn a buck by producing a play that fails. All one has to do is induce dozens of backers to invest in the play by promising them exorbitant percentages of its profits. When the play fails, there being no profits to disperse, the producer walks away with thousands of dollars that can never be claimed. Of course, the central problem he must solve is to make sure that his play is a disastrous failure. And so he hits upon an excellent idea: he will take the most tragic and grotesque story of our century—the rise of Adolf Hitler—and make it into a musical.

Because the producer is only a crook and not a fool, he as- 9 sumes that the stupidity of making a musical on this theme will be immediately grasped by audiences and that they will leave the theater in dumbfounded rage. So he calls his play *Springtime for Hitler,* which is also the name of its most important song. The song begins with the words:

> *Springtime for Hitler and Germany;*
> *Winter for Poland and France.*

The melody is catchy, and when the song is sung it is accom- 10 panied by a happy chorus line. (One must understand, of course, that *Springtime for Hitler* is no spoof of Hitler, as was, for example, Charlie Chaplin's *The Great Dictator*. The play is instead a kind of denial of Hitler in song and dance; as if to say, it was all in fun.)

The ending of the movie is predictable. The audience loves 11 the play and leaves the theater humming "Springtime for Hitler." The musical becomes a great hit. The producer ends up in jail, his joke having turned back on him. But Brooks's point is that the joke is on us. Although the film was made years before a movie actor became President of the United States, Brooks was making a kind of prophecy about that—namely, that the producers of American culture will increasingly turn our history, politics, religion, commerce, and education into forms of entertainment, and that we will become as a result a trivial people, incapable of coping with complexity, ambiguity, uncertainty, perhaps even reality. We will become, in a phrase, a people amused into stupidity.

For those readers who are not inclined to take Mel Brooks as   12
seriously as I do, let me remind you that the prophecy I attribute here to Brooks was, in fact, made many years before by a more formidable social critic than he. I refer to Aldous Huxley, who wrote *Brave New World* at the time that the modern monuments to intellectual stupidity were taking shape: Nazism in Germany, fascism in Italy, communism in Russia. But Huxley was not concerned in his book with such naked and crude forms of intellectual suicide. He saw beyond them, and mostly, I must add, he saw America. To be more specific, he foresaw that the greatest threat to the intelligence and humane creativity of our culture would not come from Big Brother and Ministries of Propaganda, or gulags and concentration camps. He prophesied, if I may put it this way, that there is tyranny lurking in a Coca-Cola bottle; that we could be ruined not by what we fear and hate but by what we welcome and love, by what we construe to be a gift from the gods.

And in case anyone missed his point in 1932, Huxley wrote   13
Brave New World Revisited twenty years later. By then, George Orwell's *1984* had been published, and it was inevitable that Huxley would compare Orwell's book with his own. The difference, he said, is that in Orwell's book people are controlled by inflicting pain. In *Brave New World,* they are controlled by inflicting pleasure.

The Coke bottle that has fallen in our midst is a corporation of   14
dazzling technologies whose forms turn all serious public business into a kind of *Springtime for Hitler* musical. Television is the principal instrument of this disaster, in part because it is the medium Americans most dearly love, and in part because it has become the command center of our culture. Americans turn to television not only for their light entertainment but for their news,

their weather, their politics, their religion, their history—all of which may be said to be their serious entertainment. The light entertainment is not the problem. The least dangerous things on television are its junk. What I am talking about is television's preemption of our culture's most serious business. It would be merely banal to say that television presents us with entertaining subject matter. It is quite another thing to say that on television all subject matter is presented as entertaining. And that is how television brings ruin to any intelligent understanding of public affairs.

Political campaigns, for example, are now conducted largely in the form of television commercials. Candidates forgo precision, complexity, substance—in some cases, language itself—for the arts of show business: music, imagery, celebrities, theatrics. Indeed, political figures have become so good at this, and so accustomed to it, that they do television commercials even when they are not campaigning. Even worse, political figures appear on variety shows, soap operas, and sitcoms. Where is the line that one ought to be able to draw between politics and entertainment? I would suggest that television has annihilated it.   15

But politics is only one arena in which serious language has been displaced by the arts of show business. We have all seen how religion is packaged on television, as a kind of Las Vegas stage show, devoid of ritual, sacrality, and tradition. Today's electronic preachers are in no way like America's evangelicals of the past. Men like Jonathan Edwards, Charles Finney, and George Whitefield were preachers of theological depth, authentic learning, and great expository power. Electronic preachers such as Jimmy Swaggart, Jim Bakker, and Jerry Falwell are merely performers who exploit television's visual power and their own charisma for the greater glory of themselves.   16

We have also seen "Sesame Street" and other educational shows in which the demands of entertainment take precedence over the rigors of learning. And we well know how American businessmen, working under the assumption that potential customers require amusement rather than facts, use music, dance, comedy, cartoons, and celebrities to sell their products.   17

Even our daily news, which for most Americans means televi-   18
sion news, is packaged as a kind of show, featuring handsome
news readers, exciting music, and dynamic film footage. Most especially, film footage. When there is no film footage, there is no
story. Stranger still, commercials may appear anywhere in a news
story—before, after, or in the middle. This reduces all events to
trivialities, sources of public entertainment and little more. After
all, how serious can a bombing in Lebanon be if it is shown to us
prefaced by a happy United Airlines commercial and summarized
by a Calvin Klein jeans commercial? Indeed, television newscasters
have added to our grammar a new part of speech—what may be
called the "Now . . . this" conjunction, a conjunction that does not
connect two things, but disconnects them. When newscasters say,
"Now . . . this," they mean to indicate that what you have just heard
or seen has no relevance to what you are about to hear or see.
There is no murder so brutal, no political blunder so costly, no
bombing so devastating that it cannot be erased from our minds by
a newscaster saying, "Now . . . this." He means that you have
thought long enough on the matter (let us say, for forty seconds)
and you must now give your attention to a commercial. Such a situation is not "the news." It is merely a daily version of *Springtime
for Hitler,* and in my opinion accounts for the fact that Americans
are among the most ill-informed people in the world. To be sure,
we know of many things; but we know *about* very little.

I do not mean to say that the trivialization of American public   19
discourse is all accomplished on television. Rather, television is
the paradigm for all our attempts at public communication. It
conditions our minds to apprehend the world through fragmented pictures and forces other media to orient themselves in
that direction. You know the standard question we put to people
who have difficulty understanding even simple language: we ask
them impatiently, "Do I have to draw a picture for you?" Well, it
appears that, like it or not, our culture will draw pictures for us,
will explain the world to us in pictures. As a medium for con-
ducting public business, language had receded in importance; it
has been moved to the periphery of culture and has been replaced
at the center by the entertaining visual image.

Please understand that I am making no criticism of the visual   20
arts in general. That criticism is made by God, not by me. You will
remember that in His Second Commandment, God explicitly
states that "Thou shalt not make unto thee any graven image, nor
any likeness of anything that is in Heaven above, or that is in the
earth beneath, or the waters beneath the earth." I have always felt
that God was taking a rather extreme position on this, as is His
way. As for myself, I am arguing from the standpoint of a symbolic
relativist. Forms of communication are neither good nor bad in
themselves. They become good or bad depending on their relationship to other symbols and on the functions they are made to
serve within a social order. When a culture becomes overloaded
with pictures; when logic and rhetoric lose their binding authority; when historical truth becomes irrelevant; when the spoken or
written word is distrusted or makes demands on our attention
that we are incapable of giving; when our politics, history, education, religion, public information, and commerce are expressed
largely in visual imagery rather than words, then a culture is in serious jeopardy.

Neither do I make a complaint against entertainment. As an   21
old song has it, life is not a highway strewn with flowers. The sight
of a few blossoms here and there may make our journey a trifle
more endurable. But in America, the least amusing people are our
professional entertainers. In our present situation, our preachers,
entrepreneurs, politicians, teachers, and journalists are committed
to entertaining us through media that do not lend themselves to
serious, complex discourse. But these producers of our culture are
not to be blamed. They, like the rest of us, believe in the su-
premacy of technological progress. It has never occurred to us that
the gods might be crazy. And even if it did, there is no mountaintop from which we can return what is dangerous to us.

We would do well to keep in mind that there are two ways in   22
which the spirit of a culture may be degraded. In the first—the
Orwellian—culture becomes a prison. This was the way of the
Nazis, and it appears to be the way of the Russians. In the second—the Huxleyan—culture becomes a burlesque. This appears
to be the way of the Americans. What Huxley teaches is that in the

Age of Advanced Technology, spiritual devastation is more likely to come from an enemy with a smiling countenance than from one whose face exudes suspicion and hate. In the Huxleyan prophecy, Big Brother does not watch us, by his choice; we watch him, by ours. When a culture becomes distracted by trivia; when political and social life are redefined as a perpetual round of entertainments; when public conversation becomes a form of baby talk; when a people become, in short, an audience and their public business a vaudeville act, then—Huxley argued—a nation finds itself at risk and culture-death is a clear possibility. I agree.

Meaning and Purpose

1. The purpose of an essay is like a goal that the writer sets. The writer has to keep the reader reminded of the purpose and pointed in the right direction. What do you think Postman's purpose is in "Future Shlock"? Does he achieve it? How does he do so, and if he doesn't, why does he fail?
2. Postman states his general thesis in a number of ways. Paragraphs 2, 3, 4, 11, and 12 have sentences that sound like thesis statements. Reread these paragraphs, and find the statement that you think best summarizes the essay as a whole.
3. What is the main point in *The Gods Must Be Crazy* example? In *The Producers* example?
4. How convincing is Postman? Does his view of our culture coincide with yours? In what ways? Do you disagree with portions of his argument?

Strategy

1. Postman often ends paragraphs with strong statements. See paragraphs 1, 2, and 3. Find other strong statements that end paragraphs and discuss the purpose they serve.

2. Why does Postman begin with a pre–World War II German example in an essay about the United States? Why does he turn away from the example without examining its causes?

3. Whom do you think Postman had in mind as his audience when he wrote "Future Shlock"? What kind of reader does he appeal to? Do you think he wants to provoke readers with his criticisms of television and American culture and intelligence? Discuss.

4. Trace the use of examples in the essay. Are they specific or typical? Extended or brief? Are different types of examples put to different uses?

Style

1. In Postman's opening example, Germany in the late 1920s, he says, "this cathedral of human reason had been transformed into a cesspool of barbaric irrationality." Comment on the effectiveness of this metaphor, especially the words "cathedral," "cesspool," and "barbaric."

2. The Coca-Cola bottle that is so vital to Postman's discussion of *The Gods Must Be Crazy* is used as a metaphor for what? Comment on the connection between these statements and the original metaphor:

   "there is tyranny lurking in a Coca-Cola bottle" (paragraph 12).

   "we could be ruined . . . by what we welcome and love" (paragraph 12).

   "The Coke bottle that has fallen in our midst is a corporation of dazzling technologies" (paragraph 14).

   "Television . . . is the medium Americans most dearly love" (paragraph 14).

3. If necessary, check a dictionary for the meaning of these words: *shlock; nemeses* (paragraph 1); *rhetorical, precipitous* (3); *preemption, banal* (14); *sacrality* (16); *paradigm* (19); *countenance* (22).

Writing Tasks

1. In paragraph 1, Postman says, "In this century, we have had some lethal examples of how easily and quickly intelligence can be defeated by any one of its several nemeses: ignorance, superstition, moral fervor, cruelty, cowardice, neglect." Have you ever seen these forces at work in your studies or in your own experience? Consider your own behavior, your friends' behavior, the workings of your city or community, national or international affairs, your college, your clubs and organizations. Write an essay about one of these forces as you have seen it at work in one or more situations. Develop your essay with either typical or specific examples.

2. Postman argues that "serious matters of public concern" have been turned into entertainment. Write an essay in which you agree or disagree with his view in regard to one serious matter of public concern. Use one or more specific, extended examples to support your assertions.

❦ Caryl Rivers ❦

Caryl Rivers, born in 1937, is a graduate of Trinity College and Columbia University and a freelance writer who has taught journalism at Boston University. She has written a number of nonfiction books and several novels, including Beyond Sugar and Spice: How Girls and Women Develop Competence; For Better, for Worse, *a humorous account of her own married life with journalist Alan Lupo;* More Joy Than Rage: Crossing Generations With the New Feminism; Slick Spins and Fractured Facts: How Cultural Myths Distort the News; She Works/He Works: How Two-Income Families Are Happy, Healthy, and Thriving; *and* Camelot.

The Issue Isn't Sex, It's Violence

Grounded in feminism, Rivers casts a critical eye on the impact of social and political experience on women. In "The Issue Isn't Sex, It's Violence," a 1985 Boston Globe *article, Rivers identifies the legitimization of violence, not sex, as the social danger embedded in some rock lyrics. Notice how effectively she uses hypothetical examples to illustrate her discussion.*

After a grisly series of murders in California, possibly inspired   1
by the lyrics of a rock song, we are hearing a familiar chorus: Don't blame rock and roll. It's all just adolescent rebellion. Kids will be kids. They love to rebel, and the more shocking the stuff, the better they like it.

There's some truth in this, of course. I loved to watch Elvis   2
shake his torso when I was a teenager, and it was even more fun when Ed Sullivan wouldn't let the cameras show him below the waist. I snickered at the forbidden "Rock with Me, Annie" lyrics by a black Rhythm and Blues group, which were deliciously naughty. But I am sorry, rock fans, that is not the same thing as hearing lyrics

269

about how a man is going to force a woman to perform oral sex on him at gunpoint in a little number called "Eat Me Alive." It is not in the same league with a song about the delights of slipping into a woman's room while she is sleeping and murdering her, the theme of an AC/DC ballad that allegedly inspired the California slayer.

Make no mistake, it is not sex we are talking about here, but   3
violence. Violence against women. Most rock songs are not violent—they are funky, sexy, rebellious and sometimes witty. Please do not mistake me for a Mrs. Grundy. If Prince wants to leap about wearing only a purple jock strap, fine. Let Mick Jagger unzip his fly as he gyrates, if he wants to. But when either one of them starts garroting, beating or sodomizing a woman in their number, that is another story.

I always find myself annoyed when "intellectual" men dismiss   4
violence against women with a yawn, as if it were beneath their dignity to notice. I wonder if the reaction would be the same if the violence were directed against someone other than women. How many people would yawn and say, "Oh, kids will be kids," if a rock group did a nifty little number called "Lynchin," in which stringing up and stomping on black people were set to music? Who would chuckle and say, "Oh, just a little adolescent rebellion" if a group of rockers went on MTV dressed as Nazis, desecrating synagogues and beating up Jews to the beat of twanging guitars?

I'll tell you what would happen. Prestigious dailies would   5
thunder on editorial pages: senators would fall over each other to get denunciations into the *Congressional Record*. The president would appoint a commission to clean up the music business.

But violence against women is greeted by silence. It shouldn't be.   6

This does not mean censorship, or book (or record) burning.   7
In a society that protects free expression, we understand a lot of stuff will float up out of the sewer. Usually, we recognize the ugly stuff that advocates violence against any group as the garbage it is, and we consider its purveyors as moral lepers. We hold our nose and tolerate it, but we speak out against the values it proffers.

But images of violence against women are not staying on the   8
fringes of society. No longer are they found only in tattered, paper-covered books or in movie houses where winos snooze and

the scent of urine fills the air. They are entering the mainstream at a rapid rate. This is happening at a time when the media, more and more, set the agenda for the public debate. They are a powerful legitimizing force—especially television. Many people regard what they see on TV as the truth; Walter Cronkite once topped a poll as the most trusted man in America.

Now, with the advent of rock videos and all-music channels, rock music has grabbed a big chunk of legitimacy. American teenagers have instant access, in their living rooms, to the messages of rock, on the same vehicle that brought them "Sesame Street." Who can blame them if they believe that the images they see are accurate reflections of adult reality, approved by adults? After all, Big Bird used to give them lessons on the same little box. Adults, by their silence, sanction the images. Do we really want our kids to think that rape and violence are what sexuality is all about?

This is not a trivial issue. Violence against women is a major social problem, one that's more than a cerebral issue to me. I teach at Boston University, and one of my most promising young journalism students was raped and murdered. Two others told me of being raped. Recently, one female student was assaulted and beaten so badly she had $5,000 worth of medical bills and permanent damage to her back and eyes.

It's nearly impossible, of course, to make a cause-and-effect link between lyrics and images and acts of violence. But images have a tremendous power to create an atmosphere in which violence against certain people is sanctioned. Nazi propagandists knew that full well when they portrayed Jews as ugly, greedy and powerful.

The outcry over violence against women, particularly in a sexual context, is being legitimized in two ways: by the increasing movement of these images into the mainstream of the media in TV, films, magazines, albums, videos, and by the silence about it.

Violence, of course, is rampant in the media. But it is usually set in some kind of moral context. It's usually only the bad guys who commit violent acts against the innocent. When the good guys get violent, it's against those who deserve it. Dirty Harry blows away the scum, he doesn't walk up to a toddler and say, "Make my day." The A Team does not shoot up suburban shopping malls.

But in some rock songs, it's the "heroes" who commit the acts. 14 The people we are programmed to identify with are the ones being violent, with women on the receiving end. In a society where rape and assaults on women are endemic, this is no small problem, with millions of young boys watching on their TV screens and listening on their Walkmans.

I think something needs to be done. I'd like to see people in 15 the industry respond to the problem. I'd love to see some women rock stars speak out against violence against women. I would like to see disc jockeys refuse air play to records and videos that contain such violence. At the very least, I want to see the end of the silence. I want journalists and parents and critics and performing artists to keep this issue alive in the public forum. I don't want people who are concerned about this issue labeled as bluenoses and book-burners and ignored.

And I wish it wasn't always just women who are speaking out. 16 Men have as large a stake in the quality of our civilization as women do in the long run. Violence is a contagion that infects at random. Let's hear something, please, from the men.

Meaning and Purpose

1. In the first paragraph of this essay, Rivers says, "Don't blame rock and roll." Obviously, rock and roll isn't the only popular music we hear. What other popular music reflects her main point in this paragraph? Give two examples of music titles, along with the messages in their lyrics, to show that this is true.

2. Rivers notes in paragraph 4 that "'intellectual' men dismiss violence against women with a yawn." Why does she put the word *intellectual* in quotes?

3. In paragraph 12, Rivers notes two ways in which violence against women is being legitimized, one of them being "the silence about

it." How does being silent about violence against women "legitimize" that violence?

4. The author says in the last paragraph of the essay that "Violence . . . infects at random." How does that claim reinforce the main topic of the essay?

5. After reading this essay, what would you say is the author's most *immediate* purpose for having written it?

Strategy

1. Why does Rivers make it a point to tell her reader, in paragraph 14, that the "heroes" in popular music should be blamed in part for violence against women?

2. The British philosopher Stephen Toulmin says that a claim is a statement of belief or truth. In your words, what claim is made in paragraph 15?

3. Paragraph 6 ends with the sentence, "It shouldn't be." What "shouldn't be"? Is the author stating a claim or a fact? How can you tell?

4. Paragraph 5 deals with an effect, anything brought about by a cause or an agent. According to the author, what is the cause or agent that has led to this effect?

5. Although this essay discusses the effects of song lyrics on their listeners, Rivers says in paragraph 11 that it is "nearly impossible, of course, to make a cause-and-effect link between lyrics and images and acts of violence." How does this statement strengthen or weaken the examples that she gives to support her main point?

Style

1. Why does the author deliberately use the trite expression "Kids will be kids" in her opening paragraph?

2. In paragraph 8, what is meant by the phrase "fringes of society"?

3. How does the word *nifty*, in paragraph 4, seem particularly appropriate in its context?
4. A rhetorical question is a question that is not meant to be answered by its reader. Why, then, does the author end paragraph 9 with a rhetorical question?
5. In paragraph 4, why does the author suggests "Lynchin" as a song title, instead of the correctly spelled term "Lynching"?

Writing Tasks

1. Each of us has listened to the kind of music that the author refers to. Write an essay in which you mention three or more currently popular song titles and their lyrics that show that what the author says is true today, not true today, or probably true today. Explain by using lyrics as examples of why your opinion is valid.
2. Using your knowledge of modern popular music, write an essay that shows by examples from lyrics, from the actions of performers, and from what takes place during performances themselves, whether on television or in person, how popular music endorses a movement or an opinion.

❦ *Responding to Photographs* ❦

Examples

Style Is the Man

What is style? If we say a certain person has style, what exactly do we mean? Is it behavior? Clothing? Speech? Posture? Grooming? All of these? Some other things? Does everyone have style or do only a few?

Style might be hard to define precisely, but we know it when we see it, right? And most people would undoubtedly agree that the young man in the photograph "Style Is the Man" has it.

Style communicates. Before interacting with a person, we form impressions based on some elements at least of his or her personal style. We may be able to trace this impression to very specific things, or we may say we just have a feeling but are unable to specify particulars. A style may be created consciously and purposefully (perhaps to deceive), or it may simply grow out of the true values and accumulated experiences of the individual.

After reviewing the material at the beginning of this chapter, complete one of the following writing tasks.

1. Using specific examples from the photograph as your method of development, write a paper that characterizes the style portrayed by the young man. Begin with a short physical description of the man leading to a generalization about his style and the attitude and values it communicates to you. Then examine various items and aspects of his appearance, and discuss each as a specific example that led you to your interpretation of his message.

2. Write a paper combining typical and specific examples. Find three photographs of humans, each showing a different sense of style. These need not be as dramatic as the style illustrated in "Style Is the Man," though they may be. As in task 1, begin with a short description of the three photographs leading to a generalization about each style and what it communicates to you. In the discussion section of your paper, point to specific examples in each photograph that support your generalization, and then relate typical examples of the expected behavior, dress, and attitudes of a member of each style group. Include the photographs when you submit your final draft.

❧ *Additional Writing Tasks* ❧
Examples

1. Write an essay on one of the general statements listed here or on a general statement that you compose. Throughout your essay, use examples to illustrate your main idea or thesis. Your discussion should include a mixture of typical and specific examples. Remember that you are not bound by any of these statements; you may rewrite them to reflect your interests, or you may compose your own.
   a. People must assume responsibility for their actions.
   b. Success comes from 5 percent talent and 95 percent hard work.
   c. Vandals control the night in local neighborhoods.
   d. Teenagers can learn both positive and negative lessons about economic survival from part-time jobs.
   e. Graffiti scrawled on walls throughout the city carry psychological messages about human behavior.
   f. Books I have read have taught me a great deal about life.
   g. Bumper stickers reveal a person's values.
   h. Public obscenity is objectionable.
   i. Life in the fast lane leads to head-on collisions.
2. Write a full essay related to one of these situations. Be sure that examples serve as the dominant essay pattern of development.
   a. Some contemporary political figures have demonstrated courage in office. Using examples from recent history, write an essay illustrating how important political courage is.
   b. Society seems to require more and more cooperation among individuals and groups to function effectively. Write an essay illustrating how cooperation is needed for success.
   c. Although society seems to require more and more cooperation among individuals and groups, the values of the "rugged individualist" are still required for success. Write an essay illustrating how much "rugged individualism" helps in becoming successful.
   d. Often the better moments in life go unnoticed. Recollect some of your better moments, and write an essay making use of them to illustrate what they have taught you.

277

    e.   Magazine advertisers attempt to entice customers to buy products not by high quality but by associating the products with selected lifestyles. Write an essay illustrating that some magazine advertisements encourage consumers to buy products for the wrong reasons.

3.   Read this paragraph from Jack Solomon's *The Signs of Our Time,* in which he generally concentrates on the messages that clothing communicates in American society.

> The complexity of the dress code in America, the astonishing range of styles that are available to us in our choice of clothing designs, directly reflects the cultural diversity of our country. Americans are differentiated by ethnic, regional, religious, and racial differences that are all expressed in the clothing they wear. Age differences, political differences, class differences, and differences in personal taste further divide us into finer and finer sub-cultures that maintain, and even assert, their sense of distinct identity through their characteristic clothing. From the severe black suits of the Amish to the safety-pinned T-shirts and chains of punk culture, Americans tell one another who they are through the articles of their dress.

Write an essay, with examples as the dominant method of development, illustrating Solomon's general observation that "Americans tell one another who they are through the articles of their dress."

6

Comparison and Contrast
Presenting Similarities and Differences

The Method

In conversation we often hear comments that could lead to **comparison and contrast**:

"I eat vegetables, fruits, grains, nuts, and dairy products. It is a lot healthier than a diet that includes red meat, fowl, and even fish."

"Strip away the rhetoric and compare their economic platforms; you will see few differences between Republicans and Democrats."

"The effects of marijuana are no more harmful than those of alcohol. In fact they may be less harmful."

No doubt in class discussions, at family gatherings, or during arguments at the local pizza parlor you have heard similar comments. How such comparisons are developed in conversation probably depends on the group's mood and analytical talent. Nevertheless, a fundamental principle is at work: We all make decisions by comparing and contrasting our options.

To compare is to point out similarities; to contrast is to point out differences. Poems and song lyrics are often similar in some ways: Both often rhyme; they are constructed on rhythmic patterns; sometimes they repeat key lines. They also have one major difference: Poems are written to be spoken; songs are written to be sung to music. Presenting similarities and differences is a common technique not only in conversation but also in all forms of writing, including essays, research papers, reports, and examinations.

Commonly, writers include informal comparisons that are merely incidental to the dominant essay pattern. Often such brief comparisons are implied rather than fully developed, merely suggesting a comparison. This paragraph opens an essay explaining the causes directing new trends in city planning.

> In southern California, historically known for its suburban sprawl, city planning seems to have come full circle. Using the concept of the traditional village, planners are designing new urban villages that feature a main street and a mix of stores, offices, town halls, and parks. They are trying

to re-create the traditional village by designing neighborhoods where thousands of residents can live and work,
where they can walk to shopping and stroll to places of entertainment.

The writer, Jack Scott, does not intend to compare traditional with
contemporary city design; he alludes to traditional design merely
to place his reader in familiar territory.

When writers use comparison and contrast as a dominant essay pattern, they explore their subjects in detail, applying several
principles to guide the composition. To sharpen your critical eye
and read as a writer reads, be aware of these general principles.

Strategies

Professional writers know they need a basis for the comparison: Any subjects they choose to compare must belong to the
same general category. If the subjects do not belong to that category, the writers have no logical reason to enumerate the similarities and differences. Usually, but not always, the general
categories are obvious. For such a discussion, consider hammerhead sharks, great white sharks, chimpanzees, and dolphins.

Comparing and contrasting a hammerhead with a great white
shark is clearly logical because although they are similar, they differ in several distinctive ways. But to compare and contrast a
chimpanzee with a great white shark is clearly illogical. Yes, they
belong to a category that we might call "living creatures," but do
you see any other basis for a comparison? The chimpanzee is a
mammal, the great white shark a fish. One lives on land, the other
in the sea. One is a hunter, the other a forager. To compare and
contrast them just would not make much sense.

To compare and contrast a dolphin and a great white shark,
however, does make sense. Even though the dolphin is a mammal, it is a marine mammal. The dolphin and the great white
shark are also shaped roughly alike, but with significant differ-

ences. Perhaps most important, both the dolphin and the great white shark are significant in sea lore. In fact, Hollywood films featuring a dolphin and a great white shark have been box-office hits, such as *Flipper* and *Jaws*.

What about comparing a dolphin and a chimpanzee? Although they are not obvious selections, both are categorized as mammals. A writer might ask whether their both being mammals makes them subjects worth comparing and contrasting. What else do they have in common? Close examination reveals that scientists are studying communication patterns of both chimpanzees and dolphins. Perhaps they are in the limited category of animals that communicate with human beings. Taking up this similarity, a writer might explore the possibility of comparing chimpanzees and dolphins.

Now we must consider an exception to the principle that subjects should belong to the same general category if they are to be logically compared. This figurative comparison is called **analogy**. Writers use analogy to explain something that is difficult to understand by describing it as if it were something familiar. A writer might choose to explain life by comparing it with a river, watching a situation comedy with taking a narcotic, or compare being in love with riding a roller coaster. Writers of analogy are interested only in using one subject to explain another; they are not out to explain the major similarities and differences of both subjects equally, as they would be when writing a typical comparison-and-contrast passage.

In this following paragraph, humorist James Thurber develops an analogy by comparing his editor Harold Ross to a skilled auto mechanic.

> Having a manuscript under Ross's scrutiny was like putting your car in the hands of a skilled mechanic, not an automotive engineer with a bachelor of science degree, but a guy who knows what makes a motor go, and sputter, and wheeze, and sometimes come to a dead stop; a man with an ear for the faintest body squeak as well as the loudest engine rattle. When you first gazed, appalled, upon an uncorrected

proof of one of your stories or articles, each margin had a thicket of queries and complaints—one writer got a hundred and forty-four on one profile. It was as though you beheld the works of your car spread all over the garage floor, and the job of getting the thing together again and making it work seemed impossible. Then you realized that Ross was trying to make your Model T or old Stutz Bearcat into a Cadillac or Rolls-Royce. He was at work with the tools of his unflagging perfectionism, and, after an exchange of growls or snarls, you set to work to join him in his enterprise.

Clearly, Thurber has stuck to the principle of analogy: He uses the familiar work of an auto mechanic to explain the unfamiliar work of a magazine editor.

Professional writers are always wary of confusing their readers. As you study comparison-and-contrast essays, notice how writers immediately orient their readers by informing them that a comparison and contrast follows.

Read the opening paragraph in Russell Baker's "From Song to Sound: Elvis and Bing." Baker quickly establishes that he will compare two eras and the popular singers who represent them.

> The grieving for Elvis Presley and the commercial exploitation of his death were still not ended when we heard of Bing Crosby's death the other day. Here is a generational puzzle. Those of an age to mourn Elvis must marvel that their elders could really have cared about Bing, just as the Crosby generation a few weeks ago wondered what all the to-do was about when Elvis died.

Baker's opening paragraph gives a clear idea that the essay is headed into comparison and contrast. Most professional writers do likewise, thus keeping their readers on the track.

Professional writers also use clear—and we stress that word—stylistic techniques to keep their readers from becoming confused. Sometimes they use parallel structure to balance the similarities and differences of their subjects. They also use such transitional words and phrases as *on the one hand, on the other hand, in contrast, like,* and *unlike,* words with which they delineate similarities and differences.

In a paragraph from an essay contrasting crows and ravens, Barry Lopez applies both transitional phrases and parallel structures.

> The raven is larger than the crow and has a beard of black feathers at his throat. He is careful to kill only what he needs. Crows, on the other hand, will search out the great horned owl, kick and punch him awake, and then for roosting too close to their nests, they will kill him. They will come out of the sky on a fat, hot afternoon and slam into the head of a dozing rabbit and go away laughing. They will tear out a whole row of planted corn and eat only a few kernels. They will defecate on scarecrows and go home and sleep with 200,000 of their friends in an atmosphere of congratulation. Again, it is only a game; this should not be taken to mean that they are evil.

In his paragraph, Lopez concentrates primarily on the crow's destructive behavior, contrasting it sharply to the raven in the two sentences describing that black bird. Usually, writers will develop both subjects in more detail. They generally employ one of two organizational strategies when comparing and contrasting: **subject-by-subject** development or **point-by-point** development.

Subject-by-Subject Development

Developing a subject-by-subject comparison is quite simple: All the details of one side of the comparison or contrast are presented first, followed by all the details of the other side. Anthropologist Edward T. Hall uses subject-by-subject development to contrast Arab and American attitudes in a paragraph from *The Hidden Dimension.*

> Another silent source of friction between Americans and Arabs is in an area that Americans treat very informally—the

manners and rights of the road. In general, in the United States we tend to defer to the vehicle that is bigger, more powerful, faster, and heavily laden. While a pedestrian walking along a road may feel annoyed he will not think it unusual to step aside for a fast-moving automobile. He knows that because he is moving he does not have the right to the space around him that he has when he is standing still. It appears that the reverse is true with the Arabs who apparently *take on rights to space as they move.* For someone else to move into a space an Arab is also moving into is a violation of his rights. It is infuriating to an Arab to have someone else cut in front of him on the highway. It is the American's cavalier treatment of moving space that makes the Arab call him aggressive and pushy.

Hall contrasts these subjects in one paragraph, but sometimes a writer will divide the subjects into separate contrasting paragraphs, as Noel Perrin does in these two discussion paragraphs from his essay "The Two Faces of Vermont."

On the one hand, it's to the interest of everyone in the tourist trade to keep Vermont (their motels, ski resorts, chambers of commerce, etc., excepted) as old-fashioned as possible. After all, it's weathered red barns with shingle roofs the tourists want to photograph, not concrete-block barns with sheet aluminum on top. Ideally, from the tourist point of view, there should be a man and two boys inside, milking by hand, not a lot of milking machinery pumping directly into a bulk tank. Out back, someone should be turning a grindstone to sharpen an ax—making a last stand, so to speak, against the chainsaw.

On the other hand, the average farmer can hardly wait to modernize. He wants a bulk tank, a couple of arc lights, an automated silo, and a new aluminum roof. Or in a sense he wants these things. Actually, he may like last-stand farming as well as any tourist does, but he can't make a living at it. In my town it's often said that a generation ago a man could raise and educate three children on fifteen cows and still put a little money in the bank. Now his son can just barely keep going with 40 cows. With fifteen cows, hand-milking was possible, and conceivably even economic; with 40 you need all the machinery you can get. But the tourists don't want to hear it clank.

Point-by-Point Development

Subject-by-subject development is effective for an essay of a few paragraphs, but when an essay is longer, the reader might lose track of the information about the first subject while reading about the second. The point-by-point development solves this shortcoming by alternately presenting each point under consideration. Alison Lurie, in a paragraph from *The Language of Clothes*, uses the point-by-point method to compare and contrast boys' and girls' clothes.

> In early childhood girls' and boys' clothes are often identical in cut and fabric, as if in recognition of the fact that their bodies are much alike. But the T-shirts, pull-on slacks and zip jackets intended for boys are usually made in darker colors (especially forest green, navy, red and brown) and printed with designs involving sports, transportation and cute wild animals. Girls' clothes are made in paler colors (especially pink, yellow and green) and decorated with flowers and cute domestic animals. The suggestion is that the boy will play vigorously and travel over long distances; the girl will stay home and nurture plants and small mammals. Alternatively, these designs may symbolize their wearers: the boy is a cuddly bear or a smiling tiger, the girl a flower or a kitten. There is also a tendency for boys' clothes to be fullest at the shoulders and girls' at the hips, anticipating their adult figures. Boys' and men's garments also emphasize the shoulders with horizontal stripes, epaulets or yokes of contrasting color. Girls' and women's garments emphasize the hips and rear through the strategic placement of gathers and trimmings.

Lurie's strategy is quite simple. She organizes the discussion around three points: the different colors of girls' and boys' clothes, the different designs that decorate them, and the different cut. She presents the details point by point, carefully balancing one with the other.

Comparison and Contrast in College Writing

Generally, in college writing, you will compare the similarities and contrast the differences of subjects for one of two reasons: to describe two subjects to clarify them or to evaluate two subjects to determine which is better. For either reason, you must consider the outstanding features of each subject, and when the purpose is evaluation, you must carefully delineate both positive and negative aspects of the subjects.

Guidelines for Writing a Comparison and Contrast Essay

1. Select two subjects from the same general category to compare and contrast (unless, of course, you are developing an analogy).
2. With each subject as a focus, use prewriting techniques to generate a list of similarities and differences.
3. Establish your purpose and develop a thesis that does the following:

   • Names the subjects being compared and contrasted and
   • Clearly indicates whether the essay will compare, contrast, or both.

4. Select the points to be compared and contrasted, and decide which should be developed in a subject-by-subject arrangement and which should be developed in a point-by-point arrangement. Organize the paragraphs by placing the most dramatic point last in the sequence.

5. Revise your essay, making sure that you've used clear transitions to keep your reader on track as you move from one subject to the other.

A Student Essay Developed by Comparison and Contrast

For a freshman composition class, Jim Cartozian responded to the following assignment:

> Write an essay with comparison and contrast as the dominant development pattern on one of the following topics:
>
> | | |
> |---|---|
> | a. two athletes | d. two writers |
> | b. two film directors | e. two politicians |
> | c. two artists | f. two newscasters |

Cartozian selected item "d" and compared and contrasted writers Ernest Hemingway and William Faulkner. He had studied them in a high school American literature course and recalled how different the two writers seemed to be. He knew that he would have plenty of material.

Two American Writers: Hemingway and Faulkner

If American writers Ernest Hemingway and William Faulkner were to attend the same party, both would command attention for different reasons. Hemingway, a big bear of a man, seemed gregarious, and liked to hold the center of attention. He was handsome, and some have said he prided himself on being a lady's man. Faulkner, a frail, soft-spoken man, tended to be reclusive. He would not seek the attention Hemingway seemed to thrive on, but would probably find a mantel to lean on. Speaking in a gentle, lilting voice, Faulkner would tell a story about the rural South while holding the attention of everyone within earshot. No two modern American writers have gained as much worldwide critical recognition as Ernest

1

Hemingway and William Faulkner; moreover, no two are so obviously different while at the same time sharing significant similarities.

They each won the coveted Nobel Prize for literature, but when the mild-mannered Faulkner won first, the boisterous Hemingway is said to have lost his temper and then sulked. Both were publishing at a young age, but Hemingway attracted popular attention early in his career while Faulkner worked in near obscurity. Hemingway became America's first modern literary media star. Magazines featured spreads of his war exploits, his African safaris, and his bullfighting adventures. Faulkner, in contrast, was never a media celebrity. Instead, he seemed to embody the lifestyle of small-town Southern gentry, spending most of his quiet existence in Oxford, Mississippi. Hemingway set his novels and stories in exotic locales like France, Spain, and Cuba; Faulkner set his works in the South, in the mythical Yoknapatawpha County. Each dealt with very different visions: Hemingway's work displays psychologically wounded characters struggling to establish a personal value code in an absurd world. Faulkner's work displays characters who are victims of history, suffering because of the sins of their ancestors, the men who wrenched the land from Native Americans and enslaved Native Africans. In 1961 Hemingway died violently by his own hand; in 1962 Faulkner died peacefully.

The qualities that made such different men successful novelists are difficult to identify. No doubt their success came from determination and hard work, for both men were dedicated to their craft. But another quality—inspiration—must be figured into the equation. Inspiration that comes from pursuing the creative process is perhaps similar to the spiritual insight that comes from participating in a mystical practice, such as meditation, which is usually performed daily in psychological isolation. Most successful novelists pursue their creative inspiration by isolating themselves, too. Faulkner and Hemingway were no different. Both created special spaces to write in. When Faulkner wrote, he isolated himself in an upstairs bedroom located in the family house. Although Hemingway was more nomadic than Faulkner, he still created a

2

3

"space apart" to write in no matter where he was living, the most famous one in the tower at his Cuban hacienda.

Too often spiritual insight and creative inspiration are 4 thought to arrive like a bolt of lightning. But mystics claim insight comes from the relentless pursuit of routines. As writers, Faulkner and Hemingway ritually pursued their routines. Hemingway would rise at first light and spend the morning writing with a hand-sharpened pencil while standing at a high desk or bookcase top. Faulkner would also rise early, but he would sit at a desk and plunk away at an old typewriter. The routines seldom varied, but perhaps it was routine pursued with the fervor of a mystic that generated their inspiration and led to their recognition.

It is the creative process that unites Hemingway and 5 Faulkner. Beneath Hemingway's distasteful machismo and existential sophistication was a sensitive and insightful artist who depicted the modern epoch full of all its horror and despair. Yet he continued to explore the value and capacity of the individual's faith in Self. Beneath Faulkner's deceptive regionalism and self-doubts was a socially committed artist who explored the impact of history's dark events on a culture and the individual psyche. Both were remarkable in their ability to connect with their readers— even readers who were born after those authors' deaths.

Reviewing with a Writer's Eye

1. One principle in writing a comparison essay is to be sure that the subjects belong to the same general category. List the categories that Ernest Hemingway and William Faulkner share.
2. Jim Cartozian's thesis statement comes at the end of paragraph 1. What principles of comparison does it embody?
3. Make two lists: one detailing how the authors are similar, the other detailing how they are different.
4. Why does Cartozian open with a specific comparison of the two authors? What effect does the comparison have?

5. Why doesn't Cartozian write a topic sentence for paragraph 2?
6. Identify examples of subject-by-subject and point-by-point development (see pp. 284–286).
7. In comparison essays, writers use parallel structure (see pp. 79–81) and overt transitions to keep writers from becoming confused. Identify examples of each technique.
8. What analogy (see pp. 282–283) does Cartozian develop? How does it function in the essay?
9. In a note, explain to Jim Cartozian the strengths and weaknesses of "Two American Writers: Hemingway and Faulkner." Pay particular attention to paragraphs 3 and 4. Do they drift too far from the assignment, or do they enrich Cartozian's essay? Briefly explain your response in your note.

Peer Review

You may be asked to write an essay about one of the readings that follow. Before you meet with your writing group, review the introduction. As you read the papers, use these general principles of comparison and contrast to help guide your comments.

1. Unless the paper is an analogy, the subjects should belong to the same general category.
2. The reader should be informed early in the paper that a comparison and contrast will follow.
3. The choice of point-by-point or subject-by-subject development (or a combination of both) should be appropriate to the content. A long paper with complex points of comparison and contrast usually requires a point-by-point method or a combination of both methods.
4. Clear transitions between subjects or points should guide the reader through the paper.

As you read the essays that follow, keep in mind that the most effective way to develop skill in comparison and contrast is to study the professionals. Analyze their choices. Ask yourself why a writer chooses point-by-point development over subject-by-subject for a particular passage. Notice how writers mix the two development patterns. Study the kinds of transitional techniques they use. This kind of careful reading—that is, reading with a critical eye—will prepare you to write your own comparisons.

❦ Bruce Catton ❦

Bruce Catton (pronounced Cayton) was one of those rare historians who could bring the past to life. Born in Michigan in 1899, he grew up hearing Civil War stories from the many Civil War veterans in his small midwestern town. After attending Oberlin College he was a reporter for newspapers in Boston and Cleveland, served as director of information for government agencies in Washington, D.C., and finally accepted a position as full-time editor and writer for American Heritage *magazine, which he kept until his death in 1978. Considered one of the foremost authorities on the American Civil War era, he published many books on the subject. The most popular of those books is* A Stillness at Appomattox, *which won both the Pulitzer Prize for history and the National Book Award.*

Grant and Lee: A Study in Contrasts

In this essay, first published in The American Story, *an anthology of essays by noted historians, Catton describes the similarities and differences in style and character between the opposing Civil War generals. It was their coming together and their ability to put aside their extreme differences that marked the end of the war and a turning point in American history.*

   Catton claims in this essay that Ulysses S. Grant and Robert E. Lee represent two different American cultures. Make sure while you read, then, to distinguish the various facets of their personalities as well as the differences of the two societies they personified.

When Ulysses S. Grant and Robert E. Lee met in the parlor of a modest house at Appomattox Court House, Virginia, on April 9, 1865, to work out the terms for the surrender of Lee's Army of Northern Virginia, a great chapter in American life came to a close, and a great new chapter began.   1

These men were bringing the Civil War to its virtual finish. To   2
be sure, other armies had yet to surrender, and for a few days the
fugitive Confederate government would struggle desperately and
vainly, trying to find some way to go on living now that its chief
support was gone. But in effect it was all over when Grant and Lee
signed the papers. And the little room where they wrote out the
terms was the scene of one of the poignant, dramatic contrasts in
American history.

They were two strong men, these oddly different generals,   3
and they represented the strengths of two conflicting currents
that, through them, had come to final collision.

Back of Robert E. Lee was the notion that the old aristocratic   4
concept might somehow survive and be dominant in American
life.

Lee was tidewater Virginia, and in his background were fam-   5
ily, culture, and tradition . . . the age of chivalry transplanted to a
New World which was making its own legends and its own
myths. He embodied a way of life that had come down through
the age of knighthood and the English country squire. America
was a land that was beginning all over again, dedicated to nothing
much more complicated than the rather hazy belief that all men
had equal rights and should have an equal chance in the world. In
such a land Lee stood for the feeling that it was somehow of advantage to human society to have a pronounced inequality in the
social structure. There should be a leisure class, backed by ownership of land; in turn, society itself should be keyed to the land as
the chief source of wealth and influence. It would bring forth (according to this ideal) a class of men with a strong sense of obligation to the community; men who lived not to gain advantage for
themselves, but to meet the solemn obligations which had been
laid on them by the very fact that they were privileged. From them
the country would get its leadership; to them it could look for the
higher values—of thought, of conduct, of personal deportment—
to give it strength and virtue.

Lee embodied the noblest elements of this aristocratic ideal.   6
Through him, the landed nobility justified itself. For four years,
the Southern states had fought a desperate war to uphold the

ideals for which Lee stood. In the end, it almost seemed as if the Confederacy fought for Lee; as if he himself was the Confederacy . . . the best thing that the way of life for which the Confederacy stood could ever have to offer. He had passed into legend before Appomattox. Thousands of tired, underfed, poorly clothed Confederate soldiers, long since past the simple enthusiasm of the early days of the struggle, somehow considered Lee the symbol of everything for which they had been willing to die. But they could not quite put this feeling into words. If the Lost Cause, sanctified by so much heroism and so many deaths, had a living justification, its justification was General Lee.

Grant, the son of a tanner on the Western frontier, was every- 7 thing Lee was not. He had come up the hard way and embodied nothing in particular except the eternal toughness and sinewy fiber of the men who grew up beyond the mountains. He was one of a body of men who owed reverence and obeisance to no one, who were self-reliant to a fault, who cared hardly anything for the past but who had a sharp eye for the future.

These frontier men were the precise opposites of the tidewater 8 aristocrats. Back of them, in the great surge that had taken people over the Alleghenies and into the opening Western country, there was a deep, implicit dissatisfaction with a past that had settled into grooves. They stood for democracy, not from any reasoned conclusion about the proper ordering of human society, but simply because they had grown up in the middle of democracy and knew how it worked. Their society might have privileges, but they would be privileges each man had won for himself. Forms and patterns meant nothing. No man was born to anything, except perhaps to a chance to show how far he could rise. Life was competition.

Yet along with this feeling had come a deep sense of belong- 9 ing to a national community. The Westerner who developed a farm, opened a shop, or set up in business as a trader could hope to prosper only as his own community prospered—and his community ran from the Atlantic to the Pacific and from Canada down to Mexico. If the land was settled, with towns and highways and accessible markets, he could better himself. He saw his fate in terms of the nation's own destiny. As its horizons expanded, so did his. He had, in other words, an acute dollars-and-cents stake in the continued growth and development of his country.

And that, perhaps, is where the contrast between Grant and   10
Lee becomes most striking. The Virginia aristocrat, inevitably, saw himself in relation to his own region. He lived in a static society which could endure almost anything except change. Instinctively, his first loyalty would go to the locality in which that society existed. He would fight to the limit of endurance to defend it, because in defending it he was defending everything that gave his own life its deepest meaning.

The Westerner, on the other hand, would fight with an equal   11
tenacity for the broader concept of society. He fought so because everything he lived by was tied to growth, expansion, and a constantly widening horizon. What he lived by would survive or fall with the nation itself. He could not possibly stand by unmoved in the face of an attempt to destroy the Union. He would combat it with everything he had, because he could only see it as an effort to cut the ground out from under his feet.

So Grant and Lee were in complete contrast, representing two   12
diametrically opposed elements in American life. Grant was the modern man emerging; beyond him, ready to come on the stage, was the great age of steel and machinery, of crowded cities and a restless burgeoning vitality. Lee might have ridden down from the old age of chivalry, lance in hand, silken banner fluttering over his head. Each man was the perfect champion of his cause, drawing both his strengths and his weaknesses from the people he led.

Yet it was not all contrast, after all. Different as they were—in   13
background, in personality, in underlying aspiration—these two great soldiers had much in common. Under everything else, they were marvelous fighters. Furthermore, their fighting qualities were really very much alike.

Each man had, to begin with, the great virtue of utter tenacity   14
and fidelity. Grant fought his way down the Mississippi Valley in spite of acute personal discouragement and profound military handicaps. Lee hung on in the trenches at Petersburg after hope itself had died. In each man there was an indomitable quality . . .

the born fighter's refusal to give up as long as he can still remain on his feet and lift his two fists.

Daring and resourcefulness they had, too: the ability to think faster and move faster than the enemy. These were the qualities which gave Lee the dazzling campaigns of Second Manassas and Chancellorsville and won Vicksburg for Grant. 15

Lastly, and perhaps greatest of all, there was the ability, at the end, to turn quickly from war to peace once the fighting was over. Out of the way these two men behaved at Appomattox came the possibility of a peace of reconciliation. It was a possibility not wholly realized, in the years to come, but which did, in the end, help the two sections to become one nation again . . . after a war whose bitterness might have seemed to make such a reunion wholly impossible. No part of either man's life became him more than the part he played in their brief meeting in the McLean house at Appomattox. Their behavior there put all succeeding generations of Americans in their debt. Two great Americans, Grant and Lee—very different, yet under everything very much alike. Their encounter at Appomattox was one of the great moments of American history. 16

Meaning and Purpose

1. The essay begins with a brief description of the negotiations at Appomattox that led to the end of the Civil War. Can you think of any countries today that are so torn by civil strife and bitterness that reunion and reconciliation seem difficult or nearly impossible? What are the differences between their condition now and that of the United States at the time of the Civil War?

2. Describe the social structure of the Confederacy that Lee defended. The author claims that Lee was also a symbol of that social order (paragraph 6). In what way was he such a symbol?

3. In paragraph 5, Catton states, "Lee stood for the feeling that it was somehow of advantage to human society to have a pronounced inequality in the social structure." Apparently, one underclass in that society consisted of the "Thousands of tired,

underfed, poorly clothed Confederate soldiers, long since past the simple enthusiasm of the early days of the struggle," but who, nonetheless, "somehow considered Lee the symbol of everything for which they had been willing to die" (paragraph 6). Discuss the apparent contradictions in this situation.
4. Describe the social structure that Grant represented.
5. How were the two men the same? What was their most important similarity? What was their key difference?
6. What is the meaning of "tidewater Virginia" (paragraph 5), and what is its significance in this essay?

Strategy

1. Identify the introduction in Catton's essay and state his thesis. How do you know where the introduction ends? How does the information in the introduction differ from that in the rest of the essay; in other words, what characterizes Catton's introductory remarks?
2. Paragraph 2 consists of four sentences. Describe the function of each.
3. What new rhetorical technique does Catton begin to apply in paragraph 13?
4. Examine the first sentence in each paragraph. What transitional devices does the author use in each? What effect do these devices have?
5. Study Catton's method or methods of comparison and contrast in the essay. Does he use the subject-by-subject method, the point-by-point method, or a combination of the two? Discuss the effectiveness of his rhetorical structure.

Style

1. In paragraph 1, Catton uses a metaphor comparing the negotiations to end the Civil War to a concluding chapter in the larger

book of American life. How effective is that metaphor? What are its implications?

2. In paragraph 12, the author says that "Lee might have ridden down from the old age of chivalry, lance in hand, silken banner fluttering over his head." What effect does this language have? Is it satirical?

3. Check the dictionary for the meaning of these words: *virtual, poignant* (paragraph 2), *chivalry, legends, myths, embodied, deportment* (5), *obeisance* (7), *static* (10), *tenacity* (11), *fidelity, indomitable* (14).

4. In the final paragraph, Catton brings the reader back to the setting that he describes in the opening paragraph. What is the stylistic effect of this technique?

5. What is Catton's attitude toward Lee and Grant? How is this attitude shown?

Writing Tasks

1. Write an essay in which you compare and contrast two historical or literary characters who represent two ways of life or value systems. The structure of your essay should include an introduction in which you set the scene for the two people you will discuss; that is, put them in the same category or on the same basis. Choose the subject-by-subject method, point-by-point method, or a combination to set up your comparison and contrast. Pay attention to transitions. Conclude your essay by bringing the two characters together again.

2. Write a brief dialogue between the two characters that you chose for the assignment above or any other two people you want to compare and contrast. Put them in a scene, and let their conversation illustrate clearly the differences and similarities between them. You might enjoy presenting this exercise as a dramatic reading with fellow students.

❧ Richard Rodriguez ❧

Richard Rodriguez was born in San Francisco in 1944 to Mexican-American parents who spoke only Spanish at home. Rodriguez nonetheless mastered the English language and went on to study at Stanford, Columbia, and the University of California at Berkeley, where he earned a Ph.D. in English literature. He also received a Fulbright fellowship to study English literature in London. In spite of several offers to teach, Rodriguez made writing and journalism his profession. His books include Hunger of Memory, Mexico's Children, Days of Obligation: An Argument with My Mexican Father, *and* Movements.

Los Otros, Mis Hermanos

This excerpt from Richard Rodriguez's 1982 autobiography, The Hunger of Memory, *portrays one of the conflicts that he felt growing up as a Hispanic in an Anglo culture. He concentrates here on his youthful sensitivity to language and how he identified his Spanish-speaking world with the comfort and security of family and the English-speaking world that surrounded him as alien and threatening.*

In the essay Rodriguez explains the different ways that language formed his identity. While you read, imagine as vividly as you can how he perceived people, and his relationship to them, in the way that they spoke. Notice the various ways he isolated in his mind the Spanish-speaking world from the English.

I grew up in a house where the only regular guests were my relations. For one day, enormous families of relatives would visit and there would be so many people that the noise and the bodies would spill out to the backyard and front porch. Then, for weeks, no one came by. (It was usually a salesman who rang the doorbell.) Our house stood apart. A gaudy yellow in a row of white bungalows. We were the people with the noisy dog. The people who raised pigeons and chickens. We were the foreigners on the block. A few neighbors smiled and waved. We waved back. But no one in the family knew the names of the old couple who lived next door; until I was seven years old, I did not know the names of the kids who lived across the street.

In public, my father and mother spoke a hesitant, accented, not always grammatical English. And they would have to strain—their bodies tense—to catch the sense of what was rapidly said by *los gringos*. At home they spoke Spanish. The language of their Mexican past sounded in counterpoint to the English of public society. The words would come quickly, with ease. Conveyed through those sounds was the pleasing, soothing, consoling reminder of being at home. 2

During those years when I was first conscious of hearing, my mother and father addressed me only in Spanish; in Spanish I learned to reply. By contrast, English (*inglés*), rarely heard in the house, was the language I came to associate with *gringos*. I learned my first words of English overhearing my parents speak to strangers. At five years of age, I knew just enough English for my mother to trust me on errands to stores one block away. No more. 3

I was a listening child, careful to hear the very different sounds of Spanish and English. Wide-eyed with hearing, I'd listen to sounds more than words. First, there were English (*gringo*) sounds. So many words were still unknown that when the butcher or the lady at the drugstore said something to me, exotic polysyllabic sounds would bloom in the midst of their sentences. Often, the speech of people in public seemed to me very loud, booming with confidence. The man behind the counter would literally ask, "What can I do for you?" But by being so firm and so clear, the sound of his voice said that he was a *gringo*; he belonged in public society. 4

I would also hear then the high nasal notes of middle-class American speech. The air stirred with sound. Sometimes, even now, when I have been traveling abroad for several weeks, I will hear what I heard as a boy. In hotel lobbies or airports, in Turkey or Brazil, some Americans will pass, and suddenly I will hear it again—the high sound of American voices. For a few seconds I will hear it with pleasure, for it is now the sound of my society— 5 a reminder of home. But inevitably—already on the flight headed for home—the sound fades with repetition. I will be unable to hear it anymore.

When I was a boy, things were different. The accent of *los*   6
gringos was never pleasing nor was it hard to hear. Crowds at Safeway or at bus stops would be noisy with sound. And I would be forced to edge away from the chirping chatter above me.

I was unable to hear my own sounds, but I knew very well   7
that I spoke English poorly. My words could not stretch far enough to form complete thoughts. And the words I did speak I didn't know well enough to make into distinct sounds. (Listeners would usually lower their heads, better to hear what I was trying to say.) But it was one thing for me to speak English with diffi- culty. It was more troubling for *me* to hear my parents speak in public; their high-whining vowels and guttural consonants; their sentences that got stuck with 'eh' and 'ah' sounds; the confused syntax; the hesitant rhythm of sounds so different from the way gringos spoke. I'd notice, moreover, that my parents' voices were softer than those of *gringos* we'd meet.

I am tempted now to say that none of this mattered. In adult-   8
hood I am embarrassed by childhood fears. And, in a way, it didn't matter very much that my parents could not speak English with ease. Their linguistic difficulties had no serious conse- quences. My mother and father made themselves understood at the county hospital clinic and at government offices. And yet, in another way, it mattered very much—it was unsettling to hear my parents struggle with English. Hearing them, I'd grow nervous, my clutching trust in their protection and power weakened.

There were many times like the night at a brightly lit gasoline   9
station (a blaring white memory) when I stood uneasily, hearing my father. He was talking to a teenaged attendant. I do not recall what they were saying, but I cannot forget the sounds my father made as he spoke. At one point his words slid together to form one word—sounds as confused as the threads of blue and green oil in the puddle next to my shoes. His voice rushed through what he had left to say. And, toward the end, reached falsetto notes, ap- pealing to his listener's understanding. I looked away to the lights

of passing automobiles. I tried not to hear anymore. But I heard only too well the calm, easy tones in the attendant's reply. Shortly afterward, walking toward home with my father, I shivered when he put his hand on my shoulder. The very first chance that I got, I evaded his grasp and ran on ahead into the dark, skipping with feigned boyish exuberance.

But then there was Spanish. *Español:* my family's language.   10
Español: the language that seemed to me a private language. I'd hear strangers on the radio and in the Mexican Catholic church across town speaking in Spanish, but I couldn't really believe that Spanish was a public language, like English. Spanish speakers, rather, seemed related to me, for I sensed that we shared— through our language—the experience of feeling apart from *los gringos.* It was thus a ghetto Spanish that I heard and I spoke. Like those whose lives are bound by a barrio, I was reminded by Spanish of my separateness from *los otros, los gringos* in power. But more intensely than for most barrio children—because I did not live in a barrio—Spanish seemed to me the language of home. (Most days it was only at home that I'd hear it.) It became the language of joyful return.

A family member would say something to me and I would   11
feel myself specially recognized. My parents would say something to me and I would feel embraced by the sounds of their words. Those sounds said: *I am speaking with ease in Spanish. I am addressing you in words I never use with los gringos. I recognize you as someone special, close, like no one outside. You belong with us. In the family.*

(Ricardo.)   12

At the age of five, six, well past the time when most other chil-   13
dren no longer easily notice the difference between sounds uttered at home and words spoken in public, I had a different experience. I lived in a world magically compounded of sounds. I remained a child longer than most; I lingered too long, poised at the edge of language—often frightened by the sounds of *los gringos,* delighted by the sounds of Spanish at home. I shared with my family a language that was startlingly different from that used in the great city around us.

For me there were none of the gradations between public and   14
private society so normal to a maturing child. Outside the house
was public society; inside the house was private. Just opening or
closing the screen door behind me was an important experience.
I'd rarely leave home all alone or without reluctance. Walking
down the sidewalk, under the canopy of tall trees, I'd warily notice
the—suddenly—silent neighborhood kids who stood warily
watching me. Nervously, I'd arrive at the grocery store to hear there
the sounds of the gringo—foreign to me—reminding me that in
this world so big, I was a foreigner. But then I'd return. Walking
back toward our house, climbing the steps from the sidewalk,
when the front door was open in summer, I'd hear voices beyond
the screen door talking in Spanish. For a second or two, I'd stay,
linger there, listening. Smiling, I'd hear my mother call out, saying
in Spanish (words): "Is that you, Richard?" All the while her sounds
would assure me: *You are home now; come closer; inside. With us.*

"*Si,*" I'd reply.   15

Once more inside the house I would resume (assume) my   16
place in the family. The sounds would dim, grow harder to hear.
Once more at home, I would grow less aware of that fact. It required, however, no more than the blurt of the doorbell to alert
me to listen to sounds all over again. The house would turn instantly still while my mother went to the door. I'd hear her hard
English sounds. I'd wait to hear her voice return to soft-sounding
Spanish, which assured me, as surely as did the clicking tongue of
the lock on the door, that the stranger was gone.

Plainly, it is not healthy to hear such sounds so often. It is not   17
healthy to distinguish public words from private sounds so easily.
I remained cloistered by sounds, timid and shy in public, too dependent on voices at home. And yet it needs to be emphasized: I
was an extremely happy child at home. I remember many nights
when my father would come back from work, and I'd hear him
call out to my mother in Spanish, sounding relieved. In Spanish,
he'd sound light and free notes he never could manage in English.
Some nights I'd jump up just at hearing his voice. With *mis hermanos* I would come running into the room where he was with my
mother. Our laughing (so deep was the pleasure!) became scream-

ing. Like others who know the pain of public alienation, we transformed the knowledge of our public separateness and made it consoling—the reminder of intimacy. Excited, we joined our voices in a celebration of sounds. *We are speaking now the way we never speak out in public. We are alone—together,* voices sounded, surrounded to tell me. Some nights, no one seemed willing to loosen the hold sounds had on us. At dinner, we invented new words. (Ours sounded Spanish, but made sense only to us.) We pieced together new words by taking, say, an English verb and giving it Spanish endings. My mother's instructions at bedtime would be lacquered with mock-urgent tones. Or a word like *si* would become, in several notes, able to convey added measures of feeling. Tongues explored the edges of words, especially the fat vowels. And we happily sounded that military drum roll, the twirling roar of the Spanish r. Family language: my family's sounds. The voices of my parents and sisters and brother. Their voices insisting: *You belong here. We are family members. Related. Special to one another. Listen!* Voices singing and sighing, rising, straining, then surging, teeming with pleasure that burst syllables into fragments of laughter. At times it seemed there was steady quiet only when, from another room, the rustling whispers of my parents faded and I moved closer to sleep.

Meaning and Purpose

1. What are Rodriguez's childhood feelings about Spanish and English? Use examples from the essay to illustrate your answer.
2. In paragraph 7 the author says that he felt differently about his own inability to speak fluent English and his parents' inability to do so. Why does he feel so differently? How strong are his feelings? Explain.
3. Rodriguez says in paragraph 8 that his parents' difficulties with English didn't matter in some ways but did in others. Explain this.
4. "I remained a child longer than most," says the author in paragraph 13. What does he mean by this? What does he consider

the characteristics of childhood? How did language affect his slow development?

Strategy

1. Where and how does the author make clear what he intends to compare and contrast?
2. Paragraph 5 is an example. What function does it serve?
3. Paragraph 9 is also an example. What is its function?
4. Paragraph 15 consists of a short, single sentence. Why does Rodriguez separate it from the preceding paragraph?

Style

1. Examine the essay closely and point out some places where Rodriguez uses point-by-point development and where he uses subject-by-subject development. Why do you think he chose those methods when and where he did?
2. Rodriguez uses Spanish words and phrases to demonstrate "private" language. Are the meanings clear in context? What effect do they create even if you are unable to translate them?
3. What does the word *gringo* mean? What are its connotations? How does the author want the word to affect you? Explain.

Writing Tasks

1. If English is not your first language, write an essay in which you compare aspects of your native culture with those of American culture. If you are a native American but have encountered foreign cultures, compare some aspects of those cultures to your own. What were things you liked or disliked? Why?
2. Think about where you grew up. Did the place, the people, and your family affect the way you learned to think of yourself? How? Write an essay in which you enumerate and describe those things that formed your sense of identity.

❦ Deborah Tannen ❦

Deborah Tannen, born in 1945, earned her doctorate in sociolinguistics at the University of California, Berkeley, and now teaches at Georgetown University. Deeply interested in how differently men and women communicate, Tannen's publications include You Just Don't Understand, That's Not What I Meant: How Conversational Style Makes or Breaks Relationships, Gender and Conversational Interaction, Talking from 9 to 5: Women and Men in the Workplace: Language, Sex, and Power, *and* The Argument Culture: Moving from Debate to Dialogue.

Sex, Lies, and Conversation

This informative essay, from You Just Don't Understand, *published in 1991, points out some of the communication features that differentiate men and women when they engage in ordinary conversation. As you read, notice how clearly Tannen shifts her focus back and forth, from discussing the ways that men talk and listen to discussing the ways that women talk and listen.*

I was addressing a small gathering in a suburban Virginia living room—a women's group that had invited men to join them. Throughout the evening, one man had been particularly talkative, frequently offering ideas and anecdotes, while his wife sat silently beside him on the couch. Toward the end of the evening, I commented that women frequently complain that their husbands don't talk to them. This man quickly concurred. He gestured toward his wife and said, "She's the talker in our family." The room burst into laughter; the man looked puzzled and hurt. "It's true," he explained. "When I come home from work I have nothing to say. If she didn't keep the conversation going, we'd spend the whole evening in silence." 1

This episode crystallizes the irony that although American men tend to talk more than women in public situations, they of- 2 ten talk less at home. And this pattern is wreaking havoc with marriage.

The pattern was observed by political scientist Andrew   3
Hacker in the late '70s. Sociologist Catherine Kohler Riessman reports in her new book *Divorce Talk* that most of the women she interviewed—but only a few of the men—gave lack of communication as the reason for their divorces. Given the current divorce rate of nearly 50 percent, that amounts to millions of cases in the United States every year—a virtual epidemic of failed conversation.

In my own research, complaints from women about their hus-   4
bands most often focused not on tangible inequities such as having given up the chance for a career to accompany a husband to his, or doing far more than their share of daily life-support work like cleaning, cooking, social arrangements, and errands. Instead, they focused on communication: "He doesn't listen to me," "He doesn't talk to me." I found, as Hacker observed years before, that most wives want their husbands to be, first and foremost, conversational partners, but few husbands share this expectation of their wives.

In short, the image that best represents the current crisis is the   5
stereotypical cartoon scene of a man sitting at the breakfast table with a newspaper held up in front of his face, while a woman glares at the back of it, wanting to talk.

Lingustic Battle of the Sexes

How can women and men have such different impressions of   6
communication in marriage? Why the widespread imbalance in their interests and expectations?

In the April issue of *American Psychologist,* Stanford Univer-   7
sity's Eleanor Maccoby reports the results of her own and others' research showing that children's development is most influenced by the social structure of peer interactions. Boys and girls tend to play with children of their own gender, and their sex-separate groups have different organizational structures and interactive norms.

I believe these systematic differences in childhood socializa-   8
tion make talk between women and men like cross-cultural communication, heir to all the attraction and pitfalls of that enticing
but difficult enterprise. My research on men's and women's conversations uncovered patterns similar to those described for children's groups.

For women, as for girls, intimacy is the fabric of relationships,   9
and talk is the thread from which it is woven. Little girls create
and maintain friendships by exchanging secrets; similarly, women
regard conversation as the cornerstone of friendship. So a woman
expects her husband to be a new and improved version of a best
friend. What is important is not the individual subjects that are
discussed but the sense of closeness, of a life shared, that emerges
when people tell their thoughts, feelings, and impressions.

Bonds between boys can be as intense as girls', but they are   10
based less on talking, more on doing things together. Since they
don't assume talk is the cement that binds a relationship, men
don't know what kind of talk women want, and they don't miss it
when it isn't there.

Boys' groups are larger, more inclusive, and more hierarchi-   11
cal, so boys must struggle to avoid the subordinate position in the
group. This may play a role in women's complaints that men don't
listen to them. Some men really don't like to listen, because being
the listener makes them feel one-down, like a child listening to
adults or an employee to a boss.

But often when women tell men, "You aren't listening," and   12
the men protest, "I am," the men are right. The impression of not
listening results from misalignments in the mechanics of conversation. The misalignment begins as soon as a man and a woman
take physical positions. This became clear when I studied videotapes made by psychologist Bruce Dorval of children and adults
talking to their same-sex best friends. I found that at every age, the
girls and women faced each other directly, their eyes anchored on
each other's faces. At every age, the boys and men sat at angles to
each other and looked elsewhere in the room, periodically glancing at each other. They were obviously attuned to each other, often mirroring each other's movements. But the tendency of men to

face away can give women the impression they aren't listening even when they are. A young woman in college was frustrated: Whenever she told her boyfriend she wanted to talk to him, he would lie down on the floor, close his eyes, and put his arm over his face. This signaled to her, "He's taking a nap." But he insisted he was listening extra hard. Normally, he looks around the room, so he is easily distracted. Lying down and covering his eyes helped him concentrate on what she was saying.

Analogous to the physical alignment that women and men   13
take in conversation is their topical alignment. The girls in my study tended to talk at length about one topic, but the boys tended to jump from topic to topic. The second-grade girls exchanged stories about people they knew. The second-grade boys teased, told jokes, noticed things in the room, and talked about finding games to play. The sixth-grade girls talked about problems with a mutual friend. The sixth-grade boys talked about 55 different topics, none of which extended over more than a few turns.

Listening to Body Language

Switching topics is another habit that gives women the im-   14
pression men aren't listening, especially if they switch to a topic about themselves. But the evidence of the 10th-grade boys in my study indicates otherwise. The 10th-grade boys sprawled across their chairs with bodies parallel and eyes straight ahead, rarely looking at each other. They looked as if they were riding in a car, staring out the windshield. But they were talking about their feelings. One boy was upset because a girl had told him he had a drinking problem, and the other was feeling alienated from all his friends.

Now, when a girl told a friend about a problem, the friend re-   15
sponded by asking probing questions and expressing agreement and understanding. But the boys dismissed each other's problems. Todd assured Richard that his drinking was "no big problem" because "sometimes you're funny when you're off your butt." And when Todd said he felt left out, Richard responded, "Why should you? You know more people than me."

Women perceive such responses as belittling and unsupport- 16
ive. But the boys seemed satisfied with them. Whereas women reassure each other by implying, "You shouldn't feel bad because
I've had similar experiences," men do so by implying, "You
shouldn't feel bad because your problems aren't so bad."

There are even simpler reasons for women's impression that 17
men don't listen. Linguist Lynette Hirschman found that women
make more listener-noise, such as "mhm," "uhuh," and "yeah," to
show "I'm with you." Men, she found, more often give silent attention. Women who expect a stream of listener-noise interpret
silent attention as no attention at all.

Women's conversational habits are as frustrating to men as 18
men's are to women. Men who expect silent attention interpret a
stream of listener-noise as overreaction or impatience. Also, when
women talk to each other in a close, comfortable setting, they often overlap, finish each other's sentences, and anticipate what the
other is about to say. This practice, which I call "participatory lis-
tenership," is often perceived by men as interruption, intrusion,
and lack of attention.

A parallel difference caused a man to complain about his wife, 19
"She just wants to talk about her own point of view. If I show her
another view, she gets mad at me." When most women talk to
each other, they assume a conversationalist's job is to express
agreement and support. But many men see their conversational
duty as pointing out the other side of an argument. This is heard
as disloyalty by women, and refusal to offer the requisite support.
It is not that women don't want to see other points of view, but
that they prefer them phrased as suggestions and inquiries rather
than as direct challenges.

In his book *Fighting for Life*, Walter Ong points out that men 20
use "agonistic" or warlike, oppositional formats to do almost anything; thus discussion becomes debate, and conversation a competitive sport. In contrast, women see conversation as a ritual
means of establishing rapport. If Jane tells a problem and June
says she has a similar one, they walk away feeling closer to each
other. But this attempt at establishing rapport can backfire when
used with men. Men take too literally women's ritual "troubles

talk," just as women mistake men's ritual challenges for real attack.

The Sounds of Silence

These differences begin to clarify why women and men have   21
such different expectations about communication in marriage. For women, talk creates intimacy. Marriage is an orgy of closeness: you can tell your feelings and thoughts, and still be loved. Their greatest fear is being pushed away. But men live in a hierarchical world, where talk maintains independence and status. They are on guard to protect themselves from being put down and pushed around.

This explains the paradox of the talkative man who said of his   22
silent wife, "She's the talker." In the public setting of a guest lecture, he felt challenged to show his intelligence and display his understanding of the lecture. But at home, where he has nothing to prove and no one to defend against, he is free to remain silent. For his wife, being home means she is free from the worry that something she says might offend someone, or spark disagreement, or appear to be showing off; at home she is free to talk.

The communication problems that endanger marriage can't   23
be fixed by mechanical engineering. They require a new conceptual framework about the role of talk in human relationships. Many of the psychological explanations that have become second nature may not be helpful, because they tend to blame either women (for not being assertive enough) or men (for not being in touch with their feelings). A sociolinguistic approach by which male-female conversation is seen as cross-cultural communication allows us to understand the problem and forge solutions without blaming either party.

Once the problem is understood, improvement comes natu-   24
rally, as it did to the young woman and her boyfriend who seemed to go to sleep when she wanted to talk. Previously, she had accused him of not listening, and he had refused to change his behavior, since that would be admitting fault. But then she learned about and explained to him the differences in women's and men's

habitual ways of aligning themselves in conversation. The next time she told him she wanted to talk, he began, as usual, by lying down and covering his eyes. When the familiar negative reaction bubbled up, she reassured herself that he really was listening. But then he sat up and looked at her. Thrilled, she asked why. He said, "You like me to look at you when we talk, so I'll try to do it." Once he saw their differences as cross-cultural rather than right and wrong, he independently altered his behavior.

Women who feel abandoned and deprived when their husbands won't listen to or report daily news may be happy to discover their husbands trying to adapt once they understand the place of small talk in women's relationships. But if their husbands don't adapt, the women may still be comforted that for men, this is not a failure of intimacy. Accepting the difference, the wives may look to their friends or family for that kind of talk. And husbands who can't provide it shouldn't feel their wives have made unreasonable demands. Some couples will still decide to divorce, but at least their decisions will be based on realistic expectations. 25

In these times of resurgent ethnic conflicts, the world desperately needs cross-cultural understanding. Like charity, successful cross-cultural communication should begin at home. 26

Meaning and Purpose

1. Tannen opens the essay with an episode that details the events of an evening. How does that device help to engage the reader?
2. A rhetorical question is a question that does not require a reply from its listener or its reader, but rather from the person who asked it. Why does Tannen open the second part of her essay with two rhetorical questions (paragraph 6)?
3. What are two important differences between the way women listen and the way men listen?
4. What are two important differences between the way men talk and the way women talk?
5. Why is it important to learn what Tannen teaches in this essay?

Strategy

1. Why does Tannen maintain that the "problem" must be understood? What problem does she mean?
2. Tannen discusses marriage in terms of communication. Why is that important to this essay?
3. In your opinion, who is the primary audience for this essay?
4. When Tannen discusses conversational habits, why does she refer to the studies of several scholars?
5. When Tannen compares and contrasts the various ways in which men and women communicate, what common features does she find?

Style

1. In paragraph 2, what does the term *crystallizes* mean?
2. Tannen remarks that "For women, as for girls, intimacy is the fabric of relationships" (paragraph 9). What does the term fabric suggest in that clause?
3. Tannen subtitles the last part of this essay "The Sounds of Silence." What is meant by that subtitle?
4. What does the phrase "physical alignment" (paragraph 13) mean in this essay?
5. Tannen uses the term *cross-cultural* several times in this essay. To what does the term refer?

Writing Tasks

1. Recall a conversation with a member of the opposite sex that led to a misunderstanding. Using information you gained from Tannen's essay, write a comparison-and-contrast essay in which you use the conversation to illustrate how men and women communicate differently.

2. In a cafeteria, a library, a shopping mall, a restaurant, or in another public place, observe a mixed-gender group of three or more people talking. Then, in the same area, observe another mixed-gender group of three or more people talking. In an essay, discuss the similarities and differences in the ways the members of the two groups interact conversationally.

❦ Ellen Currie ❦

A frequent contributor to magazines and newspapers, Ellen Currie has also published a novel, Available Light, *and a collection of short stories,* Moses Supposes.

Two Varieties of Killers

This essay, published in The New York Times *August 21, 1986, expresses Currie's concern about the changing nature of crime in our country and also about the manner in which law-abiding people react to sensational crimes.*

As you read, think about the recently reported violent crimes in your area. Would any of them fit Currie's definition of sociable?

Henry James, like many decorous and respectable people, entertained a lively interest in murder. He was a fan of the Scottish solicitor William Roughead, who wrote about real life crime for the first 40 years of this century; James once told Mr. Roughead he was interested in crime because through it "manners and morals become clearly disclosed." He urged Mr. Roughead to write about "the dear old human and sociable murders and adulteries and forgeries in which we are so agreeably at home. And don't tell me, for charity's sake, that your supply runs short." 1

Contemporary supplies of murder, adultery, and forgery remain abundant. But crime seems to me less sociable these days, if I am right in taking "sociable" to mean human and comprehensible and even sympathetic. The crimes get bigger and more horrible, and yet we are not sufficiently horrified by them; we pay less and less attention to the manners and the morals they disclose. 2

Look at the difference, for example, between the crimes of Madeleine Smith, who stirred arsenic into her lover's cocoa in 1857, and the convicted killer Theodore R. Bundy, who has been linked with the murders of 36 women he didn't even know. 3

Madeleine Smith, whose case greatly interested Henry James   4
(he called her a "portentous young person"), was the daughter of
a Glasgow architect. In 1855, when she was 19, she crossed paths
with a young Frenchman. He was handsome, Mr. Roughead
wrote, but "socially impossible." They met in secret and wrote to
each other constantly. When they became lovers Miss Smith's letters took on what Mr. Roughead described as "a tropical and abandoned tone." They were indelicate letters, naive and outspoken.
Another scholar of crime has pointed out that in a day when sex
was supposed to be no more than a woman's bounden duty,
Madeleine Smith found it a pagan festival.

Her lover kept her letters, 198 of them. When she accepted an   5
older, richer and more settled suitor, she asked for the letters' return. Wild with jealousy, her lover claimed he would return them
only to her father. That prospect drove Miss Smith mad with
shame and fear. She bought arsenic. Her lover soon died of arsenic
poisoning. She was brought to trial and conducted herself with
great dignity. The verdict: not proven.

These people are not admirable, but they are real. Their awful   6
situation is comprehensible: a blown up, highly colored version of
the kind of dilemma ordinary people face. Madeleine Smith's
crime was personal. It was a crime of passion.

The case of Ted Bundy is different. To me, it is not "socia-   7
ble," not comprehensible on any human scale. It is peculiarly
impersonal. He didn't even know his victims; they represented
an abstraction—women. His are crimes not of passion but
pathology. Our reaction to them seems to me to partake of
pathology too.   8

According to the reports I have read, some law enforcement
officials say Mr. Bundy may have killed more than 36 young
women in sexual crimes across the country. (Like Madeleine
Smith, Ted Bundy says he is innocent of any crime.) He has been
convicted of battering to death, early on Super Bowl Sunday 1978
in the Chi Omega sorority house at Florida State University, two
young women. He hideously beat two more young women in the
same house and, blocks away, savaged another young woman. He
didn't know any of them. Captured and charged, Mr. Bundy was

also indicted in the kidnapping and murder of a 12-year-old girl. He didn't know her, either. He was convicted of all charges. His execution, scheduled for July 3, was indefinitely postponed to give his lawyers time to frame an appeal.   9

The young women Ted Bundy has been convicted of killing, and is suspected of killing, resemble, an investigator said, "everyone's daughter." Their photographs show the sweet faces of their youth, the long hair of the period. Except for those who loved them, their identities overlap now, and blur. These women are not vivid and defined because they did nothing to bring about their deaths. They were not Ted Bundy's angry and discarded lovers. They did not refuse to return his disastrous, impassioned letters. They didn't know him.   10

At first all these deaths of pretty young women attracted wide public notice. But once Mr. Bundy was apprehended, the attention was all on his antics and not on the innocent dead. Bundy is a 20th century phenomenon. He is mediagenic. He is handsome, usually described as a former law student and witty, brilliant, charming, and polished. Oddly, these latter qualities do not come through in any of the several books about him. Mr. Bundy was once active in Republican politics; there are those who profess to believe that he might ultimately have been elected to high public office had he stayed the course. He has twice made dramatic escapes from custody. He has acted as his own counsel in sensational televised trials. He has been the subject of a television movie. Ted Bundy T-shirts, for, against, and smart aleck ("Ted Bundy is a one-night stand"), have enjoyed popularity. So have jingles: "Let's salute the mighty Bundy / Here on Friday, gone on Monday / All his roads lead out of town / It's hard to keep a good man down." Bundy Burgers and a Bundy cocktail had some play in a Colorado bar. Groupies have gathered at his trials. He gets a lot of mail.   11

Theodore Bundy is said by psychiatrists to be an antisocial personality, a man without conscience. In a strange, third person meditation on killings, Mr. Bundy described the rapes and murders as "inappropriate acting out."   12

Perhaps Ted Bundy doesn't labor under a conscience. But how about the rest of us? Shouldn't we feel more revulsion, more grief for those young lives? Something vile has happened to our ideas of what is valuable and what is waste. Perhaps we have seen too much evil and on too grand a scale. We are glib and dismissive of the moral issues. We think Mr. Bundy is good for a laugh. We made him a celebrity. (Richard Schickel, in his book *Intimate Strangers*, about the nature of celebrity in modern society, contends that multiple murderers have grasped the essentials of the celebrity system better than normal people.)   13

Crime does disclose on manners and on morals. If people must kill people, I have to put my dollar down on wicked Madeleine Smith. With her sexy letters, poisoned cocoa, and caddish lover, she dealt in death. But she is piercingly familiar. Ted Bundy's unspeakable crimes and our cheap reaction to them reveal us to ourselves in a strange and deathly light.

Meaning and Purpose

1. What is "sociable" murder according to Currie (paragraph 2)? Why is Ted Bundy's crime not sociable?
2. Where does Currie state the thesis of her essay?
3. Does Currie have a purpose beyond simply contrasting Madeleine Smith and Ted Bundy? What does she want us to think about besides the differences in their crimes?
4. What explanation is given for Bundy's crimes?
5. Why is Bundy called a "20th century phenomenon" (paragraph 10)? Can you think of other criminal suspects who might also be called that?

Strategy

1. Does Currie use a subject-by-subject or point-by-point approach to presenting her material? Why?
2. Currie devotes a larger portion of the essay to Ted Bundy than she does to Madeleine Smith. Why?

Style

1. In paragraph 4, Madeleine Smith's letters are described as having "a tropical and abandoned tone." Explain what this phrase means.
2. Bundy is described in paragraph 10 as being "mediagenic." What, in your view, makes a person mediagenic?
3. Madeleine's young Frenchman is called "socially impossible" in paragraph 4. Explain what that phrase means in the context of his relationship with Madeleine?
4. If necessary look up the meanings of these words in a dictionary: *portentous, bounden, pagan* (paragraph 4); *savaged* (8); *vile, glib* (12).

Writing Tasks

1. Using Currie's definition of "sociable" crime or developing a definition of your own, write a paper contrasting sociable and nonsociable crimes. Use a subject-by-subject development method. Use specific typical and/or hypothetical examples to illustrate your general statements.
2. Write a comparison-and-contrast paper using a point-by-point method of development. Choose a subject relating to your personal experience at work, at school, or at home.

🐜 Henry David Thoreau 🐜

When he was twenty-eight years old, Henry David Thoreau built a cabin in the woods by Walden Pond outside Concord, Massachusetts, and lived there alone for two years. His best-known book, Walden, *is about that experience. Born in nearby Concord, Massachusetts, in 1817, Thoreau was educated at Harvard University and was influenced by the American essayist, poet, and philosopher Ralph Waldo Emerson, who was also a close friend. Thoreau believed in the citizens' duty to act on their conscience and once spent a night in jail for refusing to pay a poll tax on the grounds that he objected to United States involvement in war with Mexico. In his famed essay, "Civil Disobedience," he outlines his philosophy of passive resistance and has often been cited in support of the American civil-rights movement.*

The Battle of the Ants

In this extended analogy from Walden, *Thoreau compares a battle between red ants and black ants that he witnessed on his woodpile, to the wars men have waged all through history. While elevating the ants by comparing them to men, Thoreau diminishes the glory of human wars by comparing them to battles among insects.*

By using an analogy that compares ant wars to human wars, Thoreau satirizes the brutality and ultimate futility of war. Take notice of all the various aspects of war making he satirizes.

One day when I went out to my wood-pile, or rather my pile   1
of stumps, I observed two large ants, the one red, the other much larger, nearly half an inch long, and black, fiercely contending with one another. Having once got hold they never let go, but struggled and wrestled and rolled on the chips incessantly. Looking farther, I was surprised to find that the chips were covered with such combatants, that it was not a *duellum*, but a *bellum*, a war between two races of ants, the red always pitted against the black, and frequently two red ants to one black. The legions of

these Myrmidons covered all the hills and vales in my wood-yard, and the ground was already strewn with the dead and dy-ing, both red and black. It was the only battle which I have ever witnessed, the only battle-field I ever trod while the battle was raging; internecine war; the red republicans on the one hand, and the black imperialists on the other. On every side they were en-gaged in deadly combat, yet without any noise that I could hear, and human soldiers never fought so resolutely. I watched a cou-ple that were fast locked in each other's embraces, in a little sunny valley amid the chips, now at noonday prepared to fight till the sun went down, or life went out. The smaller red cham-pion had fastened himself like a vise to his adversary's front, and through all the tumblings on that field never for an instant ceased to gnaw at one of his feelers near the root, having already caused the other to go by the board; while the stronger black one dashed him from side to side, and, as I saw on looking nearer, had al-ready divested him of several of his members. They fought with more pertinacity than bulldogs. Neither manifested the least dis-position to retreat. It was evident that their battle-cry was "Con-quer or die." In the meanwhile there came along a single red ant on the hillside of this valley, evidently full of excitement, who ei-ther had dispatched his foe, or had not yet taken part in the bat-tle; probably the latter, for he had lost none of his limbs; whose mother had charged him to return with his shield or upon it. Or perchance he was some Achilles, who had nourished his wrath apart, and had now come to avenge or rescue his Patroclus. He saw this unequal combat from afar—for the blacks were nearly twice the size of the red—he drew near with rapid pace till he stood on his guard within half an inch of the combatants; then, watching his opportunity, he sprang upon the black warrior, and commenced his operations near the root of his right foreleg, leav-ing the foe to select among his own members; and so there were three united for life, as if a new kind of attraction had been in-vented which put all other locks and cements to shame. I should not have wondered by this time to find that they had their re-spective musical bands stationed on some eminent chip, and playing their national airs the while, to excite the slow and cheer the dying combatants. I was myself excited somewhat even as if they had been men. The more you think of it, the less the difference. And certainly there is not the fight recorded in Concord history, at least, if in the history of America, that will bear a moment's comparison with this, whether for the numbers engaged in it, or for the patriotism and heroism displayed. For numbers and for carnage it was an Austerlitz or Dresden. Concord Fight! Two killed on the patriots' side, and Luther Blanchard wounded! Why here every ant was a Buttrick—"Fire! for God's sake fire!"— and thousands shared the fate of Davis and Hosmer. There was not one hireling there. I have no doubt that it was a principle they fought for, as much as our ancestors, and not to avoid a three-penny tax on their tea; and the results of this battle will be as important and memorable to those whom it concerns as those of the battle of Bunker Hill, at least.

I took up the chip on which the three I have particularly described were struggling, carried it into my house, and placed it under a tumbler on my window-sill, in order to see the issue. Holding a microscope to the first-mentioned red ant, I saw that, though he was assiduously gnawing at the near foreleg of his enemy, having severed his remaining feeler, his own breast was all torn away, exposing what vitals he had there to the jaws of the black warrior, whose breastplate was apparently too thick for him to pierce; and the dark carbuncles of the sufferer's eyes shone with ferocity such as war only could excite. They struggled half an hour longer under the tumbler, and when I looked again the black soldier had severed the heads of his foes from their bodies, and the still living heads were hanging on either side of him like ghastly trophies at his saddle-bow, still apparently as firmly fastened as ever, and he was endeavoring with feeble struggles, being without feelers, and with only the remnant of a leg, and I know not how many other wounds, to divest himself of them, which at length, after half an hour more, he accomplished. I raised the glass, and he went off over the window-sill in that crippled state. Whether he finally survived that combat, and spent the remainder of his days in some Hôtel des Invalides, I do not know; but I thought that his industry would not be worth much thereafter. I never learned which party was victorious, nor the cause of the war, but I felt for the rest of that day as if I had my feelings excited and harrowed by witnessing the struggle, the ferocity and carnage, of a human battle before my door.

Kirby and Spence tell us that the battles of ants have long been celebrated and the date of them recorded, though they say that Huber is the only modern author who appears to have witnessed them. "Aeneas Sylvius," say they, "after giving a very circumstantial account of one contested with great obstinacy by a great and small species on the trunk of a pear tree," adds that "'this action was fought in the pontificate of Eugenius the Fourth, in the presence of Nicholas Pistoriensis, an eminent lawyer, who related the whole history of the battle with the greatest fidelity.' A similar engagement between great and small ants is recorded by Olaus Magnus, in which the small ones, being victorious, are said to have buried the bodies of their own soldiers, but left those of their giant enemies a prey to the birds. This event happened previous to the expulsion of the tyrant Christian the Second from Sweden." The battle which I witnessed took place in the Presidency of Polk, five years before the passage of Webster's Fugitive-Slave Bill.

Meaning and Purpose

1. Have you ever stopped to observe and perhaps become fascinated by small things in nature? Explain. What in Thoreau's essay reminds you of your own experience?
2. What was Thoreau's opinion of war? Use evidence from the essay for your answer.
3. Can you find a statement or statements of Thoreau's main point, or thesis?
4. Thoreau mentions Greek heroes, great historical battles, a pope, and a President of the United States. What is his purpose in these widely different references?
5. Think of the time in which Thoreau lived. What audience do you think he is addressing?

6. Although the last paragraph in the essay seems to drift into other topics, in fact, it serves an important purpose. What is that purpose?

Strategy

1. The body of this essay is an extended analogy that parallels some activities of ants and men. What are two qualities that ants and men share in this essay? Give examples from specific sentences.
2. Late in the first paragraph, Thoreau says, "The more you think of it, the less the difference." What is he comparing? What "difference" is he talking about?
3. Toward the end of paragraph 2, Thoreau wonders whether a crippled ant survived to spend the rest of his days "in some Hôtel des Invalides." What is the analogy here?
4. Thoreau makes generous use of satire as a strategy in his analogy. What is satire, and how is it effective here?
5. Overall, how effective do you judge Thoreau's extended analogy is in comparing human battles with those of ants? Without this analogy, how might Thoreau have talked about the folly of war, and do you think his message would have been as forceful?

Style

1. Early in the essay, Thoreau says that he witnessed an "internecine war." Define that kind of war.
2. The first paragraph in the essay includes "Concord Fight!" and "Two killed on the patriots' side, and Luther Blanchard wounded!" Where do these kinds of exclamations often appear? Who might Luther Blanchard be?
3. The second paragraph in the essay includes this description: "the dark carbuncles of the sufferer's eyes shone with ferocity such as war only could excite." Is this description realistic? Is it factual? Support your answer with your own opinions.
4. Thoreau says that the soldier-ants "fought with more pertinacity than bulldogs." Look up the word *pertinacity*. It has at least two

meanings. Which meaning compares ants with men? Which meaning compares ants with bulldogs?

Writing Tasks

1. In the essay, Thoreau says, "I have no doubt that it was a principle they fought for, as much as our ancestors." Can you think of a principle many people believe in that you feel is not worth fighting or working for? Write an essay in which you use an analogy and compare that principle to something familiar to readers to show why it is not worth the struggle.
2. There are other analogies for war besides the battle of the ants. Finish the statement "War is like . . . ," listing three things to compare war to. Write a few paragraphs of analogy for each comparison you choose.

❦ Responding to Photographs ❦
Comparison and Contrast

The New Warriors

For general purposes, think of photography as having two main uses: to record private experiences and to record public experiences. A photograph of private experience—a snapshot of a family outing, a portrait of a father, a candid photo of a child—is appreciated within a private context by those who have some direct connection with the recorded event or person.

A photograph that records public experience usually has nothing directly to do with us, its viewers, but we nevertheless bring meaning to it based on our experiences.

Both private and public photographs can evoke infinite associations from the viewer's own experience. But most public photographs have a second dimension. They create social or political associations that many people share. Often they suggest discontinuity in our common social experience. As an organizing principle, photographers create discontinuity through juxtaposition—that is, they oppose contrasting elements in their photographs.

327

Select one of the following writing assignments to explore the use of contrasting elements in photographs. Before you begin, reread the material at the beginning of this chapter to review strategies for developing contrasts.

1. "The New Warriors" is a public photograph that ironically explores the ideas on which the United States is predicated. By referring to details in "The New Warriors," examine its contrasting elements and determine what social or political message it embodies. Remember that you must select details from the photograph to support your contention, presenting them to readers as if they have not seen the image.

2. Select a private photograph from your or your family's collection. Be sure to find one that embodies contrasting elements. In a brief essay, examine the contrasting elements in the photograph. Keep in mind that since your readers have not been part of your family history, you must supply background information to create a context for the photograph.

❦ Additional Writing Tasks ❦
Comparison and Contrast

1. Using comparison and contrast as the dominant pattern, write an essay on one of these tasks or one that you compose for yourself. Keep in mind that you may modify any of the tasks to fit your interests.

    a. At the library, find two advertisements for the same product: one published in the 1950s and one published within the last year. Write an essay presenting the similarities and differences in these advertisements.

    b. Select two fairy tales that have similar patterns and characters, such as children journeying into a forest, an encounter with death, the appearance of a mysterious creature, a magical transformation. Identify at least three significant elements that the tales have in common and three significant elements that are different. Write an essay comparing and contrasting the similarities and differences in these two tales.

    c. Collect several advertisements for two brands of the same product type that direct their advertising campaigns toward men and women, such as Marlboro cigarettes (men) and Virginia Slims (women). After examining the advertisements, write an essay comparing and contrasting how these advertisements appeal to male consumers and how they appeal to female consumers.

    d. Accurately and fairly, compare and contrast the arguments on both sides of a controversial issue, such as abortion, capital punishment, pornography, or gun control.

    e. Most people hold important social or political beliefs that are opposed by people close to them. Select a belief that you hold, and in an essay, contrast your attitude to the opposing attitude of one of your parents, a brother, a sister, or a close friend.

    f. Select two classes you have attended, two jobs you have held, or two vacations you have taken. Write a comparison-and-contrast essay discussing the similarities and differences of your subjects.

    g. Compare and contrast a past experience with a current experience. You might compare how you once viewed a holiday, such as Thanksgiving, Christmas, or Chanukah, with your view of it today. Or you might compare how you once viewed a special place, such as a vacation site, a fun zone, or even your bedroom, with your current view.

    h. Compare and contrast how two people from different cultures, economic situations, or age groups might perceive the same experience.

    i. Select two public figures with opposing views on one controversial issue. After familiarizing yourself with their positions, write an essay contrasting their attitudes.

    j. Select two campus groups that hold opposing social values. In an essay, compare and contrast their views and behavior.

2. Write an essay with comparison and contrast as the dominant pattern on one of these general subjects or on a subject of your own choice. By the end of your essay, the reader should know why you prefer one thing to the other.

    a. Two people who embrace different life-styles

    b. A national news program and a local news program

    c. Two methods for losing weight

    d. Female and male consumers

    e. Children's games yesterday and today

    f. Two characters from film or fiction

    g. A film created from a novel

    h. Watching a movie on television and watching it in a movie theater

    i. Coverage of a news event by television and by a newspaper

    j. Two classic films: horror, western, mystery, or romance

3. Read this quotation from social critic Morton Hunt:

> The record of man's inhumanity to man is horrifying, when one compiles it—enslavement, castration, torture, rape, mass slaughter in war after war. But who has compiled the record of man's kindness to man—the trillions of acts of gentleness and goodness, the helping hands, smiles, shared meals, kisses, gifts, healings, rescues? If we were no more than murderous predators, with a freakish lack of inhibition

against slaughtering our own species, we would have been at a terrible competitive disadvantage compared with other animals; if this were the central truth of our nature, we would scarcely have survived, multiplied and become the dominant species on earth. Man does have an aggressive instinct, but it is not naturally or inevitably directed to killing his own kind. He is a beast and perhaps at times the cruelest beast of all—but sometimes he is also the kindest beast of all. He is not all good and not perfectible, but he is not all bad and not wholly unchangeable or unimprovable. That is the only basis on which one can hope for him; but it is enough.

Hunt stresses humanity's dual nature. Write an essay with comparison and contrast as the dominant pattern that makes Hunt's general observation specific.

7

Cause and Effect

Identifying Reasons and Results

The Method

When you explain why something happened or the consequences of that happening, you are engaged in an intellectual activity that seems to be at the core of human curiosity—that is, the search for **causes and effects**.

In their simplest form, cause-and-effect relationships appear as a series of escalating events, one triggering another like a chain reaction. Consider the children's song in which a woman swallows a fly. The lively fly causes her to swallow a spider to catch the fly. She then swallows a bird to catch the spider, then a cat to catch the bird, then a dog to catch the cat, then a goat, then a cow, and finally a horse. The effect? She dies, of course.

In a more complex form, cause and effect are often at work in thrillers and mysteries. A wealthy politician falls dead during a banquet. He had been in excellent health. There seems to be no clear cause of death. Could he have been murdered in some mysterious way? The question triggers the appearance of a super-sleuth, who begins the investigation. The detective discovers clues, each of which reveals a new suspect. After an exhaustive exploration of the many reasons suspects had for wanting the victim dead, the murderer is unmasked, the mysterious murder method is explained, and the dark reasons for the murder are revealed.

Of course, mystery fans aren't consciously seeking cause or effect patterns. They're probably trying to beat the writer at his or her own game by figuring out "Whodunit?" before the final scene. But that question is not much different from "What caused it?"

If you think of causes as **reasons** and effects as **results**, you might better understand cause-and-effect patterns. Like a detective you can begin with questions: Why did something happen? What are the consequences of something's happening? When you answer the Why, you are giving reasons, that is, causes. When you answer the What, you are giving results, that is, effects. Professional writers observe this distinction when exploring the causes or effects behind any event. Generally, the distinction keeps them on the track.

Consider this question: "Why did the women's liberation movement bloom in the 1960s?" The question would lead a writer to seek reasons—that is, causes.

But the question "What were the consequences of the women's liberation movement on college campuses during the 1970s?" would lead a writer to seek results—that is, effects.

And the compound question "Why did the women's liberation movement falter in the 1980s, and what will be the consequences in the 1990s?" would lead a writer to explain the reasons and the results—that is, both causes and effects.

Strategies

When you begin analyzing the cause-and-effect relationships in a complex subject, you might feel somewhat like a detective unraveling a mystery. You must be prepared for the false starts and deceptive clues that will send you down the wrong path, but don't lose heart: You can learn by studying professional writers, who often approach cause-and-effect analysis from several angles, depending on the characteristics of their subjects. First, they may narrow their effort by concentrating only on the causes. Second, they may concentrate only on the effects. And third, they may choose to concentrate on both causes and effects. If you understand cause-and-effect development patterns and apply your knowledge critically as you read, you'll soon master the technique of analyzing cause-and-effect relationships in your own writing.

Identifying Causes

When effects are clear, writers will concentrate on causes. In 1948, Harry Truman upset Thomas Dewey, Governor of New York, for the presidency. Dewey was predicted to win by a landslide. In fact, one newspaper prematurely printed headlines announcing Dewey's victory. The political pundits were wrong: Truman won. A writer who asked, "Why did Truman win?" would not have to establish the result (Truman's victory), but he or she would concentrate on the reasons—that is, the causes—behind Truman's victory. Did his "underdog" image generate sympathy among voters? Did a last-minute whistlestop campaign through America's heartland swing the election his way? Was it a well-oiled Democratic machine that kept the party faithful in line? These and other causes would have to be explored in any analysis of the election.

In *Redoing America*, Robert Faltermayer discusses the interwoven character of American cities. In the following paragraph, Faltermayer concentrates on causes. He opens with the common assumption that the automobile has had a destructive effect on the "close knit fabric" of cities. He then presents the reasons for this phenomenon:

> The close knit fabric was blown apart by the automobile, and by the postwar middle-class exodus to suburbia which the mass-ownership of automobiles made possible. The automobile itself was not to blame for this development, nor was the desire for suburban living, which is obviously a genuine aspiration of many Americans. The fault lay in our failure, right up to the present time, to fashion new policies to minimize the disruptive effects of the automobile revolution. We have failed not only to tame the automobile itself, but to overhaul a property-tax system that tends to foster automotive-age sprawl and to institute coordinated planning in the politically fragmented suburbs that have caught the brunt of the postwar building boom.

In the opening sentence, Faltermayer establishes a relationship between automobiles and the changing character of cities and sprawling suburbs. In the next sentence he refines his focus by dismissing two possible causes: the automobile itself and the desire for suburban living. In the remainder of the paragraph he explains what he believes to be the true cause: the failure to fashion public policies that would have controlled the automobile and the building boom.

Identifying Effects

When writers select subjects with very clear causes, they will then concentrate on effects. For instance, drug merchants are expanding their operations into rural communities. Crack houses are springing up in small towns where drugs had previously been scarce. This fact has been substantiated by law-enforcement agencies across the nation. A writer who asked, "What are the consequences of increased drug use in rural communities?" would spend very little time establishing the existence of increased drug activity in small-town America because it is widely known. He or she would, however, concentrate on the effects this trend might have on rural communities. What, for instance, are the consequences for families? What will be the effects on undertrained and underbudgeted law-enforcement agencies, on social services, and on schools?

In this paragraph from *Anatomy of an Illness*, Norman Cousins uses this pattern. He quickly establishes the cause, a hypothetical injury, and then concentrates on exploring effects of pain suppressants on injured professional athletes.

Professional athletes are sometimes severely disadvantaged by trainers whose job it is to keep them in action. The more famous the athlete, the greater the risk that he or she may be subjected to extreme medical measures when injury strikes. The star baseball pitcher whose arm is sore because of a torn muscle or tissue damage may need sustained rest more than anything else. But this team is battling for a place in the World Series; so the trainer or team doctor, called upon to work his magic, reaches for a strong dose of butazolidine or other powerful pain suppressants. Presto, the pain disappears! The pitcher takes his place on the mound and does superbly. That could be the last game, however, in which he is able to throw the ball with full strength. The drugs didn't repair the torn muscle or cause the damaged tissue to heal. What they did was to mask the pain, enabling the pitcher to throw hard, further damaging the torn muscle. Little wonder that so many star athletes are cut down in their

prime, more the victims of overzealous treatment of their injuries than of the injuries themselves.

Cousins opens by establishing the direction the paragraph
will take. He then states the cause of the effects that will follow—
a hypothetical injury to a star baseball pitcher's throwing arm.
Next, he develops the effects of the injury—under pressure to
win, a trainer or team doctor prescribes a pain killer; the pitcher
plays as if he had no injury; and the ultimate effect is a career cut
short, not by injury but by the mistreatment of injury.

Identifying Causes and Effects

Writers are always cautious about assuming that readers
know the causes or effects of an event, especially when exploring
a complex subject that is not part of common knowledge. When
such a subject is discussed, they usually explain both causes and
effects. Often they will alternate causes and effects in one
paragraph.

Victor C. Cline uses this pattern in a paragraph from "How TV
Violence Damages Your Children."

> Much of the research that has led to the conclusion that
> TV and movie violence could cause aggressive behavior in
> some children has stemmed from the work in the area of im-
> itative learning or modeling which, reduced to its simplest
> expression, might be termed "monkey see, monkey do."
> Research by Stanford psychologist Albert Bandura has
> shown that even brief exposure to novel aggressive behavior
> on a *one-time basis* can be repeated in free play by as high as
> 88 percent of the young children seeing it on TV. Dr.
> Bandura also demonstrated that even a single viewing of a
> novel aggressive act could be recalled and produced by chil-
> dren six months later, without any intervening exposure.
> Earlier studies have estimated that the average child between
> the ages of 5 and 15 will witness, during this 10-year period,
> the violent destruction of more than 13,400 fellow humans.

This means that through several hours of TV-watching, a child may see more violence than the average adult experiences in a lifetime. Killing is as common as taking a walk, a gun more natural than an umbrella. Children are thus taught to take pride in force and violence and to feel ashamed of ordinary sympathy.

Cline's first sentence establishes that children learn aggressive behavior from television through modeling, or, as Cline phrases it, "monkey see, monkey do." In the second sentence he presents his first cause and first effect—even *brief exposure* to aggressive behavior (cause) can lead to children's repeating it in free play (effect). In the third sentence he presents the second cause and its effect: a *single viewing* of an aggressive act (cause) can be recalled by children six months later (effect). The next three sentences detail the violence a typical child might see over ten years, thus establishing a very dramatic cause. In his final sentence, Cline states the ultimate effect: Television teaches children to take pride in violence and to be ashamed of sympathy.

Rather than alternating causes and effects in individual paragraphs, writers will sometimes divide them into separate paragraphs. The following two paragraphs are from Frank Trippett's humorous essay "The Great American Cooling Machine." In the first paragraph, Trippett establishes that air conditioning has been overlooked as a major cause for change in U.S. society. In the second paragraph he presents three effects of air conditioning on society.

Neither scholars nor pop sociologists have really got around to charting and diagnosing all the changes brought about by air conditioning. Professional observers have for years been preoccupied with the social implications of the automobile and television. Mere glancing analysis suggests that the car and TV, in their most decisive influences on American habits, have been powerfully aided and abetted by air conditioning. The car may have created all those shopping centers in the boondocks, but only air conditioning has made them attractive to mass clienteles. Similarly, the artificial cooling of the living room undoubtedly helped turn the typical American into a year-round TV addict. Without air conditioning, how many viewers would endure reruns (or even Johnny Carson) on one of those pestilential summer nights that used to send people out to collapse on the lawn or to sleep on the roof?

Many of the side effects of air conditioning are far from being fully pinned down. It is a reasonable suspicion, though, that controlled climate, by inducing Congress to stay in Washington longer than it used to during the swelter season, thus presumably passing more laws, has contributed to bloated government. One can only speculate that the advent of the supercooled bedroom may be linked to the carnal adventurism associated with the mid-century sexual revolution. Surely it is a fact----if restaurant complaints about raised thermostats are to be believed—that air conditioning induces at least expense-account diners to eat and drink more; if so, it must be credited with adding to the national fat problem.

Identifying Immediate and Ultimate Causes and Effects

Careful writers usually distinguish between immediate and ultimate causes and effects, that is, the ones that are most apparent and those that underlie them. In the example above, Trippett, in his humorous way, presents the ultimate effects of air conditioning: bloated government, the sexual revolution, and the national fat problem. The depth to which a writer analyzes causes or effects depends upon the subject and the purpose. Exploring the ultimate causes or effects requires more effort than getting to the immediate ones because a writer must establish a foundation for the analysis.

In *The Seasons of a Man's Life,* Daniel J. Levenson studies the psychological development of men. In these two paragraphs, after establishing a solid foundation for his conclusions, he presents the ultimate effects of middle age on a man's relationships with young adults.

At around 40 a man is deeply involved in the Young/Old polarity. This developmental process has a powerful effect upon his relationships with his offspring and with young adults generally. When his own aging weighs heavily upon him, their exuberant vitality is more likely to arouse his envy and resentment than his delight and forbearance. He may be preoccupied with grievances against his own parents for damage, real or imagined, that they have inflicted upon him at different ages. These preoccupations make him less appreciative of the (often similar) grievances his offspring direct toward him.

If he feels he has lost or betrayed his own early Dream, he may find it hard to give his wholehearted support and blessing to the Dreams of young adults. When his offspring show signs of failure or confusion in pursuing their adult goals, he is afraid that their lives will turn out as badly as his own. Yet, when they do well, he may resent their success. Anxiety and guilt may undermine his efforts to be helpful and lead him instead to be nagging and vindictive.

Levenson's analysis probes deeply into the nagging relationship some middle-aged men might have with young adults. He exposes the ultimate cause and its effects—anxiety over aging, failure, and competition.

In this paragraph from *The Faces of the Enemy*, Sam Keen explores the ultimate cause of war, not the politicians who start wars or the generals who carry them out, but the "good people" who allow their leaders to act out community neuroses by waging war.

The major responsibility for war lies not with villains and evil men but with reasonably good citizens. Any depth understanding of the social function of war leads to the conclusion that it was the "good" Germans who created the social ecology that nurtured the Nazis. Lincoln said, "War is much too important to be left to the generals." But the psychological truth is much more disturbing. The generals are the (largely unconscious) agents of a (largely unconscious) civilian population. The good people send out armies as symbolic representatives to act out their repressed shadows, denied hostilities, unspoken cruelties, unacceptable greed, unimagined lust for revenge against punitive parents and authorities, uncivil sexual sadism, denied animality, in a purifying blood ritual that confirms their claim to goodness before the approving eyes of history or God. Warfare is the political equivalent of the individual process of seeking "vindictive triumph," which Karen Horney described as the essence of neurosis.

Writers keep two cautions in mind when exploring cause-and-effect relationships; be aware of them. First, writers avoid confusing process patterns with cause-and-effect patterns. The analysis of a process usually stems from a question of How? not Why? or What? "*How* did Ronald Reagan get elected to the presidency?" sends a writer into process analysis. "*Why* was Ronald Reagan elected to the presidency?" sends a writer into an examination of the causes—that is, the reasons. "*What* were the consequences of Ronald Reagan's presidency?" sends a writer to examine the effects—that is, the results.

Second, they avoid the *post hoc, ergo propter hoc* fallacy, that is, the "after this, therefore because of this" or "false-cause" fallacy. Writers commit this fallacy (argument from a false inference) by jumping to conclusions based on insufficient information. That former President Ronald Reagan was elected when the electorate's average life expectancy was increasing does not mean that an older voting population will elect older presidents.

In a variation of the false-cause fallacy, an event is identified as triggering a series of events in a cause-and-effect chain reaction, or *causal chain.* This kind of reasoning was at work in the arguments of politicians who supported the U.S. military action in Vietnam during the 1960s and 1970s. They maintained that if North Vietnam was successful in its efforts to take over South Vietnam, then the nearby Southeast Asian countries would soon be taken over by Communist regimes one at a time, like a file of falling dominoes triggered by the first domino toppling into the second. History, of course, has shown that these events did not happen.

But keep in mind that causes of complicated events are seldom simple or obvious and that predicting the future with cause-and-effect reasoning is a chancy business.

Cause and Effect in College Writing

Essays exploring cause-and-effect relationships are common in classrooms across campus. In a history class you might be asked to discuss the causes of racial discrimination following the Civil War. In an economics class you might be asked to explain the international effects of the massive United States budget deficit. In a psychology class you might be asked to discuss the causes of clinical depression and its effects or simply causes *or* effects.

Guidelines for Writing a Cause and Effect Essay

1. Select a subject that lends itself to the analysis of cause-and-effect relationships. Use prewriting techniques to develop a list of causes, effects, or both.
2. Group the causes and effects identified in your prewritten material. If appropriate, separate immediate causes from ultimate causes.
3. Decide on your approach to the subject—that is, if the causes are clear, then concentrate on the effects; if the effects are clear, then concentrate on the causes; or concentrate on both the causes and effects. Be sure to emphasize the most important causes or effects to avoid becoming distracted by the obvious or trivial. Determine which causes or effects should be developed in a single paragraph and which should be developed in two paragraphs.
4. With the general purpose of the essay in mind, write a tentative thesis that signals whether you will mainly emphasize causes, effects, or causes and effects. Write the first draft.
5. Revise your essay, avoiding the *post hoc, ergo propter hoc* fallacy.

A Student Essay Developed by Cause and Effect

Tom Kim wrote a cause-and-effect analysis in response to the following sociology assignment:

In a 900- to 1000-word essay, identify a campuswide problem and explain why it is taking place and what will result from it. Consider these possible subjects:

- Services needed by returning students
- Inadequate library support
- Lack of health professionals on campus
- Increase in student cheating
- Sexual harassment
- Tension among ethnic groups
- Lack of competitive sports
- Increase in part-time faculty

Kim decided to write on the increase in student cheating. It had become widespread, and school officials, professors, and students were concerned about it. First read the essay, then reread it and respond to the items in Reviewing with a Writer's Eye.

Cheating: A Growing Campus Problem

Five years ago, according to student government records, four students were officially charged with cheating. Each incident took place in a large lecture class: two in Psychology 100, one in Art History, and one in Economics. All four incidents seemed to be spontaneous acts that involved copying answers from another student's answer sheet and were committed "because the opportunity presented itself." Last year 206 cheating incidents were officially reported, a dramatic increase. Although most of these incidents took place in large lecture courses, many of them took place in smaller classes that require individual work. For example, a biology instructor reported two students from different classes who turned in remarkably similar projects. Two advanced psy-

1

chology professors reported several students for turning in case studies done by other students during previous semesters. Four English professors reported students who plagiarized material from professional sources or submitted essays someone else had written. Perhaps a way to approach the problem is to ask, Why do students cheat? and What are the effects? Although the reasons for cheating are not easy to identify, the effects of cheating are clear.

The rise in cheating is often attributed to two immediate causes. First, in these difficult economic times more and more students are working more hours a week but not cutting back on their course load. Currently, according to the campus records office, over ninety percent of our student body works at least twenty-five hours a week, but the average course load has not decreased. This fact suggests that students are trying to cram too much into their schedules. Once the semester is underway, they discover they must take short cuts or drop classes. Cheating is an easy shortcut. A second reason students cheat may be because of pressure to attend graduate school. Although most students can pass their courses through their own efforts, a few believe they must earn "A"s to qualify for graduate programs. These students feel that cheating will give them the grade boost they need.

A third reason is more remote, thus much less obvious to a casual observer. Cheating may have increased because a subculture of cheating has developed—when a student's friends cheat, then it is easier to cheat. Students in this subculture exchange test information, science projects, essays, and research papers. This material gets reworked and recycled from semester to semester. Rather than keeping their exploits as cheaters secret, they celebrate them, often bragging about their prowess, thus fueling the process from semester to semester.

Although the causes of cheating are difficult to identify, its immediate effects can be seen around campus. Large lecture-class professors are taking new precautions. First, they are scrambling the questions on their tests, perhaps creating as many as five different tests for one class. Second, they are using more proctors to monitor the class during the examination. One professor had ten proctors roaming the lecture hall while students took the test. Finally, they are requiring students to "check in" to get copies of the test booklet. The proctors check their driver's licenses against the roster to be sure the enrolled student is actually taking the test. The ultimate result of this intense security could be the creation of a "Big Brother" atmosphere in some classes—yet it all seems necessary.

The effect of cheating in composition classes is less   5
dramatic but equally significant. Many composition pro-fessors are assigning more in-class writing. Once the in-structor becomes familiar with a student's writing ability, then spotting plagiarized or cribbed essays is easier. For instance, if a student consistently writes "C" papers in class, then begins to write "A" papers out of class, the in-structor becomes suspicious. At this point, the instructor will usually meet in conference with the student to discuss the essay's subject and content. This discussion helps the instructor to determine if the student actually wrote the essay or had someone else write it. One English professor said she had not uncovered any cheating but believed her diligence deterred cheating.

Two other effects of cheating may ultimately damage   6
students. The first is obvious. Students who cheat will eventually reach a point where they are unable to cheat and will lack the fundamental skills for success in upper-division classes. Some might say their failure is just retri-bution. How sad. Most students can be successful if they accept the challenge of education; those who cheat are hobbling themselves unnecessarily. A second effect could possibly make serious students victims of cheaters. Students who actually struggle with course content may receive lower grades than those who cheat. This fact is discouraging, especially for those who know that some students achieved higher grades dishonestly. As a result, some students have quietly reported cheaters. This, of course, may make honest students feel as if they are be-traying their classmates, thus disrupting their sense of collegiality.

The number of students reported to be cheating is a   7
mere fraction of the 15,673 enrolled students. But cam-

pus officials believe a great deal of unreported cheating takes place. As a consequence, a committee composed of students, faculty, and campus administration is investigating cheating to develop campus guidelines to combat it. Aside from creating a more formal process to determine if a student was actually cheating, the committee is also developing a strategy to educate the entire student body about cheating and its effects on campus life. The strategy will include information that all students will receive and a detailed honor system that all professors will present the first day of classes. What will be the result of the committee's work? That is hard to predict, but the effort has already heightened student and faculty awareness.

Reviewing with a Writer's Eye

1. Review Tom Kim's writing assignment (p. 344). Explain how he succeeds or fails to meet its requirements. Identify specific paragraphs of "Cheating: A Growing Campus Problem" that address particular aspects of the assignment.

2. Develop a detailed scratch outline of Kim's essay. Begin by restating the thesis statement in your own words. Then restate the topic sentences and subpoints (see pp. 42–44).

3. Identify the immediate causes and the ultimate causes of cheating. How does Kim distinguish them (see pp. 340–343)?

4. Identify the immediate effects and the ultimate effects of cheating. How does Kim distinguish them (see pp. 340–343)?

5. Indicate where Kim explains the causes and effects of cheating and where he illustrates with examples the causes and effects of cheating. Identify the key examples.

6. What is the campuswide outcome of cheating? Write a new one-paragraph introduction to "Cheating: A Growing Campus Problem" that concentrates on the campuswide outcome and ends with a thesis statement similar to Kim's.

7. Imagine that you're a member of Kim's peer-review group. He has asked you to review the structure of his essay, paying partic-

Peer Review

You may be asked to write an essay about one of the readings that follow. Before you meet with your writing group, review this introduction. As you read the papers of your group members, use these general writing principles about cause and effect to help guide your comments.

1. The paper should not belabor the obvious; it should not present causes or effects that are already well known to most readers.
2. The causes that are discussed should clearly lead to the effects, and the effects discussed should clearly result from the causes.
3. The cause-and-effect relations should be based on sufficient information and logical reasoning.

ular attention to transitions and responding to paragraphs 2 and 3. Write a brief note, no more than 150 words, detailing your responses.

As you will see while reading the essays that follow, professional writers frequently mix example and comparison and contrast patterns into essays dominated by cause and effect. Study these professionals for their craft. Examine how they construct their discussions. Separate the causes from the effects. And separate the immediate effects from the ultimate effects. Through this kind of critical reading, you will develop your own writing skills.

❦ E. M. Forster ❦

Edward Morgan Forster was born in London in 1879 and attended King's College, Cambridge, where he studied classics and history and developed a strong interest in foreign cultures. From a family of bankers, he had no interest in business, and after finishing his education traveled to India, Greece, and Italy. He later settled in London to pursue a career as a writer. His travels in India (in 1912 and again in 1921) inspired his best-known novel, A Passage to India. *His other books include the novels* A Room with a View *and* Howard's End, *two collections of essays, and a collection of short stories. Forster died in 1970.*

My Wood

This selection is from Forster's Abinger Harvest, *a 1936 collection of essays. He opens with a reference to his novel* A Passage to India *and uses his experience in buying a piece of land to examine the effects of property ownership. He distinguishes between the unavoidable materialism of "life on earth" and the problematic desire for ownership.*

We usually associate wealth with freedom. In reading this essay, be alert to the ways in which Forster turns the common perception around to show how property ownership actually restricts freedom.

A few years ago I wrote a book which dealt in part with the difficulties of the English in India. Feeling that they would have had no difficulties in India themselves, the Americans read the book freely. The more they read it the better it made them feel, and a cheque to the author was the result. I bought a wood with the cheque. It is not a large wood—it contains scarcely any trees, and it is intersected, blast it, by a public footpath. Still, it is the first property that I have owned, so it is right that other people should participate in my shame, and should ask themselves, in accents that will vary in horror, this very important question: What is the effect of property upon the character? Don't let's

349

touch economics; the effect of private ownership upon the community as a whole is another question—a more important question, perhaps, but another one. Let's keep to psychology. If you own things, what's their effect on you? What's the effect on me of my wood?

In the first place, it makes me feel heavy. Property does have this effect. Property produces men of weight, and it was a man   2
of weight who failed to get into the Kingdom of Heaven. He was not wicked, that unfortunate millionaire in the parable, he was only stout; he stuck out in front, not to mention behind, and as he wedged himself this way and that in the crystalline entrance and bruised his well-fed flanks, he saw beneath him a comparatively slim camel passing through the eye of a needle and being woven into the robe of God. The Gospels all through couple stoutness and slowness. They point out what is perfectly obvious, yet seldom realized: that if you have a lot of things you cannot move about a lot, that furniture requires dusting, dusters require servants, servants require insurance stamps, and the whole tangle of them makes you think twice before you accept an invitation to dinner or go for a bathe in the Jordan. Sometimes the Gospels proceed further and say with Tolstoy that property is sinful; they approach the difficult ground of asceticism here, where I cannot follow them. But as to the immediate effects of property on people, they just show straightforward logic. It produces men of weight. Men of weight cannot, by definition, move like the lightning from the East unto the West, and the ascent of a fourteen-stone bishop into a pulpit is thus the exact antithesis of the coming of the Son of Man. My wood makes me feel heavy.

In the second place, it makes me feel it ought to be larger.

The other day I heard a twig snap in it. I was annoyed at   3
first, for I thought that someone was blackberrying, and depre-   4
ciating the value of the undergrowth. On coming nearer, I saw it was not a man who had trodden on the twig and snapped it, but a bird, and I felt pleased. My bird. The bird was not equally pleased. Ignoring the relation between us, it took fright as soon as it saw the shape of my face, and flew straight over the bound-

ary hedge into a field, the property of Mrs. Henessy, where it sat down with a loud squawk. It had become Mrs. Henessy's bird. Something seemed grossly amiss here, something that would not have occurred had the wood been larger. I could not afford to buy Mrs. Henessy out, I dared not murder her, and limitations of this sort beset me on every side. Ahab did not want that vineyard—he only needed it to round off his property, preparatory to plotting a new curve—and all the land around my wood has become necessary to me in order to round off the wood. A boundary protects. But—poor little thing—the boundary ought in its turn to be protected. Noises on the edge of it. Children throw stones. A little more, and then a little more, until we reach the sea. Happy Canute! Happier Alexander! And after all, why should even the world be the limit of possession? A rocket containing a Union Jack, will, it is hoped, be shortly fired at the moon. Mars. Sirius. Beyond which . . . But these immensities ended by saddening me. I could not suppose that my wood was the destined nucleus of universal dominion—it is so very small and contains no mineral wealth beyond the blackberries. Nor was I comforted when Mrs. Henessy's bird took alarm for the second time and flew clean away from us all, under the belief that it belonged to itself.

In the third place, property makes its owner feel that he ought to do something to it. Yet he isn't sure what. A restlessness comes over him, a vague sense that he has a personality to express—the same sense which, without any vagueness, leads the artist to an act of creation. Sometimes I think I will cut down such trees as remain in the wood, at other times I want to fill up the gaps between them with new trees. Both impulses are pretentious and empty. They are not honest movements towards money-making or beauty. They spring from a foolish desire to express myself and from an inability to enjoy what I have got. Creation, property, enjoyment form a sinister trinity in the human mind. Creation and enjoyment are both very, very good, yet they are often unattainable without a material basis, and at such moments property pushes itself in as a substitute, saying, "Accept me instead—I'm good enough for all three." It is not enough. It is, as Shakespeare

5

said of lust, "The expense of spirit in a waste of shame": it is "Before, a joy proposed; behind, a dream." Yet we don't know how to shun it. It is forced on us by our economic system as the alternative to starvation. It is also forced on us by an internal defect in the soul, by the feeling that in property may lie the germs of self-development and of exquisite or heroic deeds. Our life on earth is, and ought to be, material and carnal. But we have not yet learned to manage our materialism and carnality properly; they are still entangled with the desire for ownership, where (in the words of Dante) "Possession is one with loss."

And this brings us to our fourth and final point: the blackberries.   6

Blackberries are not plentiful in this meagre grove, but they are easily seen from the public footpath which traverses it, and all   7 too easily gathered. Foxgloves, too—people will pull up the foxgloves, and ladies of an educational tendency even grub for toadstools to show them on the Monday in class. Other ladies, less educated, roll down the bracken in the arms of their gentlemen friends. There is paper, there are tins. Pray, does my wood belong to me or doesn't it? And, if it does, should I not own it best by allowing no one else to walk there? There is a wood near Lyme Regis, also cursed by a public footpath, where the owner has not hesitated on this point. He had built high stone walls each side of the path, and has spanned it by bridges, so that the public circulate like termites when he gorges on the blackberries unseen. He really does own his wood, this able chap. Dives in Hell did pretty well, but the gulf dividing him from Lazarus could be traversed by vision, and nothing traverses it here. And perhaps I shall come to this in time. I shall wall in and fence out until I really taste the sweets of property. Enormously stout, endlessly avaricious, pseudo-creative, intensely selfish, I shall weave upon my forehead the quadruple crown of possession until those nasty Bolshies come and take it off again and thrust me aside into the outer darkness.

Meaning and Purpose

1. What is Forster's purpose in "My Wood," and where does he most clearly state it?
2. In paragraph 5, he says that "property makes its owner feel that he ought to do something to it." What do you own that you have done something to, just because you owned it? A pair of shoes? A jacket? A car? Briefly describe the ways in which you changed it and your reasons for changing it.
3. An allusion often refers to a historical or literary figure, event, or object. Choose one allusion from this essay, and learn more about it. If you chose "Canute," you might look it up in an unabridged dictionary, an encyclopedia, or other reference works. Select an allusion other than "Canute" and describe it briefly.
4. In paragraph 2, Forster says that owning many things restricts one's freedom. How does owning the wood restrict the author's freedom?
5. The first paragraph includes the words "blast it." Why does the author use that interjection?

Strategy

1. Study the cause-and-effect structure of the essay. Does Forster alternate cause and effect in each paragraph or develop them one at a time in separate paragraphs? Explain the effectiveness of the structure.
2. In the middle of paragraph 2 is the statement, "if you have a lot of things you cannot move about a lot, that furniture requires dusting, dusters require servants, servants require insurance stamps, and the whole tangle of them makes you think twice before you accept an invitation to dinner or go for a bathe in the Jordan." What is the cause-and-effect structure of this sentence called, and how is it used here?
3. The last paragraph in this essay says that the owner of a wood near Lyme Regis "really does own his wood." What caused that ownership? What is the effect of that kind of ownership?

4. In paragraph 6, Forster says that the fourth and final point in the essay is blackberries. But it is not. What is the fourth and final point, and why does the author tell us that it is blackberries?

Style

1. What is the occupation of the "ladies of an educational tendency," in paragraph 7, and why do you think the author describes them as he does?
2. In paragraph 4, the author says, "A little more, and then a little more, until we reach the sea." What is the author describing in this sentence?
3. Look at paragraphs 3 and 6. Why do you think each has only one sentence?

Writing Tasks

1. The American writer Henry David Thoreau said, "A man is rich in proportion to the number of things which he can afford to let alone." E. M. Forster's essay "My Wood" has much in common with Thoreau's statement. In your paper, consider being rich a cause, and discuss what you think are some of its effects. Develop each effect in a paragraph.
2. Here is a list of causes. Write about one effect of each. Develop at least one causal chain.
   Teenager watching MTV
   Landfill overflowing
   Apple trees blossoming
   Car breaking down in the fast lane during rush hour

❦ Stephen King ❦

Stephen King was born in Portland, Maine, in 1947 and graduated from the University of Maine in 1970. Before finding enormous success with his writing, King worked in a knitting mill and as a janitor, laundry worker, and high school English teacher. Since then, he has become, arguably, the world's most successful writer of horror fiction. He has published short story collections, screenplays, and nearly thirty novels that have sold over 20 million copies. Many of those novels—including Carrie, The Shining *, and* Pet Sematary*—have been made into movies. His short story "The Body," from the collection* Night Shift, *was produced as the film* Stand By Me. *His works include* Apt Pupil: A Novella in Different Seasons *and* Bag of Bones, *both published in 1998. King's original television miniseries,* Storm of the Century, *was broadcast in 1999. King also plays rhythm guitar for the Rock Bottom Remainders, a rock band composed entirely of professional writers. Amy Tan (see pp. 234–240) is a Remainderette—she sings backup vocals—with the same band.*

Why We Crave Horror Movies

In this essay, first published in Playboy *magazine, Stephen King speculates on the reasons why horror films have been so enormously popular over the years. He concludes that they not only entertain in a ghoulish way, but also serve an important psychological and social purpose.*

While you read, weigh the validity of King's conclusions against your own firsthand experience of horror films.

I think that we're all mentally ill; those of us outside the asylums only hide it a little better—and maybe not all that much better, after all. We've all known people who talk to themselves, people who sometimes squinch their faces into horrible grimaces when they believe no one is watching, people who have some hysterical fear—of snakes, the dark, the tight place, the long drop . . . and, of course, those final worms and grubs that are waiting so patiently underground.

When we pay our four or five bucks and seat ourselves at   2
tenth-row center in a theater showing a horror movie, we are daring the nightmare.

Why? Some of the reasons are simple and obvious. To show   3
that we can, that we are not afraid, that we can ride this roller
coaster. Which is not to say that a really good horror movie may
not surprise a scream out of us at some point, the way we may
scream when the roller coaster twists through a complete 360 or
plows through a lake at the bottom of the drop. And horror
movies, like roller coasters, have always been the special province
of the young; by the time one turns 40 or 50, one's appetite for
double twists or 360-degree loops may be considerably depleted.

We also go to re-establish our feelings of essential normality;   4
the horror movie is innately conservative, even reactionary. Freda
Jackson as the horrible melting woman in *Die, Monster, Die!* confirms for us that no matter how far we may be removed from the
beauty of a Robert Redford or a Diana Ross, we are still light-years
from true ugliness.

And we go to have fun.   5

Ah, but this is where the ground starts to slope away, isn't it?   6
Because this is a very peculiar sort of fun, indeed. The fun comes
from seeing others menaced—sometimes killed. One critic has
suggested that if pro football has become the voyeur's version of
combat, then the horror film has become the modern version of
the public lynching.

It is true that the mythic, "fairy-tale" horror film intends to   7
take away the shades of gray. . . . It urges us to put away our more
civilized and adult penchant for analysis and to become children
again, seeing things in pure blacks and whites. It may be that horror movies provide psychic relief on this level because this invitation to lapse into simplicity, irrationality and even outright
madness is extended so rarely. We are told we may allow our
emotions a free rein . . . or no rein at all.

If we are all insane, then sanity becomes a matter of degree. If   8
your insanity leads you to carve up women like Jack the Ripper or
the Cleveland Torso Murderer, we clap you away in the funny farm
(but neither of those two amateur-night surgeons was ever caught,

heh-heh-heh); if, on the other hand, your insanity leads you only to talk to yourself when you're under stress or to pick your nose on your morning bus, then you are left alone to go about your business . . . though it is doubtful that you will ever be invited to the best parties.

The potential lyncher is in almost all of us (excluding saints, past and present; but then, most saints have been crazy in their own ways), and every now and then, he has to be let loose to scream and roll around in the grass. Our emotions and our fears form their own body, and we recognize that it demands its own exercise to maintain proper muscle tone. Certain of these emotional muscles are accepted—even exalted—in civilized society; they are, of course, the emotions that tend to maintain the status quo of civilization itself. Love, friendship, loyalty, kindness—these are all the emotions that we applaud, emotions that have been immortalized in the couplets of Hallmark cards and in the verses (I don't dare call it poetry) of Leonard Nimoy.

When we exhibit these emotions, society showers us with positive reinforcement; we learn this even before we get out of diapers. When, as children, we hug our rotten little puke of a sister and give her a kiss, all the aunts and uncles smile and twit and cry, "Isn't he the sweetest little thing?" Such coveted treats as chocolate-covered graham crackers often follow. But if we deliberately slam the rotten little puke of a sister's fingers in the door, sanctions follow—angry remonstrance from parents, aunts and uncles; instead of a chocolate-covered graham cracker, a spanking.

But anticivilization emotions don't go away, and they demand periodic exercise. We have such "sick" jokes as, "What's the difference between a truckload of bowling balls and a truckload of dead babies?" (You can't unload a truckload of bowling balls with a pitchfork . . . a joke, by the way, that I heard originally from a ten-year-old.) Such a joke may surprise a laugh or a grin out of us even as we recoil, a possibility that confirms the thesis: If we share a brotherhood of man, then we also share an insanity of man. None of which is intended as a defense of either the sick joke or insanity but merely as an explanation of why the best horror films, like the best fairy tales, manage to be reactionary, anarchistic, and revolutionary all at the same time.

The mythic horror movie, like the sick joke, has a dirty job to   12
do. It deliberately appeals to all that is worst in us. It is morbidity
unchained, our most base instincts let free, our nastiest fantasies realized . . . and it all happens, fittingly enough, in the dark. For those
reasons, good liberals often shy away from horror films. For myself,
I like to see the most aggressive of them—*Dawn of the Dead*, for instance—as lifting a trap door in the civilized forebrain and throwing
a basket of raw meat to the hungry alligators swimming around in
that subterranean river beneath.

Why bother? Because it keeps them from getting out, man. It   13
keeps them down there and me up here. It was Lennon and
McCartney who said that all you need is love, and I would agree
with that.

As long as you keep the gators fed.   14

Meaning and Purpose

1. What is King's thesis? Is it explicitly stated or is it implied?
2. Is King serious when he claims in the opening sentence that
    "we're all mentally ill"? What exactly does he mean by this?
    Explain.
3. In paragraph 4 King asserts that horror movies are "innately con-
    servative, even reactionary," and in paragraph 11 he claims them
    to be "reactionary, anarchistic, and revolutionary all at the same
    time." Explain what he means by these claims.
4. Why, according to King, are horror movies both a psychological
    and a social good?

Strategy

1. King grabs our attention with the opening sentence. Explain how
    the meaning of that sentence relates to the rest of the essay.
2. What does King claim are the immediate causes of the popular-
    ity of horror films? What is the ultimate cause? (See pp.
    340–343.)

3. Explain how King organizes his essay around the immediate and ultimate causes for the popularity of horror films. How much time and space does he spend on each? What effect does this organizational pattern have on the reader?
4. Why does King change from the first person singular (I) in the first sentence to the first person plural (we) in the second?
5. What evidence does King offer to support his claims about the reasons for the popularity of horror movies?

Style

1. Reread the essay, paying close attention to King's use of concrete language and metaphor (see Glossary). Point out passages in which King uses these devices and comment on their effectiveness. Try translating at least two of these passages into more common usage. Which version is more lively?
2. What is King's tone (see Glossary) in the essay? How does he establish that tone? Explain.
3. Closely examine the analogy (see Glossary) King uses in paragraph 3. What idea does it explain, and how effectively does it clarify that idea?
4. If necessary, look the following words up in a dictionary: *grimaces, hysterical* (paragraph 1); *province* (3); *voyeur* (6); *penchant, psychic* (7); *exalted* (9); *twit, sanctions, remonstrance* (10); *recoil, anarchistic* (11); *morbidity, subterranean* (12).

Writing Tasks

1. Write an essay in which you explain the reasons (causes) that you attend horror films regularly, attend them only occasionally, or never attend them at all. Use King's essay as a model, in that you organize your essay so that you spend more time on ultimate causes and relatively less time on immediate causes.
2. Write an essay that examines the validity or the invalidity of

King's claims in "Why We Crave Horror Movies." Make sure that you include as much supportive evidence as you can to prove your thesis.

❧ Neal Gabler ❧

Neal Gabler, author of a history of Hollywood (An Empire of Their Own: How the Jews Invented Hollywood), a biography of Walter Winchell (Winchell: Gossip, Power and the Culture of Celebrity), and a study of U.S. popular culture (Life the Movie: How Entertainment Conquered Reality), believes that the evolution of popular theater, with its reliance on technology, has permeated our culture to the extent that entertainment is "the primary value of American life" and we now view life itself as entertainment.

How Urban Myths Reveal Society's Fears

As you read this essay, first published in the Los Angeles Times *in 1995, notice how Gabler compares urban myths with ancient myths, the stuff of folklore, to show how urban myths affect our ways of thinking.*

The story goes like this: During dinner at an opulent wedding reception, the groom rises from the head table and shushes the crowd. Everyone naturally assumes he is about to toast his bride and thank his guests. Instead, he solemnly announces that there has been a change of plan. He and his bride will be taking separate honeymoons and, when they return, the marriage will be annulled. The reason for this sudden turn of events, he says, is taped to the bottom of everyone's plate. The stunned guests quickly flip their dinnerware to discover a photo—of the bride *in flagrante* with the best man. 1

At least that is the story that has been recently making the rounds up and down the Eastern seaboard and as far west as Chicago. Did this really happen? A Washington Post reporter who tracked the story was told by one source that it happened at a New Hampshire hotel. But then another source swears it happened in 2

361

Medford, Mass. Then again another suggests a banquet hall outside Schenectady, N.Y. Meanwhile, a sophisticated couple in
Manhattan has heard it happened at the Pierre.

In short, the whole thing appears to be another urban myth,   3
one of those weird tales that periodically catch the public imagination. Alligators swarming the sewers after people have flushed
the baby reptiles down the toilet. The baby-sitter who gets threatening phone calls that turn out to be coming from inside the
house. The woman who turns out to have a nest of black-widow
spiders in her beehive hairdo. The man who falls asleep and awak-
ens to find his kidney has been removed. The rat that gets deep-
fried and served by a fast-foot outlet. Or, in a variation, the mouse
that has somehow drowned in a closed Coca-Cola bottle.

These tales are preposterous, but in a mass society like ours,   4
where stories are usually manufactured by Hollywood, they just
may be the most genuine form of folklore we have. Like traditional folklore, they are narratives crafted by the collective consciousness. Like traditional folklore, they give expression to the
national mind. And like traditional folklore, they blend the fantastic with the routine, if only to demonstrate, in the words of
University of Utah folklorist Jan Harold Brunvand, the nation's
leading expert on urban legends, "that the prosaic contemporary
scene is capable of producing shocking or amazing occurrences."

Shocking and amazing, yes. But in these stories, anything can   5
happen not because the world is a magical place rich with wonder—as in folk tales of yore—but because our world is so utterly
terrifying. Here, nothing is reliable and no laws of morality gov-
ern. The alligators in the sewers presents an image of an urban hell
inhabited by beasts—an image that might have come directly
from Hades and the River Styx in Greek mythology. The baby-
sitter and the man upstairs exploits fears that we are not even safe
in our own homes these days. The spider in the hairdo says that
even on our own persons, dangers lurk. The man who loses his
kidney plays to our fears of the night and the real bogymen who
prowl them. The mouse in the soda warns us of the perils of an
impersonal mass-production society.

As for the wedding-reception tale, which one hacker on the   6
Internet has dubbed "Wedding Revenge," it may address the
greatest terror of all: that love and commitment are chimerical and
even friendship is meaningless. These are timeless issues, but the
sudden promulgation of the tale suggests its special relevance in
the age of AIDS, when commitment means even more than it used
to, and in the age of feminism, when some men are feeling increasingly threatened by women's freedom. Thus, the groom not
only suffers betrayal and humiliation; his plight carries the hint of
danger and emasculation, too. Surely, a legend for our time.

Of course, folklore and fairy tales have long subsisted on ter-   7
ror, and even the treacly cartoons of Walt Disney are actually,
when you parse them, dark and complex expressions of fear—
from Snow White racing through the treacherous forest to
Pinnochio gobbled by the whale to Dumbo being separated from
his mother. But these crystallize the fears of childhood, the fears
one must overcome to make the difficult transition to adulthood.
Thus, the haunted forest of the fairy tales is a trope for haunted
adolescence; the witch or crone, a trope for the spent generation
one must vanquish to claim one's place in the world, and the
prince who comes to the rescue, a trope for the adult responsibilities that the heroine must now assume.

Though urban legends frequently originate with college stu-   8
dents about to enter the real world, they are different from traditional fairy tales because their terrors are not really obstacles on
the road to understanding, and they are different from folklore
because they cannot even be interpreted as cautionary. In urban
legends, obstacles aren't overcome, perhaps can't be overcome,
and there is nothing we can do differently to avoid the consequences. The woman, not knowing any better, eats the fried rat.
The baby-sitter is terrorized by the stranger hiding in the house.
The black widow bites the woman with the beehive hairdo. The
alligators prowl the sewers. The marriage in Wedding Revenge
breaks up.

It is not just our fears, then, that these stories exploit. Like so   9
much else in modern life—tabloids, exploitalk programs, real-life

crime best-sellers—urban legends testify to an overwhelming condition of fear and to a sense of our own impotence within it. That is why there is no accommodation in these stories, no lesson or wisdom imparted. What there is, is the stark impression that our world is anomic. We live in a haunted forest of skyscrapers or of suburban lawns and ranch houses, but there is no one to exorcise the evil and no prince to break the spell.

Given the pressures of modern life, it isn't surprising that we have created myths to express our malaise. But what is surprising is how many people seem committed to these myths. The Post reporter found people insisting they personally knew someone who had attended the doomed wedding reception. Others went further: They maintained they had actually attended the reception—though no such reception ever took place. Yet even those who didn't claim to have been personally involved seemed to feel duty bound to assert the tale's plausibility.   10

Why this insistence? Perhaps the short answer is that people want to believe in a cosmology of dysfunction because it is the best way of explaining the inexplicable in our lives. A world in which alligators roam sewers and wedding receptions end in shock is at once terrifying and soothing—terrifying because these things happen, soothing because we are absolved of any responsibility for them. It is just the way it is.   11

But there may be an additional reason why some people seem so willing to suspend their disbelief in the face of logic. This one has less to do with the content of these tales than with their creation. However they start, urban legends rapidly enter a national conversation in which they are embellished, heightened, reconfigured. Everyone can participate—from the people who spread the tale on talk radio to the people who discuss it on the Internet to the people who tell it to their neighbors. In effect, these legends are the product of a giant campfire around which we trade tales of terror.   12

If this makes each of us a co-creator of the tales, it also provides us with a certain pride of authorship. Like all authors, we don't want to see the spell of our creation broken—especially when we have formed a little community around it. It doesn't   13 matter whether these tales are true or not. What matters is that they plausibly reflect our world, that they have been generated from the grass roots and that we can pass them along.

In a way, then, these tales of powerlessness ultimately assert a   14
kind of authority. Urban legends permit us to become our own Stephen Kings, terrorizing ourselves to confirm one of the few powers we still possess: the power to tell stories about our world.

Meaning and Purpose

1. "The story goes like this" seems an unusually friendly way to begin an essay. Why do you suppose Gabler opens the essay this way?
2. Reread paragraphs 7 and 8. What is one important difference between how traditional tales affected their audiences and how urban myths affect their audiences?
3. Reread paragraphs 9 and 10. How can urban myths exploit our fears, according to Gable?
4. What do Walt Disney cartoons, discussed in paragraph 7, have in common with urban myths?
5. Which one of the urban myths that Gabler discusses is, in your opinion, the most convincing? Why?

Strategy

1. How can any urban myth be said to be true? Why does Gabler say that we believe in them without checking their authenticity?
2. What strategies does Gabler use to show that urban myths do in fact cause us to fear parts of our own lives?
3. Using evidence from Gabler's essay, note why we need some kind of myths, be they folklore or urban myths.
4. What main strategy in paragraph 9 does Gabler employ to persuade the reader that myths "exploit" our fears?
5. How does Gabler imply that we can, in fact, overcome our fears?

Style

1. What does the word *opulent* mean, as it is used in the first sentence of this essay? Suggest an appropriate synonym.
2. Define the phrase *in flagrante*, as it is used in the first paragraph. Why is this phrase in italics?
3. What are two current examples of "exploitalk programs" (paragraph 9) on television?
4. Why does Gabler talk about the fairy tales of our youth?
5. Of the several definitions of *terror* in a reliable college dictionary, which definition of the word *terror* is the most appropriate definition in describing urban myths? Suggest an appropriate synonym.

Writing Tasks

1. We all experience what Gabler calls "the pressures of modern life" (paragraph 10). In a cause-and-effect essay, discuss two personal pressures that you now face and the effects of those personal pressures on your academic life.
2. Like all first-year college students, you had fears—fears about failing, fears about making new friends, fears about finding your way around campus, and so forth. Write an essay in which you discuss two of those fears, being sure that you discuss them from a personal point of view, and tell your audience how those fears affected you during your first few weeks of college life.

❦ Leonce Gaiter ❦

Leonce Gaiter lives in Los Angeles and writes frequently about social issues.

The Revolt of the Black Bourgeoisie

In this essay, first published in The New York Times Magazine, Leonce Gaiter describes how he and other African-Americans have been affected by the current stereotype of blacks in the media. He then traces how that stereotype has been enforced and perpetuated.

As you read, notice how Gaiter uses specific examples to support his contentions.

At a television network where I once worked, one of my 1
bosses told me I almost didn't get hired because his superior had
"reservations" about me. The job had been offered under the network's Minority Advancement Program. I applied for the position
because I knew I was exceptionally qualified. I would have applied for the position regardless of how it was advertised.

After my interview, the head of the department told my boss I 2
wasn't really what he had in mind for a Minority Advancement
Program job. To the department head, hiring a minority applicant
meant hiring someone unqualified. He wanted to hire some semi-
literate, hoop-shooting former prison inmate. That, in his view,
was a "real" black person. That was someone worthy of the
program.

I had previously been confronted by questions of black au- 3
thenticity. At Harvard, where I graduated in 1980, a white classmate once said to me, "Oh, you're not really a black person." I
asked her to explain. She could not. She had known few black
people before college, but a lifetime of seeing black people depicted in the American media had taught her that real black people talked a certain way and were raised in certain places. In her

world, black people did not attend elite colleges. They could not stand as her intellectual equals or superiors. Any African-American who shared her knowledge of Austen and Balzac—while having to explain to her who Douglass and Du Bois were—had to be *willed* away for her to salvage her sense of superiority as a white person. Hence the accusation that I was "not really black."

But worse than the white majority harboring a one-dimensional vision of blackness are the many blacks who embrace this stereotype as our true nature. At the junior high school I attended in the mostly white Washington suburb of Silver Spring, Md., a black girl once stopped me in the hallway and asked belligerently, "How come you talk so proper?" Astonished, I could only reply, "It's proper*ly*," and walk on. This girl was asking why I spoke without the so-called black accent pervasive in the lower socioeconomic strata of black society, where exposure to mainstream society is limited. This girl was asking, Why wasn't I impoverished and alienated? In her world view, a black male like me couldn't exist.

Within the past year, however, there have been signs that blacks are openly beginning to acknowledge the complex nature of our culture. Cornel West, a professor of religion and the director of Afro-American Studies at Princeton University, discusses the growing gulf between the black underclass and the rest of black society in his book "Race Matters"; black voices have finally been raised against the violence, misogyny and vulgarity marketed to black youth in the form of gangsta rap; Ellis Cose's book "The Rage of a Privileged Class," which concentrates on the problems of middle- and upper-income blacks, was excerpted as part of a Newsweek magazine cover story; Bill Cosby has become a vocal crusader against the insulting depiction of African-Americans in "hip-hop generation" TV shows.

Yes, there are the beginnings of a new candor about our culture, but the question remains, How did one segment of the African-American community come to represent the whole? First, black society itself placed emphasis on that lower caste. This made sense because historically that's where the vast majority of us were placed; it's where American society and its laws were designed to keep us. Yet although doors have opened to us over the past 20 years, it is still commonplace for black leaders to insist on our community's uniform need for social welfare programs, inner-city services, job skills training, etc. Through such calls, what has passed for a black political agenda has been furthered only superficially; while affirmative action measures have forced an otherwise unwilling majority to open some doors for the black middle class, social welfare and Great Society style programs aimed at the black lower class have shown few positive results.

According to 1990 census figures, between 1970 and 1990 the number of black families with incomes under $15,000 rose from 34.6 percent of the black population to 37 percent, while the number of black families with incomes of $35,000 to $50,000 rose from 13.9 percent to 15 percent of the population, and those with incomes of more than $50,000 rose from 9.9 percent to 14.5 percent of the black population. 7

Another reason the myth of an all-encompassing black underclass survives—despite the higher number of upper-income black families—is that it fits with a prevalent form of white liberalism, which is just as informed by racism as white conservatism. Since the early 70's, good guilt-liberal journalists and others warmed to the picture of black downtrodden masses in need of their help. Through the agency of good white people, blacks would rise. This image of African-Americans maintained the lifeline of white superiority that whites in this culture cling to, and therefore this image of blacks stuck. A strange tango was begun. Blacks seeking advancement opportunities allied themselves with whites eager to "help" them. However, those whites continued to see blacks as inferiors, victims, cases, and not as equals, individuals or, heaven forbid, competitors. 8

It was hammered into the African-American psyche by media-appointed black leaders and the white media that it was essential to our political progress to stay or seem to stay economically and socially deprived. To be recognized and recognize oneself as middle or upper class was to threaten the political progress of 9

black people. That girl who asked why I spoke so "proper" was ac-
cusing me of political sins—of thwarting the progress of our race.

Despite progress toward a more balanced picture of black   10
America, the image of black society as an underclass remains
strong. Look at local news coverage of the trial of Damian Williams
and Henry Watson, charged with beating the white truck driver
Reginald Denny during the 1992 South-Central L.A. riots. The
press showed us an African-print-wearing cadre of Williams and
Watson supporters trailing Edi M. O. Faal, Williams's defense attorney, like a Greek chorus. This chorus made a point of standing
in the camera's range. They presented themselves as the voice of
South-Central L.A., the voice of the oppressed, the voice of the
downtrodden, the voice of the city's black people.

To anyone watching TV coverage of the trial, all blacks agreed   11
with Faal's contention that his clients were prosecuted so aggressively because they are black. Period. Reporters made no effort to
show opposing black viewpoints. (In fact, the media portrait of
the Los Angeles riot as blacks vs. whites and Koreans was a mis-
representation. According to the Rand Corporation, a research institute in Santa Monica, blacks made up 36 percent of those
arrested during the riot; Latinos made up 51 percent.) The black
bourgeoisie and intelligentsia remained largely silent. We had too
long believed that to express disagreement with the "official line"
was to be a traitor.

TV networks and cable companies gain media raves for pro-   12
grams like "Laurel Avenue," an HBO melodrama about a working-
class black family lauded for its realism, a real black family
complete with drug dealers, drug users, gun toters and basketball
players. It is akin to the media presenting "Valley of the Dolls" as
a realistic portrayal of the ways of white women.

The Fox network offers a differing but equally misleading   13
portrait of black Americans, with "Martin." While blue humor has
long been a staple of black audiences, it was relegated to clubs and
records for *mature* black audiences. It was not peddled to kids or
to the masses.

Now the blue humor tradition is piped to principally white   14
audiences. If TV was as black as it is white—if there was a fair

share of black love stories, black dramas, black detective heroes—these blue humor images would not be a problem. Right now, however, they stand as images to which whites can condescend.

Imagine being told by your peers, the records you hear, the programs you watch, the "leaders" you see on TV, classmates, prospective employers—imagine being told by virtually everyone that in order to be your true self you must be ignorant and poor, or at least seem so.

Blacks must now see to it that our children face no such burden. We must see to it that the white majority, along with vocal minorities within the black community (generally those with a self-serving political agenda), do not perpetuate the notion that African-Americans are invariably doomed to the underclass.

African-Americans are moving toward seeing ourselves—and demanding that others see us—as individuals, not as shards of a degraded monolith. The American ideal places primacy on the rights of the individual, yet historically African-Americans have been denied those rights. We blacks can effectively demand those rights, effectively demand justice only when each of us sees him or herself as an individual with the right to any of the opinions, idiosyncrasies and talents accorded any other American.

Meaning and Purpose

1. In the first two paragraphs, Gaiter describes applying for a job for which he was exceptionally qualified. Why was he nearly turned down?
2. Gaiter's "black authenticity" is questioned by a black girl in paragraph 4. Why?
3. What segments of American society, according to Gaiter, are guilty of stereotyping African-Americans?
4. What are the immediate causes of black stereotyping? The ultimate causes?
5. How do the TV programs that Gaiter cites promote the black stereotype?

6. How, according to Gaiter, can African-Americans effectively demand that they be recognized as individuals?

Strategy

1. What is the function of the first four paragraphs? What, precisely, is the point of the examples?
2. Describe the function of paragraph 5. How, specifically, does it carry the reader from one section of the essay to the next?
3. What point do the statistics in paragraph 7 support? How effective are these statistics?
4. Describe the function of paragraph 15.

Style

1. What is "blue humor" (paragraph 13)? What is the derivation of the term?
2. If necessary, look the following words up in a dictionary: *elite, salvage* (3); *pervasive, strata* (4); *misogyny, excerpted* (5); *candor* (6); *psyche, thwarting* (9); *cadre* (10); *bourgeoisie, intelligentsia* (11); *lauded* (12); *staple, relegated* (13); *condescend* (14); *peers, prospective* (15); *invariably* (16); *shards, degraded, monolith, primacy, idiosyncracies* (17).

Writing Tasks

1. Construct an essay in which you either attack or defend Gaiter's contentions about the deleterious effects of media stereotyping. But don't feel confined to the stereotyping of African-Americans. Use the stereotype with which you are most familiar, and make sure to support your points with specifics.
2. Write an essay in which you defend Gaiter's contentions by

citing further examples from the media that enforce his point of view. Or attack his position by citing contrary examples. In either case, make sure you refer to the Gaiter essay in your argument.

William Severini Kowinski

William Kowinski grew up in Pennsylvania and attended Knox College in Illinois. He spent one semester at the University of Iowa studying fiction and poetry writing. His writing career, however, has been in nonfiction. To research his book The Malling of America, *Kowinski visited malls all over both the United States and Canada. He has been a writer and editor for the* Boston Phoenix *and for* Newsworks *of Washington, D.C., and his articles have appeared in* Esquire, The New York Times, *and* The New York Times Magazine.

Kids in the Mall
Growing Up Controlled

Many American children grow up almost entirely in the controlled environments of home, school, and "the mall." What are the effects, Kowinski asks, of "growing up controlled"? The essay is from his 1985 book The Malling of America: An Inside Look at the Great Consumer Paradise.

As you read Kowinski's essay, be alert to how he moves from causes to effects. Pay particular attention to how he passes judgments on some of his effects.

Butch heaved himself up and loomed over the group. "Like it was different for me," he piped. "My folks used to drop me off at the shopping mall every morning and leave me all day. It was like a big free baby-sitter, you know? One night they never came back for me. Maybe they moved away. Maybe there's some kind of a Bureau of Missing Parents I could check with."

—Richard Peck
Secrets of the Shopping Mall,
a novel for teenagers

From his sister at Swarthmore, I'd heard about a kid in Florida

374

whose mother picked him up after school every day, drove him   2
straight to the mall, and left him there until it closed—all at his insistence. I'd heard about a boy in Washington who, when his family moved from one suburb to another, pedaled his bicycle five
miles every day to get back to his old mall, where he once
belonged.

These stories aren't unusual. The mall is a common experience for the majority of American youth; they have probably been   3
going there all their lives. Some ran within their first large open
space, saw their first fountain, bought their first toy, and read their
first book in a mall. They may have smoked their first cigarette or
first joint or turned them down, had their first kiss or lost their
virginity in the mall parking lot. Teenagers in America now spend
more time in the mall than anywhere else but home and school.
Mostly it is their choice, but some of that mall time is put in as the
result of two-paycheck and single-parent households, and the
lack of other viable alternatives. But are these kids being harmed
by the mall?

I wondered first of all what difference it makes for adolescents
to experience so many important moments in the mall. They are,   4
after all, at play in the fields of its little world and they learn its
ways; they adapt to it and make it adapt to them. It's here that
these kids get their street sense, only it's mall sense. They are
learning the ways of a large-scale artificial environment: its subtleties and flexibilities, its particular pleasures and resonances,
and the attitudes it fosters.

The presence of so many teenagers for so much time was not
something mall developers planned on. In fact, it came as a big   5
surprise. But kids became a fact of mall life very early, and the
International Council of Shopping Centers found it necessary to
commission a study, which they published along with a guide to
mall managers on how to handle the teenage incursion.

The study found that "teenagers in suburban centers are
bored and come to the shopping centers mainly as a place to go.   6
Teenagers in suburban centers spent more time fighting, drinking,
littering and walking than did their urban counterparts, but presented fewer overall problems." The report observed that "adoles-

cents congregated in groups of two to four and predominantly at locations selected by them rather than management." This probably had something to do with the decision to install game arcades, which allow management to channel these restless adolescents into naturally contained areas away from major traffic points of adult shoppers.

The guide concluded that mall management should tolerate and even encourage the teenage presence because, in the words of   7
the report, "The vast majority support the same set of values as does shopping center management." *The same set of values* means simply that mall kids are already preprogrammed to be consumers and that the mall can put the finishing touches to them as hardcore, lifelong shoppers just like everybody else. That, after all, is what the mall is about. So it shouldn't be surprising that in spending a lot of time there, adolescents find little that challenges the assumption that the goal of life is to make money and buy products, or that just about everything else in life is to be used to serve those ends.

Growing up in a high-consumption society already adds inestimable pressure to kids' lives. Clothes consciousness has invaded   8
the grade schools, and popularity is linked with having the best, newest clothes in the currently acceptable style. Even what they read has been affected. "Miss [Nancy] Drew wasn't obsessed with her wardrobe," noted *The Wall Street Journal*, "but today the mystery in teen fiction for girls is what outfit the heroine will wear next." Shopping has become a survival skill and there is certainly no better place to learn it than the mall, where its importance is powerfully reinforced and certainly never questioned.

The mall as a university of suburban materialism, where Valley Girls and Boys from coast to coast are educated in con-   9
sumption, has its other lessons in this era of change in family life and sexual mores and their economic and social ramifications. The plethora of products in the mall, plus the pressure on teens to buy them, may contribute to the phenomenon that psychologist David Elkind calls "the hurried child": kids who are exposed to too much of the adult world too quickly, and must respond with a sophistication that belies their still-tender emotional develop-

ment. Certainly the adult products marketed for children—form-fitting designer jeans, sexy tops for preteen girls—add to the social pressure to look like an adult, along with the home-grown need to understand adult finances (why mothers must work) and adult emotions (when parents divorce).

Kids spend so much time at the mall partly because their parents allow it and even encourage it. The mall is safe, it doesn't   10
seem to harbor any unsavory activities, and there is adult supervision; it is, after all, a controlled environment. So the temptation, especially for working parents, is to let the mall be their babysitter. At least the kids aren't watching TV. But the mall's role as a surrogate mother may be more extensive and more profound.

Karen Lansky, a writer living in Los Angeles, has looked into the subject and she told me some of her conclusions about the ef-   11
fects on its teenaged denizens of the mall's controlled and controlling environment. "Structure is the dominant idea, since true 'mall rats' lack just that in their home lives," she said, "and adolescents about to make the big leap into growing up crave more structure than our modern society cares to acknowledge." Karen pointed out some of the elements malls supply that kids used to get from their families, like warmth (Strawberry Shortcake dolls and similar cute and cuddly merchandise), old-fashioned mothering ("We do it all for you," the fast-food slogan), and even home cooking (the "homemade" treats at the food court).

The problem in all this, as Karen Lansky sees it, is that while families nurture children by encouraging growth through the as-   12
sumption of responsibility and then by letting them rest in the bosom of the family from the rigors of growing up, the mall as a structural mother encourages passivity and consumption, as long as the kid doesn't make trouble. Therefore all they learn about becoming adults is how to act and how to consume.

Kids are in the mall not only in the passive role of shoppers—they also work there, especially as fast-food outlets infiltrate the   13
mall's enclosure. There they learn how to hold a job and take responsibility, but still within the same value context. When *CBS Reports* went to Oak Park Mall in suburban Kansas City, Kansas, to tape part of their hour-long consideration of malls, "After the

Dream Comes True," they interviewed a teenaged girl who worked in a fast-food outlet there. In a sequence that didn't make the final program, she described the major goal of her present life, which was to perfect the curl on top of the ice-cream cones that were her store's specialty. If she could do that, she would be moved from the lowly soft-drink dispenser to the more prestigious ice-cream division, the curl on top of the status ladder at her restaurant. These are the achievements that are important at the mall.

Other benefits of such jobs may also be overrated, according to Laurence D. Steinberg of the University of California at Irvine's social ecology department, who did a study on teenage employment. Their jobs, he found, are generally simple, mindlessly repetitive and boring. They don't really learn anything, and the jobs don't head anywhere. Teenagers also work primarily with other teenagers; even their supervisors are often just a little older than they are. "Kids need to spend time with adults," Steinberg told me. "Although they get benefits from peer relationships, without parents and other adults it's a one-sided socialization. They hang out with each other, have age-segregated jobs, and watch TV." 14

Perhaps much of this is not so terrible or even so terribly different. Now that they have so much more to contend with in their lives, adolescents probably need more time to spend with other adolescents without adult impositions, just to sort things out. Though it is more concentrated in the mall (and therefore perhaps a clearer target), the value system there is really the dominant one of the whole society. Attitudes about curiosity, initiative, self-expression, empathy, and disinterested learning aren't necessarily made in the mall; they are mirrored there, perhaps a bit more intensely—as through a glass brightly. 15

Besides, the mall is not without its educational opportunities. There are bookstores, where there is at least a short shelf of classics at great prices, and other books from which it is possible to learn more than how to do sit-ups. There are tools, from hammers to VCRs, and products, from clothes to records, that can help the young find and express themselves. There are older people with 16 stories, and places to be alone or to talk one-on-one with a kindred spirit. And there is always the passing show.

The mall itself may very well be an education about the future. I was struck with the realization, as early as my first forays into Greengate, that the mall is only one of a number of enclosed and controlled environments that are part of the lives of today's young. The mall is just an extension, say, of those large suburban schools—only there's Karmelkorn instead of chem lab, the ice rink instead of the gym: It's high school without the impertinence of classes. 17

Growing up, moving from home to school to the mall—from enclosure to enclosure, transported in cars—is a curiously continuous process, without much in the way of contrast or contact with unenclosed reality. Places must tend to blur into one another. But whatever differences and dangers there are in this, the skills these adolescents are learning may turn out to be useful in their later lives. For we seem to be moving inexorably into an age of pre-planned and regulated environments, and this is the world they will inherit. 18

Still, it might be better if they had more of a choice. One teenaged girl confessed to *CBS Reports* that she sometimes felt she was missing something by hanging out at the mall so much. "But I'm here," she said, "and this is what I have." 19

Meaning and Purpose

1. What has been your experience in malls? What is your response to Kowinski's essay? Do you agree or disagree with him? Do you identify with the situations he describes?
2. What primary questions does the author attempt to answer in the essay? What is the thesis and where is it stated?
3. What negative effects does growing up in the mall have on children? Are there any positive effects?
4. Whom is Kowinski addressing in this essay? Who should hear his message?

5. Can a careful reading of the essay establish the author's values?
    What are they? Where are these attitudes evident?

Strategy

1. Paragraphs 2–4 serve as the essay's introduction. How does each
    function independently? How do they fit together to form the
    larger unit?
2. Does Kowinski talk about immediate or ultimate causes and ef-
    fects in paragraph 9? Explain.
3. Compare paragraphs 9 and 14. In paragraph 9, Kowinski de-
    scribes "the hurried child" syndrome, the negative effect on a
    child who is too quickly exposed to the adult world and must re-
    spond with a sophistication that is still beyond him or her. In
    paragraph 14, discussing how teenagers who work in malls work
    mostly with other teenagers, Kowinski cites an authority who
    claims that kids need more time in their work with adults. Do
    you see a contradiction here?
4. A related cause-and-effect structure is visible in paragraphs
    10–12. What is it and how does it work?
5. Study the structure of paragraph 18. How does it contribute to
    the essayist's main purpose of showing how stultifying and con-
    trolling malls are for teenagers?

Style

1. Comment on the effects of the final sentence in paragraph 13 on
    the rest of the paragraph. What does it say about the mall expe-
    rience as a whole?
2. What is Kowinski's attitude toward his subject? Where is this at-
    titude manifest?
3. If necessary, look up the meanings of these words: *resonances*
    (paragraph 4); *incursion* (5); *plethora* (9); *denizens* (11); *imperti-
    nence* (17); *inexorably* (18).

Writing Tasks

1. Kowinski takes a rather dim view of what happens to kids when they "grow up" in a mall. Write an essay in which you either show that mall experiences do not have such dire consequences or agree with Kowinski. Either way, draw from your own experience or that of those you know. Be sure to discuss immediate and ultimate causes and effects, either alternately in the same paragraphs or in separate paragraphs.

2. Think of a place, other than a mall, where you spent a lot of time during your teenage years—a hangout of some sort. What do you think some of the immediate and ultimate effects were and are from your having spent time there? Answer this question in a short essay. Be specific.

🍒 *Responding to Photographs* 🍒
Cause and Effect

A Woman

Noted author Sharon Curtin has criticized American attitudes toward those who are growing old. In the following quotation she expresses her own feeling about aging and projects those feelings to others:

> I am afraid to grow old—we're all afraid. In fact, the fear of growing old is so great that every aged person is an insult and a threat to society. They remind us of our own death, that our body won't always remain smooth and responsive, but will someday betray us by aging, wrinkling, faltering, failing. The ideal way to age would be to grow slowly invisible, gradually disappearing, without causing worry or discomfort to the young. In some ways that does happen. Sitting in a small park across from a nursing home one day, I noticed that the young mothers and their children gathered on one side, and the old people from the home on the other. Whenever a youngster would run over to the "wrong" side,

chasing a ball or just trying to cover all the available space, the old people would lean forward and smile. But before any communication could be established, the mother would come over, murmuring embarrassed apologies, and take her child to the "young" side.

Curtin's reflections on aging find a haunting expression in "A Woman," which features an older woman with a photograph of herself when young. Drawing on Curtin's observations and elements in the photograph, compose an essay with cause and/or effect as the dominant development pattern. Before starting your project, review the material at the beginning of the chapter; then select one of the following writing tasks as the basis for your essay.

1. Begin with the assertion that aging is the subject of "A Woman." Review Curtin's reflection on aging, and also study the photograph, allowing its imagery to work on your imagination. Identify an emotion the photograph creates. Then relate the reasons the photograph has this effect.

2. Imagine that you are a psychologist who shares Curtin's belief about growing old in our society. The young woman in "A Woman" is your client. She is beautiful, and because of her beauty, she has a deep fear of growing old. She asks you what you believe the physical and social effects of growing old will be for her. You decide to be blunt and state your feelings as directly as possible, but you decide to do so in writing. First you describe her current beauty and relate the effects of her beauty on others. Then you describe her as she will appear fifty years in the future and what will result from growing old. You then give her positive advice on how to deal with the aging process, and then you predict the effects the advice will have on her twilight years if she follows it.

❦ Additional Writing Tasks ❦
Cause and Effect

1. Using cause and effect (or one of the two alone) as the dominant development pattern, write an essay explaining something that interests you. These general questions are offered as ways to get you started. Revise them in any way that reflects your interests, and then, in a well-developed essay, answer them, using the principles of cause and effect or one of the two.
    a. Why do works by some artists, filmmakers, poets, or novelists affect you?
    b. Why do people need "idols," such as singers, athletes, actors, and politicians?
    c. Why does a television series—police drama, situation comedy, talk show—succeed?
    d. What are the effects of music lyrics that some political activists believe are obscene and condone violence?
    e. What are the effects of stand-up comedians who deliver monologues that critics claim are racist and sexist?
    f. Why are stories that repeat familiar formulas successful?
    g. Is common sense an effective way to solve complex problems?
    h. Is routine the great deadener, or do we need it to organize experience?
    i. Is homelessness a "real" problem in America?
    j. Can government solve the national-deficit problem by printing more money?
    k. Should children be seen and not heard?
    l. What results can you expect from an education?
    m. Is deceit self-destructive?
    n. Should children be made to feel guilty as a way of controlling teenage recklessness?
    o. Why should a dieter avoid eating foods that are high in fat?
    p. What causes stress, and what are its temporary and lasting effects?
    q. What are the effects of a mental illness?
    r. Why does the destruction of symbols such as the American flag enrage some people?

s. What would happen if everyone were given the college degree of his or her choice without completing course work?

2. Discuss one of these subjects in an essay using cause and effect (or one of the two) as the dominant pattern.

   a. Violence has always been a major element in action-oriented entertainment. In recent years, however, action-oriented children's television cartoons have become stripped of story line of any value and of characterization. The shows present unrelenting karate chopping and related mayhem and "us versus them" worlds with little or no complexity. Currently, some experts and a growing number of parents are beginning to worry about the possible harmful effects these shows might have upon children. In a cause-and-effect (or cause or effect alone) essay, explain the influence of action-oriented cartoons on children.

   b. David A. Goslin, Ph.D., of the American Institute for Research in Washington, D.C., which conducts behavioral and social science research, claims, "Choices do not make life easier; they make it more difficult, for all of us. As social scientists, we know that with an increase in choices, people tend to become more anxious."

     In your experience, is Dr. Goslin's comment valid? Write a cause-and-effect (or cause or effect alone) essay discussing his point of view. You might keep in mind that Americans can choose from more than 25,000 items shelved in their supermarkets. They can tune in more than fifty television channels. They can buy more than 11,000 magazines or periodicals. They are solicited by tens of thousands of special-interest groups. And now through the Internet Americans can expand their choices by linking up to a global marketplace while sitting in their living rooms. Some call this opportunity "freedom of choice," but social critics and experts are beginning to believe that the marketplace may have outsmarted itself by creating all these choices.

   c. In The *Tyranny of Malice*, Joseph H. Berke explains that "Envy is a state of exquisite tension, torment, and ill will provoked by an overwhelming sense of inferiority, impotence, and worthlessness. It begins in the eye of the beholder and is so painful to the mind that the envious person will go to almost any lengths to diminish, if not destroy, whatever or whoever may have aroused it." Basing a cause-and-effect (or cause or effect alone) essay on personal observation, discuss the sources of envy and how it might affect behavior.

d. "Think globally, act locally" was the rallying cry of environmental activism in the 1960s. This advice is as appropriate now as it was then. Just as the Greenpeace movement started almost three decades ago not with governments but at the grass roots, so today it is individuals who must occupy the front lines in protecting the environment. In a cause-and-effect (or cause or effect alone) essay, discuss individual or local-government actions that have resulted from environmental activism.

e. In "The Slaughterer," a short story by Isaac Bashevis Singer, Yoineh Meir wanted to be a rabbi. Instead, the religious authorities in his community made him the ritual slaughterer. Obediently, Meir learned the laws of slaughter as found in religious texts and followed the command of authority.

"Barely three months had passed since Yoineh Meir had become a slaughterer," Singer wrote, "but the time seemed to stretch endlessly. He felt as though he were immersed in blood and lymph. His ears were beset by the squawking of hens, the crowing of roosters, the gobbling of geese, the lowing of oxen, the mooing and bleating of calves and goats; wings fluttered, claws tapped on the floor. The bodies refused to know any justification or excuse—every body resisted in its own fashion, tried to escape, and seemed to argue with the Creator to its last breath."

Yoineh Meir's life ended in madness: "The killing of every beast, great or small, caused him as much pain as though he were cutting his own throat. Of all the punishments that could have been visited upon him, slaughtering was the worst."

Although Yoineh Meir is an extreme example, many people are forced to follow the dictates of authority against their better judgment. In an essay, describe a situation in which authority has been used to pressure an individual into action that seems contrary to his or her nature and discuss the related causes and effects.

8

Process Analysis
Explaining Step by Step

The Method

Are you, like many readers, fascinated by how things work? Are you attracted to writing that explains how to organize your life and time? You might want to understand how the stock market works or how Colombian drug producers smuggle cocaine into the United States. Perhaps your interests have to do with the mind—you might want to learn how psychotherapy works. Authors of essays or books explaining how things work use **process analysis**: They help us to better understand something by breaking it down into its components.

In some ways, process analysis comes close to narration and cause-and-effect analysis by attending to a sequence of related events. Narration, however, is meant to tell a story, and cause-and-effect analysis deals with the reasons for and results of an event or experience. In process analysis a writer examines the way in which something works. In short, narration concentrates on *what* happened; cause and effect, on *why* it happened; and process analysis, on *how* it happened.

Strategies

Careful writers distinguish between two kinds of process analysis: **directive** and **informative**. Directive process analysis explains *how* to do something. Directive process analysis is usually a practical kind of writing based on the assumption that someone will follow the directions to complete a task. Informative process analysis emphasizes *how* something works rather than *how to* do something. Informative process analysis might explain how the brain functions, how gravity holds human beings to the face of the earth, or how food is grown, processed, and merchandised, but an informative process analysis will not offer directions for completing a task.

Directive Process Analysis

Directive process analysis can range from brief instructions on a soup can label to a complicated plan for putting an astronaut on another planet. Keep in mind that directive process analysis has one clear purpose: to guide a reader to a predetermined goal by breaking down the steps required to get there. Consider this paragraph from Tom Cuthbertson's *Anybody's Bike Book*, setting out simple directions for checking bike tire pressure.

> There's a great *curb-edge test* you can do to make sure your tires are inflated just right. Rest the wheel on the edge of a curb or stair so the bike sticks out into the street or path, perpendicular to the curb or stair edge. Get the wheel so you can push down on it at about a 45 degree angle from above the bike. Push hard on the handlebars or seat, depending on which wheel you're testing. The curb should flare the tire a bit but shouldn't push right through the tire and clunk against the rim. You want the tire to have a little give when you ride over chuckholes and rocks, in other words, but you don't want it so soft that you bottom out. If you are a hot-shot who wants tires so hard that they don't have any give, you'll have to stick to riding on cleanswept Velodrome tracks, or watch very carefully for little sharp objects on the road. Or you'll have to get used to that sudden riding-on-the-rim feeling that follows the blowout of an overblown tire.

Cuthbertson's paragraph illustrates several characteristics of directive process analysis. First, he clearly establishes his purpose: to explain how to test bike tires for proper inflation. Second, he breaks the process down into simple steps and explains the final result: "The curb should flare the tire." Third, Cuthbertson addresses his reader directly by using the second person pronoun *you*, a practice that many writers adopt in directive process analysis: "There's a great curb-edge test **you** can do to make sure **your** tires are inflated just right." A fourth frequent characteristic of directive process analysis alerts the reader to possible mistakes and their consequences. Notice that Cuthbertson states the consequences of overinflated bike tires.

Now consider this passage from *The New York Times Complete Manual of Home Repair*. Bernard Gladstone gives directions for building a fire. Notice that Gladstone's passage embodies most of the common characteristics of process analysis, but he chooses not to address the reader as "you." Instead he writes in the more impersonal passive voice, which seems to create a distance between the reader and the subject.

Though "experts" differ as to the best technique to follow when building a fire, one generally accepted method consists of first laying a generous amount of crumpled newspaper on the hearth between the andirons. Kindling wood is then spread generously over this layer of newspaper and one of the thickest logs is placed across the back of the andirons. This should be as close to the back of the fireplace as possible, but not quite touching it. A second log is then placed an inch or so in front of this, and a few additional sticks of kindling are laid across these two. A third log is then placed on top to form a sort of pyramid with air space between all logs so that flames can lick freely up between them.

A mistake frequently made is in building the fire too far forward so that the rear wall of the fireplace does not get properly heated. A heated back wall helps increase the draft and tends to suck smoke and flames rearward with less chance of sparks or smoke spurting out into the room.

Another common mistake often made by the inexperienced firetender is to try to build a fire with only one or two logs, instead of using at least three. A single log is difficult to ignite properly, and even two logs do not provide an efficient bed with adequate fuel-burning capacity.

Use of too many logs, on the other hand, is also a common fault and can prove hazardous. Building too big a fire can create more smoke and draft than the chimney can safely handle, increasing the possibility of sparks or smoke being thrown out into the room. For best results, the homeowner should start with three medium-size logs as described above, then add additional logs as needed if the fire is to be kept burning.

Like Cuthbertson, Gladstone opens by clearly stating his purpose; that is, to explain the steps necessary to build a fire in a fireplace. He then follows with a series of steps—six in all—that are clearly written and easy to follow. After devoting a paragraph to directions for building a fire he presents three common mistakes people make when building a fire and their consequences, with one brief paragraph devoted to each mistake. Although Gladstone's directions for building a fire are longer than Cuthbertson's for testing air pressure in a bike tire, both follow the same general pattern. They begin with a clear statement of purpose, then present the steps necessary to complete the process, and, as is often done in directive process analysis, they identify the common mistakes people make when following the procedure.

Informative Process Analysis

Instead of guiding a reader through a series of directions to complete a task as directive process analysis does, informative process analysis explains how something happens or how it works. In this paragraph from Caroline Sutton's *How Do They Do That?* she explains how stripes are put into striped toothpaste.

> Although it's intriguing to imagine the peppermint stripes neatly wound inside the tube, actually stripes don't go into the paste until it's on its way out. A small hollow tube, with slots running lengthwise, extends from the neck of the toothpaste tube back into the interior a short distance. When the toothpaste tube is filled, red paste—the striping material—is inserted first, thus filling the conical area around the hollow tube at the front. (It must not, however, reach beyond the point to which the hollow tube extends into the toothpaste tube.) The remainder of the dispenser is filled with the familiar white stuff. When you squeeze the toothpaste tube, pressure is applied to the white paste,

which in turn presses on the red paste at the head of the tube. The red then passes through the slots and onto the white, which is moving through the inserted tube—and which emerges with five red stripes.

Sutton doesn't expect any of her readers to make a tube of striped toothpaste, but she does answer a common question, one that might have aroused your curiosity, too: "How do they get the stripes into the tube?"

An informative process analysis is usually arranged in chronological order and makes careful use of transitional techniques to guide a reader through the process. Sometimes the procedure is quite simple and easily organized in a step-by-step sequence. Often, however, the process is complex, such as a chemical reaction or human digestion, and challenges a writer's organizational skills, especially when the writer wishes to interrupt the explanation to add additional information or description.

For example, John McPhee in *Oranges* devotes a paragraph to describing the process that oranges undergo when made into concentrated juice. As you read McPhee's paragraph, notice that he interrupts to bring in related information—first to explain that oranges culled from the crop were once dumped in fields and eaten by cattle, thus accounting for the orangeade flavor of Florida milk, and later, to describe two kinds of juicing machines. Even though McPhee interrupts the process, he still guides the reader's attention with clear transitional techniques, especially phrases that create a sense of movement, such as, "As the fruit starts to move," "Moving up a conveyor belt," "When an orange tumbles in," and, finally, "As the jaws crush the outside."

> As the fruit starts to move along a concentrate plant's assembly line, it is first culled. In what some citrus people remember as "the old fresh-fruit days," before the Second World War, about forty per cent of all oranges grown in Florida were eliminated at packinghouses and dumped in fields. Florida milk tasted like orangeade. Now, with the exception of the split and rotten fruit, all of Florida's orange

crop is used. Moving up a conveyor belt, oranges are scrubbed with detergent before they roll on into juicing machines. There are several kinds of juicing machines, and they are something to see. One is called the Brown Seven Hundred. Seven hundred oranges a minute go into it and are split and reamed on the same kind of rosettes that are in the centers of ordinary kitchen reamers. The rinds that come pelting out the bottom are integral halves, just like the rinds of oranges squeezed in a kitchen. Another machine is the Food Machinery Corporation's FMC In-line Extractor. It has a shining row of aluminum jaws, upper and lower, with shining aluminum teeth. When an orange tumbles in, the upper jaw comes crunching down on it while at the same time the orange is penetrated from below by a perforated steel tube. As the jaws crush the outside, the juice goes through the perforations in the tube and down into the plumbing of the concentrate plant. All in a second, the juice has been removed and the rind has been crushed and shredded beyond recognition.

Some processes defy chronological explanation because they take place simultaneously. Here a writer must present the material in parallel stages, as McPhee does in the last three sentences of his paragraph when he describes juicing, clearly indicating with transitional markings that two or more interlocked events are taking place at once.

In a paragraph from "The Spider and the Wasp," zoologist Alexander Petrunkevitch presents the procedure a female *Pepsis* wasp follows when paralyzing a tarantula before burying it with a wasp egg attached to its belly. The challenge Petrunkevitch faced was to show both the wasp's and the spider's simultaneous behavior.

> When the grave is finished, the wasp returns to the tarantula to complete her ghastly enterprise. First, she feels it all over once more with her antennae. Then her behavior becomes more aggressive. She bends her abdomen, protruding her sting, and searches for the soft membrane at the point

where the spider's legs join its body—the only spot where she can penetrate the horny skeleton. From time to time, as the exasperated spider slowly shifts ground, the wasp turns on her back and slides along with the aid of her wings, trying to get under the tarantula for a shot at the vital spot. During all this maneuvering, which can last for several minutes, the tarantula makes no move to save itself. Finally the wasp corners it against some obstruction and grasps one of its legs in her powerful jaws. Now at last the harassed spider tries a desperate but vain defense. The two contestants roll over and over on the ground. It is a terrifying sight and the outcome is always the same. The wasp finally manages to thrust her sting into the soft spot and holds it there for a few seconds while she pumps in the poison. Almost immediately the tarantula falls paralyzed on its back. Its legs stop twitching; its heart stops beating. Yet it is not dead, as is shown by the fact that if taken from the wasp it can be restored to some sensitivity by being kept in a moist chamber for several months.

Often the success of a process analysis essay rests on clear information about the reader. The writer must estimate how much knowledge about the process the reader might already have and how much additional information must be included in the essay. If the writer's guess is wildly inaccurate, then he or she will include either too much information, which might send the reader into a fit of yawning, or too little, which may send the reader into an intellectual fog bank.

Process Analysis in College Writing

In the sciences and social sciences, process analysis is an important development pattern. In laboratory sciences you will often use directive process analysis to write reports that communicate the procedure in an experiment or research project. In courses such as geology, biology, cultural anthropology, and social psychology you will often use informative process analysis to describe such subjects as the formation of mountains, photosynthesis, initiation ceremonies, and socialization.

Guidelines for Writing Process Analysis

1. Select a subject that lends itself to either directive or informative process analysis. Be sure your subject is fresh—that is, avoid such common subjects as how to cook anything, how to put together anything, or how to find any place. Instead, look for the unusual, something from your own experience or research.
2. Decide whether your analysis will be primarily directive, informative, or a little of each. Develop a list of steps necessary to complete the process, or develop a list of key elements necessary to explain the process.
3. Use prewriting techniques to generate information necessary to understand and follow each element of the analysis. Then arrange your information in the proper order: for directive analysis, sequentially; for informative, chronologically.
4. Write your analysis. Carefully work in related information necessary to understand each step. Remember that a reader will be expected to follow the procedure in directive analysis but only to understand the process in informative analysis.
5. Revise your analysis. Pay particular attention to the transitions. Be sure they accurately guide the reader, and be sure they clearly show the connection to related information and delineate simultaneous events.

A Student Essay Developed by Process Analysis

In his Introduction to Psychology class, John Barton responded to the following writing task.

> In 550 to 600 words, write an overview of a supplemental analytic practice that attempts to show family relationships. Your essay should give a clear impression of what

is involved in the process and how it proceeds. Select one of
the following:

a. Transactional Analysis   d. Psychodrama
b. Photoanalysis   e. Hypnotherapy
c. Encounter Sessions   f. Cognitive Therapy

Barton selected item (b), photoanalysis, a subject that the lecturer
had covered only briefly. First, read Barton's process analysis,
then reread it and respond to the items in Reviewing with a
Writer's Eye.

Friendly Smile, Clenched Fist

Although many critics of psychotherapy claim that the   1
field is slow to change, some new techniques are developing. One is photoanalysis. No doubt you have heard that
"A photograph is worth a thousand words." Well, photoan-
alysts would agree, but with a slight revision, "A family
photo album is worth a thousand words." For example, a
person might be aware that he has difficulty showing affection and expressing himself. After a session with a
photoanalyst, usually a certified psychiatrist or psychologist, he could become aware that the difficulty is rooted in
his family history. Instead of spending hours verbally exploring his family relationships, a client working with a
photoanalyst would examine a family photo album where
the patterns of restraint might be documented in photographs.

Besides being trained as a therapist, a photoanalyst   2
should also be sensitive to visual images and the nonver-
bal expression they embody. But analyzing photographs to
uncover family themes is not simple. The analyst should
use group photographs taken over a number of years. A
single photograph may whet curiosity but is no more helpful in unearthing patterns of family relationship than a
crystal ball.

Most analysts begin by spreading the photographs on   3
a table. Then the analyst will study the faces to determine
the general "tone" of the relationships. Are the subjects
looking at each other or at the camera? Are their expres-

sions happy? Or severe? Or angry? Often a child's first impression of the world comes from parents. Their expressions, captured in a series of photographs, may reveal their general perceptions.

Next, the analyst will study the body language of family members. Do they seem to interact with each other or do they seem emotionally isolated from each other? Are they touching? Perhaps one has an arm around another's shoulder or a hand on another's leg. Is the hand open or clenched?

Finally, the analyst will also examine family members' proximity to each other. If they are close enough to rub elbows, they probably enjoy a warm relationship. If they put distance between themselves to avoid touching, they may shun intimacy with each other. What if males and females are clearly separated? Does this distance suggest that men and women play traditional roles within the family? An analyst will notice who takes the dominant place in the photographs. Mother? Father? A grandparent? Perhaps the children. Whoever takes a dominant place in a series of photographs probably takes the dominant role at home as well. A parent who consistently gravitates toward one child in photographs might play favorites in family relationships. A person who always chooses to stand at the outside of the group might feel like an outsider.

Throughout a photoanalysis session, the analysts should avoid narrow interpretations of the photographs, but should offer observations for the client's response. After all, the client is the one with the direct experience and therefore should have the last word in interpreting any photograph. The photoanalyst must, however, point out that a friendly smile might be masking the tension revealed by a clenched fist half hidden in a lap.

Reviewing with a Writer's Eye

1. Explain why John Barton's "Friendly Smile, Clenched Fist" is primarily either directive or informative process analysis (see pp. 389–394).

Peer Review

You may be asked to write an essay about one of the readings that follow. Before you meet with your writing group, review this introduction. As you read the papers of your group, use these general principles of process analysis to help guide your comments.

1. The paper's complexity and vocabulary should be appropriate for the intended audience.
2. A process analysis paper should proceed in clearly defined steps. In a directive paper, readers should be warned of possible missteps at appropriate places. In an informative paper, readers should be told of actions that take place simultaneously.
3. A reader's understanding of the process can be enhanced with careful use of transitional words and phrases.

---

2. What single sentence indicates Barton's general purpose?
3. List the steps a photoanalyst might follow.
4. Barton develops his essay mainly by asking questions. Why?
5. What purposes do paragraphs 2 and 6 serve?
6. In no more than 150 words, write Barton a detailed note that points out the strengths and weaknesses of his essay.

In the professional examples that follow, you will find a variety of process analysis essays to study. Each is written for a different purpose. Yet each makes use of the fundamental strategies behind directive or informative process analysis. Study them with care to learn how professionals apply these strategies.

❦ Joan Gould ❦

Joan Gould was born in 1927 in New York City and attended Bryn Mawr College. She has written a juvenile novel and the "Hers" column in The New York Times *and has contributed to major magazines such as* Esquire, Life, Sports Illustrated, *and* McCall's. *Many of her essays are very personal explorations of the experience of being a wife, a mother, a mother-in-law, and an adult daughter of an aging mother. Her book* Spirals: A Woman's Journey Through Family Life *is a collection of those essays.*

Binding Decisions

This essay was first printed in Memories *magazine in 1989. The author describes an event from her past, the ritual of getting ready for a blind date in 1950, which she uses to reveal social attitudes about women and men, marriage, and relationships at that time. The essay invites us to wonder how much attitudes like these have changed since then.*

This process comprises a set of steps, with a description of each step. As you read, separate the steps from their descriptions to find out exactly how many steps Joan Gould took to get ready for her date.

I'm out of the bathtub. I'm ready to get dressed for my date tonight, which is a blind date, serious business in this year of 1950 for any girl who's over 20 and still single. I'm 22. No matter how much money I may earn in my job, I'll never be allowed to have an apartment of my own; I'll never pay an electric bill or buy a bedspread or spend a night away from home without my parents; in fact, I'll never be a grown-up so long as I remain single. 1

How shall I dress? I want to look sexy enough to attract this unknown man, so that he'll call and ask me for another date next week. (Needless to say, I won't call him, even if my life depends on it.) On the other hand, I don't want to hide the fact that I'm what's known as a Nice Girl, addicted to Peter Pan collars and vel- 2

vet hats and white gloves, which means that I'm good wife material, and also makes it clear that he'll get nothing more than a good-
night kiss from me tonight.

And so I dress carefully. Every single item that I put on not   3
only is complicated in itself but carries an even more complicated
message.

My girdle comes first. Here's the badge, the bind, the bondage   4
of womanhood. Here's the itch of it. This is the garment that tells
me I'm not a little girl anymore, who wears only underpants, but
neither am I middle-aged like my mother, who wears a real corset
with bones that dig into her diaphragm and leave cruel sores
there. I can get away with either a panty girdle or a two-way
stretch, both of which are made of Lastex with a panel of stiff satin
over the abdomen. The basic difference is that a panty girdle, unlike a two-way stretch, covers the crotch, which was considered a
shocking—indeed obscene—idea when first introduced.
Victorian women were obliged to wear half a dozen petticoats at a
time to be respectable, but never, never would they put on anything that slipped between their thighs, like a pair of pants.

But why should I be bothering with this sausage casing when   5
I weigh a grand total of a hundred and two pounds?

I bother because being thin has nothing to do with it. A girdle   6
is a symbolic garment, and unless I want to be regarded as a child
or a slut I have to put it on. When I go out with girlfriends in the
daytime I may choose to be more comfortable in only a garter belt,
a device with four long, wiggly elastics that dangle down my
thighs like hungry snakes lunging at my stockings. When I'm with
a boy, however, it would be unthinkable—it would be downright
indecent—to let him see my rear end jiggle or let him notice that
it has two halves. (All males are called "boys," no matter what their
age, so long as they're single.) My backside is supposed to be
molded in a rigid piece that divides into two legs, like a walking
clothespin.

Besides, if I don't wear a girdle every day, the older girls warn   7
me, I'm going to "spread." Spreading is somehow related to letting
my flesh hang loose, which is in turn related to the idea of the
"loose" woman, and none of us wants to be considered loose. A

man doesn't buy a cow if he can get milk for free, our mothers tell us in dire tones. We don't point out that we're not cows, and we don't fight against girdles, which apparently do a good job of discouraging wandering hands, since most of the single girls I know are virgins.

But which girdle should I wear? If I pick the panty girdle, I'll need 10 minutes' advance notice before going to the toilet. If I wear the two-way stretch, it will ride up and form a sausage around my waist. Either way, my flesh will be marked with welts and stripes when, at that delirious moment in my bedroom, I can strip off my clothes and scratch and scratch.   8

I pick the two-way stretch but, born compromiser that I am, put underpants over it.   9

Next comes the bra. I don't dare look at myself in the mirror as I put it on. This is the era of the pinup girl, the heyday of Lana Turner and Betty Grable, when breasts bubble and froth over the rims of C-cups and a flat chest is considered about as exciting as flat champagne. Not until Twiggy appears on the scene in the 1960's will thinness become acceptable in a girl, much less desirable—but how am I supposed to survive until then? The answer is the garment I've just put on, the confession of my disgrace—a padded bra. If I wear a strapless gown, I pin foam-rubber bust pads, which are known as "falsies," in place. Occasionally one of these breaks loose during a particularly ardent conga or mambo and rises above my dress like the rim of the sun peering over a hilltop.   10

At least the bra won't show under my silk slip. Silk is expensive, of course, and no male will see my underwear unless he marries me or I'm carried off to a hospital emergency room—but then, as all the mothers warn us, accidents do happen.   11

Stockings next. During World War II, just as I became old enough to wear them, our wonderful new nylons were snatched away from us in order to make parachutes for what was known as the "war effort." What were we girls supposed to do—go out on a date in socks, like little children? If there weren't any stockings around, we'd have to create them. And so we bought bottles of makeup base and painted stockings on our legs and drew seams   12

up the back with eyebrow pencils, which was undoubtedly the
last time my seams were ever straight.

My dress, oddly enough, is easy to choose. For a woman of   13
my years, a skirt-and-sweater is out of the question on a date. The
dress mustn't be too highstyle or expensive, however, or else the
young man will think that I'm spoiled, a fatal defect in a girl who
might otherwise qualify as good wife material. Never mind that I
earned the money to buy my own clothes; I still have to show that
it won't cost much to support me once we marry and I quit my
job. For the same reason, wherever we go—which is always at his
expense, of course—I'll insist that we travel by bus or subway,
never by taxi. If he invites me out to dinner (which doesn't happen often, because of cost, and never on a first date), I'll eat a
sandwich at home before I leave, to make sure I won't be tempted
to order an appetizer or dessert in the restaurant.

Shoes. I'd like to wear my fashionable new ones, with their   14
ankle straps crisscrossing in back and fastening above the ankle
bone, but they have 3 1/2-inch heels, and I have no idea if I'll
tower over this unknown man. If I choose low heels, on the other
hand, he may think that I'm condescending. I pick the high heels
but hide a low-heeled pair in the hall closet, just in case. Blind
dates have their special hazards.

I still have to put on my makeup, which includes lots of lip-   15
stick, loose face power and an eyebrow pencil to extend my brow
line, but no eye shadow, much less liner. I also have to do my hair,
which is set with heavy lotion and rollers in the beauty parlor
every week. (At night I sleep in a cotton mesh hairnet that I tie
around my head, in order to preserve the set for at least a week.)

Speeding up the pace, I rush to equip my pocketbook with a   16
monogrammed handkerchief and some "mad money," including
several nickels for phone calls or a bus, obligatory for a blind date.
I run to my glove drawer and hunt up a pair in white kid, since
he's invited me to a concert. I won't need a hat. He'll wear one, of
course.

The doorbell rings. I dab Shalimar on a tuft of cotton, which I   17
tuck inside my bra; I check my stocking seams and move toward
the door. For an instant, my hand rests on the knob, while I won-

der what sort of person is breathing out there, only inches away from me but still unrevealed, unexplored. And then I open the door, and I see his face and hear his voice, because he's already in mid-sentence. As a matter of fact, he's in mid-story, as if it's inconceivable that anyone could be less than fascinated with what he's saying, which happens to be true, or as if he's my husband already and has waited all day, or maybe all his life, to tell me about what happened to him that afternoon.

A box of Kleenex is tucked under his arm, because he has a   18
cold, and he lays the box down on the hall table with the assurance of the rightful prince stepping into his kingdom at last. This one I'll marry or I'll marry no one, I say to myself an hour later.

Three dates—which means three weeks—later, he proposes.   19
"Wait. I have to tell you something first," I declare in distress. He waits. I'm in turmoil. I'm risking everything on candor, and candor isn't a virtue in which I've had much practice. I've never said anything like this out loud before. "You have a right to know," I announced. "I wear a padded bra."

He says he imagines he can handle that.   20

We were married three months later. I wonder, if he hadn't   21
proposed so promptly, how much longer it would have been before he discovered my secret for himself.

Meaning and Purpose

1. What significance does the title have for you after you read the essay?
2. In paragraph 6, Gould says that the girdle is "a symbolic garment." We still have symbolic garments. What is one of them? How is it symbolic?
3. The author makes sure that she "won't be tempted to order an appetizer or dessert" if she is invited by a date to eat in a restaurant (paragraph 13). Why?
4. What is Gould's purpose in writing about the procedure of getting ready for a blind date in 1950? From what perspective is she writing?

5. In paragraph 10, she talks about what could happen during "an ardent conga or mambo." To what do *conga* and *mambo* refer? Why is *ardent* an appropriately descriptive word?

Strategy

1. The process in this essay can be broken into specific steps. What are three of those steps?
2. Gould often interrupts the chronology of her process of dressing for a date to give explanations and related information. Where is one example of this strategy, and how does it work in the essay?
3. From the kind and detail of information in this essay, what decision would you say Gould has made about the knowledge her audience has of her subject?
4. The blind date is in "mid-story" as the author opens the door (paragraph 17). What does this strategy of description tell you about the blind date's mental attitude?

Style

1. The process described in this essay was carried out forty or so years ago. Why is the essay written in the present tense?
2. What is Gould's attitude toward the procedure she must go through for a date? Point out specific language that illustrates her attitude.
3. Why is the word *delirious* so appropriate, as it is used in paragraph 8?
4. How does the word *candor* in paragraph 19 serve as an ironic comment on the entire process of dressing for a blind date in the 1950s?

Writing Tasks

1. The title is quite important to this essay. The expression "binding decisions" means at least two things. Using the material in this

essay, write a paper exploring two meanings of "binding decisions": as the expression describes the process in this essay and as the expression defines the reason the author carries out that process.

2. How do you dress for a date or for some other occasion? Write a brief essay chronicling the steps in the process. If it is relevant, give background information that places your process in a larger social context.

Richard Strozzi Heckler not only holds a Ph.D. in psychology but also holds a fourth-degree black belt in Aikido, defined by its founder, Morihei Ueshiba, as "the activity of being taught by God about the echoes of the soul (tamashii) of the Universal Design (shikumi)." Dr. Heckler edited the anthology Aikido and the New Warrior, *from which the above definition comes. Currently living in the San Francisco Bay area, he is a practicing psychotherapist and consultant. He has written several articles for the* Whole Earth Review, *which first published this essay.*

Commanded by Love

In this essay, Richard Strozzi Heckler shows how it is possible to train a horse by using techniques that many readers find, ironically, to be applicable to "training" people. In fact, as you read this essay, you see that Heckler himself treats his horse humanly, even to the extent of carrying on conversations with the animal. And as a psychologist, Heckler applies his discipline's methods to his training sessions, to the point of using psychological jargon to describe parts of his and the horse's efforts to understand one another. As you read this essay, note the stages in the careful process that Heckler uses to establish the bond between him and the horse.

This morning it took ten minutes to get Rios' attention and an-   1
other twenty before he was really listening to me. First he distracted himself with two crows bickering in the cypress trees and then it was the flies that rose with the heat and dust of the day. Mostly I could feel he just wasn't with me. Perhaps he didn't feel my commitment; I was tired from a late night and not fully present when we began. When I finally got irritated, he perked up and we started to get some work done. It's been a week since we opened this new conversation and I feel we're just now beginning to listen to each other.

Rios is a young, green quarterhorse who is saddle-broke but   2
has never been formally schooled. In the human world of sports
he would be a pulling guard in football: he's muscular, quick, aggressive in turning a corner, and belligerent when he feels he's being forced or manipulated. He's not a mean or tricky horse, a
juvenile delinquent maybe, but in fact he's patient in ways that allow my year-and-a-half-old daughter to walk safely around his
legs. In any case he demands that I be present with him; if I'm not
he'll go on his merry way—bolting out of riding rings, trying to
peel me off on low-hanging limbs, turning unexpectedly in the
opposite direction. In short, he's capable of anything.

In this stage of his training I'm asking Rios to bring his head   3
down. When a horse brings his head to a vertical line he is more
able to organize around his center of gravity; this increases his potential for moving in a balanced, effortless, coherent, and powerful way. A number of techniques and aids are commonly used to
affect this behavior (and that's what it is, behavior modification)—
side reins, dropped nosebands, bit-tying—but at a deeper level
Rios and I are having a conversation about the nature of our relationship. This conversation tells a story—a table perhaps—about
a horse and a man who are exploring a definition of power. It
brings to mind Wittgenstein's observation, "To imagine a language is to imagine a form of life." The grammar of our discourse
is conveyed through skin, muscles, legs, mouth, hands, voice; the
syntax is the intention, trust, respect, and authenticity communicated between our energy fields.

What makes this conversation particularly challenging with   4
Rios is that he has a different, already-in-place story about
power. His previous owner, in asking him to respond to the
same lessons that I am, was inordinately harsh with his mouth
and bewildered him with mixed messages. Rios embodies this
story by holding his head up and by constantly reacting to the
bit in anticipation of being yanked around. His story about
power revolves around dominance and fear and goes something
like this: *The human with his whip, bit, spurs, and calculating mind
will dominate me with pain and confusion, so I'll fear him enough to
obey his commands.* What happens in this kind of story, as it did

with Rios, is that it makes a horse, or a person, neurotic and even psychotic. A crazy horse, like a crazy person, can never really be counted on to listen and respond with an open mind and heart. A story like this also confuses power, which has everything to do with enhancing one's capacity to love and be loved, with coercion. Love cannot be commanded, but we must be commanded by love.

At the beginning of our story I tell Rios that I want a relation- 5
ship with him. He's interested; the fraternal history of horse and man lives in his marbled flesh and surging neck. "But don't expect that your riding tack has any true authority," he adds. "It's only an emblem of power. You must earn the right to ride and command me. To start with, what are your assumptions about horse and rider?" he asks.

"I've never met a horse, nor a human, in which there is no love 6
that longs to emerge."

We proceed, one lesson at a time, always with the same ques- 7
tion Who are you? "How do you respond when I demand some-thing from you?" I ask.

"How do you react when I refuse?" he counters. 8

"Why would a 1,300-pound animal let me ride him in the first 9
place?" I wonder.

Curiosity is a terrifyingly open force that moves us toward 10
some unknown understanding in the future. We struggle with trust and respect. Here the story is about the opportunity to fail, consequences, and redemption. Rios has a noble heart and, like most people, takes pride in overcoming obstacles and doing something difficult well.

Despite his attitude on any given ride—pissy, aloof, commit- 11
ted—I can always sense the dark pounding blood of his line; an incontestable dignity and robust spirit. If I say I want to ride him, and then act condescendingly—as in, "If I love and coddle you enough maybe you'll do what I ask"—he won't respect me. He'll think that my soul is flabby, that my love has no teeth. "Show me your commitment, show me that you really mean what you say, give me a moral reason to want to do this with you," he asks mo-ment to moment.

"Pay attention to my seat and legs. Quit fussing on the bit and 12 come down here and listen to what I have to say," I demand.

"Are you there?" we constantly whisper back and forth, and 13 the question itself shapes us into the moment, or not.

"You were hurt once," I recognize, "but I want you to trust 14 that it is your radiance that inspires me. There is a great beauty within you that I can help summon."

"How can you know what I want?" 15

"I don't know," I confess, "but I do know that it is really me 16 who is being commanded. It is the beauty within you that commands me. We are both, once and at the same time, leader and follower. The beauty in you commands me, my love of your beauty commands you."

Then there are the moments when he brings his head down, 17 collects his power under him, and we become one. There are no more questions, no wondering, only wonder. The roles coalesce into a single mind. "This feeling is power," I say. "This is a powerful feeling," he replies. This power has no ownership, yet we both feel touched by its luminosity and splendor. It is still, yet immensely capable and alive. Then my hat blows off and I momentarily look back. Rios immediately changes gait and direction. "Does he think I have fallen out of love?" I question, "Have I?"

Rios thinks, "He demands so much of me and then leaves. He 18 must love his hat also." Days later, leaving the ring after another session, he suddenly turns and walks over to my hat, fallen much earlier and forgotten. His taking command at that moment is an act of generosity and love.

As our story unfolds, we learn that power is not a thing, or 19 something to be personally accumulated, or having someone obey us, but a capacity to surrender to something greater than either of us. Power is a reservoir of which we can partake, and to which each can lead the other. Psychology can define this power; technique and skill can take us to its threshold; but it is in a set of practices, within a living discipline of spirit and heart, that we come to the realization: it is the surrendering itself that is empowering.

There are two other characters in our story. One is the land- 20 scape—the bronze hills, the lacquer-blue sky, dust, the trees faithful in their watching, the inevitable wind. The other is the great arc of time. Our story is not finished. What we learn takes time, and it links the tedious with the dramatic and the mundane with the transcendent. Rios and I, as in human relationships, are empowered only when we are available for it, moment by moment, in our continuing, forever-changing story of who we are together.

Meaning and Purpose

1. In the first paragraph of this essay the author says, "It's been a week since we opened this new conversation." What "new conversation" does he mean?
2. The author remarks in the last line of paragraph 2 that Rios is "capable of anything." No one or no animal is "capable of anything." What does the author mean by that phrase?
3. In paragraph 4 the author says that Rios already has his own "story about power." In your words, describe Rios's "story about power" as it is described in this paragraph.
4. In paragraph 11 is the clause " my love has no teeth." Love is not usually thought of as having teeth in the first place. Why does the author use teeth as a reference for love?
5. What is the importance of the author's hat in this essay?

Strategy

1. In classical rhetoric the Latin term *significatio* ("sign") describes a phrase, passage, or statement that implies more than it says. In paragraph 2, the phrase "juvenile delinquent" is an example of *significatio*. What does that phrase imply in that paragraph?
2. Why does the author refer to his year-and-a-half-old daughter in paragraph 2?
3. Paragraph 5 mentions "the fraternal history of horse and man." How is that "history" important to that paragraph?

4. What evidence does the reader have for saying that the author of this essay is an experienced horse trainer?
5. What is the purpose of having simulated conversations between the rider and the horse in this essay?

Style

1. Why does the author begin the essay with "This morning," when obviously it is not now "this morning," the same morning as in the essay?
2. In paragraph 3, what is meant by the phrase "energy fields"?
3. One long sentence in paragraph 4 is cast in italics. Why did the author cast that sentence in italics?
4. Why is the word *coalesce*, as used in paragraph 17, important to understanding this essay?
5. Why, in your opinion, is time referred to as being an "arc" in the last paragraph of this essay?

Writing Tasks

1. Each of us has had a kinship with an animal or with an inanimate object, such as a car, a book, or a piece of sports equipment. We have all had our pets and our properties. Write an essay in which you tell about the process of caring for your pet or your property and how that process served to connect you even more closely with that pet or property.
2. Using data from "Commanded by Love," write an essay that shows the sequential steps taken by the author to change Rios's attitude toward his surroundings. Point out which steps you believe are the most important and which steps are the least important.

❧ Garry Trudeau ❧

Garry Trudeau, born in New York City in 1948, is most famous for his internationally acclaimed comic strip Doonesbury. *He attended Yale University and in 1970 was awarded a Master of Fine Arts degree from Yale's School of Art and Architecture.* Doonesbury *appears in newspapers nationwide and has been collected in numerous books. In 1975, Trudeau won the Pulitzer Prize for editorial cartooning. In 1977 he was nominated for an academy award for the animated film,* A Doonesbury Special.

Anatomy of a Joke

This short essay was first published August 1, 1993, in the opinion section of The New York Times. *In it, Trudeau traces in detail a single* Tonight Show *joke, from its inception to Jay Leno's delivery.*

As you read Trudeau's description, you might be surprised at the time, detail, and calculation that go into a seemingly impromptu and fleeting television joke. Consider why such meticulous and expensive attention would be given to something so inconsequential.

In the wake of last week's press "availabilities" of funnymen   1
Dave Letterman, Jay Leno, Chevy Chase et al., there was much
rim-shot critiquing, all of it missing the point.

The real jokes, the ones that count, occur not at press events   2
but during those extraordinary little pieces called monologues.
Despite the popular conception of the monologue as edgy and unpredictable, it is actually as formal and structured as anything
found in traditional kabuki. The stakes are too high for it to be
otherwise. Even the ad-libs, rejoinders, and recoveries are carefully scripted. While it may suit Leno's image to portray the
"Tonight" show monologue as something that's banged out over
late-night pizza with a few cronies, in fact each joke requires the
concerted effort of a crack team of six highly disciplined comedy
professionals. To illustrate how it works, let's follow an actual top-

ical joke, told the night of Monday, July 26, as it makes its way through the pipeline.

The inspiration for a topical joke is literally torn from the headlines by a professional comedy news "clipper." Comedy news reading is sometimes contracted out to consultants, but the big-budget "Tonight" show has 12 of its own in-house clippers who peruse some 300 newspapers every day. Clippers know that the idea for the joke must be contained in the headline or, at worst, the subhead. If the idea is in the body text, then the general public has probably missed it and won't grasp the reference the joke is built around. In this case, the clipper has spied an item about flood relief.

A20   FRIDAY, JULY 23, 1993

House Delays Final Flood Aid Vote

$3 Billion Package Stalls in Dispute Over Budget Limits

The Washington Post

The news clip is then passed on to a comedy "engineer," whose job is to decide what shape the joke should take. After analyzing the headline, the engineer decides how many parts the joke should have, the velocity of its build, whether it contains any red herrings (rare on the "Tonight" show), and the dynamics of the payoff and underlaughing. With Monday's joke, the engineer chose a simple interrogatory setup, which telegraphs to the often sleepy audience that the next line contains a payoff. The finished sequencing is then sent on to the "stylist."

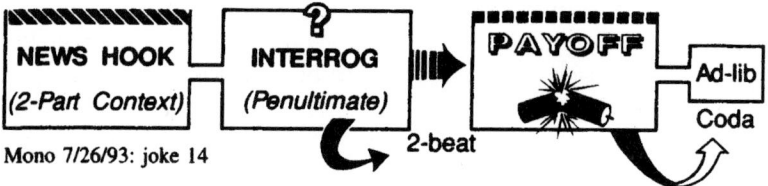

The comedy stylist is the writer who actually fashions the raw   5
joke. The stylist is the prima donna of the team, the best paid, the
worst dressed—and never in the office. The stylist, who is typically a per diem session player, is faxed the original headline, the
structural scheme, and a gross time count, and from those elements creates the rough draft for the joke. It's up to him to find
the joke's "spring," that tiny component of universal truth that
acts as the joke's fulcrum. In this case, the joke hinges on the public's resentment of Congress, a hoary but proven truism. The stylist then faxes his finished rough to the "polish man."

**1./It looks like the House of Representatives is having
trouble voting flood relief because they're worried
about where to appropriate the money from.
2./Here's my question.
3./How come when the House votes itself a pay raise,
they never worry about that appropriation?**

The polish man, usually a woman, is the joke's editor, charged   6
with burnishing the joke until it gleams. Obscure references, awkward phrasing, and puns are all removed, and any potentially offensive material is run by an outside anti-defamation consultant.
Unlike the stylist, who usually works at his beach house, the polish man is always on the premises, available in the event of emergency rewrites. For Monday's joke, the polish man adds a "fall
from the sky" coda that will allow Leno some physical business.
The decision to use it, however, ultimately rests with the "timing
coach."

The timing coach is responsible for timing out the phrasing   7
and pauses, and bringing the 21-joke routine in under its seven-
minute limit. Running over is a major no-no. During the Carson
era, a timing coach, who asked not to be identified, signed off on
a monologue that ran 13.5 seconds long, a deficit that came out of
Barbra Streisand's guest segment. The coach was summarily
sacked. Such errors are rare today, however, as the monologues

@ too long   Senate

It looks like the ~~House of Representatives~~ is
passing, @ where? for the midwest
having trouble ~~voting~~ flood relief because ~~they're~~
(some Senators are)
~~worried~~ about where ~~to appropriate~~ the money from.
is going to come
Now,
Here's my question: How come when the ~~House~~ votes
Senate
big   wonder where
itself a ~~pay~~ raise, they never ~~worry about~~ that
money's coming from ?
~~appropriation?~~   ad-libs: Ever notice that?

It just seems to fall from the sky.

---

are now digitalized on disk. A timer can modulate the phrasing pattern to within 0.01 of a second, well beyond the performance sensitivity of any comic but Robin Williams.

(6.3 sec. to pause) IT LOOKS LIKE . . . FLOOD RELIEF . . . WORRIED . . . MONEY IS GOING TO COME FROM. (.95 sec. beat) NOW, HERE'S MY QUESTION; (.6 second beat; 3.45 sec. to ad-lib) HOW COME . . . BIG PAY RAISE . . . WHERE <u>THAT</u> MONEY'S COMING FROM? (ad-lib under laugh; see menu).

The final joke is then e-mailed to the "talent," in this case Jay Leno. Leno dry-runs the joke in his office, adding spin and body movement, and locks in his ad-libs, including recovery lines in case the joke bombs. (Carson had such good recovery material that he used to commission intentionally bad jokes, but Leno has not yet reached that pinnacle of impeccability.) Once Leno approves the joke, it is transferred to a hard disk and laser-printed on cue cards with a special font to make it look hand-lettered. Finally, at exactly 5:30 P.M., California taping time, Leno walks on stage and reads it to 15 million people.

8

Meaning and Purpose

1. Now that you have read the essay, what significance does the title have for you?
2. Why are news headlines used as the bases for jokes in the *Tonight Show* monologue?
3. In paragraph 7, Trudeau says, "The timing coach is responsible for timing out the phrasing and pauses, and bringing in the 21-joke routine in under its seven-minute limit." Why are the subject, structure, and timing of a TV joke given such meticulous care?
4. What is the thesis of the essay? Where has Trudeau placed it?

Strategy

1. What is each stage of the joke process Trudeau describes?
2. Trudeau often disrupts the strict chronology of his process to give descriptions and explanations. Find two examples of this strategy. Why does he include these interruptions?
3. Trudeau is careful to use clear transitions. What transitions does he use to move the reader through each stage of the process? What other transitions does he use to clarify his ideas?
4. Why does Trudeau include visual illustrations? Do they help to clarify his ideas or not?

Style

1. Trudeau employs many colloquialisms in his essay (see *colloquial expressions* in Glossary). After finding several, determine why he uses them.
2. What specialized vocabulary does he use? Why?
3. If necessary, look up the following words in a dictionary: *anatomy* (title); *in the wake of* (paragraph 1); *kabuki, cronies, pipeline* (2); *peruse* (3); *velocity, red herrings, dynamics, interroga-*

tory (4); *prima donna, per diem, gross, fulcrum, hoary* (5); *burnishing, anti-defamation, coda* (6); *summarily, digitalized, modulate* (7); *pinnacle, impeccability* (8).

Writing Tasks

1. Choose something in your own life that lends itself to an informative process analysis (see *Informative Process Analysis*, pp. 391–394). Then write a paper in which you clearly explain how, precisely, that thing in your life happens or how it works. Take care to carry the reader along with transitional expressions. Like Trudeau, include clarifying descriptions, explanations, and examples.

2. Trudeau traces the meticulous detail and care that goes into a single, fleeting TV joke. Consider why such care would be taken for such a seemingly trivial pursuit. What would the payoff be for such time, expense, and attention? Consider other pursuits that entail similar attention to detail: many medical procedures, many aspects of the space program, the creative process (art and writing, in particular), many legal matters, much neurotic and psychotic behavior. Write a paper in which you describe one or more processes that demand a meticulous attention to detail and result in a compensating payoff for that attention.

❦ Frank Gannon ❦

Frank Gannon, born in 1952, earned his bachelor's degree, magna cum laude, *and his master's degree from the University of Georgia. His works include* Yo Poe, Vanna Karenina, *and* All About Man. *His essays have appeared in* The Atlantic, Harper's, Gentlemen's Quarterly, *and* The New Yorker. *He is also a contributing editor of* Southern. *He remarks, "At first I was influenced by Yukio Mishima. Then Hemingway and Fitzgerald."*

Rat Patrol: A Saga

This selection was originally published in Harper's Magazine *in 1996. The essay contains an anecdote, a short biographical account of an event in the author's life, as an important strategy to help clarify his reason for explaining a process. While reading this essay, try to imagine yourself relating such an anecdote to a nine-year-old child to determine whether, in your opinion, the anecdote that Gannon tells to his own child would make sense to another child.*

As a young man, I liked nothing better than playing a game   1
called Rat Patrol. It had nothing to do with rats and little to do
with patrols. What it did involve was this: when I was in eighth
grade, around 1966, there was on ABC an unpopular program
called *The Rat Patrol.* It was canceled very quickly, and I never
spent even a single minute actually watching the show. Neither
did any of my fellow Rat Patrol players. What we did see (it would
have been difficult to miss) was the thirty-second commercial for
the show. This commercial ran virtually all day, at perhaps
twenty-minute intervals. I sat in front of the television that my dad
had gotten cheap because the little square that showed the channel was on sideways, and I watched this commercial, it seemed, all
summer. It was always the same. This is how it went.

A deep "announcer" voice: 2

THEY PLAYED BY THEIR OWN RULES.

(Shot of jeeps driving very fast through the desert, making hairpin 3
turns, throwing sand all over the camera.)

WHAT OTHER MEN CALLED
THE WASTELAND, THEY
CALLED HOME.

(Shot of some grimy-faced guys with bandannas around their 4
necks. They are driving their jeeps very fast and making very abrupt
turns that throw sand into the camera.)

THIS FALL.
THE RAT PATROL.

(Shot of a really big explosion with a giant wave of sand going all 5
over everything.)

I watched it approximately five hundred times. I was not 6
alone. My associates, Andy and Paul, also watched, often in my
presence. Although very little was said, I am quite sure that we
were all forming the same word in our eighth-grade minds. That
word was "cool."

Here is how the game is played. 7

Near my home there is a big sloping hill. Because of some 8
construction work done decades ago, one whole side of the hill is
composed of sand. Regular beach-type sand. The hill inclines at
about a forty-degree angle. So there you have it. Maybe three hundred yards of nothing but sand.

This is the official playing field. 9

Next, you need the equipment. You need at least one full can 10
of lighter fluid or barbecue starter. That's easy to come by. The
rest of the equipment gets a bit trickier. You need a whole bunch
of aerosol cans. You need to keep your eyes open and your Rat
Patrol ears cocked, particularly around the women. The big sisters
and the moms are an excellent source of aerosol devices. Hair

spray is the most obvious choice, but you have many others. This was, of course, the days before Sting and Greenpeace, and everybody whacked away at the ozone level on a regular basis. Deodorants. Room fresheners. Furniture polish. Nonstick cooking spray. Bug repellent.

Dads also contributed to the Rat Patrol cause. They all had   11 those cans that they kept in the trunk of the car, canisters that were supposed to come in handy if you had a flat tire. Compressed-air devices. In the weeks of preparation for Rat Patrol, cans disappeared from Dodges and Chevys and Ramblers all over the neighborhood. After a while, we often didn't even know what we were stealing. If it had those magic words WARNING: CONTENTS UNDER PRESSURE, that was good enough for us.

The International Rules of Rat Patrol

1. You must dig a very large hole in the sand. You have to   12 take maybe a half ton of sand out of there. If in doubt, make the hole larger. The hole can't be too big.

2. Throw all of the WARNING: CONTENTS UNDER PRESSURE   13 canisters into the hole. As in the case of the hole, you cannot have too many cans. If you have a hundred cans, that's good. If you have, say, a googolplex cans, that's even better. An infinite number of cans would be infinitely good.

3. You must come up with some kind of fuse. The best kind   14 is one that burns like a sparkler, with lots of little twinkly sparks as it goes along. This is best because (a) it burns slowly enough that you can get the hell out of there before zero hour, and (b) those twinkly sparks are aesthetically pleasing. If Rat Patrol isn't going to be beautiful, then why bother?

4. You have to empty a great deal of lighter fluid into the   15 hole. Again, you can't have too much lighter fluid. Barbecue starter works just as well. A case or two of barbecue starter followed by a case or two of lighter fluid—that would maybe be the ideal formula for the platonically perfect Rat Patrol, the "Rat Patrolness" that exists in the realm of essences.

5.   After the fuse has been lit, the lighter of the fuse must run 16
away from the hole for a distance of approximately twenty-five
yards. Then he, along with his fellow players, must scream loudly
and dive face-down into the sand. All players should remain in
said position until the explosion(s) is (are) over and there are no
more flaming can fragments aloft.

6.   This is optional, but the lighter of the fuse may choose to 17
articulate some words rather than merely screaming. These are
some, but not all, of the possibilities:

A.   HIT THE DECK!

B.   THAR SHE BLOWS!

C.   THEY GOT CHARLIE!

D.   EAT LEAD, COPPER!

I have not played Rat Patrol in almost thirty years. As an adult, 18
I have found that big explosions are no longer very entertaining. I
hate action movies. There is no way on earth that anyone could
talk me into spending good money to watch Dennis Hopper or
somebody blow stuff up.

The Fourth of July is definitely the most mediocre holiday as 19
far as I'm concerned. Sitting outside at night while mosquitoes attack you, watching stuff explode in the sky, is just about as bad an
idea for a holiday as they come. I prefer Labor Day or Columbus
Day. You don't get any mail, but nothing blows up.

Last week, however, I realized that Rat Patrol is still with me. 20
I was watching a movie on TV with my son. The movie was *The
Secret Garden*. During a particularly touching moment, I looked
over at my son. He appeared to be close to nausea. I asked him
whether he liked the movie. He said no, very emphatically. I asked
him what he didn't like.

"Heartfelt moments, Dad," he said. 21

"What *do* you like?" I asked. 22

He looked right at me. 23

"Explosions," he said. "That's what I like. Lots of explosions." 24

The next day, the boy's mother asks me to have a little talk with 25
my son. He has been showing, she feels, an unhealthy interest in

explosives, detonation, carnage, destruction, and other allegedly unhealthy aspects of life. My son is nine years old, and he has the same name—first and last—as I do.

I sit in a chair that makes me look as if I have that thing they   26 call authority. It's a big purple chair with ugly stitching. A chair Goliath would have picked out at Haverty's if he had had the chance. Now we are ready to talk.

I clear my throat. Yes, I am the dad. My voice is deeper than   27 his. My tone, when I begin, is somber yet vaguely intense. I tell him the most appalling stories about explosions that I can devise. After a moment I realize that if I make the stories *too* appalling, they will have the wrong effect. So I tell stories that are appalling but also a little boring. I mention grisly details, and occasionally I veer off into narrative. I tell him about the guy in the Ripley's "Believe It or Not"—the railroad worker. Just another honest workin' man putting in his time. Maybe looking to qualify for the retirement plan. About ten o'clock, though, maybe thinking about taking a break for some coffee or something, he pounds a steel railroad spike into the ground with a sledgehammer. He has done this all day every day for ten years or fifteen years. Every time, the same thing happens: the spike goes about four or five inches into the ground. Then it's time to hit it again. Do this for about five hours and it's time for lunch.

This time, though, it's not like that. This time he hits the   28 spike, just like normal. It goes in about five inches, just like nor-mal. Then something a little different happens. This time there's a massive, ear-shattering explosion. The spike flies back at his head at an almost unimaginable speed. It hits the side of the poor guy's chin with, of course, the flat end first. The spike, which is about two and a half inches thick, goes right through the guy's head. It leaves the mother of all exit wounds. A big, tomato-size exit wound, right on the side of his head. This poor man, making the post–Civil War equivalent of $4.25 an hour, has just had a thirty-five-pound spike driven straight through his post–Civil War head.

As I tell this, my voice gets quieter, more intense, more Clint   29 Eastwood. I tell this as intensely as I can, trying with everything I have to convey the impression that things that explode are things that are bad. I think, with all due modesty, that I am doing this pretty well. I give myself at least a B-plus. I'm not Olivier, but I'm not Brad Pitt either.

Nevertheless, I detect in my son's eyes a need for further convincing. 30

I go to the big well. Vietnam. Northern Ireland. Bosnia. 31 Hiroshima. Mangled bodies. Severed limbs. Missing eyeballs. Slow decapitations. Large pieces of metal flying through tender pieces of human flesh. Fragmentation bombs dropped near elephants. Tiny babies. Sobbing women. Everywhere anguished wails and unending human torment.

And why? Why? 32

I'll tell you why, my son. Because of those things that explode, 33 that's why.

I hope I'm clear. 34

Then I realize I can add something very intense and personal 35 and powerful to all this. I pull my hair back from my forehead and point to a long scar that intersects my left eyebrow.

"See this?" I ask. 36

He leans forward. "Yeah." I can see he's interested. 37

"Let me tell you how I got this." He sits down again. I begin. 38

"When I was in college, one night a bunch of guys and me, we 39 got real bored. So we were looking around for something to do. One guy had a CO_2 capsule."

"What's that?" 40

"It's a little metal cylinder. CO_2 is carbon dioxide. They use it 41 for scientific stuff. Anyway, he had this empty one. We decided— I forget whose idea this was—to stuff it full of match heads and make a bomb."

I look at my son's eyes. He's really interested now. 42

"We kept stuffing match heads in it. Finally, we couldn't fit 43 any more in there. That's when we started pounding them in there."

I wince in recollection. 44

"We got a file and pliers and a hammer. We used the pliers to 45 hold the CO_2 capsule while another guy pounded the match heads in. Finally, it got to be like a 'guts' thing. Like who had the nerve to keep pounding those things in. At the end, a guy named Bob Foundry was holding the capsule, and I pounded the last match head in."

"Then what happened?"   46

"It exploded. It exploded so loud I really couldn't hear it, just   47 a crazy ringing. I looked over at myself in the mirror, and the whole left side of my face was covered in blood. They rushed me to the emergency room and gave me thirty-five stitches. The doctor said that if I was his son, he would have beaten the hell out of me. There were pieces of the capsule stuck an inch deep in the cinderblock walls of the dorm room. They never did get them out. They were still in the wall when we left at the end of the year. If the capsule had exploded a half inch lower, a fragment would have gone into my eye, and I'd either be blind or, more likely, dead, because the fragment would have just kept going until it entered my brain."

There's a pause. We both just sit there. I finally get up and get   48 a glass of water. My mouth has gotten very dry.

About two hours later, my son starts asking me about CO_2 49 capsule bombs. He wants to make sure he's got the details right.

Meaning and Purpose

1. An early part of this essay contains a how-to section, that is, how to make a bomb. How is that information important to Gannon's anecdote?
2. Why does it bother the author that his son does not like the "heartfelt moments" (paragraph 21) in the movie that he and his son watched together?
3. This essay deals with a moral, that which is "good" or "right" in one's conduct. In your opinion, what is the moral of this essay?
4. Why did Gannon entitle his essay "Rat Patrol: A Saga"? Specifically, what does the term *saga* convey to the reader?

Strategy

1. What is significant about Gannon's scar? What does it add to the story that he tells his son?
2. After mentioning a game that he used to play, more than thirty years ago, Gannon writes, "Here is how the game *is* played" (paragraph 7). Why does the author shift to the present tense?
3. Gannon notes that "Dads" helped his friends and him in the "Rat Patrol cause" (paragraph 11). How can you tell by reading the essay that the "Dads" did not know that they had contributed to that "cause"?
4. Why did Gannon list Vietnam, Northern Ireland, Bosnia, and Hiroshima (paragraph 31)?

Style

1. First, Gannon relates an incident about himself in this essay, and then he relates an incident about himself and his son. In terms of their style, what do the two incidents have in common?
2. When we read on a product's label the words "Warning: Contents Under Pressure," we usually exercise care with that product. Why, then, does Gannon call that warning "those magic words" (paragraph 11)?
3. In the statement "that thing they call authority" (paragraph 26), who are "they"?
4. *Harper's Magazine* has a comparatively educated readership. In your opinion, is the style of this essay a comparatively educated style?

Writing Tasks

1. In our youth, each of us has done something that could have caused us physical or psychological harm. However, at the time we did it, either we did not think about the possibly harmful

consequences or we did not care about them. In your essay, describe step by step an incident in your life that could have
harmed you or your friends, either physically or psychologically.

2. This essay begins by discussing the television series *Rat Patrol*, a
    series that began in 1966, ended in 1967, and had a total of 56
    episodes, each including a plan on how to attack the enemy or
    how to resist an attack from the enemy. Write an essay in which
    you discuss one episode of a current television series that in-
    volves its characters in some kind of planning, including the
    steps in the process involved in that planning.

❦ Donald M. Murray ❦

Donald M. Murray was born in 1924 in Boston. He has had a long and distinguished career as a writer and teacher. Murray has published fiction, nonfiction, and poetry, served as an editor of Time *magazine, and won the Pulitzer Prize for editorial writing in 1959. His teaching career at the University of New Hampshire, Durham, and the textbooks he has published on how to write—*A Writer Teaches Writing, Write to Learn, *and* Read to Write*—have established him as one of America's most influential teachers of writing. He sees the writing teacher as a coach and is convinced that a student must want to learn and be willing to exert much effort in order to write well.*

The Maker's Eye
Revising Your Own Manuscripts

Originally published in The Writer, *this essay demonstrates the process professional writers go through to revise their manuscripts. Murray distinguishes the differences in attitudes that student writers and professional writers take to the revising process and cites other professional writers to argue for the essential importance of meticulous revision.*

As you read, note any differences between the methods you use to revise a paper and the methods the professional writer uses. Jot down advice you might find helpful in improving your own writing.

When students complete a first draft, they consider the job of writing done—and their teachers too often agree. When professional writers complete a first draft, they usually feel that they are at the start of the writing process. When a draft is completed, the job of writing can begin.

That difference in attitude is the difference between amateur and professional, inexperience and experience, journeyman and craftsman. Peter F. Drucker, the prolific business writer, calls his

427

first draft "the zero draft"—after that he can start counting. Most writers share the feeling that the first draft, and all of those which follow, are opportunities to discover what they have to say and how best they can say it.

To produce a progression of drafts, each of which says more   3
and says it more clearly, the writer has to develop a special kind of reading skill. In school we are taught to decode what appears on the page as finished writing. Writers, however, face a different category of possibility and responsibility when they read their own drafts. To them the words on the page are never finished. Each can be changed and rearranged, can set off a chain reaction of confusion or clarified meaning. This is a different kind of reading, which is possibly more difficult and certainly more exciting.

Writers must learn to be their own best enemy. They must   4
accept the criticism of others and be suspicious of it; they must accept the praise of others and be even more suspicious of it. Writers cannot depend on others. They must detach themselves from their own pages so that they can apply both their caring and their craft to their own work.

Such detachment is not easy. Science fiction writer Ray   5
Bradbury supposedly puts each manuscript away for a year to the day and then rereads it as a stranger. Not many writers have the discipline or the time to do this. We must read when our judgment may be at its worst, when we are close to the euphoric moment of creation.

Then the writer, counsels novelist Nancy Hale, "should be   6
critical of everything that seems to him most delightful in his style. He should excise what he most admires, because he wouldn't thus admire it if he weren't . . . in a sense protecting it from criticism." John Ciardi, the poet, adds, "The last act of the writing must be to become one's own reader. It is, I suppose, a schizophrenic process, to begin passionately and to end critically, to begin hot and to end cold; and, more important, to be passion-hot and critic-cold at the same time."

Most people think that the principal problem is that writers   7
are too proud of what they have written. Actually, a greater problem for most professional writers is one shared by the majority of

students. They are overly critical, think everything is dreadful, tear up page after page, never complete a draft, see the task as hopeless.

The writer must learn to read critically but constructively, to cut what is bad, to reveal what is good. Eleanor Estes, the children's book author, explains: "The writer must survey his work critically, coolly, as though he were a stranger to it. He must be willing to prune, expertly and hard-heartedly. At the end of each revision, a manuscript may look . . . worked over, torn apart, pinned together, added to, deleted from, words changed and words changed back. Yet the book must maintain its original freshness and spontaneity."   8

Most readers underestimate the amount of rewriting it usually takes to produce spontaneous reading. This is a great disadvantage to the student writer, who sees only a finished product and never watches the craftsman who takes the necessary step back, studies the work carefully, returns to the task, steps back, returns, steps back, again and again. Anthony Burgess, one of the most prolific writers in the English-speaking world, admits, "I might revise a page twenty times." Ronald Dahl, the popular children's writer, states, "By the time I'm nearing the end of a story, the first part will have been reread and altered and corrected at least 150 times. . . . Good writing is essentially rewriting. I am positive of this."   9

Rewriting isn't virtuous. It isn't something that ought to be done. It is simply something that most writers find they have to do to discover what they have to say and how to say it. It is a condition of the writer's life.   10

There are, however, a few writers who do little formal rewriting, primarily because they have the capacity and experience to create and review a large number of invisible drafts in their minds before they approach the page. And some writers slowly produce finished pages, performing all the tasks of revision simultaneously, page by page, rather than draft by draft. But it is still possible to see the sequence followed by most writers most of the time in rereading their own work.   11

Most writers scan their drafts first, reading as quickly as possible to catch the larger problems of subject and form, then   12 move in closer and closer as they read and write, reread and rewrite.

The first thing writers look for in their drafts is *information*. 13 They know that a good piece of writing is built from specific, accurate, and interesting information. The writer must have an abundance of information from which to construct a readable piece of writing.

Next writers look for *meaning* in the information. The 14 specifics must build a pattern of significance. Each piece of specific information must carry the reader toward meaning.

Writers reading their own drafts are aware of *audience*. They 15 put themselves in the reader's situation and make sure that they deliver information which a reader wants to know or needs to know in a manner which is easily digested. Writers try to be sure that they anticipate and answer the questions a critical reader will ask when reading the piece of writing.

Writers make sure that the *form* is appropriate to the subject 16 and the audience. Form, or genre, is the vehicle which carries meaning to the reader, but form cannot be selected until the writer has adequate information to discover its significance and an audience which needs or wants that meaning.

Once writers are sure the form is appropriate, they must then 17 look at the *structure*, the order of what they have written. Good writing is built on a solid framework of logic, argument, narrative, or motivation which runs through the entire piece of writing and holds it together. This is the time when many writers find it most effective to outline as a way of visualizing the hidden spine by which the piece of writing is supported.

The element on which writers may spend a majority of 18 their time is *development*. Each section of a piece of writing must be adequately developed. It must give readers enough information so that they are satisfied. How much information is enough? That's as difficult as asking how much garlic belongs in a salad. It must be done to taste, but most beginning writers underdevelop, underestimating the reader's hunger for information.

As writers solve development problems, they often have to   19
consider questions of *dimension*. There must be a pleasing and effective proportion among all the parts of the piece of writing.
There is a continual process of subtracting and adding to keep the
piece of writing in balance.

Finally, writers have to listen to their own voices. *Voice* is the   20
force which drives a piece of writing forward. It is an expression
of the writer's authority and concern. It is what is between the
words on the page, what glues the piece of writing together. A
good piece of writing is always marked by a consistent, individual
voice.

As writers read and reread, write and rewrite, they move   21
closer and closer to the page until they are doing line-by-line editing. Writers read their own pages with infinite care. Each sentence, each line, each clause, each phrase, each word, each mark
of punctuation, each section of white space between the type has
to contribute to the clarification of meaning.

Slowly the writer moves from word to word, looking through   22
language to see the subject. As a word is changed, cut, or added,
as a construction is rearranged, all the words used before that moment and all those that follow that moment must be considered
and reconsidered.

Writers often read aloud at this stage of the editing process,   23
muttering or whispering to themselves, calling on the ear's experience with language. Does this sound right—or that? Writers
edit, shifting back and forth from eye to page to ear to page. I find
I must do this careful editing in short runs, no more than fifteen
or twenty minutes at a stretch, or I become too kind with myself.
I begin to see what I hope is on the page, not what actually is on
the page.

This sounds tedious if you haven't done it, but actually it is   24
fun. Making something right is immensely satisfying, for writers
begin to learn what they are writing about by writing. Language
leads them to meaning, and there is the joy of discovery, of understanding, of making meaning clear as the writer employs the
technical skills of language.

Words have double meanings, even triple and quadruple   25
meanings. Each word has its own potential for connotation and
denotation. And when writers rub one word against the other,
they are often rewarded with a sudden insight, an unexpected
clarification.

The maker's eye moves back and forth from word to phrase to   26
sentence to paragraph to sentence to phrase to word. The maker's
eye sees the need for variety and balance, for a firmer structure, for
a more appropriate form. It peers into the interior of the paragraph, looking for coherence, unity, and emphasis, which make
meaning clear.

I learned something about this process when my first bifocals   27
were prescribed. I had ordered a larger section of the reading portion of the glass because of my work, but even so, I could not contain my eyes within this new limit of vision. And I still find myself
taking off my glasses and bending my nose towards the page, for
my eyes unconsciously flick back and forth across the page, back
to another page, forward to still another, as I try to see each evolv-
ing line in relation to every other line.

When does this process end? Most writers agree with the great   28
Russian writer Tolstoy, who said, "I scarcely ever reread my published writings, if by chance I come across a page, it always strikes
me: all this must be rewritten; this is how I should have written it."

The maker's eye is never satisfied, for each word has the po-   29
tential to ignite new meaning. This article has been twice written
all the way through the writing process, and it was published four
years ago. Now it is to be republished in a book. The editors make
a few small suggestions, and then I read it with my maker's eye.
Now it has been re-edited, re-revised, re-read, re-re-edited, for
each piece of writing to the writer is full of potential and alternatives.

A piece of writing is never finished. It is delivered to a dead-   30
line, torn out of the typewriter on demand, sent off with a sense of
accomplishment and shame and pride and frustration. If only
there were a couple more days, time for just another run at it, perhaps then . . .

Meaning and Purpose

1. According to Murray, what are the differences in the ways in which professional writers and student writers view their first drafts? Do his observations ring true? Do both types of writers share any common problems?
2. What two kinds of reading skills does the author distinguish? How does the writer's reading skill differ from that of the normal readers?
3. What does Murray mean when he says, "Writers must learn to be their own best enemy" (paragraph 4)? Explain.
4. In paragraphs 12–30, Murray takes the reader chronologically through each of the elements that a writer must consider to revise a manuscript. Describe the ways in which a writer must consider each of these elements.
5. Murray distinguishes between "information" and "meaning." Explain the difference between the two.
6. Explain Murray's contention that "A piece of writing is never finished" (paragraph 30).

Strategy

1. What is the essay's thesis? Where is it stated?
2. Is the essay an example of directive or informative process analysis (see pp. 389–394)? Explain.
3. Murray cites other writers in his description of the revision process. Why?
4. Explain the author's seemingly odd statement that "most writers share the feeling that the first draft, and all of those which follow, are opportunities to discover what they have to say" (paragraph 2).
5. Murray doesn't actually begin a description of the professional writer's revision process until paragraph 12. What is the purpose of such a long introduction?

Style

1. Murray changes from the third person ("writer," "writers," "the maker") to the first person ("I") in paragraphs 23, 27, and 29. What effect does he create by this change of person?
2. Why does Murray end the essay in midsentence?
3. If necessary, use a dictionary to determine the meanings of these words: *journeyman, prolific* (paragraph 2); *euphoric* (5); *schizophrenic* (6); *connotation, denotation* (25).

Writing Tasks

1. Write an essay in which you detail the way in which you revise an essay. In the process, explain, why this method might work better for you than the method explained by Murray.
2. If you use a computer to write, explain the advantages of revising on a computer.
3. Write an essay in which you explain to the reader a process that you do regularly and well. Without being moralistic, demonstrate how this might actually benefit the reader.

❦ Responding to Photographs ❦

Process Analysis

Untitled

For some writers the act of writing can be so painful that they go to remarkable lengths to postpone the labor. They travel to the farthest stationery store for the "right" pencil, the one with the exact texture of lead that works best with the amount of pressure they apply to the paper. When they return, they might discover that they are short of the right kind of paper—you know, the yellow pads with the blue lines. Again back to the stationery store. Home once again, all those new pencils must be sharpened to a fine—a very, very fine—point.

What's the solution to this kind of procrastination?

There probably isn't one, for writing is a deeply personal process, one that is full of mystery. Probably no two people go about it exactly the same way. We all use devices to get ourselves started and to keep ourselves at the task. Nevertheless, something must get written. We must get the images and thoughts out of our heads, translate them to words, and put them on paper. Then, of course, a new process begins: the revision process.

Clearly, the untitled photograph here captures a moment in the writing process. For this essay you are to explore the writing process by completing one of the following writing tasks. Before beginning the task, reread the material at the beginning of the chapter to remind yourself of process analysis strategies.

1. Create an appropriate title for the untitled photograph. Then describe its content as capturing part of the writing process. In your essay, account for all the elements in the photograph that relate to the writing process—manuscript, pencils, coffee, calendar, stapler, glasses, desk or table, even the writer's posture.
2. Document your own writing process with photographs of its various stages. Then use the photographs to compose a "photo-essay" that concentrates on your own writing process. Use at least five photographs, each one capturing a stage in the process, and explain to your readers what the photographs signify. Keep in mind that writing is a highly personal process, so be sure your photographs and essay embody your personal writing quirks.

🍏 Additional Writing Tasks 🍏

Process Analysis

1. Develop one of these subjects (or one you create for yourself) through *directive process analysis*. Explain the process one step at a time, and be sure to provide your reader with enough detail to make each step clear.
   a. how to prepare a vegetable garden
   b. how to live without an automobile
   c. how to domesticate a wild creature, such as a falcon or rabbit
   d. how to get rid of pests without using poisons
   e. how to prepare for an acting role
   f. how to prepare a canvas for paint
   g. how to show appreciation to others
   h. how to toss a Frisbee, football, baseball, and so on
   i. how to skateboard, roller blade, roller skate
   j. how to bluff at poker
   k. how to survive Muzak
   l. how to complain effectively
   m. how to overcome shyness
   n. how to write an effective essay
   o. how to take effective notes
   p. how to outsmart a video game
   q. how to survive a natural disaster, such as an earthquake or tornado
   r. how to meditate in a crowded setting
   s. how to ride a roller coaster
   t. how to attend a concert
   u. how to run for local elected office
   v. how to win others to your point of view
   w. how to buy a used motorcycle or car

2. Develop one of these subjects (or one you create for yourself) through *informative process analysis*. Remember that this technique does not explain how to do something; it explains how something happens—it informs, often using narrative and descriptive techniques.
   a. how psychoanalysis works

b. how secret codes are broken
c. how to read detective, espionage, or suspense fiction
d. how to learn from past experience
e. how a stroke damages the brain
f. how Alzheimer's disease develops
g. how dreams work
h. how intuition works
i. how to taste wine
j. how to create a frightening film scene
k. how to create suspense
l. how to collect art, rare books, or something else
m. how to detect lies
n. how to overcome guilt
o. how to change community thinking
p. how to live as an outsider
q. how to become an insider
r. how an idea becomes accepted
s. how voodoo works

9

Classification and Division

Establishing Categories

The Method

Have you ever played Twenty Questions, a parlor game in which one participant selects a person, place, or thing and the other participants try to guess what or who it is? The participants may ask up to twenty yes-or-no questions to find the answer. To discover that answer is a difficult task—unless you understand the principles of **classification.**

The game usually begins with a series of questions that divide the world into three roughly drawn categories: animal, vegetable, or mineral. Once the correct category is determined—"animal," for our purposes—the interrogation begins, the participants moving logically from category to category.

"Does it live in water?" a questioner might ask—a sensible question, for the earth is easily divided into land and water.

"No," the person with the secret responds. But "No" means that the animal lives on land. Of course, birds may fly but may also nest on land. The process of elimination continues.

"Does it have two legs?" Another logical question, because animals can be classified by locomotion.

"No."

"Four legs?" The pace of questions quickens.

"No."

Aha! the questioner has it: "Is this creature an insect?"

"Nope!" Oops . . . must be a snake, right? But what snake? The only two large categories are venomous and nonvenomous. If the answer is venomous, the questions will take one direction, "Does it have rattles?" If the answer is nonvenomous, the questions will move in another direction, "Does it kill by coiling around and crushing its prey?" And so on, until the secret is revealed or the twenty questions are exhausted.

To classify is to divide a large subject into components and sort them into categories with common characteristics, a principle that clearly guides the search in any round of Twenty Questions. Classification is so pervasive that it must be fundamental to the human way of perceiving and understanding experience. Few things, no matter how significant or insignificant, seem to escape classification. Think how chaotic your campus library would be without a clear classification system. Your supermarket trips are probably organized by the manager's way of classifying products—first the vegetables, on to dairy products, rush to meats, march to canned goods, stalled at the register. Television shows, books, actors, restaurants, fun-zone rides—the possibilities for classification are endless because of our desire to understand and organize experience.

Keep in mind, too, that most subjects can be classified in a number of ways, depending on the purpose and who's doing the classifying. Consider the subject *college students.* For statistical purposes, a registrar might classify college students by age, sex, major, grade-point average, or region. An art teacher might classify students by their talent: painters, sculptors, ceramicists, illustrators, and print makers. A political science teacher might classify the same students by their politics: reactionary, conservative, liberal, or radical. Much of this kind of classification is done informally; but in writing, a classification system should be complete and follow consistent principles.

Writers using classification as a pattern of development begin by carefully analyzing their subject—that is, by breaking it into components. They look for qualities that some components share and that others don't share. Using the qualities they've identified, they create categories. They then sort through the various components to group them in the appropriate category. They are careful to be logical, sorting and grouping the parts in a consistent manner. They also keep in mind that their categories must be complete. It would not be complete if they divided voters into Republicans and Democrats, because some voters are registered in the Peace and Freedom and Libertarian parties, among others. But if a writer's subject is limited to elected senators, then the categories might indeed be Republicans and Democrats, because no other party is represented in the Senate. Writers also make sure that their categories do not overlap. To classify a group of congresswomen as Republicans, Democrats, and politicians would not make much sense because all are politicians.

Professional writers distinguish between the terms *division* and *classification*, yet these categories are intellectual companions in the classification procedure. Writers begin by first *dividing* a subject into manageable categories. They then *classify* the components of the subject according to the shared qualities. Consider the subject *movies*, which can be broken down into such categories as mystery, romance, horror, musical, comedy, western, and war. This step is division. Once the categories are established, a writer might evaluate several films, and sort them according to the qualities of each category. This step is classification. Remember, division breaks one subject into categories; classification groups the parts of the subject into the categories. Although this distinction may be important for understanding the intellectual procedure of classification, it is less important in reaching the result, a system that shows the relationship among parts of a subject.

The simplest form of classification is **two-part**, often called **binary**, classification. This pattern divides a subject in two, usually into positive and negative categories, such as vegetarians and non-vegetarians; smokers and nonsmokers; television viewers and non–television viewers; deaf people and hearing people; or runners and nonrunners. But two-part classification is usually inexact and skirts the edge of comparison and contrast. Most classification systems therefore have at least three categories.

Strategies

Careful writers arrange their classifications in a straightforward division, usually in blocks and according to the order that seems most appropriate. Each block is a subclass and will usually be identified by a name or phrase to keep the reader on track. In the following paragraph, anthropologist Ruth Benedict divides the ceremonial societies of the Zuñi. She clearly identifies each society—the priestly societies, the masked-god societies, and the medicine societies—before describing them.

This ceremonial life that preoccupies Zuni attention is organized like a series of interlocking wheels. The priesthoods have their sacred objects, their retreats, their dances, their prayers; and their year-long program is annually initiated by the great winter solstice ceremony that makes use of all the different groups and sacred things and focuses all their functions. The tribal masked-god society has similar possessions and calendric observances, and these culminate in the great winter tribal masked god ceremony, the Shalkado. In like fashion the medicine societies, with their special relation to curing, function throughout the year and have their annual culminating ceremony for tribal health. These three major cults of Zuni ceremonial life are not mutually exclusive. A man may be, and often is, for the greater part of his life, a member of all three. They each give him sacred possessions "to live by" and demand of him exacting ceremonial knowledge.

Writers use one of two strategies to identify their categories. They either use ready-made categories or create their own. In the next classification passage, from *Blood and Money*, Thomas Thompson uses subclasses to present his view of the personal characteristics that describe surgeons.

Among those who train students to become doctors, it is said that surgeons find their niche in accordance with their personal characteristics. The orthopedic surgeon is medicine's carpenter—up to his elbows in plaster of Paris—and tradition holds that he is a gruff, slapdash sort of man whose labor is in a very physical area of healing. Away from the hospital, the orthopedists are often hunters, boaters, outdoorsmen.

The neurosurgeon, classically, does not get too involved with his patients. Or, for that matter, with anybody. They are cool men, blunted, rarely gregarious.

Heart surgeons are thundering egotists, star performers in a dazzling operating theater packed with assistants, nurses, paramedics, and a battery of futuristic equipment which could seemingly lift the room into outer space. These are men who relish drama, who live life on the edge of the precipice.

And the plastic surgeon? He is, by nature, a man of art, and temperament, and sensitivity. "We are the artists who deal in beauty lost, or beauty that never was," said one plastic man at a national convention. "Our stitches are hidden, and so are our emotions."

Because Thompson is working with established categories, part of his task is to make his material fresh. Most readers know the professional qualities of surgeons, and so Thompson creates a sense of the person holding the scalpel by including descriptive details of each type's dominant personality trait.

In the next paragraph, Larry McMurtry uses established categories in a slightly different way. He classifies beer bars in the city of Houston according to their location: East side, West side, and North side.

> The poor have beer-bars, hundreds of them, seldom fancy but reliably dim and cool. Most of them are equipped with jukeboxes, shuffleboards, jars of pig's feet and talkative drunks. There are lots of bar burlesques, where from 3 p.m. on girls gyrate at one's elbow with varying degrees of grace. On the East side there are a fair number of open-air bars—those who like to watch the traffic can sit, drink Pearl, observe the wrecks, and listen to "Hello, Vietnam" on the juke box. Louisiana is just down the road, and a lot of the men wear Cajun sideburns and leave their shirttails out. On the West side cowboys are common. Members of the cross-continental hitch-hiking set congregate on Franklin Street, at places like The Breaking Point Lounge. Symbolic latinos slip over to the Last Concert on the North side; or, if they are especially bold, go all the way to McCarty Street, where one can view the most extraordinary example of Mexican saloon-and-whorehouse architecture north of the border.

McMurtry opens with a general description of Houston beer bars: They are dim and cool with jukeboxes, shuffleboards, jars of pig's feet, and drunks—a watering hole for blue-collar men. After rendering the general qualities of these bars, McMurtry presents the geographic categories, each with a brief description that characterizes it.

Writers often classify a subject that has no ready-made categories. They must, therefore, create their own categories and the labels that identify them. In this paragraph from "Here Is New York," E. B. White divides the population of New York into three categories according to a person's relation to the city.

> There are roughly three New Yorks. There is, first, the New York of the man or woman who was born here, who takes the city for granted and accepts its size and its turbulence as natural and inevitable. Second, there is the New York of the commuter—the city that is devoured by locusts each day and spat out each night. Third, there is the New York of the quest of something. Of these three trembling cities the greatest is the last—the city of final destination, the city that is a goal. It is this third city that accounts for New York's high-strung disposition, its poetical deportment, its dedication to the arts, and its incomparable achievements. Commuters give the city its tidal restlessness; natives give it solidarity and continuity; but the settlers give it passion. And whether it is a farmer arriving from Italy to set up a small grocery store in a slum, or a young girl arriving from a small town in Mississippi to escape the indignity of being observed by her neighbors, or a boy arriving from the Corn Belt with a manuscript in his suitcase and a pain in his heart, it makes no difference: each embraces New York with the intense excitement of first love, each absorbs New York with the fresh eyes of an adventurer, each generates heat and light to dwarf the Consolidated Edison Company.

Commuters, natives, and settlers, these are White's three categories. He uses each category to present characteristics of New York City. The commuter gives the city a sense of restlessness; the native gives it solidarity; and the settler, the category he stresses, gives it passion.

Classification in College Writing

The physical sciences, social sciences, and humanities all use classification, which some writers believe is the hardest rhetorical pattern to master. Whether the pattern is difficult or not, you can expect to use it across the academic curriculum.

Guidelines for Classification

1. Select a subject that can be divided into at least three components. Identify the chief characteristics of each component. Use the characteristics to sort and group the components into categories.
2. Examine the categories with two questions in mind: Are they complete—that is, can all the components of your subject be grouped within them? Are the categories consistent—that is, can any of your component parts be classified in more than one category? If your categories are incomplete or inconsistent, then restructure them or move on to another subject.
3. Compose a thesis that clearly indicates that you will be classifying your subject. If you use ready-made categories or name your categories, include the names as part of the thesis. Naming your categories early will prepare your readers for the shift from one category to another in the discussion.
4. Decide how to arrange your categories effectively, saving the most dramatic for last.
5. Revise your essay, making sure that each category is clearly distinguished and adequately developed.

A Student Essay Developed by Classification

For an assignment in cultural anthropology, Mark Freeman wrote a classification essay on the general topic of people who collect artifacts from popular culture. His assignment was as follows:

> · From your own experience and observation, write a 500- to 600-word essay that classifies "collectors," that is, people who collect such popular culture artifacts as baseball cards, garage-sale paintings, bottles, magazines, movie posters, bottle caps, tourist novelties, campaign buttons, and celebrity autographs.
>
> Concentrate on vertical as opposed to horizontal collectors—that is, those who collect one kind of artifact rather that several different kinds.

Freeman selected the general subject "magazines." He quickly narrowed this to the more specific subject "comic books." Since he was once an avid comic book collector, he had plenty of material to work with. First read Freeman's classification and division essay, then reread it and respond to items in Reviewing with a Writer's Eye.

In Search of the Comic

Comic book collectors represent every income level and often fit the stereotype of the computer nerd; that is, whether young or old, they tend to be pale disheveled males who wear glasses and speak a language the uninitiated seldom understand. They can be found rummaging through pile after pile of unsorted, secondhand comics in magazine marts across the country. These collectors, the serious ones, can be classified into four major groups: Antiquarians, Mercenaries, Idolaters, and Compulsive Completers.

The Antiquarian searches for classic comics only, subject matter is of no concern. He is looking for a 1933 *Funnies on Parade* or *Famous Funnies*, the first publications that are recognizable as comic books and initially used as giveaways in advertising promotions. The

Antiquarian, driven by a desire to connect with the past, will travel the country's backroads to find 1933 editions of The Spider, which was reintroduced as the Spiderman series in 1962.

The Mercenary searches for value. Certain numbers   3
and titles ring a bell in his cash-register brain and start him checking through a half-dozen price sheets. A pristine first edition of Action Comics (value $12,000) would suit him just fine. He would also hunt down early editions of Marvel Comics, especially the first publications featuring early super heroes, such as Captain America, the Punisher, and the Human Torch. The Mercenary would, no doubt, love to have first editions of <u>Batman</u> and <u>Superman</u> but, being a realist, knows they are locked in vaults.

The Idolater has little interest in age or value. He   4
searches for favorites: a <u>Sheena</u>, a <u>Flash Gordon</u>, or an <u>Incredible Hulk</u>. With little money to spend, the Idolater will usually be hiding in the corner of a comic mart, reading the comic books he cannot afford to buy. He will freely announce his dream of creating his own hero figure and is always eager to display his sketches to anyone willing to listen to his heroic tales and future visions. The Idolater will be the last one out of the mart at night and the first one back in the morning.

The most frustrated of the group is the Compulsive   5
Completer. This obsessed collector will examine and reject thousands of comics in a search for a badly needed <u>Felix the Cat</u> to complete a year's set. The Completer is usually a specialist, perhaps concentrating on comic books featuring animals, such as Mighty Mouse, a pint-sized superior who became famous when featured in cartoons shown between movies in theaters across America, or Super Rabbit, a long-eared protector of the innocent who became known during W.W. II for fighting Nazis in the pages of Marvel Comics. Compulsive Completers often become so desperate to acquire every issue published in one year they will seek bank loans to cover their costs.

Although driven by different motivations, the   6
Antiquarian, Mercenary, Idolater, and Compulsive Completer share a common trait: They love the thrill of the hunt.

Reviewing with a Writer's Eye

1. What characteristics do all members of Freeman's categories share?
2. Develop your own scratch outline (p. 42) of Mark Freeman's "In Search of the Comic." What do you believe to be Freeman's organizational strategy? Why is the conclusion composed of a single sentence?
3. Should Freeman have created a fifth category named Explorers, that is, people who buy comics, read them, and then toss them aside? Explain.
4. In the first sentence of paragraph 3, Freeman uses the word "searches" for the first time. Where else does he use the word and other words with similar meanings? Why?

Peer Review

You may be asked to write an essay about one of the readings that follow. Before you meet with your writing group, review this introduction. As you read the group papers, use these general principles of classification and division to help guide your comments.

1. A classification system should have at least three categories to distinguish it from comparison and contrast.
2. A classification paper should give a reader a fresh way of looking at a subject. Even if the categories used are already established and well known, the content describing each category should be fresh.
3. The categories chosen should not overlap and allow a component to be assigned to more than one class.
4. The categories should be complete, covering the entire subject.

5. In a brief note to Freeman, evaluate his essay by the conventions that dominate classification (pp. 440–445). In what ways does his essay succeed? In what ways does it fail?

The essays that follow show the variety of ways in which writers divide and classify subjects. Study them closely. Note the categories each writer establishes. Ask yourself whether the categories are complete and consistent, two important tests to determine whether a classification essay is successful.

❦ Alison Lurie ❦

Born in Chicago in 1926, Alison Lurie graduated from Radcliffe College. As a fiction writer, she has often been compared to Jane Austen, both for her style and for her subject matter, which has often been a particular segment of American society—that of the wealthy and educated. Since publication of her first novel, Love and Friendship, *in 1962, she has published eight more, including the 1998 publication of* The Last Resort. *Lurie received the Pulitzer Prize for her 1984 novel,* Foreign Affairs. *She has also published three children's books and a nonfiction book on the social history of clothes. Her most recent nonfiction publication is* Don't Tell the Grownups: The Subversive Power of Children's Literature.

American Regional Costume

In this excerpt from her 1981 book The Language of Clothes, *Lurie classifies American styles of dress by region and the people of those regions by the clothes they wear. She traces the historical influences of climate, landscape, economy, and life-style on various regional "costumes."*

While reading this essay, pay careful attention to the ways in which Lurie carefully describes each regional costume so that the classifications of dress do not overlap.

Even today, when the American landscape is becoming more and more homogeneous, there is really no such thing as an all-American style of dress. A shopping center in Maine may superficially resemble one in Georgia or California, but the shoppers in it will look different, because the diverse histories of these states have left their mark on costume.

Regional dress in the United States, as in Britain, can best be observed at large national meetings where factors such as occupation and income are held relatively constant. At these meetings regional differences stand out clearly, and can be checked by

1

2

looking at the name tags Americans conventionally wear to conventions. Five distinct styles can be distinguished: (1) Old New England, (2) Deep South, (3) Middle American, (4) Wild West and (5) Far West or Californian. In border areas, outfits usually combine regional styles.

Americans who do not travel much within their own country   3
often misinterpret the styles of other regions. Natives of the Eastern states, for instance, may misread Far Western clothing as indicating greater casualness—or greater sexual availability—than is actually present. The laid-back-looking Los Angeles executive in his open-chested sport shirt and sandals may have his eye on the main chance to an extent that will shock his Eastern colleague. The reverse error can also occur: a Southern Californian may discover with surprise that the sober-hued, buttoned-up New Englander he or she has just met is bored with business and longing to get drunk or hop into bed.

Northeast and Southeast: Puritans and Planters

The drab, severe costumes of the Puritan settlers of New   4
England, and their suspicion of color and ornament as snares of the devil, have left their mark on the present-day clothes of New Englanders. At any large meeting people from this part of the country will be dressed in darker hues—notably black, gray and navy—often with touches of white that recall the starched collars and cuffs of Puritan costume. Fabrics will be plainer (though heavier and sometimes more expensive) and styles simpler, with less waste of material: skirts and lapels and trimmings will be narrower. More of the men will also wear suits and shoes made in England (or designed to look as if they had been made in England). The law of camouflage also operates in New England, where gray skies and dark rectangular urban landscapes are not unknown.

The distinctive dress of the Deep South is based on a climate   5
that did not demand heavy clothing and an economy that for years exempted middle- and upper-class whites from all manual labor and made washing and ironing cheap. Today the planter's white

suits and fondness for fine linen and his wife's and daughters' elaborate and fragile gowns survive in modern form. At our imaginary national meeting the male southerners will wear lighter-colored suits—pale grays and beiges—and a certain dandyism will be apparent, expressing itself in French cuffs, more expensive ties, silkier materials and wider pin stripes. The women's clothes will be more flowery, with a tendency toward bows, ruffles, lace and embroidery. If they are white, they will probably be as white as possible; a pale complexion is still the sign of a Southern lady, and female sun tans are unfashionable except on tourists.

Midwest and Wild West: Pioneers and Cowboys

The American Midwest and Great Plains states were settled by men and women who had to do their own work and prided themselves on it. They chose sturdy, practical clothes that did not show the dirt, washed and wore well and needed little ironing, made of gingham and linsey-woolsey and canvas. From these clothes descends the contemporary costume of Middle Americans. This style is visible to everyone on national television, where it is worn by most news announcers, politicians, talk-show hosts and actors in commercials for kitchen products. A slightly dowdier version appears in the Sears and Montgomery Ward catalogues. But even when expensive, Middle American fashion is apt to lag behind fashion as it is currently understood back East; it is also usually more sporty and casual. The pioneer regard for physical activity and exercise is still strong in this part of the country, and as a result the Midwesterners at our convention will look healthier and more athletic—and also somewhat beefier—than their colleagues from the cold, damp Northeast and the hot, humid South. Their suits will tend toward the tans and browns of plowed cornfields rather than the grays of Eastern skies. More of them will wear white or white-on-white shirts, and their striped or foulard ties will be brighter and patterned on a larger scale than those purchased in sober New York and Boston.

The traditional Western costume, of course, was that of the cowboy on the range. Perhaps because of the isolation of those wide-open spaces, this is the style which has been least influenced by those of other regions. At any national convention the Wild Westerners will be the easiest to identify. For one thing, they are apt to be taller—either genetically or with the help of boots. Some may appear in full Western costume, the sartorial equivalent of a "he-went-thataway" drawl; but even the more conservative will betray, or rather proclaim, their regional loyalty through their dress, just as in conversation they will from time to time use a ranching metaphor, or call you "pal" or "pardner." A man in otherwise conventional business uniform will wear what looks like cowboy boots, or a hat with an enlarged brim and crown. Women, too, are apt to wear boots, and their jackets and skirts may have a Western cut, especially when viewed from the rear. Some may wear red or navy-blue bandanna-print shirts or dresses, or an actual cotton-print bandanna knotted round their necks.

The Far West: Adventurers and Beach Boys

The men and women who settled the Far West were a mixed and rather raffish lot. Restlessness, the wish for excitement, the hope of a fortune in gold and sometimes a need to escape the law led them to undertake the long and dangerous journey over mountains and deserts, or by sea round Cape Horn. In more than one sense they were adventurers, and often desperadoes—desperate people. California was a territory where no one would ask about your past, where unconventionality of character and behavior was easily accepted. Even today when, as the country song puts it, "all the gold in California is in a bank in the middle of Beverly Hills in somebody else's name," the place has the reputation of an El Dorado. Men and women willing to risk everything on long odds in the hope of a big hit, or eager to put legal, financial and personal foul-ups behind them, often go west. 8

Present-day California styles are still in many ways those of adventurers and eccentrics. Whatever the current fashion, the California version will be more extreme, more various and—pos- 9 sibly because of the influence of the large Spanish-American population—much more colorful. Clothes tend to fit more tightly than is considered proper elsewhere, and to expose more flesh: an inability to button the shirt above the diaphragm is common in both sexes. Virtuous working-class housewives may wear outfits that in any other part of the country would identify them as medium-priced whores; reputable business and professional men may dress in a manner which would lose them most of their clients back east and attract the attention of the Bureau of Internal Revenue if not of the police.

Southern Californians, and many other natives of what is now 10 called the Sun Belt (an imaginary strip of land stretching across the bottom of the United States from Florida to Santa Barbara, but excluding most of the Old South), can also be identified by their year-round sun tans, which by middle age have often given the skin the look of old if expensive and well-oiled leather. The men may also wear the getup known as Sun Belt Cool: a pale beige suit, open-collared shirt (often in a darker shade than the suit), cream-colored loafers and aviator sunglasses. The female version of the look is similar, except that the shoes will be high-heeled sandals.

Regional Disguise: Sunbelt Puritans and Urban Cowboys

Some long-time inhabitants of California and the other sarto- 11 rially distinct regions of the United States refuse to wear the styles characteristic of that area. In this case the message is clear: they are unhappy in that locale and/or do not want anyone to attribute to them the traits associated with it. Such persons, if depressed, may adopt a vague and anonymous mode of dress; if in good spirits they may wear the costume of some other region in order to proclaim their sympathy with it. In terms of speech, what we have then is not a regional accent, but the conscious adoption of a dialect by an outsider.

In the urban centers of the West and Far West bankers and fi- 12 nancial experts of both sexes sometimes adopt an Eastern manner of speech and a Wall Street appearance in order to suggest reliability and tradition. And today in Southern California there are professors who speak with Bostonian accents, spend their days in the library stacks, avoid the beach and dress in clothes that would occasion no comment in Harvard Yard. New arrivals to the area sometimes take these men and women for visiting Eastern lecturers, and are surprised to learn that they have lived in Southern California for thirty or forty years, or have even been born there.

The popularity of the various regional styles of American 13 costume, like that of the various national styles, is also related to economic and political factors. Some years ago modes often originated in the Far West and the word "California" on a garment was thought to be an allurement. Today, with power and population growth shifting to the Southwestern oil-producing states, Wild West styles—particularly those of Texas—are in vogue. This fashion, of course, is not new. For many years men who have never been nearer to a cow than the local steakhouse have worn Western costume to signify that they are independent, tough and reliable. In a story by Flannery O'Connor, for instance, the sinister traveling salesman is described as wearing "a broad-brimmed stiff gray hat of the kind used by businessmen who would like to look like cowboys"—but, it is implied, seldom succeed in doing so.

The current popularity of Western costume has been in- 14 creased by the turn away from foreign modes that has accompanied the recent right-wing shift in United States politics. In all countries periods of isolationism and a belligerently ostrichlike stance toward the rest of the world have usually been reflected in a rejection of international modes in favor of national styles, often those of the past. Today in America the cowboy look is high fashion, and even in New York City the streets are full of a variety of Wild West types. Some are dressed in old-fashioned, well-worn Western gear; others in the newer, brighter and sleeker outfits of modern ranchers, while a few wear spangled, neon-hued Electric Cowboy and Cowgirl costumes of the type most often seen on Texas country-rock musicians.

Meaning and Purpose

1. If you were to classify American regional dress, would you choose Lurie's categories? Why or why not? If not, what would your categories be?
2. Why does Lurie claim that large, national meetings are best for observing regional dress?
3. What is Lurie's main point, and where does she state it?
4. Why is it possible to misinterpret the dress styles of different regions?
5. How does Lurie explain the differences in dress from region to region?
6. How does Lurie account for the then current popularity of Western costume? Do you agree with her?

Strategy

1. What scheme does Lurie use to organize her categories?
2. In paragraph 2, Lurie lists five categories of style of dress, but only three subheadings cover those five categories. Why do you suppose she puts the first two and the second two together and gives the Far West its own subheading?
3. Lurie adds to classification and division other rhetorical strategies to support her categories. Look again at paragraphs 4 and 5 and at paragraph 8 and paragraph 9. What strategies does she use in these places?
4. Lurie quotes a country song in paragraph 8 and the short-story writer and novelist Flannery O'Connor in paragraph 13. What is the purpose of these quotations?

Style

1. Lurie often juxtaposes formal sociological and anthropological language with the language of casual conversation and slang.

What are some examples of this mixture? What is the effect of such juxtapositions?

2. In her categories and descriptions, is Lurie making any judgments about regional dress, or is she neutral? Support your answer with language from the essay.

3. If necessary, check a dictionary for the meanings of these expressions: *homogeneous, superficially* (paragraph 1); *Puritan* (4); *dandyism* (5); *gingham, linsey-woolsey, dowdier, foulard* (6); *sartorial* (7); *raffish* (8); *allurement* (13); *isolationism, belligerently* (14).

Writing Tasks

1. Analyze the styles of dress popular on your campus. Create four or five style categories and use as many specific examples as you can. In a classification and division essay, establish clearly the basis for your classifications.

2. Examine the ways in which popular entertainment—movies, television, rock music, and rock music stars—affects dress, speech, or hair style. Write a classification essay in which you show how these influences have produced the styles you describe.

❦ John Holt ❦

John Holt is the author of, among other famous books, How Children
Fail *and* How Children Learn. *He was born in 1923 and studied at Yale
University. His fourteen years of experience in elementary and high
school teaching led him to some radical and controversial conclusions
about the ineffectiveness of the U.S. educational system. In many of his
books he addresses this problem and offers alternative methods for helping children to learn. He was a visiting lecturer at Harvard University
and the University of California at Berkeley. After 1969 he devoted himself primarily to writing, lecturing, social activism, and playing the cello,
which he took up at age forty. He founded, edited, and published*
Growing Without Schooling, *a magazine by and for families who
choose to teach their children at home. He died in 1985.*

Three Kinds of Discipline

*This tightly organized short essay offers a general prescription for the
use of discipline by classifying into three categories. Here and in the
book where this passage first appeared,* Freedom and Beyond *(1972),
Holt argues that, to learn, children need to be left alone as much as
they need to be disciplined.*

*As you read Holt's essay, think of your own childhood and compare
the ways that you were disciplined with how Holt would like to see children disciplined.*

A child, in growing up, may meet and learn from three different kinds of disciplines. The first and most important is what we
might call the Discipline of Nature or of Reality. When he is trying
to do something real, if he does the wrong thing or doesn't do the
right one, he doesn't get the result he wants. If he doesn't pile one
block right on top of another, or tries to build on a slanting
surface, his tower falls down. If he hits the wrong key, he hears
the wrong note. If he doesn't hit the nail squarely on the head,
it bends, and he has to pull it out and start with another. If he

doesn't measure properly what he is trying to build, it won't open, close, fit, stand up, fly, float, whistle, or do whatever he wants it to do. If he closes his eyes when he swings, he doesn't hit the ball. A child meets this kind of discipline every time he tries to *do* something, which is why it is so important in school to give children more chances to do things, instead of just reading or listening to someone talk (or pretending to). This discipline is a good teacher. The learner never has to wait long for his answer; it usually comes quickly, often instantly. Also it is clear, and very often points toward the needed correction; from what happened he can not only see that what he did was wrong, but also why, and what he needs to do instead. Finally, and most important, the giver of the answer, call it Nature, is impersonal, impartial, and indifferent. She does not give opinions, or make judgments: she cannot be wheedled, bullied, or fooled; she does not get angry or disappointed; she does not praise or blame; she does not remember past failures or hold grudges; with her one always gets a fresh start, this time is the one that counts.

The next discipline we might call the Discipline of Culture, of   2
Society, of What People Really Do. Man is a social, a cultural animal. Children sense around them this culture, this network of agreements, customs, habits, and rules binding the adults together. They want to understand it and be a part of it. They watch very carefully what people around them are doing and want to do the same. They want to do right, unless they become convinced they can't do right. Thus children rarely misbehave seriously in church, but sit as quietly as they can. The example of all those grownups is contagious. Some mysterious ritual is going on, and children, who like rituals, want to be part of it. In the same way, the little children that I see at concerts or operas, though they may fidget a little, or perhaps take a nap now and then, rarely make any disturbance. With all those grownups sitting there, neither moving nor talking, it is the most natural thing in the world to imitate them. Children who live among adults who are habitually courteous to each other, and to them, will soon learn to be courteous. Children who live surrounded by people who speak a certain way will speak that way, however much we may try to tell them that speaking that way is bad or wrong.

The third discipline is the one most people mean when they   3
speak of discipline—the Discipline of Superior Force, of sergeant
to private, of "You do what I tell you or I'll make you wish you
had." There is bound to be some of this in a child's life. Living as
we do surrounded by things that can hurt children, or that children can hurt, we cannot avoid it. We can't afford to let a small
child find out from experience the danger of playing in a busy
street, or of fooling with the pots on the top of a stove, or of eating up the pills in the medicine cabinet. So, along with other precautions, we say to him, "Don't play in the street, or touch things
on the stove, or go into the medicine cabinet, or I'll punish you."
Between him and the danger too great for him to imagine we put
a lesser danger, but one he can imagine and maybe therefore
wants to avoid. He can have no idea of what it would be like to
be hit by a car, but he can imagine being shouted at, or spanked,
or sent to his room. He avoids these substitutes for the greater
danger until he can understand it and avoid it for its own sake.
But we ought to use this discipline only when it is necessary to
protect the life, health, safety, or well-being of people or other
living creatures, or to prevent destruction of things that people
care about. We ought not to assume too long, as we usually do,
that a child cannot understand the real nature of the danger from
which we want to protect him. The sooner he avoids the danger,
not to escape our punishment, but as a matter of good sense, the
better. He can learn that faster than we think. In Mexico, for example, where people drive their cars with a good deal of spirit, I
saw many children no older than five or four walking unattended
on the streets. They understood about cars, they knew what to
do. A child whose life is full of the threat and fear of punishment
is locked into babyhood. There is no way for him to grow up, to
learn to take responsibility for his life and acts. Most important of
all, we should not assume that having to yield to the threat of our
superior force is good for the child's character. It is never good
for *anyone's* character. To bow to superior force makes us feel
impotent and cowardly for not having had the strength or
courage to resist. Worse, it makes us resentful and vengeful. We
can hardly wait to make someone pay for our humiliation, yield
to us as we were once made to yield. No, if we cannot always

avoid using the discipline of Superior Force, we should at least use it as seldom as we can.

There are places where all three disciplines overlap. Any very demanding human activity combines in it the disciplines of Superior Force, of Culture, and of Nature. The novice will be told, "Do it this way, never mind asking why, just do it that way, that is the way we always do it." But it probably is just the way they always do it, and usually for the very good reason that it is a way that has been found to work. Think, for example, of ballet training. The student in a class is told to do this exercise, or that; to stand so; to do this or that with his head, arms, shoulders, abdomen, hips, legs, feet. He is constantly corrected. There is no argument. But behind these seemingly autocratic demands by the teacher lie many decades of custom and tradition, and behind that, the necessities of dancing itself. You cannot make the moves of classical ballet unless over many years you have acquired, and renewed every day, the needed strength and suppleness in scores of muscles and joints. Nor can you do the difficult motions, making them look easy, unless you have learned hundreds of easier ones first. Dance teachers may not always agree on all the details of teaching these strengths and skills. But no novice could learn them all by himself. You could not go for a night or two to watch the ballet and then, without any other knowledge at all, teach yourself how to do it. In the same way, you would be unlikely to learn any complicated and difficult human activity without drawing heavily on the experience of those who know it better. But the point is that the authority of these experts or teachers stems from, grows out of their greater competence and experience, the fact that what they do *works*, not the fact that they happen to be the teacher and as such have the power to kick a student out of the class. And the further point is that children are always and everywhere attracted to that competence, and ready and eager to submit themselves to a discipline that grows out of it. We hear constantly that children will never do anything unless compelled to by bribes or threats. But in their private lives, or in extracurricular activities in school, in sports, music, drama, art, running a newspaper, and so on, they often submit themselves willingly and wholeheartedly to very intense disciplines, simply because they want to learn to do a given thing well. Our Little-Napoleon football coaches, of whom we have too many and hear far too much, blind us to the fact that millions of children work hard every year getting better at sports and games without coaches barking and yelling at them.

Meaning and Purpose

1. What does Holt set out to say in this essay?
2. What methods of discipline have you seen in practice, and how effective do you think they are?
3. Do you agree with the statement "Thus children rarely misbehave seriously in church, but sit as quietly as they can" (paragraph 2). Does Holt make a good case for the truth of the statement? Why or why not?
4. What is Holt's attitude toward children? Where is this attitude evident in the essay?

Strategy

1. Holt divides discipline into three kinds. What is the basis for this division, and why does he identify only three kinds?
2. Does paragraph 4 describe a fourth kind of discipline? If so, does this category cause an imbalance in the essay's structure (Holt announces only three categories in the beginning)? Why or why not?
3. How does Holt make use of examples in this essay?

Style

1. Why do you think Holt capitalizes the names of the kinds of discipline he classifies?

2. What is Holt's attitude toward his subject? Is he neutral about it, or is he advocating something? How do you know?
3. If necessary, look up the meaning of these words: *wheedled* (paragraph 1); *contagious, fidget* (2); *impotent* (3); *novice, autocratic, suppleness* (4).

Writing Tasks

1. Write an essay in which you classify parents according to the kinds of discipline they use with their children. Speak from first-hand knowledge, and take Holt as a model for using specific examples.
2. Write an essay in which you classify students. You might want to use elementary, high school, or college students, or you might show how each kind of student behaves at each of the three levels of education. Make sure you use typical examples and then demonstrate them in real life with specific examples.

❦ Desmond Morris ❦

Born in England in 1928, Desmond Morris studied at Birmingham University and Oxford University. After receiving his doctorate from Oxford, he was a researcher in the zoology department there for a short time. He later worked for several years at the Zoological Society of London, first as curator of mammals and later as director of the society's television and film department. He has also been director of London's Institute of Contemporary Arts and in 1950 had a one-man show in which he exhibited his own paintings. He is best known, however, as writer of popular—if sometimes controversial—books on human behavior, including The Naked Ape *and* The Human Zoo.

Territorial Behavior

This essay is from Morris's book Manwatching *(1974), another of his works on human behavior. He supports his premise that human beings are "remarkably territorial animals" by classifying and describing three kinds of human territory, each of which induces its own form of territorial behavior.*

As you read this essay, pay close attention to how Morris uses metaphors and similes to help the reader understand each classification.

A territory is a defended space. In the broadest sense, there are   1
three kinds of human territory: tribal, family and personal.

It is rare for people to be driven to physical fighting in defense   2
of these "owned" spaces, but fight they will, if pushed to the limit.
The invading army encroaching on national territory, the gang
moving into a rival district, the trespasser climbing into an or-
chard, the burglar breaking into a house, the bully pushing to the
front of a queue, the driver trying to steal a parking space, all of
these intruders are liable to be met with resistance varying from
the vigorous to the savagely violent. Even if the law is on the side
of the intruder, the urge to protect a territory may be so strong
that otherwise peaceful citizens abandon all their usual controls

and inhibitions. Attempts to evict families from their homes, no matter how socially valid the reasons, can lead to siege conditions reminiscent of the defense of a medieval fortress.

The fact that these upheavals are so rare is a measure of the success of Territorial Signals as a system of dispute prevention. It is sometimes cynically stated that "all property is theft," but in reality it is the opposite. Property, as owned space which is *displayed* as owned space, is a special kind of sharing system which reduces fighting much more than it causes it. Man is a cooperative species, but he is also competitive, and his struggle for dominance has to be structured in some way if chaos is to be avoided. The establishment of territorial rights is one such structure. It limits dominance geographically. I am dominant in my territory and you are dominant in yours. In other words, dominance is shared out spatially, and we all have some. Even if I am weak and unintelligent and you can dominate me when we meet on neutral ground, I can still enjoy a thoroughly dominant role as soon as I retreat to my private base. Be it ever so humble, there is no place like a home territory.

Of course, I can still be intimidated by a particularly dominant individual who enters my home base, but his encroachment will be dangerous for him and he will think twice about it, because he will know that here my urge to resist will be dramatically magnified and my usual subservience banished. Insulted at the heart of my own territory, I may easily explode into battle—either symbolic or real—with a result that may be damaging to both of us.

In order for this to work, each territory has to be plainly advertised as such. Just as a dog cocks its leg to deposit its personal scent on the trees in its locality, so the human animal cocks its leg symbolically all over his home base. But because we are predominantly visual animals we employ mostly visual signals, and it is worth asking how we do this at the three levels: tribal, family and personal.

First: the Tribal Territory. We evolved as tribal animals, living in comparatively small groups, probably of less than a hundred, and we existed like that for millions of years. It is our basic social unit, a group in which everyone knows everyone else. Essentially, the tribal territory consisted of a home base surrounded by extended hunting grounds. Any neighbouring tribe intruding on our social space would be repelled and driven away. As these early tribes swelled into agricultural super-tribes, and eventually into industrial nations, their territorial defence systems became increasingly elaborate. The tiny, ancient home base of the hunting tribe became the great capital city, the primitive war-paint became the flags, emblems, uniforms and regalia of the specialized military, and the war-chants became national anthems, marching songs and bugle calls. Territorial boundary-lines hardened into fixed borders, often conspicuously patrolled and punctuated with defensive structures—forts and lookout posts, check-points and great walls, and, today, customs barriers.

Today each nation flies its own flag, a symbolic embodiment 7 of its territorial status. But patriotism is not enough. The ancient tribal hunter lurking inside each citizen finds himself unsatisfied by membership of such a vast conglomeration of individuals, most of whom are totally unknown to him personally. He does his best to feel that he shares a common territorial defence with them all, but the scale of the operation has become inhuman. It is hard to feel a sense of belonging with a tribe of fifty million or more. His answer is to form sub-groups, nearer to his ancient pattern, smaller and more personally known to him—the local club, the teenage gang, the union, the specialist society, the sports association, the political party, the college fraternity, the social clique, the protest group, and the rest. Rare indeed is the individual who does not belong to at least one of these splinter groups, and take from it a sense of tribal allegiance and brotherhood. Typical of all these groups is the development of Territorial Signals—badges, costumes, headquarters, banners, slogans, and all the other displays of group identity. This is where the action is, in terms of tribal territorialism, and only when a major war breaks out does the emphasis shift upwards to the higher group level of the nation.

Each of these modern pseudo-tribes sets up its own special 8 kind of home base. In extreme cases non-members are totally excluded, in others they are allowed in as visitors with limited rights and under a control system of special rules. In many ways they are like miniature nations, with their own flags and emblems and their own border guards. The exclusive club has its own "customs barrier": the doorman who checks your "passport" (your membership card) and prevents strangers from passing in unchallenged. There is a government: the club committee; and often special displays of the tribal elders: the photographs or portraits of previous officials on the walls. At the heart of the specialized territories there is a powerful feeling of security and importance, a sense of shared defence against the outside world. Much of the club chatter, both serious and joking, directs itself against the rottenness of everything outside the club boundaries—in that "other world" beyond the protected portals.

In social organizations which embody a strong class system,   9 such as military units and large business concerns, there are many territorial rules, often unspoken, which interfere with the official hierarchy. High-status individuals, such as officers or managers, could in theory enter any of the regions occupied by the lower levels in the peck order, but they limit this power in a striking way. An officer seldom enters a sergeant's mess or a barrack room unless it is for a formal inspection. He respects those regions as alien territories even though he has the power to go there by virtue of his dominant role. And in businesses, part of the appeal of unions, over and above their obvious functions, is that with their officials, headquarters and meetings they add a sense of territorial power for the staff workers. It is almost as if each military organization and business concern consists of two warring tribes: the officers versus the other ranks, and the management versus the workers. Each has its special home base within the system, and the territorial defence pattern thrusts itself into what, on the surface, is a pure social hierarchy. Negotiations between managements and unions are tribal battles fought out over the neutral ground of a boardroom table, and are as much concerned with territorial display as they are with resolving problems of wages and conditions. Indeed, if one side gives in too quickly and accepts the other's demands, the victors feel strangely cheated and deeply suspicious that it may be a trick. What they are missing is the protracted sequence of ritual and counter-ritual that keeps alive their group territorial identity.

Likewise, many of the hostile displays of sports fans and teenage gangs are primarily concerned with displaying their group image to rival fan-clubs and gangs. Except in rare cases, they do not attack one another's headquarters, drive out the occupants, and reduce them to a submissive, subordinate condition. It is enough to have scuffles on the borderlands between the two rival territories. This is particularly clear at football matches, where the fan-club headquarters becomes temporarily shifted from the club-house to a section of the stands, and where minor fighting breaks out at the unofficial boundary line between the massed groups of rival supporters. Newspaper reports play up the few accidents and injuries which do occur on such occasions, but when these are studied in relation to the total numbers of displaying fans involved it is clear that the serious incidents represent only a tiny fraction of the overall group behaviour. For every actual punch or kick there are a thousand war-cries, war-dances, chants and gestures.

Second: the Family Territory. Essentially, the family is a breeding unit and the family territory is a breeding ground. At the centre of this space, there is the nest—the bedroom—where, tucked up in bed, we feel at our most territorially secure. In a typical house the bedroom is upstairs, where a safe nest should be. This puts it farther away from the entrance hall, the area where contact is made, intermittently, with the outside world. The less private reception rooms, where intruders are allowed access, are the next line of defence. Beyond them, outside the walls of the building, there is often a symbolic remnant of the ancient feeding grounds—a garden. Its symbolism often extends to the plants and animals it contains, which cease to be nutritional and become merely decorative—flowers and pets. But like a true territorial space it has a conspicuously displayed boundary-line, the garden fence, wall, or railings. Often no more than a token barrier, this is the outer territorial demarcation, separating the private world of the family from the public world beyond. To cross it puts any visitor or intruder at an immediate disadvantage. As he crosses the threshold, his dominance wanes, slightly but unmistakably. He is entering an area where he senses that he must ask permission to do simple things that he would consider a right elsewhere. Without lifting a finger, the territorial owners exert their dominance. This is done by all the hundreds of small ownership "markers" they have deposited on their family territory: the ornaments, the "possessed" objects positioned in the rooms and on the walls; the furnishings, the furniture, the colours, the patterns, all owner-chosen and all making this particular home base unique to them.

It is one of the tragedies of modern architecture that there has   12
been a standardization of these vital territorial living-units. One of the most important aspects of a home is that it should be similar to other homes only in a general way, and that in detail it should have many differences, making it a *particular* home. Unfortunately, it is cheaper to build a row of houses, or a block of flats, so that all the family living-units are identical, but the territorial urge rebels against this trend and house-owners struggle as best they can to make their mark on their mass-produced properties. They do this with garden-design, with front-door colours, with curtain patterns, with wallpaper and all the other decorative elements that together create a unique and different family environment. Only when they have completed this nest-building do they feel truly "at home" and secure.

When they venture forth as a family unit they repeat the   13
process in a minor way. On a day-trip to the seaside, they load the car with personal belongings and it becomes their temporary, portable territory. Arriving at the beach they stake out a small territorial claim, marking it with rugs, towels, baskets and other belongings to which they can return from their seaboard wanderings. Even if they all leave it at once to bathe, it retains a characteristic territorial quality and other family groups arriving will recognize this by setting up their own "home" bases at a respectful distance. Only when the whole beach has filled up with these marked spaces will newcomers start to position themselves in such a way that the inter-base distance becomes reduced. Forced to pitch between several existing beach territories they will feel a momentary sensation of intrusion, and the established

"owners" will feel a similar sensation of invasion, even though they are not being directly inconvenienced.

The same territorial scene is being played out in parks and 14 fields and on riverbanks, wherever family groups gather in their clustered units. But if rivalry for spaces creates mild feelings of hostility, it is true to say that, without the territorial system of sharing and space-limited dominance, there would be chaotic disorder.

Third: the Personal Space. If a man enters a waiting-room and 15 sits at one end of a long row of empty chairs, it is possible to predict where the next man to enter will seat himself. He will not sit next to the first man, nor will he sit at the far end, right away from him. He will choose a position about halfway between these two points. The next man to enter will take the largest gap left, and sit roughly in the middle of that, and so on, until eventually the latest newcomer will be forced to select a seat that places him right next to one of the already seated men. Similar patterns can be observed in cinemas, public urinals, aeroplanes, trains and buses. This is a reflection of the fact that we all carry with us, everywhere we go, a portable territory called a Personal Space. If people move inside this space, we feel threatened. If they keep too far outside it, we feel rejected. The result is a subtle series of spatial adjustments, usually operating quite unconsciously and producing ideal compromises as far as this is possible. If a situation becomes too crowded, then we adjust our reactions accordingly and allow our personal space to shrink. Jammed into an elevator, a rush-hour compartment, or a packed room, we give up altogether and allow body-to-body contact, but when we relinquish our Personal Space in this way, we adopt certain special techniques. In essence, what we do is to convert these other bodies into "nonpersons." We studiously ignore them, and they us. We try not to face them if we can possibly avoid it. We wipe all expressiveness from our faces, letting them go blank. We may look up at the ceiling or down at the floor, and we reduce body movements to a minimum. Packed together like sardines in a tin, we stand dumbly still, sending out as few social signals as possible.

Even if the crowding is less severe, we still tend to cut down 16 our social interactions in the presence of large numbers. Careful observations of children in play groups revealed that if they are high density groupings there is less social interaction between the individual children, even though there is theoretically more opportunity for such contacts. At the same time, the high-density groups show a higher frequency of aggressive and destructive behaviour patterns in their play. Personal Space—"elbow room"—is a vital commodity for the human animal, and one that cannot be ignored without risking serious trouble.

Of course, we all enjoy the excitement of being in a crowd, 17 and this reaction cannot be ignored. But there are crowds and crowds. It is pleasant enough to be in a "spectator crowd," but not so appealing to find yourself in the middle of a rush-hour crush. The difference between the two is that the spectator crowd is all facing in the same direction and concentrating on a distant point of interest. Attending a theatre, there are twinges of rising hostility towards the stranger who sits down immediately in front of you or the one who squeezes into the seat next to you. The shared armrest can become a polite, but distinct, territorial boundary-dispute region. However, as soon as the show begins, these invasions of Personal Space are forgotten and the attention is focused beyond the small space where the crowding is taking place. Now, each member of the audience feels himself spatially related, not to his cramped neighbours, but to the actor on the stage, and this distance is, if anything, too great. In the rush-hour crowd, by contrast, each member of the pushing throng is competing with his neighbours all the time. There is no escape to a spacial relation with a distant actor, only the pushing, shoving bodies all around.

Those of us who have to spend a great deal of time in crowded 18 conditions become gradually better able to adjust, but no one can ever become completely immune to invasions of Personal Space. This is because they remain forever associated with either powerful hostile or equally powerful loving feelings. All through our childhood we have been held to be loved and held to be hurt, and anyone who invades our Personal Space when we are adults is, in effect, threatening to extend his behaviour into one of these two highly charged areas of human interaction. Even if his motives are clearly neither hostile nor sexual, we still find it hard to suppress our reactions to his close approach. Unfortunately, different countries have different ideas about exactly how close is close. It is easy enough to test your own "space reaction": when you are talking to someone in the street or in any open space, reach out with your arm and see where the nearest point on his body comes. If you hail from western Europe, you will find that he is at roughly fingertip distance from you. In other words, as you reach out, your fingertips will just about make contact with his shoulder. If you come from eastern Europe you will find you are standing at "wrist distance." If you come from the Mediterranean region you will find that you are much closer to your companion, at little more than "elbow distance."

Trouble begins when a member of one of these cultures meets 19 and talks to one from another. Say a British diplomat meets an Italian or an Arab diplomat at an embassy function. They start talking in a friendly way, but soon the fingertips man begins to feel uneasy. Without knowing quite why, he starts to back away gently from his companion. The companion edges forward again. Each tries in this way to set up a Personal Space relationship that suits his own background. But it is impossible to do. Every time the Mediterranean diplomat advances to a distance that feels comfortable for him, the British diplomat feels threatened. Every time the Briton moves back, the other feels rejected. Attempts to adjust this situation often lead to a talking pair shifting slowly across a room, and many an embassy reception is dotted with western-European fingertip-distance men pinned against the walls by eager elbow-distance men. Until such differences are fully understood, and allowances made, these minor differences in "body territories" will continue to act as an alienation factor which may interfere in a subtle way with diplomatic harmony and other forms of international transaction.

If there are distance problems when engaged in conversation, 20 then there are clearly going to be even bigger difficulties where people must work privately in a shared space. Close proximity of others, pressing against the invisible boundaries of our personal body-territory, makes it difficult to concentrate on non-social matters. Flatmates, students sharing a study, sailors in the cramped quarters of a ship, and office staff in crowded work-places, all have to face this problem. They solve it by "cocooning." They use a variety of devices to shut themselves off from the others present. The best possible cocoon, of course, is a small private room—a den, a private office, a study or a studio—which physically obscures the presence of other nearby territory-owners. This is the ideal situation for non-social work, but the space-sharers cannot enjoy this luxury. Their cocooning must be symbolic. They may, in certain cases, be able to erect small physical barriers, such as screens and partitions, which give substance to their invisible Personal Space boundaries, but when this cannot be done, other means must be sought. One of these is the "favoured object." Each space-sharer develops a preference, repeatedly expressed until it becomes a fixed pattern, for a particular chair, or table, or alcove. Others come to respect this, and friction is reduced. This system is often formally arranged (this is my desk, that is yours), but even where it is not, favoured places soon develop. Professor Smith has a favourite chair in the library. It is not formally his, but he always uses it and others avoid it. Seats around a mess-room table, or a board-room table, become almost personal property for specific individuals. Even in the home, father has his favourite chair for reading the newspaper or watching television. Another device is the blinkers-posture. Just as a horse that overreacts to other horses and the distractions of the noisy racecourse is given a pair of blinkers to shield its eyes, so people studying privately in a public place put on pseudo-blinkers in the form of shielding hands. Resting their elbows on the table, they sit with their hands screening their eyes from the scene on either side.

A third method of reinforcing the body-territory is to use per-   21
sonal markers. Books, papers and other personal belongings are scattered around the favoured site to render it more privately owned in the eyes of companions. Spreading out one's belongings is a well-known trick in public-transport situations, where a traveller tries to give the impression that seats next to him are taken. In many contexts carefully arranged personal markers can act as an effective territorial display, even in the absence of the territory

owner. Experiments in a library revealed that placing a pile of magazines on the table in one seating position successfully reserved that place for an average of 77 minutes. If a sports-jacket was added, draped over the chair, then the "reservation effect" lasted for over two hours.

In these ways, we strengthen the defences of our Personal Spaces, keeping out intruders with the minimum of open hostility. As with all territorial behaviour, the object is to defend space with signals rather than with fists and at all three levels—the tribal, the family and the personal—it is a remarkably efficient system of space-sharing. It does not always seem so, because newspapers and newscasts inevitably magnify the exceptions and dwell on those cases where the signals have failed and wars have broken out, gangs have fought, neighbouring families have feuded, or colleagues have clashed, but for every territorial signal that has failed, there are millions of others that have not. They do not rate a mention in the news, but they nevertheless constitute a dominant feature of human society—the society of a remarkably territorial animal. 22

Meaning and Purpose

1. What is the main point that Morris makes in this essay? Does it have a thesis statement?
2. Can you tell from the title what kind of essay this will be?
3. In paragraph 11 the author says, "we feel at our most territorially secure" in our bedroom. Does this statement apply to you? Where is another place in which you feel quite "territorially secure"?
4. What does Morris say we do in our large tribal territory to feel a sense of belonging?
5. Why is it "one of the tragedies of modern architecture" that so many new homes look alike?
6. In paragraph 11, Morris calls the family and its territory a "breeding unit" and "breeding ground." What does he mean by these expressions? Is he being sarcastic or judgmental?

Strategy

1. Morris begins his categories of territories in paragraph 6. How does he use the first five paragraphs?
2. What strategy does Morris use to develop the classification of "Tribal Territory"?
3. In the personal space category, Morris has some subcategories. What are they, and how do they work in the structure of this category?
4. In paragraph 4, Morris mentions a "home base." If Morris had wanted to, he could have classified several kinds of home bases. In your opinion, what are two kinds of home bases?

Style

1. How would you describe the tone of this essay? Where is the tone evident?
2. What is a *pseudo-tribe* (paragraph 8)?
3. Judging from the tone and style of this essay, whom do you think Morris has in mind for his audience?

Writing Tasks

1. Classify your "tribe's territory." How does your neighborhood, town, city, parish, county, or other easily identifiable political territory differ from others in its display? How do its looks make it different? How do its people make it different? How does its economy make it different? In what other ways does classifying your territory show that it is different from other territories in the same class?
2. Personal space is becoming more and more difficult to enjoy. What is your own definition of "personal space"? How do you separate and protect your space? How do you handle intruders into your space? How would you instruct elementary school children who tell you they would like to learn how to have more personal space?

🍂 William Lutz 🍂

William Lutz, born in 1940, holds doctorates in both English and law and is a professor and former chair of the Department of English at Rutgers University in New Jersey. He is the former editor of The Quarterly Review of Doublespeak, *a journal that examines the subject of doublespeak, "language that is carefully designed and constructed to appear to communicate when in fact it doesn't," "language designed not to lead but to mislead," "language designed to distort reality and corrupt thought." He is an expert on the use of the English language who has published numerous articles on language and has authored or coauthored fourteen books. Lutz's book* Doublespeak: From Revenue Enhancements to Terminal Living *was a best-seller; its sequel,* Why No One Knows What Anyone's Saying Anymore, *has been equally influential.*

Doublespeak

Language allows us to communicate, and the better we're able to handle language, the more clearly and effectively we can communicate—or so we like to think. But what about language that is deliberately designed to deceive and obfuscate? William Lutz, in this 1989 essay, considers such language.

In reading the essay, keep in mind the things that distinguish each kind of doublespeak from each other, as well as the things they have in common.

There are no potholes in the streets of Tucson, Arizona, just "pavement deficiencies." The Reagan Administration didn't propose any new taxes, just "revenue enhancement" through new "user's fees." Those aren't bums on the street, just "non-goal oriented members of society." There are no more poor people, just "fiscal underachievers." There was no robbery of an automatic teller machine, just an "unauthorized withdrawal." The patient didn't die because of medical malpractice, it was just a "diagnostic misadvanture of a high magnitude." The U.S. Army doesn't kill the enemy anymore, it just "services the target." And the double-speak goes on.

Doublespeak is language that pretends to communicate but   2
really doesn't. It is language that makes the bad seem good, the negative appear positive, the unpleasant appear attractive or at least tolerable. Doublespeak is language that avoids or shifts responsibility, language that is at variance with its real or purported meaning. It is language that conceals or prevents thought; rather than extending thought, doublespeak limits it.

How to Spot Doublespeak

How can you spot doublespeak? Most of the time you will rec-   3
ognize doublespeak when you see or hear it. But, if you have any doubts, you can identify doublespeak just by answering these questions: Who is saying what to whom, under what conditions and circumstances, with what intent, and with what results? Answering these questions will usually help you identify as doublespeak language that appears to be legitimate or that at first glance doesn't even appear to be doublespeak.

First kind of doublespeak

There are at least four kinds of doublespeak. The first is the   4
euphemism, an inoffensive or positive word or phrase used to avoid a harsh, unpleasant, or distasteful reality. But a euphemism can also be a tactful word or phrase which avoids directly mentioning a painful reality, or it can be an expression used out of concern for the feelings of someone else, or to avoid directly discussing a topic subject to a social or cultural taboo.

When you see a euphemism because of your sensitivity for   5
someone's feelings or out of concern for a recognized social or cultural taboo, it is not doublespeak. For example, you express your condolences that someone has "passed away" because you do not want to say to a grieving person, "I'm sorry your father is dead." When you see the euphemism "passed away," no one is misled.

Moreover, the euphemism functions here not just to protect the feelings of another person, but to communicate also your concern for that person's feelings during a period of mourning. When you excuse yourself to go to the "restroom," or you mention that someone is "sleeping with" or "involved with" someone else, you do not mislead anyone about your meaning, but you do respect the social taboos about discussing bodily functions and sex in direct terms. You also indicate your sensitivity to the feelings of your audience, which is usually considered a mark of courtesy and good manners.

However, when a euphemism is used to mislead or deceive, it 6
becomes doublespeak. For example, in 1984 the U.S. State Department announced that it would no longer use the word "killing" in its annual report on the status of human rights in countries around the world. Instead, it would use the phrase "unlawful or arbitrary deprivation of life," which the department claimed was more accurate. Its real purpose for using this phrase was simply to avoid discussing the embarrassing situation of government-sanctioned killings in countries that are supported by the United States and have been certified by the United States as respecting the human rights of their citizens. This use of a euphemism constitutes doublespeak, since it is designed to mislead, to cover up the unpleasant. Its real intent is at variance with its apparent intent. It is language designed to alter our perception of reality.

The Pentagon, too, avoids discussing unpleasant realities 7
when it refers to bombs and artillery shells that fall on civilian targets as "incontinent ordnance." And in 1977 the Pentagon tried to slip funding for the neutron bomb unnoticed into an appropriations bill by calling it a "radiation enhancement device."

Second kind of doublespeak

A second kind of doublespeak is jargon, the specialized lan- 8
guage of a trade, profession, or similar group, such as that used by doctors, lawyers, engineers, educators, or car mechanics. Jargon can serve an important and useful function. Within a group, jar-

gon functions as a kind of verbal shorthand that allows members of the group to communicate with each other clearly, efficiently, and quickly. Indeed, it is a mark of membership in the group to be able to use and understand the group's jargon.

But jargon, like the euphemism, can also be doublespeak. It   9
can be—and often is—pretentious, obscure, and esoteric terminology used to give an air of profundity, authority, and prestige to speakers and their subject matter. Jargon as doublespeak often makes the simple appear complex, the ordinary profound, the obvious insightful. In this sense it is used not to express but impress. With such doublespeak, the act of smelling something becomes "organoleptic analysis," glass becomes "fused silicate," a crack in a metal support beam becomes a "discontinuity," conservative economic policies become "distributionally conservative notions."

Lawyers, for example, speak of an "involuntary conversion" of   10
property when discussing the loss or destruction of property through theft, accident, or condemnation. If your house burns down or if your car is stolen, you have suffered an involuntary conversion of your property. When used by lawyers in a legal situation, such jargon is a legitimate use of language, since lawyers can be expected to understand the term.

However, when a member of a specialized group uses its jar-   11
gon to communicate with a person outside the group, and uses it knowing that the nonmember does not understand such language, then there is doublespeak. For example, on May 9, 1978, a National Airlines 727 airplane crashed while attempting to land at the Pensacola, Florida airport. Three of the fifty-two passengers aboard the airplane were killed. As a result of the crash, National made an after-tax insurance benefit of $1.7 million, or an extra 18¢ a share dividend for its stockholders. Now National Airlines had two problems: It did not want to talk about one of its airplanes crashing, and it had to account for the $1.7 million when it issued its annual report to its stockholders. National solved the problem by inserting a footnote in its annual report which explained that the $1.7 million income was due to "the involuntary conversion of a 727." National thus acknowledged the crash of its airplane and the subsequent profit it made from the crash, without once men-

tioning the accident or the deaths. However, because airline officials knew that most stockholders in the company, and indeed most of the general public, were not familiar with legal jargon, the use of such jargon constituted doublespeak.

Third kind of doublespeak

A third kind of doublespeak is gobbledygook or bureaucratese. Basically, such doublespeak is simply a matter of piling on words, of overwhelming the audience with words, the bigger the words and the longer the sentences the better. Alan Greenspan, then chair of President Nixon's Council of Economic Advisors, was quoted in *The Philadelphia Inquirer* in 1974 as having testified before a Senate committee that "It is a tricky problem to find the particular calibration in timing that would be appropriate to stem the acceleration in risk premiums created by falling incomes without prematurely aborting the decline in the inflation-generated risk premiums." 12

Nor has Mr. Greenspan's language changed since then. Speaking to the meeting of the Economic Club of New York in 1988, Mr. Greenspan, now Federal Reserve chair, said, "I guess I should warn you, if I turn out to be particularly clear, you've probably misunderstood what I've said." Mr. Greenspan's doublespeak doesn't seem to have held back his career. 13

Sometimes gobbledygook may sound impressive, but when the quote is later examined in print it doesn't even make sense. During the 1988 presidential campaign, vice-presidential candidate Senator Dan Quayle explained the need for a strategic-defense initiative by saying, "Why wouldn't an enhanced deterrent, a more stable peace, a better prospect to denying the ones who enter conflict in the first place to have a reduction of offensive systems and an introduction to defense capability? I believe this is the route the country will eventually go." 14

The investigation into the Challenger disaster in 1986 revealed the doublespeak of gobbledygook and bureaucratese used by too many involved in the shuttle program. When Jesse Moore, NASA's associate administrator, was asked if the performance of 15

the shuttle program had improved with each launch or if it had remained the same, he answered, "I think our performance in terms
of the liftoff performance and in terms of the orbital performance,
we knew more about the envelope we were operating under, and
we have been pretty accurately staying in that. And so I would say
the performance has not by design drastically improved. I think
we have been able to characterize the performance more as a function of our launch experience as opposed to it improving as a
function of time." While this language may appear to be jargon, a
close look will reveal that it is really just gobbledygook laced with
jargon. But you really have to wonder if Mr. Moore had any idea
what he was saying.

Fourth kind of doublespeak

The fourth kind of doublespeak is inflated language that is de-   16
signed to make the ordinary seem extraordinary; to make everyday things seem impressive; to give an air of importance to people,
situations, or things that would not normally be considered important; to make the simple seem complex. Often this kind of
doublespeak isn't hard to spot, and it is usually pretty funny.
While car mechanics may be called "automotive internists," elevator operators members of the "vertical transportation corps," used
cars "pre-owned" or "experienced cars," and black-and-white television sets described as having "non-multicolor capability," you
really aren't misled all that much by such language.

However, you may have trouble figuring out that, when   17
Chrysler "initiates a career alternative enhancement program," it is
really laying off five thousand workers; or that "negative patient
care outcome" means the patient died; or that "rapid oxidation"
means a fire in a nuclear power plant.

The doublespeak of inflated language can have serious conse-   18
quences. In Pentagon doublespeak, "pre-emptive counterattack"
means that American forces attacked first; "engaged the enemy on
all sides" means American troops were ambushed; "backloading of
augmentation personnel" means a retreat by American troops. In
the doublespeak of the military, the 1983 invasion of Grenada was

conducted not by the U.S. Army, Navy, Air Force, and Marines, but by the "Caribbean Peace Keeping Forces." But then, according to the Pentagon, it wasn't an invasion, it was a "predawn vertical insertion."

The Dangers of Doublespeak

These . . . examples of doublespeak should make it clear that doublespeak is not the product of carelessness or sloppy thinking. Indeed, most doublespeak is the product of clear thinking and is carefully designed and constructed to appear to communicate when in fact it doesn't. It is language designed not to lead but mislead. It is language designed to distort reality and corrupt thought. . . . When a fire in a nuclear reactor building is called "rapid oxidation," an explosion in a nuclear power plant is called an "energetic disassembly," the illegal overthrow of a legitimate government is termed "destabilizing a government," and lies are seen as "inoperative statements," we are hearing doublespeak that attempts to avoid responsibility and make the bad seem good, the negative appear positive, something unpleasant appear attractive; and which seems to communicate but doesn't. It is language designed to alter our perception of reality and corrupt our thinking. Such language does not provide us with the tools we need to develop, advance, and preserve our culture and our civilization. Such language breeds suspicion, cynicism, distrust, and, ultimately, hostility.

Meaning and Purpose

1. What is Lutz's thesis? Where does he state it?
2. From Lutz's point of view, what distinguishes permissible evasive or esoteric language from doublespeak?
3. What can we do to recognize doublespeak?
4. According to Lutz, what are the dangers of doublespeak?

Strategy

1. By dividing his subject of doublespeak into four different categories, Lutz makes classification and division his primary organizational pattern. What are examples of other organizational patterns in the essay?
2. How do Lutz's first two kinds of doublespeak, euphemism and jargon, differ from his second two, gobbledygook and inflated language?
3. How do paragraphs 2 and 19 reflect each other?

Style

1. Compare the quotes from Alan Greenspan in paragraphs 12 and 13. In what way are the two quotes different? What is the significance of that difference?
2. What is Lutz's tone in this essay? What is his attitude toward his subject? How can you tell?
3. If necessary, look up the following words in a dictionary: *variance, purported* (paragraph 2); *tactful* (4); *condolences* (5); *incontinent, ordnance* (7); *pretentious, esoteric, profundity* (9); *dividend* (11); *initiative* (14).

Writing Tasks

1. Find a number of television, magazine, or newspaper advertisements that you think are meant to deceive, and write an essay in which you categorize and explain the types of deception the ads use.
2. Find an example of doublespeak that you find particularly offensive. You might look for examples in television, radio, magazine, or newspaper advertisements or in editorials or articles in newspapers or journals of opinion. Then write an essay in which you analyze the doublespeak and, in doing so, point out why it is dangerous and/or offensive.

❦ Paul Sheehan ❦

A native Australian now living in Sydney, Sheehan has had his work published in The Atlantic Monthly, The New Yorker, *and the* New York Times. *Most of his writing, however, has been for the* Sydney Morning Herald. *After being a Nieman Fellow at Harvard University and having graduated from Columbia University's Graduate School of Journalism, Sheehan spent ten years in New York and Washington as a foreign correspondent.*

My Habit

The essay that follows, first published in a 1996 issue of The New Yorker, *also appears in* The Best American Essays 1997. *As you read it, follow carefully Sheehan's transitions, noting how easily he seems to move from paragraph to paragraph.*

The morning after New York's great January blizzard, I took a 1
long walk to the places where I often explore my arcane little niche of the drug world. I walked up Central Park West from the Nineties to Harlem and Morningside Park, passed under the lee of the Cathedral of St. John the Divine, and crossed over to Riverside Park. All are fertile drug sites for me.

The city looked gloriously serene and cleansed, but I was cu- 2
rious to see if my specialty, the crack trade, had paused during the previous day and night of heavy snow. The crack epidemic still rages quietly, even though it has largely slipped from public concern, and a popular myth has grown that the trade is burning itself out because so many crack addicts became zombies. But the police don't see any burnout among hard-core users. And from my peculiar perch I find that the trade seems as busy as ever. I wanted to see what the snow would reveal.

It revealed that the crack trade had not paused. In two hours, 3
I found a dozen vials newly discarded on the fresh snow. Each had

been used in the narrow space of time since the blizzard had dissipated. Most of the vials had been used outside, but a few had been thrown out of windows and had landed upright in the powdery snow, like little missiles.

Every New Yorker has stepped over empty crack vials, yet   4
most people tell me they don't even know what a crack vial looks like. I look, and so I find. During my walk after the blizzard, I also came upon a man lighting his crack pipe in Morningside Park. It was ten o'clock in the morning, and the park was filled with children and parents playing in the snow. He was clearly, as they say on the street, "thirsty."

I waited until he left, then walked to his spot and saw some-   5
thing I had hoped to find. Lying bright on a snowdrift was a small glass tube, not quite an inch long, with a blue plastic cap inserted in the top. The inside surface of the glass was coated with the white residue of crack. I don't know why the man had neatly reinserted the cap before throwing the vial away, but a lot of crack addicts have that fastidious habit. I watched him walking away, then examined the slender vial. I knew I held a totem of the quenchless thirst for crack in my hand, but I did not feel sorry for him, because he had left a type of crack vial I had not seen before. I was thrilled.

I write for a living, but I am also the owner and curator of what is   6
almost certainly the world's largest collection of crack vials. The crack vial first turned up in New York and Florida, and was invented specifically as a package for crack cocaine, which comes in a pebble form that must be handled with care. For a decade, the vials have been made illegally in an abundance of styles, and they have been discarded by the tens of thousands on the streets of New York. My collection is a measure of this abundance, and a small monument to it.

Inevitably, it has become more difficult to find new vials as   7
the collection has grown into the hundreds, so my search has widened, and the terrain has become more unfamiliar and sometimes dangerous. Last November, I was surrounded by drug dealers in the notorious Cabrini-Green housing project in Chicago. I

had gone there looking for Chicago crack vials and had not found any, and so had begun to root around the buildings, until I became an object of inspection for every lookout and enforcer at work in the project that day. They kept asking me, "Wassup, slick boy?" This was an unnecessary risk, an obsessional predicament, and all for something that most people would regard as worthless. I smiled and introduced myself as "Father Sheehan from St. Joseph's," and, with a measured, priestly gait, continued on my way out of Cabrini. (I am not a priest.) And I discovered belatedly that addicts don't use crack vials in Chicago; they use tiny plastic bags.

As I have wandered around rough neighborhoods, talking to addicts and cops and scholars, the underground world of crack has revealed some of itself to me. I learned about "mills," where heroin and cocaine are processed for street distribution. The cocaine powder is cooked into the more potent form of crack cocaine: teams of women, sometimes naked, I was told, fill hundreds of vials a day—an operation known as "bottling up." The idea that naked women are employed to fill crack vials seemed a patently absurd urban myth, but serious people, among them several urban ethnographers, assured me that it was true. Drug dealers are paranoid about pilfering. "A naked woman can't steal it, because she's got nowhere to put it" is how one source explained it.   8

I learned the street names of many of the vials: bunnies, crazies, supers, skinnies, flavors, bullets, and Taj Mahals. The word "vial" carries the heavy connotation of poison, and it is a term that users avoid, preferring to call the vials "caps." Users in need of the drug are "thirsty" or are "looking for Scotty" (as in "Beam me up, Scotty," from *Star Trek*) or looking for "rock" or "ready rock." New crack vials are usually sold in bags of fifty at grocery stores and bodegas, and the wholesale business appears to be dominated by immigrants from Yemen. "The crack-vial manufacturers have eluded us so far," Inspector William Taylor, of the New York Police Department drug squad, told me. "The information we have is that the vials are brought in from overseas." When I told him I had heard that they are brought in from the Bronx and   9

Queens, he conceded that that may also be true. The police occasionally conduct sweeps against the paraphernalia industry and confiscate display boards, which are kept under shops' counters and used to show drug dealers the available range of vials' colors and designs.

The colors can denote a selling crew or a supplier or a product or a gang territory, or they can simply be random. I have heard dealers on Amsterdam Avenue shouting "We got blue!" or "Blue is up!" to alert buyers that blue-capped crack vials are on the street. Crack is price-driven, and the price is generally three to five dollars per vial, sometimes as low as two. The whole point of crack, which in its most common form is a cooked mixture of cocaine, lidocaine (a synthetic crystalline compound used in anesthetics), and baking soda, is to create more value out of a kilo of cocaine powder by making a drug that can produce an intense high at a very low price, thus vastly expanding the market downward. The more intensely addictive quality of crack is simply a bonus.

Blue caps? I have seventy different ones, blue being the most common color in a collection that at the time of writing contains 562 different crack vials. They are displayed in five Riker Specimen Mounts, thin cases with glass fronts which can be hung on the wall; the cases were designed to hold insects. Each of my cases has a name:

1. The Main Collection. A large case densely overcrowded with plastic vials—no glass vials—representing three quarters of the collection and gathered entirely on the Upper West Side and mostly within a ten-block radius of my apartment building, on West Ninety-eighth Street, off Riverside Drive.

2. The Taj Mahal Annex. A set of fifty-six plastic vials with ornate colored caps. I originally called this collection the Crown Annex, because the caps look like little crowns, but then learned that their street name is Taj Mahals.

3. The Newark Annex. Glass vials collected during two visits to Newark. Everything there was glass, no plastic. Because glass vials break easily and perish quickly once they're discarded, they are much harder to find.

4. The Harlem Annex. A mixture of both glass and plastic

vials and caps that are unique to Harlem. They include "jumbo" vials—larger glass vials, developed for the suburban trade.

5. The Gold and Silver Annex. Thirty different vials, either 16 glass or plastic, whose caps are either gold or silver plastic. This is my favorite case.

Among the 562 vials are eighty different cap designs, possibly 17 suggesting eighty different manufacturers, and each cap is usually produced in ten or twelve different colors. The vials themselves have numerous variations—hexagonal, bullet-shaped, long, squat, thin, thick, plastic, glass—totaling more than four dozen different types, but all of them are transparent, so the contents can be seen. Vials produced a frisson of excitement in me last summer when they appeared in tinted versions for the first time: green vials, then blue, then red. Most of the cap and vial designs in the collection are no longer made and will never be on the streets again.

I clean all the vials except those which contain crack residue: 18 I don't touch that. (I also have eight vials with deep teeth indentations, which I keep in a plastic bag, out of sight.)

Why bother? What is the worthiness? Isn't this collection a 19 variation on the parasitism that crack already represents? Similar brutal questions are posed by Geoff Nicholson in *Hunters and Gatherers*, his novel about bizarre and exceptionally useless collections and collectors:

> What was collecting, anyway? You took one thing and you took another thing, you put them next to each other and somehow their proximity was supposed to create a meaning. You put certain artifacts together, drew an artificial boundary around them, and there you were with a collection. So what?
>
> As for the people themselves, I suspected that collectors were deeply inadequate human beings, compensating for a lack of personality, intelligence or love. I pictured them as a bunch of unsocial dullards: shy, oafish, unhip.

I am comfortable with these questions. I asked them myself 20 long ago, and I have the answers.

The collection began as evidence. In 1991, the West 97/98th   21
Street Block Association filed suit to block the reopening, by
Volunteers of America, of a residence for homeless people, including some who were mentally ill, at 305 West Ninety-seventh
Street. Two years later, the New York State Court of Appeals rejected a "fair share" argument that there were already thirty-eight
shelters and treatment centers between West Ninetieth Street and
West 110th Street, and almost none on the Upper East Side or on
the West Side below Ninetieth Street. Meanwhile, the center reopened in 1992, and neighborhood activists predicted that drug-
taking, panhandling, and car break-ins would increase. Whether
or not crack users did move into the building—Volunteers of
America always said they did not—I did notice more crack vials
between Ninety-seventh and Ninety-eighth Streets and began
gathering them as tangible evidence that the block association was
right. One of the denizens of West Ninety-seventh Street, a stick-
figure junkie with bleached blond hair who always seemed to be
crying, parked herself at the entrance to the Ninety-sixth Street
subway station every day and panhandled. For the first time, I
found vials on the pavement outside the entrance to my building.
I felt that the courts and the city government were pushing the
tide of drugs right to my front door.

Once I started seeing crack vials, I noticed their extraordinary   22
variety. Then the writer Allen Kurzweil came to visit, still basking
in the success of his first novel, *A Case of Curiosities*, and he suggested that I put the crack vials in a display case—a case of curiosities. He then brought me a small Riker Specimen Mount from
Maxilla & Mandible, on Columbus Avenue. After we mounted the
vials, we discovered that when crack vials are massed in multicol-
ored ranks they are charismatic. They have something to say. I put
them on the wall, and when people came by they always looked at
the crack case before even noticing any of the other art in my living room.

I can't explain why, but collecting became important to me. I   23
stopped worrying about who lived at 305 West Ninety-seventh
Street. Besides, the crying junkie had disappeared, the building
had been cleaned up, and crack vials had become rare on my

street. I felt safe wandering around some of the city's worst neighborhoods, especially after I noticed that people were calling me "Officer." Once, in Morningside Heights, a man came out of the bushes with his hands up when he saw me approaching. In Harlem, while I was on my knees sifting through a scattering of crack vials under a park bench, a young woman lolling on the bench, who was high on something, said to me, "You don't care what people think about you, do you?"

I have seen the entire panoply of New York's addiction debris: hundreds of discarded butane lighters, hypodermic needles, "cooker" bottles, tubes of glue, used condoms, empty handbags, empty bottles of Night Train, baking-soda boxes, rubbing-alcohol bottles, razor blades, and broken crack pipes.   24

In a paper that Doug Goldsmith, a New York ethnographer, delivered last year to the Society for Applied Anthropology, he compared crack vials to the detritus found at archaeological digs. Not long afterward, I spoke with him. "I've been on digs in the Southwest," he told me, "and I know those indestructible colored tops are the things that will remain behind, like pottery shards in ancient dwellings."   25

One day, there will be no more crack vials. And one day, perhaps soon, crack itself will be replaced. When the hard pebbles created by cooking cocaine were first sold, in the early 1980s, dealers used small perfume bottles or contact-lens cases to distribute them. Today's small, cheap, transparent, sturdy vials were developed as the market expanded, and the packaging of crack continues to evolve. Dealers are increasingly replacing vials with tiny Ziploc plastic bags, because they are easier to obtain, sell, carry, and, most important, conceal. When there are no more crack vials, I suppose my collection will have genuine anthropological value.   26

Artists have tinkered with drug paraphernalia to make aesthetic moral statements. The composer Philip Glass owns a work entitled *Found Dope #2*, which was made by a friend of his, and which consists of crack vials and caps stuck on parchment. The most common reaction to my collection has been that it is beautiful, so I took some of my cases of vials to a friend, a distinguished   27 art historian, because I thought he would find layers of meaning that had not occurred to me. He loved the collection. "It's like looking at a little graveyard, little tombs," he said. "Except it has these childlike colors from Toys R Us, a compound of juvenilia and death. It reminds me of the collection of Dr. Ruysch, a Dutch anatomist who draped fetuses in lace and preserved them in jars. Staggeringly horrible oxymorons. But compelling oxymorons. They ended up in the collection of Peter the Great."

Meaning and Purpose

1. The term *irony* refers to using words to express something different from, and often opposite to, a literal meaning. Now that you have read the essay, what is ironic about its title?
2. What is ironic about the statement early in the essay, "I look, and so I find" (paragraph 4)?
3. Sheehan speaks of his vial collection as being "a small monument to it" (paragraph 6). To what does the *it* refer in that phrase?
4. Sheehan has five cases filled with crack vials. He has classified them into categories. Do the categories overlap, or are they true categories in that each case contains quite different vials? Support your answer with concrete evidence.
5. Why did Sheehan begin to collect the vials?

Strategy

1. Crack addiction is not only unlawful but also life-destroying. What is Sheehan's opinion of crack users?
2. What evidence in this essay shows that Sheehan is quite serious about collecting crack vials?
3. Why did Sheehan once masquerade as a Catholic priest?
4. In your opinion, why does Sheehan clean all his vials except those that contain crack residue?

5. Some people have said that only a foreigner or a scientist could have written this essay. Why do you think they said that?

Style

1. Sheehan has a "Taj Mahal" collection (paragraph 13). What is the original Taj Mahal?
2. According to Sheehan, crack vials can be "charismatic" (paragraph 22). What does the term *charismatic* mean?
3. Sheehan says that he has seen "the entire panoply of New York's addiction debris" (paragraph 24). What does *panoply* mean? Suggest a synonym.
4. One ethnographer compared crack vials "to the detritus found at archaeological digs" (paragraph 25). What does *detritus* mean in that phrase?
5. What is an "ethnographer" (paragraph 25)? In some sense, could Sheehan be classified as an ethnographer? Why or why not?

Writing Tasks

1. Imagine that we have only three ways to classify: mostly flat, mostly round, and mostly square. Using those three classes, write an essay in which you describe the contents of any room where you live, placing each object in that room in one of the three classes and giving at least one reason for putting each object into a specific class.
2. Visit a restaurant, a cafeteria, or a fast-food franchise. Study its menu carefully, and then write an essay in which you classify each of its items into one of three categories that you yourself invent. Give at least one reason for your having classified each item into one of your categories.

❦ Responding to Photographs ❦

Classification and Division

Veterans Day

Humans are social beings. We form groups and subgroups for a variety of purposes—social, economic, vocational, political.

Some of these groups are informal and temporary: a study group for the final exam, a tour group to a vacation spot, an ad hoc committee to support a municipal bond issue. Others are more formal and longer lasting, binding together the common interests of large numbers of people across geographic and generational lines. Why do we join groups? What do we expect our membership in the group to accomplish for us or for others? Do groups provide us with a sense of identity? Of self-worth? Undoubtedly, the reasons vary from one individual to another.

The picture "Veterans Day" shows two members of a veterans' group posing in uniform with an American flag unobtrusively in the background. Their stance, legs apart and feet planted firmly, gives a solidity to their figures, which is tempered by the warmth of their smiles. They look content, happy, proud. Clearly, each has found some satisfaction in belonging to this organization.

We might wonder, though, whether the satisfaction of membership or the reason for joining this organization is the same for the woman as for the man. Wearing their uniforms and standing in the noonday sun, they represent the values of the veterans' organization. But as individuals their motivations for being there are personal, a product of their own backgrounds and experiences.

After reviewing the material at the beginning of the chapter, complete one of the following writing tasks.

1. Write a division paper that considers the woman and the man in the photograph separately. Describe the physical appearance of each. For each, determine what you believe are possible motivations for joining the armed services and, later, a veterans' organization. What do you imagine the service experience of each was like? What would the veterans' organization represent to each? What satisfactions would each receive from membership? One caution: Since there are only the two figures prominent in the picture, this will be a binary division. Don't slip into comparison and contrast, but profile the woman and the man separately.

2. Write a classification paper that presents categories of people of similar age: children, youth, young adults, older adults, seniors. Find at least five photographs of people of one age group in social situations. Describe the people in each photograph as representatives of a category of their age group. Discuss the characteristics of each category. Include the pictures when submitting your final draft.

🍒 Additional Writing Tasks 🍒
Classification and Division

1. Choose one of the following subjects and write an essay using division as the dominant pattern. Describe each component in some detail, distinguishing it from the other components. Keep your readers in mind by guiding them carefully from component to component.
   a.   A musical performance
   b.   A board game, such as chess, Monopoly, Risk, or Clue
   c.   The human mind
   d.   A ceremonial event, such as a wedding, funeral, campaign rally, banquet, or religious service
   e.   A week at a teenage vacation spot
   f.   A novel
   g.   A police drama, situation comedy, or national news broadcast
   h.   Your monthly income
   i.   Bargaining in a foreign marketplace
   j.   A meal in an expensive restaurant
2. Write an essay using classification as the dominant development method. Sort one of the following subjects into categories. Be sure the basis for your classification is clear. To direct your readers' attention, make up names for each category.
   a.   The books, records, and/or videotapes you own
   b.   Unusual sports, such as "earth games" or other sports that are seldom televised or reported in newspapers
   c.   Talk-show hosts
   d.   War toys, family-oriented toys, or intellectual toys
   e.   People who like to hunt game
   f.   Lies
   g.   Ways to read a novel or poem
   h.   Ways to watch a horror movie
   i.   Kinds of photography
   j.   Attitudes revealed by bumper stickers
   k.   Trends in dating, marriage, or divorce

l. Kinds of terror
m. Responses to a dramatic national or international event
n. New ways to learn
o. Kinds of good luck
p. Kinds of bad luck

10

Definition
Limiting Meaning

The Method

Think of how many words you hear in a day. Tens of thousands? Hundreds of thousands? Millions? Spoken words are plentiful. They are easy to produce: Just open your mouth, activate your larynx, wag your tongue, and words will take flight. Of course, spoken words are often strung together thoughtlessly. If you have any doubts about this description, just turn your television dial to a talk show and listen to the relentless babble.

But written words are different. They require work. Serious writers select them with care. Some words are so technical that only technically trained readers understand them. Some words are so rarely used that few readers know what they mean. Some have meanings so ambiguous that readers understand them differently. That is why definition is indispensable in writing.

Strategies

Professional writers approach definition in three ways: etymological, or lexical, definition; stipulative definition; and extended definition.

Etymological Definition

An etymological definition is a dictionary definition. It defines a word in a narrow way by specifying its class and its distinguishing characteristics. Consider the word *thriller*. A good college dictionary tells you that a thriller is a suspenseful work of fiction—a novel, play, or film—that deals with crime or detection. Sometimes an etymological definition includes synonyms: a thriller might be referred to as a *whodunit*.

Rather than using a ready-made dictionary definition, writers often expand dictionary information to fit the interests of their audience and requirements that suit their purposes. Consider the dictionary definition of *bird*: "a warm-blooded, two-legged, egg-laying vertebrate with a wishbone, feathers, and wings." Now imagine that a writer wishes to define *bird* for a ten-year-old reader. The definition might read something like this:

> A bird is an animal. It has a backbone, is warm-blooded, and walks on two legs, but a human being does, too. It flies, but insects and bats do, too. It lays eggs, but salamanders, some snakes, and turtles do the same.
> What then makes birds different from all other animals? Only birds have feathers and a wishbone.

Stipulative Definition

Sometimes a writer uses a common word extensively in a special or limited way. The writer then usually stipulates the meaning of the word—that is, the writer explains how the word is to be understood as it appears throughout the essay. This explanation creates the *stipulative definition.* In this paragraph from *Amusing Ourselves to Death,* educator and communications critic Neil Postman stipulates the meaning of "conversation."

> I use the word "conversation" metaphorically to refer not only to speech but to all techniques and technologies that permit people of a particular culture to exchange messages. In this sense, all culture is a conversation or, more precisely, a corporation of conversations, conducted in a variety of symbolic modes. Our attention here is on how forms of public discourse regulate and even dictate what kind of content can issue from such forms.

Social critic Don Pierstorff stipulates a meaning for "suits" when examining Michael Levine's *Deep Cover,* an exposé of the Drug Enforcement Administration (DEA).

> Who are the "suits"? They are the men and women who crowd the corridors and sit behind the desks of the Drug Enforcement Administration. They are government bureaucrats and managers. According to Michael Levine, they are

the people who have no first-hand experience of the drug war and are unwilling to listen to agents who do. They spend their days shuffling reports and briefing politicians.

Postman's paragraph stipulates the meaning of *conversation* by enlarging it to mean all the methods culture uses to communicate. Pierstorff's paragraph defines the commonly understood word *suits* by presenting its uncommon slang definition, the way in which DEA agents use it. Both authors anticipate that their readers will need to know these special definitions to understand what they are writing about.

Extended Definitions

Etymological and stipulative definitions usually are concisely written for the sole purpose of clarification. Extended definitions are much more detailed and usually employ various patterns of development to fully explain a word or concept. In this paragraph from *Hog on Ice*, C. E. Funk defines *white elephant*. He uses examples to establish its class and a brief narration about the word's origin to differentiate it from others.

> That large portrait of your wealthy Aunt Jane, given by her and which you loathe but do not dare to take down from your wall; that large bookcase, too costly to discard, but which you hope will be more in keeping with your future home; these, and a thousand other like items, are "white elephants"—costly but useless possessions. The allusion takes us to Siam. In that country it was the traditional custom for many centuries that a rare albino elephant was, upon capture, the property of the emperor—who even today bears the title Lord of the White Elephant—and was thereafter sacred to him. He alone might ride or use such an animal, and none might be destroyed without his consent. Because of that latter royal prerogative, it is said that whenever it pleased his gracious majesty to bring about the ruin of a courtier who had displeased him, he would present the poor fellow with an elephant from his stables. The cost of feeding

and caring for the huge animal that he might neither use nor destroy—a veritable white elephant—gave the term its present meaning.

In this two-paragraph passage from *Alligators in Sewers and Other Urban Legends,* Jan Harold Brunvand defines *urban legend.* Brunvand first establishes the class to which *urban legend* belongs and then distinguishes it from other members of the class. His definition goes beyond the etymological category because he develops the expression in greater detail, primarily with brief comparison and contrast and examples.

Urban legends are realistic stories that are said to have happened recently. Like old legends of lost mines, buried treasure, and ghosts, they usually have an ironic or supernatural twist. They belong to a subclass of folk narratives that (unlike fairy tales) are set in the recent past, involving ordinary human beings rather than extraordinary gods and demigods.

Unlike rumors, which are generally fragmentary or vague reports, legends have a specific narrative quality and tend to attach themselves to different local settings. Although they may explain or incorporate current rumors, legends tend to have a longer life and wider acceptance; rumors flourish and then die out rather quickly. Urban legends circulate by word of mouth, among the "folk" of modern society, but the mass media frequently help to disseminate and validate them. While they vary in particular details from one telling to another, they preserve a central core of traditional themes. In some instances these seemingly fresh stories are merely updatings of classic folklore plots, while other urban legends spring directly from recent conditions and then develop their own traditional patterns in repeated retellings. For example, "The Vanishing Hitchhiker," which describes the disappearance of a rider picked up on a highway, has evolved from a 19th-century horse-and-buggy legend into modern variants incorporating freeway travel. A story called "Alligators in the Sewers," on the other hand, goes back no further than the 1930s and seems to be a New York City invention. Often, it begins with people who bring pet baby alligators back from Florida and eventually flush them down the drain.

Both Funk's definition of *white elephant* and Brunvand's definition of *urban legend* involve much more than merely looking up the established meanings; nevertheless, they do make use of a common pattern of definition by placing a term in a class and distinguishing it from other members of the class. Funk and Brunvand can use this pattern because the words they define have been in common use for some time. But the strength of an extended definition is to introduce new terms to readers, or, more accurately, to introduce concepts that those terms represent. This kind of extended definition may be highly personal, embodying a writer's values and independent observation.

In this three-paragraph passage from *Zen and the Art of Motorcycle Maintenance*, Robert M. Pirsig defines "mechanic's feel." Clearly, his definition is based on close observation during personal experience.

The mechanic's feel comes from a deep inner kinesthetic feeling for the elasticity of materials. Some materials, like ceramics, have very little, so that when you thread a porcelain fitting you're very careful not to apply great pressures. Other materials, like steel, have tremendous elasticity, more than rubber, but in a range in which, unless you're working with large mechanical forces, the elasticity isn't apparent.

With nuts and bolts you're in the range of large mechanical forces and you should understand that within these ranges metals are elastic. When you take up a nut there's a point called "fingertight" where there's contact but no takeup of elasticity. Then there's "snug," in which the easy surface elasticity is taken up. Then there's the range called "tight," in which all the elasticity is taken up. The force required to reach these three points is different for each size of nut and bolt, and different for lubricated bolts and for locknuts. The forces are different for steel and cast iron and brass and aluminum and plastics and ceramics. But a person with mechanic's feel knows when something's tight and stops. A person without it goes right on past and strips the threads or breaks the assembly.

A "mechanic's feel" implies not only an understanding for the elasticity of metal but for its softness. The insides of a motorcycle contain surfaces that are precise in some cases to as little as one ten-thousandth of an inch. If you drop them or get dirt on them or scratch them or bang them with a hammer, they'll lose that precision. It's important to understand that the metal *behind* the surfaces can normally take a great shock and stress but that the surfaces themselves cannot. When handling precision parts that are stuck or difficult to manipulate, a person with mechanic's feel will avoid damaging the surfaces and work with his tools on the nonprecision surfaces of the same part whenever possible. If he must work on the surfaces themselves, he'll always use softer surfaces to work them with. Brass hammers, plastic hammers, wood hammers, rubber hammers and lead hammers are all available for this work. Use them. Vise jaws can be fitted with plastic and copper and lead faces. Use these too. Handle precision parts gently. You'll never be sorry. If you have a tendency to bang things around, take more time and try to develop a little more respect for the accomplishment that a precision part represents.

Pirsig's definition of "mechanic's feel" is unique. Readers have no resource to consult for a commonly accepted definition of an expression like that. Primarily relying on descriptive techniques, Pirsig carefully delineates the qualities of "mechanic's feel," right down to naming the degrees to which someone might tighten down a bolt: "fingertight," "snug," and "tight." Pirsig points out that metal has elasticity, and that someone with "mechanic's feel" must sense that quality or face the consequences—a broken assembly. Pirsig creates a sense of the soft, delicate surfaces of metal and names the tools someone should use when working on them—hammers of many materials varying in softness, as well as vise jaws fitted with soft faces. Someone with mechanic's feel is precise; in fact, the need for precision seems to be the message beneath the detail.

Definition in College Writing

You will write definitions to clarify important terms or concepts, especially in the social sciences, history, and philosophy. Usually, these will be stipulative definitions that are one or two paragraphs long and serve as part of an essay with another dominant development pattern. But sometimes an entire essay will be devoted to an extended definition. When you write an essay-length extended definition, the basic essay structure does not change: Begin with an introduction that ends with a clear statement of purpose or thesis. Write a discussion that develops the definition in several paragraphs. Write a conclusion that recalls the key points of the definition and restates the central purpose. Usually, a definition will include examples that illustrate the term or concept and comparisons to show the meaning in relation to similar terms or concepts.

Guidelines for Writing a Definition Essay

1. Select a term or concept that is currently being used in a new way or for which there is no clear etymological definition, such as a slang term or a new term from technology.
2. Develop a rough working explanation of what you will be defining. Then use prewriting techniques to generate examples and comparisons to illustrate it for your reader. If you are writing to define a special term, generate information that explains how to use it effectively and how it is misused.
3. Evaluate your prewritten material to see what you can and can't use effectively. Develop a clear purpose for your essay, one that clearly shows you will be writing a definition. Then shape the purpose into a thesis.

4. Write your essay. Organize it by moving from the general to the particular; that is, first create a broad sense of your term or concept then present particular examples, comparisons, and information to clarify it in more detail.

5. Revise your definition. Be sure your definition is clear, including everything in its category and excluding everything that isn't. Check your examples and comparisons to see that they are integrated effectively into the definition. Polish the entire definition for clarity.

A Student Essay Developed by Definition

For a freshman composition class, Chris Schneider responded to the following writing task:

> Use definition to develop any of the following topics in 500 to 600 words. You may use any number of paragraph development patterns, such as description, example, and comparison, to develop your thought.

a. commonsense	e. sign
b. code	f. saga
c. myth	g. tale
d. symbol	h. legend

Schneider selected item "c." "Myth" had taken on new significance. She had encountered the new usage in culture studies. First, read Chris Schneider's essay, then reread it and respond to the items in Reviewing with a Writer's Eye, which follows the essay.

Myth Redefined

1

Do you believe childhood is a time of innocence separated from the emotions and cares of the adult world? Do you count on science to solve the dangers of fossil-fuel shortage, ozone depletion, and toxic pollution? Do you feel that men are rational, and women are intuitive? Men are active; women, passive? Men are ambitious; women, nurturing? If you do, then you have been influenced by common American "myths," as a group of contemporary scholars and social critics known as semiologists would claim.

Semiologists are interested in the study of meaning. 2
They don't limit themselves to the meaning of words. This territory belongs to semanticists, that is, to those scholars who concentrate on linguistic significance. Semiologists may examine words, but they will also explore the ways that advertisements, television programs, films, clothes, toys, and other such things embody meaning, a kind of cultural meaning that semiologists sometimes refer to as "myth."

To most of us, the term "myth" might call to mind 3
marvelous Greek stories of disguised gods cavorting with humans. We might think of heroes wielding swords against dragons or of magicians mesmerizing entire armies. We might recall the story of Johnny Appleseed planting apple trees across the American landscape or of Rip Van Winkle sleeping for twenty years or of John Henry racing against a steam-powered spike driver. These myths are different from legends because they lack historical background and shade into the supernatural. They are also different from fables because they lack an overt moral intent. Like legends and fables they are stories, imaginative stories, that, according to one popular view, embody cultural patterns. Now semiologists are using the term "myth" in a different way.

To semiologists "myth" refers to deeply rooted cul- 4
tural beliefs, not to ancient stories. These beliefs are held by most members of any given society. Despite whatever evidence there might be to contradict the validity of a myth, semiologists do not judge it as right or wrong. They merely recognize its existence and analyze its social influence. Whether valid or invalid, a myth, therefore, is a psychological and social fact projected onto experience. We never clearly see things as they really are; we only see their reflections in our cultural beliefs.

Cultural myths are often used for manipulative pur- 5
poses. For instance, one myth embedded in cultural conscious is the myth of the rugged individual. Usually a man, the rugged individual is one who can survive on his

own in environments that would be hostile to all of us acculturated folks. Advertisers especially associate their products with the image of the rugged individual to manipulate consumers. For example, consider the Marlboro man, the lone cowboy who leads a rugged life herding steers on the open range. He calls to mind the rugged individuals cowboy actors John Wayne and Clint Eastwood play in western films, tough hombres who ride the range alone. Well, not quite alone; he has his cigarette. Of course, not everyone will respond to this myth. That's why advertisers employ many different kinds of cultural myths to sell their products.

Myths, as semiologists use the term, pervade every aspect of our cultural experience. Sometimes these belief systems are unrecognized and have a powerful influence on how we view experience. Other times, we become aware of them and through that awareness, change our perception of the world. Remember this myth: The husband is the breadwinner; the wife is the homemaker. The world has changed dramatically since that perception dominated American thinking.

6

Reviewing with a Writer's Eye

1. In "Myth Redefined," Chris Schneider writes an extended definition of the word *myth*. Develop your own scratch outline (p. 42) of Schneider's essay. Begin with the following statement: "Schneider's general purpose is to define a specialized use of the word *myth*." Then write the purpose of each paragraph that follows the introduction and briefly state the strategy she uses to achieve it.

2. Explain how Schneider arranges information from paragraph 2 through paragraph 5.

3. To define *myth*, Schneider uses several paragraph patterns. What is the primary development pattern of paragraph 2? Paragraph 3? Paragraph 5? Why does she use them?

4. Are Schneider's introduction and conclusion effective or ineffective? Why?

Peer Review

You may be asked to write an essay about one of the readings that follow. Before you meet with your writing group, review this introduction. As you read the papers of your group, use these general principles of definition to help guide your comments.

1. A definition paper should go beyond a dictionary definition to give the reader a fuller understanding of the term being defined.
2. A definition paper should have a clear purpose. The reader should be told why the term is important and how it relates to some larger picture.

---

5. Do you understand what Schneider means by the word *myth*? Write a note to Schneider that explains your understanding of *myth*. Ask her to clarify any points you don't understand.

The essays that follow are developed with definition as their main purpose. Study them. Make note of each writer's strategy. Apply what you learn to your own writing.

🦃 Judy Brady 🦃

Judy Brady was born in San Francisco in 1937. She studied painting at the University of Iowa, married and had children, and later worked as a secretary in San Francisco, having been discouraged by her male university professors from becoming a teacher. She later became very active in the feminist movement and has written numerous articles on women's roles in society and related subjects. In 1973 she went to Cuba to study social class relationships, having developed an interest in how societies change from her feminist political work.

I Want a Wife

This essay was published in the first issue of Ms. *magazine in 1971 and has been widely reprinted since. This biting description of the "ideal" wife has become a classic of feminist satire. Brady first classifies herself as a wife, then proceeds to define "wife" by explaining why she wants a wife of her own.*

I belong to that classification of people known as wives. I am   1
A Wife. And, not altogether incidentally, I am a mother.

Not too long ago a male friend of mine appeared on the scene   2
fresh from a recent divorce. He had one child, who is, of course, with his ex-wife. He is looking for another wife. As I thought about him while I was ironing one evening, it suddenly occurred to me that I, too, would like to have a wife. Why do I want a wife?

I would like to go back to school so that I can become eco-   3
nomically independent, support myself, and, if need be, support those dependent upon me. I want a wife who will work and send me to school. And while I am going to school I want a wife to take care of my children. I want a wife to keep track of the children's doctor and dentist appointments. And to keep track of mine, too. I want a wife to make sure my children eat properly and are kept clean. I want a wife who will wash the children's clothes and keep

them mended. I want a wife who is a good nurturant attendant to my children, who arranges for their schooling, makes sure that they have an adequate social life with their peers, takes them to the park, the zoo, etc. I want a wife who takes care of the children when they are sick, a wife who arranges to be around when the children need special care, because, of course, I cannot miss classes at school. My wife must arrange to lose time at work and not lose the job. It may mean a small cut in my wife's income from time to time, but I guess I can tolerate that. Needless to say, my wife will arrange and pay for the care of the children while my wife is working.

I want a wife who will take care of *my* physical needs. I want   4
a wife who will keep my house clean. A wife who will pick up after my children, a wife who will pick up after me. I want a wife who will keep my clothes clean, ironed, mended, replaced when need be, and who will see to it that my personal things are kept in their proper place so that I can find what I need the minute I need it. I want a wife who cooks the meals, a wife who is a *good* cook. I want a wife who will plan the menus, do the necessary grocery shopping, prepare the meals, serve them pleasantly, and then do the cleaning up while I do my studying. I want a wife who will care for me when I am sick and sympathize with my pain and loss of time from school. I want a wife to go along when our family takes a vacation so that someone can continue to care for me and my children when I need a rest and change of scene.

I want a wife who will not bother me with rambling com-   5
plaints about a wife's duties. But I want a wife who will listen to me when I feel the need to explain a rather difficult point I have come across in my course of studies. And I want a wife who will type my papers for me when I have written them.

I want a wife who will take care of the details of my social life.   6
When my wife and I are invited out by my friends, I want a wife who will take care of the babysitting arrangements. When I meet people at school that I like and want to entertain, I want a wife who will have the house clean, will prepare a special meal, serve it to me and my friends, and not interrupt when I talk about things that interest me and my friends. I want a wife who will have arranged that the children are fed and ready for bed before my

guests arrive so that the children do not bother us. I want a wife who takes care of the needs of my guests so that they feel comfortable, who makes sure that they have an ashtray, that they are passed the hors d'oeuvres, that they are offered a second helping of the food, that their wine glasses are replenished when necessary, that their coffee is served to them as they like it. And I want a wife who knows that sometimes I need a night out by myself.

I want a wife who is sensitive to my sexual needs, a wife who makes love passionately and eagerly when I feel like it, a wife who makes sure that I am satisfied. And, of course, I want a wife who will not demand sexual attention when I am not in the mood for it. I want a wife who assumes the complete responsibility for birth control, because I do not want more children. I want a wife who will remain sexually faithful to me so that I do not have to clutter up my intellectual life with jealousies. And I want a wife who understands that *my* sexual needs may entail more than strict adherence to monogamy. I must, after all, be able to relate to people as fully as possible.   7

If, by chance, I find another person more suitable as a wife than the wife I already have, I want the liberty to replace my present wife with another one. Naturally, I will expect a fresh, new life; my wife will take the children and be solely responsible for them so that I am left free.   8

When I am through with school and have a job, I want my wife to quit working and remain at home so that my wife can more fully and completely take care of a wife's duties.   9

My God, who *wouldn't* want a wife?   10

Meaning and Purpose

1. What are your ideas about what a wife is and does, and where do your ideas come from? How do they compare to what Brady says she wants her "wife" to be and do?
2. Brady repeats "I want a wife" many times throughout this essay. What is the purpose of that repetition?
3. Why does Brady use "of course" in paragraph 2?

4. Can you find a thesis statement in the essay? What is Brady's main point?
5. In listing a wife's duties, Brady also lists a husband's needs. What are some of these needs? Do you think Brady is fair to husbands in this essay?

Strategy

1. Do you think the first paragraph is effective as an opening? How does it serve Brady's purpose?
2. Brady defines "wife" by listing the duties she would expect her wife to perform. She arranges these duties in clusters of similar items. For each of paragraphs 3–7, label the cluster and tell what human characteristics Brady describes.
3. Classify this essay by labeling it with a name such as "informative," "political," "sarcastic," or "optimistic." Try to think of your own name—use one of those above if you must—and explain your reasons for labeling it as you have.

Style

1. Why is "A Wife" capitalized in the first paragraph?
2. What important attitude of Brady toward her "wife" does the word "replace" in paragraph 8 suggest?
3. Paragraph 4 says that the wife will not go on vacation with the author. Instead, she will go "along" on vacation. What is the difference in meaning between "going" and "going along" on vacation?
4. Why does Brady end her essay with a question? How is the question effective?

Writing Tasks

1. Brady's "wife" is an ideal one described from an exaggerated selfish male viewpoint. Who is your ideal person in some classifica-

tion of people, such as parent, boyfriend or girlfriend, sister or brother, teacher, athlete, food server, or salesperson? Write a definition essay in which you define by describing this ideal's behavior in various circumstances.

2. Give a man's counterpoint to Brady's essay by writing "I Want a Husband." Write from a first-person male point of view, and decide which categories to use. Try to imitate Brady's sarcastic and exaggerated tone.

❦ George Gilder ❦

George Gilder is a sociologist. His works include Men and Marriage, Life After Television, *and* Visible Man: A True Story of Post-Racist America. *In 1995, he published* Speaking of George Gilder, *a collection of thoughts drawn from transcripts and tapes of speeches given to Corporate America.*

Why Men Marry

This excerpt from Men and Marriage *(1992) recognizes the difficulty of defining the word "love" in a simple declarative sentence and makes no attempt to do so. Instead Gilder focuses on the psychological and biological needs that lead a man to replace the hunter love of youth with the procreative love of maturity.*

As you read, notice how Gilder uses catalogs of images to convey pictures of various aspects of love, particularly in paragraphs 1, 4 and 6.

Men marry for love. But what does this mean beyond what they got in their lives as single men: the flash of a new face, new flesh across a room. The glimpse of breasts shifting softly in a silken blouse. The open sesame of a missing ring. The excited pursuit, the misunderstood meanings, the charged meetings. The telling touch of hands. The eyes welling open to the gaze. The scent of surrender. The pillowed splash of unbound hair. The ecstatic slipping between new sheets. The race. The winning. The chase and the conquest . . . and back on the road. Definitely back on the road. Free again. Strong again. For new women, new pursuit. What more is there in life—in love—than this?

Marriage means giving it all up. Giving up love? That is how it seems to the single man, and that is why he fears it. He must give up his hunter's heart, forgo the getaway Honda growl, shear off his shaggy hair, restrict his random eye, hang up his handgun, bow down and enter the cage. At bottom, what he is is hunter. No way he will be hubby.

And yet, he will. For years he lunges at women's surfaces, but as time passes he learns of a deeper promise. For years he may not know the reasons or believe them or care. The heart, it is said, has its reasons. They spring from the primal predicament of man throughout the history of the race: the need to choose a particular woman and stay by her and provide for her if he is to know his children and they are to love him and call him father.

In procreative love, both partners consciously or unconsciously glimpse a future infant—precarious in the womb, vulnerable in the world, and in need of nurture and protection. In the swelter of their bodies together, in the shape and softnesses of the woman, in the protective support of the man, the couple senses the outlines of a realm that can endure and perpetuate their union: a pattern of differences and complements that goes beyond the momentary pleasures of reciprocal sex.

Marriage asks men to give up their essential sexuality only as part of a clear scheme for replacing it with new, far more important, and ultimately far more sexual roles: husband and father. Without these roles, a woman can bear a child, but the man is able only to screw. He can do it a lot, but after his first years it will only get him unthreaded, and in the end he is disconnected and alone. In his shallow heats and frustrations, he all too often becomes a menace to himself and his community.

There are millions of single men, unlinked to any promising reality, dissipating their lives by the years, moving from job to job, woman to woman, illusion to embitterment. Yet they are not hopeless. Many more millions have passed through the same sloughs, incurred the same boozy dreams, marijuana highs, cocaine crashes, sex diseases, job vapors, legal scrapes, wanderings. They follow the entire syndrome and then break out of it. Normally they do not escape through psychiatrists' offices, sex-education courses, VISTA or Peace Corps programs, reformatories, or guidance-counseling uplift. What happens, most of the time—the only effective thing that happens, the only process that reaches the sources of motivation and character—is falling in love.

Love is effective because it works at a deeper, more instinctual ⁷ level than the other modes of education and change. Love does not teach or persuade. It possesses and transforms. . . .

It is not just an intelligent appraisal of his circumstances ⁸ that transforms the single man. It is not merely a desire for companionship or "growth." It is a deeper alchemy of change, flowing from a primal source. It seeps slowly into the flesh, the memory, the spirit; it rises through a life, until it can ignite. It is a perilous process, full of chances for misfire and mistake—or for an ever more mildewed middle age. It is not entirely understood. But we have seen it work, and so have we seen love. Love infuses reason and experience with the power to change a man caught in a morbid present into a man passionately engaged with the future.

The change that leads to love often comes slowly. Many of the ⁹ girls a man finds will not help. They tend to go along with him and affirm his single life. But one morning he turns to the stranger sleeping next to him, who came to him as easily as a whiskey too many, and left him as heavy-headed, and decides he must seek a better way to live. One day he looks across the room over a pile of dirty dishes and cigarette butts and beer cans and sex magazines and bills and filthy laundry, and he does not see the evidence of happy carousing and bachelor freedom; he sees a trap closing in upon him more grimly than any marriage. One day while joking with friends about the latest of his acquaintances to be caught and caged, he silently wonders, for a moment, whether he really wishes it were he.

Suddenly he has a new glimpse of himself. His body is begin- ¹⁰ ning to decline, grow weaker and slower, even if he keeps it fit. His body, which once measured out his few advantages over females, is beginning to intimate its terrible plan to become as weak as an older woman's. His aggressiveness, which burst in fitful storms throughout his young life but never seemed to cleanse him—his aggression for which he could so rarely find the adequate battle, the harmonious chase—is souring now. His job, so below his measure as a man, so out of tune with his body and his inspiration, now stretches ahead without joy or relief.

His sex, the force that drove the flower of his youth, drives   11
still, drives again and again the same hard bargain—for which there are fewer and fewer takers, in a sexual arena with no final achievement for the single man, in which sex itself becomes work that is never done.

The single man is caught on a reef and the tide is running out.   12
He is being biologically stranded and he has a hopeless dream. Studs Terkel's book *Working* registers again and again men's desire to be remembered. Yet who in this world is much remembered for his job?

Stuck with what he may sense as a choice between being   13
trapped and being stranded, he still may respond by trying one more fling. The biological predicament can be warded off for a time, like Hemingway's hyena. Death often appears in the guise of eternal youth, at the ever-infatuating fountains: alcohol, drugs, hallucinogenic sex. For a while he may believe in the disguise. But the hyena returns and there is mortality in the air—diseases, accidents, concealed suicides, the whole range of the single man's aggression, turned at last against himself.

But where there is death, there is hope. For the man who is in   14
touch with his mortality, but not in the grips of it, is also in touch with the sources of his love. He is in contact with the elements—the natural fires and storms so often used as metaphors for his passions. He is a man who can be deeply and effectively changed. He can find his age, his relation to the world, his maturity, his future. He can burn his signature into the covenant of a specific life.

The man has found a vital energy and a possibility of durable   15
change. It has assumed the shape of a woman. It is the same form that has caught his eye and roiled his body all these years. But now there will be depths below the pleasing surfaces, meanings beyond the momentary ruttings. There will be a sense that this vessel contains the secrets of new life, that the womb and breasts bear a message of immortality. There will be a knowledge that to treat this

treasure as an object—mere flesh like his own, a mere matrix of his pleasure—is to defile life itself. It is this recognition that she offers a higher possibility—it is this consciousness that he has to struggle to be worthy of her—that finally issues the spark. And then arises the fire that purges and changes him as it consumes his own death. His children . . . they will remember. It is the only hope.

The man's love begins in a knowledge of inferiority, but it of-   16
fers a promise of dignity and purpose. For he then has to create, by dint of his own effort, and without the miracle of a womb, a life that a woman could choose. Thus are released and formed the energies of civilized society. He provides, and he does it for a lifetime, for a life.

Meaning and Purpose

1. Who do you think is the primary audience for this essay? What does Gilder hope to communicate to this audience?
2. According to Gilder, what is life like for men who do not marry? Be specific in your answer.
3. According to Gilder, what leads a man to give up the hunter life and seek procreative love?
4. Why, according to this essay, are a man's children more important than his work?

Strategy

1. We have included this essay as an example of extended definition, but Gilder also uses other development strategies that you have studied in earlier chapters of this text. What other strategies can you find and where are they located?
2. Gilder's essay is not a typical straightforward definition. You might say it defines more by implication than explication. How effective do you think his approach is? Support your answer with reasons.

Style

1. In writing, the word *catalogue* denotes a list composed of sentences, phrases, or words used to suggest the fullness of an idea. Most of paragraph 1, beginning with "the flash of" is an example of a catalogue. In what other places does Gilder use catalogues to convey his meaning? How effective is this technique?
2. Explain in your own words why Gilder says, "the womb and breasts bear a message of immortality" (paragraph 15).
3. In the last paragraph, Gilder says, "man's love begins in a knowledge of inferiority." What do you think this statement means? Is it valid in the context of this essay?
4. If necessary, check a dictionary for the meanings of these words: *ecstatic* (paragraph 1); *primal* (3); *procreative* (4); *sloughs, vapors* (6); *alchemy, morbid* (8); *covenant* (14); *ruttings, purges* (15).

Writing Tasks

1. For his essay, Gilder narrows the word *love* to "procreative love." Write a definition of an abstract word such as *loyalty, courage, patriotism, conservative,* or *liberal.* In your essay, do a similar thing, that is, limit your word to something more manageable. For example, *courage* might be limited to "physical courage" or "moral courage."
2. Choose a group that you believe is underprivileged, discriminated against, or misunderstood, such as illiterate adults, paraplegics, or gay parents. Define what it is to be a member of the group and the reality of what the person's life is like.

❦ Marie Winn ❦

Marie Winn was born in Czechoslovakia in 1936 and, as a child, immi-grated with her family to New York City, where she attended public schools. She pursued her education at Radcliffe College and Columbia University, graduating from the latter in 1959. An expert on culture and education, she has had numerous articles published in The New York Times Magazine, The New York Times Book Review, Smithsonian, The Wall Street Journal, *and* The Village Voice. *Her many books include* Children without Childhood, Unplugging the Plug-In Drug, *and* The Secret Life of Central Park. *Winn's most influential book is* The Plug-In Drug: Television, Children and the Family. *The book indicts Americans for their addiction to television and has been translated into French, German, Italian, Spanish, Swedish, and Japanese.*

TV Addiction

This selection from The Plug-In Drug *(orginally published in 1977 and revised in 1985), defines television addiction as a disease that is as severe and crippling as alcohol or drug addiction.*

Notice as you read how carefully Winn defines the terms addiction *and* TV addiction. *Notice, too, how the abundant examples she cites make her points clear.*

Cookies or Heroin?

The word "addiction" is often used loosely and wryly in conversation. People will refer to themselves as "mystery book addicts" or "cookie addicts." E. B. White wrote of his annual surge of interest in gardening: "We are hooked and are making an attempt to kick the habit." Yet nobody really believes that reading mysteries or ordering seeds by catalogue is serious enough to be compared with addictions to heroin or alcohol. The word "addiction" is here used jokingly to denote a tendency to overindulge in some pleasurable activity.

People often refer to being "hooked on TV." Does this, too, fall into the lighthearted category of cookie eating and other pleasures that people pursue with unusual intensity, or is there a kind of television viewing that falls into the more serious category of destructive addiction?

When we think about addiction to drugs or alcohol we frequently focus on negative aspects, ignoring the pleasures that accompany drinking or drug-taking. And yet the essence of any serious addiction is a pursuit of pleasure, a search for a "high" that normal life does not supply. It is only the inability to function without the addictive substance that is dismaying, the dependence of the organism upon a certain experience and an increasing inability to function normally without it. Thus people will take two or three drinks at the end of the day not merely for the pleasure drinking provides, but also because they "don't feel normal" without them.

Real addicts do not merely pursue a pleasurable experience one time in order to function normally. They need to *repeat* it again and again. Something about that particular experience makes life without it less than complete. Other potentially pleasurable experiences are no longer possible, for under the spell of the addictive experience, their lives are peculiarly distorted. The addict craves an experience and yet is never really satisfied. The organism may be temporarily sated, but soon it begins to crave again.

Finally, a serious addiction is distinguished from a harmless pursuit of pleasure by its distinctly destructive elements. Heroin addicts, for instance, lead a damaged life: their increasing need for heroin in increasing doses prevents them from working, from maintaining relationships, from developing in human ways. Similarly alcoholics' lives are narrowed and dehumanized by their dependence on alcohol.

Let us consider television viewing in the light of the conditions that define serious addictions.

Not unlike drugs or alcohol, the television experience allows the participant to blot out the real world and enter into a pleasurable and passive mental state. The worries and anxieties of reality are as effectively deferred by becoming absorbed in a television program as by going on a "trip" induced by drugs or alcohol. And just as alcoholics are only vaguely aware of their addiction, feeling that they control their drinking more than they really do ("I can cut it out any time I want—I just like to have three or four drinks before dinner"), people similarly overestimate their control over television watching. Even as they put off other activities to spend hour after hour watching television, they feel they could easily resume living in a different, less passive style. But somehow or other, while the television set is present in their homes, the click doesn't sound. With television pleasures available, those other experiences seem less attractive, more difficult somehow.

A heavy viewer (a college English instructor) observes: 8

"I find television almost irresistible. When the set is on, I cannot ignore it. I can't turn it off. I feel sapped, will-less, enervated. As I reach out to turn off the set, the strength goes out of my arms. So I sit there for hours and hours."   9

Self-confessed television addicts often feel they "ought" to do other things—but the fact that they don't read and don't plant their garden or sew or crochet or play games or have conversations means that those activities are no longer as desirable as television viewing. In a way the lives of heavy viewers are as imbalanced by their television "habit" as a drug addict's or an alcoholic's. They are living in a holding pattern, as it were, passing up the activities that lead to growth or development or a sense of accomplishment. This is one reason people talk about their television viewing so ruefully, so apologetically. They are aware that it is an unproductive experience, that almost any other endeavor is more worthwhile by any human measure.   10

Finally it is the adverse effect of television viewing on the lives of so many people that defines it as a serious addiction. The television habit distorts the sense of time. It renders other experiences vague and curiously unreal while taking on a greater reality for itself. It weakens relationships by reducing and sometimes eliminating normal opportunities for talking, for communicating.   11

And yet television does not satisfy, else why would the viewer   12 continue to watch hour after hour, day after day? "The measure of health," writes Lawrence Kubie, "is flexibility . . . and especially the freedom to cease when sated." But heavy television viewers can never be sated with their television experiences—they do not provide the true nourishment that satiation requires—and thus they find that they cannot stop watching.

Meaning and Purpose

1. According to Marie Winn, what are the things that are necessary for a habit to add up to an addiction?
2. Why does Winn consider addictions to such things as reading mystery books or gardening harmless, while she views an addiction to television watching as self-destructive?
3. According to the author, what distinguishes alcohol or drug addiction from TV addiction?
4. What is Winn's purpose in writing this essay? Who is her intended audience?

Strategy

1. What is the general movement in this essay, from the specific to the general or from the general to the specific? What is the effect of this movement? Explain.
2. Winn first defines *addiction* (paragraph 3–5) and then defines *TV addiction* (paragraphs 7–12). How are the two extended definitions organized? How does this organization further the author's purpose (see question 4, above)?
3. What effect does Winn's example of a college English instructor's TV addiction have in her argument?
4. What are some of the rhetorical techniques that Winn uses to develop her definitions?

Style

1. What is the tone of the essay? Explain.
2. Note the diction in the quote from E. B. White (paragraph 1) and some of the words Winn places in quotation marks: *"high," "don't feel normal"* (paragraph 3); *"trip"* (7); and *"habit"* (10). What is the significance of this diction? How does it differ from the language in the rest of the essay?
3. Winn begins paragraph 7 with a double negative. How does this reinforce the meaning of what immediately follows?
4. If necessary, look up the following words in a dictionary: *wryly, surge* (paragraph 1); *deferred, induced* (7); *sapped, enervated* (9); *ruefully* (10); *adverse* (11); *sated, satiation* (12).

Writing Tasks

1. Write an essay in which you describe and comment on an activity that fits Winn's definition of addiction. The addiction could be your own or somebody else's, and it could be any kind of compulsive behavior, such as collecting antiques, baseball cards, boyfriends, girlfriends, or anything else; hanging out at the local coffee shop; shopping; or surfing the Internet. Treat your subject seriously or humorously, but be consistent.
2. Write an essay in which you analyze the way you most often spend your free time: watching TV, going to movies, reading, hanging out at the mall. Discuss whether or not the behavior is an addiction. Consider both the positive and negative aspects of the behavior.

👣 Anna Quindlen 👣

A journalist, columnist, essayist, and novelist, Anna Quindlen was born in 1953. In 1974 she graduated from Barnard College, where she began her journalism career as a part-time reporter for the New York Post. *She wrote columns for several newspapers and, as a columnist for the* New York Times, *won the Pulitzer Prize for commentary in 1992. She has published several novels, most recently* Black and Blue. *She has also published collections of essays.*

Homeless

"Homeless" is taken from the collection Living Out Loud, *published in 1987. In this essay, Quindlen examines the painful phenomenon of homelessness, defining the term by putting it in human perspective.*

   Notice while you read how Quindlen makes the problem of home-lessness real by always painting the issue in terms of real people and things, rather than in abstract terms.

Her name was Ann, and we met in the Port Authority Bus   1
Terminal several Januarys ago. I was doing a story on homeless people. She said I was wasting my time talking to her; she was just passing through, although she'd been passing through for more than two weeks. To prove to me that this was true, she rummaged through a tote bag and a manila envelope and finally unfolded a sheet of typing paper and brought out her photographs.

   They were not pictures of family, or friends, or even a dog or   2
cat, its eyes brown-red in the flashbulb's light. They were pictures of a house. It was like a thousand houses in a hundred towns, not suburb, not city, but somewhere in between, with aluminum siding and a chain-link fence, a narrow driveway running up to a one-car garage and a patch of backyard. The house was yellow. I looked on the back for a date or a name, but neither was there. There was no need for discussion. I knew what she was trying to tell me, for it was something I had often felt. She was not adrift,

527

alone, anonymous, although her bags and her raincoat with the grime shadowing its creases had made me believe she was. She had a house, or at least once upon a time had had one. Inside were curtains, a couch, a stove, potholders. You are where you live. She was somebody.

I've never been very good at looking at the big picture, taking   3
the global view, and I've always been a person with an overactive sense of place, the legacy of an Irish grandfather. So it is natural that the thing that seems most wrong with the world to me right now is that there are so many people with no homes. I'm not simply talking about shelter from the elements, or three square meals a day or a mailing address to which the welfare people can send the check—although I know that all these are important for survival. I'm talking about a home, about precisely those kinds of feelings that have wound up in cross-stitch and French knots on samplers over the years.

Home is where the heart is. There's no place like it. I love my   4
home with a ferocity totally out of proportion to its appearance or location. I love dumb things about: the hot-water heater, the plastic rack you drain dishes in, the roof over my head, which occasionally leaks. And yet it is precisely those dumb things that make it what it is—a place of certainty, stability, predictability, privacy, for me and for my family. It is where I live. What more can you say about a place than that? That is everything.

Yet it is something that we have been edging away from grad-   5
ually during my lifetime and the lifetimes of my parents and grandparents. There was a time when where you lived often was where you worked and where you grew the food you ate and even where you were buried. When that era passed, where you lived at least was where your parents had lived and where you would live with your children when you became enfeebled. Then, suddenly where you lived was where you lived for three years, until you could move on to something else and something else again.

And so we have come to something else again, to children   6
who do not understand what it means to go to their rooms because they have never had a room, to men and women whose fantasy is a wall they can paint a color of their own choosing, to old people reduced to sitting on molded plastic chairs, their skin

blue-white in the lights of a bus station, who pull pictures of houses out of their bags. Homes have stopped being homes. Now they are real estate.

People find it curious that those without homes would rather sleep sitting up on benches or huddled in doorways than go to shelters. Certainly some prefer to do so because they are emotionally ill, because they have been locked in before and they are damned if they will be locked in again. Others are afraid of the violence and trouble they may find there. But some seem to want something that is not available in shelters, and they will not compromise, not for a cot, or oatmeal, or a shower with special soap that kills the bugs. "One room," a woman with a baby who was sleeping on her sister's floor, once told me, "painted blue." That was the crux of it; not size or location, but pride of ownership. Painted blue.

This is a difficult problem, and some wise and compassionate people are working hard at it. But in the main I think we work around it, just as we walk around it when it is lying on the sidewalk or sitting in the bus terminal—the problem, that is. It has been customary to take people's pain and lessen our own participation in it by turning it into an issue, not a collection of human beings. We turn an adjective into a noun: the poor, not poor people; the homeless, not Ann or the man who lives in the box or the woman who sleeps on the subway grate.

Sometimes I think we would be better off if we forgot about the broad strokes and concentrated on the details. Here is a woman without a bureau. There is a man with no mirror, no wall to hang it on. They are not the homeless. They are people who have no homes. No drawer that holds the spoons. No window to look out upon the world. My God. That is everything.

Meaning and Purpose

1. What is Quindlen's primary purpose in this essay?
2. According to Quindlen, what is wrong with "looking at the big picture" or "taking the global view" (paragraph 3)?

3. Explain the difference between a home as a shelter, a place to eat, and a mailing address and a home as reflected in "cross-stitch and French knots on samplers" (paragraph 3).
4. Considering how Quindlen develops her definition of "homeless," what is the meaning of her statement "Now [homes] are real estate" (paragraph 6)?
5. Describe how Quindlen's statement "We turn an adjective into a noun" (paragraph 8) explains the problem of the term "the homeless."

Strategy

1. Why is it appropriate for Quindlen to begin the essay with an anecdote?
2. How does the essay's final paragraph (9) expand and clarify the meaning of the first sentence of paragraph 3?
3. What organizational methods does Quindlen use in paragraph 3?

Style

1. Quindlen uses short sentences and phrases to conclude paragraphs 2, 4, 6, 7, and 9. What effect does this create?
2. What effect does Quindlen create with the phrase "once upon a time" in paragraph 2?
3. What do the terms *cross-stitch*, *French knots*, and *samplers* mean (paragraph 3)? In what way do they reflect the meaning of home?
4. Quindlen is careful to tie all of her ideas tightly together. What transitional devices does she use to tie all of the paragraphs together?

Writing Tasks

1. Using Quindlen's essay as a model, write a paper that defines any abstract term (such as *fear, success, beauty, family values, the privileged*) by showing what the term means in concrete examples.

2. Write an essay in which you describe what your home means to you. Use concrete language and examples to define your meaning of *home*.

❦ Francine Prose ❦

Francine Prose, born in 1947, is a novelist and essayist. Her novels in-clude Bigfoot Dreams, Primitive People, *and* Hunters and Gatherers. *Her novel* Household Saints *was made into a critically acclaimed movie in 1993. One critic has compared her latest fiction,* Guided Tours of Hell, *to the work of Mark Twain because of its acerbic social commentary. Her essays have appeared in* Mademoiselle, *Atlantic* Monthly, *the* New York Times, *and elsewhere.*

Gossip

In "Gossip," first published in the New York Times *in May, 1985, Prose plays the contrarian defining gossip in unexpected ways, by showing that her usually maligned subject serves important social and psychological functions.*

As you read, examine Prose's points with a critical eye to determine whether she really does release gossip from its normally unsavory reputation.

Once I met a woman who grew up in the small North Carolina town to which Chang and Eng, the original Siamese twins, retired after their circus careers. When I asked her how the town reacted to the twins marrying local girls and setting up adjacent households, she laughed and said: "Honey, that was *nothing* compared to what happened *before* the twins got there. Get the good gossip on any little mountain town, scratch the surface and you'll find a snake pit!" [1]

Surely she was exaggerating; one assumes the domestic arrangements of a pair of Siamese twins and their families would cause a few ripples anywhere. And yet the truth of what she said seemed less important than the glee with which she said it, her pride in the snake pit she'd come from, in its history, its scandals, [2] its legacy of "good gossip." Gossip, the juicier the better, was her heritage, her birthright; that town, with its social life freakish enough to make Chang and Eng's seem mundane, was part of who she was.

Gossip must be nearly as old as language itself. It was, I imagine, the earliest recreational use of the spoken word. First the cave man learned to describe the location of the plumpest bison, then he began to report and speculate on the doings of his neighbors in the cave next door. And yet, for all its antiquity, gossip has rarely received its due; its very name connotes idleness, time-wasting, frivolity and worse. Gossip is the unacknowledged poor relative of civilized conversation: Almost everyone does it but hardly anyone will admit to or defend it; and of these only the smallest and most shameless fraction will own up to enjoying it.

My mother and her friends are eloquent on the subject and on the distinction between gossiping and exchanging information: "John got a new job," is, they say, information. "Hey, did you hear John got fired?" is gossip; which is, they agree, predominantly scurrilous, mean-spirited. That's the conventional wisdom on gossip and why it's so tempting to disown. Not long ago I heard myself describe a friend, half-jokingly, as "a much better person than I am, that is, she doesn't gossip so much." I heard my voice distorted by that same false note that sometimes creeps into it when social strain and some misguided notion of amiability make me assent to opinions I don't really share. What in the world was I talking about?

I don't, of course, mean rumor-mongering, outright slander, willful fabrication meant to damage and undermine. But rather, ordinary gossip, incidents from and analyses of the lives of our heroes and heroines, our relatives, acquaintances and friends. The fact is, I love gossip, and beyond that, I believe in it—in its purposes, its human uses.

I'm even fond of the word, its etymology, its origins in the Anglo-Saxon term "godsibbe" for god-parent, relative, its meaning widening by the Renaissance to include friends, cronies and later what one *does* with one's cronies. One gossips. Paring away

its less flattering modern connotations, we discover a kind of synonym for connection, for community, and this, it seems to me, is
the primary function of gossip. It maps our ties, reminds us of
what sort of people we know and what manner of lives they lead,
confirms our sense of who we are, how we live and where we
have come from. The roots of the grapevine are inextricably en-
twined with our own. Who knows how much of our sense of the
world has reached us on its branches, how often, as babies, we
dropped off to sleep to the rhythms of family gossip? I've often
thought that gossip's bad name might be cleared by calling it
"oral tradition"; for what, after all, is an oral tradition but the stories of other lives, other eras, legends from a time when human
traffic with spirits and gods was considered fit material for gos-
sipy speculation?

Older children gossip; adolescents certainly do. Except in the
case of those rare toddler-fabulists, enchanting parents and sib-   7
lings with fairy tales made up on the spot, gossip may be the way
that most of us learn to tell stories. And though, as Gertrude Stein
is supposed to have told Hemingway, gossip is not literature,
some similar criteria may apply to both. Pacing, tone, clarity and
authenticity are as essential for the reportage of neighborhood
news as they are for well-made fiction.

Perhaps more important is gossip's analytical component.
Most people—I'm leaving out writers, psychologists and proba-   8
bly some large proportion of the academic and service profes-
sions—are, at least in theory, free to go about their lives without
feeling the compulsion to endlessly dissect the minutiae of human motivation. They can indulge in this at their leisure, for
pleasure, in their gossip. And while there are those who clearly
believe that the sole aim of gossip is to criticize, to condemn (or,
frequently, to titillate, to bask in the aura of scandal as if it were
one's own), I prefer to see gossip as a tool of understanding. It
only takes a moment to tell what someone did. Far more
mileage—and more enjoyment—can be extracted from debating
why he did it. Such questions, impossible to discuss without
touching on matters of choice and consequence, responsibility

and will, are, one might argue, the beginnings of moral inquiry, first steps toward a moral education. It has always seemed peculiar that a pastime so conducive to the moral life should be considered faintly immoral.

I don't mean to deny the role of plain nosiness in all this, of unadorned curiosity about our neighbors' secrets. And curiosity (where would we be without it?) has, like gossip, come in for some negative press. Still, it's understandable, everyone wants to gossip, hardly anyone wants to be gossiped about. What rankles is the fear that our secrets will be revealed, some essential privacy stripped away and, of course, the lack of control over what others say. Still, such talk is unavoidable; it's part of human nature, of the human community. When one asks, "What's the gossip?" it's that community that is being affirmed.   9

So I continue to ask, mostly without apology and especially when I'm talking to friends who still live in places I've moved away from. And when they answer—recalling the personalities, telling the stories, the news—I feel as close as I ever will to the lives we shared, to what we know and remember in common, to those much-missed, familiar and essentially beneficent snake pits I've lived in and left behind.   10

Meaning and Purpose

1. What is Prose's thesis? Does she state it explicitly, or is it implied?
2. Prose broadens the usual negative definition of gossip to include seldom-considered positive connotations of the word. What are those positive connotations? Which aspects of gossip, the negative or the positive, does Prose consider the more important? Explain.
3. In paragraph 8, Prose contends that gossip is "conducive to the moral life." Explain what she means by that.
4. What attributes do literature and gossip share? What does Prose accomplish by comparing the two?

Strategy

1. Why does Prose begin her essay with the anecdote of Chang and Eng, the Siamese twins?
2. The essay is an extended definition of the word *gossip*. What other rhetorical patterns does Prose employ to create that definition?
3. In what way does Prose's description of the etymology of *gossip* further her extended definition of the word?

Style

1. In paragraph 2, Prose uses the third person "one." More commonly throughout the essay, she uses the first person "I." Why?
2. Reread paragraph 6, looking closely at the "roots" metaphor in the fifth sentence. How does the metaphor advance Prose's definition?
3. Look up the etymology of *legend* (paragraph 6). How does the word's history lend meaning to Prose's definition of *gossip*?
4. If necessary, look up the following words in a dictionary: *adjacent* (paragraph 1); *legacy, mundane* (2); *speculate, antiquity, connotes, frivolity* (3); *scurrilous, amiability, assent* (4); *slander, fabrication* (5); *etymology, cronies* (6); *fabulists, criteria* (7); *component, compulsion, dissect, minutiae, titillate, bask, aura, conducive* (8); *rankles* (9); *beneficent* (10).

Writing Tasks

1. By giving an extended definition of the term *gossip*, Francine Prose rescues the word from its common, unsavory reputation. Choose some other common activity that has garnered a similar reputation—daydreaming, people watching, nagging, worrying, penny pinching, or the like—and write a paper in which you

make a case for its redeeming qualities by giving it an extended definition.

2. Write a paper in which you refute Prose's argument for the human value of gossip. Make sure your thesis is clear, and use an adequate number of specific examples to validate it.

❦ Responding to Photographs ❦

Definition

Touching a Snake

Symbols are visible objects or actions that communicate significance beyond their literal meaning. For example, the American flag might stir our patriotic feelings. A superstitious person might grow anxious if he breaks a mirror, predicting a streak of bad luck for himself. The flag, breaking a mirror—each is a symbol.

Often symbols have conventional meanings; for example, a heart sent on St. Valentine's Day is an emblem of affection. A wedding ring is an emblem of eternal commitment to another person. A Christian cross is an emblem of devotion. Many objects or actions do not have conventional meanings but have significance that is created by their context. For example, imagine that you observe the following scene: A woman in black stands next to a tombstone, which reads:

Harold Ross
1930–1993
May He Rest in Peace

Next to the woman, their heads bowed, stand three young children. From a few yards away you watch, believing that this is a widow and her children in mourning. After all, the grave, the tombstone, the black dress, and the bowed heads all suggest this interpretation. But then the woman turns from the grave, and you see her face. She's smiling, joyfully smiling. The children begin to skip and sing, "Who's afraid of the big bad wolf / the big bad wolf / the big bad wolf? Who's afraid. . . ." Suddenly the significance of this symbolic scene has changed. To what? Well, that's open to interpretation, which is characteristic of symbolic experience.

Frequently, a symbolic dimension is at work in photographs. Photographers carefully compose the elements of their images so we sense a symbolic dimension in a photograph. "Touching a Snake" is such a photograph. With definition as the dominant development pattern, complete one of the following writing tasks. Before beginning the task, reread the material at the beginning of the chapter to review the conventions involved in writing a definition.

1. Begin by looking up the definition of *symbol* in an unabridged dictionary or other resource material in the library. From the information you gather and from information you gleaned from the introductory comments to this assignment, develop a full definition of symbol, using examples from your experience and reading. Next, interpret the symbolic significance of "Touching a Snake." Consider several elements: the snake itself, which has a rich conventional symbolic history; the teddy bear; the generational difference between the man and the boy; the image on the man's T-shirt. In the process of developing your material, you might decide that there are several ways to interpret the photograph. Try to accommodate them in your essay.

2. Research the symbolic significance of the snake as it has appeared throughout history and in different cultures. Integrating

the various symbolic meanings your research has uncovered, define *snake* as a multidimensional symbol, integrating its various
interpretations. Finally, using one or more views of the symbolic
snake, interpret the meaning of "Touching a Snake."

🍒 Additional Writing Tasks 🍒

Definition

1. Write an essay that defines one of the following terms. Explore the subject beyond its dictionary meaning, using a variety of methods to develop your definition. As part of this or any extended definition, you can state what the subject *excludes* as a way to clarify your definition.

   a. humanity
   b. education
   c. Armageddon
   d. terror
   e. leadership
   f. honesty
   g. fad
   h. evil
   i. female liberation
   j. male liberation
   k. corruption
   l. intuition
   m. liberation theology
   n. social responsibility
   o. obsession
   p. team player
   q. sociopath
   r. maverick
   s. imagination
   t. tragedy
   u. confidence
   v. luck
   w. glamour
   x. scorched earth
   y. genocide
   z. blindsided

2. From the following list of slang terms, select one and define it in several paragraphs. After you explain the term, create a situation in which it might apply, using the term in several sample sen-

tences as a speaker might. Also include other slang that has a similar meaning.
   a. hoodwink
   b. greenhorn
   c. whoopee
   d. scam
   e. boob
   f. folknik
   g. bamboozled
   h. boodle
   i. macho
   j. bonehead
3. As a representative of a student rights organization, you have accepted the responsibility to convince a campus grievance committee composed of students, faculty, and administrators that a sexual harassment policy should be adopted as official college policy. Your first task is to define *sexual harassment* and to illustrate at least three different ways it manifests itself in behavior.
4. a. You are an environmentalist living in a major metropolitan area. You have formed an action group that is committed to protect all the natural landscapes that still exist in your city, even to the point of taking militant action against developers. You have used the phrase "urban environmentalist" to describe people who think and act as you do. In an essay, define *urban environmentalists* and describe what developers can expect from them.
    b. A group of self-designated "urban environmentalists" are disrupting development in the city. They see themselves as saviors of natural settings that exist within the urban landscape, but you regard them as "environmental terrorists." In an essay, define *environmental terrorists*, and predict what city officials can expect from them.
5. Look up the medical explanation of a debilitating ailment such as Alzheimer's disease, Down syndrome, or Hodgkin's disease. Once you understand the medical terminology, write a definition essay that explains the disease to someone who has no background in medicine. Create a case study of a person who has the disease to further explain its debilitating effects.

11

Persuasion and Argument

Convincing a Reader

The Method

An argumentative essay is an attempt to change or reinforce someone's opinion or to move someone to take action. On the one hand, the essay may be emotionally charged, appealing to a reader's feelings with emotional detail and biased language. The writing is then called *persuasion* or *persuasive argument.* On the other hand, an argumentative essay may be highly rational, appealing to a reader's intellect with logical explanation. This writing is called *argument* or *logical argument.* Political writing relies heavily on persuasion, and scientific writing on argument. Rarely, however, does an argumentative essay appeal only to emotion or only to reason. Usually, writers appeal to both, striving to convince their readers that their position is valid.

Imagine that you want to convince your readers of the merits of a vegetarian diet. You might begin by appealing to reason. First, you might contrast the high cost of meat with the low cost of grains that provide comparable protein. Second, you might point out that the grains grown for animal feed would be better used to feed the world's hungry. You might continue by presenting the danger highly marbled meat poses to health. You might then shift the appeal to emotion. You might construct an emotional description of animals being raised in pens, relating examples of force feeding and chemical injections, and describing slaughterhouse procedures. While composing the essay, you would keep an eye on your readers, anticipating their responses to your appeals by asking yourself if you are being too emotional or even too rational.

Throughout an argumentative essay a writer must carefully balance reason and emotion. A writer whose essay is so self-righteous that it ignores reason or so rational that it ignores feelings will alienate most readers. A general rule to follow is that an argumentative essay should be primarily rational or it may fail to convince critical readers. Consequently, writers of effective arguments usually present their opinions persuasively but develop ample and strong evidence throughout their essays.

544

The ancient Greeks, who formulated the underlying concepts of *logic,* identified three factors that are crucial to the construction of an effective argument:

1. *Logos,* or the quality of arguing soundly, refers to the quality of evidence—that is, examples, facts, statistics, authority statements, and reasonable interpretations.
2. *Pathos,* or the feeling dimension of language, refers to the ability to connect with a reader's emotion—that is, values, attitudes, and psychological needs.
3. *Ethos,* or credibility and honesty, refers to how writers present themselves—that is, as knowledgeable, trustworthy, and logical or as ignorant, shiftless, and erratic.

An effective argument usually blends logos, pathos, and ethos. The exact mixture varies with the audience and your purpose.

An argument is predicated on an *assertion,* that is, an opinion you want a reader to accept or an action you want a reader to take. When stated in a sentence, the assertion is referred to as a **proposition** or **thesis**.

The high-fashion fur industry should be curtailed.

The state should resume capital punishment.

Magazines featuring nudity—such as *Playboy, Penthouse,* and *Playgirl*—should be banned from community magazine stands.

The writer then supports the thesis with *evidence*, which is the proof behind the assertion.

It is the quality of evidence that goes a long way to persuade a reader to agree with a writer and reject an opposing position. Keep in mind that the evidence that writers use to develop an argument is the same as that any of us uses in oral arguments: personal experience, the experience of others, and authoritative sources.

Personal experience. Suppose you assert that police are harassing college-age drivers. You have had firsthand experience.

Several times, a patrol car has pulled you over while you were driving near campus. Each time, an officer initiated a search of your car. Once one even required you to take a field sobriety test, which you passed. At none of these times did any officer issue a traffic citation. These personal experiences could serve as legitimate evidence to support your position.

Experience of others. You might narrate a story of a friend who had a similar experience. You might also include observations by a passenger or bystander to corroborate your friend's experience.

When using the experience of others, do all you can to be sure that the information is accurate. You know how accurate a description of your experience is because you lived it, but when you use the experience of others, you are, in effect, vouching for its veracity. It is wise, therefore, to include more than one account of the same event.

Authoritative sources. An argument gains its strength from the quality of authoritative evidence a writer can marshal. You can develop some authoritative information yourself. Once again, consider the argument supporting the proposition that police are harassing college-age drivers. To support your opinion even more thoroughly, you might research police records. If the research revealed that police stopped and searched a significantly larger number of college-age drivers than older drivers, then you would use the information as evidence.

Sometimes, however, you must rely on other authoritative sources, such as encyclopedias, dictionaries, handbooks, digests, journals, and scientific research as well as people who are recognized as having extensive knowledge about a subject. When citing knowledgeable people to support an argument, be sure that their expertise is in the subject you are discussing. It will not do your argument much good to quote a well-known nuclear physicist's opinion on gun control; your reader won't accept that specialist's word as authoritative.

Facts and statistics from authoritative sources can lend a great deal of credibility to any argument. Facts are irrefutable. No matter what the source, a fact is a fact:

The Earth revolves around the sun.
John F. Kennedy, the thirty-fifth President of the United States, was assassinated on November 22, 1963.

When facts are corroborated by statistics, they exert a powerful influence on a reader. For instance:

The United States has more homicides each year than Japan, Taiwan, and the combined countries of Western Europe.

But what does this statistical fact mean? Should the government execute all convicted murderers? Do we need stricter handgun laws? Should every citizen arm for self-protection? Answering these questions involves interpretations of fact based on personal feelings and beliefs; that is, it involves opinions.

Strategies

Writers of argument essays pay particular attention to their readers. Since they can't be all things to all readers, they find it helpful to lump readers into one of three general categories and then address them appropriately

1. *Supportive readers.* They already agree with you. There's no need to overload your argument with dry facts and statistics. You can emphasize pathos over logos, that is, rely more on emotion and less on information. Touch the right emotional nerve and this crowd will carry you away on its shoulders.

2. *Wavering readers.* These uncommitted or uninformed readers are the ones you want to move through both logos and ethos, that is, by presenting solid evidence and by establishing your trustworthiness and honesty. Establish the right image and they will hop on your bandwagon.

3. *Hostile readers.* These readers are apathetic, skeptical, and maybe even downright mean. Convincing them of *anything* will be like trying to pull an angry bull's tooth with a pair of pliers. Give them just the facts—simple facts, dramatic facts, any facts that will penetrate their intransigence. Ethos won't help much, since they already see you as a low-down schemer, and pathos will be thrown back in your face. Just keep writing calmly and rely on logos. It's hard to spit in the face of truth.

Argument Essay Structure

Writers frequently structure their arguments in a thesis-evidence-conclusion pattern; that is, they state a thesis with a clear assertion in the introduction, present the evidence in the discussion, and reinforce the assertion in the conclusion. This is similar to the commonly used college essay structure.

Sometimes they will use a generalization-evidence-thesis pattern; that is, they open with a general statement of their position, withholding a succinct thesis statement until the close, develop the evidence, and then state the thesis in the close. Generally, no matter which pattern a writer chooses, an effective argumentative essay will have five elements:

1. A clear representation of the controversial issue and the writer's position on it
2. A clearly stated thesis, in either the opening or the close
3. Ample evidence and an orderly arrangement with a refuting counterargument
4. A reasonable tone with an undercurrent of emotion
5. A compelling close that emphasizes the central assertion

To be convincing, evidence in an argumentative essay must be arranged in logical sequence or risk readers rejecting the writer's conclusion. When composing an argument, writers reason through one of two processes: induction or deduction.

Argument Paragraph Structure

Like all essays, an argument essay is composed of paragraphs. In fact, a writer will usually employ a variety of paragraph modes, such as examples, comparison and contrast, cause and effect, and definition. Like all effective discussion paragraphs, these paragraphs will have a topic sentence and adequate development.

There is another paragraph structure, however, that is unique to argument: a *refutation* paragraph, which presents an opposing point and offers the writer's response. For example, in the following passage from "Politics and the English Language," George Orwell recognizes and refutes a point of argument that counters his position.

> I said earlier that the decadence of our language is probably curable. Those who deny this would argue, if they produced an argument at all, that language merely reflects existing social conditions, and that we cannot influence its development by any direct tinkering with words and constructions. So far as the general tone or spirit of a language goes, this may be true, but it is not true in detail. Silly words and expressions have often disappeared, though not through any evolutionary process but owing to the conscious actions of a minority.

Orwell's refutation paragraph follows a common structure, or sequence of sentences. He begins by establishing his position. He then states a counterargument. Next, he writes a sentence that swings the direction from the counterpoint to his response. He closes with an interpretation that supports his opinion.

Often writers employ traditional paragraph modes to develop refutation paragraphs. In the following paragraph from "Scientist: I Am the Enemy," pediatrician Ron Karpati responds to accusations made by animal rights activists with stunning brief examples. Notice how Karpati first summarizes the activists' point before countering it.

Much is made of the pain inflicted on animals in the name of medical science. The animal-rights activists contend that this is evidence of our malevolent and sadistic nature. A more reasonable argument, however, can be advanced in our defense. Life is often cruel, both to animals and human beings. Teenagers get thrown from the back of a pickup truck and suffer severe head injuries. Toddlers, barely able to walk, find themselves at the bottom of a swimming pool while a parent checks the mail. Physicians hoping to alleviate the pain and suffering these tragedies cause have but three choices: create an animal model of the injury or disease and use that model to understand the process and test new therapies; experiment on human beings—some experiments will succeed, most will fail—or finally, leave medical knowledge static, hoping that accidental discoveries will lead us to the advances.

In "The Futility of the Death Penalty," Clarence Darrow uses comparison and contrast to refute a counterargument.

It seems to be a general impression that there are fewer homicides in Great Britain than in America because in England punishment is more certain, more prompt, and more severe. As a matter of fact, the reverse is true. In England the average term for burglary is eighteen months; with us it is probably four or five years. In England, imprisonment for life means twenty years. Prison sentences in the United States are harder than in any country in the world that could be classed as civilized.

In "Letter from Birmingham Jail," Martin Luther King, Jr., uses analogy to refute a public statement made by Alabama clergymen who opposed civil rights demonstrations.

In your statement you assert that our actions, even though peaceful, must be condemned because they precipitate violence. But is this a logical assertion? Isn't this like condemning a robbed man because his possession of money

precipitated the evil act of robbery? Isn't this like condemning Socrates because his unswerving commitment to truth
and his philosophical inquiries precipitated the act by the
misguided populace in which they made him drink hemlock? Isn't this like condemning Jesus because his unique
God-consciousness and never-ceasing devotion to God's will
precipitated the evil act of crucifixion? We must come to see
that, as federal courts have consistently affirmed, it is wrong
to urge an individual to cease his efforts to gain his basic
constitutional rights because the quest may precipitate violence. Society must protect the robbed and punish the
robber.

Even process analysis can be effective in refuting a counterpoint. In "Concerning Abortion: An Attempt at a Rational
View," Charles Harshrone analyzes the function of a fertilized
egg to refute the view that the egg in this early stage is a human being.

> Anti-abortion advocates argue that human life begins at
> the moment of conception. But this is not accurate.
> The fertilized egg is an individual egg, but not an in-
> dividual human being. For such a being is, in its body, a
> multicellular organism, a *metazoan*—to use the scientific
> Greek—and the egg is a single cell. The first thing the egg
> cell does is to begin dividing into many cells. For some
> weeks the fetus is not a single individual at all, but a colony
> of cells. During its first weeks there seems to be no ground
> for regarding the fetus as comparable to an individual an-
> imal. Only in possible or probable destiny is it an indi-
> vidual. Otherwise it is an organized society of single-celled
> individuals.

Although not all argument writers state an opposing point of
argument in order to refute it, it's an effective technique. It shows
a reader that a writer has thoroughly considered the issue, thus
making an argument all the more convincing.

Inductive Reasoning

Through *inductive reasoning,* writers accumulate enough specific evidence to justify a *general conclusion.* In other words, inductive reasoning moves from the *specific* to the *general.* While growing up, we all learned to use induction. A child may bite into a hard green apple and discover that it tastes bitter. When the child tastes a hard green pear, he finds that it, too, is bitter. At another time the child bites into a hard green plum and an apricot. Both are bitter. By induction, he draws the general conclusion that hard green fruit is bitter and should not be eaten.

Argumentative essays written with inductive reasoning follow a similar pattern but with one difference: they usually begin with a *hypothesis* or question that embodies the conclusion the writer wants the reader to accept as valid. To argue that a city named Glenwood is environmentally responsible, a writer will have to present evidence that leads directly to that conclusion.

Hypothesis:	Glenwood is an environmentally responsible city. (or: Is Glenwood an environmentally responsible city?)
Evidence:	Glenwood has instituted these environmental programs:
	Curbside recycling for glass, newspaper, aluminum, and plastics;
	Disposal of household toxic waste;
	Law prohibiting release of ozone-depleting chlorofluorocarbons from air conditioners;
	Refuse landfill designed to protect ground water from toxic pollution and to generate methane gas;
	A wetlands bird habitat preserved as open space.
Conclusion:	Glenwood is environmentally responsible.

Conclusions drawn from the inductive reasoning procedure are usually referred to as *probable conclusions,* or *inferences,* for they are reached with incomplete evidence. The reader's acceptance of a conclusion that follows from inductive reasoning is often referred to as the *inductive leap.* To establish a clear connection between the evidence and the conclusion, you must be sure that the evidence you present is *relevant, sufficient,* and *representative.*

To be relevant, the evidence must support the hypothesis and contribute directly to the conclusion. To be sufficient, the evidence must amply support the conclusion. And to be representative, the evidence must represent the full range of information related to the hypothesis, not just one side or the other. By following these criteria, a writer increases the probability that the conclusion is valid, thus bridging the distance from evidence to conclusion and making the reader's intellectual passage easier.

Deductive Reasoning

Deductive reasoning is the opposite of inductive reasoning. Deductive reasoning moves from general assumptions, called premises, to a specific conclusion that follows from the general *premises.* In formal logic, this deductive pattern is called a *syllogism,* a form of organization that includes a *major premise,* a *minor premise,* and a *necessary conclusion,* one that is the logical result of the two premises. The classic example of syllogistic form comes down to us from Aristotle:

Major premise:	All humans are mortal.
Minor premise:	Socrates is human.
Conclusion:	Therefore, Socrates is mortal.

The conclusion of a syllogism is always drawn from the major and minor premises, both of which must be accurate for the conclusion to be accurate. If the premises are drawn from relevant, sufficient, and representative evidence—the same criteria used to draw sound conclusions in inductive reasoning—the conclusion of a syllogism will probably be accurate. But syllogisms can be illogical. An inaccurate major premise may make the syllogism illogical, as shown on the following page:

Major premise:	Professional gamblers carry large quant-ities of cash and drive expensive cars.
Minor premise:	John Murphy is a professional gambler.
Conclusion:	Therefore, John Murphy must carry large quantities of cash and drive an expensive car.

The major premise is inaccurate. Ask yourself, Are all professional gamblers successful enough to have large quantities of cash on their person and drive expensive cars? Because the major premise is inaccurate, the conclusion is inaccurate.

Sometimes the language of a syllogism is deceptive. Consider the use of "good American," "accept," and "change" in this flawed syllogism.

Major premise:	Every good American accepts the United States Constitution.
Minor premise:	Martin Luther King did not accept the United States Constitution because he worked to change it.
Conclusion:	Therefore, Martin Luther King was not a good American.

The phrase "good American" is vague, too vague to describe a class of people accurately. What do "accept" and "change" mean in this context? The United States Constitution has provisions for change. In fact, it has been amended many times. Anyone who accepts the Constitution accepts the possibility of changing it. Because language is used deceptively in the premises, the conclusion is meaningless.

Sometimes a syllogism is illogical because it is constructed improperly. First, examine this properly constructed syllogism:

Major premise:	All artists rely on intuition.

In a properly constructed syllogism, the subject of the major premise, in this example "artists," must appear in the minor premise and be narrowed.

Minor premise: John is an artist.

The conclusion then follows necessarily from the major and minor premises.

Conclusion: Therefore, John relies on intuition.

That syllogism is properly constructed and is valid. Now examine this invalid syllogism:

Major premise: All artists rely on intuition.
Minor premise: All psychics rely on intuition.
Conclusion: Therefore, all psychics are artists.

This syllogism is improperly constructed because the minor premise does not repeat the subject of the major premise. The conclusion, therefore, is invalid.

Like inductive reasoning, deductive reasoning can help to organize an argument. But using deduction is never quite as simple as the skeletal form of syllogisms used to illustrate it.

Imagine that the Sierra Club has established a *representative sample* of environmentally responsible cities. By extensive inductive reasoning, the Sierra Club finds several cities, including Glenwood, from our previous example, operating effective environmental programs. On the basis of its analysis of these programs, the Sierra Club defines the environmentally responsible city. A syllogism showing that a city is environmentally responsible might be constructed in this sequence:

Major premise: Cities with ecologically beneficial programs for disposal of waste, conservation of energy, and preservation of open space are environmentally responsible.
Minor premise: San Lorenzo has ecologically beneficial programs for disposal of waste, conservation of energy, and preservation of open space.

Conclusion: Therefore, San Lorenzo is environmentally responsible.

In an argumentative essay, a syllogism seldom appears in such clear form, but often its deductive structure is embedded in the text. If a writer wanted to argue that San Lorenzo is environmentally responsible, he or she might first construct a syllogism such as the one above, analyze the evidence needed to support the proposition, and then arrange the argument, incorporating syllogistic reasoning in the structure.

In the first section of the essay the writer would address the questions raised in the major premise.

1. What is an ecologically beneficial program for disposing of waste?
2. What is an ecologically beneficial program for conserving energy?
3. What is an ecologically beneficial program for preserving open space?

To answer these questions would take several paragraphs, and the writer would have to rely on the authority of the Sierra Club's definition. An ecologically beneficial program for disposing of waste would probably require recycling usable trash, disposing of toxic waste, and stringent restrictions on use of landfills. An ecologically beneficial program for conserving energy would probably mean reducing use of automobiles to save fuel and increasing use of solar energy to save electricity. An ecologically beneficial program for preserving open space would probably include protection for unique land formations and wildlife habitats. This discussion would be rather broad because the definition is based on a representative sample of many cities that may vary dramatically in size and geographic location.

To develop the second section of the essay, the writer would address the questions raised by the minor premise:

1. What specific actions has San Lorenzo taken to implement an ecologically beneficial waste-disposal program?

2. What specific actions has San Lorenzo taken to implement ecologically beneficial programs for conserving energy?
3. What specific actions has San Lorenzo taken to implement an ecologically beneficial program for preserving open space?

The purpose of this section is to present evidence that San Lorenzo does indeed meet the definition of environmentally responsible cities. In this section, which would also require several paragraphs to fully develop, the writer would present as evidence the specific environmental programs San Lorenzo has implemented, thus demonstrating the validity of the syllogism's minor premise.

In the last section of the essay, by far the shortest, the writer would conclude that San Lorenzo is an environmentally responsible city. The writer might choose to summarize the key points of the argument, but here the force of deductive reasoning would be irresistible, making it unnecessary to restate the argument in abbreviated form. But whether to develop a conclusion fully or to leave it implied is the decision of the writer, who is responsible for the argument's coherence and consistency. Risks lie in both strategies.

Examine an Argument

Philosopher Stephen Toulmin developed a simple system to examine the strength of an argument, one that helps writers to check whether they are covering everything they should. It's a simple system to use in ordinary thinking situations and reflects how most people use their minds. It's now called the Toulmin model, and it consists of three main elements:

1. The *claim* is the conclusion you draw from your examination of the information—the thesis.
2. The *grounds* are the pieces of information related to the issue—the evidence.
3. The *warrant* is the principle that links the evidence to the thesis—the assumption.

How does the Toulmin model work? Here's a simplified example: Someone suggests that you and your roommates would have fun camping over the upcoming weekend. You respond by saying, "We can't. We have an examination in freshman composition on Monday."

Claim: We can't go camping.
Ground: We have a midterm exam.
Warrant: Students should stay home and study before
           a test.

A warrant is often left unstated because it is usually so obvious that the listener will fill it in. *Students should study the weekend before a test* is a warrant that college students would agree with. But suppose someone has a different warrant, one that says *Students should relax before a test.* This person would likely insist that everyone should go camping. You might find this view strange or even unreasonable until you clarified the conflicting assumptions behind each other's thinking.

Notice that a warrant is similar to the generalization used in a syllogism (see pp. 553–557) or the conclusion of an inductive chain. You could easily show the following:

Students who have a test on Monday shouldn't camp the weekend before.

All of us have a test on Monday.

Therefore, we shouldn't go camping Friday, Saturday, and Sunday.

Toulmin's model is especially useful in argument writing. You probably won't write in syllogisms or in pure inductive arrangements. An untrained writer will usually make a claim and offer grounds to support the claim. He or she will not pay much attention to the actual reasoning process that goes into the conclusion and the assumption behind the argument. By using Toulmin's model to identify the warrant, claim, and grounds, you will see that the warrant links the claim and grounds and you can determine whether it should be stated explicitly or left implicit. The model will also help you to clarify or even qualify your claim and help you to determine whether you have enough information to convince a reader that your claim is justified.

Logical Fallacies in Writing

Logical fallacies are common mistakes in reasoning, and an argument tainted by them is ineffective. The word *fallacy* means "deception," or "a fault in reasoning." Fallacies deceive by distorting the truth and making logical conclusions unattainable. Using fallacies consciously signifies dishonesty; using them inadvertently demonstrates muddled thinking.

Study this list of eight most common fallacies. Remember that writers must scrutinize their arguments to avoid slipping into fallacious reasoning.

Overgeneralization.   Writers overgeneralize when they draw a conclusion from insufficient or unrepresentative evidence.

During the last year, three of five award-winning films concentrated on family violence. An examination of family violence was just broadcast on national television. No doubt these events indicate that family violence is on the rise.

A handful of films and a television program do not constitute a trend. The conclusion that family violence is rising could be substantiated with statistics and reports from authorities such as psychologists, sociologists, and law enforcement officers.

Oversimplification.   To oversimplify is to ignore essential information from which a conclusion is drawn. Be careful to avoid this fallacy when writing about complicated subjects. You might become too eager to offer a simple explanation to a complicated problem.

> The problems of air pollution, ozone depletion, and global warming are not really problems at all. They are merely manifestations of our educational system. We have too many scientists working in universities with nothing to do but study our environment.

Faulty Either/Or Reasoning.   The either/or fallacy is a type of oversimplification in which a writer assumes only two alternatives, black or white, when there are others, including gray. The slogan "America, love it or leave it" implies that love of country must be unqualified, which has the effect of excluding constructive criticism.

> Everyone would agree that America is being severely damaged by the sale and use of illegal drugs. The only two courses of action are these: the country's leaders can ignore the problem, or they can enforce the law to its maximum limits.

Of course, other actions are possible—initiate public education, fund rehabilitation for former drug users, develop agreements with other countries to curtail manufacturing of drugs, and even legalize use of drugs. The choice is not between doing nothing or joining a law-and-order crusade.

Post Hoc **Argument.**   The complete Latin phrase is *post hoc, ergo propter hoc,* which means "after this, therefore because of this." The assumption in this fallacious argument is that one event causes another event simply because the second follows the first in time.

> For more than a year, I have been meditating nightly for one hour. Although I usually have the flu at least once each year, I didn't have it last year. No doubt the meditation prevented me from catching the flu.

As stated, the only relationship between meditation and catching the flu is that one followed the other. Other explanations could be found: Perhaps that year had no flu epidemic, or perhaps the person was lucky enough to avoid a deadly sneeze. Time sequence alone cannot prove that a cause-and-effect relationship applies.

Non Sequitur. In Latin, *non sequitur* means "it does not follow." A *non sequitur* is a conclusion that does not logically follow from its premises.

> The city in this county that has the most crime also has the highest-paid police force. The city with the least crime has the lowest-paid police force. It does not make sense for our city to pay higher salaries to our police when doing so will not reduce crime.

The reasons for high crime rates are many, a high incidence of poverty being one of them. But we doubt that high police salaries contribute to a rising crime rate. In fact, dangerous working conditions could lead to higher wages for police.

False Analogy. Someone using a false analogy assumes that if two things are similar in one or more characteristics, then they are similar in other characteristics.

> We should not forget the lessons of Grenada and Panama, when our leaders tried to negotiate settlements and failed. Once we sent in the Marines, peace and a working relationship were restored. The best way to deal with renegade countries who act against our interests is to invade them to show other hostile governments we will not be bullied.

We are not living in the same world we lived in even five years ago. The breakup of Communist bloc countries, the danger of renegade terrorist action, the proliferation of nuclear weapons, all make the international scene too complex for rash action based on a false analogy.

Ad Hominem **Argument.** When a writer attacks a person associated with an issue rather than the argument supporting the issue, then the writer is committing an *ad hominem* fallacy, which in Latin means "to the man."

> Councilman Hunt has made a strong argument against raising the gasoline tax for revenue to build more roads. Why shouldn't he? He takes the bus to work each day, and he has the money to fly to any part of the country where he might want to vacation.

This statement ignores the argument for a tax increase and concentrates instead on the person making the argument.

Association Fallacy.   To commit the association fallacy is to claim that an act or belief is worthy or unworthy simply because of the people associated with it.

> Congressman Will is supported by some of Hollywood's leading figures. Because actors, directors, and producers know talent when they see it, you should support Congressman Will too.

Do Hollywood figures know any more about the qualities necessary to serve as an effective congressman than most other voters?

Argument in College Writing

Whether presenting examples, comparing two subjects, explaining a process, or classifying components into distinctive categories, you must think clearly and write logically. One development method, however, holds writers to the highest standard of clear thinking and logical writing: argumentation. At some point in the term, most instructors, especially those in the humanities and social sciences, will require you to take a position in relation to a particular opinion or controversial subject—that is, they will require you to write an argument.

Guidelines for Writing Argument

1. Once you select a controversial subject and decide on your position, marshal two kinds of evidence: that which supports your position and, if appropriate, that which opposes it.

2. Develop a plan that arranges the evidence in a logical progression. Use inductive arrangement if the presentation of your evidence would best be organized by arguing from specifics to a general conclusion; use deductive arrangement if the presentation of your evidence is best organized by arguing from a general conclusion to the specifics.

3. Determine who your readers are. If you perceive your readers to be committed to your position, then you will not have to establish your credibility, nor will you have to write an argument dense with facts, examples, and statistics. Your goal: to reinforce their support.

   If you perceive your readers to be uncommitted, then you must establish yourself to be a reliable source and offer a detailed presentation of the evidence, one that not only informs them but also stirs their emotion. Your goal: to win their support.

   If you perceive your readers to be hostile, then you must establish your authority, present compelling evidence—that is, indisputable facts and carefully reasoned arguments—and avoid emotional appeals, which they might perceive as an emotional attack on their beliefs. Your goal: to encourage them to question their position.

4. Write the essay. If the arrangement is inductive, begin with a stated or implied hypothesis, and lead your reader through the evidence to a reasonable conclusion.

   If the arrangement is deductive, begin with an introduction that states your position and ends with a thesis that clearly indicates an argument will follow. Develop the evidence, which should address questions your thesis raises, in an orderly, step-by-step fashion. Note, where appropriate, the position that opposes yours. Conclude by restating your thesis and reviewing the evidence to show the reader that your position is valid and should be accepted.

5. Review the essay to catch and correct any errors in reasoning you find. Look for logical fallacies, such as overgeneralization, oversimplification, faulty either/or reasoning, and flawed syllogistic reasoning embedded in your discussion.

A Student Essay Developed by Argument

Rolanda Burris received the following assignment to write an argument essay in a mass communications course.

> In an essay of 1000 to 1250 words, take a position for or against controlling what some social critics perceive to be a detriment to the public welfare that is perpetuated in popular culture. Examples include violence against authority and women in music lyrics; the display and use of weapons in cartoons; and the portrayal of drinking, smoking, drugs, or sexual relations in movies or on television.

Burris decided to convince her readers that films featuring characters who smoke should carry a warning much like the one the law requires cigarette companies to place in magazine advertisements. A movie buff, Burris enjoyed reviewing the history of films to gather evidence of the role that smoking has played. As you read her essay, notice how she uses historical examples to build her case.

Here's Looking at Reality, Kid

Among college students Humphrey Bogart is a cult figure. His films, such as <u>The Maltese Falcon, The Harder They Fall</u>, and <u>To Have and Have Not</u>, are still shown at colleges across America. Just last Saturday our Film Society sponsored a Bogart retrospective. I watched   1

<u>Casablanca</u> again. It becomes more romantic each time I
see it. <u>Casablanca</u> is set in an exotic place and time. It
features mysterious supporting characters. It concentrates
on a dilemma. The beautiful heroine must decide between
two men who love her, a political idealist and a world-
weary cynic. Bogart, the cynic, is suave. His style dominates the film. During this viewing I saw something I had
not noticed before: No actor could handle a cigarette better
than Bogart. Hanging from the corner of his mouth as he
talks or held between two fingers as he drinks, a smolder-
ing cigarette is clearly associated with the stylish image
Bogart will eternally project from the screen. Bogart the
actual man, however, was not eternal. At 58 he died from
lung cancer after a lifetime of heavy smoking. After the
movie, I asked myself how many film buffs smoke because they admired the way Bogart handled a cigarette? If
Bogart's style influenced just one filmgoer to smoke,
shouldn't <u>Casablanca</u>, in fact all films that feature characters who smoke, carry a warning about the dangers of
smoking?

Apparently cigarette manufacturers understand the 2
power of association to influence someone's decision to
smoke. In an effort to attract more smokers, Philip
Morris, the company that sells Benson and Hedges ("For
people who love to smoke") Virginia Slims ("You've come
a long way, Baby"), and Merit ("For those who want marital bliss") once paid $350,000 to have secret agent 007
James Bond smoke Larks in <u>License to Kill</u>. Philip Morris
seems to believe that many young men are too immature
to make the logical connection between smoking and death
yet do make the illogical connection between smoking and
the adventurous life James Bond leads, even though it is
not real life.

A couple of years before <u>License to Kill</u> was released, 3
Philip Morris paid a substantial amount to have Lois Lane
smoke Marlboros in <u>Superman II</u>. One movie critic raised
the question that even if Lois Lane had to smoke, why
feature a particular cigarette brand so prominently?
Philip Morris must have been counting on the power of association even then. Will every immature young woman
who sees Lois Lane lighting up conclude that if she
smokes Marlboros, her own Man of Steel will drop from

the sky? Probably not consciously, but the subconscious might associate smoking with sex appeal.

Recently, cigarette companies have had to pay billions in legal settlements for misleading consumers. A reasonable person might assume they would be chastened after their lies were exposed publicly. But selling cigarettes has little to do with reason. The industry seems to be intensifying its effort to glamorize smoking. 4

Just the other night on the Movie Channel, I watched Die Hard. There was megastar Bruce Willis smoking Marlboros and blasting away a band of terrorists. I recently watched the video of My Best Friend's Wedding. There was the stunning Julia Roberts nervously puffing on a Newport while trying to disrupt the wedding plans of a rival. But the most shocking movie display of smoking came to the public through the cinematic talents of director John Cameron. 5

In Titanic, the world's largest grossing film to date, Cameron shows every major character smoking. Teen heart-throb Leonardo di Caprio smokes. His love interest, Kate Winslet, smokes. At one point, Winslet rebelliously blows smoke in her social-climbing mother's face. Later, she snatches a cigarette from a young man's lips in an act of independence. Cameron portrays smoking as sexy, glamorous, and sophisticated. To smoke, the unstated message suggests, is to have "style"—maybe not Bogart's style, but style nevertheless. 6

Movies are rated according to who should be allowed to see them. The National Coalition on Television Violence discovered that cigarette smoking appears in 100 percent of PG-13 films. These movies have been approved for thirteen year olds who have parental permission to watch. Even if they come from families who do not smoke, young people may be influenced by powerful images that show smoking as an accepted behavior. But where is the warning in movies that smoking is a health hazard? 7

I can hear opponents now. "One more law designed to control personal freedom," they will charge. "Following this logic, if government wants to protect people, it also should put warnings about cars on films with car chases or warnings about guns on films with shoot-outs." But they would be wrong. Cars and guns don't kill people, drivers 8 and gun owners kill people. In contrast, cigarettes <u>do</u> kill people, and that's a well-documented fact. Moreover, the government has already taken action to control smoking.

Cigarette advertisements have been banned from television and radio for years. When they appear in magazines, cigarette advertisements must include the Surgeon General's warning that smoking can result in cancer, heart disease, or fetal injury in pregnant women. This legal requirement is sensible public-health policy, but where does such a warning appear in films that feature characters who smoke? Clearly cigarette companies believe that by associating cigarettes with appealing characters they will influence a person's decision to smoke. Why else would Philip Morris pay movie producers to feature its products?

The practice of featuring smokers in films is disturbing enough, but when cigarette companies actually pay to have their brands featured in films, the practice goes beyond being disturbing to being criminal. It is time government put a stop to this kind of indirect advertising just as it did with radio and television advertising. If politicians lack the courage, at the very least, they should require that films featuring smokers announce the dangers of smoking before the plot begins. Then the next time someone watches Humphrey Bogart raise a glass, squint through a cloud of cigarette smoke at Ingrid Bergman, and say, "Here's looking at you, Kid," viewers will not be seduced by the romantic image. Instead, they might be awakened to the excruciating pain Bogart must have felt while dying of lung cancer.

Reviewing with a Writer's Eye

1. Explain the irony in Rolanda Burris's title.
2. In your own words, state Burris's thesis, the proposition at the heart of her argument.
3. What kinds of evidence does Burris offer to support her thesis? (See pp. 545–547.)
4. In a few sentences, describe Burris's intended reader. What details suggest her reader? (See pp. 547–548.)

5. With a total score of 100, what percentage of Burris's argument relies on logos? On pathos? On ethos? (See p. 545.)
6. Is Burris's essay inductively or deductively arranged? Explain. (See pp. 552–557.)
7. Use the Toulmin model to clarify Burris's argument. Identify the claim, the ground, and the warrant. (See pp. 558–559.)
8. Identify Burris's refutation paragraph. (See pp. 549–551). Is it a successful refutation? Why or why not?
9. In no more than 300 words, write a brief critique of "Here's Looking at Reality, Kid" as if you were writing it to Rolanda Burris. Discuss her success or failure in meeting argument-writing conventions.

Peer Review

You may be asked to write an essay about one of the readings that follow. Before you meet with your writing group, review this introduction. As you read the group papers, use these general principles of persuasion and argument to help guide your comments.

1. As stated on page 548, an argumentation paper should have the following:

   a. a clear statement of the writer's assertion;
   b. an orderly presentation of the evidence;
   c. a clear connection between the evidence and the argument;
   d. a reasonable refutation of evidence that is counter to the writer's assertion;
   e. a conclusion that emphasizes the assertion.

2. An argumentative essay should have an appropriate balance between reason and emotion.
3. An argumentative essay should avoid logical fallacies. See pages 559–562.

❦ Joy Williams ❦

Joy Williams, born in Massachusetts in 1944, was educated at Marietta College in Ohio and at the University of Iowa. She has written three novels, State of Grace, The Changeling, *and* Breaking and Entering, *and two collections of short stories,* Taking Care *and* Escapes. *She has also contributed nonfiction pieces to a number of magazines including* Esquire, *where the following essay was first published. She lives in Key West, Florida, and has written a history and guidebook about the Florida Keys. She has recently published* Florida, *a collection of essays.*

The Killing Game

Williams's essay, presented here in a shorter version than the original in Esquire, *argues passionately against hunting. She examines the traditional reasons advanced by hunters to explain the attraction of hunting and the arguments used to justify it, rejecting each in turn. Then she advances her personal interpretation of why humans hunt. Whichever side of the argument you are on, Williams's skillful use of language is sure to hold your interest and probably elicit a strong response.*

As you read the essay, be aware of your response to each paragraph. Which of her arguments do you accept and which do you reject?

Death and suffering are a big part of hunting. A big part. Not that you'd ever know it by hearing hunters talk. They tend to downplay the killing part. To kill is to put to death, extinguish, nullify, cancel, destroy. But from the hunter's point of view, it's just a tiny part of the experience. *The kill is the least important part of the hunt,* they often say, or, *Killing involves only a split second of the innumerable hours we spend surrounded by and observing nature* . . . For the animal, of course, the killing part is of considerably more importance. José Ortega y Gasset, in Meditations on Hunting, wrote, *Death is a sign of reality in hunting. One does not*

569

hunt in order to kill; on the contrary, one kills in order to have hunted. This is the sort of intellectual blather that the "thinking" hunter holds dear. The conservation editor of Field & Stream, George Reiger, recently paraphrased this sentiment by saying, *We kill to hunt, and not the other way around,* thereby making it truly fatuous. A hunter in West Virginia, one Mr. Bill Neal, blazed through this philosophical fog by explaining why he blows the toes off tree raccoons so that they will fall down and be torn apart by his dogs. *That's the best part of it. It's not any fun just shooting them.*

Instead of monitoring animals—many animals in managed areas are tagged, tattooed, and wear radio transmitters—wildlife managers should start hanging telemetry gear around hunters' necks to study their attitudes and listen to their conversations. It would be grisly listening, but it would tune out for good the *suffering as sacrament and spiritual experience* blather that some hunting apologists employ. *The unease with which the good hunter inflicts death is an unease not merely with his conscience but with affirming his animality in the midst of his struggles toward humanity and clarity,* Holmes Rolston III drones on in his book *Environmental Ethics.*   2

There is a formula to this in literature—someone the protagonist loves has just died, so he goes out and kills an animal. This makes him feel better. But it's kind of a sad feeling-better. He gets to relate to Death and Nature in this way. Somewhat. But not really. Death is still a mystery. Well, it's hard to explain. It's sort of a semireligious thing . . . Killing and affirming, affirming and killing, it's just the cross the "good" hunter must bear. The bad hunter just has to deal with postkill letdown.   3

Many are the hunter's specious arguments. Less semireligious but a long-standing favorite with them is the vegetarian approach: you eat meat, don't you? If you say no, they feel they've got you— you're just a vegetarian attempting to impose your weird views on others. If you say yes, they accuse you of being hypocritical, of allowing your genial A&P butcher to stand between you and reality. The fact is, the chief attraction of hunting is the pursuit and murder of animals—the meat-eating aspect of it is trivial. If the hunter chooses to be ethical about it, he might cook his kill, but the meat   4 of most animals is discarded. Dead bear can even be dangerous! A bear's heavy hide must be skinned at once to prevent meat spoilage. With effort, a hunter can make okay chili, *something to keep in mind,* a sports rag says, *if you take two skinny spring bears.*

As for subsistence hunting, please . . . Granted that there might be one "good" hunter out there who conducts the kill as spiritual exercise and two others who are atavistic enough to want to supplement their Chicken McNuggets with venison, most hunters hunt for the hell of it. 5

For hunters, hunting is fun. Recreation is play. Hunting is recreation. Hunters kill for play, for entertainment. They kill for the thrill of it, to make an animal "theirs." (The Gandhian doctrine of nonpossession has never been a big hit with hunters.) The animal becomes the property of the hunter by its death. Alive, the beast belongs only to itself. This is unacceptable to the hunter. *He's yours . . . He's mine . . . I decided to . . . I decided not to . . . I debated shooting it, then I decided to let it live . . .* Hunters like beautiful creatures. A "beautiful" deer, elk, bear, cougar, bighorn sheep. A "beautiful" goose or mallard. Of course, they don't stay "beautiful" for long, particularly the birds. Many birds become rags in the air, shredded, blown to bits. *Keep shooting till they drop!* Hunters get a thrill out of seeing a plummeting bird, out of seeing it crumple and fall. *The big pheasant folded in classic fashion.* They get a kick out of "collecting" new species. *Why not add a unique harlequin duck to your collection?* Swan hunting is satisfying. *I let loose a three-inch Magnum. The large bird only flinched with my first shot and began to gain altitude. I frantically ejected the round, chambered another, and dropped the swan with my second shot. After retrieving the bird I was amazed by its size. The swan's six-foot wingspan, huge body, and long neck made it an impressive trophy.* Hunters like big animals, trophy animals. A "trophy" usually means that the hunter doesn't deign to eat it. Maybe he skins it or mounts it. Maybe he takes a picture. *We took pictures, we took pictures.* Maybe he just looks at it for a while. The disposition of the "experience" is up to the hunter. He's entitled to do whatever he wishes with the damn thing. It's dead. 6

Hunters like categories they can tailor to their needs. There   7
are the "good" animals—deer, elk, bear, moose—which are allowed to exist for the hunter's pleasure. Then there are the "bad"
animals, the vermin, varmints, and "nuisance" animals, the rabbits
and raccoons and coyotes and beavers and badgers, which are dis-
encouraged to exist. The hunter can have fun killing them, but the
pleasure is diminished because the animals aren't "magnificent."

Then there are the predators. These can be killed any time,   8
because, hunters argue, they're predators, for godssakes.

Many people in South Dakota want to exterminate the red fox   9
because it preys upon some of the ducks and pheasant they want
to hunt and kill each year. They found that after they killed the
wolves and coyotes, they had more foxes than they wanted. The
ring-necked pheasant is South Dakota's state bird. No matter that
it was imported from Asia specifically to be "harvested" for sport,
it's South Dakota's state bird and they're proud of it. A group
called Pheasants Unlimited gave some tips on how to hunt foxes.
Place a small amount of larvicide [a grain fumigant] *on a rag and
chuck it down the hole . . . The first pup generally comes out in fifteen
minutes . . . Use a .22 to dispatch him . . . Remove each pup shot from
the hole. Following gassing, set traps for the old fox who will return
later in the evening . . .* Poisoning, shooting, trapping—they make
up a sort of sportsman's triathlon. . . .

Large predators—including grizzlies, cougars, and wolves—   10
are often the most "beautiful," the smartest and wildest animals of
all. The gray wolf is both a supreme predator and an endangered
species, and since the Supreme Court recently affirmed that
ranchers have no constitutional right to kill endangered predators—apparently some God-given rights are not constitutional
ones—this makes the wolf a more or less lucky dog. But not for
long. A small population of gray wolves has recently established
itself in northwestern Montana, primarily in Glacier National
Park, and there is a plan, long a dream of conservatists, to "rein-
troduce" the wolf to Yellowstone. But to please ranchers and
hunters, part of the plan would involve immediately removing the
wolf from the endangered-species list. Beyond the park's bound-

aries, he could be hunted as a "game animal" or exterminated as a "pest." (Hunters kill to hunt, remember, except when they're hunting to kill.) The area of Yellowstone where the wolf would be restored is the same mountain and high-plateau country that is abandoned in winter by most animals, including the aforementioned luckless bison. Part of the plan, too, is compensation to ranchers if any of their far-ranging livestock is killed by a wolf. It's a real industry out there, apparently, killing and controlling and getting compensated for losing something under the Big Sky.

Wolves gotta eat—a fact that disturbs hunters. Jack Atcheson, 11 an outfitter in Butte, said, *Some wolves are fine if there is control. But there never will be control. The wolf-control plan provided by the Fish and Wildlife Service speaks only of protecting domestic livestock. There is no plan to protect wildlife . . . There are no surplus deer or elk in Montana . . . Their numbers are carefully managed. With uncontrolled wolf populations, a lot of people will have to give up hunting just to feed wolves. Will you give up your elk permit for a wolf?*

It won't be long before hunters start demanding compensa- 12 tion for animals they aren't able to shoot. . . .

Hunters' self-serving arguments and lies are becoming more 13 preposterous as nonhunters awake from their long, albeit troubled, sleep. Sport hunting is immoral; it should be made illegal. Hunters are persecutors of nature who should be prosecuted. They wield a disruptive power out of all proportion to their numbers, and pandering to their interests—the special interests of a group that just wants to kill things—is mad. It's preposterous that every year less than 7 percent of the population turns the skies into shooting galleries and the woods and fields into abattoirs. It's time to stop actively supporting and passively allowing hunting, and time to stigmatize it. It's time to stop being conned and cowed by hunters, time to stop pampering and coddling them, time to get them off the government's duck-and-deer dole, time to stop thinking of wild animals as "resources" and "game," and start thinking of them as sentient beings that deserve our wonder and respect, time to stop allowing hunting to be creditable by calling it "sport" and "recreation." Hunters make wildlife *dead, dead, dead.*

It's time to wake up to this indisputable fact. As for the hunters, it's long past check-out time.

Meaning and Purpose

1. Is Williams's essay designed to change or reinforce a reader's opinion, to move someone to action, or both? Who is the intended audience? Support your answer with evidence from the essay.
2. According to the essay, what reasons do hunters use to explain why they hunt?
3. What are the real reasons hunters hunt according to Williams?
4. What information about hunting that you were previously unaware of has this essay given you? List specific items.
5. Do you find this essay convincing? Why or why not?
6. Underlying Williams's essay, though not directly stated, is an assumption about life and nature. What is that assumption?

Strategy

1. Williams frequently quotes the apparent words of hunters. What effect does she achieve by doing this? Point to at least one such quotation and explain why you think she included it.
2. On page 544 we say, "Throughout an argumentative essay a writer must carefully balance reason and emotion." Has Williams, in your opinion, achieved that balance? Support your answer by references to specific portions of the essay.
3. Where does Williams directly state her assertion (thesis)? Why do you think she delays a direct statement for so long?
4. Williams devotes a considerable portion of her essay to the words and arguments of hunters. Why do you suppose she gives them so much space when she wants her readers to reject those ideas?

Style

1. How would you describe the tone of the essay? Point out specific examples that contribute significantly to that tone.
2. Point out examples of irony, sarcasm, and the use of emotional words and phrases.
3. What is the effect of the series of words for death in sentence 5 of the first paragraph and the three-word series in the third-to-last sentence of the essay? How do they work together?
4. If necessary look up these words in a dictionary: *fatuous* (paragraph 1); *specious* (4); *atavistic* (5); *vermin, varmints* (7); *abattoir, sentient* (13).

Writing Tasks

1. Write an argumentative essay defending hunting. Refer to Williams's arguments as appropriate and/or quote her directly and answer her charges.
2. Write an essay calling for the abolishment of something, for example, the sale of handguns, presidential primaries, a particular kind of tax, or athletic scholarships. Balance emotion and logic in your arguments.

❦ Vicki Hearne ❦

A Yale University professor and an active professional dog trainer, Vicki Hearne is the author of three volumes of poetry, Nervous Horses, In the Absence of Horses, *and* The Parts of Light: Poems, *and two books of essays,* Adam's Task: Calling Animals by Name *and* Bandit: Dossier of a Dangerous Dog. *Her collection of prose,* Animal Happiness, *was published in 1994.*

What's Wrong with Animal Rights

Originally appearing in Harper's *magazine (1991), "What's Wrong with Animal Rights" was selected by Susan Sontag for* The Best American Essays 1992. *Vicki Hearne wrote this essay to explore the meanings and other qualities of terms such as "rights," "happiness," "philosophy," "ownership," and other related signifiers as they are used, often thoughtlessly and mostly by those in the "animal rights movement" who have adopted, if not taken over, the moral high ground labeled "animal rights."*

While reading this essay, see if you can relate to Professor Hearne's comments about the worth of animals. Especially if you have a pet, try to determine whether you agree strongly with the author's comments about how we should treat animals. As soon as you can after reading the essay, contemplate the author's attitudes toward animals in terms of your own attitudes toward animals. See, if only for the moment, whether the essay has caused you to reconsider any of your previous thinking about animals and their place in the world.

Not all happy animals are alike. A Doberman going over a hurdle after a small wooden dumbbell is sleek, all arcs of harmonious power. A basset hound cheerfully performing the same exercise exhibits harmonies of a more lugubrious nature. There are chimpanzees who love precision the way musicians or fanatical housekeepers or accomplished hypochondriacs do; others for whom happiness is a matter of invention and variation—chimp

1

vaudevillians. There is a rhinoceros whose happiness, as near as I can make out, is in needing to be trained every morning, all over again, or else he "forgets" his circus routine, and in this you find a clue to the slow, deep, quiet chuckle of his happiness and to the glory of the beast. Happiness for Secretariat is in his ebullient bound, that joyful length of stride. For the draft horse or the weight-pull dog, happiness is of a different shape, more awesome and less obviously intelligent. When the pulling horse is at its most intense, the animal goes into himself, allocating all of the educated power that organizes his desire to dwell in fierce and delicate intimacy with that power, leans into the harness, and MAKES THAT SUCKER MOVE.

If we are speaking of human beings and use the phrase "animal happiness," we tend to mean something like "creature comforts." The emblems of this are the golden retriever rolling in the grass, the horse with his nose deep in the oats, the kitty by the fire. Creature comforts are important to animals—"Grub first, then ethics" is a motto that would describe many a wise Labrador retriever, and I have a pit bull named Annie whose continual quest for the perfect pillow inspires her to awesome feats. But there is something more to animals, a capacity for satisfactions that come from work in the fullest sense—what is known in philosophy and in this country's Declaration of Independence as "happiness." This is a sense of personal achievement, like the satisfaction felt by a good wood-carver or a dancer or a poet or an accomplished dressage horse. It is a happiness that, like the artist's, must come from something within the animal, something trainers call "talent." Hence, it cannot be imposed on the animal. But it is also something that does not come ex nihilo. If it had not been a fairly ordinary thing, in one part of the world, to teach young children to play the pianoforte, it is doubtful that Mozart's music would exist.

Happiness is often misunderstood as a synonym for pleasure or as an antonym for suffering. But Aristotle associated happiness with ethics—codes of behavior that urge us toward the sensation of getting it right, a kind of work that yields the "click" of satisfaction upon solving a problem or surmounting an obstacle. In his *Ethics,* Aristotle wrote, "If happiness is activity in accordance with excellence, it is reasonable that it should be in accordance with the highest excellence." Thomas Jefferson identified the capacity for happiness as one of the three fundamental rights on which all others are based: "life, liberty, and the pursuit of happiness."

I bring up this idea of happiness as a form of work because I   4
am an animal trainer, and work is the foundation of the happiness a trainer and an animal discover together. I bring up these words also because they cannot be found in the lexicon of the animal-rights movement. This absence accounts for the uneasiness toward the movement of most people, who sense that rights advocates have a point but take it too far when they liberate snails or charge that goldfish at the county fair are suffering. But the problem with the animal-rights advocates is not that they take it too far; it's that they've got it all wrong.

Animal rights are built upon a misconceived premise that   5
rights were created to prevent us from unnecessary suffering. You can't find an animal-rights book, video, pamphlet, or rock concert in which someone doesn't mention the Great Sentence, written by Jeremy Bentham in 1789. Arguing in favor of such rights, Bentham wrote: "The question is not, Can they *reason*? nor, can they *talk*? but, can they suffer?"

The logic of the animal-rights movement places suffering at   6
the iconographic center of a skewed value system. The thinking of its proponents—given eerie expression in a virtually sadoporno-graphic sculpture of a tortured monkey that won a prize for its compassionate vision—has collapsed into a perverse conundrum. Today the loudest voices calling for—demanding—the destruction of animals are the humane organizations. This is an inevitable consequence of the apotheosis of the drive to relieve suffering: death is the ultimate release. To compensate for their contradictions, the humane movement has demonized, in this century and the last, those who made animal happiness their business: veterinarians, trainers, and the like. We think of Louis Pasteur as the man whose work saved you and me and your dog and cat from rabies, but antivivisectionists of the time claimed that rabies increased in areas where there were Pasteur Institutes.

An anti-rabies public relations campaign mounted in England   7
in the 1880s by the Royal Society for the Prevention of Cruelty to

Animals and other organizations led to orders being issued to club any dog found not wearing a muzzle. England still has her cruel and unnecessary law that requires an animal to spend six months in quarantine before being allowed loose in the country. Most of the recent propaganda about pit bulls—the crazy claim that they "take hold with their front teeth while they chew away with their rear teeth" (which would imply, incorrectly, that they have double jaws)—can be traced to literature published by the Humane Society of the United States during the fall of 1987 and earlier. If your neighbors want your dog or horse impounded and destroyed because he is a nuisance—say the dog barks, or the horse attracts flies—it will be the local Humane Society to whom your neighbors turn for action.

In a way, everyone has the opportunity to know that the history of the humane movement is largely a history of miseries, arrests, prosecutions, and death. The Humane Society is the pound, the place with the decompression chamber or the lethal injections. You occasionally find worried letters about this in Ann Landers's column. 8

Animal-rights publications are illustrated largely with photographs of two kinds of animals—"Helpless Fluff" and "Agonized Fluff," the two conditions in which some people seem to prefer their animals, because any other version of an animal is too complicated for propaganda. In the introduction to his book *Animal Liberation,* Peter Singer says somewhat smugly that he and his wife have no animals and, in fact, don't much care for them. This is offered as evidence of his objectivity and ethical probity. But it strikes me as an odd, perhaps obscene underpinning for an ethical project that encourages university and high school students to cherish their ignorance of, say, great bird dogs as proof of their devotion to animals. 9

I would like to leave these philosophers behind, for they are inept connoisseurs of suffering who might revere my Airedale for his capacity to scream when subjected to a blowtorch but not for his wit and courage, not for his natural good manners that are a gentle rebuke to ours. I want to celebrate the moment not long 10 ago when, at his first dog show, my Airedale, Drummer, learned that there can be a public place where his work is respected. I want to celebrate his meticulousness, his happiness upon realizing at the dog show that no one would swoop down upon him and swamp him with the goo-goo excesses known as the "teddy-bear complex" but that people actually got out of his way, gave him room to work. I want to say, "There can be a six-and-a-half-month-old puppy who can care about accuracy, who can be fastidious, and whose fastidiousness will be a foundation for courage later." I want to say, "Leave my puppy alone!"

I want to leave the philosophers behind, but I cannot, in part because the philosophical problems that plague academicians of the animal-rights movement are illuminating. They wonder, do animals have rights or do they have interests? Or, if these rightists lead particularly unexamined lives, they dismiss that question as obvious (yes, of course animals have rights, prima facie) and proceed to enumerate them, James Madison style. This leads to the issuance of bills of rights—the right to an environment, the right not to be used in medical experiments—and other forms of trivialization.   11

The calculus of suffering can be turned against the philosophers of festering flesh, even in the case of food animals, or exotic animals who perform in movies and circuses. It is true that it hurts to be slaughtered by man, but it doesn't hurt nearly as much as some of the cunningly cruel arrangements meted out by "Mother Nature." In Africa, 75 percent of the lions cubbed do not survive to the age of two. For those who make it to two, the average age at death is ten years. Asali, the movie and TV lioness, was still working at age twenty-one. There are fates worse than death, but twenty-one years of a close working relationship with Hubert Wells, Asali's trainer, is not one of them. Dorset sheep and polled Herefords would not exist at all were they not in a symbiotic relationship with human beings.   12

A human being living in the "wild"—somewhere, say, without the benefits of medicine and advanced social organization—would probably have a life expectancy of from thirty to thirty-five years. A human being living in "captivity"—in, say, a middle-class   13 neighborhood of what the Centers for Disease Control call a Metropolitan Statistical Area—has a life expectancy of seventy or more years. For orangutans in the wild in Borneo and Malaysia, the life expectancy is thirty-five years; in captivity, fifty years. The wild is not a suffering-free zone or all that frolicsome a location.

The questions asked by animal-rights activists are flawed, be- 14 cause they are built on the concept that the origin of rights is in the avoidance of suffering rather than in the pursuit of happiness. The question that needs to be asked—and that will put us in closer proximity to the truth—is not, do they have rights? or, what are those rights? but rather, what is a right?

Rights originate in committed relationships and can be found, 15 both intact and violated, wherever one finds such relationships— in social compacts, within families, between animals, and between people and nonhuman animals. This is as true when the non-human animals in question are lions or parakeets as when they are dogs. It is my Airedale whose excellencies have my attention at the moment, so it is with reference to him that I will consider the question, what is a right?

When I imagine situations in which it naturally arises that A 16 defends or honors or respects B's rights, I imagine situations in which the relationship between A and B can be indicated with a possessive pronoun. I might say, "Leave her alone, she's my daughter" or "That's what she wants, and she is my daughter. I think I am bound to honor her wants." Similarly, "Leave her alone, she's my mother." I am more tender of the happiness of my mother, my father, my child, than I am of other people's family members; more tender of my friends' happinesses than your friends' happinesses, unless you and I have a mutual friend.

Possession of a being by another has come into more and 17 more disrepute, so that the common understanding of one person possessing another is slavery. But the important detail about the kind of possessive pronoun that I have in mind is reciprocity: if I have a friend, she has a friend. If I have a daughter, she has a mother. The possessive does not bind one of us while freeing the other; it cannot do that. Moreover, should the mother reject the daughter, the word that applies is "disown." The form of disowning that most often appears in the news is domestic violence. Parents abuse children; husbands batter wives.

Some cases of reciprocal possessives have built-in limitations, such as "my patient/my doctor" or "my student/my teacher" or "my agent/my client." Other possessive relations are extremely limited but still remarkably binding: "my neighbor" and "my country" and "my president."   18

The responsibilities and the ties signaled by reciprocal posses-   19
sion typically are hard to dissolve. It can be as difficult to give up an enemy as to give up a friend, and often the one becomes the other, as though the logic of the possessive pronoun outlasts the forms it chanced to take at a given moment, as though we were stuck with one another. In these bindings, nearly inextricable, are found the origin of our rights. They imply a possessiveness but also recognize an acknowledgment by each side of the other's existence.

The idea of democracy is dependent on the citizens' having   20
knowledge of the government; that is, realizing that the govern-
ment exists and knowing how to claim rights against it. I know this much because I get mail from the government and see its "representatives" running about in uniforms. Whether I actually have any rights in relationship to the government is less clear, but the idea that I do is symbolized by the right to vote. I obey the government, and, in theory, it obeys me, by counting my ballot, reading the *Miranda* warning to me, agreeing to be bound by the Constitution. My friend obeys me as I obey her; the government "obeys" me to some extent, and, to a different extent, I obey it.

What kind of thing can my Airedale, Drummer, have knowl-   21
edge of? He can know that I exist and through that knowledge can claim his happinesses, with varying degrees of success, both with me and against me. Drummer can also know about larger human or dog communities than the one that consists only of him and me. There is my household—the other dogs, the cats, my husband. I have had enough dogs on campuses to know that he can learn that Yale exists as a neighborhood or village. My older dog, Annie, not only knows that Yale exists but can tell Yalies from townies, as I learned while teaching there during labor troubles.

Dogs can have elaborate conceptions of human social struc-   22
tures, and even of something like their rights and responsibilities
within them, but these conceptions are never elaborate enough to
construct a rights relationship between a dog and the state, or a
dog and the Humane Society. Both of these are concepts that depend on writing and memoranda, officers in uniform, plaques and
seals of authority. All of these are literary constructs, and all of
them are beyond a dog's ken, which is why the mail carrier who
doesn't also happen to be a dog's friend is forever an intruder—
this is why dogs bark at mailmen.

It is clear enough that natural rights relations can arise be-   23
tween people and animals. Drummer, for example, can insist,
"Hey, let's go outside and do something!" if I have been at my
computer several days on end. He can both refuse to accept various of my suggestions and tell me when he fears for his life—such
as the time when the huge, white flapping flag appeared out of
nowhere, as it seemed to him, on the town green one evening
when we were working. I can (and do) say to him either, "Oh, you
don't have to worry about that" or, "Uh oh, you're right, Drum,
that guy looks dangerous." Just as the government and I—two different species of organism—have developed improvised ways of
communicating, such as the vote, so Drummer and I have worked
out a number of ways to make our expressions known. Largely
through obedience, I have taught him a fair amount about how to
get responses from me. Obedience is reciprocal; you cannot get
responses from a dog to whom you do not respond accurately. I
have enfranchised him in a relationship to me by educating him,
creating the conditions by which he can achieve a certain happiness specific to a dog, maybe even specific to an Airedale, inas-
much as this same relationship has allowed me to plumb the
happiness of being a trainer and writing this article.

Instructions in this happiness are given terms that are alien to   24
a culture in which liver treats, fluffy windup toys, and miniature
sweaters are confused with respect and work. Jack Knox, a sheep-
dog trainer originally from Scotland, will shake his crook at a
novice handler who makes a promiscuous move to praise a dog,
and will call out in his Scottish accent, "Eh! Eh! Get back, get

BACK! Ye'll no be abusin' the dogs like that in my clinic." America
is a nation of abused animals, Knox says, because we are always
swooping at them with praise, "no gi'ing them their freedom." I
am reminded of Rainer Maria Rilke's account in which the
Prodigal Son leaves—has to leave—because everyone loves him,
even the dogs love him, and he has no path to the delicate and
fierce truth of himself. Unconditional praise and love, in Rilke's
story, disenfranchise us, distract us from what truly excites our
interest.

In the minds of some trainers and handlers, praise is dishon-   25
esty. Paradoxically, it is a kind of contempt for animals that mas-
querades as a reverence for helplessness and suffering. The idea of
freedom means that you do not, at least not while Jack Knox is
nearby, helpfully guide your dog through the motions of, say,
herding over and over—what one trainer calls "explainy-wainy."
This is rote learning. It works tolerably well on some handlers, because people have vast unconscious minds and can store complex
preprogrammed behaviors. Dogs, on the other hand, have almost
no unconscious minds, so they can learn only by thinking. Many
children are like this until educated out of it.

If I tell my Airedale to sit and stay on the town green, and   26
someone comes up and burbles, "What a pretty thing you are," he
may break his stay to go for a caress. I pull him back and correct
him for breaking. Now he holds his stay because I have blocked
his way to movement but not because I have punished him. (A
correction blocks one path as it opens another for desire to work;
punishment blocks desire and opens nothing.) He holds his stay
now, and—because the stay opens this possibility of work, new to
a heedless young dog—he watches. If the person goes on talking,
and isn't going to gush with praise, I may heel Drummer out of his
stay and give him an "Okay" to make friends. Sometimes something about the person makes Drummer feel that reserve is in order. He responds to an insincere approach by sitting still, going
down into himself, and thinking, "This person has no business
pawing me. I'll sit very still, and he will go away." If the person
doesn't take the hint from Drummer, I'll give the pup a little
backup by saying, "Please don't pet him, he's working," even
though he was not under any command.

The pup reads this, and there is a flicker of a working trust   27
now stirring in the dog. Is the pup grateful? When the stranger
leaves, does he lick my hand, full of submissive blandishments?
This one doesn't. This one says nothing at all, and I say nothing
much to him. This is a working trust we are developing, not a mutual congratulation society. My backup is praise enough for him;
the use he makes of my support is praise enough for me.

Listening to a dog is often praise enough. Suppose it is just af-   28
ter dark and we are outside. Suddenly there is a shout from the
house. The pup and I both look toward the shout and then toward
each other: "What do you think?" I don't so much as cock my
head, because Drummer is growing up, and I want to know what
he thinks. He takes a few steps toward the house, and I follow. He
listens again and comprehends that it's just Holly, who at fourteen
is much given to alarming cries and shouts. He shrugs at me and
goes about his business. I say nothing. To praise him for this performance would make about as much sense as praising a human
being for the same thing. Thus:

A. What's that?
B. I don't know. [Listens] Oh, it's just Holly.
A. What a gooooooood human being!
B. Huh?

This is one small moment in a series of like moments that will   29
culminate in an Airedale who on a Friday will have the discrimination and confidence required to take down a man who is attacking me with a knife and on Saturday clown and play with the
children at the annual Orange Empire Dog Club Christmas party.

People who claim to speak for animal rights are increasingly   30
devoted to the idea that the very keeping of a dog or a horse or a
gerbil or a lion is in and of itself an offense. The more loudly they
speak, the less likely they are to be in a rights relation to any given
animal, because they are spending so much time in airplanes or
transmitting fax announcements of the latest Sylvester Stallone
anti-fur rally. In a 1988 *Harper's* forum, for example, Ingrid
Newkirk, the national director of People for the Ethical Treatment

of Animals, urged that domestic pets be spayed and neutered and ultimately phased out. She prefers, it appears, wolves—and wolves someplace else—to Airedales and, by a logic whose interior structure is both emotionally and intellectually forever closed to Drummer, claims thereby to be speaking for "animal rights."

She is wrong. I am the only one who can own up to my   31
Airedale's inalienable rights. Whether or not I do it perfectly at any given moment is no more refutation of this point than whether I am perfectly my husband's mate at any given moment refutes the fact of marriage. Only people who know Drummer, and whom he can know, are capable of this relationship. PETA and the Humane Society and the ASPCA and the Congress and NOW—as institutions—do have the power to affect my ability to grant rights to Drummer but are otherwise incapable of creating conditions or laws or rights that would increase his happiness. Only Drummer's owner has the power to obey him—to obey who he is and what he is capable of—deeply enough to grant him his rights and open up the possibility of happiness.

Meaning and Purpose

1. How does the author distinguish between people and animals in this essay?
2. Why does the author refer to the Declaration of Independence in paragraph 2?
3. What is the overall importance to this essay of Jeremy Bentham's "Great Sentence," in paragraph 5?
4. Why does the author mention her husband in this essay?

Strategy

1. What point does the author make by using the information contained in paragraphs 12 and 13?

2. Why does the author want to leave philosophers behind, as she maintains in paragraph 10? Why can't she?
3. In your own words, tell how "Obedience is reciprocal," as the author maintains in paragraph 23. Do you agree with this concept? Why or why not?
4. Why does the author use *being* in paragraph 17? Why doesn't she use a word such as *man, woman,* or *person,* for example?

Style

1. What does the word *calculus* mean, as it is used in paragraph 12?
2. Many people have noticed that in this essay, the author treats dogs in at least one respect the same way that most people treat other people. In what way or ways does the author treat dogs like people?
3. What does the author mean by "Helpless Fluff" and "Agonized Fluff" in paragraph 9?
4. Why does the author describe the government and herself as "two different species of organism," in paragraph 23?

Writing Tasks

1. Write an essay in which you agree with Hearne's position on animal rights. Strengthen your essay by using your personal examples and other outside examples of how animals are far better off than certain groups would have you believe.
2. Argue against Hearne's position on animal rights. Strengthen your essay by using your personal examples and other outside examples of how animals suffer at the hands of people and therefore should be freed or allowed to have rights.

❦ Stephanie Coontz ❦

Born in Seattle, Stephanie Coontz currently teaches history and family studies at Evergreen State College in Olympia, Washington. She has also taught at Kobe University in Japan and the University of Hawaii at Hilo. Her research and publications have placed her at the center of the "family values" debate in American politics. Her articles and reviews have appeared in The New York Times, The Wall Street Journal, The Washington Post, Newsweek, Harper's, Vogue, Mirabella, *and other national publications and academic journals. Her seven books include* The Way We Never Were: American Families and the Nostalgia Trap *and* The Way We Really Are: Coming to Terms with American Changing Families.

A Nation of Welfare Families

This essay, adapted from The Way We Never Were, *was published in the October 1992 issue of* Harper's *magazine. In it, Stephanie Coontz pokes some holes in many of the inflated myths that are widely believed about government welfare for American families.*

Notice, as you read, Coontz's careful reasoning and the examples she cites to back up her contentions.

The current political debate over family values, personal responsibility, and welfare takes for granted the entrenched American belief that dependence on government assistance is a recent and destructive phenomenon. Conservatives tend to blame this dependence on personal irresponsibility aggravated by a swollen welfare apparatus that saps individual initiative. Liberals are more likely to blame it on personal misfortune magnified by the harsh lot that falls to losers in our competitive market economy. But both sides believe that "winners" in America make it on their own, that dependence reflects some kind of individual or family failure, and that the ideal family is the self-reliant unit of traditional lore—a family that takes care of its own, carves out a

1

future for its children, and never asks for handouts. Politicians at both ends of the ideological spectrum have wrapped themselves in the mantle of these "family values," arguing over why the poor have not been able to make do without assistance, or whether aid has exacerbated their situation, but never questioning the assumption that American families traditionally achieve success by establishing their independence from the government.

The myth of family self-reliance is so compelling that our actual national and personal histories often buckle under its emotional weight. "We always stood on our own two feet," my grandfather used to say about his pioneer heritage, whenever he walked me to the top of the hill to survey the property in Washington State that his family had bought for next to nothing after it had been logged off in the early 1900s. Perhaps he didn't know that the land came so cheap because much of it was part of a federal subsidy originally allotted to the railroad companies, which had received 183 million acres of the public domain in the nineteenth century. These federal give-aways were the original source of most major western logging companies' land, and when some of these logging companies moved on to virgin stands of timber, federal lands trickled down to a few early settlers who were able to purchase them inexpensively.

Like my grandparents, few families in American history— whatever their "values"—have been able to rely solely on their own resources. Instead, they have depended on the legislative, judicial and social-support structures set up by governing authorities, whether those authorities were the clan elders of Native American societies, the church courts and city officials of colonial America, or the judicial and legislative bodies established by the Constitution.

At America's inception, this was considered not a dirty little secret but the norm, one that confirmed our social and personal interdependence. The idea that the family should have the sole or even primary responsibility for educating and socializing its members, finding them suitable work, or keeping them from poverty and crime was not only ludicrous to colonial and revolutionary thinkers but dangerously parochial.

Historically, one way that government has played a role in the   5
well-being of its citizens is by regulating the way that employers
and civic bodies interact with families. In the early twentieth century, for example, as a response to rapid changes ushered in by a
mass-production economy, the government promoted a "family
wage system." This system was designed to strengthen the ability
of the male breadwinner to support a family without having his
wife or children work. This family wage system was not a natural
outgrowth of the market. It was a *political* response to conditions
that the market had produced: child labor, rampant employment
insecurity, recurring economic downturns, an earnings structure
in which 45 percent of industrial workers fell below the poverty
level and another 40 percent hovered barely above it, and a system in which thousands of children had been placed in orphan-
ages or other institutions simply because their parents could not
afford their keep. The state policies involved in the establishment
of the family wage system included abolition of child labor, government pressure on industrialists to negotiate with unions, federal arbitration, expansion of compulsory schooling—and
legislation discriminating against women workers.

But even such extensive regulation of economic and social in-   6
stitutions has never been enough: Government has always supported families with direct material aid as well. The two best
examples of the government's history of material aid can be found
in what many people consider the ideal models of self-reliant families: the western pioneer family and the 1950s suburban family.
In both cases, the ability of these families to establish and sustain
themselves required massive underwriting by the government.

Pioneer families, such as my grandparents, could never have   7
moved west without government-funded military mobilizations
against the original Indian and Mexican inhabitants or state-spon-
sored economic investment in transportation systems. In addition, the Homestead Act of 1862 allowed settlers to buy 160 acres
for $10—far below the government's cost of acquiring the land—
if the homesteader lived on and improved the land for five years.
In the twentieth century, a new form of public assistance became
crucial to western families: construction of dams and other feder-

ally subsidized irrigation projects. During the 1930s, for example, government electrification projects brought pumps, refrigeration, and household technology to millions of families.

The suburban family of the 1950s is another oft-cited example   8
of familial self-reliance. According to legend, after World War II a new, family-oriented generation settled down, saved their pennies, worked hard, and found well-paying jobs that allowed them to purchase homes in the suburbs. In fact, however, the 1950s suburban family was far more dependent on government assistance than any so-called underclass family of today. Federal GI benefit payments, available to 40 percent of the male population between the ages of twenty and twenty-four, permitted a whole generation of men to expand their education and improve their job prospects without foregoing marriage and children. The National Defense Education Act retooled science education in America, subsidizing both American industry and the education of individual scientists. Government-funded research developed the aluminum clapboards, prefabricated walls and ceilings, and plywood paneling that comprised the technological basis of the postwar housing revolution. Government spending was also largely responsible for the new highways, sewer systems, utility services, and traffic-control programs that opened up suburbia.

In addition, suburban home ownership depended on an un-   9
precedented expansion of federal regulation and financing. Before the war, banks often required a 50 percent down payment on homes and normally issued mortgages for five to ten years. In the postwar period, however, the Federal Housing Authority, supplemented by the GI Bill, put the federal government in the business of insuring and regulating private loans for single-home construction. FHA policy required down payments of only 5 to 10 percent of the purchase price and guaranteed mortgages of up to thirty years at interest rates of just 2 to 3 percent. The Veterans Administration required a mere dollar down from veterans. Almost half the housing in suburbia in the 1950s depended on such federal programs.

The drawback of these aid programs was that although they   10
worked well for recipients, nonrecipients—disproportionately

poor and urban—were left far behind. While the general public financed the roads that suburbanites used to commute, the street-
cars and trolleys that served urban and poor families received
almost no tax revenues, and our previously thriving rail system
was allowed to decay. In addition, federal loan policies, which
were a boon to upwardly mobile white families, tended to system-
atize the pervasive but informal racism that had previously characterized the housing market. FHA redlining practices, for
example, took entire urban areas and declared them ineligible for
loans, while the government's two new mortgage institutions, the
Federal National Mortgage Association and the Government
National Mortgage Association (Fannie Mae and Ginny Mae),
made it possible for urban banks to transfer savings out of the
cities and into new suburban developments in the South and
West.

Despite the devastating effects on families and regions that did   11
not receive such assistance, government aid to suburban residents
during the 1950s and 1960s produced in its beneficiaries none of
the demoralization usually presumed to afflict recipients of government handouts. Instead, federal subsidies to suburbia encouraged family formation, residential stability, upward occupational
mobility, and rising educational aspirations among youth who
could look forward to receiving such aid. Seen in this light, the
idea that government subsidies intrinsically induce dependence,
undermine self-esteem, or break down family ties is exposed as no
more than a myth.

I am not suggesting that the way to solve the problems of   12
poverty and urban decay in America is to quadruple our spending
on welfare. Certainly there are major reforms needed in our current aid policies to the poor. But the debate over such reform
should put welfare in the context of *all* federal assistance programs. As long as we pretend that only poor or single-parent families need outside assistance, while normal families "stand on their
two feet," we will shortchange poor families, overcompensate rich
ones, and fail to come up with effective policies for helping out
families in the middle. Current government housing policies are a
case in point. The richest 20 percent of American households re-

ceives three times as much federal housing aid—mostly in tax subsidies—as the poorest 20 percent receives in expenditures for low-income housing.

Historically, the debate over government policies toward families has never been over *whether* to intervene but *how:* to rescue or to warehouse, to prevent or to punish, to moralize about values or mobilize resources for education and job creation. Today's debate, lacking such historical perspective, caricatures the real issues. Our attempt to sustain the myth of family self-reliance in the face of all the historical evidence to the contrary has led policymakers into theoretical contortions and practical miscalculations that are reminiscent of efforts by medieval philosophers to maintain that the earth and not the sun was the center of the planetary system. In the sixteenth century, leading European thinkers insisted that the planets and the sun all revolved around the earth—much as American politicians today insist that our society revolves around family self-reliance. When evidence to the contrary mounted, defenders of the Ptolemaic universe postulated all sorts of elaborate planetary orbits in order to reconcile observed reality with their cherished theory. Similarly, rather than admit that all families need some kind of public support, we have constructed ideological orbits that explain away each instance of middle-class dependence as an "exception," an "abnormality," or even an illusion. We have distributed public aid to families through convoluted bureaucracies that have become impossible to track; in some cases the system has become so cumbersome that it threatens to collapse around our ears. It is time to break through the old paradigm of self-reliance and substitute a new one that recognizes that assisting families is, simply, what government does.

Meaning and Purpose

1. What is Coontz's thesis? Where does she state it?
2. What is it that both liberals and conservatives agree on concerning American families and government welfare?

3. What was the attitude of early Americans to the idea families must rely on government assistance to some degree?
4. The western pioneer family and the 1950s suburban family have been held up as ideal models of self-reliant families. How did these models benefit from government assistance?
5. How and why did government assistance to middle-class suburbanites harm the poor?
6. What ideas have been used to argue that government subsidies are harmful to their recipients? How does Coontz counter those ideas?

Strategy

1. In the first two paragraphs, what words does Coontz use to cast doubt on the validity of the idea of family self-reliance?
2. What is the point of Coontz's extended comparison in paragraph 13?
3. Coontz uses extensive examples to back up her points. Is she convincing? Why or why not?

Style

1. Coontz places some of her words in quotation marks: "winners" and "family values" in paragraph 1 and "exception" and "abnormality" in paragraph 13, for example. Why does she do this?
2. What are some of the meanings of the word *myth*? In what sense does Coontz use the word in paragraphs 2, 11, and 13?
3. If necessary, look up the following words in a dictionary: *entrenched, aggravated, apparatus, saps, lore, spectrum, mantle, exacerbated* (paragraph 1); *heritage, subsidy, allotted, domain* (2); *inception, ludicrous, parochial* (4); *rampant, abolition, arbitration, compulsory* (5); *legend, clapboards, prefabricated, comprised* (8); *unprecedented* (9); *recipients, boon, pervasive, redlining* (10); *beneficiaries, afflict, intrinsically, induce* (11); *intervene, perspective, car-*

icatures, contortions, reminiscent, Ptolemaic universe, postulated, reconcile, convoluted, cumbersome, paradigm (13).

Writing Tasks

1. Stephanie Coontz concludes her essay by saying that "assisting families is, simply, what government does." Write an argumentative essay in which you either agree or disagree with her point of view. Make sure to account for her major points, whatever point of view you take.

2. Write an argumentative essay about social welfare programs in which you compare, contrast, and evaluate the opposing points of view of Stephanie Coontz in *A Nation of Welfare Families* and David Kelley in *The End of Welfare as We Know It?* Make sure to have a clearly stated thesis to hold your argument together.

❦ David Kelley ❦

David Kelley, born in 1941, was awarded a Ph.D. in philosophy from Princeton University in 1975. Since that time, he has taught courses in philosophy and cognitive sciences at Vassar College and Brandeis University. He has written widely on social issues and public policy. His articles have appeared in Barron's, Harper's, The Sciences, Harvard Business Review, *and elsewhere. His books include* The Evidence of the Senses, *a treatise on perception;* The Art of Reasoning, *a college textbook on logic;* Truth and Toleration, *an essay on the principles of intellectual exchange; and* Unrugged Individualism: The Selfish Basis of Benevolence. *Kelley founded and is currently executive director of the Institute for Objectivist Studies, a center for the study of Objectivism, a philosophy created by Ayn Rand and associated with the political philosophy of libertarianism that espouses the principles of individual liberty and limited government.*

The End of Welfare as We Know It?

This essay is taken from Kelley's latest book, A Life of One's Own: Individual Rights and the Welfare State *(1998), in which he argues that government welfare programs undermine individual freedoms and values, as well as the economic stability of society.*

In his argument, Kelley compares private and public values. Notice the differences that Kelley points out between the two and his unspoken assumption that the values of the two should be the same.

In our personal lives, most of us realize that the world doesn't 1 owe us a living. Whatever our individual circumstances, we know that we are responsible for doing what it takes to get the things we want in life. We're responsible for earning a living that provides for both current and future needs. We're responsible, not just for doing our jobs day by day, but for finding a job in the first place and for acquiring the knowledge and skills it takes to find a job. We're responsible, not just for paying current expenses like rent and groceries, but for saving some portion of our income for long-term needs like retirement and for unexpected ones like an incapacitating illness. We're responsible, not just for getting the kids on the school bus in the morning, but for making sure they are learning what they will need to know in life. And we're responsible for choosing to bear children in the first place, knowing the long-term commitment it involves and the investment of time and money we might have devoted to other pursuits.

Yet in our public lives we have accepted an obligation to provide food, shelter, jobs, education, pensions, medical care, child support, and other goods to every member of society. The premise of the welfare state—the sprawling network of programs for transferring wealth from taxpayers to recipients—is that the world *does* owe us a living. If someone is unable or unwilling to support himself, the government will provide food stamps, housing subsidies, and possibly cash assistance as well. If someone is laid off, the government will provide unemployment compensation. If an unmarried teenager has a baby she can't support, she is eligible for cash benefits, Medicaid, and other poverty programs. If someone fails to save for retirement, the Social Security system provides a pension and Medicare covers the doctor's bills. In those and other ways, the welfare state confers entitlements to goods independent of the process of earning them. It elevates needs and downplays responsibility. The result is a public morality at odds with our personal standards.

In our personal lives we know that people sometimes suffer through no fault of their own. We recognize a place in life for generosity and mutual aid. If a stranger is hurt in the street, we call the ambulance and see to his needs. If a neighbor's house burns down, we do what we can to help. But we choose to do so voluntarily, weighing such needs against the other demands on our resources, and we expect some measure of gratitude in recognition of our help. If a stranger appeared at our door demanding a place to live, or help with his medical bills, or a contribution to his retirement fund or to his kid's education—if he demanded it as a matter of right, regardless of whether we were willing and able to help, and without any obligation to thank us for helping—we would take offense. We would recognize it as a monumental act of presumption.

Yet in our public life we accept such demands as a matter of   4
course. The beneficiaries of social welfare programs, and those who speak on their behalf, put forward their needs as claims on the public purse, and thus on the productive members of society who pay taxes. Those claims are not always successful. They may be opposed for economic reasons; they may fail to win political support. But they are rarely challenged as illegitimate. The operating assumption in debates about social welfare programs is that the needs of recipients take precedence over the rights of producers: those with the ability to produce are obliged to serve, while those with needs are entitled to make demands. The result, once again, is a public morality at odds with our private standards.

Federal budget deficits, and comparable fiscal problems at the   5
state level, have come to seem intractable because food stamps, Social Security, Medicaid and Medicare, public housing, unemployment compensation, and other benefits have been provided as entitlements. Casting those benefits as rights has bred intransigence among recipients and thus made the prospect of benefit cuts all the more difficult for legislators to contemplate publicly. When the Massachusetts legislature voted in early 1995 to cut welfare benefits and require that recipients work, for example, welfare recipients marched through the statehouse protesting the new restrictions.

The spirit of entitlement is not peculiar to poverty programs.   6
In New York City, students dressed in black held a mock funeral march from Battery Park to City Hall to protest cuts in federal spending on student loans and grants. Speaking of Social Security, Norman Ornstein, a political scientist at the American Enterprise Institute, observed,

> Talk to almost any audience of elderly people, and it be-
> comes clear that the widespread public view is that recipi-
> ents are "entitled" to these programs—and any cutbacks or
> changes are thus illegitimate. . . . A capped entitlement, of
> course, is like a partial pregnancy; the cap or limitation be-

comes increasingly difficult to maintain because one either has a right or one doesn't.

The concept of a right to the goods and services provided by   7
the welfare state is the chief source of disparity between our private and our public morality. A right is something an individual can demand as his due without apology for asking and without gratitude for receiving. When that concept is extended to the provision of social welfare, the necessary result is to empower those who make claims on public provision and silence those who do the providing. Since the New Deal, and especially during the three decades since the creation of the Great Society programs, the legal framework of entitlements has given rise to a public *spirit* of entitlement, a sense that the world does owe us a living.

Across its length and breadth, the welfare state is facing a crisis.   8
In part, it is a social crisis, as the pathologies bred by dependence on welfare become more and more severe. In part, it is a financial crisis, as the costs of entitlements rise faster than the revenues available. At root, however, the crisis is moral—it is a crisis of legitimacy—and the fundamental issue in this crisis is whether people do indeed have a right to public support. Never before in the 60-year history of the welfare state have so many problems broken out across such a broad front. And none of the problems can be addressed coherently without tackling the fundamental issue: Do we have a right to be taken care of by others, or do we not?. . .

Some will say, "So what?" As a vast engine for transferring   9
wealth, the welfare state has created enormous vested interests. Lobbies for the elderly will never agree to let Congress cut back Medicare or Social Security benefits. The poverty bureaucrats will fight to the death any major change in the industry that feeds and clothes them. It is naive idealism to think that the lack of a moral justification represents any sort of danger to the welfare state.

Maybe so. But the cynics have been proven wrong time and   10
again, most recently in the collapse of communism. That system was backed by forces much more powerful than lobbies and bureaucratic inertia. The Soviet state had its secret police. It owned

all the media; indeed it owned the entire economy. Yet it collapsed when the central sanctifying myth—the myth of a worker's paradise to be created by collective ownership and economic planning—had lost all credibility. The welfare state has likewise been sustained by nothing more than myth, and it is likewise vulnerable to collapse.

Meaning and Purpose

1. According to David Kelley, what distinguishes our private lives from our public lives? Comment on the validity of his distinction.
2. In paragraph 2, Kelley claims that the welfare state "elevates needs and downplays responsibility. The result is a public morality at odds with our personal standards." What, precisely, does he mean by that statement? Is the statement necessarily true? Explain.
3. Other than public aid to the needy, what kinds of welfare does Kelley cite? What negative effects does he think this state aid creates? What might happen if these kinds of public assistance were eliminated?
4. Why does Kelley think the welfare state might collapse?

Strategy

1. What is the primary organizational pattern that Kelley uses to advance his argument? What are the different ways in which he uses that pattern?
2. What does Kelley imply when he says that welfare programs transfer "wealth from taxpayers to recipients" (paragraph 2) and that the "beneficiaries of social welfare programs" unfairly burden "the productive members of society who pay taxes" (paragraph 4)? What effect does he strive for with these statements?
3. In what ways does Kelley's argument appeal to emotion? In what ways does it appeal to logic and reason?

Style

1. Point out words and phrases Kelley uses to cast a negative light on the position he opposes.
2. What twofold effect does Kelley create by comparing welfare to Communism in paragraph 10? Is the comparison a valid one? Explain.
3. What are some of the meanings of the word *myth*? What does the word mean as used in paragraph 10?
4. If necessary, look up the following words in a dictionary: *incapacitating* (paragraph 1); *recipients, compensation, entitlements, elevates* (2); *monumental, presumption* (3); *beneficiaries, precedence, obliged* (4); *fiscal, intractable, intransigence* (5); *disparity* (7); *pathologies, legitimacy, coherently* (8); *naive* (9); *inertia, sanctifying, myth, credibility, vulnerable* (10).

Writing Tasks

1. Write an argumentative essay in which you either agree or disagree with David Kelley's basic contention that social welfare programs undermine individual freedoms and values as well as the economic stability of society. In your discussion, make sure to consider welfare to all segments of society: aid to the poor and handicapped (food stamps, unemployment compensation, Medicaid, etc.); aid to the middle class (college grants and loans, social security, Medicare, etc.); aid to the wealthy (tax subsidies, corporate bailouts by government, etc.).
2. Write an argumentative essay about social welfare programs in which you compare, contrast, and evaluate the opposing points of view of David Kelley in *The End of Welfare as We Know It?* and Stephanie Coontz in *A Nation of Welfare Families*. Make sure to have a clearly stated thesis to hold your argument together.

❦ Andrew Klavan ❦

Andrew Klavan, born in 1954, is a two-time Edgar Award–winner who writes under three names. As Keith Peterson and Margaret Tracy he writes detective novels, mysteries, and thrillers. Some of these include the highly acclaimed John Wells mysteries: The Trapdoor, There Fell a Shadow, The Rain, *and* Rough Justice. *As Andrew Klavan, he is a well-known screenwriter and journalist. His most recent novel is* Hunting Down Amanda. *A former resident of New York City, Klavan now lives in Great Britain with his wife and family.*

The Shrieking of the Lambs

This essay, first published in the June–September 1994 issue of the Boston Review, *contends that fictional violence, now under constant attack by would-be censors, must not be defended. Rather, fictional violence must be celebrated.*

Klavan's point of view is, if anything, unconventional. Read his essay critically to determine how convincing the points of his argument are.

I love the sound of people screaming. Women screaming— 1
with their clothes torn—as they run down endless hallways with some bogeyman in hot pursuit. Men, in their priapic cars, screaming as the road ends, as the fender plummets towards fiery oblivion under their wild eyes. Children? I'm a little squeamish about children, but okay, sure. I'll take screaming children too. And I get off on gunshots—machine gun shots goading a corpse into a posthumous jitterbug; and the coital jerk and plunge of a butcher knife; and axes; even claws, if you happen to have them.

Yes, yes, yes, only in stories. Of course; in fictions only: nov- 2
els, TV shows, films. I've loved the scary, gooey stuff since I was a child. I've loved monsters, shootouts, bluddy murther; Women In Jeopardy (as they say in Hollywood); the slasher in the closet; the intruder's shadow that spreads up the bedroom wall like a stain.

And now, having grown to man's estate, I make a very good living writing these things: thriller novels like *Don't Say A Word,* which begins with a nice old lady getting dusted and ends with an assault on a child, and *The Animal Hour* which features a woman's head being severed and stuffed into a commode.

Is it vicious? Disgusting? Sexist? Sick? Tough luck, it's my imagination—sometimes it is—and it's my readers' too—always, for all I know. And when they and I get together, when we dodge down that electric alleyway of the human skull where only murder is delight—well then, my friend, it's showtime.   3

But enough about me, let's talk about death. Cruel death, sexy death, exciting death: death, that is, on the page and on the screen. Because this is not a defense of violence in fiction, it's a celebration of it. And not a moment too soon either.   4

Hard as it is for a sane man to believe, fictional violence is under attack. Again. Floundering in a mean street America where bigots and enablers dither while the malicious play catch with live ammo, where one interest group calls a machine gun a hunting weapon and another calls a kitchen knife a form of feminist expression, where children are stolen from their houses and killed and tourists are executed for the crime of getting lost on their way to Disneyworld, the folks back home have understandably panicked, and the unerring eye of political opportunism has once more found its scapegoat: those good people who make up scary stories to help you pass the time. This year's list of would-be censors trying to shoulder their way to the trough of celebrity is hardly worth enumerating: their 15 minutes might be up by the time I'm done. Film critic Michael Medved says cinematic violence is part of a pop culture "war on traditional values"; Congressman Edward Markey says television violence should be reduced or regulated; some of our less thoughtful feminists tried to quash the novel *American Psycho* because of its descriptions of violence toward women and even some more thoughtful, like Catherine MacKinnon, have fought for censorship in law, claiming that written descriptions of "penises slamming into vaginas" deprive actual human beings of their civil rights.   5

It's nonsense mostly, but it has the appeal of glamour, of flash.   6
The "issue" of fictional violence lifts crime out of the impoverished, muddy-minded, rage-filled milieus in which it usually occurs, and superimposes it on the gaudy images manufactured in
Hollywood and Manhattan. Instead of trying to understand the
sad, banal, ignorant souls who generally pull the trigger in our society, we get to discuss Hannibal Lecter, Ice-T, penises, vaginas. It
makes for good sound bytes, anyway—the all-American diet of 15
second thoughts.

But Britain—where I've come to live because I loathe real guns   7
and political correctness—is far from exempt. Indeed, perhaps
nowhere has there been a more telling or emblematic attack on
fictional violence than is going on here right now. It is a textbook
example of how easily pundits and politicians can channel honest
grief and rage at a true crime into a senseless assault on the innocent tellers of tales.

It began here this time with the killing of a child by two other   8
children. On 12 February, Jamie Bulger, a two-year-old toddler,
was led out of a Merseyside shopping mall by two ten-year-olds—
two little boys. The boys prodded and carried and tugged the increasingly distraught baby past dozens of witnesses who did not
understand what they were seeing. When they reached a deserted
railroad embankment, the two boys tortured, mutilated, and finally killed their captive for no reasons that anyone has been able
to explain.

The explicit testimony at the trial last November verged on   9
the unbearable. Even the more restrained newspapers could not
be read without nausea and tears. And looking at the photographs
of the killers—two sweetly mischievous Just William faces, Lords
of the Flies in their Sunday best—there arose, in me, in everyone
I spoke to, the desperate urge to understand, to grasp, to know:
What? What is it? What rough beast, its hour come round at last?

At first, the pundits did their best to answer but the answers   10
seemed miserably inadequate. Psychiatrists noted the fierce sib-
ling rivalry felt by one of the killers; sociologists noted the broken
homes, the poverty, the family violence; columnists talked about

the breakdown of society; one gay writer blamed everything on the pressures of heterosexual manhood; even the usually brilliant Martin Amis weighed in with a rather sleepy piece on the dissipation of moral energy in the west. And it wasn't just the media flailing about. At dinner parties, we daringly ventured to talk about Evil, and then let our voices trail off to nothing. At home, we tried to be nicer to our children—until the little pests caught on and began to run riot. And in almost any pub, you could hear it explained how the murderers were demon freaks of nature—an opinion that seemed a lot less ridiculous and a lot more comforting than by any rights it should've done.

But the nation's search for an answer, its grief and disgust, its sense of social despair, did not resolve themselves upon a single issue until the trial judge pronounced sentence. "It is not for me to pass judgment on their upbringing," Mr. Justice Morland said of the boys as he sentenced them to be detained at Her Majesty's pleasure. "But I suspect exposure to violent video films may in part be an explanation." 11

No one knew why he said such a thing. There had been speculation in some of the papers that *Child's Play 3*, which had been rented by one of the killers' fathers, had given the son ideas. But there was no testimony at the trial, no evidence presented showing that the boy had seen it or that it had had a contributing effect. Detective Superintendent Albert Kirby, who headed the investigation into the murder, said "the area of videos was one we looked very closely at" but that no link had been established by the police at all. 12

It didn't matter. As far as journalists were concerned, as far as public debate was concerned, "video nasties," as they are called here, became the central issue of the case. Forget the subconscious, the broken home, the poverty, the family cruelty, the breakdown of western society, even the trials of masculinity and the moral energy stuff. For the next few days, the newspapers were splattered with stories about *Child's Play 3* as writers combed the film for tenuous connections between the rampages of the movie's devil doll Chucky and the savage attack perpetrated by the Merseyside rails. In the aftermath, the British opening of the 13 film *The Good Son,* starring Macauley Culkin as an evil child, was canceled. The video release of *Reservoir Dogs* was indefinitely postponed. Twenty-five doctors and academics who had previously dismissed the effects of screen violence made front page news with a mea culpa report saying their liberal ideals had made them naive. Action was called for, and Liberal Democrat MP David Alton answered the call on the run. With the backing of rebel Tories, Alton nearly pushed through a proposal that even the country's chief censor said would prevent the video release of "half the films made in the last quarter century and some of the greatest films ever made." The Alton bill was only tabled when Home Secretary Michael Howard reluctantly agreed to implement some Draconian restrictions of his own. From hereon in, if you rent *My Cousin Vinny* to an 11-year-old, you're looking at jail time, mate.

And why not? Now, thanks to Mr. Justice Morland and an eager press, we finally know what we are seeing when we look upon the rampaging fire of violence in our society: we are seeing the effects of fiction on us. Got it? Our leaders are either mindless ideologues or soulless bureaucrats. Our cultural heritage is under attack by morons who stand on the shoulders of giants and think that they can fly. Our moral verities are crumbling by the hour. Our families are shattering. Our gods are dead. The best lack all conviction while the worst are full of passionate intensity.	14

And it's all Chucky's fault.	15

The instinct to censor is the tragic flaw of utopian minds. "Our first job," said Plato in his classic attack on the democratic system, "is to oversee the work of the story-writers, and to accept any good stories they write, but reject the others." Because the perfectibility of human society is a fiction itself, it comes under threat from other, more believable fictions, especially those fictions which document and employ the cruel, the chaotic, the Dionysian for their thrills. It's a form of homeopathic magic really. (A point once made by the magician Teller of Penn and Teller in an op-ed piece in *The New York Times.*) The chants and rituals of that old witchcraft are gone, but the template of belief remains in	16 the censor's mind: if you erase the image, he tells us, you will magically erase the thing itself.

And this superstitious fallacy plays into some prevailing fallacies of academic and political theory: the idea that language is the way we understand the world, that metaphor generates consciousness and imagery fashions our feelings and choices, that a work, an author, a reader are wholly constructed of the influences they wreak upon each other. Under such theories, literature becomes an action taken with potentially harmful or beneficial effects on the society and politics of the age (rather than, say, a sight to be seen like a sunset or a mountain range). Again, with their isomorphic links between image and reality, such theories can lead to a sort of homeopathic magic in materialist guise. 17

Yet one can understand the appeal of these intricate alchemies. With their emphasis on interpretation, they allow critics to sublimate their frustration at not being artists. With their urgent dashes for control of the shaping culture, they allow artists to feel they are engaged in struggles of great pith and moment. In general, they allow all of us who sit in lonesome rooms fiddling with language to feel a little bit more like Vaclav Havel and a little bit less like Bobo the Juggling Clown. Very tempting stuff, especially in a nation which largely refuses to make martyrs of its literati and so deprives them of political heroism; leaves them instead to splash about like trained seals in the shallow waters of commercial failure and success. 18

Fortunately for our purposes, however, a seal's life is exactly the life for me. I'm just a simple barefoot spinner of yarns plying my wares from town to town. I don't know nothing about birthing a perfect society. For me to engage the latterday Platos on their own materialist, political terms would be to be sucked in to a form of dialogue that does not reflect the reality I know—and know I know. Because personally, I understand the world not through language but through an unfathomable spirit and an infinite mind. I sit down through an urge and with a talent as basic to my personality as inborn personality itself. With language as a rude tool I try to convey a shadow of the world my imagination makes of the world at large. I do this for money and pleasure and to win 19 the admiration of women. And when, in an uncertain hour, I crave the palliative of meaning, I remind myself that people's souls run opposite to their bodies and grow more childlike as they mature—and so I have built, in my work, little places where those souls can go to play.

The proper response to anyone who would shut these play-   20
grounds down for any reason—to anyone who confuses these playgrounds with the real world—is not the specious language of theory or logic or even the law. It's the language of the spirit, of celebration and screed, of jeremiad and hallelujah. Of this.

Now I would not say that my fictions—any fictions—have no   21
effect on real life. Or that books, movies and TV are mere regurgitations of what's going on in the society around them. These arguments, frequently advanced by violence-meisters such as *Death Wish* director Michael Winner, strike me as disingenuous and self-defeating. Rather, the relationship between fiction and humanity's unconscious is so complex, so resonant, and even stichomythic that it is impossible to isolate one from the other in terms of cause and effect. The gentle family man enjoys a day at the beach with *Red Dragon*, the assassin cuddles up with *Catcher In The Rye*. Writers in Ceausescu's murderous Roumania weren't allowed to admit that homegrown murder even existed while the civilized and liberalizing high Victorians made a bestseller out of *Dracula,* in which babies are devoured by women and women are devoured by wolves. (Interestingly, Bram Stoker made virtually the same argument in favor of censoring pornography as has Catherine MacKinnon. He feared it would incite the susceptible sex to crime: "Women are the worst offenders in this form of breach of moral law," said Bram.)

Perhaps it is true that children, sociopaths, and American   22
academics should be protected, in their emotional immaturity, from the more vicious and explicit imagery of fiction. I know I wouldn't want any of them reading my books, and would support sane and limited measures to keep them out of their hands. But for the rest of us, who can honestly say why a film like *Psycho* inspires a sort of moral mourning in me, whereas the Bible inspires David

Koresh to be, well, David Koresh? The studies are always suspect and seem to change with the political winds. Last week, a new study here purported to show a relation between child violence and video nasties. This week, a new study claimed to show that criminals watched the same things as everyone else. It all depends on how you slice it, as it were.

So fiction and reality do interact, but we don't know how, not at all. And since we don't understand the effect of one upon the other—or, that is, the effect seems to be so individualistic, to depend so much upon the specific work and person at the moment they connect—whence arises this magical certainty that violence in fiction begets violence in real life like one of those old 3D films that promised to "leap off the screen?" 23

The answer seems to come straight out of the pages of Sigmund Freud. Or St. Paul if you prefer: "Wherein thou judgest another, thou condemnest thyself." It's *Psychology 1A,* but that doesn't negate the truth of it: that pleasure which is unknowingly repressed is outwardly condemned. The censor always attacks the images that secretly appeal to him or her the most. The assault on violent fiction is not really an attempt to root out the causes of violence—no one can seriously believe that. The attempt to censor fictional violence is a guilt-ridden slap at ourselves, in the guise of a mythical *them,* for taking such pleasure in make-believe acts that, in real life, would be reprehensible. How—we seem to be asking ourselves—how, in a world in which Jamie Bulger dies so young, can we kick back with a beer at night and enjoy a couple of hours of *Child's Play 3?* How can a man who has to fear so for his wife or daughter read *American Psycho* with such a goofy simper? How can a woman who tries to teach her children to negotiate the world in peace cheer like a maniac for the marauding cruelties of *Thelma and Louise?* 24

How can we enjoy this stuff so much? So very much. 25

Not all of us perhaps. I'm forever being told that there are people who'd rather not take violence with their fiction—although I wonder how many would say so if you included the delicate violence of an Agatha Christie or the "literary" violence of, say, Hemingway and Faulkner. But even if we accept the excep- 26 tions, even if we limit the field to real gore, it does seem to me that the numbers are incredible, the attraction truly profound.

For instance, in the years when we could not afford to go to   27 the movies, my wife and I would read aloud to each other: a mutual entertainment that could be stretched over several days. Once, I picked out what looked like a cheap horror novel by an author I'd never heard of. We began reading it right after dinner. Around nine o'clock, we hit the scene where a little boy was sacrificed and gutted by the factotum of a vampire. It was about four a.m. before we reached the part where a priest was forced to guzzle the spurting blood from the vampire's chest. Long after dawn, hoarse and wide-eyed, we reached the novel's apocalyptic conclusion. Even my wife—who generally does avoid this sort of thing—agreed that it was one of the most wonderfully ugly and frightening things we'd ever read.

For months afterward, I asked every reader I knew if they had   28 ever heard of the book, *Salem's Lot,* or its author, Stephen King. None of them had. It had been nicely published but largely unpublicized. Later, the movie *Carrie* helped launch what has to be one of the most successful novelistic careers since Dickens. But even before that, all over the country, all over the world eventually, readers like me and my wife were steadily discovering the nausea and mayhem and terror of the man's vision.

The moral, I mean, is this: To construct a bloodsoaked night-   29 mare of unrelenting horror is not an easy thing. But if you build it, they will come.

And so the maker of violent fiction—ho, ho—he walks   30 among us in Nietzschean glee. He has bottled the Dionysian whirlwind and is selling it as a soft drink. Like the *hausfrau* who charmed her babes with descriptions of the dismembered brides in *The Robber Baron,* like deep-browed Homer, when he told of a spear protruding from a man's head with an eyeball fixed to the point, the violent storyteller knows that that gape of disgust on your respectable mug is really the look of love. You may denounce him, you may even censor him. You may just wrinkle your nose and walk away. But sooner or later, in one form or another, he knows you'll show up to see and listen to him—and if you don't, your children will, in droves.

Nothing can be more cruelly risible than watching experts debate a piece of fictional violence on American television, always pretending that they are above and exempt from the sweet glee that fiction provides. Is *American Psycho* an eroticized attack on womankind or an exploration of modern madness? Is *Falling Down* an incitement to murder minorities or a warning against the promptings of urban rage? The idea seems to be that whoever can impose a meaning on the fiction—a meaning which will support his cause or career—wins. 31

But fiction, like life, is not about its meanings. Like life, any good story can support any number of interpretations, many of them mutually exclusive, and many of them at odds with the author's purposes and peccadilloes. This is precisely why fiction causes single-minded political thinkers to stomp and gnash so much. Fiction lives or dies, not on its messages, but on the depth and power of the emotional experience it provides. And from the *gravitas* of the Aristotelian notion of catharsis to the pseudoscientific palaver of modern literary theory, an enormous amount of intellectual energy seems to have been expended in a failed attempt to suppress the central, disturbing and irreducible fact of this experience: it's fun. Like sex: it's lots of fun. We watch fictional people love and die and screw and suffer and weep for our pleasure. It gives us joy. 32

And we watch them kill too. And this seems to give us as much joy as anything. 33

All right, I suppose you can talk about the catharsis of terror, or the harmless release of our violent impulses. Those are plausible excuses, I guess. It doesn't take a genius to notice how often—practically always—it's the villain of a successful piece of violent art who becomes its icon. Hannibal Lecter and Leatherface, Freddy Kreuger and Dracula—these are the posters that go up on the wall, the characters that we remember. Several commentators have been disturbed by the fact that modern thrillers seem more and more to take the point of view of the bad guy rather than the 34 hero, but perhaps that's just our increasing honesty about the nature of what's repressed. Plenty of kids have built plastic models of Frankenstein's monster, but I don't know a single one who's ever built a model of a Tyrolean peasant with a torch.

So I suppose, if you must, you could say these creatures represent our buried feelings. Whether it's Medea or Jason (from *Friday The 13th*), the character who commits acts of savage violence always has the appeal of a Caliban: that thing of darkness that must be acknowledged as our own. Not that people are essentially violent, but that they are violent among other things and the violence has to be repressed. After all, if I could shoot my kids every time they were snotty and beat my wife every time she was right, I'd probably be St. Francis of Assisi in my spare time. But if you want to have a civilization, you've got to roll with the discontents. Some emotions must be repressed and repressed emotions return via the imagination in distorted and inflated forms: that's the law of benevolent hypocrisy, the law of civilized life. It is an unstated underpinning of utopian thought—what Nietzsche keenly called Socratic thought—that the repressed can be eliminated completely or denied or happily freed or remolded with the proper education. It can't. Forget about it. Cross it off your list of things to do. The monsters are always there in their cages. As Stephen King says, with engaging simplicity, his job is to take them out for a walk every now and then.

But again, this business of violent fiction as therapy—this modern-jargon version of Aristotle—it's a defense, isn't it, as if these stories needed a reason for being. In order to celebrate violent fiction—I mean, *celebrate* it—it's the joy you've got to talk about. The joy of cruelty, the thrill of terror, the adrenaline of the hunter, the heartbeat of the deer—all reproduced in the safe playground of art. A joy indeed.

Americans don't seem to like that word much: joy. Every day, some newspaper seems to publish some doctor's or sociologist's reasons why we should or shouldn't take our pleasure. It deadens our brain cells, it cleans our heart, it makes us live longer, it kills us. We need to know that smoke or drink or sport, sex or entertainment, is somehow medicinal before we allow it to take the edge off the miseries of existence. Even more, Americans, culturally puritanical and yet committed to the ideal of tolerance, like to tie themselves in knots trying to show that your pleasures are not good for *them,* that is, the society at large. As a culture, we seem unable to accept the words of our great philosopher, Dr. Seuss, who said—though admittedly in a wholly other context—"These things are fun, and fun is good."

When it comes to our messier, our somehow unseemly, plea- 38 sures, like fictional gore, we are downright embarrassed by our delight. But delight is certainly what it is. Nubile teens caught out in *flagrante* by a nutcase in a hockey mask? You bet it's erotic. Whole families tortured to death by a madman who's traced them through their vacation photos. Ee-yewwww. Goblins who jump out of the toilet to devour you ass first. Delightful stuff.

I remember when *The Exorcist* (still unavailable on video in 39 the UK) first came out over 20 years ago. The hype was extensive. The film's dramatization of a neurotic Catholic view of menarche was genuinely disgusting. Excitement in the seats ran high. Toward the climax of the picture, it all got to be too much. The fellow sitting next to me suddenly started to hyperventilate and I had to carry him out into the lobby. It was like a battlefield out there: girls sobbing, guys with their heads in their hands—a funny little mustachioed theater manager hopping from victim to victim with a stick of smelling salts. The lines to get in to the next show went around the block. I mean, we were having a *good* time now.

And we've always been that way. The myths of our ancient 40 gods, the lives of our medieval saints, the entertainments of our most civilized cultures have always included healthy doses of rape, cannibalism, evisceration, and general mayhem. Critics like Michael Medved complain that never before has it all been quite so graphic, especially on screen. We are becoming "desensitized" to bloodshed, he claims, and require more and more gore to excite our feelings. But when have human beings ever been particularly "sensitized" to fictional violence? The technology to create the illusion of bloodshed has certainly improved, but read *Titus Andronicus* with its wonderful stage direction. "Enter a messenger

with two heads and a hand," read the orgasmic staking of Lucy in
Dracula, read de Sade, for crying out loud. There were always
some pretty good indications of which way we'd go once we got
our hands on the machinery.

Because we love it. It makes us do a little inner dance of ex-   41
citement, tension, and release. What pains we go to to disguise
that. With a "serious" violent work, like *Time's Arrow* or
Goodfellas, we tell ourselves it's important, we say we thought it
was good but we didn't really enjoy it—whatever that means.
When we read the accounts of the Jamie Bulger case, when we
watch the latest victims being dragged in pieces from the marketplace of Sarajevo, when we follow the next installment of the
Menendez trial or the Amy Fisher case, we say we're out for information, a spur to political action, an insight into life—it's the *news*
after all; it's really happening.

But violent fiction with its graver purposes, if any, con-   42
cealed—fiction unadorned with overt messages or historical significance—rubs our noses in the fact that narratives of horror,
murder, and gore are a blast, a gas. When Freddy Krueger disembowels someone in a geyser of blood, when Hannibal Lecter
washes down his victim with a nice Chianti, even when the vicar
merely shoots the colonel in the drawing room—the only possible
reason for this non-real, non-meaningful event to occur is that it's
going to afford us pleasure. Which leaves that pleasure obvious,
exposed. It's the exposure, not the thrill, the censors want to get
rid of. Again: celebration is the only defense.

And yet—I know—while I celebrate, the new, not-very   43
much-improved Rome is burning.

Last year sometime, I had a conversation with a highly intelli-   44
gent Scottish filmmaker who had just returned from New York.
Both of us had recently seen Sylvester Stallone's mountaineering
action picture *Cliffhanger.* I'd seen it in the placid upper class
neighborhood of South Kensington, he'd seen it in a theater in
Times Square. I had been thrilled by the movie's special effects
and found the hilariously dopey script sweetly reminiscent of the
comic books I'd read as a child. My friend had found the picture

grimly disturbing. The Times Square theater had been filled with rowdy youths. Every time the bad guys killed someone, the youths cheered—and when a woman was murdered, they howled with delight.

I freely confess that I would have been unable to enjoy the movie under those circumstances. Too damned noisy for one thing. And, all right, yes, as a repression fan I could only get off on the cruelty of the villains insofar as it fired my anticipation of the moment when Sly would cut those suckers down. Another audience could just as easily have been cheering the murders of Jews in *Schindler's List* or of blacks in *Mississippi Burning*. I understand that, and it would be upsetting and frightening to be surrounded by a crowd which seemed to have abandoned the non-negotiable values.   45

Michael Medved believes—not that one film produces one vicious act—but that a ceaseless barrage of anti-religion, anti-family, slap-happy gore films and fictions has contributed to the erosion of values so evident on 42nd Street. I don't know whether this is true or not—neither does he—but, as with the judge's remarks in the Bulger case, it strikes me as a very suspicious place to start. The postwar generation, in which these values went openly to the wall, was raised, after all, not on the films and books that are available now, but on the value-bloated pabulum of the 1950s. And Medved's old-fashioned values, to go by the interviews he gives, have not been noticeably eroded, though he's in the business of watching these things. Surely, the Scotsman's story illustrates that the problem lies not on the screen but in the seats, in the lives that have produced that audience. Fiction cannot make of people what life has not, good or evil. "Nothing ever becomes real till it is experienced," said Keats. "Even a proverb is no proverb to you till your Life has illustrated it."   46

But more to the point: though the Times Square crowd's reaction was scary—rude too—it was not necessarily harmful in itself, either to them or me. For all I know, it was a beneficial release of energy and hostility, good for the mental health. And in any case, it took place in the context of their experience of a fiction and so (outside of the unmannerly noise they made) was beyond my   47 right to judge, approve, or condemn. Nobody has to explain his private pleasures to me.

Because fiction and reality are different. It seems appalling 48 that anyone should have to say it, but it does need to be said. Fiction is not subject to the same moral restrictions as real life. It should remain absolutely free because, at whatever level, it is, like sex, a deeply personal experience engaged in by consent in the hope of anything from momentary release to satori. Like sex, it is available to fools and creeps and monsters, and that's life; that's tough. Because fiction is, like sex, at the core of our individual humanity. Stories are the basic building blocks of spiritual maturity. No one has any business messing with them. No one at all.

Reality, on the other hand, needs its limits, maintained by 49 force if necessary, for the simple reason that there are actions that directly harm the safety and liberty of other people. They don't merely offend them; they don't just threaten their delicate sense of themselves; they *hurt* them—really painfully, a lot. Again, it seems wildly improbable that this should be forgotten, but Americans' current cultural discussions show every evidence that it has been. Just as fictions are being discussed as if they were actions (as when MacKinnon recently made the loony tune claim that she had been effectively raped in print), actual crimes and atrocities are being discussed as if they were cultural events, subject to aesthetic considerations. Trial lawyers won a lesser conviction for lady-killer Robert Chambers by claiming his victim was promiscuous; columnists defended dick-chopper Lorena Bobbit, saying it might be all right to mutilate a man in his sleep, provided he was a really nasty guy. The fellows who savaged Reginald Denny during the L.A. riots claim they were just part of the psychology of the mob. And the Menendez brothers based much of their defense on a portrayal of themselves as victims, a portrayal of their victims as abusers. These are all arguments appropriate to fiction only. Only in fiction are crimes mitigated by symbolism and individuals judged not for what they've done but because of what they represent. We can allow our sympathies with fictional characters to be excited more easily by illustrative circumstances because our sympathies depend upon the fact that *no one has really gotten hurt.*

Our thrills depend upon that as well. The woman who cheers 50 when Louise (or is it Thelma?) shoots a would-be rapist who has already put his hands up and his penis down is not the same as the columnist who supports such an act in real life, where it would be cold-blooded murder. The man who sports a hard-on after reading Bret Ellis's meticulous eviscerations is not the same as the guy who says "she asked for it," when hearing of an actual rape. To say that the reaction to fiction and the reaction to reality are on a continuum is moral nonsense. Every thought is on a continuum with every other. Reasonable distinctions along the continuum are the only moral game in town.

And fiction and real life must be distinguished from one an- 51 other. The radical presumption of fiction is play, the radical presumption of real life is what Martin Amis called "the gentleness of human flesh." If we have lost the will to defend that gentleness, then God help us, because consigning Chucky to the flames is not going to bring it back.

One of the very best works of violent fiction to come along in 52 the last few years is Thomas Harris's novel, *The Silence of the Lambs.* The story, inspired, like *Psycho,* by the real-life case of murderer Ed Gein, concerns the hunt for the serial killer Jame Gumb, a failed transsexual, who strips his female victims' flesh in order to create a woman costume in which he can clothe himself. Expertly worked as an entertainment, the novel brings us face to face with the necessary corollaries to the century's materialist, non-spiritual approach to the human body. Gumb, in his obsession with the outline of his own body, treats other people as outlines as well, as shapes, things, that he can use and transform at his will. But more than that, the book calls up our own materialist reactions to the flesh. All the ugliest violence in the book is committed against women who are already dead. Our disgust is excited not by the taking of human life, but only by the butchery of flesh that used to be human life. Even the victims themselves only balk at obeying the killer's commands when they realize what's going to happen after they're gone. And yet, what moral difference does it make what Gumb does to people once he's shot them? The horror of it is nightmarish, but its moral value is nil. Our reactions seem almost to confirm Gumb in his attitudes, and underscore our flirtation with the rationalist cannibal Hannibal Lecter, the ultimate believer in humanity as meat.

When Harris introduces the killer's next victim—Catherine   53
Martin—he presents us with a character whom we aren't meant to like very much. Rich, spoiled, arrogant, dissolute, Catherine is admirable only for the desperate cleverness she shows in her battle to stay alive. But for the rest of the novel—the attempt to rescue Catherine before it's too late—Harris depends on our fear for her, our identification with her, our deep desire to see her get out of this in one piece. The killer refers to Catherine as "It." But Harris has the artistic intelligence to know that we, the reader, will care and worry for her; if we don't, the story simply won't be any fun.

Harris allows us the forbidden kick of our identification with   54
the *übermensch* Lecter whose intelligence, wit, and appreciation of fine music in no way prevent him from killing and feeding on the human race. At the same time, he relies on our irrational—spiritual—conviction that Catherine, irritating though she may be, must not be killed because . . . for no good reason: because she Must Not. Harris knowingly taps in to the purely emotional imperative we share with the book's heroine, Clarice Starling: like her, we won't be able to sleep until the screaming of innocent lambs is stopped. Harris makes pretty well sure of it.

At the end, in the only injection of auctorial opinion in the   55
book, Harris wryly notes that the scholarly journals which include articles on the Gumb case never use the words *crazy* or *evil* in their discussions of the killer. The intellectual world is uncomfortable with the inherent Must-Not, the instinctive absolute, and the individual responsibility those words ultimately suggest. In short, though not killers themselves, these materialist thinkers share the moral blindness of their brilliant colleague Lecter, who really, in the end, has logic on his side. Harris, I think, is trying to argue that if we don't trust our mindless belief in the sanctity of human

life, we produce monsters that the sleep of reason never dreamed of. *The Silence of the Lambs,* as the title suggests, is a dramatization of a world in which the spirit has lost its power to speak.

We live in that world, no question. "Destitute of faith, and ter- 56 rified at skepticism": Carlyle's phrase still applies. With our culture atomizing, we think we can make up enough rules, impose enough restrictions, inject enough emptiness into our language to replace the shared moral conviction that's plainly gone. I think all stories—along with being fun—have the potential to humanize precisely because the richest fun of them is dependent on our identification with their characters; in order to have a really good time, we have to stretch the muscles of the I-and-Thou. But stories can't do for us what experience hasn't. They're just not that powerful. No murderous sexual psychopath is going to walk out of *The Piano* with a new-found respect for womankind; no decent bloke is going to close *The Silence of the Lambs* and start digging an oubliette—it doesn't matter how many times these experiences are repeated: the lives of the audience will out. And if some people are living lives in our society that make them unfit for even the most shallow thrills of fiction, you can't solve that problem by eliminating the fiction; it doesn't even begin to make sense. By allowing politicians and pundits to turn our attention to "the problem of fictional violence," we are really allowing them to make us turn our backs on the problems of reality. We know it too, down deep, where we're in despair. After a crime like the Jamie Bulger murder, we should be asking ourselves a million questions: about our abandonment of family life, about our approach to poverty and unemployment, about the failures of our educational systems—about who and what we are and the ways we treat each other, the things we do and omit to do. These are hard, sometimes boring questions. But when instead we let our discussions devolve, as they have, into this glamour-rotten debate on whether people should be able to enjoy whatever fiction they please, then we make meaningless the taking of an individual's life. And that's no fun at all. And it's no fun to sit back and watch it happen.

Meaning and Purpose

1. According to Klavan, those who claim that fictional violence contributes to real violence really make the situation worse, not better. How? Why?
2. Klavan uses a work of fiction (*The Silence of the Lambs*) to support his contentions about how critics of fictional violence blur the distinctions between fiction and reality. Describe how this is so. What irony is created by this blurring?
3. Klavan claims that current attempts to censor media violence is "nonsense mostly" (paragraph 6), yet these attempts have popular appeal. Why?
4. What points of Klavan's argument does the story of the Jamie Bulger murder (paragraph 8–15) support?
5. Klavan, on one level, seems to accept the argument that fictional violence is psychologically healthy (paragraphs 34–35). On another level, he dismisses that argument. Explain.
6. Klavan claims that no one can seriously believe that attempts to censor fictional violence are attempts "to root out the causes of violence" (paragraph 24). How does he explain these attempts at censorship?
7. What final reason does Klavan give for antisocial behavior? Where must we look for the real causes and cures?

Strategy

1. What attitude does Klavan strike against those with opposing viewpoints? How is this attitude designed to impress readers?
2. What opposing arguments does Klavan recognize? How does he dispose of them?
3. Explain Klavan's comparison of media violence to sex.
4. Paragraphs 15, 25, 33, and 43 are extremely short and undeveloped. What are their functions?
5. What evidence does Klavan cite to show that fictional violence has an honorable history and is, in fact, often respectable?

Style

1. In paragraph 42, Klavan calls the scene in *Silence of the Lambs* in which Hannibal Lecter eats his victim and washes him down with wine a "nonreal, nonmeaningful event." Explain.
2. What is the tone of the essay? Does the tone of the language change in the essay? To what purpose?
3. What is the connotation (see *Connotation* in the Glossary) of the phrase "trough of celebrity" (paragrpah 5)? How does that connotation affect the phrase's meaning in context?
4. If necessary look up the following words in a dictionary: *priapic, plummets, oblivion, squeamish, goading, posthumous, jitterbug, coital* (1); *jeopardy, estate, dusted, commode* (2); *quash* (5); *milieus, banal* (6); *emblematic, pundits* (7); *distraught, mutilated* (8); *tenuous, mea culpa, Draconian* (13); *rampaging, verities* (14); *utopian* (16 and 35); *Dionysean* (16 and 30); *homeopathic, template* (16); *fallacy, isomorphic* (17); *alchemies, sublimate, pith, literati* (18); *unfathomable, palliative* (19); *specious, screed, jeremiad, hallelujah* (20); *resonant, stichomythic* (21); *sociopaths* (22); *guise* (24); *factotum* (27); *mayhem* (28); *hausfrau, denounce* (30); *risible* (31); *peccadilloes, gravitas, catharsis, palaver, expended* (32); *icon* (34); *benevolent* (35); *nubile, in flagrante, goblins* (38); *menarche* (39); *evisceration* (40); *disembowels, geyser* (42); *placid* (44); *satori* (48); *atrocities, aesthetic, promiscuous, mitigated* (49); *consigning* (51); *corollaries* (52); *übermensch* (54); *auctorial* (55); *atomizing, humanize, bloke, oubliette, devolve* (56).

Writing Tasks

1. Write an essay that argues against Klavan's contention that fictional violence has no real negative effect on real life. In order to do that you will have to effectively dispose of Klavan's argument. You will also have to cite evidence that convincingly shows the relationship of fictional and real violence.
2. Write an essay defending Klavan's point of view. In doing so, dispose of Michael Medved's argument in "Denial Behavior" (pages 622–631) in more detail than Klavan did. Make sure you use specific examples in the development of your thesis.

❦ Michael Medved ❦

Michael Medved graduated with honors from Yale University and is a film critic for the New York Post *and the Public Broadcasting System. He has written several nonfiction books including* What Really Happened to the Class of '65 *(coauthored with David Wallechinsky),* Hospital: The Hidden Lives of a Medical Center Staff, *and* Hollywood vs. America. *His most recent work is* Saving Childhood: Protecting our Children from the National Assault on Innocence.

Denial Behavior

In this selection, taken from Hollywood vs. America *(1993), Medved is critical of the film and television industries for denying that the content of their films and programs influence the behavior of their audiences.*

As you read, take particular note of what Medved is claiming and what he is not claiming in regard to the media's influence on us.

A Cultural Nuthouse

In the wake of the horrifying riots in Los Angeles, thoughtful observers of every political persuasion began taking a fresh look at the connection between media messages and antisocial behavior. 1

"Now we live in a cultural nuthouse, a mad world of blood, torture and murder that surrounds us in the movies and follows us home when we turn on T.V. 'entertainment,' " editorialized A. M. Rosenthal in *The New York Times* (May 5, 1992)".. .Violence made fashionable in the cause of a buck is unworthy of people of talent. Aren't those who do that becoming ashamed of themselves? Haven't they discovered that ketchup can become blood?" 2

In their most recent responses to such charges, leaders of the entertainment industry frankly acknowledge the appalling ele- 3 ments in the "cultural nuthouse" they have built, but they refuse to accept the idea that this ominous structure has significantly influenced society.

Instead of defending the content of their work, they simply deny its impact. . . . 4

The industry apologists insist that popular entertainment is by its very nature inconsequential, and that no one is seriously damaged by the fleeting images or subtle themes in a movie, TV show, or popular song. As the Hollywood establishment never tires of pointing out, several decades of research by social scientists have failed to produce conclusive, irrefutable proof that brutality and promiscuity in a product of the mass media can cause destructive behavior in the real world. . . . 5

Hollywood 4, Straw Men 0

In March 1992, I took part in a well-publicized panel discussion on the global impact of popular culture sponsored by the American Enterprise Institute in Washington. Seated to my immediate right at the long table of participants was Mr. Jack Valenti, the unfailingly articulate and courtly president of the Motion Picture Association of America, and the most prominent spokesman for the Hollywood establishment. In the course of an occasionally heated exchange of views, Mr. Valenti made an emphatic statement that neatly summed up the industry's first line of defense in all discussions of its impact on society. "I have examined the archives of people who write on socological things in this country and sociologists, and I've found that social scientists are like psychiatrists in a murder trial," Valenti declared. "The prosecution has one . . . and the defense has one. . . . *But I haven't found anybody who has said that movies cause anybody to do anything.*" 6

Along similar lines, Mike Medavoy, chairman of TriStar Pictures and one of the most thoughtful and respected of all motion picture executives, told a 1991 meeting of Hollywood political activists that even though he personally disliked watching 7 violence on screen, "to make a claim that films are *responsible* for violence in society is ludicrous."

In January 1992, *Los Angeles Times* columnist Robert A. Jones offered a more detailed explanation of film's allegedly limited ability to influence its audience. "The truth is this: the power of a movie tends to last only as long as the lights are down and the screen flickers," he wrote. "While you're watching, it owns you. But as soon as you walk out of the theater and the cold air hits your face, the movie starts to evaporate, almost like it's leaking through your skin. By the time you reach the parking lot, it's mostly gone."

This reassuring notion turns up time and again in the industry's efforts to confound its critics. An especially eloquent and effective attack on those of us who try to draw a connection between media violence and its real-world counterpart came from Teller, one half of the celebrated Penn and Teller magic-and-comedy duo, who wrote an Op-Ed piece for *The New York Times* in January 1992. In it, he derided those

> who seem to think that if we stop showing rape in movies people will stop committing it in real life. Anthropologists call this "magical thinking." It's the same impulse that makes people stick pins in voodoo dolls, hoping to cripple an enemy. It feels logical, but it does not take into account that rape predates home video by thousands of years.
>
> Zealots have long tried to prove that "evil" fiction causes wickedness in the real world. But the facts fail to cooperate. . . . Those who want us to give up our freedom disagree. They claim people are not smart enough to tell make-believe from reality. Give us a break! When one pays seven dollars to go into a theater to see big pictures moving on a wall, one does not have to be a mental giant to realize you are watching a movie. It makes you wonder how they explain the millions of people who saw Psycho without stealing bankrolls or bumping off blondes.

With this elegant flourish, the magician brought off a rhetorical sleight of hand, imputing to his ideological opponents opinions that they do not hold and demolishing positions that they had never advanced.

To the best of my knowledge, none of the prominent partici- 11 pants in the current national debate on media values has ever suggested that "if we stop showing rape in movies people will stop committing it in real life"; nor has anyone seriously suggested that "people are not smart enough to tell make-believe from reality."

Instead of confronting the substantive concerns of those who 12 question Hollywood's excesses, what Teller and the other commentators quoted above have done is to set up convenient and highly vulnerable straw men. Naturally, their self-contained debate against these phantoms allows them to achieve a magnificent victory, with a final score reading Hollywood 4, Straw Men 0.

Essential Distinctions

In an attempt to avoid the application of such deceptive tac- 13 tics to the arguments advanced in this book, I want to leave no room for confusion about what I am saying—and what I am *not* saying—about the popular culture's impact on society.

All future disputants in this controversy, please take note: 14

- I do not claim that media messages *cause* destructive be- 15 havior, but I do contend that they *encourage* it. I have never suggested that Hollywood is single-handedly responsible for America's social problems, but I do believe that the entertainment industry exacerbates them and that it has become an important contributing factor in many of our current difficulties.

- At the same time, I never stress the pernicious power of 16 *one* movie, or one TV show, or one hit song; what concerns me is the accumulated impact of irresponsible messages that are repeated hour after hour, year after year. The most significant problems of the popular culture stem from the pervasive presence of antisocial material, not from a few isolated examples of offensiveness.

With these essential distinctions in mind, I believe that some   17
of the most outspoken critics of Hollywood's values make a serious mistake when they try to indict the industry by emphasizing a
handful of shocking episodes in which unbalanced individuals injured themselves or others by imitating behavior they saw on
screen.

We have all read lurid press accounts of such cases, describ-   18
ing the tragic toll of twenty-six people who killed themselves in
games of Russian roulette shortly after The *Deer Hunter* aired on
national TV; or the fourteen-year-old girl who meticulously
copied the murders she saw in the movie *Heathers* (1990) by organizing a game of croquet and a picnic in which she poisoned
two of her best friends; or the two sixteen-year-olds who put bullets through their heads while listening again and again to Ozzy
Osbourne's "Suicide Solution"; or the four Oklahoma high school
dropouts who recently gang-raped and battered two of their classmates while repeatedly playing a tape of the rap song "Gangster of
Love"—which specifically glorifies just such an assault.

These and many similar incidents are most certainly dramatic   19
and disturbing, but the lawsuits and public controversy surrounding them only serve to distract attention from the more significant questions about Hollywood and society.

The most profound problem with the popular culture isn't its   20
immediate impact on a few vulnerable and explosive individuals,
but its long-term effect on all the rest of us. The deepest concerns
about Hollywood go beyond the industry's role in provoking a
handful of specific crimes and involve its contribution to a general
climate of violence and self-indulgence.

A Clear Consensus

The entertainment establishment responds to these concerns   21
by supplementing its standard rhetorical tricks with a few laughably bald-faced lies. On May 18, 1992, Barbara Dixon, Jack
Valenti's colleague as spokesperson for the Motion Picture
Association of America, told the *Los Angeles Times:* "We have dealt
with this issue for a long time and have looked at a number of

studies. According to the First Amendment lawyers who have handled the issue for us, none of [the studies] say that motion picture violence affects the behavior of people."

If Ms. Dixon has accurately summarized the report she received from her lawyers, then she should immediately seek more competent legal representation: in fact, more than three thousand research projects and scientific studies between 1960 and 1992 have confirmed the connection between a steady diet of violent entertainment and aggressive and antisocial behavior.   22

In a comprehensive 1982 report, published along with five thick volumes of social science surveys, the Surgeon General of the United States concluded that "there is a clear consensus among most researchers that television violence leads to aggressive behavior." Or, as the American Psychological Association declared in a 1991 resolution following a five-year task-force investigation: "The conclusion drawn on the basis of twenty-five years of research . . . is that viewing televised violence may lead to increases in aggressive attitudes, values, and behavior, particularly in children."   23

Corporate Arrogance

In a stunning display of corporate arrogance, the major entertainment conglomerates disregard the conclusions of all the leading researchers and continue to insist that their work has no harmful impact on society.   24

With almost ritualized regularity, their official representatives repeat the claim that scientific investigations show "mixed" results on the question of media influence. "There are so many yesses and nos in the literature that it's confusing," declared CBS vice president David Blank in one typical statement in 1978. In a striking demonstration of wishful thinking, he then added, "I'm not sure anyone will ever solve the problem."   25

Meanwhile, the entertainment industry greatly encourages the confusion described by Dr. Blank by spending literally millions of dollars to commission its own studies which—surprise!—usually demonstrate that the media exert no influence on anyone. CBS,   26

ABC, and NBC have all sponsored such projects with great fan-
fare, and the resulting research is regularly dusted off and trotted
out whenever the industry wants to demonstrate divided opinion
among the experts on the question of the pop culture's impact.

The fact that such studies are taken seriously at all is itself a   27
scandal: the industry-originated surveys deserve no more respect
or consideration than we grant to all the many research reports
commissioned by the tobacco industry to prove that the Surgeon
General is wrong and that cigarette smoking is actually good for
you.

The claims that Hollywood's messages do nothing to shape at-   28
titudes and behavior are equally ludicrous, and on occasion the
truth is so obvious that not even the generous expenditure of industry funds can guarantee the research results the moguls desire.
In 1978, CBS invested $290,000 on a six-year study on the effect
of television on teenage boys conducted by the Survey Research
Centre of the London School of Economics. William Belson, who
supervised the project, concluded from his examination that "the
evidence is very strongly supportive of the hypothesis that long-
term exposure to violence increases the degree to which boys engage in violence of a serious kind. The same goes for violence of
the less serious kind, such as swearing and the use of bad language, aggressiveness in sport or play, threatening to use violence
on another boy, writing slogans on walls, and breaking windows."

Predictably enough, when confronted with these unexpected   29
and unwelcome results, CBS managed to keep its enthusiasm
firmly under control. The network's embarrassed spokesman,
David Blank, did his level best to downplay the value of the find-
ings his own company had financed, announcing that "Belson's
study was interesting, but has come along after a lot of other work
has been done and adds nothing of consequence from our standpoint."

The Height of Hypocrisy

As representatives of the television business continue to   30
stonewall, insisting that their programming has no power what-

ever to influence the public, no one seems to have noticed that this utterly implausible position contradicts the most basic assumptions of their industry.

In 1982, ABC released a commissioned study in which the hired-gun experts declared that "the research does not support the conclusion that television significantly cultivates viewer attitudes and perceptions of social reality." 31

If the executives at ABC sincerely believe this nonsense and agree that their broadcasts fail to "cultivate viewer attitudes," then the network should prepare to refund all the billions of dollars of advertising revenue that it has collected under false pretenses. 32

The mighty mechanism of commercial television is based entirely on the premise that broadcast advertising can alter the buying behavior of a significant segment of the huge viewing audience. That is why hardheaded corporations will gladly invest millions of dollars in a few thirty-second commercials, secure in the knowledge that even this sort of fleeting exposure can make an important difference in the public's point of view. 33

It is the height of hypocrisy that the same network executives who accept—and demand—this lavish payment for the briefest moments of broadcast advertising simultaneously try to convince us that all their many hours of programming do nothing to change the attitudes of the audience. In short, they have adopted the outrageously illogical assumption that a sixty-second commercial makes a more significant impression than a sixty-minute sitcom. 34

On the one hand we're told that an hour of television programming does nothing to shape the sentiments of the public, and on the other we're asked to believe that the brief spots that interrupt this program are powerful enough to change perceptions of anything from canned goods to candidates. The underlying idea appears to be the bizarre notion that the average viewer ignores or shrugs off the televised entertainment he has chosen to watch, while sitting up in his chair and paying close attention only when the commercials come on. 35

The industry simply cannot have it both ways: if it claims a near magical ability to sell products or politics, planting lasting images in just a few quick seconds, then it must acknowledge the 36

long-term impact of its prime time programs, with their frequently violent and antisocial themes.

The motion picture business faces a similarly absurd internal   37
contradiction in its refusal to acknowledge the influence of the
movies it makes.

In recent years, what Hollywood calls "product placement"   38
has played an increasingly prominent role in the production
process, with corporate logos and brand names frequently displayed in the course of every major film. This process helps the
producers defray the astronomical costs of filmmaking, as the advertiser provides props or sets or costumes, or agrees to help sell
the film by mounting a tie-in promotional campaign at the time of
its release. As the *Wall Street Journal* reports: "Friendly producers
send scripts . . . weeks and even months before filming starts, and
the company analyzes them scene by scene to see if it can place a
product—or advertising material, a billboard perhaps—on, under, or behind the stars."

According to most estimates, these efforts result in several   39
million dollars in benefits to the producers of a typical major studio film. Writing in the *Atlantic Monthly,* Mark Crispin Miller reports that the 1989 James Bond entry, *License to Kill,* featured a
scene in which 007 ostentatiously smokes Larks—a magical moment for which Philip Morris paid $350,000. In the Michael
Keaton comedy *Mr. Mom* (1983), Miller identified plugs for
McDonald's, Domino's pizza, Terminix exterminators, Folger's
coffee, Lite beer, Jack Daniel's, Van Camp's chili, Ban deodorant,
Windex, Tide, Spray 'n Wash, Borax, Clorox 2, and Downy fabric
softener.

Corporate marketing experts invest considerable effort and   40
expense in these placements because their research indicates that
they are highly effective. Even if the viewer registers the name of
the product only in an unconscious manner, the association between a familiar brand and a glamorous star will make a measur-
able difference in future sales.

This is an established principle in the motion picture busi-   41
ness—accepted without question when it comes to taking the
money of eager advertisers. At the same time that everyone agrees
that a two-second glimpse of a box of Tide can help the manufac-

turer, there is no acknowledgment that two hours of graphic gore can hurt the audience.

Imagine a forthcoming feature film with a torrid sex scene between two charismatic stars. On the night stand beside the bed is a subtle product placement—say a bottle of mouthwash, with its label turned toward the camera. The current logic of the motion picture business suggests that the typical member of the audience turns his eyes away from two naked, gorgeous bodies in transports of passion and instead focuses all attention on the bottle of mouthwash at the edge of the frame. How else can one explain the assumption that the mouthwash label will influence the viewers' future behavior, but the vivid sex scene will not? 42

In short, the industry's position is both flagrantly dishonest and lavishly illogical. 43

Meaning and Purpose

1. What is Medved claiming about the impact of popular culture on society?
2. Some critics attack the entertainment industry by pointing to copycat crimes that imitate the action in certain movies. Does Medved agree?
3. According to Medved, do research studies show any connection between violent entertainment and aggressive and antisocial behavior?
4. How does Medved relate television advertising and product placement in movies to the entertainment industry's denial that their products influence human behavior?
5. What is the main point of this selection and where is it stated?

Strategy

1. Why does Medved quote from Valenti, Medavoy, Jones, and Teller in the second section of this selection, "Hollywood 4, Straw Men 0"?

2. What is a straw man? How does Medved use the concept of the straw man to his advantage?
3. Why does Medved place his argument about advertising and product placement at the end of this selection?
4. Where does Medved most concisely state the view of the entertainment industry as to the effect on society of violence in the media?
5. What argument does Medved present solely through reasoning? How effective is this argument?

Style

1. Find at least five examples of Medved's use of emotional language to sway his audience.
2. If necessary, use a dictionary to look up the meaning of the following words: *zealots* (paragraph 9); *exacerbates* (15); *pernicious* (16); *lurid* (18); *conglomerates* (24); *moguls* (28); *hypocrisy* (34); *charismatic* (42).

Writing Tasks

1. Write an essay supporting or denying Medved's contention that "antisocial material" is pervasive in American culture. Base the paper on your personal knowledge of recent movies, television programs, books, and popular music.
2. Imagine that you are a spokesperson for the entertainment industry. Write an essay refuting Medved's essay. You may want to draw ideas from the essay by Klavan (pages 602–619).

❦ Responding to Photographs ❦
Persuasion and Argument

Saturday Morning—USA

What is the impact of television violence on children? Does television violence cause aggressive behavior? Research has not conclusively proven that it does or does not teach children to use force or violence in their relationships with other children. But most researchers agree that when children watch hours of television they participate in "imitative learning" or "modeling." In simple terms, watching television creates a "monkey-see, monkey-do" effect.

Research has even shown that onetime exposure to televised aggressive behavior can be repeated in children's play by as many as 88 percent of the children who have seen it. Moreover, a single experience viewing a dramatic aggressive act can be recalled and reenacted by children six months after the viewing. Earlier studies indicate that the average child between 5 and 15 will witness during this ten-year period the violent deaths of more than 13,400 humans. Surely the accumulated impact of television violence must influence monkey-see, monkey-do behavior. Or does it?

"Saturday Morning—USA" captures a moment when television generates "imitative learning." Drawing on details from the photograph and from the discussion here, compose an argument based on one of the following assignments. Before beginning your first draft, reread the material at the beginning of the chapter to review the conventions of a sound argument.

1. Compose an inductive or deductive argument that leads your reader to conclude that children should be prevented from watching television violence. Here are a few suggestions to get you started. Include a description of "Saturday Morning—USA" that leads to the conclusion that television has a powerful modeling effect. You might also include some of your own observations of children modeling violent television behavior. You might then point out what research suggests about the effect of television violence on play, thus leading your reader to an obvious conclusion.

2. Compose an inductive or deductive essay that takes the opposing position called for in option 1; that is, the viewing of television violence should not be curtailed because it, like all television viewing, stimulates creative play. Here are a few suggestions to get you started. In this approach, you will describe the contents of "Saturday Morning—USA" but interpret the photograph as an indication that television stimulates imaginative play, not actual violent behavior. You might also draw on your own experience modeling television violence during play, but point out that you and your friends are not criminals or violent people. You might state and agree with the research alluded to in the opening discussion of the writing task, but you would interpret it in a way that supports your point; that is, modeling is a powerful teacher, but children have the ability to separate television behavior from reality.

❦ Additional Writing Tasks ❦

Persuasion and Argument

1. Write an argument in which you express one of your own deeply felt opinions. If the subject you select has undergone extensive public discussion, assume that your reader is familiar with the general elements of the debate, and develop specific evidence based on your own observations, reading, and experience. Use the following list to stimulate your thinking, but do not feel bound by the subjects.

   a. Fraternities
   b. Sororities
   c. Hiring quotas
   d. Euthanasia
   e. Prayer in schools
   f. Giving birth control advice to teenagers
   g. Sex education
   h. Legalized drugs
   i. Capital punishment
   j. Smoking in public buildings
   k. Public profanity
   l. Disruptive behavior in public places
   m. Requiring people on public assistance to work for the city
   n. Animal rights
   o. Student code of conduct
   p. Violence on television
   q. Movie ratings
   r. Subliminal messages in music
   s. Emotional advertising in political campaigns
   t. Censorship

2. Plastic disposable diapers are becoming a significant problem. Each year Americans toss approximately eighteen billion diapers—containing an estimated 2.8 million tons of excrement and urine—in the trash. Every one of these disposable diapers takes up to five hundred years to decompose. Aside from the solid waste issue, there are also growing concerns about infectious material seeping into our soil and ground water, wasted natural resources,

the rising costs of diaper production, "disposal," and increasing risks of severe rashes and toxic shock syndrome in children.

Write an argument essay in opposition to disposable diapers. Direct your essay to new parents.

3. Many people find junk mail entertaining, something to thumb through during a leisure moment. You, however, believe that junk mail is not only a nuisance but also a hazard. For example, all the junk mail you receive this year will have consumed the equivalent of one and a half trees. One year's junk mail sent in the United States amounts to a hundred million trees.

Write an essay arguing against junk mail. Here are some commonly known facts you might want to use:

a. Almost two million tons of junk mail are sent each year.
b. Over 40 percent of all junk mail is never opened.
c. Junk mail receives special postage rates—currently 10.1 cents per piece if arranged in presorted batches.
d. The average American will spend eight months of his or her life just opening junk mail.
e. The junk mail sent to a million people means the destruction of 1.5 million trees.

4. A radical counterculture has emerged in Germany's inner cities. They are the *autonomen,* a term that means the same as "autonomous" in English. The *autonomen,* who wear masks at demonstrations, are composed of squatters and street people. They see themselves as the last hope of revolutionary activism. The group refuses to participate in any political or social system, and its brand of activism is usually spontaneous, unorganized, and often violent.

The *autonomen* have no counterpart on the American social scene, but some social psychologists predict that our government's failure to solve the problems of homelessness, drug abuse, and street gangs will lead to the formation of groups like the *autonomen* to express the anger and alienation the inner-city underclass already feels.

Write an essay in which you argue that inner-city life must be improved or city governments will soon be dealing with groups like Germany's *autonomen.* You might begin by using the *Readers' Guide to Periodical Literature* to find background information on these groups.

12

The Artful Essay

Exploring Experience

In Chapter 1 we wrote that "the essay is often described as a well-organized nonfiction composition in which the author concentrates on a single aspect of a subject." We went on to write that this kind of essay is usually "designed to convey information." Do you remember that passage?

In Chapter 2 we laid out a plan for writing a traditional college essay, that is, a thesis-support essay:

Step 1. Write an introduction that introduces a thesis.
Step 2. Write a discussion of several paragraphs that supports the thesis.
Step 3. Write a conclusion that restates the thesis and reviews the supporting discussion.

In Chapters 3 through 11 we presented the common patterns of development writers tend to use. If you have mastered the college essay and development patterns, you will have gone a long way toward achieving success in writing assignments throughout your college years. But now is the time to consider essay writing from a broader perspective.

As we've indicated throughout the text, not all essays fall into neat patterns—that is, they are not always arranged in a thesis-support pattern, and they cannot be easily classified as description, narration, examples, comparison and contrast, cause and effect, and so on. In actual practice, most writers employ a mixture of development patterns, depending on what they need to accomplish in a particular passage. If you, for example, were critiquing a novel, your essay would probably include narration, as you would have to represent the plot; description, to create a feel for the characters; cause and effect, to show the relationship among events; comparison, to relate the work to other works; and argument, to convince your reader of the novel's merit. You would therefore be mixing development patterns.

Do you recall what else we wrote when defining the essay? That essays can also do more than convey information. Essays can be impressionistic or exploratory and they can express personal feelings or attitudes based on a writer's experience. Such essays

638

usually, though not necessarily, abandon a subject-thesis structure. Moreover, they are often distinguished from other essays because they have stood the test of time. That is, they've come to be appreciated as works of the imagination, not because they are fictions—they are not—but because they open the world for readers, much as poetry opens the world. We choose to call such essays *artful essays*. If you like to lean on definitions, you can think of the artful essay as a short nonfiction composition that explores from a subjective perspective a topic that shapes itself out of deep personal experience.

Let us be a little more specific. Here are some common characteristics of artful essays.

Meaning and Purpose

Artful essays often grow out of a writer's curiosity. They tend to be reflective, not necessarily informative. Writers often write to explore subjects that mystify them. The essay allows them to probe their own knowledge and to reflect on various aspects of whatever makes them curious. As a result of this reflective process, artful essays tend to be open ended—that is, writers will not necessarily clarify what an issue means. It is up to the reader to interpret the essay. So there is meaning and there is purpose, but they are never packaged in a neatly phrased sentence.

Strategy

Given the personal and reflective character of the artful essay, writers tend to place themselves in the foreground. They want it to be very clear that their essays are written by living, breathing human beings, not by writing mechanics spewing information and conventional wisdom. They also tend, but not always, to write as if they are casually conversing with their readers. Often an artfully written essay follows the twists and turns of a casual conversation, the writer's thought unspooling onto the page.

This tendency to present the mind at work, or perhaps at play, affects the structure of artfully written essays. Indeed, they may march straight ahead from beginning to end—many of them do; but more frequently, they find their own way, that is, have their own unique structure. Memory is the fuel for reflection, and memory fuels many artfully written essays, too. While our lives move to the relentless tick-tock-tick-tock of the clock, our minds graze in the meadows of the past and transcend time by projecting into the future. Artfully written essays, then, do not fall neatly into formulaic structures. Each essay requires a new strategy.

Style

It is style that truly distinguishes artfully written essays. Style—we all know what it is when we see it, but to explain it is another matter. This is where you as a reader need to develop an *ear* for writing. Odd, isn't it, to develop an inner ear that *hears* words on the page?

Style involves a distinctive use of words, sentences, and figurative language. But perhaps the single characteristic that artfully essays share is a unique tone, or voice. Each writer has a unique voice, a quality that speaks in your mind, that whispers beneath the page, an aural signature that, once identified, will never be mistaken for any other voice.

Many of the essays in the earlier chapters are distinguished by voice and embody exceptional imaginative qualities, such as Maxine Hong Kingston's "Photographs of My Parents," Maya Angelou's "Finishing School," Amy Tan's "Mother Tongue," and Phyllis Rose's "Tools of Torture," to name just a few, from Chapters 3, 4 and 5. Review them, listen to their voices, and figure out how the writers are able to create a distinctive tone.

Essayists must develop a voice. It does not come naturally, but only with desire, effort, and experience. To begin, the writers must have the burning desire to learn about themselves by recasting their experience into written language. Few of us come willingly to writing, but those who do come to it with a passion, as if an irresistible force draws them to paper, pen in hand. Then they must write—and write a lot. Writing is somewhat like playing a musical instrument. Maybe the novice can play a few notes in sequence, but that's not *real* playing. Real playing takes years of practice for no other purpose but to play well and distinctively.

To give you a taste of artfully written essays, we've selected six frequently anthologized writers who are generally considered to be masters of the essay form. Read them with care, keeping in mind the loose characteristics of the artful essay.

❦ Jonathan Swift ❦

Born in Ireland in 1667 to English parents, Swift attended Trinity College in Dublin and Oxford University in England. He moved from Ireland to England at an early age, studied for the priesthood, and was ordained an Anglican priest in 1694. While living in England, he was active in both religion and politics and, among other things, wrote pamphlets for the Tory Party. Frustrated for many years in his attempts to gain advancement in the church, Swift returned to Ireland in 1713 as Dean of St. Patrick's Cathedral, a minor post that he accepted reluctantly. He was appalled by the conditions in Ireland and by the cruelty of English rule, which reduced most of the native Irish to abject poverty. Increasingly, he devoted himself to writing satire that exposed England's injustices against the Irish. His Drapier Letters, *in which he openly attacked the English for their abuses, made him a national hero in Ireland. His satirical masterpiece,* Gulliver's Travels, *in which he attacks the stupidity of much of human conduct, is his most famous work. When Swift died in 1745, three years after being declared of unsound mind, his estate went to found a hospital for the insane.*

A Modest Proposal

When Swift wrote and anonymously published A Modest Proposal *in 1729, Ireland was destitute. It had just suffered three years of famine, and its people were literally starving to death. At the same time, they were overtaxed by the English government and charged excessive rents by British absentee landlords. The English Parliament ignored the problem.* A Modest Proposal *is Swift's scathing response to the cruel inhumanity of England's Irish policy.*

Because the essay follows the typical format of a classical argument—it first defines the problem and the need for change by giving multiple examples, then offers the "modest proposal" for solving the problem, and finally lists the advantages of the proposal over its alternatives—many first readers took it at face value. Don't fall into that trap. The voice of the narrator is not the voice of Jonathan Swift.

Notice the disparity between the reasoned and reasonable tone of the narrator and the actual madness of his proposal. Compare that dis-

parity to the disparity between the "reasonableness" of British political
policy and the actual suffering it caused.
*   Notice that underneath his sense of irony, Swift pleads for charity*
and compassion.

It is a melancholy object to those who walk through this great   1
town or travel in the country, when they see the streets, the roads,
and cabin doors, crowded with beggars of the female sex, followed by three, four, or six children, all in rags and importuning
every passenger for an alms. These mothers, instead of being able
to work for their honest livelihood, are forced to employ all their
time in strolling to beg sustenance for their helpless infants, who,
as they grow up, either turn thieves for want of work, or leave
their dear native country to fight for the Pretender in Spain, or sell
themselves to the Barbados.

I think it is agreed by all parties that this prodigious number   2
of children in the arms, or on the backs, or at the heels of their
mothers, and frequently of their fathers, is in the present de-
plorable state of the kingdom a very great additional grievance;
and therefore whoever could find out a fair, cheap, and easy
method of making these children sound, useful members of the
commonwealth would deserve so well of the public as to have his
statue set up for a preserver of the nation.

But my intention is very far from being confined to provide   3
only for the children of professed beggars; it is of a much greater
extent, and shall take in the whole number of infants at a certain
age who are born of parents in effect as little able to support them
as those who demand our charity in the streets.

As to my own part, having turned my thoughts for many years   4
upon this important subject, and maturely weighed the several
schemes of other projectors, I have always found them grossly
mistaken in their computation. It is true, a child just dropped
from its dam may be supported by her milk for a solar year, with
little other nourishment; at most not above the value of two
shillings, which the mother may certainly get, or the value in

scraps, by her lawful occupation of begging; and it is exactly at one year old that I propose to provide for them in such a manner as instead of being a charge upon their parents or the parish, or wanting food and raiment for the rest of their lives, they shall on the contrary contribute to the feeding, and partly to the clothing, of many thousands.

There is likewise another great advantage in my scheme, that   5
it will prevent those voluntary abortions, and that horrid practice of women murdering their bastard children, alas, too frequent among us, sacrificing the poor innocent babes, I doubt, more to avoid the expense than the shame, which would move tears and pity in the most savage and inhuman breast.

The number of souls in this kingdom being usually reckoned   6
one million and a half, of these I calculate there may be about two hundred thousand couples whose wives are breeders; from which number I subtract thirty thousand couples who are able to maintain their own children, although I apprehend there cannot be so many under the present distress of the kingdom; but this being granted, there will remain an hundred and seventy thousand breeders. I again subtract fifty thousand for those women who miscarry, or whose children die by accident or disease within the year. There only remain an hundred and twenty thousand children of poor parents annually born. The question therefore is, how this number shall be reared and provided for, which, as I have already said, under the present situation of affairs, is utterly impossible by all the methods hitherto proposed. For we can neither employ them in handicraft nor agriculture; we neither build houses (I mean in the country) nor cultivate land. They can very seldom pick up a livelihood by stealing till they arrive at six years old, except where they are of towardly parts; although I confess they learn the rudiments much earlier, during which time they can however be looked upon only as probationers, as I have been informed by a principal gentleman in the county of Cavan, who protested to me that he never knew above one or two instances under the age of six, even in a part of the kingdom so renowned for the quickest proficiency in that art.

I am assured by our merchants that a boy or a girl before   7
twelve years old is no salable commodity; and even when they

come to this age, they will not yield above three pounds, or three pounds and half a crown at most on the Exchange; which cannot turn to account either to the parents or the kingdom, the charge of nutriment and rags having been at least four times that value.

I shall now therefore humbly propose my own thoughts, 8 which I hope will not be liable to the least objection.

I have been assured by a very knowing American of my ac- 9 quaintance in London, that a young healthy child well nursed is at a year old a most delicious, nourishing, and wholesome food, whether stewed, roasted, baked, or boiled; and I make no doubt that it will equally serve in a fricassee or a ragout.

I do therefore humbly offer it to public consideration that 10 of the hundred and twenty thousand children, already computed, twenty thousand may be reserved for breed, whereof only one fourth part to be males, which is more than we allow to sheep, black cattle, or swine; and my reason is that these children are seldom the fruits of marriage, a circumstance not much regarded by our savages, therefore one male will be sufficient to serve four females. That the remaining hundred thousand may at a year old be offered in sale to the persons of quality and fortune through the kingdom, always advising the mother to let them suck plentifully in the last month, so as to render them plump and fat for a good table. A child will make two dishes at an entertainment for friends; and when the family dines alone, the fore or hind quarter will make a reasonable dish, and seasoned with a little pepper or salt will be very good boiled on the fourth day, especially in winter.

I have reckoned upon a medium that a child just born will 11 weigh twelve pounds, and in a solar year if tolerably nursed increaseth to twenty-eight pounds.

I grant this food will be somewhat dear, and therefore very 12 proper for landlords, who, as they have already devoured most of the parents, seem to have the best title to the children.

Infant's flesh will be in season throughout the year, but more 13 plentiful in March, and a little before and after. For we are told by a grave author, an eminent French physician, that fish being a prolific diet, there are more children born in Roman Catholic countries about nine months after Lent, than at any other season; therefore, reckoning a year after Lent, the markets will be more glutted than usual, because the number of popish infants is at least three to one in this kingdom; and therefore it will have one other collateral advantage, by lessening the number of Papists among us.

I have already computed the charge of nursing a beggar's child (in which list I reckon all cottagers, laborers, and four fifths of the farmers) to be about two shillings per annum, rags included; and I believe no gentleman would repine to give ten shillings for the carcass of a good fat child, which, as I have said, will make four dishes of excellent nutritive meat, when he hath only some particular friend or his own family to dine with him. Thus the squire will learn to be a good landlord, and grow popular among the tenants; the mother will have eight shillings net profit, and be fit for work till she produces another child. 14

Those who are more thrifty (as I must confess the times require) may flay the carcass; the skin of which artificially dressed will make admirable gloves for ladies, and summer boots for fine gentlemen. 15

As to our city of Dublin, shambles may be appointed for this purpose in the most convenient parts of it, and butchers we may be assured will not be wanting; although I rather recommend buying the children alive, and dressing them hot from the knife as we do roasting pigs. 16

A very worthy person, a true lover of his country, and whose virtues I highly esteem, was lately pleased in discoursing on this matter to offer a refinement upon my scheme. He said that many gentlemen of his kingdom, having of late destroyed their deer, he conceived that the want of venison might be well supplied by the bodies of young lads and maidens, not exceeding fourteen years of age nor under twelve, so great a number of both sexes in every country being now ready to starve for want of work and service; and these to be disposed of by their parents, if alive, or otherwise by their nearest relations. But with due deference to so excellent a friend and so deserving a patriot, I cannot be altogether in his sentiments; for as to the males, my American acquaintance assured 17

me from frequent experience that their flesh was generally tough
and lean, like that of our schoolboys, by continual exercise, and
their taste disagreeable; and to fatten them would not answer the
charge. Then as to the females, it would, I think with humble sub-
mission, be a loss to the public, because they soon would become
breeders themselves; and besides, it is not improbable that some
scrupulous people might be apt to censure such a practice (although indeed very unjustly) as a little bordering upon cruelty;
which, I confess, hath always been with me the strongest objection against any project, how well soever intended.

But in order to justify my friend, he confessed that this expe-   18
dient was put into his head by the famous Psalmanazar, a native of
the island Formosa, who came from thence to London above
twenty years ago, and in conversation told my friend that in his
country when any young person happened to be put to death, the
executioner sold the carcass to the persons of quality as a prime
dainty; and that in his time the body of a plump girl of fifteen,
who was crucified for an attempt to poison the emperor, was sold
to his Imperial Majesty's prime minister of state, and other great
mandarins of the court, in joints from the gibbet, at four hundred
crowns. Neither indeed can I deny that if the same use were made
of several plump young girls in this town, who without one single
groat to their fortunes cannot stir abroad without a chair, and appear at the playhouse and assemblies in foreign fineries which
they never will pay for, the kingdom would not be the worse.

Some persons of a desponding spirit are in great concern   19
about that vast number of poor people who are aged, diseased, or
maimed, and I have been desired to employ my thoughts what
course may be taken to ease the nation of so grievous an encum-
brance. But I am not in the least pain upon that matter, because it
is very well known that they are every day dying and rotting by
cold and famine, and filth and vermin, as fast as can be reasonably
expected. And as to the younger laborers, they are now in almost
as hopeful a condition. They cannot get work, and consequently
pine away for want of nourishment to a degree that if any time
they are accidentally hired to common labor, they have not

strength to perform it; and thus the country and themselves are happily delivered from the evils to come.

I have too long digressed, and therefore shall return to my subject. I think the advantages by the proposal which I have made are obvious and many, as well as of the highest importance. 20

For first, as I have already observed, it would greatly lessen the number of Papists, with whom we are yearly overrun, being the principal breeders of the nation as well as our most dangerous enemies; and who stay at home on purpose to deliver the kingdom to the Pretender, hoping to take their advantage by the absence of so many good Protestants, who have chosen rather to leave their country than to stay at home and pay tithes against their conscience to an Episcopal curate. 21

Secondly, the poorer tenants will have something valuable of their own, which by law may be made liable to distress, and help to pay their landlord's rent, their corn and cattle being already seized and money a thing unknown. 22

Thirdly, whereas the maintenance of an hundred thousand children, from two years old and upwards, cannot be computed at less than ten shillings a piece per annum, the nation's stock will be thereby increased fifty thousand pounds per annum, besides the profit of a new dish introduced to the tables of all gentlemen of fortune in the kingdom who have any refinement in taste. And the money will circulate among ourselves, the goods being entirely of our own growth and manufacture. 23

Fourthly, the constant breeders, besides the gain of eight shillings sterling per annum by the sale of their children, will be rid of the charge for maintaining them after the first year. 24

Fifthly, this food would likewise bring great custom to taverns, where the vintners will certainly be so prudent as to procure the best receipts for dressing it to perfection, and consequently have their houses frequented by all the fine gentlemen, who justly value themselves upon their knowledge in good eating; and a skillful cook, who understands how to oblige his guests, will contrive to make it as expensive as they please. 25

Sixthly, this would be a great inducement to marriage, which all wise nations have either encouraged by rewards or enforced by 26 laws and penalties. It would increase the care and tenderness of mothers toward their children, when they were sure of a settlement for life to the poor babes, provided in some sort by the public, to their annual profit instead of expense. We should see an honest emulation among the married women, which of them could bring the fattest child to the market. Men would become as fond of their wives during the time of their pregnancy as they are now of their mares in foal, their cows in calf, or sows when they are ready to farrow; nor offer to beat or kick them (as is too frequent a practice) for fear of a miscarriage.

Many other advantages might be enumerated. For instance, 27 the addition of some thousand carcasses in our exportation of barreled beef, the propagation of swine's flesh, and improvements in the art of making good bacon, so much wanted among us by the great destruction of pigs, too frequent at our tables, which are no way comparable in taste or magnificence to a well-grown, fat, yearling child, which roasted whole will make a considerable figure at a lord mayor's feast or any other public entertainment. But this and many others I omit, being studious of brevity.

Supposing that one thousand families in this city would be 28 constant customers for infants' flesh, besides others who might have it at merry meetings, particularly weddings and christenings, I compute that Dublin would take off annually about twenty thousand carcasses, and the rest of the kingdom (where probably they will be sold somewhat cheaper) the remaining eighty thousand.

I can think of no one objection that will possibly be raised 29 against this proposal, unless it should be urged that the number of people will be thereby much lessened in the kingdom. This I freely own, and it was indeed one principal design in offering it to the world. I desire the reader will observe, that I calculate my remedy for this one individual kingdom of Ireland and for no other that ever was, is, or I think ever can be upon earth. Therefore, let no man talk to me of other expedients: of taxing our absentees at five shillings a pound: of using neither clothes nor household furniture except what is of our own growth and manufacture: of utterly rejecting the materials and instruments that promote foreign luxury: of curing the expensiveness of pride, vanity, idleness, and gaming in our women: of introducing a vein of parsimony, prudence, and temperance: of learning to love our country, in the want of which we differ even from Laplanders and the inhabitants of Topinamboo: of quitting our animosities and factions, nor acting any longer like the Jews, who were murdering one another at the very moment their city was taken: of being a little cautious not to sell our country and conscience for nothing: of teaching landlords to have at least one degree of mercy toward their tenants: lastly, of putting a spirit of honesty, industry, and skill into our shopkeepers; who, if a resolution could now be taken to buy only our native goods, would immediately unite to cheat and exact upon us in the price, the measure, and the goodness, nor could ever yet be brought to make one fair proposal of just dealing, though often and earnestly invited to it.

Therefore, I repeat, let no man talk to me of these and the like expedients, till he hath at least some glimpse of hope that there will ever be some hearty and sincere attempt to put them in practice. 30

But as to myself, having been wearied out for many years with offering vain, idle, visionary thoughts, and at length utterly despairing of success, I fortunately fell upon this proposal, which, as it is wholly new, so it hath something solid and real, of no expense and little trouble, full in our own power, and whereby we can incur no danger in disobliging England. For this kind of commodity will not bear exportation, the flesh being of too tender a consistence to admit a long continuance in salt, although perhaps I could name a country which would be glad to eat up our whole nation without it. 31

After all, I am not so violently bent upon my own opinion as to reject any offer proposed by wise men, which shall be found equally innocent, cheap, easy, and effectual. But before something of that kind shall be advanced in contradiction to my scheme, and offering a better, I desire the author or authors will be pleased maturely to consider two points. First, as things now stand, how they will be able to find food and raiment for an hundred thousand useless mouths and backs. And secondly, there being a round million of creatures in human figure throughout this kingdom, whose 32 sole subsistence put into a common stock would leave them in debt two millions of pounds sterling, adding those who are beggars by profession to the bulk of farmers, cottagers, and laborers, with their wives and children who are beggars in effect; I desire those politicians who dislike my overture, and may perhaps be so bold to attempt an answer, that they will first ask the parents of these mortals whether they would not at this day think it a great happiness to have been sold for food at a year old in this manner I prescribe, and thereby have avoided such a perpetual scene of misfortunes as they have since gone through by the oppression of landlords, the impossibility of paying rent without money or trade, the want of common sustenance, with neither house nor clothes to cover them from the inclemencies of the weather, and the most inevitable prospect of entailing the like or greater miseries upon their breed forever.

I profess, in the sincerity of my heart, that I have not the least 33 personal interest in endeavoring to promote this necessary work, having no other motive than the public good of my country, by advancing our trade, providing for infants, relieving the poor, and giving some pleasure to the rich. I have no children by which I can propose to get a single penny; the youngest being nine years old, and my wife past childbearing.

❦ George Orwell ❦

George Orwell, whose real name was Eric Arthur Blair, was born in India in 1903 and died in England in 1950. While attending Eton, a famous English preparatory school, he published his first writings in college periodicals. Instead of accepting a scholarship to a university, he followed his family's tradition by going to Burma (now Myanmar), where he served in the Indian Imperial Police. Orwell recounted his experiences in Burma and his unfavorable opinions of imperial rule in two famous autobiographical essays, "Shooting an Elephant" and "A Hanging," later reprinted in Orwell's collection, Shooting an Elephant and Other Essays *(1950). Both are recognized as prose classics. In 1927, Orwell decided to live in England, noting that the barriers of race and caste had kept him from mingling with the Burmese. Orwell's first novel,* Burmese Days, *portrays a sensitive person who is emotionally isolated and at odds with an oppressive or dishonest political atmosphere. Orwell was a democratic socialist all his life, but in 1937, after having fought in the Spanish Civil War with the communists against the fascist forces, he returned to England with a lifelong dread of totalitarianism. Orwell's* Animal Farm, *a fierce satire of totalitarianism, made him famous and, for the first time in his life, prosperous. His essay "Politics and the English Language" explores the ways that language is used to conceal political realities. His last novel,* 1984, *which warns about the great dangers of totalitarianism, is Orwell's best-known work.*

A Hanging

This essay seems simple on the surface; however, it deals deeply with the complexities of Orwell's personal involvement in the British occupation of India in the early part of this century. A straightforward chronological narrative, "A Hanging" illustrates Orwell's deep sympathy for the oppressed in society.

Notice how Orwell uses simple, understated language to convey the political and social contrasts between the natives and the imperialists.

Notice also how the essay's presentation is calm, a seeming combination of newspaper reportage and objective commentary, a strategy that emphasizes the horror of the event.

Notice the ways in which the essay's narrator gradually comes to see the hideousness of what is occurring.

It was in Burma, a sodden morning of the rains. A sickly light, like yellow tinfoil, was slanting over the high walls into the jail yard. We were waiting outside the condemned cells, a row of sheds fronted with double bars, like small animal cages. Each cell measured about ten feet by ten and was quite bare within except for a plank bed and a pot for drinking water. In some of them brown, silent men were squatting at the inner bars, with their blankets draped round them. These were the condemned men, due to be hanged within the next week or two.

One prisoner had been brought out of his cell. He was a Hindu, a puny wisp of a man, with a shaven head and vague liquid eyes. He had a thick, sprouting mustache, absurdly too big for his body, rather like the mustache of a comic man on the films. Six tall Indian warders were guarding him and getting him ready for the gallows. Two of them stood by with rifles and fixed bayonets, while the others handcuffed him, passed a chain through his handcuffs and fixed it to their belts, and lashed his arms tight to his sides. They crowded very close about him, with their hands always on him in a careful, caressing grip, as though all the while feeling him to make sure he was there. It was like men handling a fish which is still alive and may jump back into the water. But he stood quite unresisting, yielding his arms limply to the ropes, as though he hardly noticed what was happening.

Eight o'clock struck and a bugle call, desolately thin in the wet air, floated from the distant barracks. The superintendent of the jail, who was standing apart from the rest of us, moodily prodding the gravel with his stick, raised his head at the sound. He was an army doctor, with a grey toothbrush mustache and a gruff voice. "For God's sake, hurry up, Francis," he said irritably. "The man ought to have been dead by this time. Aren't you ready yet?"

Francis, the head jailer, a fat Dravidian in a white drill suit and gold spectacles, waved his black hand. "Yes sir, yes sir," he bub-

bled. "All iss satisfactorily prepared. The hangman iss waiting. We
shall proceed."

"Well, quick march, then. The prisoners can't get their break-   5
fast till this job's over."

We set out for the gallows. Two warders marched on either   6
side of the prisoner, with their rifles at the slope; two others
marched close against him, gripping him by arm and shoulder, as
though at once pushing and supporting him. The rest of us, mag-
istrates and the like, followed behind. Suddenly, when we had
gone ten yards, the procession stopped short without any order or
warning. A dreadful thing had happened—a dog, come goodness
knows whence, had appeared in the yard. It came bounding
among us with a loud volley of barks and leapt around us wagging
its whole body, wild with glee at finding so many human beings
together. It was a large woolly dog, half Airedale, half pariah. For
a moment it pranced around us, and then, before anyone could
stop it, it had made a dash for the prisoner, and jumping up tried
to lick his face. Everybody stood aghast, too taken aback even to
grab the dog.

"Who let that bloody brute in here?" said the superintendent   7
angrily. "Catch it, someone!"

A warder detached from the escort, charged clumsily after the   8
dog, but it danced and gambolled just out of his reach, taking
everything as part of the game. A young Eurasian jailer picked up
a handful of gravel and tried to stone the dog away, but it dodged
the stones and came after us again. Its yaps echoed from the jail
walls. The prisoner, in the grasp of the two warders, looked on in-
curiously, as though this was another formality of the hanging. It
was several minutes before someone managed to catch the dog.
Then we put my handkerchief through its collar and moved off
once more, with the dog still straining and whimpering.

It was about forty yards to the gallows. I watched the bare   9
brown back of the prisoner marching in front of me. He walked
clumsily with his bound arms, but quite steadily, with that bobbing gait of the Indian who never straightens his knees. At each
step his muscles slid neatly into place, the lock of hair on his
scalp danced up and down, his feet printed themselves on the
wet gravel. And once, in spite of the men who gripped him by

each shoulder, he stepped lightly aside to avoid a puddle on the path.

It is curious; but till that moment I had never realized what it   10
means to destroy a healthy, conscious man. When I saw the prisoner step aside to avoid the puddle, I saw the mystery, the unspeakable wrongness, of cutting a life short when it is in full tide. This man was not dying, he was alive just as we are alive. All the organs of his body were working—bowels digesting food, skin renewing itself, nails growing, tissues forming—all toiling away in solemn foolery. His nails would still be growing when he stood on the drop, when he was falling through the air with a tenth-of-a-second to live. His eyes saw the yellow gravel and the grey walls, and his brain still remembered, foresaw, reasoned—even about puddles. He and we were a party of men walking together, seeing, hearing, feeling, understanding the same world; and in two minutes, with a sudden snap, one of us would be gone—one mind less, one world less.

The gallows stood in a small yard, separate from the main   11
grounds of the prison, and overgrown with tall prickly weeds. It was a brick erection like three sides of a shed, with planking on top, and above that two beams and a crossbar with the rope dangling. The hangman, a greyhaired convict in the white uniform of the prison, was waiting beside his machine. He greeted us with a servile crouch as we entered. At a word from Francis the two warders, gripping the prisoner more closely than ever, half led, half pushed him to the gallows and helped him clumsily up the ladder. Then the hangman climbed up and fixed the rope around the prisoner's neck.

We stood waiting, five yards away. The warders had formed   12
in a rough circle round the gallows. And then, when the noose was fixed, the prisoner began crying out to his god. It was a high, reiterated cry of "Ram! Ram! Ram! Ram!" not urgent and fearful like a prayer or cry for help, but steady, rhythmical, almost like the tolling of a bell. The dog answered the sound with a whine. The hangman, still standing on the gallows, produced a small cotton bag like a flour bag and drew it down over the prisoner's face. But the sound, muffled by the cloth, still persisted, over and over again: "Ram! Ram! Ram! Ram! Ram!"

The hangman climbed down and stood ready, holding the 13
lever. Minutes seemed to pass. The steady, muffled crying from
the prisoner went on and on, "Ram! Ram! Ram!" never faltering
for an instant. The superintendent, his head on his chest, was
slowly poking the ground with his stick; perhaps he was counting
the cries, allowing the prisoner a fixed number—fifty, perhaps, or
a hundred. Everyone had changed colour. The Indians had gone
grey like bad coffee, and one or two of the bayonets were wavering. We looked at the lashed, hooded man on the drop, and listened to his cries—each cry another second of life; the same
thought was in all our minds; oh, kill him quickly, get it over, stop
that abominable noise!

Suddenly the superintendent made up his mind. Throwing 14
up his head he made a swift motion with his stick. "Chalo!" he
shouted almost fiercely.

There was a clanking noise, and then dead silence. The pris- 15
oner had vanished, and the rope was twisting on itself. I let go of
the dog, and it galloped immediately to the back of the gallows;
but when it got there it stopped short, barked, and then retreated
into a corner of the yard, where it stood among the weeds, looking timorously out at us. We went round the gallows to inspect
the prisoner's body. He was dangling with his toes pointed
straight downwards, very slowly revolving, as dead as a stone.

The superintendent reached out with his stick and poked the 16
bare brown body; it oscillated slightly. "*He's* all right," said the superintendent. He backed out from under the gallows, and blew
out a deep breath. The moody look had gone out of his face quite
suddenly. He glanced at his wrist-watch. "Eight minutes past
eight. Well, that's all for this morning, thank God."

The warders unfixed bayonets and marched away. The dog, 17
sobered and conscious of having misbehaved itself, slipped after
them. We walked out of the gallows yard, past the condemned
cells with their waiting prisoners, into the big central yard of the
prison. The convicts, under the command of warders armed with
lathis, were already receiving their breakfast. They squatted in
long rows, each man holding a tin pannikin, while two warders
with buckets marched around ladling out rice; it seemed quite a

homely, jolly scene, after the hanging. An enormous relief had come upon us now that the job was done. One felt an impulse to sing, to break into a run, to snigger. All at once everyone began chattering gaily.

The Eurasian boy walking beside me nodded towards the way we had come, with a knowing smile: "Do you know, sir, our friend (he meant the dead man) when he heard his appeal had been dismissed, he pissed on the floor of his cell. From fright. Kindly take one of my cigarettes, sir. Do you not admire my new silver case, sir? From the boxwallah, two rupees eight annas. Classy European style." 18

Several people laughed—at what, nobody seemed certain. 19

Francis was walking by the superintendent, talking garrulously: "Well, sir, all has passed off with the utmost satisfactoriness. It was all finished—flick! Like that. It iss not always so—oah, no! I have known cases where the doctor was obliged to go beneath the gallows and pull the prissoner's legs to ensure decease. Most disagreeable!" 20

"Wriggling about, eh? That's bad," said the superintendent. 21

"Ach, sir, it iss worse when they become refractory! One man, I recall, clung to the bars of hiss cage when we went to take him out. You will scarcely credit, sir, that it took six warders to dislodge him, three pulling at each leg. We reasoned with him, 'My dear fellow,' we said, 'think of all the pain and trouble you are causing to us!' But no, he would not listen! Ach, he wass very troublesome!" 22

I found that I was laughing quite loudly. Everyone was laughing. Even the superintendent grinned in a tolerant way. "You'd better all come out and have a drink," he said quite genially. "I've got a bottle of whisky in the car. We could do with it." 23

We went through the big double gates of the prison into the road. "Pulling at his legs!" exclaimed a Burmese magistrate suddenly, and burst into a loud chuckling. We all began laughing again. At that moment Francis' anecdote seemed extraordinarily funny. We all had a drink together, native and European alike, quite amicably. The dead man was a hundred yards away. 24

❦ E. B. White ❦

Known to nearly all readers as simply "E. B. White," Elway Brooks White (1899–1985) was one of America's greatest essayists. After being graduated from Cornell University in 1921, E. B. White was a reporter and freelance writer before joining The New Yorker *magazine in 1927 as a writer and contributing editor. His three books for children,* Stuart Little, Charlotte's Web, *and* The Trumpet of the Swan, *are considered classics. Among professional writers, however, he may be best known for having revised and published* The Elements of Style, *a text originally written by William Strunk, Jr., under whom White had studied at Cornell. That small work has become a standard style manual for writing in the English language. If a manual on style can be said to have a thesis, the thesis of* The Elements of Style *is that no one-to-one relationship exists between big words and good writing. On the contrary, the best words are those that combine in sentences to convey their messages to the readers, while they themselves do not intrude. Good writers write to inform, not to impress; good writers are not theatrically serious. In his foreword to* Essays of E. B. White, *E. B. White wrote that the essayist "can pull on any sort of shirt, be any sort of person, according to his mood or his subject matter—philosopher, scold, jester, raconteur, confidant, pundit, devil's advocate, enthusiast." At one time or another in White's writing career, he was each of these.*

Once More to the Lake

This essay was first published in Harper's *in 1941 and collected in* One Man's Meat *(1944). In the essay, White uses the force of reminiscence to add grace and vitality to the meticulous description of a recent event, which to most readers is common enough: a fishing trip to a lake by a father and his young son.*

However, as you read this essay, notice that the details meld in time: What is recorded of the trip blends with White's memories of his own boyhood experiences at the same lake.

Also notice how White eases naturally from time present to time past, and then forward to time present, and then back to time past. Once readers are made aware of these time shifts, they seem self-evident. But

*most hurried readers are apt to miss them, so well does White deal with
transitions.*

*Notice, too, how the essay eases from a reminiscence about taking his
young son on a fishing trip to the shock of recognition that the essayist is
growing old.*

August 1941

One summer, along about 1904, my father rented a camp on   1
a lake in Maine and took us all there for the month of August. We
all got ringworm from some kittens and had to rub Pond's Extract
on our arms and legs night and morning, and my father rolled
over in a canoe with all his clothes on; but outside of that the vacation was a success and from then on none of us ever thought
there was any place in the world like that lake in Maine. We returned summer after summer—always on August 1 for one
month. I have since become a salt-water man, but sometimes in
summer there are days when the restlessness of the tides and the
fearful cold of the sea water and the incessant wind that blows
across the afternoon and into the evening make me wish for the
placidity of a lake in the woods. A few weeks ago this feeling got
so strong I bought myself a couple of bass hooks and a spinner
and returned to the lake where we used to go, for a week's fishing
and to revisit old haunts.

I took along my son, who had never had any fresh water up   2
his nose and who had seen lily pads only from train windows. On
the journey over to the lake I began to wonder what it would be
like. I wondered how time would have marred this unique, this
holy spot—the coves and streams, the hills that the sun set behind, the camps and the paths behind the camps. I was sure that
the tarred road would have found it out, and I wondered in what
other ways it would be desolated. It is strange how much you can
remember about places like that once you allow your mind to return into the grooves that lead back. You remember one thing,
and that suddenly reminds you of another thing. I guess I remembered clearest of all the early mornings, when the lake was cool

and motionless, remembered how the bedroom smelled of the lumber it was made of and of the wet woods whose scent entered through the screen. The partitions in the camp were thin and did not extend clear to the top of the rooms, and as I was always the first up I would dress softly so as not to wake the others, and sneak out into the sweet outdoors and start out in the canoe, keeping close along the shore in the long shadows of the pines. I remembered being very careful never to rub my paddle against the gunwale for fear of disturbing the stillness of the cathedral.

The lake had never been what you would call a wild lake. There were cottages sprinkled around the shores, and it was in farming country although the shores of the lake were quite heavily wooded. Some of the cottages were owned by nearby farmers, and you would live at the shore and eat your meals at the farmhouse. That's what our family did. But although it wasn't wild, it was a fairly large and undisturbed lake and there were places in it that, to a child at least, seemed infinitely remote and primeval. 3

I was right about the tar; it led to within half a mile of the shore. But when I got back there, with my boy, and we settled into a camp near a farmhouse and into the kind of summertime I had known, I could tell that it was going to be pretty much the same as it had been before—I knew it, lying in bed the first morning, smelling the bedroom and hearing the boy sneak quietly out and go off along the shore in a boat. I began to sustain the illusion that he was I, and therefore, by simple transposition, that I was my father. This sensation persisted, kept cropping up all the time we were there. It was not an entirely new feeling, but in this setting it grew much stronger. I seemed to be living a dual existence. I would be in the middle of some simple act, I would be picking up a bait box or laying down a table fork, or I would be saying something, and suddenly it would be not I but my father who was saying the words or making the gesture. It gave me a creepy sensation. 4

We went fishing the first morning. I felt the same damp moss covering the worms in the bait can, and saw the dragonfly alight on the tip of my rod as it hovered a few inches from the surface of the water. It was the arrival of this fly that convinced me beyond 5 any doubt that everything was as it always had been, that the years were a mirage and that there had been no years. The small waves were the same, chucking the rowboat under the chin as we fished at anchor, and the boat was the same boat, the same color green and the ribs broken in the same places, and under the floorboards the same fresh-water leavings and débris—the dead hellgrammite, the wisps of moss, the rusty discarded fishhook, the dried blood from yesterday's catch. We stared silently at the tips of our rods, at the dragonflies that came and went. I lowered the tip of mine into the water, tentatively, pensively dislodging the fly, which darted two feet away, poised, darted two feet back, and came to rest again a little farther up the rod. There had been no years between the ducking of this dragonfly and the other one—the one that was part of memory. I looked at the boy, who was silently watching his fly, and it was my hands that held his rod, my eyes watching. I felt dizzy and didn't know which rod I was at the end of.

We caught two bass, hauling them in briskly as though they 6 were mackerel, pulling them over the side of the boat in a businesslike manner without any landing net, and stunning them with a blow on the back of the head. When we got back for a swim before lunch, the lake was exactly where we had left it, the same number of inches from the dock, and there was only the merest suggestion of a breeze. This seemed an utterly enchanted sea, this lake you could leave to its own devices for a few hours and come back to, and find it had not stirred, this constant and trustworthy body of water. In the shallows, the dark, water-soaked sticks and twigs, smooth and old, were undulating in clusters on the bottom against the clean ribbed sand, and the track of the mussel was plain. A school of minnows swam by, each minnow with its small individual shadow, doubling the attendance, so clear and sharp in the sunlight. Some of the other campers were in swimming, along the shore, one of them with a cake of soap, and the water felt thin and clear and unsubstantial. Over the years there had been this person with the cake of soap, this cultist, and here he was. There had been no years.

Up to the farmhouse to dinner through the teeming, dusty 7 field, the road under our sneakers was only a two-track road.

The middle track was missing, the one with the marks of the hooves and the splotches of dried, flaky manure. There had always been three tracks to choose from in choosing which track to walk in; now the choice was narrowed down to two. For a moment I missed terribly the middle alternative. But the way led past the tennis court, and something about the way it lay there in the sun reassured me; the tape had loosened along the backline, the alleys were green with plantains and other weeds, and the net (installed in June and removed in September) sagged in the dry noon, and the whole place steamed with midday heat and hunger and emptiness. There was a choice of pie for dessert, and one was blueberry and one was apple, and the waitresses were the same country girls, there having been no passage of time, only the illusion of it as in a dropped curtain—the waitresses were still fifteen; their hair had been washed, that was the only difference—they had been to the movies and seen the pretty girls with the clean hair.

Summertime, oh summertime, pattern of life indelible, the   8
fade-proof lake, the woods unshatterable, the pasture with the sweetfern and the juniper forever and ever, summer without end; this was the background, and the life along the shore was the design, their tiny docks with the flagpole and the American flag floating against the white clouds in the blue sky, the little paths over the roots of the trees leading from camp to camp and the paths leading back to the outhouses and the can of lime for sprinkling, and at the souvenir counters at the store the miniature birch-bark canoes and the postcards that showed things looking a little better than they looked. This was the American family at play, escaping the city heat, wondering whether the newcomers in the camp at the head of the cove were "common" or "nice," wondering whether it was true that the people who drove up for Sunday dinner at the farmhouse were turned away because there wasn't enough chicken.

It seemed to me, as I kept remembering all this, that those   9
times and those summers had been infinitely precious and worth saving. There had been jollity and peace and goodness. The arriving (at the beginning of August) had been so big a business in it-

self, at the railway station the farm wagon drawn up, the first smell of the pine-laden air, the first glimpse of the smiling farmer, and the great importance of the trunks and your father's enormous authority in such matters, and the feel of the wagon under you for the long ten-mile haul, and at the top of the last long hill catching the first view of the lake after eleven months of not seeing this cherished body of water. The shouts and cries of the other campers when they saw you, and the trunks to be unpacked, to give up their rich burden. (Arriving was less exciting nowadays, when you sneaked up in your car and parked it under a tree near the camp and took out the bags and in five minutes it was all over, no fuss, no loud wonderful fuss about trunks.)

Peace and goodness and jollity. The only thing that was wrong   10 now, really, was the sound of the place, an unfamiliar nervous sound of the outboard motors. This was the note that jarred, the one thing that would sometimes break the illusion and set the years moving. In those other summertimes all the motors were inboard; and when they were at a little distance, the noise they made was a sedative, an ingredient of summer sleep. They were one-cylinder and two-cylinder engines, and some were make-and-break and some were jump-spark, but they all made a sleepy sound across the lake. The one-lungers throbbed and fluttered, and the twin-cylinder ones purred and purred, and that was a quiet sound, too. But now the campers all had outboards. In the daytime, in the hot mornings, these motors made a petulant, irritable sound; at night, in the still evening when the afterglow lit the water, they whined about one's ears like mosquitoes. My boy loved our rented outboard, and his great desire was to achieve single-handed mastery over it, and authority, and he soon learned the trick of choking it a little (but not too much), and the adjustment of the needle valve. Watching him I would remember the things you could do with the old one-cylinder engine with the heavy flywheel, how you could have it eating out of your hand if you got really close to it spiritually. Motorboats in those days didn't have clutches, and you would make a landing by shutting off the motor at the proper time and coasting in with a dead rudder. But there was a way of reversing them, if you learned the trick, by cutting the switch and putting it on again exactly on the final dying revolution of the flywheel, so that it would kick back against the compression and begin reversing. Approaching a dock in a strong following breeze, it was difficult to slow up sufficiently by the ordinary coasting method, and if a boy felt he had complete mastery over his motor, he was tempted to keep it running be- yond its time and then reverse it a few feet from the dock. It took a cool nerve, because if you threw the switch a twentieth of a sec- ond too soon you would catch the flywheel when it still had speed enough to go up past center, and the boat would leap ahead, charging bull-fashion at the dock.

We had a good week at camp. The bass were biting well and the sun shown endlessly, day after day. We would be tired at night and lie down in the accumulated heat of the little bedrooms after the long hot day and the breeze would stir almost imperceptibly outside and the smell of the swamp drift in through the rusty screens. Sleep would come easily and in the morning the red squirrel would be on the roof, tapping out his gay routine. I kept remembering everything, lying in bed in the mornings—the small steamboat that had a long rounded stern like the lip of a Ubangi, and how quietly she ran on the moonlight sails, when the older boys played their mandolins and the girls sang and we ate dough- nuts dipped in sugar, and how sweet the music was on the water in the shining night, and what it had felt like to think about girls then. After breakfast we would go up to the store and the things were in the same place—the minnows in a bottle, the plugs and spinners disarranged and pawed over by the youngsters from the boys' camp, the Fig Newtons and the Beeman's gum. Outside, the road was tarred and cars stood in front of the store. Inside, all was just as it had always been, except there was more Coca-Cola and not so much Moxie and root beer and birch beer and sarsaparilla. We would walk out with the bottle of pop apiece and sometimes the pop would backfire up our noses and hurt. We explored the streams, quietly, where the turtles slid off the sunny logs and dug their way into the soft bottom; and we lay on the town wharf and fed worms to the tame bass. Everywhere we went I had trouble making out which I was, the one walking at my side, the one walking in my pants.

One afternoon while we were there at that lake a thunder-   12
storm came up. It was like the revival of an old melodrama that I had seen long ago with childish awe. The second-act climax of the drama of the electrical disturbance over a lake in America had not changed in any important respect. This was the big scene, still the big scene. The whole thing was so familiar, the first feeling of op-pression and heat and a general air around camp of not wanting to go very far away. In mid-afternoon (it was all the same) a curious darkening of the sky, and a lull in everything that had made life tick; and then the way the boats suddenly swung the other way at their moorings with the coming of a breeze out of the new quar-ter, and the premonitory rumble. Then the kettle drum, then the snare, then the bass drum and cymbals, then crackling light against the dark, and the gods grinning and licking their chops in the hills. Afterward the calm, the rain steadily rustling in the calm lake, the return of light and hope and spirits, and the campers running out in joy and relief to go swimming in the rain, their bright cries perpetuating the deathless joke about how they were getting simply drenched, and the children screaming with delight at the new sensation of bathing in the rain, and the joke about get-ting drenched linking the generations in a strong indestructible chain. And the comedian who waded in carrying an umbrella.

When the others went swimming, my son said he was going   13
in, too. He pulled his dripping trunks from the line where they had hung all through the shower and wrung them out. Languidly, and with no thought of going in, I watched him, his hard little body, skinny and bare, saw him wince slightly as he pulled up around his vitals the small, soggy, icy garment. As he buckled the swollen belt, suddenly my groin felt the chill of death.

❦ Martin Luther King, Jr. ❦

Born in Atlanta, Georgia, in 1929, Martin Luther King, Jr., was the son of a Baptist minister. At the age of eighteen, he became an ordained minister himself. He went on to study at Morehouse College, Crozer Theological Seminary, and Boston University, where he earned a Ph.D. He became the acknowledged leader of the U.S. civil rights movement, having gained national recognition in 1955 by organizing a successful boycott of the segregated bus system of Montgomery, Alabama. He was arrested and jailed more than a dozen times as a civil rights leader, once for eight days, during which time he wrote the now famous letter reprinted here. King founded and acted as president of the Southern Christian Leadership Conference, through which he promoted a philosophy of nonviolent resistance to racial discrimination that has often been compared to Gandhi's. In 1964, King was awarded the Nobel Prize for Peace, the youngest person ever so honored. In 1968 he was assassinated in Memphis, Tennessee.

Letter from Birmingham Jail

King's letter was written in response to a public statement by white Birmingham clergymen who opposed the demonstrations King was leading to protest against the city's segregated public transportation system. The argument is backed by examples from history, philosophy, theology, and literature, but the power of the writing lies equally in King's rhetorical style.

The letter is a well-reasoned defense of civil rights demonstrations. Notice the reasons King cites to justify those demonstrations.

The letter is also a reasoned argument for the necessity of civil disobedience to oppose unjust laws. Notice the distinctions King makes between just and unjust laws. Notice, too, the justifications that he asserts to advocate the breaking of unjust laws.

The letter demonstrates a careful balance between persuasion and logical argument. Notice the places King where appeals to emotion and where he appeals to reason. Consider why he uses each appeal where he does.

My Dear Fellow Clergymen:

While confined here in the Birmingham city jail, I came across   1
your recent statement calling my present activities "unwise and
untimely." Seldom do I pause to answer criticism of my work and
ideas. If I sought to answer all the criticisms that cross my desk,
my secretaries would have little time for anything other than such
correspondence in the course of the day, and I would have no
time for constructive work. But since I feel that you are men of
genuine good will and that your criticisms are sincerely set forth,
I want to try to answer your statement in what I hope will be patient and reasonable terms.

I think I should indicate why I am here in Birmingham, since   2
you have been influenced by the view which argues against "out-
siders coming in." I have the honor of serving as president of the
Southern Christian Leadership Conference, an organization operating in every southern state, with headquarters in Atlanta,
Georgia. We have some eighty-five affiliated organizations across
the South, and one of them is the Alabama Christian Movement
for Human Rights. Frequently we share staff, educational, and financial resources with our affiliates. Several months ago the affili-
ate here in Birmingham asked us to be on call to engage in a
nonviolent direct-action program if such were deemed necessary.
We readily consented, and when the hour came, we lived up to
our promise. So I, along with several members of my staff, am
here because I was invited here. I am here because I have organizational ties here.

But more basically, I am in Birmingham because injustice is   3
here. Just as the prophets of the eighth century B.C. left their villages and carried their "thus saith the Lord" far beyond the boundaries of their home towns, and just as the Apostle Paul left his
village of Tarsus and carried the gospel of Jesus Christ to the far
corners of the Greco-Roman world, so am I compelled to carry the
gospel of freedom beyond my own home town. Like Paul, I must
constantly respond to the Macedonian call for aid.

Moreover, I am cognizant of the interrelatedness of all com-   4
munities and states. I cannot sit idly by in Atlanta and not be concerned about what happens in Birmingham. Injustice anywhere is

a threat to justice everywhere. We are caught in an inescapable network of mutuality, tied in a single garment of destiny. Whatever affects one directly, affects all indirectly. Never again can we afford to live with the narrow, provincial "outside agitator" idea. Anyone who lives inside the United States can never be considered an outsider anywhere within its bounds.

You deplore the demonstrations taking place in Birmingham.   5
But your statement, I am sorry to say, fails to express a similar concern for the conditions that brought about the demonstrations. I am sure that none of you would want to rest content with the superficial kind of social analysis that deals merely with effects and does not grapple with underlying causes. It is unfortunate that demonstrations are taking place in Birmingham, but it is even more unfortunate that the city's white power structure left the Negro community with no alternative.

In any nonviolent campaign there are four basic steps: collec-   6
tion of the facts to determine whether injustices exist; negotiation; self-purification; and direct action. We have gone through all these steps in Birmingham. There can be no gainsaying the fact that racial injustice engulfs this community. Birmingham is probably the most thoroughly segregated city in the United States. Its ugly record of brutality is widely known. Negroes have experienced grossly unjust treatment in the courts. There have been more unsolved bombings of Negro homes and churches in Birmingham than in any other city in the nation. These are the hard, brutal facts of the case. On the basis of these conditions, Negro leaders sought to negotiate with the city fathers. But the latter consistently refused to engage in good-faith negotiation.

Then, last September, came the opportunity to talk with   7
leaders of Birmingham's economic community. In the course of the negotiations, certain promises were made by the merchants—for example, to remove the stores' humiliating racial signs. On the basis of these promises, the Reverend Fred Shuttlesworth and the leaders of the Alabama Christian Movement for Human Rights agreed to a moratorium on all demonstrations. As the weeks and months went by, we realized that we

were the victims of a broken promise. A few signs, briefly removed, returned; the others remained.

As in so many past experiences, our hopes had been blasted, 8
and the shadow of deep disappointment settled upon us. We had
no alternative except to prepare for direct action, whereby we
would present our very bodies as a means of laying our case before
the conscience of the local and the national community. Mindful
of the difficulties involved, we decided to undertake a process of
self-purification. We began a series of workshops on nonviolence,
and we repeatedly asked ourselves: "Are you able to accept blows
without retaliating?" "Are you able to endure the ordeal of jail?"
We decided to schedule our direct-action program for the Easter
season, realizing that except for Christmas, this is the main shopping period of the year. Knowing that a strong economic-
withdrawal program would be the by product of direct action, we
felt that this would be the best time to bring pressure to bear on
the merchants for the needed change.

Then it occurred to us that Birmingham's mayoral election 9
was coming up in March, and we speedily decided to postpone action until after election day. When we discovered that the
Commissioner of Public Safety, Eugene "Bull" Connor, had piled
up enough votes to be in the run-off, we decided again to postpone action until the day after the run-off so that the demonstrations could not be used to cloud the issues. Like many others, we
waited to see Mr. Connor defeated, and to this end we endured
postponement after postponement. Having aided in this community need, we felt that our direct-action program could be delayed
no longer.

You may well ask, "Why direct action? Why sit-ins, marches, 10
and so forth? Isn't negotiation a better path?" You are quite right
in calling for negotiation. Indeed, this is the very purpose of direct
action. Nonviolent direct action seeks to create such a crisis and
foster such a tension that a community which has constantly refused to negotiate is forced to confront the issue. It seeks so to dramatize the issue that it can no longer be ignored. My citing the
creation of tension as part of the work of the nonviolent-resister

may sound rather shocking. But I must confess that I am not afraid of the word "tension." I have earnestly opposed violent tension, but there is a type of constructive, nonviolent tension which is necessary for growth. Just as Socrates felt that it was necessary to create a tension in the mind so that individuals could rise from the bondage of myths and half-truths to the unfettered realm of creative analysis and objective appraisal, so must we see the need for nonviolent gadflies to create the kind of tension in society that will help men rise from the dark depths of prejudice and racism to the majestic heights of understanding and brotherhood.

The purpose of our direct-action program is to create a situation so crisis-packed that it will inevitably open the door to negotiation. I therefore concur with you in your call for negotiation. Too long has our beloved Southland been bogged down in a tragic effort to live in monologue rather than dialogue.   11

One of the basic points in your statement is that the action that I and my associates have taken in Birmingham is untimely. Some have asked: "Why didn't you give the new city administration time to act?" The only answer that I can give to this query is that the new Birmingham administration must be prodded about as much as the outgoing one, before it will act. We are sadly mistaken if we feel that the election of Albert Boutwell as mayor will bring the millennium to Birmingham. While Mr. Boutwell is a much more gentle person than Mr. Connor, they are both segregationists, dedicated to maintenance of the status quo. I have hoped that Mr. Boutwell will be reasonable enough to see the futility of massive resistance to desegregation. But he will not see this without pressure from devotees of civil rights. My friends, I must say to you that we have not made a single gain in civil rights without determined legal and nonviolent pressure. Lamentably, it is an historical fact that privileged groups seldom give up their privileges voluntarily. Individuals may see the moral light and voluntarily give up their unjust posture; but, as Reinhold Niebuhr has reminded us, groups tend to be more immoral than individuals.   12

We know through painful experience that freedom is never voluntarily given by the oppressor; it must be demanded by the   13 oppressed. Frankly, I have yet to engage in a direct-action campaign that was "well timed" in the view of those who have not suffered unduly from the disease of segregation. For years now I have heard the word "Wait!" It rings in the ear of every Negro with piercing familiarity. This "Wait" has almost always meant "Never." We must come to see, with one of our distinguished jurists, that "justice too long delayed is justice denied."

We have waited for more than 340 years for our constitutional 14 and God-given rights. The nations of Asia and Africa are moving with jetlike speed toward gaining political independence, but we still creep at horse-and-buggy pace toward gaining a cup of coffee at a lunch counter. Perhaps it is easy for those who have never felt the stinging darts of segregation to say, "Wait." But when you have seen vicious mobs lynch your mothers and fathers at will and drown your sisters and brothers at whim; when you have seen hate-filled policemen curse, kick, and even kill your black brothers and sisters; when you see the vast majority of your twenty million Negro brothers smothering in an airtight cage of poverty in the midst of an affluent society; when you suddenly find your tongue twisted and your speech stammering as you seek to explain to your six-year-old daughter why she can't go to the public amusement park that has just been advertised on television, and see tears welling up in her eyes when she is told that Funtown is closed to colored children, and see ominous clouds of inferiority beginning to form in her little mental sky, and see her beginning to distort her personality by developing an unconscious bitterness toward white people; when you have to concoct an answer for a five-year-old son who is asking, "Daddy, why do white people treat colored people so mean?"; when you take a cross-country drive and find it necessary to sleep night after night in the uncomfortable corners of your automobile because no motel will accept you; when you are humiliated day in and day out by nagging signs reading "white" and "colored"; when your first name becomes "nigger," your middle name becomes "boy" (however old you are) and your last name becomes "John," and your wife and mother are never given the respected title "Mrs."; when you are harried by day and haunted by night by the fact that you are a

Negro, living constantly at tiptoe stance, never quite knowing what to expect next, and are plagued with inner fears and outer resentments; when you are forever fighting a degenerating sense of "nobodiness"—then you will understand why we find it difficult to wait. There comes a time when the cup of endurance runs over, and men are no longer willing to be plunged into the abyss of despair. I hope, sirs, you can understand our legitimate and unavoidable impatience.

You express a great deal of anxiety over our willingness to break laws. This is certainly a legitimate concern. Since we so diligently urge people to obey the Supreme Court's decision of 1954 outlawing segregation in the public schools, at first glance it may seem rather paradoxical for us consciously to break laws. One may well ask: "How can you advocate breaking some laws and obeying others?" The answer lies in the fact that there are two types of laws: just and unjust. I would be the first to advocate obeying just laws. One has not only a legal but a moral responsibility to obey just laws. Conversely, one has a moral responsibility to disobey unjust laws. I would agree with St. Augustine that "an unjust law is no law at all." 15

Now, what is the difference between the two? How does one determine whether a law is just or unjust? A just law is a man-made code that squares with the moral law or the law of God. An unjust law is a code that is out of harmony with the moral law. To put it in the terms of St. Thomas Aquinas: An unjust law is a human law that is not rooted in eternal law and natural law. Any law that uplifts human personality is just. Any law that degrades human personality is unjust. All segregation statutes are unjust because segregation distorts the soul and damages the personality. It gives the segregator a false sense of superiority and the segregated a false sense of inferiority. Segregation, to use the terminology of the Jewish philosopher Martin Buber, substitutes an "I-it" relationship for an "I-thou" relationship and ends up relegating persons to the status of things. Hence segregation is not only politically, economically, and sociologically unsound, it is morally wrong and sinful. Paul Tillich has said that sin is separation. Is not segregation an existential expression of man's tragic separation, 16 his awful estrangement, his terrible sinfulness? Thus it is that I can urge men to obey the 1954 decision of the Supreme Court, for it is morally right; and I can urge them to disobey segregation ordinances, for they are morally wrong.

Let us consider a more concrete example of just and unjust   17
laws. An unjust law is a code that a numerical or power majority group compels a minority group to obey but does not make binding on itself. This is *difference* made legal. By the same token, a just law is a code that a majority compels a minority to follow and that it is willing to follow itself. This is *sameness* made legal.

Let me give another explanation. A law is unjust if it is in-   18
flicted on a minority that, as a result of being denied the right to vote, had no part in enacting or devising the law. Who can say that the legislature of Alabama which set up that state's segregation laws was democratically elected? Throughout Alabama all sorts of devious methods are used to prevent Negroes from becoming registered voters, and there are some counties in which, even though Negroes constitute a majority of the population, not a single Negro is registered. Can any law enacted under such circumstances be considered democratically structured?

Sometimes a law is just on its face and unjust in its application.   19
For instance, I have been arrested on a charge of parading without a permit. Now, there is nothing wrong in having an ordinance which requires a permit for a parade. But such an ordinance becomes unjust when it is used to maintain segregation and to deny citizens the First-Amendment privilege of peaceful assembly and protest.

I hope you are able to see the distinction I am trying to point   20
out. In no sense do I advocate evading or defying the law, as would the rabid segregationist. That would lead to anarchy. One who breaks an unjust law must do so openly, lovingly, and with a willingness to accept the penalty. I submit that an individual who breaks a law that conscience tells him is unjust, and who willingly accepts the penalty of imprisonment in order to arouse the conscience of the community over its injustice, is in reality expressing the highest respect for law.

Of course, there is nothing new about this kind of civil dis-   21
obedience. It was evidenced sublimely in the refusal of Shadrach,

Meshach, and Abednego to obey the laws of Nebuchadnezzar, on the ground that a higher moral law was at stake. It was practiced superbly by the early Christians, who were willing to face hungry lions and the excruciating pain of chopping blocks rather than submit to certain unjust laws of the Roman Empire. To a degree, academic freedom is a reality today because Socrates practiced civil disobedience. In our own nation, the Boston Tea Party represented a massive act of civil disobedience.

We should never forget that everything Adolf Hitler did in   22
Germany was "legal" and everything the Hungarian freedom fighters did in Hungary was "illegal." It was "illegal" to aid and comfort a Jew in Hitler's Germany. Even so, I am sure that, had I lived in Germany at the time, I would have aided and comforted my Jewish brothers. If today I lived in a Communist country where certain principles dear to the Christian faith are suppressed, I would openly advocate disobeying that country's anti-religious laws.

I must make two honest confessions to you, my Christian   23
and Jewish brothers. First, I must confess that over the past few years I have been gravely disappointed with the white moderate. I have almost reached the regrettable conclusion that the Negro's great stumbling block in his stride toward freedom is not the White Citizen's Counciler or the Ku Klux Klanner, but the white moderate, who is more devoted to "order" than to justice; who prefers a negative peace which is the absence of tension to a positive peace which is the presence of justice; who constantly says, "I agree with you in the goal you seek, but I cannot agree with your methods of direct action"; who paternalistically believes he can set the timetable for another man's freedom; who lives by a mythical concept of time and who constantly advises the Negro to wait for a "more convenient season." Shallow understanding from people of good will is more frustrating than absolute misunderstanding from people of ill will. Lukewarm acceptance is much more bewildering than outright rejection.

I had hoped that the white moderate would understand that   24
law and order exist for the purpose of establishing justice and that

when they fail in this purpose they become the dangerously structured dams that block the flow of social progress. I had hoped that the white moderate would understand that the present tension in the South is a necessary phase of the transition from an obnoxious negative peace, in which the Negro passively accepted his unjust plight, to a substantive and positive peace, in which all men will respect the dignity and worth of human personality. Actually, we who engage in nonviolent direct action are not the creators of tension. We merely bring to the surface the hidden tension that is already alive. We bring it out in the open, where it can be seen and dealt with. Like a boil that can never be cured so long as it is covered up but must be opened with all its ugliness to the natural medicines of air and light, injustice must be exposed, with all the tension its exposure creates, to the light of human conscience and the air of national opinion, before it can be cured.

In your statement you assert that our actions, even though peaceful, must be condemned because they precipitate violence. But is this a logical assertion? Isn't this like condemning a robbed man because his possession of money precipitated the evil act of robbery? Isn't this like condemning Socrates because his unswerving commitment to truth and his philosophical inquiries precipitated the act by the misguided populace in which they made him drink hemlock? Isn't this like condemning Jesus because his unique God-consciousness and never-ceasing devotion to God's will precipitated the evil act of crucifixion? We must come to see that, as the federal courts have consistently affirmed, it is wrong to urge an individual to cease his efforts to gain his basic constitutional rights because the quest may precipitate violence. Society must protect the robbed and punish the robber. 25

I had also hoped that the white moderate would reject the myth concerning time in relation to the struggle for freedom. I have just received a letter from a white brother in Texas. He writes: "All Christians know that the colored people will receive equal rights eventually, but it is possible that you are in too great a religious hurry. It has taken Christianity almost two thousand years to accomplish what it has. The teachings of Christ take time to come to earth." Such an attitude stems from a tragic miscon- 26 ception of time, from the strangely irrational notion that there is something in the very flow of time that will inevitably cure all ills. Actually, time itself is neutral; it can be used either destructively or constructively. More and more I feel that the people of ill will have used time much more effectively than have the people of good will. We will have to repent in this generation not merely for the hateful words and actions of the bad people, but for the appalling silence of the good people. Human progress never rolls in on wheels of inevitability; it comes through the tireless efforts of men willing to be co-workers with God, and without this hard work, time itself becomes an ally of the forces of social stagnation. We must use time creatively, in the knowledge that the time is always ripe to do right. Now is the time to make real the promise of democracy and transform our pending national elegy into a creative psalm of brotherhood. Now is the time to lift our national policy from the quicksand of racial injustice to the solid rock of human dignity.

You speak of our activity in Birmingham as extreme. At first I 27 was rather disappointed that fellow clergymen would see my nonviolent efforts as those of an extremist. I began thinking about the fact that I stand in the middle of two opposing forces in the Negro community. One is a force of complacency, made up in part of Negroes who, as a result of long years of oppression, are so drained of self-respect and a sense of "somebodiness" that they have adjusted to segregation; and in part of a few middle-class Negroes who, because of a degree of academic and economic security and because in some ways they profit by segregation, have become insensitive to the problems of the masses. The other force is one of bitterness and hatred, and it comes perilously close to advocating violence. It is expressed in the various black nationalist groups that are springing up across the nation, the largest and best-known being Elijah Muhammad's Muslim movement. Nourished by the Negro's frustration over the continued existence of racial discrimination, this movement is made up of people who have lost faith in America, who have absolutely repudiated Christianity, and who have concluded that the white man is an incorrigible "devil."

I have tried to stand between these two forces, saying that we need emulate neither the "do-nothingism" of the complacent nor the hatred and despair of the black nationalist. For there is the more excellent way of love and nonviolent protest. I am grateful to God that, through the influence of the Negro church, the way of nonviolence became an integral part of our struggle. 28

If this philosophy had not emerged, by now many streets of the South would, I am convinced, be flowing with blood. And I am further convinced that if our white brothers dismiss as "rabble-rousers" and "outside agitators" those of us who employ nonviolent direct action, and if they refuse to support our nonviolent efforts, millions of Negroes will, out of frustration and despair, seek solace and security in black-nationalist ideologies—a development that would inevitably lead to a frightening racial nightmare. 29

Oppressed people cannot remain oppressed forever. The yearning for freedom eventually manifests itself, and that is what has happened to the American Negro. Something within has reminded him of his birthright of freedom, and something without has reminded him that it can be gained. Consciously or unconsciously, he has been caught up by the *Zeitgeist*, and with his black brothers of Africa and his brown and yellow brothers of Asia, South America, and the Caribbean, the United States Negro is moving with a sense of great urgency toward the promised land of racial justice. If one recognizes this vital urge that has engulfed the Negro community, one should readily understand why public demonstrations are taking place. The Negro has many pent-up resentments and latent frustrations, and he must release them. So let him march; let him make prayer pilgrimages to the city hall; let him go on freedom rides—and try to understand why he must do so. If his repressed emotions are not released in nonviolent ways, they will seek expression through violence; this is not a threat but a fact of history. So I have not said to my people, "Get rid of your discontent." Rather, I have tried to say that this normal and healthy discontent can be channeled into the creative outlet of nonviolent direct action. And now this approach is being termed extremist. 30

But though I was initially disappointed at being categorized as   31
an extremist, as I continued to think about the matter I gradually
gained a measure of satisfaction from the label. Was not Jesus an
extremist for love: "Love your enemies, bless them that curse you,
do good to them that hate you, and pray for them which despite-
fully use you, and persecute you." Was not Amos an extremist for
justice: "Let justice roll down like waters and righteousness like an
ever-flowing stream." Was not Paul an extremist for the Christian
gospel: "I bear in my body the marks of the Lord Jesus." Was not
Martin Luther an extremist: "Here I stand; I cannot do otherwise,
so help me God." And John Bunyan: "I will stay in jail to the end
of my days before I make a butchery of my conscience." And
Abraham Lincoln: "This nation cannot survive half slave and half
free." And Thomas Jefferson: "We hold these truths to be self-
evident, that all men are created equal. . . ." So the question is not
whether we will be extremists, but what kind of extremists we will
be. Will we be extremists for hate or for love? Will we be extremists for the preservation of injustice or for the extension of justice?
In that dramatic scene on Calvary's hill three men were crucified.
We must never forget that all three were crucified for the same
crime—the crime of extremism. Two were extremists for im-
morality, and thus fell below their environment. The other, Jesus
Christ, was an extremist for love, truth, and goodness, and
thereby rose above his environment. Perhaps the South, the nation, and the world are in dire need of creative extremists.

I had hoped that the white moderate would see this need.   32
Perhaps I was too optimistic; perhaps I expected too much. I suppose I should have realized that few members of the oppressor
race can understand the deep groans and passionate yearnings of
the oppressed race, and still fewer have the vision to see that injustice must be rooted out by strong, persistent, and determined
action. I am thankful, however, that some of our white brothers in
the South have grasped the meaning of this social revolution and
committed themselves to it. They are still all too few in quantity,
but they are big in quality. Some—such as Ralph McGill, Lillian
Smith, Harry Golden, James McBride Dabbs, Anne Braden, and

Sarah Patton Boyle—have written about our struggle in eloquent and prophetic terms. Others have marched with us down nameless streets of the South. They have languished in filthy, roach-infested jails, suffering the abuse and brutality of policemen who view them as "dirty nigger-lovers." Unlike so many of their moderate brothers and sisters, they have recognized the urgency of the moment and sensed the need for powerful "action" antidotes to combat the disease of segregation.

Let me take note of my other major disappointment. I have 33
been so greatly disappointed with the white church and its leadership. Of course, there are some notable exceptions. I am not unmindful of the fact that each of you has taken some significant stands on this issue. I commend you, Reverend Stallings, for your Christian stand on this past Sunday, in welcoming Negroes to your worship service on a nonsegregated basis. I commend the Catholic leaders of this state for integrating Spring Hill College several years ago.

But despite these notable exceptions, I must honestly reiterate 34
that I have been disappointed with the church. I do not say this as one of those negative critics who can always find something wrong with the church. I say this as a minister of the gospel, who loves the church; who was nurtured in its bosom; who has been sustained by its spiritual blessings and who will remain true to it as long as the cord of life shall lengthen.

When I was suddenly catapulted into the leadership of the 35
bus protest in Montgomery, Alabama, a few years ago, I felt we would be supported by the white church. I felt that the white ministers, priests, and rabbis of the South would be among our strongest allies. Instead, some have been outright opponents, refusing to understand the freedom movement and misrepresenting its leaders; all too many others have been more cautious than courageous and have remained silent behind the anesthetizing security of stained glass windows.

In spite of my shattered dreams, I came to Birmingham with 36
the hope that the white religious leadership of this community would see the justice of our cause and, with deep moral concern,

would serve as the channel through which our just grievances could reach the power structure. I had hoped that each of you would understand. But again I have been disappointed.

I have heard numerous southern religious leaders admonish 37 their worshipers to comply with a desegregation decision because it is the law, but I have longed to hear white ministers declare: "Follow this decree because integration is morally right and because the Negro is your brother." In the midst of blatant injustices inflicted upon the Negro, I have watched white churchmen stand on the sideline and mouth pious irrelevancies and sanctimonious trivialities. In the midst of a mighty struggle to rid our nation of racial and economic injustice I have heard many ministers say: "Those are social issues, with which the gospel has no real concern." And I have watched many churches commit themselves to a completely otherworldly religion which makes a strange, unBiblical distinction between body and soul, between the sacred and the secular.

I have traveled the length and breadth of Alabama, 38 Mississippi, and all the other southern states. On sweltering summer days and crisp autumn mornings I have looked at the South's beautiful churches with their lofty spires pointing heavenward. I have beheld the impressive outlines of her massive religious-education buildings. Over and over I have found myself asking: "What kind of people worship here? Who is their God? Where were their voices when the lips of Governor Barnett dripped with words of interposition and nullification? Where were they when Governor Wallace gave a clarion call for defiance and hatred? Where were their voices of support when bruised and weary Negro men and women decided to rise from the dark dungeons of complacency to the bright hills of creative protest?"

Yes, these questions are still in my mind. In deep disappoint- 39 ment I have wept over the laxity of the church. But be assured that my tears have been tears of love. There can be no deep disappointment where there is not deep love. Yes, I love the church. How could I do otherwise? I am in the rather unique position of being the son, the grandson, and the great-grandson of preachers. Yes, I see the church as the body of Christ. But, oh! How we have blemished and scarred that body through social neglect and through fear of being nonconformists.

There was a time when the church was very powerful—in the   40 time when the early Christians rejoiced at being deemed worthy to suffer for what they believed. In those days the church was not merely a thermometer that recorded the ideas and principles of popular opinion; it was a thermostat that transformed the mores of society. Whenever the early Christians entered a town, the people in power became disturbed and immediately sought to convict the Christians for being "disturbers of the peace" and "outside agitators." But the Christians pressed on, in the conviction that they were "a colony of heaven," called to obey God rather than man. Small in number, they were big in commitment. They were too God-intoxicated to be "astronomically intimidated." By their effort and example they brought an end to such ancient evils as infanticide and gladiatorial contests.

Things are different now. So often the contemporary church is   41 a weak, ineffectual voice with an uncertain sound. So often it is an archdefender of the status quo. Far from being disturbed by the presence of the church, the power structure of the average community is consoled by the church's silent—and often even vocal—sanction of things as they are.

But the judgment of God is upon the church as never before.   42 If today's church does not recapture the sacrificial spirit of the early church, it will lose its authenticity, forfeit the loyalty of millions, and be dismissed as an irrelevant social club with no meaning for the twentieth century. Every day I meet young people whose disappointment with the church has turned into outright disgust.

Perhaps I have once again been too optimistic. Is organized   43 religion too inextricably bound to the status quo to save our nation and the world? Perhaps I must turn my faith to the inner spiritual church, the church within the church, as the true *ekklesia* and the hope of the world. But again I am thankful to God that some noble souls from the ranks of organized religion have broken loose from the paralyzing chains of conformity and joined us as active partners in the struggle for freedom. They have left their secure congregations and walked the streets of Albany, Georgia, with us. They have gone down the highways of the South on tortuous rides for freedom. Yes, they have gone to jail with us. Some have been dismissed from their churches, have lost the support of their bishops and fellow ministers. But they have acted in the faith that right defeated is stronger than evil triumphant. Their witness has been the spiritual salt that has preserved the true meaning of the gospel in these troubled times. They have carved a tunnel of hope through the dark mountain of disappointment.

I hope the church as a whole will meet the challenge of this 44 decisive hour. But even if the church does not come to the aid of justice, I have no despair about the future. I have no fear about the outcome of our struggle in Birmingham, even if our motives are at present misunderstood. We will reach the goal of freedom in Birmingham and all over the nation, because the goal of America is freedom. Abused and scorned though we may be, our destiny is tied up with America's destiny. Before the pilgrims landed at Plymouth, we were here. Before the pen of Jefferson etched the majestic words of the Declaration of Independence across the pages of history, we were here. For more than two centuries our forebears labored in this country without wages; they made cotton king; they built the homes of their masters while suffering gross injustice and shameful humiliation—and yet out of a bottomless vitality they continued to thrive and develop. If the inexpressible cruelties of slavery could not stop us, the opposition we now face will surely fail. We will win our freedom because the sacred heritage of our nation and the eternal will of God are embodied in our echoing demands.

Before closing I feel impelled to mention one other point in 45 your statement that has troubled me profoundly. You warmly commended the Birmingham police force for keeping "order" and "preventing violence." I doubt that you would have so warmly commended the police force if you had seen its dogs sinking their teeth into unarmed, nonviolent Negroes. I doubt that you would so quickly commend the policemen if you were to observe their ugly and inhumane treatment of Negroes here in the city jail; if you were to watch them push and curse old Negro women and young Negro girls; if you were to see them slap and kick old Negro men and young boys; if you were to observe them, as they did on two occasions, refuse to give us food because we wanted to sing our grace together. I cannot join you in your praise of the Birmingham police department.

It is true that the police have exercised a degree of discipline   46
in handling the demonstrators. In this sense they have conducted themselves rather "nonviolently" in public. But for what purpose? To preserve the evil system of segregation. Over the past few years I have consistently preached that nonviolence demands that the means we use must be as pure as the ends we seek. I have tried to make clear that it is wrong to use immoral means to attain moral ends. But now I must affirm that it is just as wrong, or perhaps even more so, to use moral means to preserve immoral ends. Perhaps Mr. Connor and his policemen have been rather nonviolent in public, as was Chief Pritchett in Albany, Georgia, but they have used the moral means of nonviolence to maintain the immoral end of racial injustice. As T. S. Eliot has said, "The last temptation is the greatest treason: To do the right deed for the wrong reason."

I wish you had commended the Negro sit-inners and demon-   47
strators of Birmingham for their sublime courage, their willingness to suffer, and their amazing discipline in the midst of great provocation. One day the South will recognize its real heroes. They will be the James Merediths, with the noble sense of purpose that enables them to face jeering and hostile mobs, and with the agonizing loneliness that characterizes the life of the pioneer. They will be old, oppressed, battered Negro women, symbolized in a seventy-two-year-old woman in Montgomery, Alabama, who rose up with a sense of dignity and with her people decided not to ride segregated buses, and who responded with ungrammatical profundity to one who inquired about her weariness: "My feets is tired, but my soul is at rest." They will be the young high school and college students, the young ministers of the gospel and a host of their elders, courageously and nonviolently sitting in at lunch counters and willingly going to jail for conscience' sake. One day the South will know that when these disinherited children of God

sat down at lunch counters, they were in reality standing up for what is best in the American dream and for the most sacred values in our Judaeo-Christian heritage, thereby bringing our nation back to those great wells of democracy which were dug deep by the founding fathers in their formulation of the Constitution and the Declaration of Independence.

Never before have I written so long a letter. I'm afraid it is   48
much too long to take your precious time. I can assure you that it would have been shorter if I had been writing from a comfortable desk, but what else can one do when he is alone in a narrow jail cell, other than write long letters, think long thoughts, and pray long prayers?

If I have said anything in this letter that overstates the truth   49
and indicates an unreasonable impatience, I beg you to forgive me. If I have said anything that understates the truth and indicates my having a patience that allows me to settle for anything less than brotherhood, I beg God to forgive me.

I hope this letter finds you strong in faith. I also hope that cir-   50
cumstances will soon make it possible for me to meet each of you, not as an integrationist or a civil-rights leader but as a fellow clergyman and a Christian brother. Let us all hope that the dark clouds of racial prejudice will soon pass away and the deep fog of misunderstanding will be lifted from our fear-drenched communities, and in some not too distant tomorrow the radiant stars of love and brotherhood will shine over our great nation with all their scintillating beauty.

Yours for the cause of Peace and Brotherhood,
MARTIN LUTHER KING, JR.

❦ Lewis Thomas ❦

Lewis Thomas (1913–1994) studied at Princeton University and Harvard Medical School. He had a distinguished career as a research pathologist, medical doctor, biologist, professor, and writer but is best known for his collections of essays, many of which first appeared in the New England Journal of Medicine. *He was professor of pathology and medicine at the Cornell University Medical School and served as both president and executive officer of the Memorial Sloan-Kettering Cancer Center in New York City. His first collection,* The Lives of a Cell: Notes of a Biology Watcher, *won the National Book Award and was followed by* The Medusa and the Snail: More Notes of a Biology Watcher, *and by his memoir,* The Youngest Science. *This he followed with three more essay collections:* Late Night Thoughts on Listening to Mahler's Ninth Symphony, Etcetera, Etcetera, *and* The Fragile Species.

On Natural Death

In this short essay from The Medusa and the Snail *(1979), Lewis Thomas invites the reader to consider a new way of thinking about death. His examples are taken from his own observations and from medical research, from the professional realm as well as the personal, from the extraordinary and the mundane.*

Keep in mind the essay's title as you read. Apply the title to each paragraph to determine exactly how convincing Thomas's contentions about death are.

Pay close attention to the examples Thomas uses to support his ideas. How effective are they?

Consider as you read why Thomas devotes four paragraphs to his thoughts about the details of a mouse's death and only one to the death of two soldiers.

There are so many new books about dying that there are now 1 special shelves set aside for them in bookshops, along with the health-diet and home-repair paperbacks and the sex manuals.

Some of them are so packed with detailed information and step-by-step instructions for performing the function that you'd think this was a new sort of skill which all of us are now required to learn. The strongest impression the casual reader gets, leafing through, is that proper dying has become an extraordinary, even an exotic experience, something only the specially trained get to do.

Also, you could be led to believe that we are the only creatures 2 capable of the awareness of death, that when all the rest of nature is being cycled through dying, one generation after another, it is a different kind of process, done automatically and trivially, more "natural," as we say.

An elm in our backyard caught the blight this summer and 3 dropped stone dead, leafless, almost overnight. One weekend it was a normal-looking elm, maybe a little bare in spots but nothing alarming, and the next weekend it was gone, passed over, departed, taken. Taken is right, for the tree surgeon came by yesterday with his crew of young helpers and their cherry picker, and took it down branch by branch and carted it off in the back of a red truck, everyone singing.

The dying of a field mouse, at the jaws of an amiable house- 4 hold cat, is a spectacle I have beheld many times. It used to make me wince. Early in life I gave up throwing sticks at the cat to make him drop the mouse, because the dropped mouse regularly went ahead and died anyway, but I always shouted unaffections at the cat to let him know the sort of animal he had become. Nature, I thought, was an abomination.

Recently I've done some thinking about that mouse, and I 5 wonder if his dying is necessarily all that different from the passing of our elm. The main difference, if there is one, would be in the matter of pain. I do not believe that an elm tree has pain receptors, and even so, the blight seems to me a relatively painless way to go even if there were nerve endings in a tree, which there are not. But the mouse dangling tail-down from the teeth of a gray cat is something else again, with pain beyond bearing, you'd think, all over his small body.

There are now some plausible reasons for thinking it is not 6 like that at all, and you can make up an entirely different story about the mouse and his dying if you like. At the instant of being trapped and penetrated by teeth, peptide hormones are released by cells in the hypothalamus and the pituitary gland; instantly these substances, called endorphins, are attached to the surface of other cells responsible for pain perception; the hormones have the pharmacologic properties of opium; there is no pain. Thus it is that the mouse seems always to dangle so languidly from the jaws, lies there so quietly when dropped, dies of his injuries without a struggle. If a mouse could shrug, he'd shrug.

I do not know if this is true or not, nor do I know how to   7
prove it if it is true. Maybe if you could get in there quickly enough and administer naloxone, a specific morphine antagonist, you could turn off the endorphins and observe the restoration of pain, but this is not something I would care to do or see. I think I will leave it there, as a good guess about the dying of a cat-chewed mouse, perhaps about dying in general.

Montaigne had a hunch about dying, based on his own close   8
call in a riding accident. He was so badly injured as to be believed dead by his companions, and was carried home with lamentations, "all bloody, stained all over with the blood I had thrown up." He remembers the entire episode, despite having been "dead, for two full hours," with wonderment:

> It seemed to me that my life was hanging only by the tip of
> my lips. I closed my eyes in order, it seemed to me, to help
> push it out, and took pleasure in growing languid and letting
> myself go. It was an idea that was only floating on the surface
> of my soul, as delicate and feeble as all the rest, but in truth
> not only free from distress but mingled with that sweet feel-
> ing that people have who have let themselves slide into
> sleep. I believe that this is the same state in which people
> find themselves whom we see fainting in the agony of death,
> and I maintain that we pity them without cause. . . . In order
> to get used to the idea of death, I find there is nothing like
> coming close to it.

Later, in another essay, Montaigne returns to it:

> If you know not how to die, never trouble yourself: Nature
> will in a moment fully and sufficiently instruct you; she will
> exactly do that business for you; take you no care for it.

The worst accident I've ever seen was on Okinawa, in the   9
early days of the invasion, when a jeep ran into a troop carrier and
was crushed nearly flat. Inside were two young MPs, trapped in
bent steel, both mortally hurt, with only their hands and shoulders visible. We had a conversation while people with the right
tools were prying them free. Sorry about the accident, they said.
No, they said, they felt fine. Is everyone else okay, one of them
said. Well, the other one said, no hurry now. And then they died.

Pain is useful for avoidance, for getting away when there's   10
time to get away, but when it is end game, and no way back, pain
is likely to be turned off, and the mechanisms for this are wonderfully precise and quick. If I had to design an ecosystem in
which creatures had to live off each other and in which dying was
an indispensable part of living, I could not think of a better way to
manage.

❦ Joan Didion ❦

Born in 1934 in Sacramento, California, Joan Didion was graduated from the University of California at Berkeley in 1956. From 1956 to 1963 she worked for Vogue *magazine as a copywriter and later as an editor. Didion is known for her lucid prose style and her keen depictions of social and psychological disintegration. Her first novel,* Run River, *explores the social and personal dissolution of a California family. Her collection of magazine columns published as* Slouching Towards Bethlehem *established her reputation as an essayist and confirmed her abiding interest in the forces of social, political, and psychological decay. As one who has incisive reflections and a unique vision of American life, Didion is also an epitome of ethics in that she often, as a writer, examines herself, not flinching from what she finds, both the good and the not so good. The major way in which Didion explores herself is by keeping a notebook, which to her is not merely an exercise in jotting down birthdays, anniversaries, names, and addresses, but instead is a recording of the running record of her life, which, like all lives, comprises a series of events, both large and small. Upon reflection, some of the small events are more important to Didion than she had first thought.*

On Keeping a Notebook

This essay, from Slouching Towards Bethlehem *(1968), is not simply a procedure, a set of directions for how to keep a notebook—far from it. As Didion herself notes in the preface to* Slouching Towards Bethlehem, *"Writers are always selling somebody out."*

Notice how Didion "sells herself out" to herself, in that throughout the essay she passes strong critical judgments on what she has written in her own notebook. Didion does not fear facing parts of herself that she herself condemns.

Notice that Didion asks many rhetorical questions, the kind of questions that do not require replies from her reader, and notice that her own replies to those questions are often not anticipated by her reader.

Notice also that Didion carefully distinguishes between a diary and a notebook.

" 'That woman Estelle,' " the note reads, " 'is partly the rea-   1
son why George Sharp and I are separated today.' *Dirty crêpe-de-
Chine wrapper, hotel bar, Wilmington RR, 9:45 A.M. August Monday
morning.*"

Since the note is in my notebook, it presumably has some   2
meaning to me. I study it for a long while. At first I have only the
most general notion of what I was doing on an August Monday
morning in the bar of the hotel across from the Pennsylvania
Railroad station in Wilmington, Delaware (waiting for a train?
missing one? 1960? 1961? why Wilmington?), but I do remember
being there. The woman in the dirty crêpe-de-Chine wrapper had
come down from her room for a beer, and the bartender had
heard before the reason why George Sharp and she were separated
today. "Sure," he said, and went on mopping the floor. "You told
me." At the other end of the bar is a girl. She is talking, pointedly,
not to the man beside her but to a cat lying in the triangle of sunlight cast through the open door. She is wearing a plaid silk dress
from Peck & Peck, and the hem is coming down.

Here is what it is: the girl has been on the Eastern Shore, and   3
now she is going back to the city, leaving the man beside her, and
all she can see ahead are the viscous summer sidewalks and the 3
A.M. long-distance calls that will make her lie awake and then
sleep drugged through all the steaming mornings left in August
(1960? 1961?). Because she must go directly from the train to
lunch in New York, she wishes that she had a safety pin for the
hem of the plaid silk dress, and she also wishes that she could forget about the hem and the lunch and stay in the cool bar that
smells of disinfectant and malt and make friends with the woman
in the crêpe-de-Chine wrapper. She is afflicted by a little self-pity,
and she wants to compare Estelles. That is what that was all about.

Why did I write it down? In order to remember, of course, but   4
exactly what was it I wanted to remember? How much of it actually happened? Did any of it? Why do I keep a notebook at all? It
is easy to deceive oneself on all those scores. The impulse to write
things down is a peculiarly compulsive one, inexplicable to those
who do not share it, useful only accidentally, only secondarily, in
the way that any compulsion tries to justify itself. I suppose that it

begins or does not begin in the cradle. Although I have felt compelled to write things down since I was five years old, I doubt that my daughter ever will, for she is a singularly blessed and accepting child, delighted with life exactly as life presents itself to her, unafraid to go to sleep and unafraid to wake up. Keepers of private notebooks are a different breed altogether, lonely and resistant rearrangers of things, anxious malcontents, children afflicted apparently at birth with some presentiment of loss.

My first notebook was a Big Five tablet, given to me by my mother with the sensible suggestion that I stop whining and learn to amuse myself by writing down my thoughts. She returned the tablet to me a few years ago; the first entry is an account of a woman who believed herself to be freezing to death in the Arctic night, only to find, when day broke, that she had stumbled onto the Sahara Desert, where she would die of the heat before lunch. I have no idea what turn of a five-year-old's mind could have prompted so insistently "ironic" and exotic a story, but it does reveal a certain predilection for the extreme which has dogged me into adult life; perhaps if I were analytically inclined I would find it a truer story than any I might have told about Donald Johnson's birthday party or the day my cousin Brenda put Kitty Litter in the aquarium.

So the point of my keeping a notebook has never been, nor is it now, to have an accurate factual record of what I have been doing or thinking. That would be a different impulse entirely, an instinct for reality which I sometimes envy but do not possess. At no point have I ever been able successfully to keep a diary; my approach to daily life ranges from the grossly negligent to the merely absent, and on those few occasions when I have tried dutifully to record a day's events, boredom has so overcome me that the results are mysterious at best. What is this business about "shopping, typing piece, dinner with E, depressed"? Shopping for what? Type what piece? Who is E? Was this "E" depressed, or was I depressed? Who cares?

In fact I have abandoned altogether that kind of pointless entry; instead I tell what some would call lies. "That's simply not true," the members of my family frequently tell me when they come up against my memory of a shared event. "The party was not for you, the spider was *not* a black widow, *it wasn't that way at all.*" Very likely they are right, for not only have I always had trouble distinguishing between what happened and what merely might have happened, but I remain unconvinced that the distinction, for my purposes, matters. The cracked crab that I recall having for lunch the day my father came home from Detroit in 1945 must certainly be embroidery, worked into the day's pattern to lend verisimilitude; I was ten years old and would not now remember the cracked crab. The day's events did not turn on cracked crab. And yet it is precisely that fictitious crab that makes me see the afternoon all over again, a home movie run all too often, the father bearing gifts, the child weeping, an exercise in family love and guilt. Or that is what it was to me. Similarly, perhaps it never did snow that August in Vermont; perhaps there never were flurries in the night wind, and maybe no one else felt the ground hardening and summer already dead even as we pretended to bask in it, but that was how it felt to me; and it might as well have snowed, could have snowed, did snow.

How it felt to me: that is getting closer to the truth about a note-   8
book. I sometimes delude myself about why I keep a notebook, imagine that some thrifty virtue derives from preserving everything observed. See enough and write it down, I tell myself and then some morning when the world seems drained of wonder, some day when I am only going through the motions of doing what I am supposed to do, which is write—on that bankrupt morning I will simply open my notebook and there it will be, a forgotten account with accumulated interest, paid passage back to the world out there: dialogue overheard in hotels and elevators and at the hatcheck counter in Pavillon (one middle-aged man shows his hat check to another and says, "That's my old football number"); impressions of Bettina Aptheker and Benjamin Sonnenberg and Teddy ("Mr. Acapulco") Stauffer; careful *aperçus* about tennis bums and failed fashion models and Greek shipping heiresses, one of whom taught me a significant lesson (a lesson I could have learned from F. Scott Fitzgerald, but perhaps we all

must meet the very rich for ourselves) by asking, when I arrived to interview her in her orchid-filled sitting room on the second day of a paralyzing New York blizzard, whether it was snowing outside.

I imagine, in other words, that the notebook is about other people. But of course it is not. I have no real business with what one stranger said to another at the hatcheck counter in Pavillon; in fact I suspect that the line "That's my old football number" touched not my own imagination at all, but merely some memory of something once read, probably "The Eighty-Yard Run." Nor is my concern with a woman in a dirty crêpe-de-Chine wrapper in a Wilmington bar. My stake is always, of course, in the unmentioned girl in the plaid silk dress. *Remember what it was to be me:* that is always the point.

It is a difficult point to admit. We are brought up in the ethic that others, any others, all others, are by definition more interesting than ourselves; taught to be diffident, just this side of self-effacing. ("You're the least important person in the room and don't forget it," Jessica Mitford's governess would hiss in her ear on the advent of any social occasion; I copied that into my notebook because it is only recently that I have been able to enter a room without hearing some such phrase in my inner ear.) Only the very young and the very old may recount their dreams at breakfast, dwell upon self, interrupt with memories of beach picnics and favorite Liberty lawn dresses and the rainbow trout in a creek near Colorado Springs. The rest of us are expected, rightly, to affect absorption in other people's favorite dresses, other people's trout.

And so we do. But our notebooks give us away, for however dutifully we record what we see around us, the common denominator of all we see is always, transparently, shamelessly, the implacable "I". We are not talking here about the kind of notebook that is patently for public consumption, a structural conceit for binding together a series of graceful *pensées;* we are talking about something private, about bits of the mind's string too short to use, an indiscriminate and erratic assemblage with meaning only for its maker.

And sometimes even the maker has difficulty with the mean-   12
ing. There does not seem to be, for example, any point in my
knowing for the rest of my life that, during 1964, 720 tons of soot
fell on every square mile of New York City, yet there it is in my
notebook, labeled "FACT." Nor do I really need to remember that
Ambrose Bierce liked to spell Leland Stanford's name "£eland
$tanford" or that "smart women almost always wear black in
Cuba," a fashion hint without much potential for practical application. And does not the relevance of these notes seem marginal at
best?:

> In the basement of the Inyo County Courthouse
> in Independence, California, sign pinned to a mandarin
> coat: "This MANDARIN COAT was often worn by Mrs.
> Minnie S. Brooks when giving lectures on her TEAPOT
> COLLECTION."

> Redhead getting out of car in front of Beverly Wilshire Hotel,
> chinchilla stole, Vuitton bags with tags reading:
> MRS LOU FOX
> HOTEL SAHARA
> VEGAS

Well, perhaps not entirely marginal. As a matter of fact, Mrs.
Minnie S. Brooks and her MANDARIN COAT pull me back into
my own childhood, for although I never knew Mrs. Brooks and
did not visit Inyo County until I was thirty, I grew up in just such
a world, in houses cluttered with Indian relics and bits of gold ore
and ambergris and the souvenirs my Aunt Mercy Farnsworth
brought back from the Orient. It is a long way from that world to
Mrs. Lou Fox's world where we all live now, and is it not just as
well to remember that? Might not Mrs. Minnie S. Brooks help me
to remember what I am? Might not Mrs. Lou Fox help me to remember what I am not?

But sometimes the point is harder to discern. What exactly   13
did I have in mind when I noted down that it cost the father of

someone I know $650 a month to light the place on the Hudson in which he lived before the Crash? What use was I planning to make of this line by Jimmy Hoffa: "I may have my faults, but being wrong ain't one of them"? And although I think it interesting to know where the girls who travel with the Syndicate have their hair done when they find themselves on the West Coast, will I ever make suitable use of it? Might I not be better off just passing it on to John O'Hara? What is a recipe for sauerkraut doing in my notebook? What kind of magpie keeps this notebook? "*He was born the night the* Titanic *went down.*" That seems a nice enough line, and I even recall who said it, but is it not really a better line in life than it could ever be in fiction?

But of course that is exactly it: not that I should ever use the 14 line, but that I should remember the woman who said it and the afternoon I heard it. We were on her terrace by the sea, and we were finishing the wine left from lunch, trying to get what sun there was, a California winter sun. The woman whose husband was born the night the *Titanic* went down wanted to rent her house, wanted to go back to her children in Paris. I remember wishing that I could afford the house, which cost $1,000 a month. "Someday you will," she said lazily. "Someday it all comes." There in the sun on her terrace it seemed easy to believe in someday but later I had a low-grade afternoon hangover and ran over a black snake on the way to the supermarket and was flooded with inexplicable fear when I heard the checkout clerk explaining to the man ahead of me why she was finally divorcing her husband. "He left me no choice," she said over and over as she punched the register. "He has a little seven-month-old baby by her, he left me no choice." I would like to believe that my dread then was for the human condition, but of course it was for me, because I wanted a baby and did not then have one and because I wanted to own the house that cost $1,000 a month to rent and because I had a hangover.

It all comes back. Perhaps it is difficult to see the value in having one's self back in that kind of mood, but I do see it; I think we are well advised to keep on nodding terms with the people we used to be, whether we find them attractive company or not.

Otherwise they turn up unannounced and surprise us, come hammering on the mind's door at 4 A.M. of a bad night and demand to know who deserted them, who betrayed them, who is going to make amends. We forget all too soon the things we thought we could never forget. We forget the loves and the betrayals alike, forget what we whispered and what we screamed, forget who we were. I have already lost touch with a couple of people I used to be; one of them, a seventeen-year-old, presents little threat, although it would be of some interest to me to know again what it feels like to sit on a river levee drinking vodka-and-orange-juice and listening to Les Paul and Mary Ford and their echoes sing "How High the Moon" on the car radio. (You see I still have the scenes, but I no longer perceive myself among those present, no longer could even improvise the dialogue.) The other one, a twenty-three-year-old, bothers me more. She was always a good deal of trouble, and I suspect she will reappear when I least want to see her, skirts too long, shy to the point of aggravation, always the injured party, full of recriminations and little hurts and stories I do not want to hear again, at once saddening me and angering me with her vulnerability and ignorance, an apparition all the more insistent for being so long banished.

It is a good idea, then, to keep in touch and I suppose that   16
keeping in touch is what notebooks are all about. And we are all on our own when it comes to keeping those lines open to ourselves: your notebooks will never help me, nor mine you. "*So what's new in the whiskey business?*" What could that possibly mean to you? To me it means a blonde in a Pucci bathing suit sitting with a couple of fat men by the pool at the Beverly Hills Hotel. Another man approaches, and they all regard one another in silence for a while. "So what's new in the whiskey business?" one of the fat men finally says by way of welcome, and the blonde stands up, arches one foot and dips it in the pool, looking all the while at the cabana where Baby Pignatari is talking on the telephone. That is all there is to that, except that several years later I saw the blonde coming out of Saks Fifth Avenue in New York with her California complexion and a voluminous mink coat. In the harsh wind that day she looked old and irrevocably tired to me, and even the skins in the mink coat were not worked the way they

were doing them that year, not the way she would have wanted them done, and there is the point of the story. For a while after that I did not like to look in the mirror, and my eyes would skim the newspapers and pick out only the deaths, the cancer victims, the premature coronaries, the suicides, and I stopped riding the Lexington Avenue IRT because I noticed for the first time that all the strangers I had seen for years—the man with the seeing-eye dog, the spinster who read the classified pages every day, the fat girl who always got off with me at Grand Central—looked older than they once had.

It all comes back. Even that recipe for sauerkraut: even that   17
brings it back. I was on Fire Island when I first made sauerkraut, and it was raining, and we drank a lot of bourbon and ate the sauerkraut and went to bed at ten, and I listened to the rain and the Atlantic and felt safe. I made the sauerkraut again last night and it did not make me feel any safer, but that is, as they say, another story.

Writing Task: The Artful Essay

To give you a taste of what it's like to reflect on your experience in writing, we've created a five-week sequence of informal notebook entries that will prepare you to write a reflective essay based on personal experience. We hope that completing the sequence will awaken your curiosity about the possibilities of self-exploration through writing. We also hope that you will become engaged in a creative process many writers experience while they pursue the artful essay.

Reflecting on Experience

Many writers keep a writer's notebook. It is generally a sketchbook of some kind or a looseleaf notebook. They use the writer's notebook as a way to collect material for their writing projects. Of course not every entry will be used, but the process of recording details from their lives seems to connect them to their work. Joan Didion, for example, in "On Keeping a Notebook," explains why she keeps a writer's notebook and how she uses it (see pp. 689–697). If you are interested in developing an artful touch when writing, keeping a notebook is a good way to start. But sustaining a writer's notebook is often difficult for beginning writers. They make the mistake of concentrating on what is happening in their immediate experience. Soon the process bogs down in repetition. To avoid getting bogged down, we suggest that you complete the following five weeks of notebook-keeping exercises. They are designed to plunge you into your life in ways you might not have thought of and to help you collect a body of informal writing that can be used in writing reflective essays.

Guidelines for Notebook Entries

1. Think of your entries as freewriting. No one but you will read them. Don't revise them. The goal is to merely collect experience.
2. Write for at least thirty minutes, five days a week.
3. Don't stop to correct your grammar or punctuation. Just write, and write in concrete detail.
4. Date your entries, and leave space between them so that they are clearly delineated.
5. Think of your notebook as an artist thinks of a sketchbook. It will be filled with fragments, random images, and scribbles.

    As part of your notebook writing experience, you might also keep a dream log. There, you can record any dreams you remember.

Five Weeks of Notebook Entries

Week 1: Current Life

Begin by concentrating on your current life. In the words of Henry David Thoreau, you will begin a "simple and sincere account" of your life. He writes:

I, on my side, require of every writer, first and last, a simple and sincere account of his own life, and not merely what he has heard of other men's lives; some such account as he would send to his kindred from a distant land; for if he has lived sincerely, it must have been in a distant land to me.

The distant land to which Thoreau alludes is the land of the mind. None of us sees, smells, touches, or hears the world as anyone else does. This is what makes each mind a unique landscape.

Day 1.   This entry is to capture where you are in your life. It might be a good idea to begin with a comment on your general situation as you sense it. Begin with a broad comment, then let your mind sweep through your recent life. Record specifics, bits of dialogue, frustrations, pleasures, questions, fantasies—everything that comes to you.

Second Day.   In the previous entry you described where you are in your current life. Today you are going to record impressions of where you live. Try to capture fleeting impressions and details. Let your mind loose, recording the associations it makes. Perhaps your mind will connect with other places where you have lived; work those details into your entry, but always come back to your immediate surroundings. Remember, be specific. Never let your mind linger for long in general statements such as this:

> I live in a pretty white house with a big lawn and some palm trees near the center of town. I like it here. The neighbors are. . . .

Instead, get to the details and the associations they bring:

> My front lawn has gone brown from the drought, but it still has two fat palms about two stories high with drooping limbs. I used to swing on them I was a kid: Ahhhhhh—Tarzan. People could hear my scream all over town (at least my mom said they could). Ahhhhhhh, ahhh, ahhhhhhhh! But now things are different. I've gotten older and the house. . . .

Be specific. Capture the details.

Day 3.   List personal items in your possession. Don't just name individual items; include brief descriptions and associations you have with them. Start by emptying the contents of your wallet or purse. Arrange the items in whatever way suits you, then study them. Hold them. Read the writing on the ones that have writing. Smell the ones that have smells. In your own time, make the list.

As an alternative, go to the medicine cabinet, cosmetic drawer, or refrigerator. List jars, bottles, cans, and individual items. List your associations with these items.

Day 4.   List activities you do: attend classes, read, write papers, take tests; drive, walk, bike, or ride a bus or subway to school; sleep and roll out of bed in the morning; talk with friends, teachers, parents; hold a job or play sports.

Begin by drawing up a list of your activities. Then from the list, select one or two to write about. Record everything that comes to you: how it feels to do them, why you like doing them, how long you've been doing them. Record the associations you have with them. Use specific language.

For example, this student entry about jogging starts off fuzzy, a way many writers begin, then goes past the general comments to the particulars of the experience:

> I like jogging because it makes me feel good. After I finish jogging, I relax. My body is limber—limber, reminds me of lumber. That's how I start in the mornings, my legs like pieces of lumber—I lumber along. But after I run for a while, I feel limber, like a birch tree in the wind. I like the sound of my feet slapping the asphalt and the sound of breathing deep in my chest. I like to jog on cold mornings. Once there was frost on the grass. I ran across the park. Crunch, crunch, crunch.

Day 5.   Write about special places in your current life. Randomly list places that come to mind. These special places need not be your favorite spots, ones that you associate with pleasure; they may also be places you associate with discomfort, such as a doctor's or dentist's office. Perhaps one or two places on your list will be secret places, spots you may visit for a moment or two when the world seems to be coming down around your shoulders, such as a rock overlooking a field, a window looking out to a yard or street, or a couch in a quiet place in your home.

For example, here is a part of one student's list of special places:

- Mountains: love the cool breezes that hum through the pines.
- Beach: but not with people—people everywhere, an anthill.
- Restaurants: Salernos—ummmmm! El Torito, but only on Fridays between four and six. El Tapito: carnitas, jalapenos, flautas.

I like

- My shower
- The park in early morning
- Sitting in the quad
- My granddad's garage—cans of old paint, rusted tools, pipes, bicycle parts, at least a dozen alarm clocks—all waiting to be fixed.

Notice the phrases that follow some of the items. They add the concrete details; often they are lists themselves.

Take a few minutes to draw up your list of special places and record some associations with them. Then select one or two to write about more completely.

Week 2: Life Experiences

You will continue with the exploration of your experience, but this week you will concentrate on the past.

Make a series of brief entries in the form of an extended list that spontaneously captures memories from your past. The key word is spontaneously; the goal here is not to capture only the most important events in your life—although they may be on your list—but to let the memories and images from your past come uncalled. Here is a list of notebook entries by a student who has returned to college to earn a second degree in psychology. They might seem fragmented, as if written in a personalized code:

- I remember walking to school on a cold morning. It had rained—puddles covered with thin ice. Mountains with snow. Graduating from high school. The speech seemed like hours. Fear. Thought I could never do it.
- Running on the mountain trail. A trip with dad. A cabin. Fishing. Hated the smell on my hands.
- Living in the city. Once a man stopped me on the way to school. "Got a quarter, missy? Give me your lunch money." I ran.
- My first real date. Must have taken three hours to get ready. Spilled a Coke in my lap.
- Flunked geometry—the end of the world. Thought all hell would break loose. Mom shrugged her shoulders. Dad said to take it over.
- Mom and dad divorced. Took me a year before I could say the word.
- Away to school. Mixed feelings. Couldn't wait to get out of the house. Yet scared.

This writer dips deeply into her past. In fact, the list appears to stretch from early memories to more recent ones. The list also includes the ups and downs of experience. Often when making life history lists of this sort, writers tend to consciously exclude difficult times. But if the mind finds its own course, the list will include both good and bad memories.

Day 1. For the first half-hour session, develop a list of memories from your past. Begin by sitting quietly and reflecting on the past. Then record in two or three lines a half dozen to a dozen of the strongest memories that come to you. They may not be big events in your life, but for the moment they will hold your interest. Be sure to write legibly enough to reread your entries, and leave plenty of space around them. Finally, after you finish the list, reread it and write the approximate dates when the events took place.

Days 2–5.   During the rest of this week's writing sessions, expand four entries from your list. In a way, each memory you've listed is like a doorway to your past. To write a brief entry is to open the door just a crack. To expand the entry is to swing the door open wide. Behind it will be a story or interesting detail that you might have forgotten.

Week Three: Portraits

Day 1.   Spend your practice time today developing a list of people to use for possible portraits. You can go about doing this in two ways. First, you might draw together a memory list by sitting quietly and allowing your mind to roam throughout your life history. As the names of people come to you, jot them down.

Another way to draw up a list is by browsing through your previous entries to find references to others who might be important to you. Put these people on your list. Remember to add brief comments about the relationship and the experiences you've shared with them. In other words, this is to be an extended list, full of detail and observations.

- Martha K: See her often. Sometimes we walk down University where the sycamores drop their leaves. No real commitment, just comfortable with her. We sometimes have lunch—introduced me to lox and cream cheese on bagels.
- Old Ben: Vietnam. Playing with blocks, Lego blocks. Fishing at the jetty. Taught me about death.

- John C: Three years together on the football team—left and right halfbacks. Everyone called us Heckle and Jeckle. "He's Jeckle," we both once said, while pointing at each other.

Notice that this partial list includes specific detail. The writer does not merely record a few general comments on the page and leave it at that.

Days 2–5. Each day, select one person from your list. Spend your practice time describing the person and the relationship you've shared with the person. Remember to include more than physical details. Include all that comes to you about the relationship. Try to develop a specific event that embodies some aspect of the person's character. Create some tension in the portrait.

Week Four: Paintings and Photographs

Days 1–5. Use paintings and photographs to prompt notebook entries. Select several images of paintings from art books or personal photographs that span your life, and write about them. We suggest that you paste the image, or a photocopy of the image, into your notebook. If that isn't possible, write brief descriptions of the images as part of your entries.

What follows is part of a philosophical response to a photographic slide of Salvador Dali's "Persistence of Memory":

> This morning in art history I saw a slide of a Dali painting. A crazy thing. It was filled with melting pocket watches—pocket watches that looked more real than real watches. These watches were melting in a desert wasteland with some strange trees in the background. One watch had thousands of ants crawling out of it. Another was melting over a strange amoeba-shaped object covered with hair and with a tongue hanging out of an opening.
>
> The painting reminded me of words from an old song:

"Time, time, time—what's to become of me. . . ." And I began to wonder about how time worked in my life. Time is a funny thing to be thinking about, but I can't get the thought out of my mind. I wonder how time works. I know I live in time that moves forward, that is, I was born, I went to grammar school, junior high school, and high school. I know all this education has led to college, but in my mind I can be in all these places at once. Time in my mind seems to melt together.

Whereas this writer chose to write about a well-known painting, the following writer chose to record his responses to a series of childhood photographs. His response to a photograph of himself as a baby being held by his father starts like this:

When I look at this picture, I feel very strange. I know the man standing next to the birch tree is my father and I know the baby he holds wrapped in a blanket is me. But for some reason I can't emotionally accept the thought. My father seems so young, not any older than I am now, and I find imagining him at my age is difficult.

Did he feel at 22 what I feel?

At that age he had a child—me. It makes me feel he had his life under control. But here I am at 22 without an idea of what I'll be doing four years from now.

My father now, compared to the picture, seems so much older. So changed. Once he was thin, athletic. Now he has a paunch and looks as if he never sees the sun. His hair, once full and wavy, is now thin. His face was smooth, now wrinkled.

At this moment I wonder if somewhere there exists a photograph of him and his father. I wonder if he has ever compared himself to his dad's image. Where does this lead, this photographing, this photographing of fathers and sons?

Where?

Back, back, back. And forward—into the future. The never-ending future. But somehow I feel there's knowledge to be gained from studying these images.

The key to responding to images, whether paintings or personal photographs, is to avoid trying to figure out what you are going to write before you write it. Instead, concentrate on the image and just write.

Week 5: Self-Reflection

For several weeks you have been exploring a subject that is close to you: your life. We hope you are beginning to sense the scope of self-exploration. People, places, memories, feelings, objects, events, books, films, music, dreams, even unharnessed thoughts—all fall into the vast, partially charted territory of your life. We also hope that you have made some discoveries.

We want to lead you a few steps down the path of self-examination, or, as we prefer to call it, self-reflection.

Instead of making a direct assault on yourself, you'll follow a gentler course by merely rereading your entries and recording any responses or insights you have. Novelist Anaïs Nin, after years of keeping diaries, reflected on her recorded experiences:

> In the early diaries I speak of my feeling that I am playing many roles demanded of woman, which I have been programmed to play. But I know also that there is a part of myself that stands apart from that and wants some other kind of life, some other kinds of authenticity. R. D. Laing [a contemporary psychiatrist] describes this authenticity as a process of constantly peeling off the false selves. You can do this in many ways but you can also do it by looking at it, for there is so much that we don't want to look at.

Reflecting on notebook entries need not always lead to deep insights. Often a thought will come that's related to your current life. Or you might feel as if you have reexperienced what you've already described. You might then want to extend it. After rereading a dream that she recalled while recording her past, one student wrote:

Returned to the cave dream. The whole experience came back to me, almost as if I were in the dream again. When I finished I felt I was still standing at the cave's mouth. Afraid, unable to move, just staring into the darkness. This is crazy, I thought, why am I scared of going in there. Then I began to imagine I went in. I told myself there was no reason to be afraid of the unknown. Unknown! The word sounded in my mind like a scream. Unknown! That's what the cave was. So I imagined I walked into the darkness. I had to put my hands in front of my face the cave was so black. I felt my way around a turn and there was a blue light ahead—a soft hazy glow. In a moment I was at the edge of an underground pond—more the size of a lake than a pond. It was beautiful. It seemed to glow. It was worth the journey through the dark. This entire imaginary journey took only a second, but I saw some truth in it. It told me that I'm often too timid when I face something I don't know or understand. Thinking the word "unknown" made me realize I'm frightened of it, but if I move ahead with some caution, it will be okay.

The sequence of this entry is simple. The writer reflects on the dream, which led her to again face the dream dilemma: to enter or not enter the cave. She suddenly realizes what the dream suggests to her—the unknown—and then does in fantasy what she was unable to do while dreaming. She finally gains the insight that facing unknowns in her life needn't frighten her.

Whether or not her insight will have any lasting significance is not the point. What's important is that she looked at a part of her life and came away with a message. She's been engaged in self-reflection.

Days 1–5. During this final week of directed notebook entries, spend each day's session both rereading previous entries and recording your responses to them. You might reread several entries before you have a response. That's fine. The appropriate way to do this task is the way that works best for you. Think in terms of what you have learned. Ask yourself whether the lesson could be passed on to someone else in writing.

Writing a Reflective Essay

To write a reflective essay requires a more creative touch than writing a typical college essay. The reflective essay follows no clear pattern; therefore, we can't give you hard—and—fast rules. What we can do is give you some general guidelines.

First, turn to your writer's notebook. Your entries represent the initial phase of a prewriting process. They are probably unedited fragments, that is, bits and pieces of experiences that passed swiftly from your memory to the page. Although some fragments will be nothing more than fleeting thoughts, others will capsulize significant events in your life, events from which you can gain some meaning. Such events might trigger deep emotions. They might hold some mystery. Perhaps one event will represent a milestone in your life. Or perhaps an event that seemed insignificant when it took place has become meaningful over time. Notebook entries that capture such events can launch a reflective essay.

Begin by browsing through your notebook. Look for entries that remind you of previous events that you can now see from a new perspective. Find an event that is meaningful. Such events don't have to be earth-shattering. Often an event that might appear ordinary to others might hold tremendous significance for you. These are "symbolic" events, ones that will reveal some personal insight if you explore them.

Second, after you've identified a meaningful event, make a list of memories you associate with it. Some might already be recorded in your notebook; others will need to be sketched out in new entries. In this prewriting phase, you shouldn't waste time evaluating the associations; you should only identify them without judgment.

Third, after collecting the raw material, you need to shape the whole essay. Like all essays, a reflective essay will have a beginning, a middle, and an end. But unlike a basic college essay, a reflective essay will seldom be organized by a thesis. Instead, the beginning of an reflective essay will usually set the stage for what will follow. It will typically suggest where the writer is headed. It will also include background information, much like the information a fiction writer includes in the opening of a story.

The middle of a reflective essay often weaves together memories of past experiences connected with the central event. The paragraphs, though less rigidly structured than traditional patterns, should begin with sentences that give readers a sense of order. Never let readers stumble in disordered associations, but guide them each step of the way.

The end of the essay reveals the insight you've gained from the experience. This revelation, however, should be suggested, not flatly stated, as the meaningful result of your experience.

Such suggestion is often hard to achieve. To make writing the conclusion easier, we suggest you use an image or thought that leads a reader to reflect on a detail in the essay, one that resonates with significance.

A Student Essay Developed by Reflection

By way of illustration, we offer the following reflective essay. While a freshman student in the 1980s, Larry Swanson, currently a practicing psychotherapist in Southern California, relates an experience he had returning to the home and neighborhood where he was born and raised. His parents were moving to a new house, and his former home was to be destroyed.

Swanson uses the experience to indirectly communicate his feelings about change and to share an insight that comes to him through the encounter. As you read, notice that Swanson never flatly states the purpose behind his essay. Instead, he suggests his feelings by describing early memories he associates with growing up in the old neighborhood. The use of suggestion creates subtle suspense and prepares readers for the final insight.

First read Swanson's opening comment on the piece; then read the entire piece. Finally, reread the essay with Swanson's marginal comments.

My goal for this essay was very clear—I wanted to communicate what "home"and "change" mean to me. By "home" I mean all those deep feelings, often confused feelings, that seem to be located just below consciousness. By "change" I mean a sense of loss and separation.

I recall developing the essay from various notebook entries. Of course, the entries were incomplete in themselves; I had to polish and add information to make everything fit.

One detail I developed while doing the final draft was the use of "Allie, Allie Oxen Free" in the closing section. In children's games of hide and seek, the phrase means the players can come "home" safely, but in the essay I wanted these words to suggest that childhood was over, symbolized by the fact that I would have no childhood home to return to.

Allie, Allie Oxen Free

In the middle of my freshman year in college I returned to my hometown to visit the old neighborhood. It was the last time I could go home. Home—the word has a deep meaning for me.   1

Driven out by a severe drought, my parents came from the cornfields of Nebraska to the house where they lived for thirty-five years. I was born in the back bedroom because, as my mother said, "there just wasn't enough time to get to a hospital." My earliest memories center on playing in that house: pushing trucks over the hardwood floors, my pajama knees mopping up the morning dust; rummaging through my mother's pan drawers and banging them on the linoleum; and hiding behind the over-stuffed couch whenever I was called for lunch. The backyard seemed to stretch the length of a football field and was the place I would chase my older brother and sisters until I fell down, breathless and sweating. Before I started grammar school, I knew all the neighborhood's marvelous places: the avocado tree where my friends and I used to climb to an ancient treehouse that had been built by children before us, the park where the old-timers would sit on benches and laugh at our wild games, the   2 abandoned garage where we used to spy at the neighborhood through knotholes.

All that came back to me as I drove to pick up my parents for a final visit. You see, my home and the surrounding two blocks were to be destroyed. The City Council, those faceless champions of change, had condemned the neighborhood and planned to replace it with a civic center. 3

As I turned onto the street where my parents had bought a tract home, I saw my father, a little stooped since retiring after years of hard labor, standing before the recently seeded lawn that was beginning to sprout slivers of grass. In work boots, khaki trousers, and plaid shirt, which had become faded and thin from too much sun and too many washings, he didn't seem to belong to the stucco house packed with all the modern conveniences I knew my parents had avoided most of their lives. I pulled to the curb and he climbed in. 4

"Where's Mom?" I asked. 5

"Not coming," he said. "Let's go." 6

That was all he had to say to make me understand that Mom didn't want to make a final visit to the old place and to make me realize I didn't either. 7

As we drove, he filled his pipe, lit it, and began puffing—the smoke carrying the smell of Sugar Barrel, a smell I will always associate with him. We chatted about nothing important. "How're classes?" he asked and I answered routinely, knowing that neither of us wanted to say much about losing our home. Then we were on the old street, and the memories seemed to rise in my blood. 8

I first saw the store the Hungarian couple used to run. The advertisements were peeling off the walls, the windows had been boarded up, and the screen door dangled stiffly from one hinge—empty, abandoned. But I remembered how I once spent summer afternoons sitting in front of it and playing Monopoly with my friends or chess with old man Jefferson, a retired sailor. The car seats we used to lounge on were still there, but the stuffing had been torn out and only the springs remained. 9

Then we passed Mr. Salling's house. Tall and bony, Salling was the neighborhood's mysterious figure. The few times I saw him in the sunlight he wore a gray suit and 10 had gray hair and skin. But more often I saw him moving behind the curtains where he paced the darkened parlor or rocked in a creaky chair. I was told he had been "that way" since "losing his wife." He wanted only to be left alone. One morning I learned that he had "left" the night before. I never heard of him again.

We drove past the vacant lot that had been the scene   11 of many of my childhood joys. Each Independence Day the neighborhood fathers would set up a fireworks display and thrill us kids for hours. In the spring we held war games there. Costumed in makeshift army uniforms and wearing plastic helmets and carrying plastic rifles, we dodged through the tall grass and dove into foxholes, shouting "TATATATATA, Gotcha! C'mon you're dead!" During the summer, the lot served as the center for our nightly game of hide-and-seek. As my father and I drove past, I imagined hearing Billy Kieler's voice, the loudest and most melodic among us, echoing throughout the neighborhood, "ALLIE, ALLIE OXEN FREE! ALLIE, ALLIE OXEN FREE!" Billy was the first of my childhood friends to move away. How much had his life changed, I wondered. Yes, how much?

Then we were in front of our old wood-frame home.   12 My father climbed from the car. I looked straight ahead. "Coming?" he said. But before I knew I had made a decision, I said no. I turned in time to see him walk the five steps up to the front porch, unlock the door, and step inside. No, I just could not bring myself to see the house empty, abandoned.

I sat staring at the front lawn and recalled how I   13 had spent hundreds of Saturday mornings mowing the grass, trimming the hedges, and hoeing around the rose bushes. I had hated to spend my Saturday mornings in such labor since I hadn't inherited my dad's love of growing and caring for things. Now the grass was brown and the hedges and rose bushes were dying and I missed the unvarying routine those secure Saturday mornings brought.

In a few moments Dad was returning, lugging a heavy   14 toolbox in each hand. I saw he breathed a little heavy. I went to help him.

"Hard going?" I asked.   15

"It's the last time for me," he said as we hefted the   16
boxes into the car.

At first I didn't make the connection between his   17
words and mine. I had referred to the difficulty he had
carrying the boxes. He referred to much more. He referred
to the illusion I wished to keep. I glanced up the street to
the vacant lot and wished I could hear those comforting
words that meant everything was okay, that the game was
over and I could return home: ALLIE, ALLIE OXEN FREE!

Did you notice how muted Swanson's essay seems, yet how it
still communicates a great deal of emotion? He steadily develops
the scene and memories through description that suggests a
deeper meaning than he reveals overtly. When he does comment it
is done in a quiet way.

Guidelines for Writing a Reflective Essay

The primary methods of development for a reflective essay are
narration and description, so you might want to review Chapters
3 and 4. You will also need to work in some background information and responses, but the main intent is to suggest the meaning
of the experience, not to explain it.

Even though reflective essays are developed by the unique requirements of their subjects, we do recommend that you use the
following procedure:

1. Select an event that means a great deal to you and that brought
    you some personal insight.
2. Use your writer's notebook to trigger memories you associate
    with the experience. Collect the raw material in extended lists.
3. Decide what you wish to communicate to readers. Use it as the
    essay's guiding purpose.
4. Write the essay by beginning with the main experience. Follow
    with a development of the experience while weaving in the asso-
    ciations you've collected.
5. Round off the essay by stating or implying how you feel or what
    you've learned from the experience.

Glossary

Abridgment   A shortened version of a work, but one in which the compiler attempts to include all pertinent parts of the longer work.

Abstract   Abstract words or terms describe ideas, concepts, or qualities, as opposed to **concrete** entities. Sample abstract words and expressions are *philosophy, remorse, happiness, beauty, honor, peace, organizational climate, achievement motive,* and *burden of proof (see* **concrete***)*.

Acronym   A word formed by combining the first letters or syllables of words, to form a new word. An example is BASIC, the word that names a computer language; it is an acronym meaning "Beginner's All-purpose Symbolic Instruction Code."

Ad hominem argument   *See* **Logical fallacies**.

Allusion   An allusion briefly and often casually refers to something the writer believes is common knowledge. If you write that your neighbor's fence "looks like the Berlin Wall," you allude to the state of the Berlin Wall, which is in ruins. "Future Shlock," the title of the Neil Postman essay in Chapter 5, is an allusion to Alvin Toffler's *Future Shock*, a book about what to expect in the future. A Robert Frost poem about the sudden death of a boy is titled " 'Out, Out—,' " an allusion to lines from Shakespeare's *Macbeth*:

> Out, out, brief candle!
> Life's but a walking shadow, a poor player
> That struts and frets his hour upon the stage,
> And then is heard no more. (V,v,23)

Analogy   An analogy is an imaginative comparison between two things, one less familiar than the other, usually intended to clarify a description of the less familiar one. In his novel *The Red and the Black*, the French author Stendhal (Marie Henri Beyle) wrote, "A novel is a mirror that strolls along a highway. Now it reflects the blue of the skies, now the mud puddles underfoot," clarifying his concept of the novel by imaginatively comparing it to a common, familiar item.

Analysis   In an analysis, a writer examines a piece of writing by paying special attention to its elements of thought. An analysis is based on the premise that some ideas or concepts are actually combinations formed of other ideas or concepts. An analysis of an idea or concept as incorporated in an extended piece of writing often shows that many smaller thoughts have been combined into larger thoughts. Analyzing the Pledge of Allegiance to the Flag shows that it includes a definition of an ideal republic, which has its roots in classical Greek philosophy.

Anecdote   An anecdote is an incident, or **narration**, which reveals a facet of character, most often about a well-known person.

Argument   An argument is meant to persuade an audience to accept the qualities of a proposition (a statement to be supported), so that the audience will be convinced of the proposition's truth or falsity. In his commentary on rhetoric, Aristotle spoke of "artistic proofs," so called because they are invented in the sense of being thought up or devised for the specific purpose of swaying an audience to an orator's point of view.

   Aristotelian proofs as they are used when writing arguments appeal to the audience in one of three ways: rationally, emotionally, or ethically. A rational appeal (*logos*) appeals to the audience's reason: an emotional appeal (*pathos*) appeals to the audience's emotions or passions; an ethical appeal (*ethos*) appeals to the audience's confidence in the writer's character or credentials. Today, an argument commonly includes more than one of these proofs, and may also embody such nonartistic proofs as statistics, results of polls, scientific data, and other scientifically verifiable statements.

Association fallacy   *See* **Logical fallacies**.

Audience   An audience is a reader or a class of readers whom writers keep in mind while they write and particularly while they revise their writing. Writers determine as much as they can about their audiences, including their expertise, their education, their biases, their political and cultural background, their assumptions, and their interests. Writers deal with many kinds of audiences, including those who already share the writer's convictions. Each audience affects the writer's way of casting the writing.

Knowing as much as they can about their audiences helps writers determine which **strategies** to use, such as sentence structure, reasoning, **definition**, **emphasis**, organization, and **style**.

Audiences also affect writers' **diction**. A writer aiming at an audience of experienced amateur sailors would use words such as *pulpit* and *roach*, but for an audience knowing nothing of nautical terminology, the writer would use "the platform on the forward part of the ship from which sailors handle and change sails," instead of *pulpit*, and "the curved portion of a sail closest to the rear end of the ship," instead of *roach*.

Body   The main part of a piece of writing is its body. Here, events are dramatized, dialogue is sustained, **conflicts** are developed, and other **strategies** are applied to sustain the reader's involvement.

Categories   Classes or divisions in an organized **classification**. Under the classification *general education requirements*, a writer could list the categories humanities, foreign languages, and sciences. Further, the writer could subcategorize by listing *foreign languages* such as French, Latin, German, and Japanese.

Cause and effect   A cause is that which came before an effect, the effect being the result of that cause. Combined, *cause and effect* is a useful way of analyzing reasons for actions and for the results of those actions. In the sentence, "Because Gwen did not study, she failed the calculus examination," one can see the immediate cause and the immediate effect. But what ultimate cause was behind Gwen's not studying? Not even Gwen can be absolutely sure, because most causes in our daily lives are probable, not certain. Aware of this uncertainty, writers use with caution the cause-and-effect strategy.

Circumlocution   Circumlocution in writing fails to make a point clearly or evades a point because many words are used where fewer would have sufficed. The sentence, "What is the cause of the source of his pain cannot be other than his appendix, which seems to be less than healthy," illustrates circumlocution. The sentence could have been recast as, "His pain is probably caused by appendicitis."

Claim The philosopher and rhetorician Stephen Toulmin devised a model of reasoning similar to the **syllogism**. One of the Toulmin model's primary elements is *claim*, which is the conclusion. The other two elements are *data*, which form the evidence, and *warrant*, which is the supporting argument. This sentence briefly illustrates the Toulmin model: Jasmah is a physicist (*data*); therefore, Jasmah is intelligent (*claim*) because all physicists are intelligent (*warrant*).

Classification Classification is a system for sorting things into distinct categories, or classes. A music lover might want to organize her cassettes. After sorting them, she sees that she can classify them into these categories, according to types of music: jazz, classical, and country and western. Later, perhaps when she wants to write a paper about her jazz cassettes, she can classify them into categories according to the musical styles of the featured artists on her tapes, making sure that each category is described clearly so that it is distinct from other categories.

Cliché In French the *cliché* is an outmoded system for making metal printing plates with which to print the same thing again and again. In English the name describes words and phrases that have been used again and again so that they have become worn out, tired. Examples abound: A person can be "as old as the hills." A night can be "as black as coal." We can be "afraid of our own shadow." Someone can have "an ax to grind." A child can be "a chip off the old block." A trend can be "here today; gone tomorrow." An employee can be "a square peg in a round hole." A project can "start from scratch." When revising, writers "keep an eye peeled" for clichés so that they can replace those with fresh, colorful expressions of their own **invention**.

Climax In a **narration** essay the climax is the conclusion, the highest point of interest. In other kinds of writing the climax, or peak of interest, marks the turning point in the action.

Coherence Coherence clearly, consistently, and logically connects the parts in a piece of writing. It is the glue that holds together all vigorous, effective writing. Among other techniques, coherence invokes **transitions** to show introductory relationships among ideas, paragraphing to signal shifts in thought, sentences that follow reasonably from those which came before them, and **diction** appropriate to the **audience**.

Colloquial expressions   Colloquial expressions, such as "Don't even try to psych out Professor Sherman" and "Ralph crammed all his stuff into his closet" characterize informal (and often playful) speaking and writing. Therefore they have limited use in formal writing because their very casualness can distract readers.

Comparison and contrast   A comparison involves similarities; a contrast involves differences. Combining these two ways of judging qualities can lead to discoveries about two things formerly thought to be ordinarily alike or unalike. A writer who compares and contrasts an electric typewriter and a computer discovers that whatever an electric typewriter can do, a computer with a word-processing program and printer can do more efficiently (a comparison). The writer will also discover the many things that a computer, equipped with various programs, can do that a typewriter cannot possibly do, such as maintaining a continuous record of household expenditures (a contrast). On the other hand, the writer will discover that both machines can be used for writing brief informal notes, but a computer can also retain easily correctable copies of those notes on a disk (comparison and contrast).

Conclusions   Conclusions are ways of ending essays. The way in which an essay is concluded depends in great part on the content of the essay itself. An essay arguing for or against gun control is likely to end by restating the reasons for taking one position or another. An essay explaining one of the complex relationships between human beings and nature might conclude by warning the reader that the relationship is endangered. An essay with several examples of how the world's economies are intertwined might end with one sterling example of an economy that is vitally connected to our own. An essayist offering information about an inexpensive medicine for a common disease might conclude by recommending that readers consult their personal physicians for more information.

Conclusions do not drift into other topics, nor do they shift an essay's emphasis away from its own topic. A writer would not end an essay taking a firm stand against showing pornographic movies on television by writing something like, "It all depends on each person's tastes."

So-called cute conclusions suggest to the audience that the writer was not deeply involved in thinking about the essay's content. They should be avoided.

Conclusions grow logically and sufficiently from the essay, and they should bring an essay to a satisfying close.

Concrete   Concrete words or expressions refer to things experienced by the senses, as opposed to **abstractions**. These words and expressions are concrete: *chair, perfume, music, automobile, bitter, cardboard box, dictionary, window,* and *refrigerator.*

Conflict   In writing, a conflict is a struggle that grows from two opposing beliefs, values, characters, and so on, which are developed in the **body** of the piece.

Connotation   The word *connotation* describes the implied meanings that become attached to words. *Skinny* and *slender* both mean thin or slight, but the first has negative connotations (emaciation and perhaps ill health), and the latter implies grace, even elegance.

The descriptive phrase *cheap furniture* carries connotations of shoddy workmanship and poor quality. The phrase *inexpensive furniture,* however, implies only the furniture's low cost. Although *cheap* and *inexpensive* are dictionary synonyms, the meaning implied in *cheap* sets it apart from *inexpensive.* Careful writers keep in mind what words mean according to dictionaries and what those same words may imply beyond their dictionary definitions.

Data   The proofs in Stephen Toulmin's model of reasoning are *data.* They are the evidence that supports the model's **claim**, or conclusion.

Data are also nonartistic proofs (see **argument**) used in other models of reasoning. These kinds of data come from scientific observations, record keeping, or statistics—facts or figures from which conclusions can be inferred, and information from credible, reliable sources.

Deduction   A deduction is the result of reasoning from a general statement to a specific instance. If your college requires that all prospective students be tested in a foreign language before they are enrolled, then you can reason that Pat, who sits next to you in

English class, has taken a test in a foreign language. Deductions are not always that clear-cut, though.

One might think that all small cars get good gas mileage and then buy a small car to save money on fuel, only to find that this car gets poor mileage. The original assumption, then, was false.

Definition   A definition outlines, limits, or states the meaning of a word, term, phrase, or concept.

A formal definition puts a term into a class and then shows how it differs from other members of the same class. A trumpet (term) is a brass musical wind instrument (class) consisting of a tube in an oblong loop or loops, with a flared bell at one end, a curved mouthpiece at the other, and three valves for making tonal changes (difference).

An extended definition, a form of **exposition**, not only defines in the senses above but also explains issues by employing rhetorical strategies, such as **narration, description, example,** and **classification.**

Denotation   The term *denotation* applies to the literal, lexical meaning of a word—that which is explained in a good dictionary.

Description   The technique of making pictures with words is *description.* An effective description includes clear evidence that appeals to one or more of the senses—sight, touch, taste, smell, or hearing—as well as **explanation.** Henry David Thoreau's "The Battle of the Ants," in Chapter 6, demonstrates this combination of description and explanation: "his own breast was all torn away, exposing what vitals he had there to the jaws of the black warrior, whose breastplate was apparently too thick for him to pierce; and the dark carbuncles of the sufferer's eyes shone with ferocity such as only war could excite."

Diction   Diction is deliberate choice of words. Writers conscientiously choose words and the ways in which they use them, being guided by their audience and their purpose. Writers make their selections from various levels of usage, including **standard English, slang,** conversational expressions, regionalisms (choosing among "spigot," "tap," and "faucet"), and scientific and technical **jargon.**

Consider these sentences:

1. "Christine resigned her position."
2. "Chris quit her job."
3. "Chris told him he could take his job and shove it!"

What determines which of these sentences is correct? The audience and the purpose.

Sentence 1 is appropriate for a formal audience and a formal purpose. Perhaps the writer's audience was college-level readers and the purpose was to describe her best friend's employment difficulties.

Sentence 2 might have been for a semiformal audience and a semiformal purpose, such as writing an essay for the readers of a college alumnae newsletter to help graduates keep track of their classmates.

Sentence 3 might have been for an informal audience and purpose, such as writing an essay for other members of a composition class to explain how one of them had reacted to being treated poorly by the manager of a local pizza parlor.

Whoever the audience and whatever the purpose, writers are guided by their own sense of propriety and by dictionaries and a thesaurus. They rarely use a thesaurus, however, without also consulting a dictionary to be sure that the words they have chosen from the thesaurus are in fact appropriate for their audience and purpose.

Directive process analysis   A directive process analysis tells how to do something. It is a sequence of directions to guide a reader who wants to complete a specific task. Such an analysis tells how to plant a tree, but *not* how a tree grows, the latter topic being an **informative process analysis**.

Division   Division is a subclass of **classification**. Writers divide a classification into logical parts, usually for description or explanation. Let's say that a writer wanted to describe a personal computer. First, you would classify it, telling how it differs from mainframe computers, from large industrial computers, and from laptop computers. Then you would divide the home computer into its logical parts: the keyboard, the central processing unit, and the video monitor. After making that division, you would describe each of these components. By your division you help the reader to see one component at a time, rather than try to imagine an entire home computer all at once.

Dominant impression   The dominant impression is the main sensation or conception that the author strives to fix in the reader's mind, by carefully shaping the details of a **description**.

Effect   It is part of **cause and effect**, the result or outcome of an occurrence or action, but the word *effect* also refers to the impression that writing—whether a word, sentence, paragraph, essay, or larger work—makes on its audience.

Emphasis   With emphasis, writers emphasize or highlight the things they want their readers to see as most important in their writing. Writers use such **strategies** as **diction**, sentence structure, position, active voice, repetition, and mechanics to emphasize their main points.

Diction: A writer who wanted to emphasize a negative opinion of a newly opened restaurant could write, "This restaurant has food fit to eat only if you are starving."

Sentence structure: If you wanted to emphasize your opinion of the food itself, you could write a periodic sentence, which moves from supporting details to the main idea. "With lukewarm coffee, half-cooked cold chicken, salty mashed potatoes, and burned vegetables, my meal was barely edible." You could emphasize your description of the food by writing a loose sentence, in which the supporting details follow the main idea: "I had a barely edible meal of lukewarm coffee, half-cooked cold chicken, salty mashed potatoes, and burned vegetables."

Position: That which we read last, we remember longest, whether chapters in a book, groups of words in a sentence, or paragraphs in an essay. Commenting on an unsavory experience in a restaurant, you might begin a paper by describing how you had read about the restaurant in a respectable tourist guide, where it had been awarded three stars. Then you might devote a short paragraph to the small problem you had in finding the place because it was in a part of the city unfamiliar to the taxicab driver, who had been profusely apologetic. You then might describe the restaurant's décor, a delightful amalgam of French Provincial and

Early American, and your waitress, a pleasant young lady dressed in a peasant frock, who was also attending law school at the nearby university. Finally, because you had been shocked at the poor quality of the food, in utter contrast to the treat you had been expecting, you might conclude the essay with a paragraph meant to shock your readers as well, thus emphasizing the most important point in your experience by putting it last.

Active voice: Verbs in active voice—"This restaurant serves poorly prepared food"—are more emphatic than those in passive voice: "Poorly prepared food is served by this restaurant."

Repetition: "I spent a valuable hour of my vacation sipping the lukewarm coffee at Harry's Restaurant, chewing Harry's half-cooked chicken, tasting the salty mashed potatoes at Harry's, and staring at the vegetables Harry burned. Never again will I eat in Harry's Restaurant."

Mechanics: Usually, the least appropriate way to emphasize formal writing, mechanics include underlining, quotation marks, and exclamation points: "When I was served the 'food' I had ordered in this 'restaurant,' I was *shocked* to see how *poorly* it had been prepared!" Such devices must be used sparingly. Your emphasis will be more successfully communicated with diction, sentence structure, position, active voice, and repetition.

Essay   The word *essay* is from the French *essai*, meaning "attempt" or "experiment." In English, an essay is a relatively short piece of nonfiction prose on a specified topic. It is an attempt by a writer to persuade, inform, explain, argue, describe, narrate, expose, or in some other way organize and develop a topic to interest an **audience**.

Essays are occasionally defined as informal or formal, although the definitions admittedly are vague. Generally, however, a formal essay includes **diction** appropriate to a serious audience, has a serious **tone**, and is focused on a serious topic. An informal essay, on the other hand, often has a light, perhaps humorous tone and informal language, and is focused on a personal, perhaps frivolous topic.

Evaluation   An evaluation determines the worth or quality of a work. If you are revising your own work or reading someone else's, you try to evaluate it objectively, to see how well it fulfills its purpose. Usually, those who evaluate a work look to see how well its thesis is stated and supported, how strongly its proofs support its claims, how clearly it is organized, whether or not its language is clear, and whether or not it is appropriately written for its intended audience.

Evidence   Evidence is support for a theory, claim, or **thesis**. The commonest kinds of evidence are obvious evidence, manifest evidence, and clear evidence. Obvious evidence, usually scientific, is readily perceived or easily inferred. If $6 + 2 + x = 9$, then the evidence is obvious that $x = 1$. Manifest evidence is immediately clear to the understanding, often by intuition. If you see water in its solid state, then you know almost without thinking that it is frozen. Clear evidence, the kind essayists use most often, supports and clarifies a reader's understanding of the writer's thesis. If the writer's thesis is that marriage vows are hopelessly outmoded, then you must offer clear evidence to support that thesis. You must examine and clarify the vows, compare them with the spousal responsibilities in modern marriages, illustrate how those vows conflict with reality, and so on.

Examples   An example is an instance that follows and illustrates the assertion in a statement. Among the more usual are specific examples, typical examples, and hypothetical examples. Specific examples amplify one experience, event, incident, or fact. They clarify in detail your earlier statement. Typical examples illustrate many experiences, events, incidents, or facts. They clarify generally your earlier statement, so that they will be representative. Hypothetical examples are imagined or supposed representations. They clarify the probability of your earlier statement.

Exposition   An exposition is a detailed explanation of the content of an idea, an object, an attitude, or a position. An exposition exposes, makes something accessible to a reader, by using any of a number of **strategies**, including examples, comparisons and contrasts, analogies, and classifications. Most essays in this book are expository, as are most essays written in college.

False analogy   *See* **Logical fallacies.**

Faulty either/or reasoning   *See* **Logical fallacies.**

Figures of speech   Tropes, or figures of speech, make a clear style vivid by adding **connotations** to statements, which appeal to the reader's imagination. The most used figures of speech are metaphor, simile, personification, hyperbole (overstatement), litotes (understatement), synecdoche, metonymy, and paradox.

A *metaphor* is an implied comparison between two dissimilar things: "Jamie is the tiger on the team." Tigers are noted for their speed, intelligence, and strength—the attributes that this metaphor gives to Jamie.

A *simile* is an explicit comparison between two dissimilar things, using the word *as* or *like:* "Jamie is as southern as Georgia."

Personification gives human qualities to inanimate objects or abstract ideas: "Six tall, menacing pine trees guard our campus at night."

Hyperbole (overstatement) is deliberate exaggeration used for emphasis: "It was raining so hard that I almost drowned while driving to school."

Litotes (understatement) is deliberate understatement used for emphasis: "Getting a D on my history test was not my greatest birthday present."

Synecdoche substitutes part of something for the whole: "Two hands left the ship just before it sailed." In this example, *hands* substitutes for "sailors."

Metonymy substitutes the whole for a part of something: "The Pentagon said today that, except for Near Eastern flareups, fewer troops will be needed in the next decade." In this example, *The Pentagon* substitutes for "a spokesperson for the army."

A *paradox* appears to be contradictory, but in fact carries some truth: "The wealthier you are, the poorer you may be." Wealth is not always measured by money. It is also measured by wisdom, knowledge, morality, love, and other qualities.

Focus   In photography a subject that is in focus is sharply defined. That is also true in writing. Writers who focus on their subject bring it into sharp detail. They begin by thinking about a large unfocused topic, such as "crime in the streets." Then they may decide to focus on some part of crime in the streets—"street crime in our city." After they have found their focus, they may narrow it even more—to "street crime in my neighborhood."

How sharply they focus on a subject often depends on their **audience** and **purpose**.

General and specific   General words are names for broad classes of things, from which you can move to words that designate members of those classes. One broad class is *automobiles*. A term that designates a member of that class is *sports car*. A designation for a more specific member of the sports-car class is *Alfa Romeo*. Writers are guided by their **audience** and by their **purpose** when they choose among general and specific names.

Generalization   A generalization is a broad statement that rests on personal observation or acquired information. The sentence "Children usually follow their parents' advice" suggests that its writer has experience with raising children and from that experience has written a generalization that includes all children.

   Writers sometimes begin with generalizations and then move toward conclusions based on their generalizations. But to avoid hasty generalizations, they often use qualifiers in their conclusions: "She has a degree in English, and so she *probably* knows a lot about Shakespeare." Or "She has a degree in English, and so she *might* know *something* about Shakespeare." *See also* **induction**.

Hyperbole   *See* **Figures of speech**.

Hypothetical examples   *See* **Examples**.

Image   An image appeals to the imagination through the senses. It is a **strategy** many writers apply to help readers "see" what they are reading. The sentence, "Her ancient face was a sheaf of small etched road maps to nowhere," is an image that describes an old and wrinkled countenance. The sentence, "He sings the songs of an old man's childhood, the golden past that never was," describes a person who reminisces about former times, which seem far more attractive now ("the golden past") than they were then.

Induction   An induction is the result of reasoning that interprets limited evidence to arrive at a general truth. A person who has owned three or four friendly and alert cocker spaniels over the years may reason that all cocker spaniels are friendly and alert.

   Inductive reasoning is useful in writing because it is a powerful persuader. Writers who want to persuade readers of a gen-

eral truth use enough sound evidence to make their claims reasonably acceptable. If you wanted to persuade readers of the
benefits in jogging, you might offer as evidence all your healthy
friends who jog, newspaper articles that endorse jogging as a
healthy activity, well-known athletes who jog, your doctor's saying that jogging promotes health, and so on. The more sound evidence you present, the more apt the reader is to accept your
persuasive **argument**.

Informative process analysis   With an informative process analysis, you tell how something is done. You describe sequentially
the steps in a natural procedure that does not involve interven-
tion. An informative process analysis might tell how a tree grows,
but *not* how to plant a tree, the latter topic being a **directive
process analysis**.

Introduction   An introduction begins a piece of writing. An effective introduction establishes the essay's topic, tone, and territory. It leads directly into the main idea or issue discussed
in the **body** of the paper. Its purpose is to engender readers'
interest. To achieve that purpose, writers include such **strategies** as **rhetorical questions**, unusual facts, **anecdotes**, and
personal comments.

The length of an introduction depends on the essay's **purpose** and its intended **audience**.

Invention   Writers use invention to develop their subjects. It includes planning the piece of writing, thinking of ways of organizing material, of presenting material, and of deciding how to
handle questions that you anticipate readers will raise

Irony   A difference between appearance and reality creates irony.
When it compliments, it is ironically condemning. When it
condemns, it is ironically complimenting. The sentence "What
a magnificent car," when used to describe a rusting hulk sitting in a junkyard, is ironic. The sentence "It's not a bad paint
job," when used to describe Michelangelo's Sistine Chapel ceiling, is ironic. When the irony is not subtle but is intended to
cause deliberate offense, it is called **sarcasm**. If someone says,
"Thank you. It's just what I've always wanted," when reacting
to the ketchup stain you accidentally put on her new blouse,
she is using sarcasm.

When they are contrary to our anticipation, situations can also be ironic. You might discover that you were not hired for a job because you failed a company's mandatory typing test, only to learn that the job for which you applied required no typing at all.

Jargon   Jargon is technical vocabulary that is appropriate only among experts in a field. As a kind of shorthand, it saves time in their communication. Among themselves lawyers use such expressions as "caveat," "entrapment," "estoppel," "the M'Naghten Rule," and "mens rea," knowing that they all understand legal jargon. To a lay listener, however, the words mean little. For lay audiences, writers use jargon sparingly, and when they do use it, they include definitions.

Another kind of jargon, sometimes called bureaucratese, is nothing more than pompous **diction** used more to impress readers than to inform them. The sentence "Our consumer demand analysis precludes our implementation of the proposed planning stage"—which means, by the way, "We don't need to plan to produce something that no one wants to buy"—typifies the jargon of pomposity.

Litotes   *See* **Figures of speech**.

Logical fallacies   Mistakes in reasoning that lead to faulty conclusions are logical fallacies or fallacious reasoning.

An *ad hominem argument* attacks a person rather than the issue that is being considered.

The *association fallacy* suggests that an act or belief is worthy or unworthy merely because of the people who are associated with it.

A writer falls into *false analogy* by presuming that if two things are alike in one or more ways, then they must be alike in other ways as well.

The *either/or fallacy* is a type of oversimplification in which a writer assumes only two alternatives are possible when in fact many others should be considered.

A *non sequitur* is a conclusion that does not follow from the premise.

A writer making an *overgeneralization* draws a conclusion from insufficient or unrepresentative evidence.

With an *oversimplification*, we draw a conclusion while ignoring information essential to the subject.

Someone who accepts the *post hoc* argument assumes that if one event occurred before another, then the second event was caused by the first.

Metaphor *See* **Figures of speech**.

Metonymy *See* **Figures of speech**.

Narration A narration tells a story and often includes extensive **description**. Narrations, usually chronological, include among their purposes entertaining, informing, and instructing. Some narrations have a plot, a story line that moves toward an insight about the principal character in the narration.

Narrative effect The main **effect** from reading a **narration** is named the *narrative effect*. Each narration incorporates a reason for being. Writers decide the main effect that their narrative should have on their readers, and then form the narrative so as not to depart from their decision.

Non sequitur *See* **Logical fallacies**.

Nonstandard English Words and expressions that are often spoken but rarely written except when the writer has a clear reason for using them sometimes include nonstandard English. Some examples are *ain't, nohow, irregardless, theirselves, hisself, we'uns, could care less* (for "could not care less"), and *them* (instead of *those*), as in *Them people ain't got no smarts*, instead of "Those people do not seem intelligent."

Objective and subjective Objective writing is designed to be a distanced, factual account presented in language that is plain, direct, and free of value judgments. Pure objectivity is hard to achieve because people's perceptions are almost always colored by their experiences, their values, and their biases. But in writing such as scientific papers and technical reports, authors strive for objectivity. Subjective writing is more personal, more indicative of the writer's thoughts, feelings, and attitudes. The emphasis here is on the writer's relationship to the topic rather than the topic itself. Very few essays are exclusively objective or subjective. Most often, writings combine the two.

Opening   An opening is the first part of a three-part narrative essay. The other two parts are the body and the climax. The beginning sentences usually capture the reader's attention without giving away the outcome. The opening may hint at the purpose of the story about to unfold, but may not actually reveal it.

Order of ideas   Ideas can be arranged in various ways, but all are derived from the subject and the writer's purpose. The order may be spatial, moving from top to bottom, side to side, or background to foreground. Or the order may simply be chronological, as in a narrative. The writer may work from least important to most important. The sequence of ideas should always be well thought out, chosen for its greatest effect.

Overgeneralization   *See* **Logical fallacies**.

Oversimplification   *See* **Logical fallacies**.

Paradox   *See* **Figures of speech**.

Paragraph   The paragraph is the basic unit in an essay. It is composed of a group of closely related sentences that together develop one of the essay's main ideas. The main or unifying idea of a paragraph is usually stated in a topic sentence, often found at the beginning of the paragraph. All other sentences in the paragraph relate directly to the topic sentence, thus establishing unity and coherence. But occasionally, a unified and coherent paragraph has no topic sentence. The paragraph then undoubtedly has a leading idea that is strongly implied in every sentence. Paragraphs also work visually in an essay, graphically demonstrating the progress of ideas and also providing visual relief to the reader.

Parallel structure   The repetition of similar grammatical elements within or between sentences makes a parallel structure. Logic dictates that grammatical elements with equal value in a sentence be constructed in the same grammatical form. Thus "I prefer running, jumping, and to swim" does not exhibit parallelism, but does have awkwardness. "I prefer running, jumping, and swimming" demonstrates parallelism and logic. Parallel structure is also a stylistic technique that is often used to create emphasis and drama. The long fourth sentence in paragraph 14 of Martin Luther King, Jr.'s "Letter from Birmingham Jail" (Chapter 12) is a particularly effective example of parallel structure.

Paraphrase   A paraphrase is a restatement of another person's words in your own words. This technique is particularly necessary in writing any essay in which you use others' ideas or words as evidence supporting your own argument. Often, you paraphrase instead of using a direct quotation in order to more easily mold the idea to fit your argument. The sense of the original, as well as the tone and order of ideas, remains the same. In either a paraphrase or a direct quotation you must give credit to your source. In a more informal paper you incorporate the credit into your text: "According to Charles Neerland, being a Minneapolitan means being cold much of the year." In more formal writing, such as a research paper, footnoting is required.

Person   The grammatical distinction between the speaker (first person: I, we); the person spoken to (second person: you, singular and plural); and the subject spoken about (third person: he, she, it, or they) is labeled *person*.

Persona   A fictional speaker in an essay or the fictional narrator of a story is its persona. The character, attitudes, and ideas of the persona are often different from those of the author. In fact, it is often the persona's character, attitudes, and ideas that are held up for criticism. The persona of Swift's "A Modest Proposal" (Chapter 12) voices ideas that Swift obviously finds abhorrent.

Personification   *See* **Figures of speech**.

Persuasion or persuasive argument   Persuasive writing is an attempt to win readers to a point of view and, often, move them to action. It appeals primarily to the emotions, as opposed to *argument*, which is meant to win the reader by reason and logic. Most often, the two are used together.

Plagiarism   Presenting someone else's words or ideas as if they were your own is plagiarism. It is a serious offense in the academic world and can lead to consequences such as failure and expulsion from school. Whenever you use someone else's words or ideas you must give that person credit in your own text or by citation (*see* **paraphrase**).

Point-by-point and subject-by-subject development   These are the two basic methods for developing a comparison-and-contrast essay. Point-by-point development alternately presents each point being considered. Subject-by-subject development presents all the details about one side of the argument first and follows with all the details about the other side.

Point of view   In an argumentative essay the point of view is the author's opinion or the thesis the writer hopes to advance. In expository essays it is the physical or mental vantage point from which the author views the subject. An essay on professional football told from a player's firsthand experience would be approached differently from that of the team's owner (whose interest may be exclusively financial) or from that of a newspaper reporter. Each would approach the subject with a different kind of authority. And that authority would mean a difference in vocabulary, style, and tone. The player might use first **person** to capture immediacy. The owner might want to involve the reader in experiencing her financial woes and so use second person. Or, to create a mood of objectivity, the reporter might use the third person. The point of view in an essay must remain consistent. An inconsistent point of view can leave the reader confused and disconcerted.

Post hoc argument   *See* **Logical fallacies**.

Premise   A deductive **syllogism** is composed of two premises and a conclusion. The first or major premise is an assumption, and the second or minor premise is a fact or another assumption based on evidence: All mammals are animals (first premise is an assumption). Raccoons are mammals (second premise is a fact). Therefore, all raccoons are animals (conclusion is logically deduced from the two premises).

Prewriting   All the activities a writer goes through before actually beginning to write are part of *prewriting*. These might consist of brainstorming for a subject, doing background reading, narrowing the subject, devising a thesis, planning the essay—everything, in other words, that leads to the actual writing.

Probable conclusions   Conclusions arrived at by inductive reasoning and from incomplete evidence are *probable conclusions*. The reader's acceptance of a conclusion that follows from inductive reasoning is often referred to as the *inductive leap*. To establish a clear connection between the evidence and the conclusion, the writer must be sure to present **relevant evidence, sufficient evidence**, and **representative evidence**.

Proposition or thesis   In argument the proposition or thesis is a written assertion, the opinion the writer wants a reader to accept, or an action the writer wants a reader to take.

Psychological time   Arranging events in a narrative so as to show how they are connected in memory, shifting back and forth in time while keeping a sense of forward movement, creates *psychological time*.

Purpose   The goal the writer wants to achieve is the *purpose*. The clearer the writer's purpose, the more clarity, coherence, and unity the essay will have. If the writer's purpose is muddled, the essay too will be muddled. All kinds of purposes are possible: to entertain with an amusing story; to inform; to convince readers of a point of view and move them to action. These purposes can be achieved by using the rhetorical modes: narration, description, exposition, and argument. In an essay you may use them alone or in combination.

Qualification   Tempering broad statements to make them more logically acceptable is the technique called *qualification*. In qualifying a statement, the writer admits that exceptions to that assertion are possible or probable, thereby indicating that the statement is not oversimplified. In these days with much emphasis on physical fitness, the statement "Physical exercise is good" might, at first blush, seem valid. But exercise may, in fact, be detrimental to some people. Therefore the statement needs qualifying. "Exercise is good for most people" might be a more acceptable statement.

Reason and result   Another way of saying **cause and effect**.

Refutation   The attempt to counter an opposing argument by revealing its weaknesses is called *refutation*. You must refute the opposition's argument if it is obvious and is strong or logical enough to be a real alternative to your own. The refutation usually is done early in an argumentative essay to get it out of the way so that you can proceed with your own argument. The three most usual strategies are pointing our weaknesses in the opposition's evidence, questioning the argument's relevance, and pointing out errors in logic. Refutation indicates that the writer is aware the issue is complex and is willing to consider opposing opinions. To be effective, refutation must always be done in a moderate tone and must always be accurate in representing the opposing argument. To do otherwise is to risk being judged harshly by the reader for sounding intemperate and for treating the opposition unfairly.

Relevant evidence   You can directly support the essay's thesis and contribute directly to its conclusion with relevant evidence (*see* **representative evidence** and **sufficient evidence**).

Representative evidence   Representative evidence covers the full range of information related to an essay's thesis, not just one side or the other. An argument cannot be convincing unless evidence from every point of view is admitted (*see* **relevant evidence** and **sufficient evidence**).

Representative sample   A representative sample is a typical example chosen from examples that exhibit similar characteristics.

Rhetoric   Rhetoric is the study and art of using prose effectively. The various methods of prose discourse described and exemplified in this textbook—narration, description, exposition, and argument—are rhetorical forms.

Rhetorical question   A rhetorical question is posed for effect and no answer is expected. It is a question meant to provoke thought or to launch the writer into the subject to be discussed in the writing.

Satire   The form of writing using wit, irony, and ridicule to attack foolish and vicious human behavior and the institutions and customs that promote such behavior is *satire*. Two main types of satire are at the writer's disposal: social satire, which is used to attack foolish but not dangerous behavior and does it by invoking laughter and sympathy and ethical satire, which is far sharper and points with anger and indignation at social corruption and evil (*see* Jonathan Swift's "A Modest Proposal" in Chapter 12).

Sentimentality   Sentimental writing overemotionalizes its subject and thus becomes ineffective. Sentimentality is often emotion displayed for the sake of emotion, losing connection with the actuality of the thing that supposedly caused the emotion. Sentimental writers risk readers' ridicule because they don't fully acquaint the reader with that actuality and thus appear to overreact.

Simile   *See* **Figures of speech**.

Slang   Colorful and humorous expressions, mostly short-lived and often peculiar to a group of people, are called *slang*. Almost always informal, slang is unacceptable in formal writing except in quotations and for creating special effects.

Specific examples   *See* **Examples**.

Standard English   The English language in its most widely accepted form, written and spoken by educated people in both formal and informal contexts, and having universal currency though it incorporates regional differences, is *standard English*.

Strategy   The means by which writers effectively accomplish their purpose is *strategy*, which involves evaluating the audience, narrowing the subject, choosing a dominant rhetorical pattern such as narration, description, examples, comparison and contrast, and definition, among others.

Style   The distinctive way in which a writer writes creates an individual *style*. Choice of words, structure of sentences, use or nonuse of figurative language—all contribute to a writer's style. Two writers may write about the same subject, have the same attitude toward the subject (*see* **tone**), and yet "sound" distinctly different. Style is a writer's writing personality and can be developed with practice.

Subject-by-subject development   *See* **Point-by-point development**.

Sufficient evidence   In an argumentative paper you must supply ample evidence to convincingly support your conclusion (*see* **relevant evidence** and **representative evidence**).

Summary   A summary is a comprehensive and usually brief recapitulation of previously stated facts or statements. Summarizing your main points is one way of concluding a paper.

Suspense   The pleasurable uncertainty or excitement we feel when anticipating what will happen next as we read a story is *suspense*. This tactic is most evident in mystery or detective stories but is less dramatically present in much narration.

Syllogism   A form of deductive reasoning composed of two premises and a conclusion is the *syllogism*. The first premise (major premise) is an assumption and the second (minor premise) is a fact or another assumption based on **evidence**. The conclusion is logically deduced from the two premises: All human beings are animals (major premise is an assumption). Ephraim is a human (minor premise is a fact). Therefore, Ephraim is an animal (conclusion is logically deduced from the two premises).

Symbol   A symbol is any concrete thing that means something beyond itself. Many symbols are, on the surface, clear-cut and readily acceptable. The flag, of course, represents country and elicits patriotic feeling. But ideas and attitudes differ about what constitutes patriotism and what things conjure patriotic feelings. Some people become proud when their country asserts itself militarily. Others find their patriotic values in freedom, tolerance, fairness, and compassion. The flag, a rather simple symbol as symbols go, therefore has a complex of powerful meanings beyond itself. Symbols are employed most in fiction and poetry, less in exposition and argument. But they can be used in the latter to express meaning concisely and palpably.

Synecdoche   *See* **Figures of speech**.

Thesis   The thesis is the main point in expository writing, an idea that all the other ideas and facts in an essay should point to and support. A thesis can be either clearly stated or implied. It is most commonly found at the end of an early paragraph. A thesis cannot be a statement of fact, because facts do not need proving. A thesis, therefore, must have an argumentative edge, a point of view that will be proven or demonstrated in some way somewhere in the paper.

Tone   Diction, sentence variety, figurative language, and anything else that establishes the writer's attitude toward the subject forms the tone, which can vary extensively. A writer's tone can be amused, angry, exasperated, approving, surprised, sarcastic. It can, in other words, run the gamut of human emotions. But tone should be consistent, for it must inform the entire essay and lead the reader to the response the writer desires.

Topic sentence A topic sentence states the main idea of a paragraph. All other sentences in the paragraph support the topic sentence. Most often, it appears at the beginning but can be placed anywhere in the paragraph.

Transitions Transitions are words, phrases, sentences, and paragraphs that link ideas. Because a reader cannot get into the writer's head, it is the writer's responsibility to make sure that the ideas are clearly stated and that relationships between the ideas are clear. The first way to ensure that clarity is to organize ideas so that they flow logically from one to another. But even sturdier bridges are needed to carry the reader from sentence to sentence and from paragraph to paragraph. For this continuity you will need to use transitional devices such as these:

1. In the first sentence of a paragraph, repeat some words or phrases from the last sentences in the preceding paragraph.
2. Use pronouns to refer to nouns in the preceding paragraph. You must be careful here to make precisely clear which words the pronouns refer to.
3. Use transitional expressions to carry the reader.
   Addition: also, in addition, too, moreover, and besides, further, furthermore, equally important, next, then, finally.
   Example: for example, for instance, thus, as an illustration, namely, specifically.
   Contrast: but, yet, however, on the other hand, nevertheless, conversely, in contrast, on the contrary, still, at the same time.
   Comparison: similarly, likewise, in like manner, in the same way, in comparison.
   Concession: of course, to be sure, certainly, naturally, granted.

Result: therefore, thus, consequently, so, accordingly.

Summary: as a result, hence, in short, in brief, in summary, in conclusion, finally, on the whole.

Time sequence: first, second, third, fourth, next, then, finally, afterward, before, soon, later, during, meanwhile, subsequently, immediately, at length, eventually, in the future, currently.

Place: at the front, in the foreground, at the back, in the background, at the side, adjacent, nearby, in the distance, here, there.

Two-part classification Often called *binary*, two-part classification is the simplest way of breaking a subject down. This pattern divides the subject in two, usually into positive and negative categories, such as vegetarians and nonvegetarians; smokers and nonsmokers; television viewers and nonviewers of television, and so on. But two-part classification is usually inexact and skirts the edge of comparison and contrast. Most classification systems therefore have at least three categories.

Typical examples *See* **Examples**.

Understatement (Litotes) *See* **Figures of speech**.

Unity In a paragraph, every idea and every sentence relates directly to and helps support the main idea, usually stated in the topic sentence. Likewise, in the essay as a whole, every unified paragraph points to and supports the essay's main idea expressed in the thesis.

Warrant Warrant is the supporting argument in Toulmin's model of reasoning (*see* **Claim**).

Writing process The various tasks a writer must perform to produce a piece of writing are called the writing process. **Prewriting** entails a series of activities that pave the way for the actual writing. Only after this stage can the writer make the first draft, revise it into a number of subsequent drafts, and then polish it to achieve the final product.

Acknowledgments

"What You See Is the Real You" by Willard Gaylin, from *The New York Times,* October 7, 1977, OP-ED. Copyright © 1977 by the New York Times Co. Reprinted by permission.

"Photographs of My Parents" from *The Woman Warrior* by Maxine Hong Kingston. Copyright © 1975, 1976 by Maxine Hong Kingston. Reprinted by permission of Alfred A. Knopf, Inc.

"Hyena" by Joanna Greenfield. First published by *The New Yorker,* November 11, 1996. Reprinted by permission of International Creative Management, Inc. Copyright © 1996 Joanna Greenfield.

Excerpt from "Cop Diary" by Marcus Laffey. Adapted from an article originally published by *The New Yorker,* November 10, 1997. Copyright © 1997 by Marcus Laffey. Reprinted by permission of William Morris Agency, Inc. on behalf of the Author.

"The War Room at Bellevue" by George Simpson. Originally published by *New York Magazine,* 1983. Reprinted by permission of the author.

Excerpt from *Match to the Heart* by Gretel Ehrlich. Copyright © 1994 by Gretel Ehrlich. Reprinted by permission of Pantheon Books, a division of Random House, Inc.

"Finishing School" from *I Know Why the Caged Bird Sings* by Maya Angelou. Copyright © 1969 by Maya Angelou. Reprinted by permission of Random House, Inc.

"The Masked Marvel's Last Toehold" from *Confessions of a Knife* by Richard Selzer (New York: William Morrow, 1979). Copyright © 1979 by David Goldman and Janet Selzer, Trustees. Reprinted by permission of Georges Borchardt, Inc. for the author.

"The Lady of the Ring" by Rene Denfeld, from *The New York Times Magazine,* August 24, 1997, Section 6. Reprinted by permission of the author. Rene Denfeld is the author of *The New Victorians* and *Kill the Body, the Head Will Fall.*

"Trapped in Another Life" by Art Harris, © 1990, The Washington Post. Reprinted with permission.

"Los Pobres," excerpted from *Hunger of Memory* by Richard Rodriguez. Reprinted by permission of David R. Godine, Publisher, Inc. Copyright © 1982 by Richard Rodriguez.

"Mother Tongue" by Amy Tan, first published in *The Threepenny Review,* 1990. Reprinted by permission of the Author.

"Black Men and Public Spaces" by Brent Staples, originally published by *Ms. Magazine.* Reprinted by permission of Brent Staples. Brent Staples writes editorials for *The New York Times* and is author of the memoir, *Parallel Time: Growing Up in Black and White.*

"The Shrieking of the Lambs" by Andrew Klavan. Originally published by *Boston Review*, June–September 1994. Copyright © 1994 by Andrew Klavan. Reprinted by permission of the Author.

Excerpt from "Denial Behavior" from *Hollywood vs. America* by Michael Medved. Copyright © 1992 by Michael Medved. Reprinted by permission of HarperCollins Publishers, Inc.

"A Hanging" from *Shooting an Elephant and Other Essays* by George Orwell, copyright 1950 by Sonia Brownell Orwell and renewed 1978 by Sonia Pitt-Rivers, reprinted by permission of Harcourt Brace & Company.

"Once More to the Lake" from *One Man's Meat* by E. B. White. Copyright 1941 by E. B. White. Reprinted by permission of HarperCollins Publishers, Inc.

"Letter from Birmingham Jail" by Martin Luther King, Jr. Reprinted by arrangement with The Heirs to the Estate of Martin Luther King, Jr., c/o Writer's House, Inc. as agent for the proprietor. Copyright 1963 by Martin Luther King, Jr., copyright renewed 1991 Coretta Scott King.

"On Natural Death," pp. 102–5, copyright © 1979 by Lewis Thomas, from *The Medusa and the Snail* by Lewis Thomas. Used by permission of Viking Penguin, a division of Penguin Putnam Inc.

"On Keeping a Notebook" from *Slouching Towards Bethlehem* by Joan Didion. Copyright © 1966, 1968 and copyright renewed © 1996 by Joan Didion. Reprinted by permission of Farrar, Straus & Giroux, Inc.

Photo Credits

Chapter 1, © Michael McGovern/The Picture Cube; Chapter 2, © Walter S. Silver/The Picture Cube; Chapter 3, © Fredrick Bodin/Stock, Boston; Chapter 4, © Jerry Howard/Stock, Boston; Chapter 5, © Spencer Grant/The Picture Cube; Chapter 6, © Rick Smolan/Stock, Boston; Chapter 7, © Glen Korengold/Stock, Boston; Chapter 8, © Jerry Howard/Stock, Boston; Chapter 9, © Lionel Delevingne/Stock, Boston; Chapter 10, © Gale Zucker/Stock, Boston; Chapter 11, © Michael Weisbrot/Stock, Boston; Chapter 12, © Jean-Claude LeJeune/Stock, Boston.

Instructor's Manual for

The Longwood Reader

Fourth Edition

Edward A. Dornan
Orange Coast College

Charles W. Dawe
Late of Orange Coast College

Allyn and Bacon

Boston London Toronto Sydney Tokyo Singapore

ISBN 0-205-31052-4

Printed in the United States of America

10 9 8 7 6 5 4 3 2 1 RRDV 02 01 00 99

Contents

10 / Definition   IM-106

11 / Persuasion and Argument   IM-117

12 / The Artful Essay   IM-144

Preface to the
Instructor's Manual

On the following pages we have provided commentary on the professionally written essays in Chapters 3–12. For the essays in Chapters 3–11, we have included Teaching Suggestions, Notes, and Possible Answers, which respond to the questions following each essay and intended to enrich the teaching experience. The treatment of essays in Chapter 12 we have left open-ended by only offering suggestions for addressing the purpose and meaning, strategy, and style of each essay.

Our suggestions for teaching are just that—merely suggestions. You will find that they often give some background information to help set the stage for class discussion and then refer to the essay itself.

Following each teaching suggestion, we have provided a series of notes arranged sequentially through the paragraphs of the essay. These notes are chock-full of observations on writing strategies, comments about allusions, information about references, and musings on culture. Their main purpose is to save you time.

Following the notes, we offer possible answers to the questions that follow each essay.

We have tried to be helpful. We hope you will find this material useful and interesting.

—————— *3 / Description* ——————

Photographs of My Parents
Maxine Hong Kingston

Teaching Suggestions

Rarely will an author attempt to develop an essay by focusing readers' attention on description primarily, as Kingston does in "Photographs of My Parents." Ostensibly describing meager biographical artifacts, Kingston outlines her mother's life, from young adult to aged matriarch, obliquely including remnants of her own life.

Archeology scientifically studies ancient lives and cultures, in part by examining artifacts excavated at the sites of ancient civilizations. You might begin an "archeological exercise" by asking the class to discuss one famous person: a politician, a movie star, a world leader, or the like. Then ask them to imagine that thousands of years from now, archeologists discover the site where this famous person thrived. The question for discussion is this: "What five artifacts—any objects made by human beings—would best represent or symbolize this person's qualities?"

After such a discussion, students see that much can be learned about people by scrutinizing their possessions; they can create a carefully contrived descriptive essay by concentrating on the artifacts that go into the essay, rather than on characters, actions, or settings.

Notes

Paragraph 1

"joy": The word *joy* is represented in "abstract" Chinese ideographs; that is, the classical ideographs themselves have been shaped into a form combining message and ornamentation.

During the Chinese Civil War (1945–1949) between the communist troops of Mao Tse-Tung and the nationalist troops of Chiang Kai-Shek, many Chinese fled China for Hong Kong.

"bat": In China, the bat is emblematic of happiness and long life.

"Canton, Hong Kong . . .": Kingston mentions four predominantly Chinese regions in the Far East, each having its distinct politics and customs; all are Chinese, nonetheless.

Paragraph 2

The National Republic of China, under Chiang Kai-Shek, was formally recognized by the United States in 1928.

"A stork and . . .": The stork-brings-the-baby myth can be traced to an Old Norse legend. To account for the mother's bed rest after giving birth, children were told that the stork bit the mother just before he departed. The stork has long been a symbol of filial devotion: The Romans enforced *Lex Ciconaria*, the "Stork's Law," compelling children to care for their aged parents.

"Ex-assistant etranger . . .": Literally, "Former foreign teacher (ex-assistant) at the surgical and maternity clinic of the University of Lyons."

Chop is from Hindi *chap*, "impression, stamp." A chop is an official stamp or seal; also, a person's "signature stamp," used in many parts of Asia.

Paragraph 3

The small mystery about the mother's true age heightens interest in this descriptive passage.

Paragraph 5

The white chrysanthemum has a long and fabled history in both China and Japan. The famous haiku poet Basho wrote that the white chrysanthemum "remains immaculate," even under intense scrutiny.

"dartless": In tailoring, a dart is a short, stitched fold meant to make a garment fit closely while conforming to the natural shape of the body.

"My mother has eyes . . .": Earlier, Kingston's mother had "spacy eyes, as all people recently from Asia have." Now the eyes have become "accustomed" to America, and the description gives Kingston a chance to comment obliquely on her mother's life.

Paragraph 6

The beginning of a *flashback*, a device with which writers present a scene or incident that happened before some preceding scene or incident in the work.

Fred Astaire (1899–1987) starred in such musical comedies as *Top Hat* (1935) and *Shall We Dance?* (1937). His graceful and original tap dancing was famous.

Paragraph 9

The photographs are described as if they were ordinary identification or passport photos.

"sea bird": A sea bird painted on a ship's bow may be a traditional emblem of protection, but it is also interesting that a bird, according to Jungian theory, is a beneficent creature representing spirits or angels, supernatural aid, or thoughts and flights of fancy.

"Two quilts": Notice that Kingston's mother took one quilt for each of them.

Possible Answers

Meaning and Purpose

1. Encourage students to discuss how they feel about old photographs. Ask them to describe some photographs in as much detail as Kingston does.
2. The Chinese in the photographs are nearly expressionless because "Chinese do not smile for photographs" (3), and Kingston "can't tell if [her mother] is happy" (4). The Chinese-Americans in the photographs are "always laughing" (6), and they pose as westerners do.
3. The seals and words over the photographs of Kingston's mother show that the photographs were official. They are not taken for pleasure, or to capture fun or happiness, as those of Kingston's father are.
4. Kingston's father is happy-go-lucky in some photographs. He works in a laundry, watches American movies, adapts an American custom about "stomping on straw hats" (6), and pursues a course of study. He seems to combine fun, work, and ambition.
5. The women were unaccustomed to decoration, and the dresses did not conform to the female figure. The flowers therefore seem out of place, and were pinned on awkwardly.
6. The bat is a symbol of happiness and long life in China.

Strategy

1. Kingston organizes her essay as the contents of the metal tube are organized: she describes the three scrolls as they appear, one inside another. The transitions from one section to the next are the second sentence in paragraph 2, and the first sentences in paragraphs 4 and 9.
2. Some examples of sensory details are: *smell*—"The smell of China flies out, a thousand-year old bat . . . brain" (1) (metaphor); *sight*—"Her naturally curly hair is parted on the left, one wavy wisp tendrilling off to the right" (3) (image); and "flowers that look like gears for a gold machine" (1) (simile). Examples of *impression* or *feeling* are: "Most of the graduates are girls whose faces have not yet formed . . . happy" (4), and "She wears a scholar's white gown and she is not thinking about her appearance" (3).
3. This is a subjective essay, told from the author's point of view.
4. Kingston describes the tube in careful details that evoke China: the "joy" ideographs, the flowers, and the stamps. The tube was damaged in the mail but still carries the smell of China. These details already suggest a contrast between East and West and prepare readers for the depth of detail that follows.

Style

1. Kingston is nostalgic about the China of her mother's younger life when she describes, in paragraph 1, the smell flying out of the tube, and in paragraph 9, "In China, there was time to complete feelings." She describes her mother with affectionate detail.
2. Kingston's mother embodies the essence of China, as the tube does. She is rigid and contained, and her Chinese customs are "damaged" by life in the West, like the tube.
3. *Ophthalmology*, specialty in eyes; *pediatrics*, specialty in children's medicine; *gynecology*, specialty in women's medicine; *dermatology*, specialty in the skin; *therapeutics*, specialty in remedies.

Hyena
Joanna Greenfield

Teaching Suggestions

Because this essay describes the horror of the unexpected, students often become engaged in its action. Also, after being queried, many students remember when they themselves have had experiences that were not what they had anticipated, especially experiences that were based on assumed trust, which resulted in unexpected outcomes. Have students first consider briefly and then discuss the kinds of ordinary experiences based on trust that can lead to results not at all anticipated. Even an experience so ordinary as expecting one's friend to collaborate on studying for a test, only to find out that the friend totally relies on luck to pass a test, will serve this purpose, that of demonstrating that unexamined trust can lead to unanticipated consequences.

Notes

Paragraph 1
The essay begins *in medias res,*a term from Horace, literally meaning "in the middle of things." Greenfield will now move, in the next paragraph, to providing information about earlier facts—in this case, a bit of history about hyenas.

Paragraph 2
Greenfield describes the hyena, partly subjectively and partly objectively.

Paragraph 3
Greenfield shifts back to the hyena described in paragraph 1, noting particularly its strong, natural sense of possession. This paragraph partly foreshadows the major event in the essay in that it shows the hyena in charge of its surroundings.

Paragraph 4
The reference to Hiroshima is of course an allusion to the aftereffects of the dropping of the atomic bomb on the Japanese city of that name in September 1945.

Paragraph 6
A savanna is a tropical or subtropical grassland containing scattered trees and drought-resistant undergrowth. The zoological information about the hyena gives the reader both information about hyenas and information that Greenfield knows a bit about them, establishing her expertise.

Paragraph 7
Further descriptive information about hyenas, this paragraph's main interest lies in its condensed description of the activities of hyenas.

Paragraph 8
Returning to autobiography, Greenfield recounts an anecdote about the actions of hyenas, which she once witnessed. The reader gains more information about Greenfield's expertise.

Paragraph 9
From this autobiographically cast paragraph, readers learn a good deal about Greenfield and her surroundings, including her educational background, how she came to work on an Israeli wildlife preserve, and why the wildlife preserve was established.

A kibbutz is a communal farm or settlement in Israel.

Paragraph 10
Greenfield here introduces the reader to Efa—his description, his genealogy, his eating habits, and her high opinion of him.

Paragraph 11
Here and in paragraph 12, Greenfield describes in depth all that one would need to know about Efa. He moves from being loving, to being complacent, to becoming hostile. These paragraphs strengthen the foreshadowing that began in paragraph 3.

Paragraph 13
Here and in paragraph 14, Greenfield describes, unknown to her at the time, what will be the arguable motive for Efa's later actions.

Paragraph 15
In this, the attack paragraph, Greenfield describes what she should have done, what she did instead, what happened as a result of her action, maintaining a detached tone while recounting a horrible action. Notice, too, that she comments generally on the response of the human mind to such an immediately shocking event.

Paragraph 16

Greenfield describes the results of the attack, maintaining her detached demeanor. She describes her personal agony objectively, which causes the reader to see the action rather than to commiserate with its unwilling participant.

Paragraph 17

Greenfield's extraordinarily compact paragraph includes (1) a continuing description of the current action; (2) a reflection on the time when she took a self-defense class; (3) a note about her losing hope; (4) a fact about how hyenas usually kill their prey; (5) a description of how this dramatic event could possibly conclude; (6) and a psychological statement about her ordinary state of mind. It then returns to the present, to the action at hand, an adept handling of time present, time past, and then back to time present.

Paragraph 18

Greenfield solidly returns to the present, describing in detail Efa's trying to kill her, yet she feels no pain.

Paragraph 19

In this lead-in to paragraph 20, Greenfield gives the reason that she intends to attack Efa.

Paragraph 20

Note why Greenfield defends herself, not for herself alone but also for her friends and family.

The Negev desert lies 60 miles south of Jerusalem, in Israel.

Paragraph 21

This paragraph is an example of *dénouement*: in literature, the explanation or outcome of a plot; in an essay, the explanation or outcome of an event. Notice that Greenfield inserts a moral to her event, that such an experience teaches people much about themselves. Then she returns to describing her struggle with the hyena.

Paragraph 22

Greenfield feels a primitive attachment to Efa in this paragraph. Efa started the assault. Greenfield believes that the assault will end here, a fight that Efa and Greenfield have silently, momentarily, agreed to finish. Then in her wisdom, she retreats.

Paragraph 23

The insight here is that when one is absorbed in an extremely dangerous activity, he or she becomes oblivious to the surroundings.

Paragraph 24

This conjecture paragraph recounts the events from the distance of time and its corollary—thought. Here, Greenfield does not believe that Efa intended to kill her without reason, that reason being one of frustration.

Paragraph 25

This insert paragraph, along with insert paragraph 26, breaks the tone of the description, moving the text to an overview of how various animals, including hyenas, deal in nature with their prey. It provides the reader a break from the intense action in the main text of the essay.

Paragraph 27

A descriptive anecdote that serves to verify Greenfield's earlier assertions about hyenas, this paragraph also strengthens the essay by alluding to Greenfield's broad experience, practical and historical, with her subject.

Paragraph 28

Along with paragraphs 29 and 30, this is a paragraph of relief: the main action has ceased; all that remains is the process of taking care of Greenfield. Note how Greenfield now comments on herself generally, both autobiographically and psychologically.

Paragraph 31

Note that the expert in treating Greenfield's wounds is not the doctor, but the reserve's veterinarian, who is schooled more about the nature of wild animal bites than is the physician.

Paragraph 32

Combined with paragraphs 33, 34, and 35, this part of the text moves back and forth, from describing human flesh in general to Greenfield's flesh specifically and her thoughts about its wounds. Note Greenfield's philosophical remarks about her life and life in general, now that she has faced almost certain death.

Paragraph 36

Notice how Greenfield broadens her perspective in this paragraph, moving from the elements of her personal experience to the philosophical import of working in nature with wild animals.

Paragraph 37

One cannot fail to note the sense of sadness Greenfield feels about how Efa died after she last saw him, when he looked just as natural as before he had attacked her.

Paragraph 38

Along with the concluding paragraph 39, Greenfield brings her reader up to date on her life. Notice how her Israeli experience with Efa helped her to decide her future.

A *matatu* bus, mentioned in paragraph 38, is a bus rigged from a vehicle such as a jeep or a weapons' carrier, usually driven by its owner.

Possible Answers

Meaning and Purpose

1. Answers vary, but not widely. Usually, students mention the hyena's sense of territory, the hyena's shape, and the hyena's general attitude.
2. As noted in paragraph 9, Greenfield volunteered to work in Israel because she was interested in helping to set up a breeding site in that country. However, when that project was postponed, she took a volunteer job at another reserve "cleaning enclosures," because it had to do with wild animals.
3. Efa had been Shlomi's ward from Efa's birth; thus, he had bonded with Shlomi, as noted in paragraphs 10 and 11. Also, Shlomi is described as being "the gentlest" worker. By contrast, Greenfield was the volunteer cage cleaner, having little personal engagement with Efa or any other animal on the reserve.
4. As noted in paragraph 14, the first defense lesson that Greenfield learned was "Poke the cockroach in the eyes." Greenfield's poking Efa in his eyes probably saved her life.
5. Throughout the essay, Greenfield moves from describing the attack to objectively describing hyenas, noting that attacking its prey is a natural attribute of the animal. See particularly paragraphs 1, 2, 3, 6, 10, 15, 17, and 21.

Strategy

1. Sharks and hyenas share the singular characteristic of being the "vacuum cleaners" of their domains. Each will eat whatever is edible, in the broadest sense of that term; therefore, each performs the valuable task of cleaning its ecosystem.

2. Paragraph 15 recounts the actual attack offhandedly, Greenfield's noting that she does not remember Efa's biting deeply into her arm. The attack seems sudden because of how two sentences are juxtaposed in paragraph 15. Greenfield makes a short statement about human minds in general, followed by "It shut off during the attack. . . ." The paragraph's lacking a prelude or a clearly stated motive adds shock to the immediacy of the attack.

3. As the term is used in paragraph 35, *dichotomy* refers to that which has seemingly contradictory qualities. Appropriate synonyms include "division," "split," "rift," and "partition," according to students, who have often given arguable reasons for their choices.

4. According to Greenfield, hyenas are productive without waste, consuming even the bones of their prey. An apt word for that attribute is *efficient*.

5. By noting in paragraph 26 that hyenas eat the bones of the animals that they kill, Greenfield strongly hints at what could have happened to her had she been killed by the hyena, adding tension to the essay.

Style

1. Greenfield moves back and forth from describing her life-or-death encounter with a hyena to describing hyenas zoologically, from the elements of personal drama to the elements of objective information. This interweaving results in the reader's understanding that no matter how first perceived, the attack by the hyena was a natural reaction.

2. Answers vary, but mildly. Most students, struck by the inactivity of the tourists and by the apparent inability of the soldiers to shoot the hyena, describe the witnesses as being uninvolved.

3. Depending on whether students focus on the attack or on the calm reportage or on a combination of the two, students describe the tone as being, for example, "cold," "tense," "objective," "scientific," or "informative."

4. Greenfield makes an important statement in her title, "Hyena," that becomes apparent after reading the essay. Although one hyena attacked her, that hyena did what any hyena would have done under similar circumstances. Being wild animals, all hyenas share nearly identical characteristics, Efa being no exception. To title the essay "The Hyena" would have singled out one hyena, perhaps then suggesting to the naive reader that this hyena is not representative but unique.

5. This episode takes place in Israel; therefore, one can assume that the caretakers' native language is Hebrew. It follows that they would shout "Lo!" the Hebrew word for *no,* rather than its English equivalent.

Cop Diary
Marcus Laffey

Teaching Suggestions

Laffey describes his job deceptively in that his essay deals with the routine of being a police officer, a routine that to others is anything but orderly. Have students consider their opinions of "cops" before reading the essay by asking them if they have any reflex opinions about police officers: When they hear the word *cop*, what quick description do they have of that profession? Then have them identify several police officers in movies and in television series, again asking them to contribute quick verbal descriptions of those "cops." This exercise stimulates students' interest in reading an essay describing a real police officer's brief diary and readies them for writing their own descriptive essays.

Notes

Paragraph 1
Laffey quickly and thoroughly establishes himself as the authority for the purpose of writing this essay while also showing that he is quite equipped to write descriptive prose.

Paragraph 2
Laffey points out a central difference between appearance and reality in police work. Witnesses see police officers arresting people, but rarely do they see what led to the arrest.

Paragraph 3
Note the equation of social authority and social trust, indicating Laffey's strong ethical stance.

Paragraph 4
Laffey's quick description of his beat informs the readers of the routine and the ruin of a New York City area.

Paragraph 5
This transitional paragraph reminds the reader that no matter the area, most people are living the lives ordinarily expected of ordinary people. By and large, Laffey enjoys his beat, being able to see all that is good in his assigned neighborhood.

Paragraph 6
Laffey has no ax to grind. In fact, as this paragraph says, people are glad that police officers walk the beat. Note that Laffey uses himself symbolically, representing the protection of all police officers who walk beats.

Paragraph 7
In this descriptive autobiography, which ends with paragraph 9, note how Laffey describes himself objectively and, by doing so, also describes all other New York City police officers who walk beats.

Paragraph 10
Laffey now describes the usual procedures that New York City police officers must use, depending on circumstances and on the personalities of the perpetrators ("perps"), a description that ends with paragraph 11.

Paragraph 12

This description, which continues to the end of paragraph 14, is an overview of how "perps" are put through the New York City penal system, from officers' booking suspects to doing the paperwork preliminaries that lead to a suspect's courtroom appearance.

Paragraph 15

Laffey's description of how police officers hope and train for arrests that, surprisingly, lead to acquittals, foreshadows the events described in the subsequent paragraph.

Paragraph 16

This paragraph begins the anecdote that concludes the essay, which ends with the frustrating event of seeing an obviously guilty man being freed by the system. Or is the man guilty? Laffey uses the cause-and-effect strategy to strongly suggest that he was guilty: His description of the rapist matched the "perp's," and when the perp left the area, the rapes stopped. The strength of this ending is that Laffey retains as much objectivity about this rapist and his crimes as a police officer can be asked to retain, his personal opinion notwithstanding.

Possible Answers

Meaning and Purpose

1. In the first paragraph of this essay, Laffey amply evidences his expertise, beginning with the first sentence of the essay, in which he says that he has handcuffed more than one hundred people in one year. In addition to citing that fact, students often point to specific passages in paragraphs 4 and 5, those that contain references to Laffey's daily activities.

2. Paragraph 2 says that Laffey views handcuffs as "tools of the trade," and goes on to defend police officers who sometimes appear brutal by noting that spectators rarely see what led up to that incident, for example, the brutality of beating up an old man.

3. It develops that the pleasure noted is not so much the actual pleasure of the activity of taking away freedom, as Laffey puts it, but the activity of seeing that the person who violated the law has been caught. Consequently, society has one less chance of violence occurring on the street. Just as a surgeon cuts open a patient not for the surgeon's pleasure but for the patient's relief, Laffey "takes away someone's freedom" so that freedom might continue for the rest of Laffey's neighborhood.

4. Laffey is describing his uniform and equipment, as he readily makes apparent in the beginning clause of this paragraph, "When I'm working. . . ."

5. Laffey is describing how it feels to deal as a police officer with a legal system so complex that sometimes a criminal will go free because, as it appears to the officer, every judge automatically favors the opposition—in this case, the suspect.

Strategy

1. Paragraphs 12 and 13 seem nearly interminable in their listing of all the legalistic forms that officers must complete. This strategy breaks the tone in the essay, taking it from the assumed occasional excitement of a police officer's day to the unassumed drudgery of a police officer's being almost overwhelmed with paperwork.

2. The element of humor in this strategic simile cannot be overlooked. Just as one is never sure exactly what one is going to experience on a blind date, a police officer cannot assume what to expect from arresting someone.

3. Particularly in paragraphs 12, 13, and 14, Laffey uses the strategy of listing the many boring activities, particularly those involving paperwork, in which a police officer must engage. He handles his prose in these paragraphs in such a way that the reader momentarily tires of reading about all the forms and procedures with which an officer must deal, which is precisely what Laffey intends, suggesting that if it is boring to read about, then how boring must it be to do?

4. Laffey strongly suspects that the person he arrested, described in paragraph 16, is a rapist. However, he obviously cannot say directly that he is a rapist because the man has never been tried for the crime. Therefore, Laffey gives the reader the information to infer conclusively that the man is indeed the rapist.

Style

1. In that phrase, *montage* refers to a rapid succession of radio messages, none of them logically connected to any of the others, yet all combining to form a mental picture of the moment. A suitable synonym, therefore, might be *chaotic,* although students have come up with several other interesting replacements.

2. As far back as 1613, the term *collared* referred to a person's, being seized by the neck or by the collar, as students usually figure out by analogy. Nowadays, it is a slang term for a police officer's detaining a person suspected of having committed a crime.

3. The term *baroque* refers to that which is characterized by extravagance, complexity, grotesqueness, or flamboyance. Good substitutes for *baroque* in this essay, to describe Laffey's opinion of the legal system, are *complex, elaborate,* and *intricate,* although students find others readily.

4. Answers vary, of course, but they all hinge on the idea that compared to the high points of excitement in an officer's life, the low points, the ordinary points, are low indeed. Coming directly from a high point of excitement to a normal state of affairs is quite a psychological drop.

5. The word *emblem* as it is used in this essay to describe handcuffs refers to that which signifies restraint or the symbol of restraint. Depending on contexts, of course, *emblem* can refer to a set of verses meant to teach a moral, a symbolic object used as a heraldic device, such as a bronze eagle, and a figure used as an identifying mark, such as a tribal tattoo.

The War Room at Bellevue
George Simpson

Teaching Suggestions

Reportorial description, the "see-it, write-it" detached yet energetic prose of the experienced observer, appeals to the reader's imagination because it displays little of the writer's own imaginative commentary, allowing readers to explore freely their own reactions. The fewer the writer's remarks about descriptions, the more readers can conjure their own remarks, a vital force behind all "appearance-versus-reality" prose.

Sometimes we look, but we do not see. Instructors can take advantage of this fact when introducing the article by asking students to look around, to see the classroom itself, often for the first time. How would the room seem to the outside observer?

Students often reply that the room is no more than "just a room." "Yes," you can reply, "and to medical personnel experienced in trauma, a battered woman is just a battered woman, a corpse is just a corpse, and a gunshot wound or a stabbing is just that. No more." To illustrate your point, you can then introduce this essay.

Notes

Paragraph 1
Bellevue: The author lists the word's *connotations*, the implications or emotional surroundings that words in context carry, as distinguished from their denotative or lexical meanings. Simpson reinforces the connotations by quoting a nurse about Bellevue's rumored reputation.

Paragraph 2
Bedlam: In London, an old insane asylum, later a hospital for the mentally ill.

"Chance for survival": Bellevue has a world-class reputation for its trauma center.

Paragraph 3
A "typical" Friday night in Bellevue begins and all is routine, down to deciding who will go for coffee.

Simpson foreshadows events by showing the shock and seriousness of what has already happened.

"stiletto": A stiletto's blade is slender and tapering, designed for use as a weapon.

Paragraph 4
"Emergent!": In trauma-care jargon, *emergent* means "sudden, or unforeseen."

"Catheter": A catheter is a tube passed through the body for evacuating or injecting fluids from or into body cavities. This paragraph mirrors the standard operating procedure for trauma victims, which includes first aid for shock, test for blood type, and quick evaluation of internal organs.

Paragraph 5
Medically, shivers are slight tremors of the skin, as from cold or fear. To a nonmedical person like Simpson, perhaps it suggests shock, which is marked by paleness of skin.

The doctor tries to determine the depth of the wound and its nearness to bone, nerves, and other parts or systems of the human body. The yellow disinfectant probably is a tincture of iodine.

Paragraph 6
Juxtaposing the wounded man and the derelict suggests the spectrum of patients treated by Bellevue's staff.

Paragraph 7
Again, coupling examination of the Hispanic girl with that of the old white woman helps illustrate the kinds of patients who go to Bellevue. Notice that each woman is attended by a specialist.

Paragraph 8

"tetanus": Tetanus is an acute infectious disease that causes painful muscle spasms. Because its first sign is stiffness of the jaw, it is sometimes called "lockjaw." It is usually, but not always, fatal. Gamma globulin is a protein formed in the blood; it and other proteins, concentrated, resist infection.

Paragraph 9

"methadone": Methadone hydrochloride is a habit-forming, synthetic, analgesic drug with potency equal to that of morphine, but with weaker narcotic action. Under careful supervision, methadone hydrochloride is used to treat people who are dependent on drugs derived from opium, such as heroin.

Paragraph 11

The story of the suicide continues. Simpson shows that Bellevue becomes one setting for the drama of many people's lives.

Paragraph 12

Emergency room. Simpson's descriptions of people include a representative spectrum from military personnel to members of minority groups to children to battered women.

Paragraph 13

While preparing for a shift change, the conversations are normal. No one recounts a specific incident that happened during her shift. The implication is that no matter what happens, it is "normal" for Bellevue.

Paragraph 14

"triage": A triage nurse screens and classifies sick and injured people to determine the most efficient way of using medical and nursing personnel, equipment, and facilities. In emergency rooms, the triage nurse ranks patients in order of importance for treatment.

"IV's": Intravenous infusions. Solutions such as those containing saline, dextrose, or potassium chloride are injected into veins in an attempt to produce immediate results, when treating hemorrhage, shock, or collapse.

The casual comment at the end of this paragraph is not to be taken as a cold, unfeeling statement. People who work daily in trauma centers have learned to mask their feelings. The alternative is to destroy their careers by becoming psychologically involved with their work.

Paragraph 15

An appearance-versus-reality paragraph. The midnight episode quickly reminds other patients that their problems, in the harsh, comparative light of reality, may not be so serious after all.

Paragraph 16

Another appearance-versus-reality paragraph, this time comparing patients' view of the various emergencies with the Bellevue staffers' view of them.

Paragraph 17

Just as the drama of the suicide had a follow up paragraph earlier, the murder drama has its follow-up—Simpson's method of showing that life goes on, desperately or otherwise, despite the deaths at Bellevue.

Paragraph 18

"0 to 60": Simpson compares the quickness of the Bellevue trauma staff with that of an automobile that can accelerate from 0 to 60 miles an hour in five seconds, which is remarkably fast.

"Collapsed right lung": Although normal in a fetus, a collapsed lung in a mature adult is serious, often caused (though not in this case) by the rupture of a bleb (an "internal blister") on the pleural (membrane) surface of the lung, which then becomes airless or nearly so.

"As the nurses work . . .": Again, the nurses deal realistically with their lives while treating the lives of others. This healthy way of handling a job that could be emotionally painful distinguishes expert trauma center personnel from those who do not last long as employees there.

Paragraph 19

The last paragraph strongly reinforces what Simpson has been describing and commenting about all along: Although unnerving for lay visitors, emergencies are routine for the medical experts at a trauma center, particularly at Bellevue.

Possible Answers

Meaning and Purpose

1. Give students a chance to relate their own experiences in hospital emergency rooms and compare theirs to those Simpson describes.
2. Simpson's purpose is to expose a vital feature of Manhattan representing its people, violence, and trauma. He also wants to praise the emergency team by showing them in action.
3. At Bellevue injured people have a good chance for survival (2). Bellevue is a "monstrous complex" (2) like an "indoor war zone" (1). Some think it's only "for crazy people" (1). The emergency staff are highly trained and efficient. Simpson's details of the varied cases that come to them illustrate their expertise. "'This is nothing, about normal, I'd say,' concludes the head nurse. 'No big deal'" (19).
4. From the emergency ward Manhattan looks like a violent, harsh city with a wide racial and ethnic mixture. "A policeman . . . twisted his knee struggling with an 'alleged perpetrator.'" (10). "A Hispanic man complains of pains in his side." (12).
5. "Bedlam" is capitalized because it is a variant of "Bethlehem"—the Hospital of St. Mary of Bethlehem, an old insane asylum in London. Bedlam: a state of uproar and confusion, a wild and frantic condition.

Strategy

1. Two introductory paragraphs set the scene and describe the hospital's reputation. Paragraphs 3–18 describe the typical activity of the emergency room from 9:00 P.M. Friday to 1:20 A.M. Saturday. The suicide story (8) has a follow-up in paragraph 11, and the gunshot victim (14–15) in paragraph 17. The final paragraph telescopes the activity till morning. This structure is clear and easy to follow. The sections by time suggest the methodical and orderly running of the emergency room.
2. Other stimulus-response patterns: the gunshot victim arrives (14), and the stab victim arrives (18).
3. Transitions indicating simultaneous action: "Meanwhile in the lobby" (6); "A young Hispanic man interrupts" (7); "The pace continues to increase" (9); and "Meanwhile, patients arrive in the lobby" (12).
4. The present tense creates an immediacy that conveys the quick action and intensity of the emergency room.

5. A panoramic view of admitting desk, waiting room, and emergency room, where "one man sleeps fitfully" (3). A far-to-near arrangement shows when the ambulance arrives, the "glass doors burst open," and a man is put on the treatment table (4). Another visual sweep takes the eye from trauma room to examination rooms to hallway (8).

Style

1. The intense emergency-room activity shows in the depth of detail—"After a few seconds another doctor inserts his finger into the wound. It sinks in all the way to the knuckles" (5). Simpson is objective and detached; "Another woman breaks down in hysterics; everywhere young Hispanics are crying and comforting each other" (15), and "The young woman of the stairs is getting stitches in a small gash over her left eye" (18).

2. Words suggestive of battle are "war zone," "wounded and bleeding," "harried doctors," "rush from stretcher to stretcher," "crushing number of injured," "battlefield," and "survival."

3. The closing paragraph quickly surveys the time from 1:20 a.m. to "the morning hours." Simpson catalogues the cases even more dispassionately, not even specifying who has which injuries. This activity is routine. The tone conveys a less harried, less immediate, less alarming atmosphere. The narrator has pulled back from the situation.

4. The sound words are "whistle has blown," "mutter of voices," "sit quietly," "tiny bleep," and "nurses can hear." Paragraph 4 has mostly touch words, and paragraph 14, sound words.

Struck by Lightning
Gretel Ehrlich

Teaching Suggestions

A successful gambit is to invite the students to talk about personal experiences to which they responded. You can open the discussion by noting that all of us have hundreds of small experiences daily; however, we remember only those to which we respond. For example, we might drive to school down a particular road, street, freeway, or expressway every day. We become so used to doing it that we rarely remember our drive to school. But one day, a car swerves directly into our path, we jam on the brakes, skid, and our car comes within inches of the other car's rear bumper. Our reaction to that experience will cause us to remember that experience for a long, long time.

Introduce this activity by telling the students that however else they describe their experiences, they should include as much of the "how, what, when, where, who, and why" details that they remember—in other words, be descriptive enough to help their listeners mentally recreate the experience. You should have quite a good time with this activity because many students have had rather touching experiences and some have had hilarious ones. After a few student examples of descriptive responses, go to the essay itself, to see how a master describer, Ehrlich, recounts a fantastic personal journey.

Notes

Paragraph 1

"Deep in an ocean": Ehrlich begins her essay with reference to one of the oldest symbols in literature—water. Limitless and immortal, water in many religions and philosophies is the beginning and the end of all things on earth. Modern psychology has interpreted water as a symbol of the unconscious, that is, of the non-formal, dynamic, motivating, female side of the personality.

"liquid clouds of dust": This is an example of *synaeceosis*, a condensed paradox. Logically, either "liquid" or "dust" would be part of this phrase; ordinarily, we can't have it both ways. Compare Milton's "darkness visible," for example.

"the continent of the body": The word *microcosm* has several definitions, one being "human beings, humanity, or the like viewed as an epitome of the world." Ehrlich's phrase exemplifies that definition.

Paragraph 2

"Blue trickles in": Ehrlich refers to blood, which turns red when exposed.

Paragraph 3

"Blue water": Freud's *Introduction to Psycho-Analysis* points out that in dreams, birth is usually expressed through water imagery.

Paragraph 4

"My two beloved dogs": Dogs have long been emblems of faithfulness. In Christian symbolism, the dog is empowered with guarding and guiding the sheep, the flock.

Paragraph 5

Here the reader learns why the opening of this essay has been eerily mystical. Ehrlich has been struck by lightning; what has come before this paragraph describes in abundant physical and metaphysical detail her return to consciousness.

Paragraph 6

"its blue path": Compare this "blue" with the *blue* in paragraphs 2 and 3, where the color is the product of the signs of blood and birth. The *blue* in this paragraph is the blue that attends the cause of the author's earlier statements containing that color.

"I had been walking": Here, the author takes the reader to the beginning of the events leading to her being struck by lightning. One might point out to students that this clause is a fine example of a "lead-in," a phrase or clause that helps the reader to try to predict what information will follow.

Paragraph 7

"you're okay as long as you're with me": The *irony*, the outcome of events contrary to what was expected, is that the dogs ultimately help Ehrlich to be "okay."

Paragraph 8

"I woke in a pool": The unpredictable shift from paragraph 7 to paragraph 8, without a transitional marker, mirrors the unpredictable shift from safety to disaster. One minute the author was "okay"; the next minute she "woke up in a pool of blood."

"dark pools in sand": The author begins and ends the paragraph with blood imagery, her rhetorical questions rendered into blood that turns the sand into "dark pools."

Paragraph 10

"Buddhist": The Buddha (566?–c.480), also called Siddhartha or Prince Siddhattha, founded Buddhism, which holds that life is filled with suffering caused by desire. The way to end the suffering is by enlightenment, which empowers one to halt the sequence of births and deaths to which one is otherwise subjected.

"sutra": *Sutra* refers to a Hindu collection of aphorisms on how to conduct one's life. In the Pali Hindi dialect, *sutta* refers to any of the sermons of Buddha.

"paradox": This term, from the Greek meaning "contrary to opinion or expectation," describes a seemingly self-contradictory statement that sometimes in a surprising way is true: "The night was dark until she smiled."

Paragraph 11
"the gate on the ranch": The ranch gate leading to nowhere mirrors the author's quizzical attitude towards her own fate.

Paragraph 12
"To be struck by lightning": Note the grim humor from juxtaposing *lightning* and *enlightened.*

"such terrible pain": In moments of terrible pain, the body feels as if it is disconnected from the mind; this is one of the feelings that denote shock.

Paragraph 13
"I loved those dogs": As noted in another context, the dog symbolizes faithfulness. In this sense, it appears often at the feet of women in the engravings on medieval tombs.

"until I faced east": The east, because it is where the sun rises, symbolizes spiritual illumination; to turn towards the east is to turn in spirit to the source of intellectual or spiritual enlightenment.

Paragraph 14
"I considered my options": The author is collecting her thoughts. She became again rational as she "calmly assessed what might be wrong" with her.

Paragraph 15
"To be struck again": Defying all odds, the author has actually been struck by lightning twice, at two different locations. She has a strong reason to wonder why.

Paragraph 16
"my brain was torn": Note that this image, often taken at face value by quick readers, actually refers to the author's state of mind.

Paragraph 18
"refulgence": That which shines radiantly. The intermediate description, linked as it is to the final clause, "I wondered when I would no longer be able to breathe," provides strong evidence that the author indeed believed that she was dying.

Paragraph 20
"tatami": From the Japanese: Thick, woven, straw mats, usually about three feet by six feet.

"EMT": Emergency medical technician, a person trained in techniques of administering emergency care.

Paragraph 21
"Sam and Yaki": Coincidentally, *Yaki* is Japanese for "broil," which suggests how the author sometimes seemed to feel—as if she had been broiled.

"IVs": In medical care, I.V. is jargon for any fluid being injected intravenously, within or into a vein.

Paragraph 22
"Cody": A town in Wyoming named after William Frederick ("Buffalo Bill") Cody.

Paragraph 23
"EKG": Abbreviation for the German *elektrokardiogramm.* Here, the term refers to a device that records the electrical activity of the heart. The electrocardiogram gives important information concerning the spread of excitation to the different parts of the heart, which helps in diagnosing cases of abnormal cardiac rhythm, for example.

Paragraph 24

"ventricular fibrillation": A ventricle is a small cavity, in this case in the heart. A fibrillation is a quivering contraction of individual muscle fibers. Ventricular fibrillation, the quivering contractions of muscle fibers in a heart cavity, may be caused by mechanical injury to the heart; the common, loose definition of a heart attack.

"medullary": The medullary centers of the brain are the innermost portions, in contrast to the outer portion or cortex.

"comatose": In a condition of coma, an abnormal deep stupor occurring in illness, as a result of it, or due to an injury.

"apneic": From *apnea*, a temporary cessation of breathing.

"circulatory collapse": Shock occurring when the peripheral blood flow is inadequate to return sufficient blood to the heart for normal function.

Paragraph 25

"aura": In medical parlance, *aura* refers to a subjective sensation preceding a paroxysmal (sudden or periodic) attack.

"ER or ICU": *ER* is medical jargon for "emergency room" (and for "external resistance"); *ICU* is medical jargon for "intensive care unit."

"kerauno": This Greek prefix means lightning.

Paragraph 26

"hematocrit": A measure of the cellular portion of a blood sample.

"osmolality": The characteristics of a solution determined by the ionic concentration of the dissolved substances per unit of solvent. (An ion is a particle containing an electrical charge.)

Paragraph 27

"gurney": A litter equipped with wheels, used in hospitals to transport patients.

Paragraph 28

"cool gold": From the Golden Fleece to the Holy Grail, world literature abounds with gold symbolizing hidden or elusive treasure of one kind or another; consequently, gold signifies all that is superior.

"dead face tipped backwards toward the moon": The symbolism of the moon, ancient and complex, often negatively alludes to error, arbitrary fantasy, or imaginative sensitivity.

Paragraph 31

"CAT scan": CAT is an acronym for "computerized axial tomography." A CAT scan is a non-invasive technique of showing detailed images of structures, in this case within the human body. It differs from an X-ray in that a CAT scan shows detailed images by blurring images in all other planes.

Paragraph 32

"arrhythmias": Irregularity or loss of rhythm, especially of the heartbeat.

Paragraph 34

"A rattlesnake": Throughout world literature, the snake has been imbued with energy. In India, cults of the snake are connected with the symbolism of the waters of the sea. Snakes also guard the springs of life and of immortality, from Adam and Eve to Jason and Medea, or vice versa.

Paragraph 35

"the dogs came back": In this final paragraph, the dogs clearly symbolize the best of defense in the name of faithfulness. Interestingly, in mythology the dog often appears as the companion of the dead on their final voyage.

Possible Answers

Meaning and Purpose

1. The casting of the answers will vary. Many students indicate one way or another that the first paragraph describes (or seems to describe) an embryo; this might be the beginning of a thorough description of how it feels to be a fetus. Others say that it could depict another kind of life beginning, perhaps at the bottom of the sea. The strength of the answers depends of course on their evidence.

2. The author, in fact, survived a kind of explosion. She attempts here to make some sense of it, and the first explosions she might remember are fictional ones, the mind's attempt to restore order from chaos. As quickly as she realizes what she is thinking, she wants to laugh.

3. Ample evidence shows that the reader has abiding interest in non-Western thought. Probably the strongest evidence is contained in paragraph 10, with its discussion of the "Buddhist instruction regarding dying." The author also has tatami in her house (20), and one of her dogs has a Japanese name (*Yaki* = "broil").

4. Given their diction, sentence structure, and style, these paragraphs are obviously from a medical text. They might have been inserted by the author as an efficient way to inform her audience about the symptoms and treatment of lightning victims.

Strategy

1. By putting those "heartbeat sentences" so far away from each other, the author is emphasizing just how slowly her heart was beating. In fact, as it says later in the essay, her body was slowly recovering from a heart attack at that time.

2. The dogs are both faithful and unquestionably loyal at a time when even nature seems chaotic and untrustworthy. They function as a steady foil to the disorder that permeates the essay, thus illustrating by contrast how much confusion existed.

3. Although the doctor "had never completed a residency and had been barred from ER or ICU work in the hospitals of Florida," the author was fortunate because he had had much experience dealing with patients who had been struck by lightning.

4. Paragraph 27, with its three-wheeled gurney slamming the patient into a wall, also notes that neither doctor nor nurse had cleaned the cuts in the patient's head. She was finally cleaned up by her friend Laura. Other evidence is in paragraph 28, where the author is said to be the only patient, and in paragraph 31, where "no one had bothered to find out why" the patient had lost consciousness, for example.

Style

1. The author humorously links "lightning" and "enlightened," as if a cause-and-effect sequence obviously existed. However and clearly, *enlightened* refers to one who has received intellectual or spiritual knowledge, not a massive electrical shock.

2. Answers vary interestingly: Based on the definition in the textbook's glossary, many students say that the question is clearly rhetorical, citing the part of the

definition that says a rhetorical question is posed for effect, not to elicit an answer. Others, however, have argued that it must be something else because the question does not provoke thought in the reader. Instead, it is a question from the author to herself, posed in wonder. If that's the case, then the question is in the form of an *apostrophe*, a breaking off of discourse to address directly (in this instance) the author herself. How the student supports the answer usually determines its worth.

3. The author is describing how she is not fully in control of her faculties, to the extent that she can not even control her voice.

4. This phrase is a quick way to describe ten miles of the road. Those ten miles are not paved. This curt description might indicate her opinion of that part of the road, as well.

4 / Narration

Finishing School
Maya Angelou

Teaching Suggestions

One possible lead-in to assigning this selection is to briefly discuss how much personal names matter: How do we feel when people mispronounce or forget our names? Do some names suggest personality or character traits? Do our names influence our behavior? Do the names parents select for children suggest (at least to the parents) qualities the parents want their children to have? Why are names so important? Such a discussion should help prepare students for reading Maya Angelou's narrative.

After students have read the story, discussion might turn to structure. Have students notice the careful and thorough attention the narrator gives to presenting background information: first, about herself in paragraphs 1 and 2, and then about Mrs. Cullinan, her house, and her family in paragraphs 3 through 12. After setting up this background, the narrator presents three brief incidents: the speckled-faced woman's suggestion that "Margaret" be shortened to "Mary," Mrs. Cullinan's first use of the name "Mary," and the climactic incident of Marguerita's breaking the china. Have students discuss the purposes of each. Finally, have them discuss how effective the last two paragraphs are.

Notes

Paragraphs 1 and 2
These paragraphs set the stage for the narration by contrasting early training of white girls with that of black girls.

"munching along": Just getting by.

"mid-Victorian values": Values of middle-class respectability, which would include a high degree of class consciousness.

Paragraph 3

The physical description of Mrs. Cullinan, though brief, allows the reader to picture her quite accurately.

Paragraph 4 and 5

Students should notice the value attached to things and their names at Mrs. Cullinan's house, an ironic contrast to the way in which names of the servants are changed for convenience.

Paragraph 8

All mentions of Mr. Cullinan remark on his insignificance to the girl and even to Mrs. Cullinan.

Paragraph 9

The next few paragraphs establish the girl's consideration and loyalty until Mrs. Cullinan does the unforgivable.

Paragraph 13

The suggestion of a name change in this incident is the turning point in the girl's sympathy for Mrs. Cullinan.

Paragraph 21

This incident illustrates Mrs. Cullinan's thoughtfulness about her white neighbors and her casual disregard of her black servants.

Paragraph 26

This paragraph emphasizes how greatly names affect a sense of personal dignity.

Paragraph 27

Miss Glory's acceptance of her name change represents the older ways of accommodation. In contrast, the girl finds the name change intolerable and resolves to leave.

Paragraph 32

Two paragraphs of transition lead to the last incident.

Paragraph 33

The final incident, the result of a deliberate plan to get fired, once again reveals Mrs. Cullinan's values. It also illustrates Bailey's wise understanding of how vulnerable these values are.

Paragraph 39 and 40

The two short paragraphs close the narrative on a defiant and triumphant note.

Possible Answers

Meaning and Purpose

1. Give students time to explore their experiences of being angered or humiliated when treated unfairly. Did they feel powerless? Did they seek revenge? Be sure they compare their experiences with Angelou's.

2. Before Mrs. Cullinan calls her Mary, Marguerita is critical but cooperative, and even sympathetic, about her inability to have children ("For weeks after I arrived early, left late and tried very hard to make up for her barrenness" [12]). After Mrs. Cullinan calls her Mary, Marguerita is justifiably angry and deliberately breaks precious dishes to take revenge and get herself fired.

3. Angelou wants readers to feel as she feels about Mrs. Cullinan. Angelou also gives information about how a young black girl was expected to be trained and what she had to deal with in the world of privileged whites.

4. Angelou's audience could be people of all colors who want to hear about her experiences and perhaps be made to think about how blacks were—and are—treated. They are people who want to understand why Angelou writes what she writes. Her readers are educated and aware.

5. Angelou says the blacks "had a hellish horror" of not being called by their correct names because of the abusive names they have been called for centuries. Even in calling her Margaret, Mrs. Cullinan doesn't use Angelou's correct name.

6. Glory accepted and even preferred having her name changed by whites, just as most blacks then were docile and submissive. Marguerita rebelled against being called Mary and would not accept the role Glory accepted. The contrast between the two women emphasizes Angelou's point about names.

Strategy

1. The payoff for the reader is the lesson in how prejudice affects one young black girl, and, by extension, all minorities. The moral is that prejudice is evil and should be rebelled against.

2. The introduction recounts for readers first how Angelou gets into the story she tells (a white woman asked Angelou about her hometown and then made the remark about a "debutante" [1]). Then Angelou gives general information about the differences between how white and black girls were trained in domestic arts. The second paragraph has some details about what black girls learned and then gets Angelou into the setting of her narrative. After reading these two paragraphs, readers know something about the larger context for the story that begins in paragraph 3.

3. Obviously Angelou is telling this story from the perspective of an adult looking back on herself at age ten. Her memory is perhaps fuzzy because the events happened a long time ago, and they happened fast. Her credibility is not in question because an adult is usually a more reliable narrator than a child. Rather, her saying she can't remember exactly what happened is honest, and true to her adult perspective.

4. Some transitional phrases are: "On our way home one evening" (9); "For weeks after" (12); "That evening I decided" (20); "Then Bailey solved my dilemma" (33). These and others keep the story flowing through its chronological order.

5. The last sentence emphasizes that Mrs. Cullinan is in fact not right in most things she says about her young black servant, including her correct name, which is not Margaret. Mrs. Cullinan does not understand her own actions and Marguerita's feelings. The one thing she finally does understand—that Marguerita's name is not going to be Mary—is a victory for Marguerita. This sentence reminds readers of the differences in training between white and black girls that Angelou talks about in her first two paragraphs.

Style

1. Paragraph 30 is a good example of Angelou's telling us Marguerita's thoughts. They reveal that Marguerita understands, even at age ten, the abuse and unfairness in Glory's not being called by her given name. And the thoughts show that Marguerita plans to get out of her job for good cause. Marguerita is shrewd and smarter than her employer.

2. a. The irony is that the white woman's kitchen could never teach anyone how to be a "debutante"; she also makes sure she is "finished" with this finishing school. b. Marguerita is expected to learn names that Mrs. Cullinan values, but Mrs. Cullinan doesn't bother to learn Marguerita's name. c. Mrs. Cullinan is melodramatic about her situation, and in fact is probably not lonely and in pain. Marguerita's sympathy is misdirected toward someone who cannot sympathize with her not wanting to be called Mary. d. Mrs. Cullinan doesn't get the point at all about the broken dishes. She is disturbed only about losing something she valued that Marguerita scorned.
3. In paragraph 9, "She was keeping herself embalmed" refers, in a humorous and sad way, to Mrs. Cullinan's drinking habit. Marguerita's explanation of the habit fits the perspective of a ten-year-old. Paragraph 11 is a humorous description of what Marguerita thinks Mr. Cullinan's daughters must look like—beautiful and with straight hair, unlike herself. That Marguerita says "Poor Mrs. Cullinan" shows her naiveté, and the reader gets the benefit of the humor.

The Masked Marvel's Last Toehold
Richard Selzer

Teaching Suggestions

Profitable areas of discussion for this selection might concentrate on Selzer's way of blending description and action and his tying the three sections of the essay together by repeating phrases and images. His skill as a writer is evident in both techniques. A third possibility is a discussion of figurative language and irony.

In some ways, this essay is a shocker. It allows us to see the same man at two stages in his life—once vigorous and successful and somewhat famous, at the end he is anonymous, diabetic, and facing amputation of his second leg. These are the changes that time has wrought. Students may not be old enough to have witnessed such changes in those they know, but perhaps they saw the equally shocking juxtaposition of pictures of Greta Garbo as a young actress and as she appeared months before her death. At any rate, Selzer's essay will work on their imaginations.

Notes

Paragragh 1
The first paragraph establishes the setting and the series of questions establishes an empathy that the narrator maintains throughout the essay.

Paragraph 4
The conversation between doctor and patient reveals who the patient is (or has been) and, in effect, answers the questions in the first paragraph. Elihu has been thinking proudly about his past as a contrast to the present.

Paragraph 23
The essay's long middle section recaptures an evening of wrestling from the doctor's childhood. Seen through the boy's eyes, it is marvelous and full of excitement. The memories of that evening heighten Elihu's plight now as his identity is revealed.

Paragraph 32

"bosselated": Characterized by lumps and protuberances.

Paragraph 33

Have students notice how some phrases in this section echo phrases in the first section. The same thing will occur in the third section closely binding the three though they take place years apart.

Paragraph 34

Selzer blends physical description and action to create an exciting narrative.

Paragraph 43

"carnal": Of the natural as opposed to the spiritual world.

Paragraph 47

The short third section is especially full of echoes from the second section that heighten our perception of the irony in Elihu's fate.

Possible Answers

Meaning and Purpose

1. Without either leg, The Masked Marvel can't be held in a toehold. The title is made significant because the doctor breaks the last toehold by amputating the second leg. Elihu Koontz has lost his hold on what he was—a wrestler.

2. This essay is about loss and pain. Selzer relates a memory that connects him to a patient. He dramatizes, with narrative, who Elihu Koontz once was, and how the surgeon has come to appreciate his role in the former wrestler's life. If the memory of the Masked Marvel can be alive in the surgeon's mind, then Koontz will always be the wrestler the boy was in awe of. He won't really lose what he was.

3. This sentence describes the pain during the wrestling match: "The Masked Marvel does not hide his agony, but pounds and slaps the floor with his hand, now and then reaching up toward the Angel in an attitude of supplication" (35). As a patient, Elihu Koontz had "pain so great as to set him apart from all other men in a red-hot place where he had no kith or kin." (1). The wrestler's pain sounds fake compared to the pain of gangrene. The surgeon is keenly aware of how his patient suffers and was sensitive to the look of pain even as a boy.

4. Uncle Max gets so excited at the wrestling match, shouting for a leg, that he turns gray and has to take a pill. He chuckles at the boy's fear for The Masked Marvel. The boy, future doctor that he is, is solicitous of his uncle and tells him to take a pill. And the boy takes the wrestling match seriously and doesn't see it as a performance, as the uncle does. The contrast in their reactions shows the point of view of the adult looking back and emphasizes the irony in the essay.

5. The surgeon says, "I am masked" (47), "And I think that forty years later I am making the catch" (48), and "I step forward to break The Masked Marvel's last toehold" (49). These details put the surgeon in the wrestler's place and unify the essay by bringing readers back to the scene at the match, by recalling Koontz's identifying himself as The Masked Marvel, and by restating the title.

Strategy

1. The first section takes place two years before the last section, and the middle section takes place forty years before the first, when the narrator was a boy.

Selzer makes the most of putting readers in a situation, going back in time to a memory that connects to that situation, then making the story both ironic and poignant in the end. Chronological order would diminish the effect of the irony, at least.

2. The repeated details in section two are about The Masked Marvel's breasts (33), and his "bed of pain" (46). In section three the repeated details are: "*I am masked*," "Elihu Koontz pinned," "beats feebly at the side of the operating table," "Tear off a leg. Throw it up here," "It's not fair," and "to break The Masked Marvel's last toehold." The repetition unifies the language and makes the essay rich in irony, especially in the last section, where the surgeon becomes like the wrestler who subdued The Masked Marvel.

3. In paragraph 22, Koontz is going through old photographs and clippings, and Selzer says, "and I remember." Then comes a space break, and he begins the memory, "It is almost forty years ago" (23). At the end of the second section, Selzer pulls us back to the first section with, "All this I remember as I stand at the bedside of Elihu Koontz" (46). Section three begins after a space break, "Once again I am in the operating room" (47), and it is two years after the opening scene. These transitions make the time order clear. The reader is always in the "present" of his narrator.

4. As a surgeon in the first section, the narrator is compassionate and patient: "I do not withdraw from this loving" (6), and "He *wants* me to remember" (16). As a boy he is sympathetic and aware of the wrestler's pain and his uncle's state of health: "I have never seen such suffering" (35); "'Sit down, Uncle Max,' I say, 'Take a pill please'" (38); and "'Stop him. Please, somebody, stop him'" (44). The last section shows the surgeon observant and aware of the painful irony: "It seems to me that I have never seen such misery" (47), and "It's not fair" (49).

Style

1. The dialogue makes scenes immediate and dramatic and puts readers in the scenes. Without dialogue, the essay would be full of exposition and probably dull. Selzer would be telling, not showing.

2. Each section is written in present tense, making the scenes vivid and real. Because transitions to the different times are so clear, readers easily distinguish the times, even though each is in present tense.

3. In the final section, the surgeon is in the operating room and imagines it as an amphitheater. He hears Uncle Max yelling for a leg and realizes that he, the boy who was awed by The Masked Marvel, is now the surgeon who will literally tear a leg off.

The Lady of the Ring
Rene Denfeld

Teaching Suggestions

This essay's unusual topic, a female boxer's experiences with men in the boxing ring, almost automatically interests first-year English composition students. One of the better ways to introduce this essay, therefore, is to ask the students if any of them has ever seen a women's boxing match, in person or on television. Usually, the answer is no. Then ask them whether they believe it is "proper" for a woman to engage in a "man's sport." This question prompts all sorts of responses, most of them vaguely positive. Then ask your students if they believe that women should box men professionally, or for that matter, if they believe that women should compete with men in any sport, as an individual or on a team. Finally, to enliven the conversation, ask them if they believe that we should have only those college sports that include equal numbers of men and women players, at the expense of sports that have only male teams and only female teams, such as soccer, softball, and basketball. The conversation by this time usually moves to an interesting plateau, just the place to start reading Denfeld's essay.

Notes

Paragraph 1
"fantasy": A fantasy is a creation of the imagination. Denfeld's imagination propelled her into boxing.

Paragraph 2
Denfeld's fantasy is quickly shattered by reality. Interestingly, the reality surpassed the fantasy.

Paragraph 3
Jess, who feels uneasy around Denfeld, is unlike television's stereotypical trainer. He does not get angry with Denfeld because she wants to box; instead, he is shy.

Paragraph 4
"macho": One who exhibits machismo; that is, a strong sense of masculine pride or an exaggerated masculinity. Denfeld discovered a difference between how typical young Mexican male immigrants are portrayed and how they are in fact.

Paragraph 5
"changed flags": Because one Mexican fighter has an American trainer, others consider him a kind of traitor.

"gringo": Originally, a gringo was a foreigner in Spain or in Latin America, especially an English or American foreigner. Nowadays, the term is often used disparagingly to denote a non-Hispanic person.

Paragraph 6
"changed flags": In paragraph 5, this term refers to a boxer who did not do what the other boxers expected him to do. Here, the term refers to Denfeld's not doing what she suspects male boxers, and perhaps other women, would expect her to do.

"dilemma": Often used as a synonym for "problem," this word refers to one's having two choices, each of them equally undesirable.

Paragraph 7
While sparring with men, Denfeld wonders at her discovery about their psychological makeup, extending her discovery to a remark about men in general.

"malignant": This word describes that which is aggressively malicious, sometimes to the point of causing death.

Paragraph 8
In paragraph 1, Denfeld says that she became interested in boxing because of her fantasy. Here, she says that her fantasy has been replaced by a reality that has altered her "perceptions of the sexes," which in turn has given her a deep-seated confidence.

Paragraph 9
This short paragraph illustrates Denfeld's compassion for her fellow boxers.
Paragraph 10
Denfeld calls into question the whole idea of male superiority, not only the alleged physical superiority but also the alleged inner-strength, or psychological, superiority.
Paragraph 11
Denfeld has become her own dream: a fine boxer who has won a title fight against a male boxer. The "opponent" in this passage is her boxing opponent and perhaps also her internal "opponent," her former belief that somehow she could not be as good a boxer as a man could be.
Paragraph 12
An ironical ending in that Denfeld not only learned about the toughness of being a boxer but also about the softness of being a human being.

Possible Answers

Meaning and Purpose

1. The term *lark* in this context refers to something done solely for fun or adventure or for both. Denfeld means that she had no serious reason to start boxing.
2. As noted in paragraph 3, Jess is the titular head of the family, a position he held because of his vast personal experience as a boxer, his renown as a trainer, and, of course, his age.
3. Students occasionally point out that this phrase means that Denfeld is a traitor to women because she tried to act like a man; however, "I had changed flags" in this context means figuratively only that she moved into a social territory not usually thought of as a place where women would want to go.
4. As pointed out in paragraph 6, the male boxers faced a dilemma: Either they could spar softly with Denfeld, thus risking getting hurt by Denfeld, or they could hit Denfeld as hard as they could hit a man, thus risking being called a bully.
5. As pointed out in paragraph 9, the greatest challenges that the male boxers faced were in fact those that could grow from Denfeld's discovering that men are vulnerable.

Strategy

1. In the last two paragraphs of the essay, by using the strategy of discovery, Denfeld shows that she has succeeded in both ways as a boxer: She won a title fight, and she found that she was as vulnerable as she had earlier discovered the men to be.
2. Answers vary, according to how deeply students want to explore this question. In fact, using the strategy of juxtaposition, Denfeld begins paragraph 1 with a description of her fantasy and begins paragraph 2 with a description of the end of her fantasy. However, evidence abounds in the essay to show that Denfeld's discovery was ongoing.
3. The myth of "male superiority in strength and aggressiveness" is discussed in this essay, particularly in paragraph 10. As it is used in paragraph 10, the word *myth* refers to a popular belief that has survived without evidence to support it. Denfeld discovered that the "myth" quoted earlier is without evidence.

4 In paragraph 11, we see that Denfeld's "fighter of my dreams" started out as Denfeld herself, the fantasy fighter mentioned in paragraph 1.

5. The dream fighter was replaced by the real fighter, which is ironically Denfeld herself, as a better person than the fantasy fighter because of her boxing experience.

Style

1. As used in paragraph 6 of this essay, the word *dilemma* refers to one's having two choices, each of them equally undesirable. Depending on students' interpretations of the word's context, they select such synonyms as "problem," "difficulty," "concern," "obstacle," and "constraint."

2. As seen in paragraph 9, the fighters wonder if Denfeld will "breathe a sigh of relief, or laugh in contempt." The purpose of the question is to illustrate Denfeld's compassion and her insight into the minds of the male boxers.

3. In paragraph 4 is contained the phrase "careful gang attire," referring to the notion that all gang members have identifying clothing that must be worn a certain way. For example, some gangs demand that their members wear a certain color baseball cap with its bill at a specific angle. Another gang dress code specifies that a pair of pants must have its cuffs at a certain height.

4. In paragraph 8, Denfeld shows us that she has entered the world of reality, where she has come to discover that male stereotyping needs to be reviewed in the light of her personal experiences.

5. Paragraph 3 contains the comment that Jess "shipped out during World War II." The phrase "to ship out" means "to engage to serve on shipboard." The phrase's past-tense version is "shipped out."

Trapped in Another Life
Art Harris

Teaching Suggestions

Students will find this story of Pamela Rodgers's two lives engrossing. Undoubtedly, they will have differing opinions about the proper disposition of the case. After discussing the content and the law-enforcement dilemma, you may wish to have students examine the way in which Harris uses different rhetorical patterns—comparison and contrast, cause and effect, description, and chronological narration—to tell Pamela's story. It is a good time to emphasize that essays are not usually written in one "pure" rhetorical pattern. In any one essay a writer may use many patterns as they become appropriate.

Notes

Paragraph 1
Harris begins with a contrast between prison life and life outside and between Kay and her former self.
Paragraph 4
Beginning here, Harris goes to the more distant past, then relates her recent past in paragraphs 5–9.

Paragraph 10
Continuing the chronological sequence, Harris relates the most immediate past and describes her present situation.
Paragraphs 16–19
The next four paragraphs contrast two views about her possible pardon.
Paragraph 20
Returning to the chronological, Harris now goes to the far distant past, relating her background up to her committing criminal acts, using a cause-and-effect pattern.
Paragraph 34
The next six paragraphs continue the cause-and-effect pattern leading up to her jail sentence and her escape.
Paragraph 50
This next section, to paragraph 69, details the recent past and her new life.
Paragraph 70
Paragraphs 70–78 report the events leading to her arrest again.
Paragraph 79
The final section relates the present situation as she and her family await word of a possible parole.

Possible Answers

Meaning and Purpose

1. Crime doesn't pay, but neither is our justice system always fair. Even though Kay seemed to have left her criminal life behind, the law caught up with her. Harris's purpose is to show her struggle to live a decent life after her misguided early life and to question the justice of her returning to prison. Perhaps Harris hopes that telling Kay's story sympathetically in the newspaper will rally support for her release and pardon.
2. Though Kay changed her life when she married Ray, she "remained haunted by the past and present" (70). Back in prison, she says, "There wasn't any freedom for the last ten years, not for anyone with a conscience" (81). The two lives she had were starkly different, and her earlier life kept her trapped.
3. Harris draws a sympathetic portrait of Kay in the first fifteen paragraphs and so leads readers to favor Hassett's statement. Harris describes Kay's exemplary life and quotes a person who says how conscientious she was. Being taken back to prison seems wrenching and unfair after these descriptions.
4. Max Factor is a cosmetics company. The phrase refers to makeup and how little Kay wore. Harris equates her use of little makeup with her new life of decency and moral uprightness.
5. Each description sounds like fiction, a stereotype. They contrast sharply, and readers will feel disbelief that both could describe the same person, will feel intrigued, even skeptical, and will want to know more.

Strategy

1. Paragraphs 1–3 describe a scene and place readers in it. Enough mystery hovers about the scene ("a devoted but baffled brood") to arouse interest. Not calling Kay by name till paragraph 3 delays this necessary information and gives Harris time to create an impression before readers know who she is. The contrasting descriptions of her in paragraph 3 have readers interested enough to read on.

2. This is a newspaper article and readers want information fast. A survey of Kay's life lets readers know the gist, then they can read on for details. If Harris had begun with her early life, readers would have a harder time sympathizing with her, and Harris's points would not be as effectively—and dramatically—made.

3. The essay is mostly a summary of events, giving highlights and leaving out a lot of details. The two sentences, "She remembers her father's belt, his guns, his whiskey, his temper" (20), and "With six or so months left to serve, in January, 1978, she hitched as far as Glen Burnie, Maryland, rented a room, took a job as a waitress in a Greek diner" (50), summarize events but do not dramatize them in a scene.

4. Harris is careful to put present events in the present tense, as in the opening scene in prison. He tells of her past life in past tense ("Somehow she managed to keep it together as she lived in fear and hid her past, even from her husband" [9]), but he again intersperses the present tense for her present life ("She wears a purple prison jumpsuit" [13] and "Family and friends have canvassed the community" [15]). The direct quotations are in present tense ("Kay says of her father" [23]).

Style

1. Harris sympathizes with Kay from the start when he paints a stark, lonely picture of her in prison. He highlights events that show her as victim, as in paragraph 28 when Danny slaps her, and in paragraph 31. When Harris describes her reformed life, he tells of good and generous things she did. The tipoff to her identity as a fugitive is inadvertently given by her son—she did nothing to draw the attention of the law. All these details arouse sympathy in readers and question the justice of putting Kay back in prison.

2. Though these words are fairly understandable in context, they are jargon, and Harris's audience might be readers unfamiliar with trucking. But any audience could understand this essay.

3. The language is concise and fast-paced, but Harris doesn't care about being objective. He portrays Kay as victimized in her young life, now trying to live a decent life, and recently yanked away from her family and thrust back into prison. Harris intends readers to see the irony when he reports that Kay "was classified by Maryland prison officials as a security risk" (14). Clearly, Harris thinks she should be released and pardoned, and his article is like a plea for this action.

Los Pobres

Richard Rodriguez

Teaching Suggestions

This selection is a good example of narrative used as a springboard to serious thoughts. A summer job serves as a growth experience for the narrator because he is aware of his own thoughts and emotions. Have students notice how much self-examination Rodriguez includes in this piece. It begins in the first paragraph and continues throughout. But it is not self-absorption. He is always aware of the others and his relationship to them.

The narrative covers a long time (an unspecified number of years), but the heart of the experience is in a few awkward moments Rodriguez spent attempting to converse with a group of Mexican alien workers. The narrator carries those moments with him as he examines his life since that summer.

Notes

Paragraph 1
The first paragraph introduces the narrator and his situation. The narrator pictures himself as a nontypical student in some characteristics: almost an outsider, not quite as sophisticated as his classmates.

Paragraph 6
This passage is required for the reader's understanding that it is not distaste for manual labor that separates the narrator from *los pobres*.

Paragraph 7
The brief incident recalled in paragraphs 7, 8, and 9 gives the narrator the insight that a summer job will not really admit him to the world of the laborer and prepares the reader for the larger insight that follows in paragraphs 20–24.

Paragraph 10
The narrator discovers the diversity among American workers and finds himself at ease in their company. The comfort contrasts with the coming description of his uneasiness in addressing the Mexican aliens.

Paragraph 16
The man's glance over the narrator's shoulder toward *el patrón* tells the narrator that he is seen only as a messenger from the boss and dashes his hopes for a bond between him and the Mexican workers.

Paragraphs 18 and 19
These paragraphs take us to a more recent past and confirm the narrator's acceptance of his membership in a privileged class.

Paragraphs 20–24
The final paragraphs sum up his understanding of what the earlier experience means. The fundamental distinction between the narrator and *los pobres* is an attitude that grows from different experiences.

Beginning the last two paragraphs with the same sentence emphasizes the Mexican workers' compliance and vulnerability and leaves us with wonder at the chasm between the classes.

Possible Answers

Meaning and Purpose

1. Rodriguez is observant of his fellow students and believes they are wealthier and more privileged than he. He feels inferior, more kin to the Mexican-American janitors and gardeners, and he is sensitive about his dark skin. He doesn't think he is appealing physically: he "didn't linger in mirrors" (1).
2. Rodriguez had never done hard physical labor, as his father had. Wanting to rise above the working class, he was surprised when "desire uncoiled"

(2) in him for the construction job. Challenged by physical labor, he didn't want his parents to think he'd taken a job beneath him, or that he had no ambition.

3. Rodriguez's main point is realizing what makes people *los pobres*. In paragraph 21 he says, "What made me different from them was an attitude of *mind,* my imagination of myself." He worked with white laborers who had college degrees and with Mexican laborers who were silent, compliant, and vulnerable (24). It was not occupation but his perception of himself, and the voice his education had given him, which would keep him from ever being one of *los pobres* (21).

4. The insight is that Rodriguez cannot "gain admission to the world of the laborer" (9) just by working at a summer construction job. He was not bound to the job and could savor the sensation of fatigue. The connection with "But I was not one of *los pobres*" (21) is that his body might be capable of physical labor and his hands as "tough as theirs" (21), but his "attitude of mind" (21) and his education keep him from being poor.

5. Being paid as a group eliminates their individuality as men. The contractor takes advantage of their alien status and their inability to bargain for themselves.

6. The Mexican workers are silent because they have no union, no grounds, no "public identity" (23). They depend on others' good will. Finally their silence brings Rodriguez "face to face with *los pobres*."

Strategy

1. The order is chronological, so that Rodriguez can show his early naiveté about class and life-style, then his later sophistication and ability to understand his summer.

2. The summer job, core of the narrative, requires details to make the point about Rodriguez's realizing what it means to be poor. Sections two and three compress time and summarize the life-style he later lived and now lives. These two sections don't describe just one event but show Rodriguez looking back through post-college experiences that help him understand that summer.

3. Rodriguez uses both summary and scene. The summer job is presented more as scene, a drama acted out with characters and dialogue. (" 'Don't make your back do so much work,' he instructed. I stood patiently listening" [8]). But some of it is summarized: "I labored with excitement the first morning—and all the days after" (6). Section two is summary about his physical condition and the clothes he wears (18–19). And in section three, he also summarizes (20). The summary parts have little or no dialogue and no scenes are acted out.

4. Rodriguez uses first person to tell his own story, but he is looking back from his thirties on the summer job in college. With this point of view he can show how he came to understand what it is to be poor. Examples that show this effectiveness are: "The more I remember that summer, the more I realize that there was no single *type* of worker" (10); "And I can still hear the quiet, indistinct sounds of the Mexican, the oldest, who replied . . . " (17).

Style

1. In the last sentence of paragraph 10, *los pobres* is what the middle-class construction workers just described are not. A *bracero* (5) is "no longer afraid," but a strong worker. The *patrón* (13), or the contractor, gives orders to the Mexicans. *Gringo* (17) comes right after the description of how the contractor pays the Mexicans, and how "loudly confident" his voice is. *Gringo* is a disparaging name for whites.

2. Three fragments in the first two paragraphs are: "Less tortured perhaps"; "But still kin"; "Nothing too hard." These fragments create the informal, conversational tone of the opening, and they are emphatic in their brevity.

3. Rodriguez re-creates life, especially in describing the Mexican workers, who seem immediate and real, even in their anonymity.

5 / Examples

Mother Tongue
Amy Tan

Teaching Suggestions

One entrance into this essay is to have your students describe situations in which the subjects of their conversations and the language they use vary. That is, what do they talk about when they are with friends of the same sex? Friends of both sexes? What do they talk about when with people they don't know well? With their co-workers? With their parents? Does their language change with the subject matter? How? Point out to them that when they give examples, particularly examples that entail some narrative, they are following the format that Tan uses in her essay.

Notes

Paragraphs 1 and 2

At the outset, Tan establishes that what follows will not be a scientific examination of language. Indeed, her evidence will be anecdotal and, therefore, inappropriate for scientific discourse. She does, however, establish her authority over her subject matter in the second paragraph since she is a professional writer and a lifelong lover of language.

Paragraph 3

Tan begins with a story that introduces us to one of her "Englishes," standard English.

Paragraph 4

She now tells another story to introduce us to her family language of intimacy that will be her primary focus.

Paragraph 5

Here Tan summarizes her mother's story that she will then quote verbatim in paragraph 6.

Paragraph 8

The body of the essay, which begins here, is an extended examination of her mother's "limited" English and the effects it has had on her, Tan.

Paragraph 9

The conclusion of paragraph 8 leads to Tan's consideration of the various ways her mother's language had limited both of them.

Tan uses general examples to demonstrate why her perceptions of her mother were limited.

Paragraphs 10–13

These paragraphs constitute a humorous extended anecdote that demonstrates her mother's recognition of her own language limitations.

Paragraph 14

Another anecdote, this time a more serious one, further illustrates her mother's acute awareness of her limitations.

CAT (computerized axial tomography) scan: a method for diagnosing disorders of the brain, lung, liver, spleen, and other soft tissue using a computerized combination of many X-ray photographs taken by a special instrument that displays computerized cross-sectional images of the body.

Paragraphs 15–17

These paragraphs concentrate on the ways Tan herself was limited.

Paragraph 18

In the first paragraph of this concluding section, Tan considers the possibility that the personal limitations she described in the previous three paragraphs can be extended to other Asian-Americans.

Paragraph 19

Tan now contracts her focus to herself—how she became a writer and the writing of her first novel, *The Joy Luck Club*.

Paragraph 21

After concentrating on limitations, Tan ends with a near paean to her mother, a respect and love that has been implicit in all of her anecdotes.

Paragraph 22

Appropriately, Tan's mother becomes her most telling critic.

Possible Answers

Meaning and Purpose

1. Tan states her thesis in the last sentence of the second paragraph.
2. Tan's mother exhibits a keen understanding of language by reading *Forbes*, listening to *Wall Street Week*, conversing with her stockbroker, and reading Shirley MacLaine's books—the last a tongue-in-cheek example (7). She also understands how her own English limits her and has a firm grasp of the predicaments which that inability puts her in. Tan gives two examples of this understanding. The first is the humorous story about her stockbroker (10–13), the second a serious anecdote about the results of a CAT scan (14).

3. As a girl Tan was embarrassed by her mother's English, thinking her defective language reflected defective thinking. This embarrassment severely limited Tan's perception of her mother (9).
4. Tan believes that the language spoken by the family, especially insular immigrant families, shapes the language of the child more than sociologists and linguists think. She thus was a higher achiever in math than she was in English (15) and conjectures this influence may account for the former paucity of Asian-American writers (18).

Strategy
1. A narrative essay usually has a single story line. Tan's anecdotes are individual stories that illustrate individual points.
2. Tan's examples are always specific, written in concrete language, and are often humorous, or poignant, or both.
3. Tan divides her essay into three parts. The first section (1–7) introduces the reader to the idea that she uses several "Englishes" and describes in detail her "family" English. The second section (8–17) is more reflective and examines the ways her mother's English have been limiting. The final section (18–21) describes why she became a writer and how she writes. The three sections serve as the essay's introduction, body, and conclusion.

Style
1. Most students will be able to decipher the gist of the story, and many may recognize it as colorful and perceptive. Tan's childhood assessment that this stumbling English reflected defective thinking was certainly faulty.
2. Tan's "Englishes" can be placed in two categories: the English she grew up with: "simple" English, "broken" English, "watered down" English; standard English that she ". . . had learned in school and through books. . . ."
3. The line is awkward, the diction pretentious. As an exercise you might have your students translate the line into plain English. "That was the beginning of my uncertainty," is a possibility.
4. *Wrought*: worked; *nominalized*: to have converted another part of speech into a noun, as in changing the adjective *lowly* to *the lowly*, or to have converted an underlying clause into a noun phrase, as in changing he *drinks* to *his drinking*; *transcribed*: made a written copy; *belies*: shows to be false, contradicts; *empirical*: derived from or guided by experience; *guise*: general external appearance; *impeccable*: faultless; *benign*: not malignant; *insular*: detached, isolated; *semantic*: arising from the different meanings of words; *quandary*: a state of perplexity or uncertainty; *nascent*: beginning to exist or develop.

Black Men and Public Spaces
Brent Staples

Teaching Suggestions
Staples's essay can be used effectively to demonstrate the necessity of using concrete examples to back-up generalizations, thereby giving those generalizations meaning

and life. The essay is full of examples—general examples, specific examples, and anecdotes—that give concrete meaning and vivid life to Staples's points. Question 3 under *Strategy* is designed to get the students to do their own analyses of the essay's structure. But, whether or not you have the students do that question on their own, it might be a good idea to lead them through the essay paragraph-by-paragraph, discussing the number and kinds of examples Staples uses, as well as the skillful way he mixes them up to give the essay variety. You may or may not choose to use the answer to question 3 of *Strategy* in this manual as a guide.

The essay could also be used in conjunction with Leone Gaiter's "The Revolt of the Black Bourgeoisie" (pp. 367–373) to get at Staples's meaning and the social and psychological ramifications of his observations. While Staples states that he has merely "inherited" his ability "to alter public space," Gaiter conjectures some specific reasons why young, black men have inherited this dubious power. Using the two essays together might lead to a lively and thoughtful discussion.

Notes

Paragraph 8
"perilous flavor": The first sentence of this paragraph serves as the topic sentence for the three anecdotes that follow. The three anecdotes lead to the general truth in the last sentence of paragraph 10, the conclusion to this three-paragraph section of the essay.

Paragraph 12
Beethoven: Ludwig von Beethoven (1770–1827), German composer. Beethoven began his career as a classical composer who used Haydn and Mozart as his models (Haydn was his teacher). His music became more powerfully emotional as he grew older, and he thus became the first and greatest of the romantic composers. One of the greatest geniuses in the history of western music, Beethoven was deaf for a good portion of his composing career.

Vivaldi: Antonio Vivaldi (c. 1675–1741), baroque Italian composer and violinist, known familiarly as *il prete rosso* (the red-haired priest). Vivaldi wrote more than four hundred concertos for various instruments and combinations of instruments, thirty-eight operas, and church music, of which the *Gloria* (c. 1726) is well known. The *Four Seasons* is his most popular and most recognizable secular piece.

Possible Answers

Meaning and Purpose

1. Staples describes himself in the first paragraph as young, black, large, and male. Simply by being so, he causes fear in others, particularly women, and particularly at night. He claims this questionable power to be an "unwieldy inheritance" (2), something he has simply by being a young, black man. He gives a partial explanation for this when he observes that "Women are particularly vulnerable to street violence, and young black males are drastically overrepresented among the perpetrators of that violence" (5). But this observation certainly cannot account for the fear projected onto virtually all young, black males by non-blacks. (Leonce Gaiter gives one explanation for this disturbing phenomenon in "The Revolt of the Black Bourgeoisie," pp. 367–372.) So, implicitly underlying the entire essay is the specter of racism.

2. The first time Staples fully recognizes that he has "the ability to alter public space in ugly ways" (2) he feels "surprised, embarrassed, and dismayed all at once" (2), because he has been unjustifiably associated with "the muggers who occasionally seeped into the area" (2). He learns "the language of fear" (3) thoroughly, in two different ways, in fact. Because he is automatically feared in certain situations, he is himself placed in danger, and so knows fear from two sides. And because he is "ever the suspect, a fearsome entity with whom pedestrians avoid making eye contact" (5), he becomes profoundly alienated. All of this results in a "rage [he] felt at so often being taken for a criminal" (11), a rage that he must smother so he can assume an attitude and demeanor that whites will find nonthreatening (11–12).
3. Staples offers no solutions. So while the essay ends on a relatively light and humorous note, that humor has a decidedly dark edge to it.
4. Staples speaks for all black males who have had to behave similarly. We know this because all of the examples he gives in the essay, both general and specific, can be applied to all young, black men.

Strategy

1. The first paragraph grabs the reader with the first sentence. Staples plays with stereotypes he's going to use later—a woman who is about to become the victim of a young, black man in an isolated park at night—to create an immediate tension. That tension gives the anecdote drama. Staples builds both the tension and, therefore, the drama by narrating the event in an ever-quickening pace. He further dramatizes the event by describing himself in the third person ("the youngish black man") so that we see him from the frightened woman's point of view, over her shoulder. Ironically, the anecdote ends anticlimactically with the woman running safely away from a man who offers her no danger. The anecdote, then, becomes emblematic of the sad, racial ironies Staples presents in the rest of the essay. A most skillful and effective beginning.
2. Staples tells us in the second paragraph that the incident he narrated in the first paragraph happened more than ten years before, when he was only twenty-two. Now, more mature, he is able to reflect on the incident, to recollect in tranquility, as it were, and consider its meaning, significance, and ramifications. The second paragraph, therefore, explains the first.
3. Staples develops his essay by using examples that make explicitly clear what he means by "the ability to alter public space." He opens with a personal anecdote. He then uses general examples in paragraphs 2, 3, 4, 5 and 7. He uses personal anecdotes in paragraphs 8 and 9, and an anecdote about another black man in paragraph 10. His conclusion, paragraphs 11 and 12, is replete with general examples. By varying the kinds of examples, Staples creates an interesting pattern instead of a repetitious laundry list.

Style

1. Staples's language is always controlled, tempered. The situations he describes are full of fear, alienation, rage, and potential violence. The discrepancy between the language and the situations the language describes creates a tension that effectively reflects the tension in the situations themselves.

2. The woman in the opening paragraph has nothing to fear from Staples, even though she perceives herself as his potential victim. In fact, it is Staples and all other law-abiding, black men who are victimized by a society that sees all black men as potentially violent and threatening.

3. The analogy is particularly apt because, in a single example, it captures the irony of the entire essay. As a young, black man, Staples is feared. Being feared, he is constantly placed in situations that are dangerous to him, not to the people who fear him. So, when he whistles a melody from Vivaldi, he alleviates the fear in others that could actually threaten him, just as a hiker's bell mitigates the potential danger to the innocent hiker by frightening the bears away.

4. *Affluent*: having an abundance of wealth; *mean*: inferior in quality; *impoverished*: reduced to poverty; *discreet*: modest, unobtrusive; *unwieldy*: not easily handled or managed; *quarry*: any object of pursuit or attack; *dicey*: unpredictable, risky, uncertain; *foyer*: the entrance or lobby of a building; *taut*: tense; *warrenlike*: like a warren, an area containing many tenants in limited or crowded quarters; *bandolier*: a broad belt worn over the shoulder by soldiers and having a number of small loops or pockets for holding cartridges; *forge*: to move ahead slowly, steadily; *solace*: comfort in sorrow, misfortune or trouble; *bravado*: a pretentious, swaggering display of courage; *ad hoc*: for the special purpose or end presently under consideration; *labyrinthine*: complicated, torturous; *cursory*: hasty; *skittish*: uncertain, shy; *constitutionals*: walks taken for the benefit of one's health; *steely*: resembling steel in strength and hardness; *warbling*: singing or whistling with trills, quavers, or melodic embellishment.

Tools of Torture
Phyllis Rose

Teaching Suggestions

A discussion of this essay might begin by considering the various kinds of torture Rose describes. Students can be asked to contribute their own examples from books they have read or movies they have seen. Then ask how they react to a discussion of torture methods. Why do such devices often fascinate us? Why are there exhibits of torture instruments like the one in Paris that Rose mentions?

From there a discussion might move to the assertions Rose makes about institutionalized torture and how people are led to accept torture as a reasonable tool in the service of a noble cause (6, 7). Do Rose's explanations conform with the view of torture presented in modern books and films? If not, how do they differ? Why are we so seldom asked to be on the side of the torturer in current fiction and films? Are we ever asked to believe torture is natural and acceptable? Paragraph 8 can be examined in this context.

Finally, what do students think of Rose's suggestion that we "refuse to allow the nobly abstract to seduce us from the sweetness of the concrete" (9)?

Notes

Paragraph 1

The first sentence of the paragraph serves as the topic sentence and emphasizes the idea that even without modern technology the human imagination has devised a horrendous variety of torture devices. Rose goes on to a lengthy series of grotesque examples.

The Inquisition was a Roman Catholic ecclesiastical tribunal instituted by Pope Innocent III in the thirteenth century to suppress heresy and punish heretics. The inquisitor's chair was one of the tortures devised to further this end, as were most of the other devices described in the essay. That is the reasoning behind the claim in paragraph 6 that human torture has been instituted, condoned, and "vetted" hand-in-hand by church and state.

Paragraph 4

The French colonized Algeria in 1830. The native Muslim Algerians, like all conquered peoples, continually smarted under foreign rule and finally rebelled, attaining independence in 1962. In the last convulsions of the revolution, the French tortured Algerians with electrodes and other devices to elicit information. Having ruled Algeria for so long, the French involved in the atrocities considered their acts both patriotic and necessary.

Paragraph 6

After explaining why so many instruments of torture are to be found, the author proposes to move to the even more important question of why they were invented in the first place.

Paragraph 7

Stanley Milgram: Milgram's experiments reinforce the idea that sadists are not responsible for institutionalized human cruelty. On the contrary, ordinary people can be convinced that the pain they inflict is for some higher cause, this time for scientific learning. Milgram also cites Hannah Arendt's 1963 book, *Eichmann in Jerusalem*. She contends that the prosecution's assertion that the Nazi Eichmann was a sadist monster, responsible for the murder of thousands of Jews, was wrong. Rather, she claims, he came closer to being a dull bureaucrat who simply sat at his desk and followed orders (Stanley Milgram, *Obedience to Authority*, 1974).

Paragraph 8

Benthamite: Jeremy Bentham (1748–1832) was an English philosopher who promoted utilitarianism, the ethical doctrine that asserted actions are right or good in proportion to their usefulness or as they tend to promote happiness. The doctrine claimed that the end and criterion of public action is the greatest happiness of the greatest number. Thus, human happiness becomes the one and only measure of right and wrong.

Paragraph 9

Marie Antoinette (1755–1793), queen of France, was the wife of Louis XVI, whom she married when she was fifteen. As daughter of Maria Theresa of Austria, she sought Austria's aid against French revolutionaries. In 1791 she counseled Louis to flee from France, an attempt that ended in their imprisonment. They were regarded as traitors and Marie Antoinette was guillotined on October 16, 1793. Her personal charm, her naive ignorance of practical life, her extravagance, and her frank and courageous honesty contributed to her unpopularity both at court and with the

French masses. When she was told that a revolution was threatening because the people had no bread, she is said to have replied, "Let them eat cake."

Possible Answers

Meaning and Purpose

1. Paragraph 1, sentences 2–4.
2. Rose gluts her readers with names and descriptions of torture devices, much as her eyes may have been glutted with them in the exhibit she mentions. The list of examples also elaborates her topic immediately and leaves the reader under no illusion that she will deal with the topic gently. Students may or may not think this opening a good one, depending on their responses to the topic.
3. When connected with food, the word "unthinkable" is positive, indicating imaginative power dedicated to gustatory pleasure. Connected with torture, however, the word's severe negative connotations come into play: when the power of the imagination is applied to evil, the results are too horrible.
4. Legal, social, and religious institutions working in unison create torture in order to perpetuate themselves (6). Feeling the need to belong, people become convinced that their actions against others, normally considered morally abhorrent, contribute to society's greater good. Torture thus becomes a patriotic duty (6). Rose cites the French torture of Algerians (4), the Nazis and the French again (8), and the Milgram experiments (7).
5. Because allegiance to abstract ideals leads people to torture, its precise opposite, the absolute pursuit of sensual pleasure, is torture's natural antidote (9).

Strategy

1. Electricity vastly expands the potential for human torture, but even without it the fertility of the human imagination applied to torture is impressive.
2. One specific example is Milgram's experiment (7). It supports the topic (first) sentence of paragraph 1 and is concrete: it actually happened. In one typical example, Rose describes how a person might have been tortured on the wheel (3). The example is effective because it suggests that this torture was used many times on nameless, and helpless, victims.
3. Paragraph 7 is focused on the Milgram experiments. Rose reminds us that cruelty was accepted before the enlightenment; thus, Milgram's experiments would have been meaningless at that time (8). Recent history suggests, however, that the enlightenment's ideals have not really taken hold. She considers the possibility that cruelty may have drifted to the margins of society, leading to her conclusion that radical hedonism may be the cure for abstract idealism (9).
4. Some readers might consider the graphic examples an assault on the senses. Rose does not back away from her topic and make torture seem less terrible than it is or was. This honest tone gives her argument strength and her voice as a writer credibility.

Style

1. Because one of Rose's themes is that the French have a unique talent for creating ways to give "loving attention to the body," it is appropriate to use the

French rather than English word in order to capture the French flavor. *Parfumerie* means perfume store (the author gets her massage in one). *Soins esthétiques* means beauty care.

2. The final paragraph sums up Rose's belief that Paris can be considered the "capital of pleasure." She has already given specific examples (4, 5). Ending the essay with her thoughts on the pleasures of modern Paris is a neat connection to her having begun with thoughts on the opposite sensation (pain) in medieval Paris.

3. Because the puritans shunned the flesh, the idea that beauty radiates from the inner self must be puritanical. The French, according to the author, will have none of that thinking.

4. *benign:* showing or expressive of gentleness or kindness; *aesthetician:* a person who is versed in aesthetics, the branch of philosophy dealing with such notions as the beautiful, the ugly, the sublime, and the comic as applicable to the fine arts; *malevolent:* evil, harmful, injurious; *vetted:* to have appraised, verified, or checked for accuracy, authenticity, validity, and so on; *inalienable:* not transferable to another or capable of being repudiated; *transitory:* not lasting, enduring, permanent, or eternal; *touchstone:* a test or criterion for the quality of a thing.

Future Shlock
Neil Postman

Teaching Suggestions

Postman is provocative, though easy to understand. His remarks about the show-business mentality in politics, religion, education, and news programs should elicit strong responses from students. Some will think he exaggerates. Others will be eager to provide additional examples. A good beginning is a discussion of student responses to the overall message.

Don't miss the opportunity to discuss the strategies Postman employs to keep the reader interested and to present his challenging views as reasonable.

Notes

Paragraph 1
The first three sentences plunge us directly into the subject. If you assign this essay as outside reading, it might be useful to read these sentences aloud in class first and ask if students are inclined to agree or disagree at first thought.

The long example of Germany prior to World War II may need amplification, briefly identifying the men listed:

Albert Einstein (1879–1955). Physicist; theory of relativity. Nobel Prize, 1921. Became United States citizen in 1940.

Sigmund Freud (1856–1939). Founder of modern psychoanalysis.

Thomas Mann (1875–1955). Novelist and critic. Nobel Prize, 1929. Came to United States in 1937.

Stefan Zweig (1881–1942). Austrian dramatist, critic, novelist.

Konrad Lorenz (1903–1989). Ethologist. Nobel Prize, 1973.

Werner Heisenberg (1901–1976). Physicist. Nobel Prize, 1932.

Martin Heidegger (1889–1976). Philosopher and writer.

Gerhardt Hauptmann (1862–1946). Dramatist, novelist, poet. Nobel Prize, 1912.

Marcel Proust (1871–1922). French novelist.

André Gide (1869–1951). French novelist, poet, critic. Nobel Prize, 1947.

Emile Zola (1840–1902). French novelist.

Jack London (1876–1916). United States novelist and short-story writer.

Upton Sinclair (1878–1968). United States novelist.

The paragraph ends with an emphatic clincher sentence. Postman often uses this device to drive a point home or to look ahead to the next paragraph. See paragraphs 2–4, 11, 14, 15, 18, and 22.

Paragraph 2

Having evoked the memory of pre-World War II Germany, an easy-to-accept example, Postman challenges his readers by saying that a similar erosion of intelligence could happen in the United States. This contrast between America's past and Postman's perception of its present condition gives his readers a measure of how much he feels has been lost.

Paragraph 3

Land-Grant Act: The Land Grant Act of 1862 was a federal government act that financed the establishment of state colleges.

Henry Steele Commager: (1902–1997). United States historian and author.

"Shlock": Of inferior quality, cheap, junk (also spelled *schlock*).

Paragraph 4

The first sentence is a fairly direct statement of Postman's thesis. (A fuller statement is at the end of paragraph 11.)

For readers who are saying to themselves that the United States is different from Germany, Postman accepts the objection, but argues that similar methodology is not necessary. He picks up this contrast later in discussing Orwell's *1984* and Huxley's *Brave New World.*

Have students comment on the effectiveness of the three sentences that begin with "a culture" and the shock value of the word "stupidity" in the last sentence.

Paragraphs 5 and 6

Many students will be familiar with *The Gods Must Be Crazy* first shown in the United States in 1984 and frequently offered on cable. In paragraph 5, he presents the situation in the movie, and in paragraph 6, he explains the bottle's disrupting effect: "The people begin to love their bottle more than they love themselves."

Paragraph 7

Before moving to the second movie example, you might want to make sure that students understand Postman's point: A new technology should be examined carefully and rejected if necessary.

Paragraph 8

The second movie example illustrates a different point: We are in danger of so trivializing dignified, serious, and important aspects of life that they will become mere entertainment.

Paragraph 12

Aldous Huxley: (1894–1963). English novelist and critic.

Big Brother, the television image in Orwell's *1984*, as well as "Ministries of Propaganda," "gulags," and "concentration camps" represent the tyranny of force.

The Coca-Cola bottle is used as a symbol of new technologies.

Paragraph 13
George Orwell [Eric Blair] (1903–1950) was an English novelist and essayist.
Paragraph 14
This paragraph marks the culmination of Postman's interpretation of the current situation. His examples thus far have pointed to the insufficiently examined power of show business (particularly, but not exclusively, television) to trivialize serious discourse.
Paragraph 15
Beginning with paragraph 15, Postman turns to examples of this trivialization in politics, religion, education, and news in the next four paragraphs.
Paragraph 16

Jonathan Edwards (1703–1758). Clergyman and theologian.
Charles Finney (1792–1875). Clergyman and educator.
George Whitefield (1714–1770). Methodist revivalist.
Jimmy Swaggart (born 1935). Television evangelist.
Jim Bakker (born 1948). Former television evangelist.
Jerry Falwell (born 1933). Television evangelist.

Paragraph 18
How do your students take to the accusation leveled against all of us at the end of this paragraph?
Paragraph 19
In three paragraphs (19,20,21), Postman tells us he is not blaming television alone, nor is he attacking the visual arts or entertainment in themselves.
Paragraph 21
This paragraph restates his belief that "entertainment" has permeated the serious aspects of our culture and reminds us, using the words "the gods must be crazy," about the message of that film: The effects of new technology must be examined carefully.
Paragraph 22
In the concluding paragraph he reminds us again that America seems to have chosen the Huxleyan rather than the Orwellian road.

Postman offers no specific way out of the situation he describes. In fact, paragraph 21 ends with a discouraging note: "there is no mountaintop from which we can return what is dangerous to us."

Possible Answers

Meaning and Purpose

1. Postman's purpose is to warn us about the "rapid erosion of our own intelligence" as a result of the trivialization of serious matters: politics, education, religion, and news. He simply informs us; he does not offer solutions. The last sentences in paragraphs 20–22 discourage hope. Students should be able to support their opinions about whether or not the purpose succeeds.
2. Paragraph 11 includes the statement that seems most nearly complete.
3. *The Gods Must Be Crazy* example shows that new technologies profoundly affect cultures, and they should be examined and discarded if necessary. *The Producers* example shows how serious matters can be trivialized.
4. Perhaps only a few students will agree with Postman completely. Some may feel he exaggerates; others will strongly resist his intensely critical message.

Strategy

1. This sentence—"We will become, in a phrase, a people amused into stupidity"—summarizes the lengthy sentence preceding it and provides shock value with the word "stupidity" (11).

   "And that is how television brings ruin. . . ." The uncompromising harshness of "ruin" conveys the seriousness of his charge in the preceding sentence (14).

   "I would suggest that television has annihilated it." The word annihilated means total erasure of the line, thus conveying Postman's contention that politics has become entertainment (15).

   "To be sure, we know *of* many things; but we know *about* very little." The parallelism used here to contrast *of* and *about* creates a memorable phrasing, reinforcing his point that television news is not really educating people (18).

   "I agree." Coming after a long (sixty-word) sentence developed with parallel structure, the punchiness of this two-word sentence is emphatic (22).

2. Germany is, first, a notorious example of unexplained "madness." Therefore, it is easy for a reader to accept the example and the conclusion. When he moves in the next paragraph to the United States example, the reader has already, at least in part, accepted his credibility.

3. Postman appeals to an intelligent, aware audience that can understand many of his historical references, or know how to look them up. Yet he probably knows that some of his readers get most of their information from television, even though he criticizes this habit. He surely intends to be provocative and make readers think and perhaps reevaluate.

4. In the first half of the essay (through paragraph 13), he uses specific, extended examples: Germany, the United States, *The Gods Must Be Crazy*, *The Producers*, and *Brave New World*, as well as a brief mention of *1984*.

   In the second half of the essay the examples are brief and both specific and typical (see paragraph 18 for a good illustration).

Style

1. *Cathedral* may be loosely applied to any large church. The connotation here is of spiritual authority, suggesting dedication, piety, learning, reverence, love, aspiration—the best human qualities.

   A *cesspool* is a drainage hole for sewage. It brings to mind filth, foul smells, disease, and waste.

   Barbarian originally meant anyone who belonged to a group outside one's own culture, and *barbaric* denoted such a person's behavior, whatever it might be. Now the word commonly indicates lack of learning, lack of restraint, wild, uneducated, uncivilized, and uncultured—a person living without reasonable values and behaviors.

   The metaphor moves from the lofty to the debased and characterizes the change as a retreat to less than civilized behavior.

2. The Coca-Cola bottle is a metaphor for new technologies. The quotations, in turn, mean a new technology can become tyrannical, recall the bottle's effect on the tribe, connect television with the Coke bottle, and restate the original metaphor.

3. *Shlock*: shoddy; *nemeses* (plural of nemesis): a powerful rival, one who inflicts destruction; *rhetorical*: use of words for persuasion; *precipitous*: steep;

preemption: acquisition or appropriation of something beforehand; *banal*: predictable, trite; *sacrality*: religious rites; *paradigm*: a model; *countenance*: appearance.

The Issue Isn't Sex, It's Violence
Caryl Rivers

Teaching Suggestions

Students can become quite animated when discussing this essay because of its conscious-raising potential. Many of them have, of course, heard the lyrics of popular songs, but it often develops in conversation that they have not thought about them, particularly those lyrics having to do with violence towards women. Occasionally, therefore, a few students become mildly defensive, commenting that "after all, it's 'only music,'" a comment that causes other students to respond warmly with such remarks as "Aren't the lyrics to religious songs also 'only music'?" Have your students discuss such commentary, perhaps prodding them a bit by asking if they have any favorite lyrics to current music and by asking them if they know the lyrics to any song that accompanies a television commercial.

Notes

Paragraph 1
Rivers's first sentence includes what I. A. Richards called an "aim of discourse," introducing the effect that the essay is intended to achieve on the reader, with its "possibly inspired by the lyrics of a rock song." Also note the use of the word *chorus,* here meaning people's comments about the murders, but also alluding to music.

Paragraph 2
Rivers identifies with "kids" by noting that she once was just like them in her appreciation of lyrics, though it was in the 1950s. Then she reminds or informs her reader that modern lyrics are much more sexually graphic. Note the comparison between her memories of Elvis Presley and the alleged realities of the AC/DC ballad.

Paragraph 3
This is the shift paragraph, the paragraph that gets the reader into the heart of the essay. It contains an ethical statement that draws a moral line between, for example, the sight of a singer's gyration and the spectacle of a woman's being sodomized.

Paragraph 4
Note the quotation marks surrounding *intellectual,* Rivers's sarcasm coming across to the reader. This paragraph contains a "what-if" analogy: What would happen if the lyrics concerned subjects other than violence against women? It's a strategy that triggers the awareness of her readers.

Paragraphs 5 and 6
These short paragraphs answer the question posed by the "what-if" analogy in paragraph 4, and then they introduce a central point for discussion in the essay.

Paragraph 7
Rivers points out that she, too, recognizes that freedom of speech not only exists, but also must be protected. At the same time, free speech means that we can and should speak out against that which offends us.

Paragraph 8

This paragraph points out the obvious, which is often so obvious as to be over-looked: We have come to accept the media as truth-bringers that lend credibility to whatever they present, no matter the form of the presentation.

Paragraph 9

The media legitimacy noted in paragraph 8 has grown to include media presentations of rock music, and the current generation has been raised (or left alone) to accept unquestioningly the "truth" that is offered to them, particularly by television programs.

Paragraph 10

This paragraph lends authorial credence to the essay. Rivers has had sympathetic experiences with her topic that add personal substance to her comments.

Paragraph 11

Realistically, this paragraph notes that one cannot prove beyond a doubt that song lyrics and television images are responsible for violence against women. Nevertheless, this possible cause-and-effect relationship is well worth pondering.

Paragraph 12

This paragraph points out the danger of remaining silent about the essay's topic, for silence has become synonymous with endorsement.

Paragraph 13

Although violence on television is by no means rare, it is nearly always not gratuitous; instead, it provides a means to show that good eventually prevails.

Paragraph 14

Unlike the kind of violence, villains, and heroes mentioned in paragraph 13, the violent person in some popular songs is portrayed as the hero, not the villain.

Paragraph 15

This is an ethical appeal from the writer to the reader. Rivers is not saying that "we" should do such-and-such. Instead, she points out clearly and forcefully what she herself believes should be done.

Paragraph 16

The ethical statement that springs from paragraph 16 is expanded to appeal to men, particularly, it seems, to those who control what is available on the media.

Possible Answers

Meaning and Purpose

1. Students' answers will vary, of course, depending on the music that they hear. Therefore, the strength of their answers depends on what they say about the lyrics of the songs that they prefer.
2. By using quotations marks to surround *intellectual,* Rivers mocks the attitudes held by certain kinds of men who would rather theorize than act.
3. Silence is a cultural way of condoning a condition or an action. By remaining silent about a topic, we imply that we are willing to accept it or that it does not bother us to the point of our taking action against it.
4. The main topic of this essay is that violence against women is being condoned by silence, but many people fail to realize that the kind of violence discussed is not geographically, socially, or economically determined. It could happen to any woman at any time, for no reason. Therefore, Rivers's call to action is a call to all of us to act.

5. Answers vary mildly, but most students agree that they were quite affected by Rivers's having taught students who were victimized by violence. They claim with some warrant that Rivers wrote the essay because of her students' being violated.

Strategy

1. Readers automatically assume that a hero is anyone who is admired for achievements and noble qualities, hence a hero is a leader, whether or not the hero relishes that role. Because the "heroes" in modern music speak lyrically of violence against women, it follows that some of their fans would in fact tolerate such violence, or, and what is worse, become violent themselves because their heroes are portrayed as violent.
2. The claim in paragraph 15, clearly implied, is that unless we all, particularly members of the media, become vocally involved in a fight against the problem of the media's portraying violence against women as a legitimate activity culturally condoned, then crimes of violence against women will increase.
3. Violence against women shouldn't be greeted by silence. As much as we all might agree with this statement, it nevertheless is presented in this essay as a personal opinion, as evidenced by the verb should(n't), used in its auxiliary function to express an obligation as the author sees it.
4. The cause or agent is a supposed one. If a person or a group favored, for example, random and immediate physical violence against African-Americans, then the media and politicians would take immediate action against that person or that group. The supposition is that violence against women is not nearly so newsworthy.
5. Answers vary interestingly, with most students stating, one way or another, that whether they agree or disagree with the statement is moot; the fact is that Rivers has caused them to think about the possibility that a cause-and-effect relationship does exist between lyrics and images and acts of violence.

Style

1 This trite expression pushes the "ho-hum" everyday idea that what is, is the way it is supposed to be, no matter the action. Rivers uses it to emphasize the public's probable lack of interest in her thesis.
2. The fringes of society comprise those people who have no political interests, who survive daily with little thought for the future, who are voiceless by choice.
3. The word *nifty* is outdated slang, meaning at one time "very attractive." Rivers uses it to emphasize the age of the people whom she addresses in this paragraph. They are mature adults, not impressionable teenagers.
4. Rivers ends the paragraph with a rhetorical question because she wants the reader to pause, to think about what the writer has just covered. The question appeals more to one's sense of morality than to one's sense of logic.
5. In the current vernacular of much pop music, it is fashionable to clip the pronunciations of as many words as practicable to lend an aura of authenticity to the lyrics, making them seem as if they were being sung by gang members instead of highly paid performers.

- 6 / *Comparison and Contrast* -

Grant and Lee: A Study in Contrasts
Bruce Catton

Teaching Suggestions

You might want to start by discussing how some current civil conflicts (Bosnia, Serbia, Kosovo, or Rwanda, perhaps) resemble our Civil War and how they differ. Outlining these similarities and differences can lead to discussion of the essay's structure: the first three paragraphs as introduction; paragraphs 4–6 describing the attributes of Robert E. Lee and the society he represented; paragraphs 7–9 describing Ulysses S. Grant and the values he represented; paragraphs 10 and 11 paired against each other; point-by-point contrast in paragraph 12; paragraph 13 a transition moving from contrast to comparison; and paragraphs 14, 15, and 16 showing the similarities of the two men, moving from the least important to the most important.

From there you might ask students to evaluate the contrary social ideals the two men represented.

Notes

Paragraph 1
The contrast between the closing of "a great chapter in American history" taking place in "the parlor of a modest house" emphasizes the enormity of the occasion.

Paragraph 2
"poignant": After students have looked up this word, you might discuss why it is so fitting here, why it is better than *teary, sad*, or *touching*, for instance.

Paragraph 3
Not only does this sentence serve as the essay's thesis, but it also has a metaphor that emphasizes the strength of the two men's personalities and characters and the power of the two societies they represented; that is, they were "two conflicting currents" so powerful that when they met the "collision" was "final."

Paragraph 4
This sentence is a kind of mini-thesis that controls the essay's next section, paragraphs 5 and 6.

Paragraph 5
It was the Virginia tidewater where the very first permanent English settlers landed and founded Jamestown, well before the *Mayflower* (1620). Ironically, in fact, the *Mayflower* was headed there but veered off course and landed at Plymouth instead. These first settlers brought with them medieval English ideals (chivalry and all the aristocratic and ritualistic courtesies that went with it, including idealization of women) and a feudal social structure, described in the rest of the paragraph.

Paragraph 6
The implication here seems to be that as the war wore on to an end and it became more and more apparent that the Confederacy itself would fall, the Confederate soldier found it psychologically necessary to personify his ideals in a living man. Lee, thus ironically, became a symbol, an abstraction.

Paragraph 7
The first sentence, the topic sentence, immediately draws the distinctions between Lee and Grant. Grant, a product of the frontier rather than the settled and aristocratic East Coast, differed from Lee in everything. The rest of the paragraph lists some primary differences.

Paragraph 11
Whereas Lee's commitment to community was local and insular, Grant's was national and even expansionist.

Paragraph 13
This paragraph serves as a transition, carrying the reader from the differences between the two men to a comparison of their likenesses.

Paragraph 14
The topic sentence cites their first similarity and is followed by examples.

Paragraph 16
After citing the qualities that made them great warriors, Catton points out that their greatest virtue was their ability to be men of peace after the fighting was over.

Catton's phrasing of the last two sentences recalls that of the thesis sentence in paragraph 3, thus bringing the essay to a satisfying close.

Possible Answers

Meaning and Purpose

1. Recall some of the economic and social differences between the North and South that Catton cites as the cause of the United States Civil War. Lead students to discuss in detail the major differences between the Civil War and modern conflicts in other regions. Currently, civil strife exists in Bosnia and seems endless in the Middle East and Northern Ireland.

2. In paragraph 5, Catton describes a social system in which privilege was based on land ownership, inspiring a strong sense of obligation to the community. Lee, embodying "the noblest elements of this aristocratic ideal" (6), became a symbol of that ideal for the soldiers who had been willing to die to preserve it.

3. Throughout history, wars have been fought for emotional attachment to ideals rather than intellectual understanding of realities. Ask students for examples of this tendency (the Crusades, Vietnam). Even poor southerners saw Lee as a hero who could save the integrity of the southern way of life. The romance in backing such a cause was stronger, for many, than the fear of deprivation and death.

4. Grant represented a society with great hope for the future and disregard for the past. He stood for democracy, with privilege based on what a man did for himself, not on landed birthright (8).

5. Both Lee and Grant had virtues that made them great soldiers, such as "tenacity," "fidelity," and the "ability to think" (14,15). Greatest among these virtues was their ability to become men of peace after the war (16). Their pivotal difference was the kind of society each represented: Grant stood for a modern, expanding one; Lee an established, stagnant one.

6. The expression "tidewater Virginia" refers to the tidal flats, up to the Piedmont Plateau, where all the rivers met. Here grew the quintessential southern plantations where slavery began, and where the Virginia aristocracy was founded.

Strategy

1. The first three paragraphs form the introduction, which ends with the thesis (3); the next paragraph begins the body of the essay with a discussion of Lee. The rest of the essay is structured as a comparison and contrast; the introduction is not. In the introduction, Catton gives background facts about the meeting between the two generals at the close of the Civil War, and sets the basis for comparison.

2. The first and second sentences tell us that Lee and Grant, "these men" (the transition from the preceding paragraph), have brought the war to a virtual end, the key word being virtual. The third confirms that the war is essentially over, and the fourth, which concludes the paragraph, points forward to the body of the essay, the contrasts between the two men and the societies they represented.

3. Catton uses paragraph 13 as a transition from contrasting the differences between the two men to comparing their likenesses.

4. The first sentence in each paragraph uses a clear transition that tightly connects it with the preceding paragraph, thus giving the entire essay solid coherence.

5. Catton uses the subject-by-subject method in paragraphs 4 to 11. Paragraph 13 begins point-by-point comparison of similarities between the two men until the conclusion in paragraph 16. The subject-by-subject structure gives, uninterrupted, all the background on each man that Catton needs to make his point-by-point comparisons in the second half.

Style

1. The metaphor suggests that the unfolding history of the United States is a story—a narrative that could be written and read—and that the close of the Civil War is a natural ending to one chapter and beginning of another. The metaphor is effective because Catton goes on to tell the "story" of Lee and Grant.

2. Lee, as a knight in shining armor, may represent a lost cause and a social ideal that has been bypassed by history, but to interpret such a description satirically would miss the tone of the essay, which is entirely laudatory.

3. *Virtual*: being in effect, though not actually or expressly; *poignant*: keenly distressing to the feelings; *chivalry*: the medieval institution and principles of knighthood, the ideal qualities of which include courage, generosity, and courtesy; *legends*: nonhistorical or unverifiable stories handed down by tradition from earlier times and popularly accepted as historic; *myths*: stories or beliefs that are attempts to explain basic truths; *embodied*: given a concrete form; *deportment*: demeanor, conduct, behavior; *obeisance*: a movement of the body expressing deep respect or deferential courtesy, as before a superior; *static*: pertaining to or characterized by a fixed or stationary condition; *tenacity*: holding fast; *fidelity*: loyalty; *indomitable*: unable to be subdued or overcome.

4. Ending the essay in the same place as it began brings it full circle and reconnects the reader to the situation described in the first paragraph. This technique is structurally satisfying because in the body of the essay Catton has given background on and expanded the meaning of the scene in the Court House.

5. Though Lee and Grant represent two entirely different social ideals, Catton admires them both. Both were, in their own ways, admirable. Even when the author contrasts them, he always does so on positive terms. When comparing them, he speaks only of virtues: tenacity and faithfulness (14); daring, resourcefulness, and the ability to think quickly (15); and, ultimately, the capacity to be men of peace (16).

Los Otros, Mis Hermanos
Richard Rodriguez

Teaching Suggestions

You might begin by asking your students for whom English is their second language, or who come from a bilingual household, to compare their experiences with language to those of Rodriguez. Ask native speakers to relate their experiences with languages other than English. Were there situations for both groups that made them feel discomfort or frustration? From that discussion you might lead the students to a consideration of some of the elements of the essay's construction: the point-by-point development of paragraphs 2 and 3, for instance, and the subject-by-subject development of 7 and 8. You might want to teach the essay in conjunction with the other Rodriguez essay, "Los Pobres," or with Maya Angelou's "Finishing School."

Notes

Paragraph 1
All of the opening images set Rodriguez, his family, and his house apart from his neighbors: the size of the family, the color of the house, the animals.

Paragraph 2
In the opening two paragraphs Rodriguez uses both parallel structure and clear transitions to keep his contrasts clear. The phrases "In public" (sentence 1) and "At home" (sentence 3) are participial phrases that begin their respective sentences and clearly distinguish the subject of each. The opening prepositional phrase of the second paragraph's opening sentence connects the time of the paragraph with that in the opening paragraph and thus serves as a transition.

Paragraph 3
The compound sentence is balanced by the semicolon, with thesis (hearing) in the first part and antithesis (replying) in the second.

Paragraph 4
Paragraphs 4, 5, 6, and the first half of 7 concentrate on the child's lack of ability to speak and understand English.

Paragraph 7
"But" in the middle of the paragraph is an emphatic transition that brings the reader's attention from the child's language difficulties to his parents' and the consequent change of attitude he has.

Paragraph 8
The first half of the paragraph shows how his parents' language problems didn't really matter when he looks at the situation from an adult perspective. But after the

transitional "And yet . . ." he shows how their language struggles meant something significant to him as a child.

Paragraph 9

Here Rodriguez uses a general example to illustrate how the power of English and his parents' difficulties in dealing with it caused him to lose confidence in them.

Paragraph 10

These next two paragraphs concentrate on the comforts he found in his family's language, *Español*. For him his family becomes extended to anyone who speaks Spanish. Paragraph 10 begins with the oppositional transition "But," and the two paragraphs contrast with the preceding three.

Paragraph 13

Because his private and public worlds remained so separate, Rodriguez believes his psychological development was retarded.

Paragraph 16 and 17

While the final two paragraphs are full of the comforting images of home, family, and native language, he makes the negative moral judgment that such extended separation of public and private language is not healthy (first sentence, paragraph 17).

Possible Answers

Meaning and Purpose

1. Spanish, for the youthful Rodriguez, is the language of home and family. In all of the examples he gives, he associates Spanish with the comfort and protection of home, a safe oasis that protects him from the surrounding and alien world of *los gringos*. English, the language of the public world that surrounds him, he finds threatening. Both he and his parents struggle to understand and speak English, but they must do so just to function in the Anglo world in which they live. Even the sounds of English he finds alien and grating: "The accent of *los gringos* was never pleasing nor was it hard to hear" (6). So Spanish, the language of home and protection, becomes an escape from the frightening and alien public world of English. "It [Spanish] became the language of joyful return" (10).

2. As a child Rodriguez views his own insecurity and fear as natural. His security lies with his parents. So when he sees them stumble in their attempts to speak English in the public world, his insecurity is heightened and he is, in a sense, embarrassed. He recognizes the surety of the native English speakers, compared to his parents, in their voices' volume: "I'd notice, moreover, that my parents' voices were softer than those of *gringos* we'd meet" (7).

3. As an adult Rodriguez recognizes that his parents' English language insufficiencies made no practical difference in either his or their lives. They could handle the language well enough to manage everyday problems. But as a child his trust in their authority diminished because he perceived his own security was threatened by their English language deficiencies in the public world.

4. For the native English speaker, the language of family and the language of the other, "public" world are the same, so the two worlds become connected early. For the non-native speaker, like Rodriguez, his Spanish-speaking

home becomes a refuge from the ubiquitous English-speaking world outside of his home and the larger Spanish speaking community that he considers family. He therefore remains psychologically dependent on his family longer than would a native speaker.

Strategy

1. The first paragraph introduces the reader to the general contrast between his home and family and the outside world represented by a salesman and his neighbors. He then focuses in on the differences in his perceptions of Spanish and English in the second paragraph with point-by-point development.
2. The illustration contrasts Rodriguez's attitudes toward English as an adult to when he was a child. Now, when he is abroad, English stands out because it is different from the language that predominates in the area, just as English stood out when he was a Spanish-speaking child in an English-speaking world. But he finds hearing English in such a context comforting now because English makes up his world. The entire paragraph, except for the transitional opening two sentences, contrasts with the preceding paragraph.
3. The example illustrates Rodriguez's last point in the preceding paragraph: When he heard his parents struggle with English, his ". . . trust in their protection and power weakened."
4. Rodriguez emphasizes the sentence by making it a separate paragraph. It dramatizes the boy's relief in returning home from the threatening world of *los gringos* with an emphatic affirmation.

Style

1. The author uses point-by-point development to quickly emphasize the differences between his two childhood worlds. He uses subject-by-subject development in two different ways. In the first, he contrasts individual paragraphs. The stumbling and insecure English of his parents and himself described in paragraph 7, for instance, is contrasted against the confidence of native English speakers in paragraphs 3 and 4. He also uses subject-by-subject development within paragraphs, as when he contrasts the two different ways he felt about his parents' English insufficiencies (8).
2. The sense of the Spanish words, if not all of their precise meanings, should be clear to any reader. Almost all students will know the meaning of *los gringos*, though they may be unclear about the phrase's connotations. Rodriguez translates *inglés* for us in paragraph 3. They may not know the exact meaning of *los otros* (the others), but it is clearly associated with "my separateness" and "*los gringos*" that precedes and follows it (10). It is clear, too, in paragraph 17 that *mis hermanos* (my brothers) refers to his siblings.
3. *Gringo* means foreigner, especially one of U.S. or English descent, and is usually used disparagingly. But the pejorative connotation seems muted in this piece, since the boy views his surrounding world of *los gringos* as threatening rather than hostile.

Sex, Lies, and Conversation
Deborah Tannen

Teaching Suggestions

This essay is particularly effective in a first-year English composition class because it delineates and defines formally what most students already intuitively suspect, that when it comes to verbal communication, women and men differ radically in their approaches. A fruitful way to introduce this essay is to ask the class to take a moment to think about whether they have ever had a discussion with a member of the opposite sex that degenerated into a quarrel that seemed at the time a confusing descent into anger. Then ask them to think for a minute about whether they have a working definition of "eye contact" and "body language." Then have each member of the class look into the eyes of the student closest to them, but only for few a seconds. Finally, ask each member of the class to jot down quickly on a slip of paper his or her immediate emotional reaction to that experience, making sure to tell the class not to write their names on the slips of paper. Finally, collect the slips of paper and read to the class several of the more interesting responses. This exercise in immediate awareness can provide a delightful introduction to Tannen's essay.

Notes

Paragraph 1
Tannen begins the essay with an interesting anecdote, a short amusing narrative in this case, sure to attract her reader.

Paragraph 2
This paragraph sets forth the main thrust of the essay, the irony produced by the obvious. When the obvious is overlooked, the result can be marital ruin.

Paragraph 3
A scholar herself, Tannen in this paragraph gives her readership an academic sense of involvement, asserting in part how she knows what she knows, thereby establishing herself as the informed writer.

Paragraph 4
Tannen moves from speaking of the research of others to speaking of her own work, which permits her to move also to introduce society's more immediate need to concern itself with the problems of verbal communication.

Paragraph 5
This stock cartoon scene exemplifies Tannen's theme: If the communication problem did not exist, then the cartoon would be meaningless.

Paragraph 6
These dual rhetorical questions combine to form a mental outline in the reader's mind of what to look for in the subsequent paragraphs.

Paragraph 7
Again, Tannen uses external sources so that her reader will not think that her opinions are idiosyncratic. Note that the author uses "gender" and "sex" interchangeably.

Paragraph 8
Now Tannen moves to noting the products of her own research, which are compatible with the research of other specialists.

Paragraph 9

This paragraph, concerned mainly with how girls and women communicate verbally, contains focused, metaphorical definitions of *intimacy* and *talk,* definitions that Tannen assumes her reader will carry mentally through the rest of the essay. She also points out that, to a woman, the topic of a conversation is not as important as its verbal methods of conveyance, which leads to the woman's bringing certain expectations into her marriage.

Paragraph 10

The essential communication distinction between boys and girls, pointed out in this paragraph, is that boys are primarily doers with their friends and girls are primarily talkers with their friends.

Paragraph 11

Tanner here offers an explanation of why boys differ from girls, a difference that can provoke strife in their later relationships with members of the opposite sex.

Paragraph 12

This centric paragraph not only points out the clear physical differences inherent in the ways that men and women talk and use body language, but also points out the ways that those differences have been discovered. Ending with an anecdote, the paragraph brings the essay's focus back to ordinary people talking under ordinary circumstances.

Paragraph 13

Not only do males and females differ in their body language, but they also differ in how they deal with their topics of conversation.

Paragraph 14

Body language, unless understood, conveys perceptions that often mislead members of the opposite sex.

Paragraph 15

The underlying message here, as it involves male-female verbal interaction, is that encoding, like body language, conveys perceptions that can lead to misunderstandings.

Paragraph 16

The distinction between woman-woman conversation and man-man conversation drawn here is that women console while men extol.

Paragraph 17

Interestingly, this notion of "listener-noise" is mandatory in the Japanese language—both sexes engage in it culturally.

Paragraph 18

The distinction drawn here is that women and men have different senses of what it means to participate in conversations.

Paragraph 19

This paragraph, topically compatible with its predecessor, illustrates another cultural discrepancy between how men talk to men versus how women talk to women, a discrepancy that can provide sparks to an already volatile man-woman conversational relationship.

Paragraph 20

The word *agonistic,* used as far back as the seventeenth century to describe the athletic contests of ancient Greece, is used here as a powerfully connotative replacement for *argumentative*. Note also that the "rituals" described here are culturally determined and sexually distinguished.

Paragraph 21

This paragraph serves to explain partially the ills that beset many marriages. Note the use of *orgy*, which has among its definitions "secret ceremonial rites held in honor of an ancient Greek or Roman deity." In ordinary parlance nowadays, the term usually means "lack of control or moderation."

Paragraph 22

This paragraph swings the reader mentally to the anecdote beginning the essay, offering a fuller analysis of the actions contained in that anecdote, an analysis that will now be clearer to the reader.

Paragraph 23

Now that the differences between how men and women communicate verbally have been clarified, Tannen moves to the prelude of pointing toward a possible solution to the problem engendered by culturally based communication distinctions mutually misunderstood by both men and women.

Paragraph 24

To clarify a problem moves us toward *understanding* a problem. To understand a problem moves us toward *solving* a problem. Tannen notes here that solving this culturally generated communication problem comes naturally, once the problem is understood.

Paragraph 25

This closing paragraph offers realistic hope by saying that if communicatively aware couples do decide to divorce, then they will divorce for reasons other than linguistic incompatibility.

Paragraph 26

This closure paragraph reminds the reader that if we can understand and solve culturally microcosmic communication problems, then we might move fruitfully toward solving macrocosmic communication problems, particularly those caused by cultural misunderstandings.

Possible Answers

Meaning and Purpose

1. This device of using an ordinary episode to begin the essay functions as a relaxing, informal introduction to a quite complex topic and at the same time entices the reader to continue reading the essay because of its mundane introduction, one with which most readers can identify.
2. These two rhetorical questions serve as a stimulating introduction to the focus of the topic in the second part of the essay and serve to clarify the meaning and the purpose of that which follows the questions. They are therefore attention-getting devices that serve to keep the reader dedicated to the direction of the essay.
3. Answers vary, of course, depending on the differences that students find most interesting. They include differences in body language, verbal expression, and, in the case of men particularly, competitive drive.
4. Again, answers vary, but most students dwell on the differences between eye contact and the differences between how women listen to other women's problems compared with how men listen to other men's problems.
5. Best shown in the final paragraphs, if we all learn the cultural differences that form the basis of how men and women communicate, then we can move toward a better understanding of how to get along.

Strategy

1. In paragraph 24, Tannen points to the "problem" in paragraph 23, that of being unable to communicate across culturally determined gender lines because neither men nor women know that differences in communication habits in fact exist and are normal to each sex. As she says in paragraph 24, after we understand the problem, then we will naturally solve it.

2. Using marriage as a vehicle to discuss the topic of communication adds immediate interest for the reader because marriages, as Tannen points out, have been known to founder on the shoals of culturally based miscommunication. This strategy is so important to Tannen that she uses it to begin and to end the essay.

3. Using evidence that appears in the first paragraph of the essay along with that which appears passim throughout the essay, one can make a fine case for saying that the audience is a lay adult audience, especially women, particularly perhaps those who are recently married, those who are having some difficulties in their marriages, or both. Students have also argued and provided solid support for their arguing that although the essay is probably directed more to women than to men, Tannen herself in the final two paragraphs makes the point that we must somehow all learn together.

4. Tannen refers to the studies of several scholars besides herself because she wants to lend credence to her own theories of cultural communication. Without the references to those studies, Tannen's essay might appear to some readers to be one writer's unsupported opinions.

5. The common features of communication shared by men and women include an open mind, although not readily apparent cross culturally; concern with being heard and understood; the willingness to listen closely; and confusion at not being understood by members of the opposite sex. Evidence to support these common features appear throughout the essay, and many students have been quite adept at discovering the evidence for those features.

Style

1. The term *crystallizes,* as used in paragraph 2, means "to cause to take a definite form," allied with the connotation of that form's being consummately clear in terms of thought.

2. In paragraph 9, the term *fabric* refers to "the underlying structure" of relationships, with *structure* itself comprising both the physical (body language, in this case) and the abstract (conversation, in this case).

3. The title of part three of the essay refers to the fact that women are silent publicly while men are silent privately and vice versa. Just as women and men differ culturally when maintaining conversation between the sexes, so also do they differ culturally when location becomes a determinant. Therefore, silence itself conveys a message, a sort of sound.

4. Physical alignment, discussed in some depth in paragraph 12, refers to "body language," the set of physical tangibles that communicates to its perceiver based on the cultural background (either linguistically determined or sexually determined) of that perceiver.

5. As Tannen uses the term *cross-cultural,* it does not refer to differences between what we commonly assume to be cultures—Chinese culture and

American culture, for example. Instead, it refers to the linguistic "culture" of women and the linguistic "culture" of men, and how those cultures need to be recognized as separate and distinct so that we will know when misunderstandings are caused by a failure to bridge the two cultures.

Two Varieties of Killers
Ellen Currie

Teaching Suggestions

You might begin by asking the class if they remember the Ted Bundy case (he was executed by the State of Florida in 1989) or can recall any other cases where the accused was accorded similar attention. After listening to their examples, turn the discussion to, Why? Why do we give such cases this kind of attention? Why the jokes? Why the T-shirts? Why the not infrequent offers of support? Why the tendency to forget the victims? You may not arrive at definitive answers to these questions, but some examination of them may lead to a general awareness that such cases affect people in some important way. Some of our reactions may be attempts to distance us from the horror of the crimes. Some reactions may be motivated by desires to make connections with something, almost anything. From there the discussion might broaden into other aspects of popular culture: radio and television talk shows, tabloid newspapers and television programs, or new age spiritualism, all of which also seem to be ways to reassure us or shield us or give us something to attach our lives to.

Notes

Paragraph 1
Henry James (1843–1916), an American born writer who later became a British subject. The author of numerous novels, short stories, sketches and critical essays. One of his recurring themes is the contrast between American and European character, which he explored in the novels *Wings of the Dove* (1902), *The Ambassadors* (1903), and *The Golden Bowl* (1904).

By quoting James about "manners and morals" and "human and sociable" crimes, Currie gives weight to her use of such terms in the discussion of Smith and Bundy.

Paragraphs 2 and 3
Here Currie tells us she will be contrasting crimes (2) and announces which specific crimes (3).

Paragraphs 4, 5, and 6
These paragraphs state the facts about Madeleine Smith's crime and describe it as a personal crime, one of passion, one of the kind Henry James liked.

Paragraph 7
This paragraph serves as a transition to Bundy by reversing the idea of paragraph 6: his crime was not personal, not a crime of passion.

Paragraphs 8 and 9
Currie describes Bundy's crimes, as she did for Smith in paragraphs 4 and 5.

Paragraph 10
Here Currie shifts to the public reaction to the trial.

Paragraph 11 and 12

These paragraphs explain Bundy's behavior (he is antisocial) and then question the reasons for the behavior of the rest of us.

Paragraph 13

The last paragraph sums it up: Smith's crime is not good, but it is understandable. Bundy's crimes are not understandable, nor is our reaction to him.

Possible Answers

Meaning and Purpose

1. Sociable crimes are "human and comprehensible and even sympathetic" (2).
2. Her thesis is stated at the end of paragraph 2: "The crimes get bigger and more horrible, and yet we are not sufficiently horrified by them; we pay less and less attention to the manners and the morals they disclose."
3. Yes. She wants us to think primarily about our reaction to them. In her last paragraph she says, "Ted Bundy's unspeakable crimes and our cheap reaction to them reveal us to ourselves in a strange and deathly light."
4. Bundy is "an antisocial person, a man without conscience." (11)
5. Bundy is all image. He creates a picture of himself as charming, witty, handsome, articulate, polished, capable (he is his own attorney and twice escaped from custody). He is mediagenic and has been the subject of a television movie.

Strategy

1. Currie uses a subject-by-subject organization. The contrast between Smith and Bundy is not complicated, so it's easy for a reader to keep Smith's case in mind as she reads about Bundy. The subject-by-subject method also emphasizes the dramatic difference between the two crimes.
2. Ted Bundy's crimes and our reaction to his case are Currie's main concerns. Smith's case is offered merely to show the difference between a "sociable murder" and the "20th century phenomenon."

Style

1. "Tropical" means hot and humid, by association with the climate of the tropics; "abandoned" means freed from restraints; in this case, the restraints of properly modest feminine behavior.
2. A mediagenic person, at a minimum, would be physically attractive, articulate, more aggressive than passive, and have a story to tell, the more unusual the better.
3. Apparently "socially impossible" refers to class distinctions. Madeleine is the daughter of a Glasgow architect, presumably of some prominence in the community, and Madeleine is later betrothed to an "older, richer, and more settled suitor."
4. *Portentous*: significant; *bounden*: obligatory; *pagan*: hedonistic; *savaged*: assaulted; *vile*: highly offensive or objectionable; *glib*: superficially or insincerely fluent; unconstrained.

The Battle of the Ants
Henry David Thoreau

Teaching Suggestions

This essay extends an analogy, like tentacles, into several allied topics, but the body of the analogy remains clear. Our modern battles are usually no more important, though just as exciting to an objective observer, as the battle of the ants. Students occasionally need reminding that each recent generation has had a war: World War II in the 1940s, the Korean War in the 1950s, the Vietnam War in the late 1960s and early 1970s. What about the 1990s? For openers, we have Desert Storm and Kosovo.

Thoreau's ants mirror the actions of two peoples at war. Thoreau's ants are fighting for a principle, the author remarks sarcastically. No war, at least according to propaganda, was ever fought except for a principle. But some of the principles are as trivial as that which caused the Trojan War, the kidnaping of one person.

Students like to brainstorm principles. List several words on the chalk board and then discuss whether those words in fact name principles. Truth? Honesty? Art? Ethics? The discussion invariably leads to analogies, for students will use analogies to explain their thinking about each "principle."

Notes

Paragraph 1

Thoreau, a legendary master of diction, using words precisely, did not "see" the ants; he "observed" them. The analogy between ants and soldiers becomes obvious in the description in sentence 1: the ants are not "fighting"; they are "fiercely contending." This strategy of *personification*, writing about something as if it were human, permeates the essay.

"chips": The chips are left over from Thoreau's chopping wood. A *duellum* is a duel; a *bellum* is a war. The "races" of ants remind us that Thoreau's America was militantly divided over slavery, and Thoreau was strongly against it.

Myrmidons: The Myrmidons were ants, changed into warriors by Zeus, supreme deity of the ancient Greeks. They accompanied Achilles to the Trojan War.

"a couple": The soldier ants "fast locked in each other's embraces" remind students that lovers, not warriors, are usually so described. The next sentence heightens that ironic comparison by moving us from lovers' to warriors' language. The writer's almost microscopic view of ants in battle alludes to the notion that all wars are petty and that nature itself carries on benignly.

"Divested him of several of his members": Notice that Thoreau's euphemism here substitutes inoffensive words for some that could be distasteful ("tore off his legs"). This phrase also contributes to the mock heroic tone.

"Conquer or die": A Roman motto, *aut vincere aut mori*, literally "either to conquer or to die," was intended to inspire soldiers going into battle.

"In the meanwhile . . .": Have students notice the personification, the human qualities of the red ant.

"Whose mother . . .": The mothers of Sparta, an ancient Greek city state, told their sons, "Return with your shield or (carried) upon it," literally, "Win or die trying."

Achilles: A Greek hero in the Trojan Wars; Patroclus was his friend slain in those wars. From Homer's *Iliad*.

The movement from ant wars to human wars, reinforces the analogy.

Austerlitz, Dresden: Two bloody battles won in the early 1800s by Napoleon's armies.

The Battle of Concord Bridge, 1775, involved few soldiers (including "Davis and Hosmer") but became famous in American history.

"Three-penny tax": A reference to the Boston Tea Party, December 16, 1773, when the colonists defied the English crown. The British won the battle of Bunker Hill, fought in June 1775, but suffered enormous casualties.

Paragraph 2

Notice the calm, objective curiosity here, contrasted with the furious life-and-death battle being studied. The description that follows depicts graphically and minutely the thirty-minute struggle.

Hotel des Invalides: A home for old soldiers, in Paris, and the actual tomb of Napoleon I, as well.

Paragraph 3

Kirby, Spence, and Huber were three leading specialists in the study of insects.

Eugenius the Fourth (1383–1447): Pope from 1431 to 1447.

Nicholas Pistoriensis (1490–1558): Swedish Roman Catholic ecclesiastic and historian who wrote a Swedish history that was long accepted in Europe as authoritative.

Olaus Magnus (1481–1559): Called "The Cruel." King of Denmark and Norway, 1513–1523. Showed extreme cruelty against the Swedes massacring their nobility (1520). Imprisoned for life in 1532.

James Knox Polk (1795–1849) was eleventh president of the United States (1845–1849). Thoreau published his first book, *A Week on the Concord and Merrimac Rivers*, in 1849.

The Fugitive-Slave Bill required that slaves who escaped to the North be captured and returned to their owners in the South.

Possible Answers

Meaning and Purpose

1. Encourage students to explore first their personal responses to Thoreau's essay. Ask them to be specific in connecting their responses to statements or ideas in the essay.
2. Thoreau considered war a far from noble pursuit, beneath human dignity, to be fought by ants if fought at all. This extended analogy between ants and soldiers is evidence of this opinion, as are his numerous and satiric examples of wars fought throughout history.
3. Thoreau buries his thesis statements well into the first paragraph: "I was myself excited somewhat even as if they had been men. The more you think of it, the less the difference." The next sentence might also be considered part of his main point.
4. Thoreau's commentary is timeless. With mockery, he raises the battle of the ants to such "heights" as comparing it to an ancient Greek war and a patriotic American war. Of course, he is mocking our seeing wars as glorious, serving his purpose (satire), and extending his analogy.
5. Thoreau wrote mostly for an educated male readership. Most who could then read were well educated men, many holding authority in government or church. Thoreau used this essay to mock the very thing most learned men admired, and to point out to them the folly in their thinking.

6. Thoreau extends the analogy through history by showing that such battles have been noteworthy for centuries. With great mocking, Thoreau raises the battle of the ants to the level of recorded human history and compares it to other ant battles celebrated in writing. He ends the extended analogy by poking fun at academic historians, whose style he mocks here.

Strategy

1. Ants and men in this essay share cruelty, tenacity, courage, bravery, and other qualities associated with combat.
2. The comparison is between soldiers and ants. He has been personifying ants and talking about them as if they were men. He realizes that he is as excited as if they were human and that the ant–human differences are less than he thought. Of course Thoreau is making fun here.
3. The analogy is between a wounded ant and a wounded soldier who spends his days in a home for old soldiers, trying to keep the glory of the war alive. Of course, the analogy is factually weak, but it is ironic.
4. Satire is a literary technique or style that combines humor and wit with a critical attitude for the purpose of improving human institutions or actions. The satirist pokes fun not so much to tear down as to inspire remodeling of the subject being satirized. Jonathan Swift's famous "A Modest Proposal" is a good example of satire to place alongside Thoreau's essay.
5. Students should evaluate Thoreau's use of satire on his subject. Without the analogy's mockery, Thoreau might have written a more formal, pedantic, or sermonlike treatise on war and principles and how thinly they disguise petty human squabbles. Such a hypothetical essay probably would have been boring by comparison, not as attention-getting, amusing, or successful in making his points.

Style

1. An internecine war is mutually destructive, full of slaughter, with enormous casualties on both sides. It is a "no-win" war.
2. These kinds of exclamations appear in newspaper headlines. Luther Blanchard, in the headline's context, is an American who fought at Concord.
3. This could have been a factual description of a man-soldier, but not an ant-soldier. Ants do not have the eyes described here, or the kind of body that permits a carbuncle. By analogy, however, it is a realistic description imaginatively comparing ant with man.
4. *Pertinacity* means "the quality of holding firmly to a belief or purpose," and "the quality of being hard to get rid of, physically." The first meaning compares ants with men, the second with bulldogs.

——— 7 / *Cause and Effect* ———

My Wood
E. M. Forster

Teaching Suggestions

One way to introduce students to the ideas of this essay is to ask, "What responsibilities go with material wealth?" The answers will be mixed, many students saying that materially wealthy people should care for the homeless and the hungry, others saying that the affluent have few responsibilities beyond caring for themselves and their own families. The follow-up question is, "Does material wealth cause a restriction of one's freedom?" Usually, students reply, "No," almost in unison.

But wait! Many materially wealthy people must wear specific kinds of clothing; otherwise, they will risk being outcasts from their own society. How about cars? Don't materially wealthy people have to drive expected makes and models? What about friends? Can materially wealthy people afford to have poor friends? What about bodyguards? Security gates? Special places in which to live?

After students see that one effect of material wealth is lack of social freedom, they are better able to grasp the points made in Forster's essay.

Notes

Paragraph 1

The British have been in India since 1600. India became independent in 1947, after many years of strife. Forster's *A Passage to India* chronicles life among the British in India before its independence. Mention the British and American English differences: Many American dialects have "woods" for *wood*, and Americans spell *cheque* "check." Notice the simple cause-and-effect statement in the first paragraph. Forster's check allows him to buy the wood. The interjection "blast it" is Forster's momentary opinion of the public footpath in his wood. The paragraph's last sentence introduces the psychological cause-and-effect topic of the essay.

Paragraph 2

"Kingdom of Heaven": See New Testament, Matthew 19:24: "It is easier for a camel to go through the eye of a needle, than for a rich man to enter into the kingdom of God." Forster follows that verse with a coupling of the religious and secular cause-and-effect possibilities. Leo Tolstoy (1828–1910), social and moral philosopher and Russian mystic, wrote *War and Peace* (1865–1869), among other great works. He emancipated his serfs in 1861. *Stone*: a unit of weight in Great Britain equal to 14 pounds. The stout bishop weighs 196 pounds.

The first and last lines of the paragraph end with the same four words, for effective emphasis: "makes me feel heavy." Forster, too, feels stout.

Paragraph 3

"In the second place" is the clearest kind of transition, as the author moves from the psychological effect of weight, caused by owning his property, to that of size. The property Forster acquired has caused him to want more.

Paragraph 4

"The other day" begins Forster's example displaying how the psychological effect of wanting more property has caused him to view his surroundings—greedily. King Ahab in the Old Testament, the seventh king of Israel (c. 875–853 B.C.), greatly expanded his territories, especially by marrying Jezebel, daughter of the king of Sidon. In Herman Melville's *Moby Dick*, Captain Ahab's obsession was to find and kill the white whale, at whatever cost. Forster discusses his growing obsession for getting more land. Canute II of Denmark (994?–1035), subject of many legends, conquered England and was chosen king in 1017 by the *witan*, the king's council of Anglo-Saxons. Alexander the Great (356–323 B.C.), said to have wept after he had no more worlds to conquer, directed enormously successful campaigns in Greece, Persia, northern India, Syria, and Egypt, among others. Sirius, the Dog Star, is the brightest star in the constellation Canis Major. Forster's imaginary domain is boundless, a cause of sadness when he compares it with his real, limited domain. The bird reminds us of nature's "definition" of property. We "own" only ourselves.

Paragraph 5

"In the third place . . .": Owning property causes us to want to change it, to make it clearly ours. This psychology of ownership—nothing really belongs to us until we change it, pseudo-creatively—deeply bothers Forster. We want to mold our property into an extension of our personality, but without a creative motive. Shakespeare's Sonnet 129 begins, "The expense of spirit in a waste of shame / Is lust in action. . . ." The "internal defect" is our inability to accept ourselves as we are, just as we are unable to accept our property for what it is. As Forster uses *carnal*, the word relates to the body as the seat of physical appetites, without intellectual or moral influence. Our life on earth should be carnal and material, yet managed by the intellect and morality. Ironically, however, our desire for ownership manages our intellect and morality. Dante Alighieri (1265–1321) wrote *The Divine Comedy*.

Paragraph 6

Forster's homely transition detaches us from his deeply philosophical paragraph.

Paragraph 7

The natural products of Forster's wood attract people. Foxgloves have long spikes of thimble like flowers. A medicine made from their leaves (digitalis) is used as a heart stimulant. Bracken are large, coarse, weedy ferns. All the public activity causes Forster to question the definition of ownership. Does the owner own the property, or does the property own the owner? For Dives, see the parable of the selfish rich man, Luke 16:19–31; Lazarus is the poor diseased man in the same parable.

"possession": To make his "quadruple crown of possession," Forster weaves together the four subtopics in this essay: worldly wealth, greed, false creativity and selfishness.

"[N]asty Bolshies": Bolsheviks are Communists or, loosely used, any radicals.

Possible Answers

Meaning and Purpose

1. Forster intends to explore the questions he poses in the first paragraph: "What is the effect of property upon the character?" and "What's the effect on

me of my wood?" These two sentences are his thesis in question form; he is asserting that ownership does affect a person.

2. Encourage students to share their stories about things they have owned and done something to. Be sure they account for clear causes and effects, such as "I painted an American flag on my leather jacket because I want people to know that I am patriotic."

3. Students are free to select their own allusions. Occasionally reading and discussing the better papers in class is an exercise that helps students realize this essay's depth.

4. The author's freedom is restricted by his imagined obligations to himself and his possession, which stem from his owning the wood in the first place. Now that he has the wood, he feels obliged to enlarge it, improve it, and protect it.

5. The interjection "blast it" sums up his opinion of the wood's being publicly and easily accessible by the footpath. This is the first clue that Forster will feel possessive about his wood.

Strategy

1. Forster gives the cause in paragraph 1: the acquiring of money that enabled him to buy the wood. In subsequent paragraphs, he develops one effect at a time. This structure is effective because it is clear and makes his reasoning easy to follow. Giving one long paragraph to each effect allows him to single it out and explore it in depth.

2. The statement quoted is an example of a causal chain, or a series of things, one triggering the next, in chronological order. This technique here exaggerates Forster's point that owning property is heavy or cumbersome. He imagines that ownership will cause slowness, having things "you cannot move about," until you'd better think twice before you "bathe in the Jordan." Forster is using humor to stress one danger of ownership.

3. The ownership was caused by the high stone walls that the owner built on both sides of the path. The effect is that those walls have imprisoned the owner.

4. The fourth and final point is selfishness. Forster means that blackberries lure people in until he is tempted to "wall in and fence out . . . property. [acts that are] Enormously . . . selfish" (7).

Style

1. The ladies are probably elementary school teachers, and the author thinks little of them for "grubbing" in his wood just to show the children toadstools.

2. Forster extends his need to enlarge the boundary of his wood all the way to the sea to keep out noise and children. This exaggeration stresses his point that once he is an owner, his greed will know no bounds.

3. These two paragraphs are transitions from discussion of one effect to the next. They are clear statements of Forster's chronology in presenting his points. And they are stylistically effective because they are short and rather abrupt between two long paragraphs. They catch attention and bring the reader back on track.

Why We Crave Horror Movies
Stephen King

Teaching Suggestions

A lively discussion of King's essay might be initiated by inviting students to list their favorite horror films and the specific aspects of each film that made it particularly effective. What were the students' reactions to the film? Did those reactions correspond to King's speculations about why horror films have been, and are, so popular? From this discussion you might try to then focus attention on the essay's form: how King grabs our attention with the first sentence; how he dispenses rather quickly and amusingly with the first three reasons for the popularity of horror films in the first five paragraphs; and, finally, how he spends the entire rest of the essay exploring what is, in his opinion, the most important cause of the film genre's popularity. There's a lesson here on how effectively to proportion an essay, allotting the most space to the most important points.

We think King's use of metaphoric language is also worth noting, for it certainly lends vibrancy to his prose. Question 1 in *Style* deals with this.

In a longer project you might want to teach the essay in conjunction with Andrew Klavan's "The Shrieking of the Lambs," which argues the efficacy of film violence, and Michael Medved's "Denial Behavior," which argues against it.

Notes

Paragraph 4
Die, Monster, Die: A 1965 film with Boris Karloff, Nick Adams, and Freda Jackson, based on a story by H.P. Lovecraft (1890–1937), an American writer of horror tales in the tradition of Poe. In the film, Karloff is a recluse who discovers a meteor which gives him strange powers. It was remade as *The Curse* in 1987.

Paragraph 8
Jack the Ripper: Name given to the unknown murderer of at least seven women, all prostitutes, in the East End of London, from August 7 to November 10, 1888. All but one of his victims were killed while soliciting customers on the street. In each instance the woman's throat was cut, and the body then mutilated in a way that indicated the murderer had a considerable knowledge of human anatomy. The Ripper was history's first recorded pattern killer and sexual psychopath. One of the most famous unsolved mysteries of English crime, the case has retained its hold on the popular imagination.

Cleveland Torso Murderer: One of the names given to an unknown murderer of at least twelve people in Cleveland, Ohio, from the fall of 1935 to the spring of 1942. Newspapers at the time also called him The Mad Butcher and The Headhunter. He preyed, for the most part, on obscure or anonymous people, many thought to have been residents of the hobo jungles of the Great Depression. The murderer beheaded and dismembered his victims with surgical precision. He was, arguably, America's first serial killer.

Paragraph 9
Leonard Nimoy: An American actor (b. 1931) in TV, films, and theater. He is best known as Paris in the TV series *Mission Impossible* and Dr. Spock in both the TV series and movie *Star Trek*. He has published two books of poetry self-illustrated with

photographs, *You and I* (1973) and *Will I Think of You* (1974)—neither much appreciated, obviously, by King.

Paragraph 12

Dawn of the Dead: The 1978 sequel to *The Night of the Living Dead* (1968), which has been called the touchstone modern horror film. In it, seven people barricade themselves inside a farmhouse while an army of flesh-eating zombies roams the countryside. In the sequel, the zombie population has increased, and four people set up a quasi-Utopian existence in a barricaded shopping mall.

Paragraph 13

Lennon and McCartney: John Lennon (1940–1980) and Paul McCartney (1942–   ), two of the four original Beatles, an English musical group that enjoyed worldwide adulation in the 1960s. McCartney wrote most of the lyrics to their songs while Lennon wrote most of the music.

Possible Answers

Meaning and Purpose

1. King never explicitly states his thesis, but it is, nonetheless, implicitly clear: there are four reasons (causes) why "we crave horror movies," why they have been so popular over the years: to show "that we are not afraid" (3); "to re-establish our feelings of essential normality" (4); "to have fun" (5); to give vicarious release to our destructive, antisocial emotions (6–14).

2. King claims that all people have hostile, antisocial emotions, but it is only those who act out those aggressive emotions in the most horrendous ways (Jack the Ripper or the Cleveland Torso Murderer, paragraph 8) who must be institutionalized. The rest of us manifest those emotions in less drastic ways: talking to ourselves, picking our noses in public (8), or getting back at our "pukey" sister simply for being "pukey" (10). It is in this sense that he is serious and reflects the self observation of the Roman playwright, Terence (c. 190–159 B.C.): "I am a man: nothing human is alien to me" (*The Self-Tormentor*).

3. Horror films are conservative or reactionary in that they "re-establish our feelings of essential normality" (4). They are anarchistic or revolutionary in that they display antisocial—or, as King says, "anticivilization" (11)—emotions.

4. Horror movies serve as a safe outlet for our hostile emotions. King, in claiming that these emotions need such an outlet for both psychological and social health, reflects, among others, English poet William Blake (1757–1827) who wrote, "He who desires but acts not, breeds pestilence" and, "Sooner murder an infant in its cradle than nurse unacted desires" (*The Marriage of Heaven and Hell*), and Freud.

Strategy

1. King's opening statement is indeed bold, and grabbing. He modifies the statement immediately, but if we accept his premise, however haltingly, we will be more open to his argument that we all need an acceptable outlet for our antisocial impulses, the ultimate reason for the popularity of horror films.

2. King offers four causes for the popularity of horror films. The first three are "simple and obvious" (3) and are the immediate causes: "to show we are not afraid" (3); "to re-establish our feelings of essential normality" (4); "to have fun" (5). The ultimate cause is the psychological and social need to face up to our dark sides.

3. King gets rid of the three immediate causes quickly, in five short paragraphs. The ultimate cause, and the focus of his argument, he spends the rest of the essay exploring. By eliminating the immediate causes so quickly, he reinforces his claim that they are "simple and obvious" (3). Conversely, he emphasizes the importance of the ultimate cause by using the bulk of the essay to explore it in detail.

4. King begins with the first person singular to establish the seemingly outlandish opening statement as a personal conviction. He immediately switches to the plural to group his readers with himself among those who aren't mentally ill enough to be institutionalized.

5. King offers no evidence, not even anecdotal evidence. He relies on the readers recognizing themselves in the group of the insane who "squinch their faces into horrible grimaces" (1), or who "talk [to themselves] when [they're] under stress" (8). For if they accept the premise that they are insane, at least to a degree, they can then easily accept his conclusions.

Style

1. King's use of concrete and metaphoric language informs the entire essay, transforming what in less skillful hands could be dry and academic. Instead of saying, for instance, that the problem he poses begins to become difficult to fully understand, he says, instead, that "the ground starts to slope away" (6). Instead of fearing death, we fear "those final worms and grubs that are waiting so patiently underground" (1). And horror movies, instead of breaking through our conscious mind to satisfy the dark fears of our unconscious mind, are presented as "lifting a trap door in the civilized forebrain and throwing a basket of raw meat to the hungry alligators swimming around in that subterranean river beneath" (12).

2. King's tone, though informal, never becomes extremely slangy. Nor does he ever deviate into psychological jargon or the stylistic flourishes of formal prose. He calls two brutal murderers "amateur night surgeons" and even imitates a deranged cackle, "heh, heh, heh" (8) when he tells us they're still at large. He calls our little sisters (notice his assumption that his readers are male) "rotten little puke[s]" (10). But underneath this informal language, language appropriate for his *Playboy* audience, is a seriousness of intention. In his conclusion, for instance, when he tells us that horror movies solve our most aggressive, unconscious impulses, he skillfully uses the colloquial "man," a word that, in context, keeps his informal language consistent and emphasizes, as well, the seriousness of his message: "Because it [horror movies feeding our subterranean alligators] keeps them from getting out, man" (13).

3. King's rollercoaster analogy aptly objectifies the swirl of emotions a horror movie can elicit, emotions that include fear and fun at the same time.

4. *Grimaces*: facial expressions, often ugly or contorted, that indicate disapproval, pain, etc.; *hysterical*: uncontrollably emotional; *province*: a sphere of authority; *voyeur*: a person who gets sexual gratification by looking at sexual objects or acts, especially secretly; *penchant*: a strong inclination, taste, or liking for something; *psychic*: mental, as opposed to physical; *exalted*: raised or elevated, as in rank or character; *twit*: to taunt, tease, or ridicule; *sanctions*: penalties for disobedience; *remonstrance*: disapproval; *recoil*: to draw or shrink back, as in

alarm, horror, or disgust; *anarchistic:* promoting disorder or revolt against any
established order or rule; *morbidity:* the state of being unwholesomely gloomy,
sensitive, or extreme; *subterranean:* existing or operating out of sight, hidden.

How Urban Myths Reveal Society's Fears
Neal Gabler

Teaching Suggestions

This essay quickly interests a number of students because they have heard many
urban myths, some of which they know are false, some of which they suspect are
false, and some of which they strongly doubt but about which they remain uncertain.
Instructors have discovered that many radio and television talk-show hosts have dealt
with urban myths in some detail, to the point of assuring their audiences that a few of
these myths are true, yet "the government" does not want you to know that they are
true. Ask your students if they have heard about unidentified flying objects (UFOs),
about large rats and cockroaches that swarm various cafeterias after dark, and about
the impending doom that starts precisely at midnight, December 31, 1999 (the Year
2000 Crisis). Encourage them to proffer the "facts" that they have heard to support
the contentions that such statements as those above are true.

Notes

Paragraph 1
Gabler begins his essay as if he were having a chat with a live audience, rather
than writing an essay, an interesting strategy in that it immediately involves the
reader, who cannot wait to see how the "story goes."

Paragraph 2
This transitional paragraph gets us to the periphery of the essay, that this wedding story has been floating all over the East Coast, thereby being automatically
suspect.

Paragraph 3
In this defining paragraph, Gabler clarifies the phrase "urban myth" and then
follows that clarification with five or, with a variation, six examples.

Paragraph 4
Gabler here condemns the whole notion of urban myths while also accounting
for them, noting that they are our late-twentieth-century folklore and giving reasons
for that notion, the main one being that urban myths express "the national mind."

Paragraph 5
Gabler partially explains the concept of urban myths by noting that nowadays,
because we have nothing reliable, we are terrified. We need explanations, no matter
how bizarre.

Paragraph 6
Gabler exemplifies his statement in paragraph 5 when saying again that an urban
myth is an explanation, a "legend" that we need to explain our actions to ourselves.

Paragraph 7
Gabler cannot ignore the obvious, so he grapples with it, the fact that we have
had Disneyland's characters for more than forty years, and we had folklore and fairy

tales long before that. However, he points out that those characters and tales serve to explain childhood terrors to children, not adult terrors to adults.

Paragraph 8

Gabler here distinguishes carefully between the contents and contexts of fairy tales and urban myths, pointing out that the latter offer no hope to their audiences, thereby exploiting them.

Paragraph 9

Gabler moves beyond the topic of exploitation, pointing out that we are so fearful that we are willing to believe nearly any story that serves to strengthen our fears.

Paragraph 10

In this paragraph and in paragraph 11, Gabler moves to a partial explanation of our fears: We have given in to the pressures of our lives, which causes us to cling to our urban myths, no matter our own questions about whether they contain any element of truth.

Paragraph 12

Interestingly, as Gabler points out, an ironic result of urban myths is that they help us to come together, to participate with one another, even though the magnet of our participation attracts nothing immediately reasonable.

Paragraph 13

In this paragraph and in paragraph 14, we see what Gabler sees, that our campfire telling and retelling of these urban myths causes us to terrorize ourselves. We add emphasis to our own terror. Yet the grand tradeoff, as noted in paragraph 14, is that we are still storytellers; we still have the power to explain. And since we still have that power, then we still have the power to reexamine our urban myths.

Possible Answers

Meaning and Purpose

1. Gabler immediately engages his audience the way that any story teller engages an audience, which is appropriate because he is, after all, telling stories. This opening could well have been changed to "Once upon a time. . . ."
2. As clarified in paragraphs 7 and 8, the important difference between traditional tales and urban myths is that traditional tales made life bearable ("explained") for their audiences, but urban myths make heavier the unbearable ("unexplained") for their audiences.
3. Urban myths exploit our fears, according to Gabler, by pointing out what we already believe we know: The world is a fearful place. He also points out what we might not know, that we ourselves keep those fears alive.
4. Walt Disney cartoons share the features of fears and challenges, the differences being that the cartoons concern overcoming fears and challenges while the urban myths concern succumbing to fears and challenges.
5. Answers to this question vary, of course, but a large number of students have unequivocally embraced the "alligators in the sewers" myth.

Strategy

1. Gabler is bringing up the interesting concept of the repeated strategy, the idea that if a story is repeated enough times in enough places by enough people, then it is true de facto. It therefore follows that we believe in them merely because we want to believe in them; they help us believe that our own fears are well founded.

2. Gabler uses the repeated strategy, mentioned in question 1 as well as the strategy of embellishment, the strategy of examples, and the strategy of commentary throughout the essay. For example, when we hear an urban myth, we do not say that we doubt it, according to Gabler; instead, we comment on it, thus lending credence to the myth.

3. Answers differ, but the usually acceptable ones include the ideas that we need explanations for what we think, what we believe, and what we do, and that we need myths to help us explain our actions to others as well as to ourselves.

4. Gabler uses here the strategy of exclusion. The paragraph's content allows for no reason other than the reason given, "an overwhelming condition of fear and to a sense of our own impotence within it," to explain the urban myth. Interestingly, this paragraph closely resembles a myth in that it allows no argument except its own stated one.

5. As Gabler notes in the last two paragraphs of the essay, urban myths keep us together. In an unusual way, yes, but together, nonetheless. And so long as we are together, then we are talking. So long as we talk, we communicate, and our communication has so far prevented us from completely submerging ourselves beneath the fears borne by our urban myths.

Style

1. In the first sentence of this essay, the term *opulent* refers to that which is characteristic of worldly wealth. Students have chosen with reason to substitute "rich and decorative," "substantial," "affluent," "eye-catching," and "moneyed." Other choices remain, obviously.

2. The phrase *in flagrante,* as used in the first paragraph of this essay, is a short version of *in flagrante delicto,* "in the midst of sexual activity." The phrase is in italics because some writers still consider it a foreign phrase, and therefore to be italicized. Most dictionaries have quietly let this distinction lapse.

3. Depending on one's locale and television reception, the answers are nearly countless, including *The Oprah Winfrey Show, The Jerry Springer Show, The Jenny Jones Show,* and so forth.

4. The main reason Gabler talks about fairy tales is their tone. They all have abiding kindness underlying whatever childhood fears they exploit. In fairy tales, we all "live happily ever after."

5. Depending on each student's dictionary, the definitions of *terror* will vary, but only slightly, all of them approaching a definition such as, "a state of intense fear." Suggested appropriate synonyms have included "horror," "distress," "dread," "fright," and "angst."

The Revolt of the Black Bourgeoisie
Leonce Gaiter

Teaching Suggestions

A discussion of the perniciousness of social stereotyping might be initiated by asking your students to list other media sources of the stereotype of the underclass black who stands for all blacks. A rather lengthy list may result. Then ask them to list the characteristics that make up that stereotype and how the stereotype is represented on each item in the list. Then ask them to list TV programs that present middle class African-Americans, or black artists and intellectuals. The two lists may appear a bit unbalanced. This could lead to a discussion of the stereotyping of other racial groups in the media and how stereotyping, because it oversimplifies and plays to popular prejudices, demeans those it represents.

In an even larger project, you might teach the essay in conjunction with Maya Angelou's "Finishing School" or Brent Staples's "Black Men and Public Spaces." Each deals with specific ways African-Americans cope in a racially divided society.

We think the structure of Gaiter's essay is also worth exploring: how paragraphs 1–3 give examples of how he has been affected by whites stereotyping blacks; how paragraph 4 shows how blacks have accepted the stereotype themselves; how he uses paragraph 5 as a transition from the effects of stereotyping to a discussion of the causes of the stereotype in paragraphs 6–14; how he rather quickly dispenses with the two immediate causes of black stereotyping in paragraphs 6–8; how he explores the ultimate cause extensively (9–14); and how he concludes the essay in three paragraphs by summarizing the effects of stereotyping (15), and by offering remedies (16–17).

Notes

Paragraph 3

Austen: Jane Austen (1775–1817), English novelist, regarded by many as the greatest of women novelists. Her world was rather narrow and parochial, but from that world she fashioned such great novels as *Sense and Sensibility, Pride and Prejudice, Mansfield Park, Emma, Northanger Abbey,* and *Persuasion,* all distinguished by their satirical wit and brilliant comedy, and their complex view of human nature. *Persuasion* and *Sense and Sensibility* have recently been made into popular films, and there are three versions of *Emma* currently being filmed. The plot of *Clueless,* a recent teenage film, is loosely based on *Emma.* The BBC made a six part serial of *Pride and Prejudice,* enormously popular in England, which then played on Cable TV's A&E in the U.S.

Balzac: Honoré de Balzac (1799–1850), French novelist. He wrote more than ninety novels and tales, combining realistic details and ordinary situations with the flagrantly romantic qualities of melodramatic plots, violent passions, and rhetorical passages. His characters, too, are romantic in the extreme. Some of his finest novels include *Eugénie Grandet* and *Le Père Goriot. La Comedié Humaine,* an attempt to present a complete social history of France in a thorough and scientific manner, is generally considered his masterpiece.

Douglass: Frederick Douglass (1817?–1895), American abolitionist, orator, and journalist. The son of a slave and a white father, Douglass escaped to the North in 1838. He delivered a speech at an anti-slavery convention in Nantucket in 1841 that was so eloquent that he was soon in great demand as a speaker. He described being mobbed and beaten because of his views in his forthright autobiography, *Narrative of the Life of Frederick Douglass* (1845). He lived for two years in Great Britain where he earned enough money to buy his freedom in this country. He founded *The North Star,* a newspaper he published for seventeen years and in it advocated the use of black troops during the Civil War and civil rights for freed men. He held a number of public offices after the war.

Du Bois: W[illiam] E[dward] B[urghardt] Du Bois (1868–1963), American civil rights leader, writer, editor and teacher. The descendant of a French Huguenot and an African slave, he was trained as a sociologist, receiving his B.A., M.A., and Ph.D. degrees from Harvard. Among the first important leaders to advocate complete economic, political, and social equality for blacks, Du Bois cofounded in 1909 the National Negro Committee, which later became the NAACP. He taught history and economics at Atlanta University from 1897 to 1910 and again from 1932 to 1944. *The Souls of Black Folk* (1903), a collection of essays, is his best known work.

Paragraph 12

Valley of the Dolls: A novel by Jacqueline Susann (1921–1974). A sensationalistic best seller in 1966, the novel is about three women: Anne starts as a theatrical attorney's secretary and later becomes a nationwide glamour figure selling cosmetics; Neely wins quick success as a singer, then alternates between stage glories and sanitariums; Jennifer, always seeking a true romance, gains fame in French-made nude movies and later commits suicide. The novel was made into a prodigiously inept film in 1967.

Possible Answers

Meaning and Purpose

1. Gaiter was almost denied a job for which he was "exceptionally qualified" (1) because he didn't fit the department head's idea of what a black man should be, his idea of a "real" black man a stereotype based on popular TV characters.

2. Ironically, many black people, just like white people, have accepted the stereotype of a black as illiterate and impoverished. Thus, a junior high girl questions Gaiter's black credentials.

3. Gaiter indicts all segments of society for racial stereotyping. He was accused by a white classmate in college of not being "really a black person" (3). He claims she had to have black people fit her stereotype so she could feel superior. White liberals, he says, are as racist as white conservatives, because, in trying to help disadvantaged blacks, they do so to bolster their own sense of superiority (8). And many blacks themselves either accept the racial stereotype out of ignorance, like the junior high girl already cited (4), or to advance their own political agendas (9–11).

4. Gaiter asserts two immediate causes for black stereotyping: black society placing emphasis on the lower class because that's where most were placed (6); white liberals seeing blacks as inferiors, not equals (8). The ultimate cause of racial stereotyping is the media, particularly TV programs, that Gaiter examines in the bulk of the essay (10–14).

5. Gaiter cites news programs that give a skewed view of black society (10–11), dramas that are praised for presenting the underbelly of black life (12), and a comedy that showcases risque humor (13–14). It's not that these representations are necessarily untrue; it's that they give only one view of a black society that is in reality far more diverse and complex.

6. African-Americans must, according to Gaiter, see to it that their children are not burdened with the idea that they are "invariably doomed to the under-

class" (16) by seeing themselves, and demanding that others see them as well, as individuals (17).

Strategy

1. As the essay's introduction, the first four paragraphs graphically illustrate the effects racial stereotyping has had on real people, both blacks and whites.
2. Paragraph 5 serves as a transition from the real effects racial stereotyping has had on real people to the question of how a stereotype of just one segment of black society has come to represent the whole (6), to an examination of the causes of that phenomenon (6–14). It does this by citing specific examples of the revolt of the "black bourgeoisie" against inaccurate stereotyping.
3. The statistics Gaiter cites are meant to support his final two points in paragraph 6: that affirmative action policies have opened "some doors for the black middle class," and that "social welfare and Great Society-style programs aimed at the black lower class have shown few positive results." Superficially, the statistics seem to bear out his contentions. The percentage of blacks with poverty level incomes has grown by 2.4 percent while the percentage of middle income blacks has grown an insignificant 1.1 percent. But he leaves unexplained the reasons for the 4.6 percent increase in the number of upper income blacks. And because the income statistics are the only evidence Gaiter offers, he seems to imply that income is the only measure of the success of affirmative action or social welfare programs. Indeed, there may be other measures.
4. Paragraph 15 indignantly sums up how the stereotype of the underclass black is perpetuated (its causes) and its effects on African-Americans. In so doing, the paragraph is the first of a three paragraph conclusion.

Style

1. "Blue humor" is lewd, lascivious, somewhat obscene, erotic humor. The term had become a colloquialism by about 1900. Its derivation is obscure. *The Dictionary of American Slang* (1960), compiled and edited by Wentworth and Flexner, suggests the erotic association of the term may be because the color blue is associated with burning brimstone. Your students may have a difficult time finding the term, but its meaning is easily enough derived from its context in the essay.
2. *Elite*: the choice or best of anything considered collectively; *salvage*: the act of saving anything from danger; *pervasive*: spread out through all parts; *strata*: layers or levels; *misogyny*: hatred, dislike, or mistrust of women; *excerpted*: having taken a passage from; *candor*: frank, open, and sincere in speech and expression; *psyche*: the human soul, spirit, or mind; *thwarting*: successfully preventing or frustrating; *cadre*: a group of trained or otherwise qualified personnel capable of forming, training, or leading an expanded organization like a political or religious faction; *bourgeoisie*: the middle class; *intelligentsia*: intellectuals considered as a group or a class; *lauded*: praised or extolled; *staple*: a basic feature or part; *relegated*: sent or consigned to an inferior position or place; *condescend*: to behave as if one is conscious of descending from a superior position, rank, or dignity; *peers*: a person equal to another; *prospective*: potential; *invariably*: con-

stantly; *shards*: fragments; *degraded*: lowered in dignity or estimation; *mono-lith*: something having a uniform, massive quality; *primacy*: being first in order, rank, importance; *idiosyncracies*: characteristics, mannerisms, habits, etc., that are peculiar to an individual.

Kids in the Mall: Growing Up Controlled
William Severini Kowinski

Teaching Suggestions

Many, if not most, of your students will have had first-hand and extensive mall experience. They can testify to the validity of Kowinski's observations, therefore, from immediate, first-hand knowledge—not always from an unbiased or critical perspective, perhaps, but from an extensive background nonetheless. Starting off by asking students to respond to the first two paragraphs can serve several purposes in getting them to evaluate the essay critically. First, because they will have personal knowledge, they will, we're sure, be able to add examples to those that Kowinski gives in paragraphs 1 and 2. This examination could turn into a discussion of the author's strategy in the first three paragraphs to convince the reader of the importance of thinking about what spending so much time in the mall does to teenagers. Most students will probably agree with Kowinski's early observations. Many, no doubt, will object to his later, critical commentary. The question could then be asked: If his early factual observations seem on target, how does he go wrong in evaluating this behavior later on? No doubt some students will remain adamant in their uncritical acceptance of the behavior Kowinski describes. Others may start looking more objectively at his evaluation.

Notes

Paragraphs 1 and 2
The examples the author gives are second-hand evidence, but this origin doesn't diminish their validity. On the contrary, they indicate that the author's observations are not isolated but widespread.

Paragraph 3
The first sentence serves as a transition and leads into the description of typical teenage mall activities. The examples are arranged chronologically to show typical stages in teenage development The question at the end of the paragraph tells us that a cause-and-effect discussion will follow.

Paragraph 4
"Street sense" connotes hard-won practical knowledge; "mall sense" connotes a knowledge that is somehow separated and protected from the real world.

Paragraphs 5, 6, and 7
These paragraphs show how mall developers were originally unprepared for the incursion by teenagers, how they then studied the phenomenon, and how, finally, the

malls became finishing schools for kids who had already been indoctrinated into the consumer ethic.

Paragraph 9

Kowinski cites authority to demonstrate that the seemingly benevolent mall of the preceding paragraph can actually be psychologically damaging.

Paragraph 12

The real psychological growth that involves active acceptance of responsibility is contrasted with the mall's promotion of passive consumption. This passivity is further emphasized in the opening sentence of the next paragraph.

Paragraph 14

The meaninglessness of teenage mall employment in the preceding paragraph is assaulted a second time by citing academic authority.

Paragraph 15

"curiosity, initiative . . .": Because the author has already established that mall teenagers have been conditioned as consumers before they ever became mall denizens and have now completed their consumer higher education, the likelihood is slight that they will ever assimilate this list of deeper values.

Paragraph 16

A sad irony colors this entire paragraph. Though the mall has objects with educational value, they will never be bought or used by mall children. And though older people with stories are there—knowledge used to be handed down from the old to the young in stories—the stories will not be heard. Instead, teenagers will just watch the "passing show."

Possible Answers

Meaning and Purpose

1. Most students will probably have experiences to relate about shopping malls. Encourage them to compare their experiences with the situations Kowinski talks about.

2. Kowinski asks, "Are these kids being harmed by the mall?" (3). His thesis is the last sentence in paragraph 4. The thesis does not completely answer the question because he has yet to explore the values of the mall environment and the extent of their effects on kids.

3. Kowinski points out all through the essay that mall life hones to a fine edge kids' already accepted false assumptions that life's primary goal is to buy and consume (7). Probably the most damaging effect the mall has on our kids is serving as a surrogate nurturing mother and family (10–12). All the mall's positive effects are described ironically.

4. Teenagers themselves would probably have their eyes opened by some of the facts Kowinski presents. But certainly the parents of mall teenagers would benefit most from reading this article. The information, the language, and the authorities cited suggest that adults are the target audience.

5. Kowinski's values can be determined by simply inverting the values he finds disconcerting—in his title, in his discussion of consumerism, and particularly in his description of the mall serving as a surrogate family (10–12). More explicitly, he lists attitudes he finds valuable that are not made in the mall: "curiosity, initiative self-expression, empathy, and disinterested learning" (15).

Strategy

1. Kowinski cites two specific examples, both tinged with dark humor, of kids who live at malls (2). He switches to typical examples to show how many children have gone through typical milestones of development at the mall (3). He speculates about all that important experience happening in an artificial environment and states his thesis in the final sentence (4).

2. The immediate cause is the "plethora of products in the mall, plus the pressure on teens to buy them." The effect from this cause is both immediate and ultimate—"the hurried child"—who must grow up too fast. This child learns how to shop in the short term, but in the longer term, he or she is pressured to look like an adult and to understand adult finances and emotions.

3. Superficially the two examples seem contradictory, but they are almost totally unlike. First, children are pressured to act in adult ways sexually and emotionally far beyond their own emotional development. Second, children just beginning to face responsibilities in the public work force need adult models on which to base their own behavior.

4. The cause of kids' spending time in the mall is that parents allow or encourage it (10). Kids' spending time at the mall becomes a cause of the mall's role of surrogate parent, which is the effect, but then this role itself becomes a cause (11) of structure being imposed on kids and elements of family life. Because kids crave structure and family life, they are drawn to cuddly merchandise and "home cooking." These elements in turn are causes, and their effects are that kids embrace passivity and consumerism. The whole progression is a causal chain.

5. Paragraph 18 is divided into two parts. The first two sentences describe how frighteningly insulated a child's mall existence is and how, therefore, every place becomes the same place. The next two sentences project that this is actually a good preparation for the future they face. In the first part, Kowinski looks back at the essay and encapsulates the experience he has just described, and in the second he looks forward to an ominous future.

Style

1. After describing how a teenage girl's major ambition was to learn how to put the perfect swirl on an ice-cream cone in order to gain a promotion in the company she worked for, and then to call that "achievement," makes a mockery of the emptiness and vapidity of the entire mall experience. Compare that to the achievement of "attitudes" (15).

2. Kowinski seems sympathetic toward his subject. He both acknowledges and understands the problem of teenagers in malls (first sentence in 4, 8, and 10). Still, he sees the dangers and hopes for a better choice for teenagers (7; first sentence, 19).

3. *Resonances*: the states or qualities of resounding or echoing; *incursion*: a hostile entrance into or invasion of a place or territory, especially a hostile one; *plethora*: overabundance, excess; *denizens*: inhabitants, residents; *impertinence*: unmannerly intrusion or presumption, insolence; *inexorably*: unyieldingly, unalterably.

——— 8 / *Process Analysis* ———

Binding Decisions
Joan Gould

Teaching Suggestions

To some members of the class, 1950 designates a time in the dark ages. To help students make historical connections between then and now, occasionally teachers mention a few facts about the 1950s: In 1950, World War II had been over for only five years. Harry S Truman was president of the United States. George VI was king of England. Josef Stalin was still heading Russia. The Korean War ("police action") was fought from 1950 to 1953. And the contraceptive pill was not developed until 1955. (By the end of 1961, 500,000 American women were on "the pill.")

A good way to engender discussion is to ask both male and female students how long the process of dressing for a date takes them. As a follow-up question, you might want to ask if the procedure takes longer for a blind date than for a date already known. For that matter, do we "dress for" a date now, or do we mostly dress for ourselves? One way to fire the discussion is to ask a question like this: Would you favor returning to the dress code of 1950? Why or why not?

Notes

Paragraph 1
The author not only sets the stage, but she also comments on cultural affairs in 1950. A single woman over twenty should be worried about being unmarried. Being single means not being grown up. A woman cannot call a man for a date. She must signal that she is a "nice girl."

Paragraph 2
Culturally significant in 1950, each item of clothing carries its own signal, which she hopes will be received properly by the man.

Paragraph 4
The process begins: step 1. Notice that each step is descriptively, personally, and culturally explained. These paragraphs hold a wealth of information beyond the description of girdles. The cultural process described here reflects the lock-step 1950s thinking in Gould's element of society. Gould fits her process to the symbolism required by each social situation because such modifications are expected by her mother and her friends, who themselves are bound to the same symbol-laden process. Gould finally compromises, but not to the point of innovation. Betty Friedan says about the generation following Gould's in *The Feminine Mystique* (1963), "When she stopped conforming to the conventional picture of femininity, she finally began to enjoy being a woman" (Chapter 14).

Paragraph 10
Lana Turner and Betty Grable, voluptuous American movie stars and pinup girls during World War II, predated Twiggy, the British model thin almost to emaciation,

by more than twenty years. The padded bra was first advertised in nineteenth-century Paris. The first modern bra was designed and made by socialite Mary Phelps Jacobs, in 1913. Notice the mother's warning. Some things never change.

Paragraph 12
Nylon stockings were again available in 1950. Gould reminisces about "stockings" during World War II. The Du Pont chemical company had invented nylon in 1938 and sent spools of nylon to selected hosiery manufacturers in 1940. Chosen stores received nylon stockings only if they agreed not to sell them before May 15, 1940, "Nylon Day"; riots nearly broke out as women all over the United States rushed hosiery departments. By the end of 1940, 36 million pairs of nylons had been sold—only because no more could be had.

Paragraph 13
Notice how Gould embodies her times. Although the man is obliged socially to pay for everything on the date, Gould is obliged to do all that society expects from a woman who "needs" to marry.

Paragraph 14
Her process of dressing for the occasion is consciously based on 1950s social requirements for a date.

Paragraph 15
Tell the class about this 1770 legislation in the British Parliament: "That women of whatever age, rank, or profession, whether virgins, maids, or widows, who shall seduce or betray into matrimony, by scents, paints, cosmetic washes, artificial teeth, (or) false hair, shall incur the penalty of the law as against witchcraft, and that the marriage shall stand null and void." The bill was defeated.

Paragraph 16
Her process of getting ready for the date is almost complete. In this entire essay, Gould has mentioned only two requirements for her blind date: that he pay all expenses incurred on the date and that he wear a hat, as befits the occasion.

Paragraph 17
Shalimar: A popular scent by Guerlain, developed in 1925. Its name is from Sanskrit, meaning "temple of love." Notice that the process is completed with the opening of the door. Her blind date, oblivious to her careful preparations for the evening, concentrates on himself and his cold. She wears Shalimar; he carries Kleenex.

Paragraph 19
All the planning and process itself lead to the man's proposing, after the proper length of time has passed, of course. Before she gives him her answer, she injects candor, in a sense revealing part of the process.

Paragraph 21
The process works! Notice the element of small mystery in the last line.

Possible Answers

Meaning and Purpose

1. Gould devotes several paragraphs to the subject of girdles (4–9). The "Binding" of the title relates first to what girdles do to the body (sentence 2, paragraph 4). A bra, which Gould describes choosing, is also binding. Dressing for a date in 1950 bound young women to a rigid set of behaviors and values. The word "Decisions" in the title is ironic because young women

then were not free to choose not to follow the rules of dating, courtship, and marriage; they could make only decisions that were ultimately insignificant and superficial, such as which girdle to wear.

2. Students may choose any symbolic garment, including white wedding gown, veil, necktie, vest, and hat. Their reasoning provides the key to judging the answer to this question.

3. She might want to show that she is "naturally" frugal, or she might want to keep down her date's expenses. Either way, she will be more appealing as a wife.

4. We know from Gould's mention of Twiggy in the 1960s (10) that Gould is looking back from more than a decade in the future of 1950. Her article captures a particular social etiquette in a particular time and intimates the values of the whole decade. This period-piece article can be useful for comparison with any current dating preparations and social values.

5. The conga originated in Latin America; the mambo in Cuba; both are energetic dances quite popular in the 1950s. *Ardent* means "warm or intense in feeling; passionate." The author feared becoming too intense during either dance, and therefore forgetful.

Strategy

1. Three of the steps are: choosing a girdle (8); putting on a padded bra (10); and "Stockings next" (12).

2. In describing her choice of a girdle, Gould begins with "My girdle comes first" (4). From here through 7, she digresses about girdles that older women wear, girdles that Victorian women wore, the girdle as a symbolic garment (6), and the consequences of not wearing a girdle (7). Gould then resumes the chronology of dressing (8).

3. Gould does not spare details about dressing for a date, or other relevant facts. She assumes her readers may be younger than herself, may not have firsthand experience with the procedure she describes, and may know little about dating and women's clothes in the 1950s. On the other hand, readers who were dating in the 1950s might be amused and carried back by her details. The information thus is not necessarily too much for an audience of Gould's peers.

4. The young man seems nervous, intent on talking to himself, and not attentive to his date.

Style

1. Written in present tense, the essay has a tone of immediacy, of excitement. The author is reliving her own past. This tone fits the essay's process—of dressing symbolically and appropriately, with anxiety, for a blind date who later becomes the author's husband.

2. Gould, even at the time of the date, is less than pleased with the rigmarole she has to go through. But her perspective from a future time also shows that she considered the ritual false and unnecessary, even humorous. Some language that illustrates her attitude: paragraph 4, "Here's the itch of it"; paragraph 5, "sausage casing"; paragraph 6, "like a walking clothespin"; and paragraph 10, "rises above my dress like the rim of the sun peering over a hilltop." Ask students for other examples.

3. The word *delirious* means, among other definitions, "wildly excited." The author is ecstatic because she can now "scratch and scratch," and be relieved of the binding girdle.

4. The word candor refers to "sharp honesty or frankness in expressing oneself." The author's candor serves as counterpoint to the masquerade imposed by society on her choice of clothing, here, the padded bra. Custom restricted her from using candor until now.

Commanded by Love
Richard Strozzi Heckler

Teaching Suggestions

A good way to begin your discussion is by having the class consider the apparent inconsistency between the title's two main words, *commanded* and *love*. Ordinarily, the two are not considered partners: One either commands or one loves. So how can one "command" by "love"? This question elicits all sorts of responses, ranging from "My parents love me, yet they command me to do things," to "If a person shows love, then a command does not seem too harsh." "Nevertheless," you might prod, "a command is a command, and love is love, so how can the two concepts intertwine?" Also, one might add, is it possible to have a command-love relationship between two people? Or is this kind of relationship successful only when it is obvious that one actor, in the final analysis, is far more powerful than the other, yet chooses not to exercise that power? Questions such as these often lead to worthy discussions of how people do or do not exercise self-control and of whether self-control is part of a process that is linked to self-esteem.

Notes

Paragraph 1
"Rios," the name of the horse, means "rivers" in Spanish. Note that this paragraph establishes the attitude of the author towards Rios. Noting that the horse is "distracted" and that he perhaps did not feel Heckler's "commitment," the author shows the close, almost entirely human relationship between the two. Also, by saying that "I feel we're just now beginning to listen to each other," the author further implies the close and kindly association between him and the horse.

Paragraph 2
A "quarterhorse" is one of a breed of strong saddle horses developed in the western United States, called a "quarterhorse" because it was originally trained to race up to a quarter of a mile.

"has never been formally schooled": Here we see again the tight focus that the author maintains for us to see clearly that his relationship with the horse resembles one's relationship with a child.

"trying to peel me off on low-hanging limbs": Rios occasionally treats his rider-trainer as if that rider-trainer were of no more consequence than a particularly bothersome scab.

Paragraph 3

"behavior modification": This phrase refers to the psychological concept of shaping behavior by manipulating reinforcements to obtain the desired behavior. Behavior therapy itself is based on the theory that hypothetical emotional factors and mental states are useless data in the study of psychopathology.

Wittgenstein: Meaning is studied in modern linguistics by making detailed analyses of how words and sentences are used in specific contexts. Scholars in other disciplines share this approach, one of the most notable being the Austrian philosopher Ludwig Wittgenstein (1889–1951).

"grammar": As well as referring to a systematic study of language, grammar can also refer to the basic principles of any area of knowledge.

"syntax": Though almost always associated with the study of language, this word has a more inclusive definition, the systematic arrangement of nearly anything. One can discuss the "syntax" of algebra or music as clearly as one can discuss the syntax of a language.

Paragraph 4

This paragraph describes the process by which Rios' previous owner attempted to teach him, by combining commands and dominance to produce obedience.

"neurotic": From the word *neurosis*, this loosely used term is applied to a variety of comparatively mild disorders.

"psychotic": From the word *psychosis*, this word denotes a mental disorder that interferes seriously with the usual functions of life.

Paragraph 5

This paragraph begins the staged dialogue between Rios and his rider. Notice the horse's personality here, as brought out by his "speech": He remains independent and leery of custom.

Paragraphs 6, 7, 8, and 9

In these short paragraphs, we have queries closely akin to *koans*, paradoxical or nonsensical questions originally from Zen philosophy, whose answers require stressing the kind of meditation that can bring forth philosophical illumination.

Paragraph 10

"like most people": Note the deliberate ambiguity in that sentence. The author combines Rios with people in terms of what motivates both.

Paragraph 11

"moral reason": Jean Piaget (1896–1980), the Swiss psychologist who studied the cognitive development of children, held that moral realism is the attitude characteristic of small children: Morality is inherent in an act as an objective fact and is observable to all. The moral reason that Rios requests in this paragraph resembles Piaget's moral realism.

Paragraph 16

At this point, we see the commingling of the commanded and that which commands. The reciprocity between beauty and love commands the rider and the horse to be both "at the same time, leader and follower."

Paragraph 17

After reinforcing the proposition in paragraph 16, that the leader and follower have become one, the author introduces the emblem of the hat and how it, too, has become integral to their relationship.

Paragraph 18

Here, the author uses an anecdote of the hat to show how much he and Rios have become commanded by one another.

Paragraph 19

We see in this paragraph what in classical rhetoric is called *diatyposis*, recommending useful precepts to someone else: Empowering and surrendering are by no means antonymous.

Paragraph 20

A reiteration of the precept contained in paragraph 19, this paragraph reminds the reader that time is measured in moments, each moment bringing an opportunity for conscious empowerment.

Possible Answers

Meaning and Purpose

1. He means, of course, the "new conversation" between him and Rios, the horse. The thoughtful student might well write that the new conversation is between the author and himself, acting out the character of Rios. The point of the answer is to establish the fact that the author begins the essay on a highly personal note, as if the horse had human attributes.

2. This is an example of a *hyperbole*, a deliberate exaggeration used to emphasize the author's point. Again, students often detail the notion that while of course no one is "capable of anything," in fact, that is how we use the language when we want to clarify or reinforce a statement.

3. Answers vary, of course, but the core of the answer is that Rios has learned from experience with a previous owner who used raw power to attempt to train Rios; therefore, the horse's "story of power" is a story that includes being dominated and fearful.

4. In this context, teeth symbolize an almost prehistoric rawness, the brute force of the jungle, a metaphor for strength. The author combines *teeth* and *love* to produce a statement implying that love without strength to support it, is love without worth.

5. The author's hat blows from his head just as the author and Rios magnetize into a kinship of one, in paragraph 17. This incident breaks the mood of the moment. In paragraph 18, Rios associates the author's love for him with the author's love for his hat, which helps us to see that the author himself draws no distinctions between love for the animate and for the inanimate. Love is love. Finally, Rios shows that he understands his new relationship with his owner, in paragraph 18, by walking over to the fallen hat, which the author had by that time forgotten. As the author says in the last line of that paragraph, "His taking command at that moment is an act of generosity and love."

Strategy

1. The phrase "juvenile delinquent" implies a young person who exhibits antisocial or criminal behavior. The phrase implies that Rios himself has become a juvenile delinquent for some of the reasons that young people become juvenile delinquents, such as having a less-than-pleasant home life, a dysfunctional "parent," and, consequently, mixed messages about how he should act.

2. The author's having a year-and-a-half old daughter sends the message that the author can deal with younger "children." The daughter herself can walk safely around Rios' legs, which shows that Rios can be patient when he realizes that he needs to be patient.

3. The word *fraternal* ordinarily refers to that which pertains to brothers. Horses and men have been combined for centuries in story and myth; in this essay, this horse and this man are brothers in the sense of being on equal levels of learning. The phrase is important in this paragraph because it shows that Rios is, partially, a historical product of his close relationship to man. The problems Rios faced earlier in his life were caused by one man's not honoring that fraternity and by Rios' not being able to feel that fraternity.

4. Answers vary according to the data the students retrieve from the essay. For example, many students use material taken mostly from paragraph 3, where the author discusses horse training in general terms, using jargon not commonly used by lay people, including "side reins," "dropped nosebands," "bit-tying." Other students note that the author starts the essay by talking about its being just another day, whereas a less experienced person would have talked about nervousness and anxiety.

5. By having this simulated conversation, Heckler reminds his readers early and often that to him, no communication boundaries exist between animals and people. What goes on in the mind of a person is just as apt to go on in the mind of an animal.

Style

1. The author establishes a sense of timelessness by beginning his essay "This morning." As the essay goes on to demonstrate, all days are the same; it is what a person does during each day that is significant. Also, by beginning with "This morning," the author establishes a sense of immediacy, putting the reader into the action now.

2. In physics, a *field* is a region of space characterized by some physical property; *energy* is the work that a physical system can do in changing from its actual state to a specified reference state. The energy fields in the essay are the two psychic regions, the author's and the horse's, in which the author and the horse work to change their relationship with one another.

3. The author italicized this sentence to emphasize its great importance: It is the summation of Rios' autobiography before meeting the author, and shows why he behaves as he does early in his new relationship.

4. If it were possible to use only one word as a synonym-summary of the essay's style, it would be *coalesce*, which means, "to blend or come together." Using such strategies as personification, metaphor, simile, and hyperbole, Heckler brings himself and the horse to an equal realization that, as he says in paragraph 19, "it is the surrendering itself that is empowering." He and the horse have coalesced into a single psychic unit comprising commanding and loving.

5. Answers vary, depending on the student's perception of *arc*. For example, some see it geometrically, as any unbroken part of the circumference of a circle or other curved line, and reason from that definition to the idea that the

word as it is used here suggests that time is timeless, that it can not be "broken." Other students see an arc as being bow-shaped, and reason from that perception that time resembles age in that we all are born, reach our heights, and then descend. Either way, students usually agree that time is a realistic character in the essay, and many of them have mentioned that until reading this essay, they had not thought of time's being a character in their own lives as well.

Anatomy of a Joke
Garry Trudeau

Teaching Suggestions

Producers take great care to give the viewers of television programs like *The Tonight Show* the impression that the opening monologue, though certainly scripted, is nonetheless "edgy and unpredictable" (2). No doubt students will be surprised to learn how minutely planned a single joke is, and how much time and money is invested in a triviality that averages about fifteen seconds to tell. You might initiate a discussion by asking what payoff is expected for such expensive attention to detail. Such a discussion could lead into the consideration of the corporate nature of commercial television, that it is possible to assert the position that all television broadcasting is solely designed to sell products. Ask students to take a position on such an assertion and then line up their reasons to justify their position. Ask them what other pursuits entail the same meticulous attention to detail and what payoffs are expected for each. What values underlie such hard work in each case?

Notes

Paragraph 1
Trudeau refers to a time when Letterman, Leno, and Chase were all competing against each other. Their ad-lib jokes, "rim-shot critiquing," during press conferences missed the point because the "real jokes, the ones that count" (2), are all carefully planned.

Paragraph 2
Trudeau states his thesis in the second sentence by contrasting popular belief with actuality.

Paragraphs 3–8
Each of these paragraphs describes one of the six phases in the making and delivery of a fleeting, trivial joke.

Possible Answers

Meaning and Purpose
1. Student answers will vary, of course, but the term *anatomy* certainly has a scientific denotation (the dissection of something to determine its structure) as well as an equally formal connotation. And Trudeau certainly focuses his analytic eye on a seemingly inconsequential *Tonight* show joke.
2. News headlines lend the jokes topicality and will probably be the most widely recognized source material for the audience.

3. Trudeau gives a clue to how important a single joke is when he says in paragraph 2, "The stakes are too high for it [the carefully formalized structure of a joke] to be otherwise." But he is never explicit about just what those stakes are, so the reader must surmise. The term *commercial television* is really the answer. Television exists for the commercials, because it is the commercials that make the money. Television advertisers pay the networks, and viewers buy the products advertised. In this kind of ethic, a monologue becomes the all-important lead-in to the point of it all—the commercial. That is why a "timing coach" was "summarily sacked" when he allowed a monologue to run 13.5 seconds long (7).

4. Trudeau states his thesis in paragraph 2: "Despite the popular conception of the monologue as edgy and unpredictable, it is actually as formal and structured as anything found in traditional kabuki."

Strategy

1. Each monologue joke goes through six stages, and Trudeau spends a single paragraph on each, sequentially: 3, 4, 5, 6, 7, and 8. The first two paragraphs serve as his introduction.

2. The diversions that disrupt Trudeau's strict description of the joke process gives color and human interest in what could otherwise be dull analysis. When he tells us, for instance, that the "comedy stylist" is a prima donna and is the best paid and worst dressed of the comedy team (5), or that the "polish man" is usually a woman (6), or that a "timing coach" was fired for allowing a monologue to run 13.5 seconds long (7), he is not telling the reader anything about the process itself, but is adding an interesting, human dimension to that process.

3. Trudeau uses the terms that describe the people at the center of each phase of the joke process as transitions. For instance, he ends paragraph 4 with the word *stylist* and begins the next paragraph with the phrase "The comedy stylist." He also employs words and phrases that indicate chronology in the process, such as "The news clip is then passed on . . ." (4).

4. The four illustrations give visual emphasis to the fact that the joke is being constantly refined. Student responses to whether or not the illustrations clarify Trudeau's ideas will, no doubt, vary.

Style

1. Colloquialisms, such as "banged out over late-night pizza with a few cronies" (2), or having a monologue running long described as a "major no-no" (7), are associated with the popular, and false, assumption described in the first half of Trudeau's thesis: "Despite the popular conception of the monologue as edgy and unpredictable . . ." (2).

2. All the jargon in the essay refers to the technical process of refining a joke and is associated with the second half of the thesis, that a monologue joke "is actually as formal and structured as anything found in traditional kabuki."

3. *Anatomy:* the dissection of all or part of an animal or plant (and by extension, anything else) to determine its structure; *in the wake of:* as a result of; *kabuki:* a popular drama of Japan characterized by stylized acting, music, and dancing; *cronies:* close friends or companions; *pipeline:* a route along which something passes at a steady rate; *peruse:* to read with thoroughness

and care; *velocity:* swiftness; *red herrings:* misleading clues; *dynamics:* driving forces; *interrogatory:* conveying or expressing a question; *prima donna:* a temperamental person; *per diem:* paid by the day; *gross:* complete; *fulcrum:* a prop or support; *hoary:* tedious from familiarity, stale; *burnishing:* polishing; *anti-defamation:* opposing unjustified injury; *coda:* a concluding part; *summarily:* immediately; *digitalized:* converted to numerical form; *modulate:* regulate or adjust; *pinnacle:* the highest or culminating point; *impeccability:* flawlessness.

Rat Patrol: A Saga
Frank Gannon

Teaching Suggestions
Gannon's connection with his son is timeless, the do-as-I-say, not-as-I-did connection that all students understand. Ask your students if their parents or guardians have ever given them advice based on the parents' or guardians' personal experiences. Then ask them if they followed that advice. Follow that question by asking them if their parents or guardians accidentally made their own stories so enticing that the students emulated the parents or guardians, just to see what would happen. This technique often results in a lively discussion that helps to interest students in Gannon's topic.

Notes
Paragraph 1
This autobiographical paragraph establishes Gannon as the authority on his topic as well as provides its readers, many of whom are younger, with a bit of television history. The ABC television series *Rat Patrol* ran for two seasons in 1966 and 1967. It still has its adherents, who conduct lively discussions on websites.
Paragraphs 2, 3, 4, and 5
These short paragraphs cover clearly the seemingly neverending string of commercials that advertised this series, which was fictionally located in the North African desert during World War II.
Paragraph 6
"nearly five hundred times": Notice the hyperbole of youth here, the deliberate exaggeration so characteristic of youngsters' conversations.
"eighth-grade minds": Gannon and his friends are apparently about thirteen years old.
"cool": When Gannon was young, this term was synonymous with "excellent." It might still be, again.
Paragraph 7
This one-sentence paragraph introduces the process much the same way that a cookbook introduces directions for a recipe.
Paragraph 8
Note that this paragraph describes the locale, which is important because to a thirteen-year-old, it would resemble the locale of *Rat Patrol*.

Paragraph 9

A bit of sarcasm here, with Gannon's calling three hundred yards of sand an "official" field.

Paragraph 10

Notice the "you" in the first sentence of this paragraph, an opening pronoun that mechanics, plumbers, and other crafts people use when they are giving directions. In this paragraph, Gannon talks in the present tense to the general reader, as if the reader needs or wants to know this process.

"excellent source": Note how cleverly Gannon skirts the notion of theft.

"Sting" and "Greenpeace": A well-known pop singer, and a political group, respectively, the latter being interested in ecological preservation.

Paragraph 11

"contributed": A tense change from that in paragraph 10, Gannon also skates around any notion of thievery.

"weeks of preparation": Note that this "game" is not an everyday source of entertainment.

"Ramblers": Small automobiles manufactured by the Nash Motor Car Company, now defunct.

"magic words": Note the humor in this phrase.

Paragraph 12

This paragraph begins the numbered sequence of specific directions in the process.

"half ton of sand": Again, note the hyperbole of youth.

Paragraph 13

"googolplex": The figure 1 followed by a "googol" of zeroes; in other words, it is 10 to the power of 10 to the power of 100, representing a large number indeed!

Paragraph 14

"aesthetically pleasing": Another humorous phrase, considering the results of following this process.

Paragraph 15

"ideal formula": Here Gannon touches humorously on the notion of the Platonic doctrine found in English literature: Through thought and action, beauty and virtue become identified. Compare this short description of Platonic doctrine with the subject matter of the essay.

Paragraph 16

"in said position": Note the ersatz formality in this sentence.

Paragraph 17

Note the dramatic possibilities here. Gannon covers the verbal-warning range from a warship under fire to (1) an oil well's release of pressure to (2) a comrade's shocked comment to (3) an old-movie criminal's words to (4) a police officer, indicating the crossover from *The Rat Patrol* to movies and television series that the youngsters have watched.

Paragraph 18

The paragraph that updates the reader to Gannon's present. In his forties now, his tastes have changed.

"Dennis Hopper": A Hollywood actor who has played in several action movies.

Paragraph 19

Gannon pushes the idea he established in the paragraph above, that he now prefers calmer ways to spend his time.

Paragraph 20

The Secret Garden: A poignant love story, usually rated in the B category, that ends sadly.

"close to nausea": Gannon's son reacts the way youngsters usually react to such scenes.

"same name": Here, as in the one-line paragraphs 21, 22, 23, and 24, Gannon overtly establishes his close identity with the son.

" 'Explosions' ": This word connects Gannon and his son in a quasi-historical way.

Paragraph 25

"same name": Again, Gannon emphasizes the close familial relationship he has with his son, not stressing the emotional attachment.

Paragraph 26

"Goliath": The giant mentioned in the Bible (I Samuel 17), now a term signifying anyone gigantic. One might note also that David slew the biblical Goliath.

"Haverty's": A furniture store chain on the East Coast.

Paragraph 27

"Ripley's 'Believe It or Not' ": Once a popular daily sidebar in many newspapers, it told of the strange, the macabre, and the nearly unbelievable by illustrating one such story each day.

Paragraph 28

"post Civil-War equivalent": Gannon alludes to the money printed in the South during the Civil War, which was worthless after the war.

Paragraph 29

"Olivier": Sir Lawrence Olivier, a famous British Shakespearean actor and movie star, Academy Award winner who was knighted for his long-time prowess as an actor.

"Brad Pitt": An American movie actor now in his thirties, a current heartthrob.

Paragraph 31

"Vietnam . . . Hiroshima": Gannon notes the currently discussed areas of the world, historical and present, that are (or were) sites of mass brutal carnage.

Paragraph 35

Seeing that his historical tack did not work with his son, Gannon begins his autobiographical tale with a visual image, which captures immediately his son's attention.

Paragraph 40

"CO_2": Carbon dioxide. During the days that Gannon attended college, a number of toys were available, including toy cars and toy rocket ships, that were propelled by carbon dioxide under pressure in a metal capsule about the size of a shotgun shell. When one pierced the end of the capsule, the carbon dioxide exited at great force, acting as the driver for the toy. These capsules were easily purchased at any drugstore, toy store, or grocery store.

Paragraph 47

After Gannon explains, perhaps inadvertently, how to make a bomb, he tells his son what happened as the result of the bomb he tried to construct. Compare this story with the "Believe It or Not" story in paragraph 28.

Paragraph 48

Gannon's dry mouth alludes to the truth of his story.

Paragraph 49

Gannon almost curtly ends his essay, having made his point that his nine-year-old son is more interested in making a bomb than in digesting a moral.

Possible Answers

Meaning and Purpose

1. The "how-to" section early in the essay refers to Gannon's escapade as a youngster. Gannon's later anecdote, paragraphs 39 through 47, refers to Gannon's escapade as a college student, showing that no matter our age (to a certain point), we are susceptible to the excitement of the unpredictable.
2. It occurs to Gannon here that the age gap between him and his son affects their points of view. Of course the son is much younger than the parent, but the parent has come to rediscover that a young person's emotional attitude differs significantly as well.
3. The moral of this essay for Gannon's son is meant "Don't do what I did," but the moral for the reader is that young people react the same way, no matter the times in which they were born. They do not often take their parents' or guardians' advice.
4. The term *saga* ordinarily refers to legendary, historical accounts of heroic adventures. As used in Gannon's title, the word suggests satire, being reduced in meaning to signify the manufactured excitement, rather than heroic adventure, of young boys.

Strategy

1. Gannon's scar proves visually to his son that what he is about to say is true. It adds to his story by holding his son's attention, as visual aids do to all young people.
2. The author shifts to the present tense for an interesting psychological reason. He is telling a "war story," that which happened to him. As he begins the story, his mind shifts to the present, showing that he is reliving his experience as he recounts it.
3. The "Dads" are never mentioned as being actors in this drama. Instead, they are mentioned only as owning the materials that the boys stole from them.
4. To an adult, these are well-known examples of twentieth-century areas of mindless brutality. In his futile attempt to give examples of horror to his son, Gannon relies on historical and current events, forgetting that few nine-year-olds keep up on the news or are aware of history on a deep level.

Style

1. The common stylistic features of these incidents are that they are cast clearly to prove the same thing: that neither the son nor the father, when he was the son's age and older, learned much from their experiences. No pontificating intrudes. This combination of the personal and the journalistic style helps the reader to see that regardless of the style, in this case, Gannon's son does not respond the way Gannon had hoped.
2. In the context of the early part of the essay, any product with a warning label was a product containing the kind of dangerous ingredients so sought by the boys for their bomb. Reading the warning label was more efficient than reading the marketing label to see what kind of product the boys were stealing.

3. The "they" in this essay is the universal "they" of authority and supposed wisdom. "They" say "this," and "they" say "that." Every reader would realize that this "they" signifies the unknown authority that lingers in our language.

4. What would attract an educated readership is the universality of the "moral," that youth never changes, it only ages, a moral that Gannon presents in the simple style befitting the obvious moral.

The Maker's Eye:
Revising Your Own Manuscripts
Donald M. Murray

Teaching Suggestions

The essay can be approached in a variety of ways. You can treat it, of course, as a fine example of informative process analysis (see pp. 391–394). In the first ten paragraphs, Murray details the skills writers must develop and the problems they must overcome in order to revise their manuscripts. He then details chronologically the process professional writers go through to improve their texts. But you might want to ignore analyzing the essay's form, or combine that analysis with a lesson on revision. The essay could serve as your very first lesson in revision or as a follow-up lesson after the students have completed a paper or two. If this is the case, have them take a paper they have completed earlier and now revise it again following the Murray process step-by-step. The changes may prove instructive.

Notes

Paragraph 2
Peter F. Drucker (born 1909) was born in Vienna and emigrated to the United States in 1937. He has taught in several U.S. universities and authored books on business, technology, and society. He has contributed articles to *Harper's*, the *Wall Street Journal*, the *New York Times*, and *Public Interest*.

Paragraph 5
Ray Bradbury (born 1920), an American science fiction writer, is known for his fantastic tales that combine acute social criticism with fanciful science fiction. He is best known for his short story collections *The Martian Chronicles* (1950), *Dandelion Wine* (1957), and *I Sing the Body Electric!* (1969). He also wrote screenplays and plays as well as the novels *Fahrenheit 451* (1953) and *Something Wicked This Way Comes* (1962).

Paragraph 6
Nancy Hale (1908–1988), born in Boston, was a painter, journalist, and author. She published nineteen volumes of fiction, biography, memoirs, and many short stories documenting changing upper-class American manners. She was the first woman reporter for the *New York Times*.

John Ciardi (1916–1985) was an American poet, teacher, and critic. He was poetry editor of the *Saturday Review* for many years and wrote numerous essays on the art of reading and enjoying poetry. He published many volumes of his own poetry and made a notable translation of Dante's *Inferno* into idiomatic English to recall Dante's use of the vernacular.

Paragraph 8

Eleanor Estes (1906–1988), born in New Haven, Connecticut, was a prolific children's author. She is best known for her earliest work, family stories based on her own childhood.

Paragraph 9

Anthony Burgess (1917–1993) was an English novelist and critic. A prolific, versatile, and comic writer, Burgess had an extraordinary facility with language, a talent he admired in James Joyce, the subject of one of his works, *Joysprick: An Introduction to the Language of James Joyce* (1973). Probably the best known of his many novels is *A Clockwork Orange* (1962), in which he envisions a future state terrorized by teenage gangs who speak Nadsat, a language created by Burgess from British and American slang, and Russian.

Roald Dahl (1916–1990) was a Welsh-born fiction and screen writer. He is best known for his macabre short fiction and children's books, the latter including *Charlie and the Chocolate Factory* and *Chitty Chitty Bang Bang*, both later adapted to film. He also wrote the script for the James Bond movie, *You Only Live Twice.*

Paragraph 11

Murray here, in a single paragraph, disposes of the minority of professional writers who do not meticulously revise draft by draft. Notice that although their methods may be untypical, they nonetheless include extensive revision.

Paragraph 17

Here Murray uses an analogy, comparing a piece of writing structure to a body's supporting spine.

Paragraph 18

He uses another analogy here, comparing the amount of information needed to make a point both satisfying and convincing to the amount of garlic needed to make a salad just right. Garlic lovers know there is no such thing as too much garlic.

Paragraph 24

Here Murray repeats an idea he stated in paragraph 2: Writers don't know what they think until they actually write about it. The concept is almost totally alien to most student writers.

Paragraph 28

Count Leo Tolstoy (1828–1910) was a Russian novelist and moral philosopher. Best known for his novels, Tolstoy also wrote short stories, plays, and essays. Together with another great nineteenth-century Russian novelist, Fyodor Dostoyevsky, Tolstoy, according to many literary critics, made the realistic novel a literary genre that ranks in importance with classical Greek tragedy and Elizabethan drama. *War and Peace* and *Anna Karenina* are probably his two greatest works.

Possible Answers

Meaning and Purpose

1. Many students might object to Murray's claim that student writers consider their first draft their final draft (1), especially if they do any revision at all. But most will certainly agree that the extensive revision a professional writer

does goes far beyond their efforts. Both student writers and professionals share the problem of being overcritical of their work (7).

2. "Normal" readers read what they believe to be a finished piece of writing. Writers, on the other hand, read their own drafts with the possibility of change always in their consciousness (3).

3. Writers must accept both the praise and criticism of others and be suspicious of both at the same time. They must remain detached from their own work in order to work on it objectively (4).

4. It might be worthwhile here to lead the students through these eight elements of writing to make sure they genuinely understand what Murray means by them.

5. Information does not exist for its own sake, but is structured for a purpose, leading the reader to an understanding, a meaning.

6. All of the information in this essay leads the reader to the understanding that for a writer a piece of writing is never complete. It can always be reworked to make it more effective.

Strategy

1. The thesis is stated in the opening paragraph: For a professional writer a draft is just the beginning of writing. Murray restates the thesis, in somewhat different form, in paragraph 10.

2. Ostensibly, Murray is writing an informative process analysis, showing ". . . the sequence followed by most writers most of the time in rereading their own work" (11). But the information is so explicit that it could certainly be used as a guide for revision. If followed, it would be directive process analysis.

3. Murray quotes other authors to give authority to his contention that the biggest part of writing is rewriting.

4. This is another version of the story told about a writer who, when asked what he thought about a subject replied, "How should I know? I haven't written about it yet." This points up the idea that writing forces the writer to make connections about things that he could never make without going through the writing process, an idea that most beginning writers have a hard time understanding.

5. Murray first establishes the importance of the process for effective writing. He distinguishes between the attitudes of professional and amateur writers, explains how writers must read with a different eye than readers who don't write, establishes a common problem shared by amateurs and professionals, and cites several writers as to not only the importance, but the necessity, of revision. Only then does he describe the typical process itself.

Style

1. In these three paragraphs Murray personalizes the revision process to make it more real for the reader. Before this he was speaking in typical terms, and now he shows how he personally applies some of the elements of the process. We think the anecdote of paragraph 27 is particularly effective.

2. Since the thrust of the entire essay is that professional writers feel a near compulsion to revise and tinker with their work continually, it is wholly appropriate for the essay to end without ending.

3. *Journeyman*: a person who has served an apprenticeship at a trade or hand-icraft and is certified to work at it assisting or under another person; *prolific*: highly productive; *euphoric*: being in a state of happiness, confidence, or well-being; *schizophrenic*: a state characterized by the coexistence of contra-dictory or incompatible elements; *connotation*: the associated or secondary meaning of a word; *denotation*: the explicit or direct meaning of a word as distinguished by the ideas or meanings associated with it or suggested by it.

9 / Classification and Division

American Regional Costume
Alison Lurie

Teaching Suggestions

In the essay Lurie classifies Americans according to their styles of dress and divides the country into five distinct regions that represent these styles. She offers historical, geographic, climatic, political, and economic explanations for the evolution of regional dress. You might begin by asking your students how valid these classifica-tions appear to them. Is an element of stereotyping involved here? Does Lurie take into account other factors that might influence dress? What classifications in dress could be identified at your college or university?

The last question could lead to a discussion of how division and classification help us make sense of complex issues. Both methods separate large subjects into smaller and more comprehensible units. Both methods make large issues easier to understand.

Notes

Paragraph 1
Lurie begins with the immediate claim that America has no typical dress, that the varied histories of various regions have left an indelible mark on styles of dress.

Paragraph 2
After establishing where distinctions of regional dress can best be observed, Lurie states her thesis that five distinct styles of dress can be seen in the United States.

Paragraph 3
She now explains how styles can be misinterpreted by someone alien to a region. This confusion bolsters her contention that dress styles reflect history, geography, and climate rather than social mores or personal morals.

Paragraph 4
Here Lurie begins the paragraph with its topic sentence and then cites examples to establish its validity.

Paragraph 5
She again begins with a topic sentence and proceeds with examples. Now, though, the often elaborate dress of the Deep South is contrasted with the severer dress of New England described in the preceding paragraph.

Paragraph 6

Lurie uses the first two sentences to introduce her next classification, midwestern dress, and to lead to her topic sentence, the third. After describing midwestern dress, she compares it to dress in New England and the South to even more clearly distinguish it.

Paragraph 7

She now describes dress in the Wild West and claims that the language as well as the dress of the Wild Westerners reflects a ranching background.

Paragraph 8

First Lurie gives a brief historical background on California's development and then shows how the present reflects the past.

El Dorado was a legendary treasure city in South America sought by early Spanish explorers. By extension, then, it is any place promising great wealth.

Paragraph 9

To emphasize the sometimes outlandish California dress, Lurie shows how that dress might be interpreted in other parts of the country.

Paragraph 10

Lurie now connects southern Californians with others in the Sun Belt and gives two more examples that distinguish them from those of other regions.

Paragraph 11

In the last section of the essay, Lurie explains why some people who live in a region refuse to dress typically and why some styles are popular in all regions. She begins by giving some general examples of people who choose to dress outside the norm.

Paragraph 12

She now offers examples.

Paragraph 13

Lurie introduces two other factors that influence the popularity of a regional style and offers examples from the past.

Paragraph 14

She concludes with an explanation of the current popularity of western costume and gives present-day examples.

Possible Answers

Meaning and Purpose

1. Encourage students to examine their own ideas about what regional American dress is, as well as where those ideas come from and what attitudes they might reflect.

2. Attendees of national meetings generally come from similar occupational and economic backgrounds. Their dress would vary not because of social and economic status, but because of the regions they come from (2).

3. Lurie's thesis is that Americans have five distinct kinds of dress, as she states (2).

4. Regional styles are determined by the region's history and climate and do not reflect moral attitudes. Someone from outside a region may misinterpret the dress of that region by reading moral values into the style of dress (3).

5. She claims that history, local interests, geography, and climate account for the differences in regional dress styles.

6. The current popularity of western costume reflects recent far-right politics and isolationism and a turning away from foreign modes (14).

Strategy

1. Lurie's organizational scheme follows the historical development of the United States from the Northeast to the South, the Midwest to the Southwest, and, finally, to the Far West.
2. Lurie's first two subheadings pair adjacent regions, and the two style categories under each are markedly different. The Far West gets its own subheading because it is traditionally big and bold enough to stand alone. California is usually set apart from other regions.
3. Cause and effect.
4. The quotations show that the kinds of dress she describes are reflected in popular and literary culture. These facts bolster the validity of her thesis.

Style

1. Some examples: "homogeneous" (1), "factors such as occupation and income are held relatively constant" (2), "laid-back-looking" and "hop into bed" (3). The casual language gives the impression that she's talking about real people.
2. Lurie makes no explicit judgments, but some of her descriptive language sounds opinionated or stereotypical.
3. *Homogeneous*: composed of parts or elements that are all of the same kind; *superficially*: externally or outwardly; *Puritan*: a member of a group of Protestants that arose in the sixteenth century within the Church of England, demanding simpler doctrine and worship and stricter religious discipline; many Puritans migrated to New England; *dandyism*: excessive attention to clothes and appearance; *gingham*: yarn dyed, plain-weave cotton fabric, usually striped or checked; *linsey-woolsey*: a coarse fabric woven from linen warp, or sometimes cotton and coarse wool filling; *dowdier*: to be dowdy is to be out of style, drab, old-fashioned, untidy; *foulard*: a soft, lightweight silk, rayon, or cotton of plain or twill weave with printed design; *sartorial*: of or pertaining to clothing or style or manner of dress; *raffish*: mildly or sometimes engagingly disreputable or nonconformist; *allurement*: fascination, charm; *isolationism*: the policy or doctrine of isolating one's country from the affairs of other nations by declining to enter alliances, foreign economic commitments, international agreements, and so on; *belligerently*: warlike, aggressively hostile.

Three Kinds of Discipline
John Holt

Teaching Suggestions

The essay could be used for discussing both childrearing and learning. The students' own backgrounds will undoubtedly determine their attitudes toward each of the kinds of discipline Holt describes, especially that of Superior Force. Encourage students to give specific examples to back up their opinions, demonstrating that specifics are always needed to be convincing.

Notes

Paragraph 1
Holt begins with examples that immediately illustrate the Discipline of Nature.
"This . . . good teacher": He then shows why this kind of discipline is important in schools: it is a good teacher.

Paragraph 2
After explaining the Discipline of Culture, Holt gives examples to show that it works in the real world.

Paragraph 3
Holt begins the paragraph using the same format as the last, a brief explanation of the Discipline of Superior Force followed by examples.

He then cautions that this kind of discipline should be used sparingly and goes on to explain why.

Paragraph 4
With an extended example of ballet training Holt illustrates how all three disciplines often overlap.

Possible Answers

Meaning and Purpose

1. Holt says that children will "meet and learn" from discipline. His first sentence is his thesis. He goes into detail about three kinds of discipline and how children may learn best from them.
2. Give students time to talk about discipline they have observed and their opinions about it. Encourage them to compare their observations to some of Holt's descriptions.
3. Students will have their own opinions about this statement. Holt's point is that children usually imitate the adults around them and that example is the best teacher. He says, "They watch very carefully what people around them are doing and want to do the same" (2). The evidence he offers is general and perhaps idealistic, but his argument is effective.
4. He believes children are basically good and easily trained, and also that they will naturally strive for the best. The penultimate sentence in the essay illustrates this attitude.

Strategy

1. Holt's classification system has to do with the kinds of things in the world outside the self that he thinks impose discipline on children. He chooses nature, culture, and force as three large areas of influence. Another social scientist might choose three other categories, or more than three. Holt's categories result from his own observations and opinions.
2. Paragraph 4 describes where his categories overlap. He doesn't say this is a fourth category, but rather sums up the three and brings them together. In practice, his kinds of discipline don't always occur in isolation. The essay is

not imbalanced but balanced by this last paragraph, tied up neatly and brought to an end.
3. Each paragraph contains a series of brief, typical examples illustrating Holt's general statements.

Style
1. The names are capitalized because they are formal labels of each division.
2. Holt appreciates the value of all three kinds of discipline while trusting the child to grow naturally without excessive adult interference. He is clearly advocating an approach to teaching in its broadest sense: allow the child to learn from hands-on experiences; provide good examples for the child to imitate; and protect the child from danger, but do not underestimate his or her ability to understand its real nature.
3. *Wheedled:* to have endeavored to influence a person by smooth, flattering, or beguiling words or acts; *contagious:* tending to spread from person to person; *fidget:* to move about restlessly, nervously, or impatiently; *impotent:* lacking power or ability; *novice:* a person who is new to the circumstances in which he is placed; *autocratic:* tyrannical, despotic, domineering; *suppleness:* the condition of being flexible, pliant.

Territorial Behavior
Desmond Morris

Teaching Suggestions

Excepting a few who may have had a sociology or social anthropology course, students do not often encounter the social-scientific methods of classification used by Morris. Some say that humankind is not to be treated like other animals. But what of athletes? We classify them like tools—according to their uses, not their intrinsic worth as people. Tribal, family, and personal territories are often thought of as occupying the whole planet, a thought decried by ecologists.

Territory carries responsibility. Do we protect the territory that we display as ours? Or do we ruin it as part of our displaying that it is ours?

While Morris examines territorial behavior, it enlivens the class discussion to add the concept of responsibility to that behavior. Explore the question of whether we should protect for ourselves what is ours alone or whether we should keep our territory in trust. If we keep it in trust, how far are we willing to go to protect it? As far as war? War destroys territory. Are we willing to be constantly vigilant politically to protect territory? And from whom are we protecting it?

Notes

Paragraphs 1–5
Morris begins by dividing human territory into three classifications. Before he expands those classifications, he discusses their sociology. First, he describes the penalties for violating the territories of others. Next, he discusses briefly the healthy reasons for having "owned space." Then he tells how we mark our territories.

Paragraph 6

Returning to the first of his classifications, Morris develops it by the strategy of cyclic expansion. That is, he starts at the center, the small group, and expands outward, each circle of expansion larger: The tribe's home base expands, finally, to become the capital city of a nation.

Paragraph 7

The nation itself, fixed by borders, holds so many people that individuals begin to lose their tribal identity. They compensate by forming subgroups, social tribes, to gain a sense of belonging, which includes the territorial signals such social tribes agree to use.

Paragraph 8

Notice that this classification is as cyclic as the strategy Morris uses to describe it. As the tribe expands, members of the tribe circle back to making efforts to form a subgroup, keeping their own membership small enough to be comfortably identifiable.

Paragraph 11

Moving down as they read, from the tribe classification to the family classification, students are occasionally shocked to see the family defined as a "breeding unit" and the family's territory as a "breeding ground." They might be reminded that Morris is not being cavalier with the family unit; instead, he is using the neutral terminology of the social scientist.

Morris's "typical house" is typical for the author's area, but houses differ in this country, according to cost and location. Because his house can be described as "ideal Victorian," students from other kinds of homes might need to be reminded that he is using a model here to represent reality, not to define it.

Paragraph 12

Morris's comments on modern architecture can deeply affect students, particularly if they live in apartments, condominiums, or in some older tracts of homes that were built quickly and identically. Teachers often break here, to discuss with their students the ways in which we mark our property as our own, with plants, paint, lawns, fences, pets, trees, and so on. A stimulating question is: "How much do we mark our territory as being comfortably ours before we begin to mark it as a warning to others not to trespass?" It is one thing to build a white picket fence around our house, quite another to build a six-foot chain-link fence, for example.

Paragraph 13

So also with temporary territory: Here is a good place to discuss the worth of Morris's comments. Does it really happen as he describes it? Do we stake out territory in the mountains, at the park, the river, the lake, or near the ocean? What happens when our territory is violated? Does it make a difference what kind of people violate our territory? If an old woman and an old man sit quite near our territory, do we feel differently than we would if a teenage boy and girl violated our territory?

Paragraph 15

The third classification, the personal space, brings us to the subject many students call the "rights" of the individual. They should notice that Morris is not talking about rights; he is precisely describing the results of socioscientific observations. Determining where we sit and how we protect our personal space is the cultural manifestation of our tribe's territorial habits.

Paragraph 16

The higher the density, the less we socially interact. This behavior surprises students until they test its validity by observation.

Paragraph 17

Notice the differences between "crowds and crowds": the spectator crowd has a special, collective goal. The rush-hour crowd has diverse goals, a fact that might lead to disputes.

Students are often interested in discussing this observation as it might be applied to driving their cars. Is rush-hour traffic more frenetic because the drivers are focusing on diverse goals? On freeways, expressways, thoroughfares, and toll roads, why does it seem that cars travel in packs, like crowds?

Paragraph 18

Adjusting to crowds takes a combination of practice, patience, and observation.

"Space reaction": Morris is discussing *proxemics* here, both sociologically and linguistically. Sociologically, proxemics describes human spatial requirements and the effects of population density on behavior. Linguistically, proxemics describes how far apart people in conversation stand, depending on their degree of intimacy.

Paragraph 19

Students from Latin America usually stand closer to each other when talking than students from western Europe. You might want to ask your students to observe proxemics in practice throughout the campus or at their jobs.

Paragraph 20

"cocooning": Libraries are sometimes crowded. Workers often are assigned carrels. Students often share apartments with roommates. They all "cocoon," carving out their own privacy in one way or another.

Morris thoroughly discusses by example each part of this classification. Students are often eager to investigate some of these examples. Do your students have their own territories, favorite chairs in the library or favorite tables in the cafeteria? Do they have favorite parking places that they feel territorially belong to them? How do they react when that territory is "invaded"?

Paragraph 21

You might want to discuss with students the various methods they use to let others know they have already claimed a space. Do they use the "favored object" (20), the "personal marker," or the "reservation effect"? With what success? Do they have other peaceful ways of claiming their own territory?

Paragraph 22

Morris points out that we hear about the exceptions to territorial respect, that most of us respect the other person's "territory," be it the temporary space of a library chair or the more lasting space of a home.

Time permitting, you might want to ask your students whether their city or neighborhood is running out of space that each person or household can call its own. If space is becoming scarce, then you might want to discuss ways of redefining territory or creating respect for territory so that we can keep strife from getting out of hand.

Possible Answers

Meaning and Purpose

1. Morris's main point is that we are territorial animals, and territory by definition must be defended. The thesis is implicit in a general way in the very first sentence. The fourth sentence in paragraph 3 is the thesis, and the last sentence in paragraph 5 narrows the thesis.

2. The title is neutral-sounding and could signal an academic and informative essay (which this is), or the title could be ironic or humorous, depending on the content of the essay. In other words, the title isn't much help in knowing the content of the essay absolutely before reading it.
3. A number of students mention the bathroom! Some include their place of work (the backroom or storage areas), and others specify attics, basements, garages, and the like.
4. We form subgroups (7) in our large tribal territories to feel a sense of belonging. We choose a "splinter group" to identify with, such as a union or political party.
5. Because so many homes look alike, people have more difficulty displaying theirs as a particular home in an attempt to feel secure and "at home" (12).
6. Morris's words are the neutral terminology of social science.

Strategy

1. Morris discusses the sociology of the three categories of territory, including the penalties for violating someone else's territory, and the reasons for having "owned space" (3). The first five paragraphs give background and definitions so that readers know Morris's basis for classification.
2. The strategy of development is a kind of cyclic expansion. Morris starts with the small group at the center, expands it outward to hunting grounds, and eventually the home base becomes the capital city. When nations become too big for people to feel personal belonging, people circle back to form small groups that they can belong to.
3. Morris talks about the distances at which people stand from each other in conversation and labels three categories: fingertip, wrist, and elbow distance (18). He also discusses how people in crowded places stake out personal space. He calls the strategy "cocooning" (20), and names three kinds: small private office or studio, favored object such as a chair or alcove, and personal markers (21) such as books or jackets. All these subdivisions help organize and order Morris's information so that it is clear and understandable to readers.
4. A home base can be one of a number of areas, depending on the student's perspective. It could be a play area, a favored street corner, one side of a fence, or a car.

Style

1. The tone is formal and academic, and people are labeled clinically—this is a social-science essay. Almost any sentence demonstrates this tone, such as the first in paragraph 3: "The fact that these upheavals are so rare is a measure of the success of Territorial Signals as a system of dispute prevention."
2. A "pseudo-tribe" is a modern imitation of the historical tribes mentioned earlier in the essay (8). The prefix *pseudo* means "fictitious, pretending, or falsely seeming."
3. Morris's audience probably consists of readers who have read academic writing before, for he doesn't talk down to them. But they are not necessarily social scientists. His language is understandable and readable for lay readers, and he is careful to define his terms in context.

Doublespeak
William Lutz

Teaching Suggestions

Have your students prepare for a class discussion of "Doublespeak" by first searching out their own examples of doublespeak. They might find their examples on television, in magazine or newspaper advertisements, or in editorials or articles in newspapers or journals of opinion. Have them discuss in class how and why their examples fit into one or more of Lutz's doublespeak categories and whether they are examples of benign euphemisms or jargon, or whether they exemplify the more dangerous forms of doublespeak. Such a discussion should help students more easily recognize and understand the dangers of doublespeak, and should also aid them in organizing their material for a classification essay, if they were to do one of the writing tasks designed for this essay.

Notes

Paragraph 1
Lutz begins with a series of contrasts between terms of inflated language ("The Fourth Kind of Doublespeak") and their plain English translations.
Paragraph 2
The essay's thesis.
Paragraph 4
Lutz contrasts two kinds of euphemisms—the first benign, the second malignant.
Paragraph 5
The first sentence is a clear topic sentence and is followed by a series of examples.
Paragraph 6
This paragraph has a parallel pattern to the preceding one: a clear topic sentence followed by a series of examples.
Paragraph 12
Have students attempt to translate Greenspan into plain English. We suggest what he says is untranslatable, because it is meaningless.
Paragraph 14
Have students compare Quayle's gobbledygook to Greenspan's. Is Quayle being as duplicitous as Greenspan, or does he simply get lost in both the idea and the language?
Paragraph 19
Lutz repeats his thesis in the essay's conclusion.

Possible Answers

Meaning and Purpose

1. Lutz states his thesis in the first sentence of the second paragraph. In the rest of the paragraph, he further refines the thesis. He restates his thesis in his conclusion, paragraph 19.
2. For Lutz, two kinds of doublespeak are irredeemable, gobbledygook or bureaucratese (12–15) and inflated language (16–18). Both are always used

to deceive and can have serious consequences. Both euphemisms and jargon, however, are often used for distinctly different reasons. Both can be used to deceive; when used for this purpose, they become forms of doublespeak. Euphemisms, however, can be used tactfully in order to protect the feelings of others. And jargon can help those in the same profession communicate quickly and clearly with each other. Used for these purposes, neither are doublespeak (4–11).

3. Most of the time, doublespeak is easily recognizable. When in doubt, one can ask and answer four questions: "Who is saying what to whom, under what conditions and circumstances, with what intent, and with what results?" (3).

4. Lutz's conclusion summarizes the dangers of doublespeak: "Such language does not provide us with the tools we need to develop, advance, and preserve our culture and our civilization. Such language breeds suspicion, cynicism, distrust, and, ultimately, hostility" (19).

Strategy

1. Lutz *defines* each of the four types of doublespeak (4, 8, 12, 16). He does this primarily through the use of examples. He uses comparison/contrast when he translates some of the euphemisms, jargon, and inflated language into plain English (6, 7, 9, 16, 17).

2. Euphemisms and jargon can both be used for legitimate communication; gobbledygook and inflated language, when used purposefully, are always meant to deceive.

3. Paragraph 2 states Lutz's thesis as an introduction to the essay, while paragraph 19 restates the thesis as a conclusion.

Style

1. Greenspan's language quoted in paragraph 12 is indecipherable gobbledygook, incapable of being translated into plain English. His language in paragraph 13 is plain English, and perfectly clear. Because he is capable of speaking plain English (unlike, perhaps, Dan Quayle in paragraph 14), his gobbledygook is clearly meant to deceive.

2. Lutz's language is almost entirely even-handed and objective. Rather than being polemical, he allows the weight of his examples to show the validity of his clear and reasoned condemnation of doublespeak. Only twice in the essay does he deviate from this reasoned, objective language: when he says that "Mr. Greenspan's doublespeak doesn't seemed to have held back his career" (13) and that "you have to wonder if Mr. Moore had any idea what he was saying" (15). In both cases Lutz is mildly derisive.

3. *Variance:* in a state of difference or disagreement; *purported:* reputed or claimed; *tactful:* sensitively appropriate; *condolences:* expression of sympathy with someone who is experiencing sorrow; *incontinent:* lacking moderation; *ordnance:* all kinds of military weapons with their equipment and ammunition; *pretentious:* characterized by an assumption of dignity or importance; *esoteric:* understood by or meant for the select few with special knowledge; *profundity:* having depth of thought or insight; *dividend:* a sum of money paid to shareholders out of corporate earnings; *initiative:* an introductory act or step.

My Habit
Paul Sheehan

Teaching Suggestions

Psychologists, sociologists, and child-care specialists all seem to agree that at one time or another, children collect things, ranging from nails to horseshoes to dolls to marbles to toy soldiers to comic books . . . the list goes on and on. However, one wonders if anyone other than Sheehan has such an unusual collection. Ask your students if they have ever collected anything, and then, as a follow-up question, ask them "Why?" Usually, you will get a standard answer, such as "Because I like to," but upon further questioning, teachers have been quite taken by some of the reasons that students have for their collections. (For example, one student in an urban area of Los Angeles collected shell casings every Monday morning, casings left over from gang clashes during the weekend!) After they see that others have collected items, usually when much younger, students open up to try to explain their own reasons for collecting, as well as their methods for organizing their collections, a discussion that provides a fine way to introduce this essay as an example of an interesting way to employ classification and division.

Notes

Paragraph 1
"arcane little niche": Those familiar with New York City will realize that Sheehan's niche encompasses several acres of less-than-desirable real estate.

Paragraph 2
"crack": Highly purified cocaine in small chips, crack is used illegally, usually by smoking.

Paragraph 3
"missiles": Although crack vials come in a number of shapes and sizes, they are characteristically elongated, resembling toy missiles. This is a most appropriate word: Since the seventeenth century, missiles have been used in warfare.

Paragraph 4
"I look, and so I find": Note the pseudo-scientific import of this sentence. Sheehan conveys an objective sense of discovery.

Paragraph 5
"totem of quenchless thirst": A totem is an object serving as the emblem of a family or class. Here, the vial is the totem of a "family" of drug addicts, those who use crack.

Paragraph 6
After his opening anecdote, Sheehan gives his reader a brief glimpse into his personal life and a brief history of the crack vial.

"small monument": Usually a memorial stone or building erected in remembrance of a person or event, Sheehan's monument memorializes part of the macabre residue of crack addiction.

Paragraph 7
"Chicago": Sheehan is quite serious about his collecting, to the point of traveling to other cities for the specific purpose of obtaining crack vials.

Paragraph 8

Again, as in paragraph 6 and later in paragraph 9, the reader is treated to information about crack, illustrating some of the authority that Sheehan has for writing this essay.

Paragraph 9

"Taj Mahals": The Taj Mahal is a renowned monument to love constructed (1632–1654) at Agra in Uttar Pradesh, India, as a mausoleum for Mumtaz Mahal, the favorite wife of the emperor Shah Jahan. Built of white marble and inlaid with semi-precious stones and mosaic work, it is a world heritage site. A huge central dome surrounded by four smaller domes surmounts the main structure, which is flanked by four slim minarets. The whole is mirrored in an ornamental pool.

Paragraph 10

"simply a bonus": Note Sheehan's dry wit in this passage.

Paragraph 11

"cases were designed to hold insects": This is the use of irony that refers to an incongruity between what is expected and what is actual. In their own ways, the vials themselves symbolize parasites.

"a name": Note the classification here. Sheehan carefully distinguishes the various kinds of vials, describing each group so that it differs visibly from the other four groups.

Paragraph 12

Note the pride of Sheehan, the collector, in this paragraph, particularly in the last sentence.

Paragraph 13

"teeth indentations": Interestingly, Sheehan keeps out of sight those vials that clearly show the effects of crack addiction.

Paragraph 14

This paragraph exemplifies pragmatic information, logical information or seemingly logical information not otherwise available to the reader in any other part of the text. Sheehan justifies his collection by reference to a passage in a novel, making, therefore, his reference a fictional representation of reality.

Paragraph 15

The questions to which Sheehan refers are the questions asked in the work of fiction cited in paragraph 14, an interesting lead-in to the journalistic story that follows, in paragraph 16.

Paragraph 16

Sheehan moves from his justifying the reasons for his collection on a work of fiction to justifying the reasons autobiographically. He lived in one of the buildings near the building that had reopened as a residence for homeless people. His collection began as evidence for proving that the drug traffic increased after the residence reopened.

Paragraph 17

Sheehan's original prosaic collecting gradually took on a life of its own. As he became more and more interested in the vials for their own sake, he also discovered that his friends became interested in his displays of them, as if the vials were works of art.

Paragraph 18

Sheehan's collecting had become a bit obsessive. What started out as a routine collecting of evidence became an ongoing hunt for the various kinds of vials, for which Sheehan searched in the worst areas of New York City.

Paragraph 19

As a result of his collecting vials, Sheehan was introduced deeply into a part of New York City that he had heretofore known only superficially.

Paragraph 20

"ethnographer": A person who studies and systematically records concrete evidence of human cultures.

"detritus": Loose material such as rock fragments or organic particles that result directly from disintegration.

Paragraph 21

"genuine anthropological value": Note that this paragraph signals an ambiguous change in tone: Sheehan perhaps hopes that crack addiction will disappear—or perhaps fears that crack addiction will be replaced with an even more vile addiction.

Paragraph 22

"oxymorons": An oxymoron is a rhetorical figure in which two contradictory terms are brought together. The oxymorons here bring together youth and death, thus generating an ambiguity in the final paragraph. Sheehan's collection suggests such an oxymoron because many addicts die young, yet his oxymoron pales beside the oxymoron noted by the art historian, that of pairing lace and fetuses.

Possible Answers

Meaning and Purpose

1. Sheehan's "My Habit" refers to the author's habit of collecting crack vials, and the vials themselves are the residue of addicts who themselves have a drug habit. Therefore, the word *habit* in the title ironically refers to one person's habit of collecting crack vials, which are the residue of other people's collective habit of using crack.

2. The irony in this statement is that it is both concretely true and abstractly true. Sheehan collects vials because he looks for vials. And because he looks for vials, he will find vials not only in the concrete sense but also in the sense of projecting, externalizing his wish for collecting to the point of distorting reality.

3. The *it* in that phrase, which appears in paragraph 6, refers to the abundant number of styles of crack vials.

4. The answers to this question vary greatly, each answer requiring a great deal of thought based on logic. The usually successful answer depends on the student's ability to defend his or her premise of what constitutes a realistic category. Some students have argued well for true categories; others have argued equally well for crossover categories.

5. As Sheehan says in paragraph 16, he began to collect the vials as evidence for proving that his neighborhood was being overrun by crack addicts because the shelter for the homeless had been reopened.

Strategy

1. Sheehan never openly condemns crack addicts, but he does condemn the sellers, as in paragraph 8. His descriptions of addicts, which appear throughout the essay, are for the most part objective.

2. Compelling evidence for Sheehan's seriousness about his collecting looms throughout the essay, but most clearly in the late paragraphs, where he

attempts to justify his collecting and to show the worth of his collection. Students' answers will vary accordingly.

3. In paragraph 7, Sheehan speaks of masquerading as a Catholic priest to protect himself from being harmed by the criminals around him.

4. Students' answers vary, ranging from their suspecting Sheehan's fear of infecting himself to Sheehan's fear of addicting himself.

5. Throughout the essay, the reader feels that Sheehan treats his collecting, his views of addicts, his views of people in general almost clinically—excepting when he fears his neighborhood is being invaded—as if he were an objective scientific observer or someone new to the country who had found a place to live and to protect. He often speaks as if from the plateau of indifference.

Style

1. Depending on their research resources, answers will vary, but as noted in the annotation of paragraph 9, the original Taj Mahal is a renowned monument to love constructed (1632–1654) at Agra in Uttar Pradesh, India, as a mausoleum for Mumtaz Mahal, the favorite wife of the emperor Shah Jahan. Built of white marble and inlaid with semiprecious stones and mosaic work, it is a world heritage site. A huge central dome surrounded by four smaller domes surmounts the main structure, which is flanked by four slim minarets. The whole is mirrored in an ornamental pool.

2. *Charismatic*, as it is used in paragraph 17, refers to a description of that which has an extraordinarily magnetic charm or appeal.

3. The word *panoply*, as it is used in paragraph 19, refers to an impressive array. Students have suggested such synonyms as *glory, luxury, majesty, spectacle, grandeur,* and *brilliance,* some of their choices perhaps better argued than others.

4. The term *detritus*, as it is used in paragraph 20, refers to loose material such as rock fragments or organic particles that result directly from disintegration.

5. An ethnographer is a person who studies and systematically records concrete evidence of human cultures; therefore, it could be argued in some sense that Sheehan is an unsuspecting ethnographer, but only time will tell.

—— 10 / *Definition* ——

I Want a Wife
Judy Brady

Teaching Suggestions

Though this essay is two decades old, it still triggers lively classroom discussions about the modern roles of husbands and wives. It can also lead to provocative discussions about today's roles of fathers and mothers.

The essay is written from a feminist point of view, but most people will recognize the duties presented here as fairly accurate traditional expectations. What are the traditional expectations for husbands? Have both traditions changed in the years since the essay was written?

Notes

Paragraph 3
Beginning here Brady defines a wife by listing expected duties and behaviors.

This paragraph and paragraphs 4–7 present these duties and behaviors in clusters of related items.

The first cluster: caring for the children as well as working outside the home.

Paragraphs 4 and 5
The second cluster: housekeeping and cooking.

The third cluster: being emotionally supportive without expecting support in return.

Paragraph 6
The fourth cluster: assuming the duties of a social secretary.

Paragraph 7
The fifth cluster: being the ideal lover (but respecting the double standard).

Possible Answers

Meaning and Purpose

1. Let students explore their notions about what being a wife means and where these notions come from. A comparison of their ideas with Brady's should show how traditional or progressive your students are.

2. Repeating "I want a wife" emphasizes the focus of the essay, which is on the elements in Brady's definition, rather than on a simple description. It also sounds demanding, and many men demand that their wives do all the things on Brady's list.

3. Brady's view is that men expect women to assume all domestic duties, so "of course" the duty to care for children stays with the wife after a divorce. The use is sarcastic.

4. No one statement asserts Brady's main point. Instead, her thesis is implied in all her details about what a wife is and does: that it is ridiculous and grossly unfair to expect wives to be superwomen who see to the needs of husbands and families who do far less work than a wife—and yet they are expected to perform thus. In her last sentence she asks a rhetorical question that implies her thesis.

5. The husband's needs are implicitly stated with the wife's duties in sentences such as, "I want a wife who will keep my clothes clean, ironed, mended, replaced when need be and who will see to it that my personal things are kept in their proper place so that I can find what I need the minute I need it" (4). Students may think Brady describes extremes when she stereotypes roles, but students probably know men who are this demanding and self-centered. Stereotypes are never fair, but these serve Brady's point that wives are expected to do far too much for their husbands.

Strategy

1. The first paragraph announces the classification "wives" as the subject of the essay, and also establishes Brady's authority to talk about wives because she

is one. This opening is strong and direct, and it informs the reader, giving a context.

2. These are possible labels and characteristics: Paragraph 3: label—worker outside the home and primary caretaker for the children; characteristics—organized, fastidious, thrifty. Paragraph 4: label—personal maid; characteristics—neat, good cook, patient. Paragraph 5: label—therapist; characteristics—patient, good listener. Paragraph 6: label—hostess; characteristics—organized, gracious. Paragraph 7: label—perfect lover; characteristics—selfless, responsible.

3. Answers will vary. Students should support their choice of label with statements from the essay. An appropriate label would be sarcastic.

Style

1. The expression "A Wife" is capitalized because it is used as a formal label.
2. The word "replace" suggests that a wife is an expendable piece of equipment rather than a person. The word also suggests that husbands are fickle about wives and don't care about who they are, only about what they do.
3. When people are "going on" vacation, they are going together. The person who "goes along" with another person is not altogether that person's equal.
4. The question is rhetorical, which means that it requires no answer—it has already been answered. It emphasizes Brady's sarcastic attitude about what men expect wives to do and her own frustrations about being expected to be such a wife. Questions are effective because they usually address readers directly and provoke thought.

Why Men Marry
George Gilder

Teaching Suggestions

When students are asked to write definition papers, love is a popular choice of topic. But the term is so elusive that few of us can do more than repeat a few popular banalities. You might begin a discussion by asking the students to consider why love is such a difficult word to define. One major reason, of course, is that we apply the word so casually to so many situations. But even when we confine our attempts at definition to a limited scope we still have difficulty applying the common definition techniques to this word. Such a discussion may prepare students for a reading of Gilder's essay which approaches the word through a combination of comparison and contrast, cause and effect, description, and process techniques, all done in a rather poetic way.

Notes

Paragraph 1
The short first sentence with its matter-of-fact finality begs to be challenged, but the rest of the paragraph takes the air out of any such challenge by promising to go

beyond the image that first comes to mind at mention of "love." The catalog of images begins with complete sentences then moves to fragments as the images pile up faster and faster.

Paragraph 2
Gilder continues the catalog related to a popular definition of love, this time focusing on what it would be like to give it up.

Paragraph 3
This paragraph introduces the central idea of the essay: that a man will eventually want to settle on one woman and have children.

Paragraphs 4 and 5
Here Gilder discusses the nature of procreative love.

Paragraph 6
Gilder returns to the cataloging technique to describe the lives of men without love.

Paragraphs 7 and 8
These paragraphs move toward a definition of love.

Paragraphs 9–14
These paragraphs describe the process of changing from a desire for hunter love to a desire for the deeper meaning of procreative love.

Studs Terkel, radio and television interviewer, has written several books based on oral history including *Division Street* (1966), *Hard Times* (1970), and *Working* (1977).

"Hemingway's hyena": From Ernest Hemingway's short story, "The Snows of Kilimanjaro." As a man lies dying from gangrene, a hyena, a symbol of death, can be seen and heard on the perimeter of the campsite.

Paragraph 15
This paragraph completes the definition of procreative love.

Paragraph 16
This last paragraph shows the importance of choosing procreative love.

Possible Answers

Meaning and Purpose

1. Although the essay may be read profitably by anyone, the primary audience seems to be young men. Gilder wants to convey the power of the desire for procreative love and show that to marry, sire children, and care for a family is a meaningful life achievement.

2. The attractive, but superficial and temporary, side of the unmarried life is described in paragraph 1, but the main point Gilder makes is in paragraph 6.

3. The fundamental reason is for a kind of immortality: to be remembered beyond one's time because one has children to carry life into the future. "The need to choose a particular woman and stay by her and provide for her if he is to know his children and they are to love him and call him father" (3); "both partners consciously or unconsciously glimpse a future infant" (4); "the couple senses the outlines of a realm that can endure and perpetuate their union" (4); "His children . . . they will remember. It is the only hope" (15).

   Secondary, but related reasons: 1) being alone and disappointed with life (5 and 6), and 2) the souring of the hunter life (9–12).

4. Children are more important because they will remember him (15) and because few are remembered for their jobs (12).

Strategy

1. Comparison and contrast: paragraphs 1 and 6 and paragraphs 1 and 15. Cause and effect: paragraphs 3, 8, 10–12, 15. Description: paragraph 9. Process: paragraphs 9–13.

2. As students write about or discuss this question, make sure they go beyond "Well, that's my opinion," and cite relevant passages in the essay's text as well as explain their reasons for their conclusions about Gilder's approach. Some students may argue that the essay would be a better example of cause and effect or comparison and contrast than it is of definition. They may be right. It's a good time to remind students that writer's usually use more than one strategy in an essay and the important thing is not to label an essay but to be aware of the possible strategies available to them as writers.

Style

1. Other catalogs are in paragraph 6 beginning with "Many more millions . . ." and in paragraph 9 beginning with "One day he looks across . . . ."
2. The unborn child is carried in the womb, the infant is suckled at the breast, and being remembered by one's children is a kind of immortality.
3. A woman does not need the roles of husband and father to bear children (5) and thus achieve a kind of immortality, but a man does need the roles of mother and wife to achieve the same thing. In the context of this essay, the statement is valid.

    Paragraph 3: "if he is to know his children and they are to love him and call him father."

    Paragraph 5: "a woman can bear a child, but the man is able only to screw."

    Paragraph 6: "There are millions of single men, unlinked to any promising reality, dissipating their lives by the years, moving from job to job, woman to woman, illusion to embitterment."

    Paragraph 10: "His body," "His aggressiveness," "His job" are all failing him.

    Paragraph 15: "this consciousness that he has to struggle to be worthy of her."
4. *Ecstatic*: characterized by sudden, intense feeling; *primal*: first, fundamental; *procreative*: that which brings into being, begats offspring; *sloughs*: conditions of despair, of helplessness; *vapors*: mental depression; *alchemy*: the process of transforming something of little value to something of great value; *morbid*: of an unhealthy mental state, gloomy; *covenant*: an agreement between two or more persons; *ruttings*: sexual excitements; *purges*: cleanses, purifies.

TV Addiction
Marie Winn

Teaching Suggestions

As a starting point, have students discuss the differences between the act of reading and the act of watching television. Reading, by its very nature, is a rather sophisticated act of intellect and imagination. First, a reader must be able to translate markings on a page, markings that have no necessary connection to the sounds, things, or ideas they represent, into words that have common meaning. The reader must then recognize grammatical structures that add another level of meaning. The reader must then connect these mental constructs to the "real" world. In this process, there is no way for a reader to be passive. The very act of reading necessitates mental engagement. If thinking itself is considered a worthwhile act, it would be difficult—but not impossible—for habitual reading to become a destructive addiction, as defined by Winn. Television viewing, on the other hand, more often than not is passive. As far as content is concerned, very little television programming engages or stimulates the intellect or imagination.

Pursuing such a discussion could lead into a discussion of the two writing tasks for this essay.

Notes

Paragraph 1
Winn begins her extended definition of addiction by citing benign activities sometimes jokingly—and wrongly—placed into the category of addiction.

Paragraph 2
Winn begins her definition proper with the inferred negation that television addiction cannot be placed into the same benign category as cookie eating.

Paragraphs 3–5
In these three paragraphs Winn defines a destructive addiction.

Paragraph 6
A transitional single sentence paragraph that carries the reader from the attributes that make up destructive addictions to those that compose television addiction.

Paragraphs 7–12
An extended definition of televison addiction.

Paragraphs 8–9
Many consider television viewing a mindless activity, particularly habitual viewing. So Winn uses the example of an addicted college English instructor, someone necessarily involved in intellect, to reinforce the idea that anyone can get "hooked" on television.

Paragraph 12
Lawrence Kubie, *Neurotic Distortion and the Creative Process*, 1958. Kubie wrote extensively on psychiatry and psychoanalysis.

Possible Answers

Meaning and Purpose

1. For a mere habit to become an addiction, it must begin as a pleasurable activity (2), entail "a search for a 'high' that normal life does not supply" (3), cre-

ate the inability of the addicted person to function normally without it (3), and create the need to repeat the experience over and over again because it never really satisfies (4). Finally, all serious addictions are "distinctly destructive" (5).

2. Unlike addictions to alcohol, drugs, or television, addictions to such things as reading or gardening can be fulfilling, pleasurable, and harmless.

3. The author cites no differences among addictions to alcohol, drugs, or television. In fact, it is her purpose to point out their similarities. She doesn't mention, however, that, unlike television, alcohol and drugs can create chemical dependencies, as well as a psychological dependence.

4. Winn's purpose is to jar the reader, presumably a television watcher, into the awareness that uncontrolled television watching is an addiction as severe and personally debilitating as addictions to alcohol or drugs.

Strategy

1. Every paragraph begins with a controlling topic sentence followed by the particulars that validate it. Internally, therefore, the paragraphs move from the general to the specific. There is a similar movement in the essay as a whole. Winn begins by discussing some harmless habits, sometimes mislabeled as addictions, then narrows her focus to define *addiction* and, finally, narrows her focus further to define *television addiction*.

2. The two definitions are constructed in a parallel way. First Winn defines *addiction* by listing all those things that make a habitual activity an addiction: an activity that is innately pleasurable, but which must be continually repeated because it can never really satisfy, and is always self-destructive. She then shows, point by point, how television addiction follows precisely the same pattern. Her logical analysis forces the reader to recognize that there is no significant difference between television and alcohol or drug addiction.

3. Winn cites a television addicted college English instructor to demonstrate that television addicts are not just the mindless. On the contrary, even a person whose profession demands a certain amount of mental acuity can be addicted to television just as easily as anyone else.

4. Winn develops her definition by classification when she divides various addictions into categories. Also, in her definition of *addiction* (3–5), she contrasts destructive addictions to the harmless pursuits she mentioned earlier. She then compares these addictions to television addiction in that definition (7–12). And her entire essay is replete with examples, both general and specific.

Style

1. Although it is Winn's point of view that television addiction is as self-destructive as drug or alcohol abuse, she is never polemical. Her language is controlled. She allows logic and the aptness of her examples to make her case. She therefore gives the reader the impression of objectivity, which is ultimately more persuasive than polemics.

2. Winn separates slang terms associated with drug and alcohol addiction from the Standard English of the rest of the essay by putting them in quotes.

3. Winn has just pointed out the deleterious effects of drug and alcohol addiction and is about to show how television addiction has the same negative results. The double negative reinforces that negativity.

4. *Wryly:* humorously ironic; *surge:* a strong rush or sweep forward; *deferred:* put off to a future time; *induced:* caused; *sapped:* exhausted; *enervated:* without vigor, force, or strength; *ruefully:* regretfully; *adverse:* opposing one's interests or desires; *sated:* glutted; *satiation:* state of being glutted.

Homeless
Anna Quindlen

Teaching Suggestions

By defining the homeless in terms of real people who suffer because they are without real homes, Quindlen forces the reader to move from the consideration of a problem in the abstract, where it can become a purely mental exercise, to the consideration of the problem in terms of concrete particulars, where the reader is forced to react viscerally as well as intellectually. Leading the students through Quindlen's essay paragraph by paragraph, pointing out the concreteness of her examples and diction, might lead to a fruitful discussion of how any abstraction is meaningless unless it is defined in concrete terms. In turn, this could lead to a discussion of how such a mental process (moving from the abstract or the general to the particular) can be translated into a definition paper (see Writing Tasks for this essay).

Notes

Paragraph 1

By beginning with an anecdote that introduces the reader to Ann, a real homeless person, Quindlen immediately demonstrates in concrete terms what will be her thesis: The problem of the homeless can only be defined in terms of real people.

Paragraph 2

Notice that in the first sentence Quindlen describes even what is not there in concrete terms.

Paragraph 3

"the legacy of an Irish grandfather": For hundreds of years many native Irish were prevented by the ruling British from owning property in their own country. Many Irish, therefore, have a heightened sense of place and property.

Paragraphs 5 and 6

Quindlen moves the reader progressively in these two paragraphs from a time when the home was the center of all family activity to the present, when many people are without homes, and homes themselves have become mere economic commodities, or "real estate."

Paragraph 7

Organized by cause and effect, the paragraph shows why many homeless would rather sleep on benches outdoors rather than in shelters, the most important reason saved for last.

Paragraphs 8 and 9

In her two paragraph conclusion, Quindlen succinctly sums up the reasons why and how thinking of the homeless problem in the abstract separates us from the problem and, thus, perpetuates it. Just as people become emotionally attached to material things in a home, so that those things gain meaning beyond themselves, so, too, we can truly understand the problem of the homeless only if we see it in terms of the real people who are deprived of a real home.

Possible Answers

Meaning and Purpose

1. Quindlen attempts to make her readers realize that there is no such thing as the homeless in the real world because the term is a mere abstraction. There are, instead, only individual human beings who are without homes.
2. When we look at the "big picture" or take the "global" view, we see "the problem" in the abstract, instead of the suffering of real people.
3. While a home is a necessary place that serves as a shelter, a place to eat, and a mailing address, it is not really a home until those living in it have emotional ties to it, emotions typically expressed in "cross-stitch and French knots on samplers."
4. For Quindlen, a home is a real physical place whose very physicality establishes the emotional ties with the people who live there. In paragraphs 5 and 6, Quindlen traces the dissolution of those ties from a time when a home was a place where families lived and worked to the present when homes have become a mere means for developers and absentee landlords to make money: "Now they [homes] are real estate" (6).
5. When adjectives (e.g., "poor," as in "poor people") are turned into nouns, real things ("poor people") are transformed into abstractions ("the poor"). We thus lose sight of the fact that "the homeless" are actually real people: "Ann or the man who lives in the box or the woman who sleeps on the subway grate" (8).

Strategy

1. Since Quindlen's essay defines "the homeless" in terms of living people and real homes, it is not only appropriate, but rhetorically effective as well, to begin with the story of a real homeless person, Ann.
2. The final paragraph explains in concrete terms what Quindlen means when she says that she has "never been very good at looking at the big picture" or "taking the global view."
3. Quindlen sets up the paragraph by contrasting the global view with the particular. Then, through cause/effect, she explains why she is inclined to take the particular view. She also uses specific examples to demonstrate those things that comprise a home.

Style

1. Quindlen ends 5 of the 9 paragraphs in her essay with short sentences and one phrase to give quick, dramatic emphasis to what she has just said. Sometimes the sentences are ironic, as in "She was somebody" (1), referring to Ann when she had a home. Now homeless, Ann has become a nobody.
2. The phrase "once upon a time" is the typical beginning of a fairy tale that often takes place in the hazy, distant past. Thus, when the phrase refers to the homeless Ann, it gives the reader the impression that her attachment to a real home, too, was in a distant, fairy tale–like past.
3. Cross-stitch and French knots are two different kinds of embroidery. In the nineteenth and early twentieth centuries, girls were taught embroidery and

would often display their skills of doing different kinds of stitching on "samplers." These often spelled out things such as "Home Sweet Home," and were framed and hung on a wall. "Home" in this context, then, is associated with old-fashioned, sentimental values.

4. Students should easily be able to pick out the words and phrases in the opening sentences of most of the essay's paragraphs that refer to words and ideas in the previous paragraph.

Gossip
Francine Prose

Teaching Suggestions

Prose makes a rather strong case for gossip as an essential human activity. Have students consider the idea that gossip can really be an affirmation of human community, probably an idea most have never considered. Have them cite examples from their own lives to show how Prose's contentions about the necessity of gossip and its ultimate salubrious and moral effects may be true. Then have them consider the idea that television talk shows, such as *The Jerry Springer Show*, are sad examples of gossip that connect people whose real communities have broken down. Such discussions could lead to provocative ideas that could be explored in papers.

Notes

Paragraph 1
Prose begins her essay with an attention getting anecdote. And the anecdote, really, is gossip about the nature of gossip—most apt.

The term *Siamese twins* originally referred to Chang and Eng, born in 1811 of Chinese parents in Siam (now Thailand), who were joined by a ligament from breastbone to naval. As adults, Chang and Eng each married and raised several children.

Paragraph 3
This paragraph begins with Prose's speculation about the origins and nature of the first gossip, the speculation itself a form of the "good gossip" she later describes in paragraph 9.

Paragraph 5
This is the keystone paragraph of the essay. Prose first defines "bad gossip," and then contrasts that with her definition of "good gossip"—for which she admits her loving commitment.

Paragraph 6
Prose uses the etymology of gossip to get at the word's core meaning, as well as its essential human functions—ideas not commonly considered.

Paragraph 7
"Gertrude Stein": (1874–1946), American poet, novelist, and critic. For many years a prominent expatriate in Paris, she was the center of a celebrated literary and artistic circle that included Hemingway.

"Hemingway": Ernest Hemingway (1899–1961), an American novelist and short story writer.

Paragraph 10

The term *snake pits* brings the essay full circle by returning the reader to the last words of the first paragraph. "beneficent snake pits": an oxymoron.

Possible Answers

Meaning and Purpose

1. The entire essay is an extended definition of the word *gossip*, in which Prose includes the usual negative connotations of the word, but then expands its meaning to include seldom considered, and from her point of view, more important positive connotations. Paragraph 5 comes closest to an actual statement of thesis in that it admits the destructive aspects of gossip but then contrasts that with its positive "purposes" and "human uses."

2. Prose elucidates the positive meanings of gossip in paragraphs 6–8. First, she uses the word's history to demonstrate that it is a kind of synonym for "connection" and "community," that the main function of gossip is to establish human connections (6). And if done right, gossip can become an art form (7). Further, gossip has an "analytical component" that serves as a "tool of understanding" (8). Finally, because gossip oftentimes asks questions of basic human values, it is "conducive to the moral life" (9).

3. Because gossip, through its analytical and speculative properties, leads us to consider values in human actions, it can be a moral force.

4. Both gossip and fiction deal in narratives that rely for their effectiveness on pacing, tone, clarity, and authenticity. Notwithstanding Gertrude Stein's assessment to the contrary, Prose implies that gossip, if done well, can be a kind of art form.

Strategy

1. The anecdote of Chang and Eng is innately interesting and thus serves as a hook for the reader. It is also, really, gossip about the nature of gossip and, therefore, works as an apt beginning for Prose's definition of gossip.

2. Prose begins with an anecdote, compares and contrasts good and bad gossip, and uses examples throughout the essay.

3. Prose begins her definition of good gossip by tracing the history of the word to its origins, and that original meaning becomes central to her definition. Common to all positive aspects of the word is human connectedness.

Style

1. Paragraph 2 is an analysis of the anecdote that precedes it. The use of the more formal "one," therefore, is appropriate for the paragraph's objective tone. Prose uses "I" throughout much of the rest of the essay to establish her personal commitment to good gossip ("I love gossip," [5]) and to connect herself personally with the reader. Several of her examples she tells from firsthand experience, a way of establishing her personal authority.

2. The roots of a grapevine metaphor reinforce the idea of the natural, organic unity of the original meaning of gossip, as well as the connectedness of the community that gossip can promote.

3. Toward the end of the thirteenth century, a collection of stories about saints' lives was published. The actual title was *Legenda Sanctorum*, literally, "things to be read of the saints." But the book became popularly known as *Legenda*

Aurea or *Golden Legends*. The stories were basically factual, though through the years the original facts became magnified and distorted. Subsequent stories of the lives of the saints, following the model set by this book, became more and more fanciful and imaginative. The consequence was that the stories began to be viewed with skepticism. Hence the word *legend*, originally "something to be read," came to denote a story that, though apparently historical, was actually traditional and lacking in authenticity. Like the word *gossip*, therefore, the word *legend* began with positive connotations that have declined with time.

4. *Adjacent*: adjoining, neighboring; *legacy*: anything handed down from the past; *mundane*: common, ordinary; *speculate*: to indulge in conjectural thought; *antiquity*: being of great age; *connotes*: signifies or suggests additional meanings to the primary meaning; *frivolity*: the quality of lacking sense or seriousness; *scurrilous*: grossly or obscenely abusive; *amiability*: pleasantness, good naturedly personable; *assent*: to agree or concur; *slander*: defamation; *fabrication*: a made-up, untruthful statement; *etymology*: the derivation and history of a word; *cronies*: close friends or companions; *legends*: non-historical or unverifiable stories handed down by tradition from earlier times and popularly accepted as historical; *fabulists*: people who invent fables, short tales that teach moral lessons; *criteria*: the plural form of *criterion*, a standard of judgment or criticism; *component*: a constituent part; *compulsion*: the act of compelling; *dissect*: to cut something apart to examine its structure; *minutia*: precise details; *titillate*: to excite or arouse agreeably; *bask*: to lie in or be exposed to pleasant warmth; *aura*: a pervasive or distinctive quality or character; *conducive*: tending to produce; *rankles*: continues to cause irritation or bitter resentment within the mind; *beneficent*: doing good or causing good to be done.

11 / *Persuasion and Argument*

The Killing Game
Joy Williams

Teaching Suggestions

Portions of this selection are likely to bring vehement denials from some members of the class. If so, you might want to let discussion continue for a time in a freewheeling fashion, then stop to examine the nature of some of the comments of class members. Are they primarily based on logic or emotion? We predict the answer will be emotion, and then it's time to turn directly to the essay itself and see what the balance is between logic and emotion there. Examine Williams's use of emotional words and phrases and ask if a more logical approach would have had greater or lesser impact.

Then ask if the students think the nature of the subject itself leads more naturally to emotional arguments or logical ones. Are there other current issues of public debate that are usually argued emotionally? Whatever the outcome of this discussion, you will probably want to leave some time to examine specific sentences and word choices that give the piece its emotional power.

Notes

Paragraph 1

The first four sentences announce the subject of hunting and establish Williams's scornful attitude toward it though no thesis is stated.

The rapid listing of five words for death focuses attention on the seriousness of the subject.

The remainder of the first paragraph begins the attack on the hunters' point of view with the use of emotional words and phrases: "intellectual blather," "fatuous," "philosophical fog," "blow the toes off," "torn apart."

José Ortega y Gasset (1883–1955) was a Spanish critic and philosopher best known in the United States for his *Revolt of the Masses* (1930), which expresses his fear of the rising political power of the working classes.

Paragraphs 2 and 3

These paragraphs continue the attack on lofty justifications for hunting, dismissing them as the "blather" of "apologists."

Rolston is a professor of philosophy at Colorado State University. "Environmental Ethics" was published in 1987.

Paragraphs 4 and 5

These paragraphs reject the idea that hunting is done to provide food.

Paragraph 6

Beginning here, Williams shifts from refuting the hunters' arguments to advancing her own: Hunters pursue pleasure (thrills) and power (control or possession).

"Mohandas K(aranchand) Gandhi", (1869–1948), known for his ascetic way of life and his use of civil disobedience and nonviolence as political weapons in India.

"Beautiful creatures": Note the irony. Apparently the beauty of an animal adds to the thrill of destroying it.

Williams frequently uses the apparent words of hunters to convict them of unthinking cruelty.

Paragraph 8

Irony again: These animals are predators, but so are the humans that hunt them.

Paragraph 9

A specific example of a concerted attack on a particular predator. The red fox is killed so hunters will have more ducks and pheasant to shoot.

Paragraphs 10 and 11

Another specific example of hunters protecting "their" game from natural predators.

Paragraph 12

The inductive arrangement of the essay leads to a strong assertion (thesis) in sentence 2 that is rephrased and amplified in the remainder of the paragraph.

Note the use of parallel structure and the repetition of the word *time* in sentences 5 and 6. "Time" is echoed in the last phrase of the essay, "check-out time."

Possible Answers

Meaning and Purpose

1. Obviously, the essay is not addressed to hunters—it would only anger them—though we can easily imagine Williams enjoying the possibility that some hunters may read it. It is addressed to a broader group of nonhunters or only occasional hunters, presumably male, since it first appeared in *Esquire*. Like most argumentative essays, it probably appeals most to those whose opinions it reinforces, but the passion of the argument suggests her desire to change opinions too. It's not a call to action except in the most indirect sense: Someone should make hunting illegal. Evidence to support this answer is in practically every paragraph: the emotional language; the sarcasm; the fact that she never addresses hunters, only refers to them; and the fact that she doesn't outline a plan of action for any reader to take.

2. Hunters say they hunt to relate to Death and Nature, to become a part of nature, for the nobility of the activity itself, and for the less "semireligious" reasons that man needs meat for subsistence and that hunting is a service (ridding an area of predators).

3. Williams says hunters hunt for fun, recreation, play, entertainment, thrills, to make the animals "theirs" (trophies), and to establish dominance and control.

4. The answer depends entirely on the readers, but probably most didn't know that the state bird of South Dakota was imported for "harvest" or about the political maneuvers behind the reintroduction of wolves to Yellowstone.

5. Here, too, the answer is personal. Some may complain that the essay is too intemperate in tone and would prefer a more thorough, logical argument. Others may more readily accept the emotional nature of the issue itself and find the essay convincing because it counters each of the hunters' arguments in turn.

6. The assumption is that life itself is of paramount value and should be left to its natural destiny. Williams comes closest to saying it directly in her last paragraph when she refers to animals as "sentient beings who deserve our wonder and respect." The series "put to death, extinguish, nullify, cancel, destroy" in the first paragraph and the repetition "dead, dead, dead" in paragraph 13 also reflect this assumption.

Strategy

1. She includes such quotations either to ridicule and dismiss them as she does with Ortega y Gasset, George Reiger (1), and Holmes Rolston III (2) or to let the words serve as self convictions as she does with Bill Neal (1) and Jack Atcheson (11).

2. Williams has made little attempt to balance logic and emotion. Her argument is emotional, but it proceeds from the assumption mentioned in question 6 under *Meaning and Purpose*. If that assumption is accepted, her emotional defense of it is understandable and more acceptable.

3. The assertion is directly stated in the second sentence of the last paragraph: "Sport hunting is immoral; it should be made illegal." The essay is arranged inductively—all the previous paragraphs make this conclusion inevitable. To state her assertion at the outset would be to risk losing readers who, without having read the other paragraphs, might dismiss the essay out of hand.

4. The words of the hunters, some apparently hypothetical, some identified, some not, have been carefully selected to support her view that their arguments are fatuous, unthinking, or cruel, so she runs no risk using them.

Style

1. A variety of adjectives might be used to describe the tone: caustic, mordant, ironic, sarcastic, truculent, scathing, sardonic. Supporting examples will vary.
2. A few examples of each: *Irony*: the hunters' appreciation of beautiful creatures which they then destroy (6); hunters prey on predators, but not for food (8); the state bird of South Dakota, the ring-necked pheasant, was actually imported from Asia to be hunted (9). *Sarcasm*: Mr. Neal "blazed through this philosophical fog" (1); "it's just the cross the 'good' hunter must bear" (3); "supplement their Chicken McNuggets with venison" (5); "We took pictures, we took pictures" (6). *Emotional words and phrases*: "intellectual blather" (1); "pursuit and murder" (4); "rags in the air, shredded, blown to bits" (6); "conned and cowed" and "pampering and coddling" (13).
3. The series in sentence 5 emphasizes the finality and horror of what hunters do and discredits in advance the first quotation: "The kill is the least important part of the hunt." The repetition of "dead, dead, dead" at the end of the essay recalls the opening series and achieves the same effect even more starkly.
4. *fatuous*: foolish or inane; *specious*: seemingly plausible, but actually not valid; deceptive; *atavistic*: the reappearance of a characteristic after several generations of absence; *vermin and varmints*: disgusting or objectionable animals or insects; *abattoir*: a slaughterhouse; *sentient*: conscious, aware, having sense perceptions.

What's Wrong with Animal Rights
Vicki Hearne

Teaching Suggestions

A good way to begin discussing this essay is with the title. This title is a clause. It has a subject and a predicate. If it were punctuated with a question mark, then it could lead the reader to believe that she was going to read a defense of rights. For example, if one were to see the essay title "What's Wrong with Capital Punishment?" then it wouldn't be hard to figure out that the essay probably *endorses* capital punishment. On the other hand, if one were to see the essay title "The Wrongs of Capital Punishment," then it would not be difficult to guess that the essay argues *against* capital punishment. Ask your students if the title suggests that the writer is going to endorse animal rights, if the author is not going to endorse animal rights, or if the author probably intends only to discuss animal rights generally. By attempting to answer this question, students will enter into the realm of *ambiguity*, doubtfulness or uncertainty of meaning or intention, learning first-hand that what might seem clear at first glance is indeed often suspect upon reflection.

Notes

Paragraph 1
"Not all happy animals are alike": Note the curious echo of Tolstoy's line in *Anna Karenina* (1875–1877; pt.I, Ch 1): "Happy families are all alike; every unhappy family is unhappy in its own way."

Secretariat: Winner of the Kentucky Derby in 1973.

Paragraph 2
"emblems": As used here, this word refers to "symbolizing a quality, state, or class; an allegorical picture."

Declaration of Independence: The "inalienable rights" noted in the Declaration of Independence are "life, liberty, and the *pursuit* of happiness," not happiness alone.

"*ex nihilo*": Latin, "out of nothing."

Paragraph 3
"Ethics, Aristotle": Here the author refers to *Nicomachean Ethics* by Aristotle (384–322 B.C.E.), in which he writes, "Every science and every inquiry, and similarly every activity and pursuit, is thought to aim at some good" (bk.I, ch.1).

Thomas Jefferson: Third president of the United States (1801–1809).

Paragraph 4
"cannot be found in the lexicon": The first clear clue that gives the reader a sense of the direction the essay is going to go.

"they've got it all wrong": Note how smoothly this clause leads the reader into the beginning of the next paragraph.

Paragraph 5
Jeremy Bentham: (1748–1832), British jurist, social reformer, and philosopher who wrote *Introduction to the Principles of Morals and Legislation* (1789).

Paragraph 6
"iconographic center": The term *iconography* refers to symbolic representation, especially to conventional meanings being attached to an image or images.

"conundrum": Anything that puzzles.

"apotheosis": Often misused, this term refers to an ideal example, an epitome.

Louis Pasteur: (1822–1895), French chemist and bacteriologist who discovered that certain foods including milk and milk products could be exposed to an elevated temperature for the period of time that it takes to destroy certain microorganisms that can produce disease or cause food spoilage.

"antivivisectionists": People who oppose *vivisection*, the practice of subjecting living animals to cutting operations, especially to advance physiological and pathological knowledge.

Paragraph 8
"Ann Landers's column": Ann Landers is a columnist who responds to letters from her readers, that concern their worries or personal problems, which she tries to alleviate or help to solve.

Paragraph 9
The last sentence of this paragraph attacks an argument interestingly: Hearne says that Peter Singer and others use their ignorance of animals as argumentative proof of their devotion to animals, a cyclic and therefore meaningless argument at best.

Paragraph 10
Notice how vividly Hearne compares the thinking and actions of her Airedale to the thinking and actions of those she describes in paragraph 9.

Paragraph 11

"particularly unexamined lives": Compare with this line from Plato's *Apology*: "The life which is unexamined is not worth living."

James Madison: Fourth president of the United States (1809–1817). Noted for his work on the Bill of Rights and for his writings in *The Federalist.*

Paragraph 12

"calculus": As used here, the term refers to a highly systematic method of treating a problem.

Paragraph 13

"orangutans": In Malay, *orangutan* means "jungle man."

Paragraph 14

Again, as was exemplified in paragraph 4, notice how smoothly the last line of this paragraph serves as a transition to the first line of the next paragraph.

Paragraph 15

"Rights": As ordinarily denoted, a *right* is that which conforms to some fact, truth, reason, or to some standard or principle.

Paragraph 16

Here and in the next paragraph (17), notice the classical use of the analogy, when *analogy* means "reasoning or arguing from parallel cases."

Paragraph 19

It develops that "rights" are not only reciprocal but also binding; one cannot have rights without recognizing what supports those rights, which are responsibilities for acknowledging other "animals'" existence.

Paragraph 20

"Miranda warning": A Supreme Court ruling (Miranda v. Arizona, 1966) that requires law-enforcement officers to warn a person who has been taken into custody of his or her rights to remain silent and to have legal counsel.

Paragraph 21

"Yalies from townies": Hearne lightens her topic for a moment, while at the same time strengthening her point in this paragraph, that dogs recognize reciprocity, as do cats and Hearne's husband (one presumes).

Paragraph 22

"elaborate enough": The conceptions that animals have about their "rights" never move to the level of academic abstractions, such as those often embedded in texts and icons.

Paragraph 23

"Obedience is reciprocal": Note how often this theme pervades the essay. All that we do and all that is done to us, says Hearne in so many ways throughout this essay, demands of us some sort of reciprocity.

Paragraph 24

"Rainer Maria Rilke's account": In *Letters to a Young Poet*, Rilke (1875–1926) says, "Love consists in this, that two solitudes protect and touch and greet each other."

Paragraph 25

"Many children": Note the last line, where Hearne comments obliquely and negatively on a common way to "teach" children.

Paragraph 26

"correction blocks one path": The author carefully distinguishes between correction and punishment.

Paragraph 28

"What a goooooood human": Here the author employs a novel form of personification to make her point.

Paragraph 30

"People who claim to speak": What follows, though it might ultimately weaken Hearne's position, is an example of *argumentum ad ignorantiam*, a classic fallacy of noting that an argument is true if it has not been proved false. Whether the argument is weakened or strengthened by this strategy greatly depends on the audience's mood or opinion before the strategy is employed.

Paragraph 31

"perfectly my husband's mate": Note Hearne's deft use of analogy in this passage, "analogy" referring to that form of reasoning in which a thing is inferred to be similar to another thing in a certain respect, on the basis of the known similarity between the things in other respects.

Possible Answers

Meaning and Purpose

1. Answers vary, of course, but no answer should range too far afield from the idea that Hearne strongly equates all living creatures, paying particular attention in this essay to the combination of features shared by dogs and humans. Depending on which parts of the essay the students use for their reasoning, they might illustrate their answers with reference to many of the people named, including Hearne's husband, and to many of her dogs, whom she also names.

2. Relying on students' knowing that we do not have a right to happiness, but rather a right to the *pursuit* of happiness, which she points out at the end of paragraph 3, Hearne suggests that this kind of happiness is abstract, in the realm of philosophy. Animals do not operate in the realm of philosophy.

3. This sentence, according to the essay, has become, knowingly or not, the rallying cry of the kind of animal-rights' activists whom the author deplores. This series of three rhetorical questions cannot be answered, but they can be used to call people to the task of "liberating" animals.

4. Associating her husband with her dogs, as Hearne does several times, makes the point for the reader that she loves both strongly, but not equally. This important point helps the reader to see that love itself does not have a single shade of meaning.

Strategy

1. By using statistics and other recoverable information here, the author points out that "captivity" does not equate with "cruelty." As she illustrates with this information, nature can be crueler than humans.

2. The author would like to leave out the philosophers because they deal with abstractions not appropriate to the topic, which itself is concrete: Either we do keep animals in some sense of *keep*, or we do not. At the same time, she cannot rid herself of the philosophers because, unfortunately, the question of animal rights has evolved into several philosophical questions that must be grappled with; otherwise, the author cannot come to terms with animal rights as they are now conceived, philosophically.

3. Answers will vary to this personal question, with most students agreeing one way or another that one must "give to get." After they have finished reading this essay, students usually agree with the premise that no person can be above another person, but some will argue that dogs and humans do not have enough in common to be thought of in terms of reciprocity.
4. If a "correct" answer exists for this question, then it grows from how closely the student reads paragraph 17. In that paragraph and based on other evidence preceding and following it, *being* need not automatically refer to a person. It can just as well refer to any living creature.

Style

1. As used in paragraph 12, the word *calculus* means "a carefully systematic way or structure designed to solve a problem," or words to that effect.
2. Answers vary depending on how much information the students offer, but almost all answers have a common thread: Hearne intertwines people and dogs to the extent that one can come away from the essay believing, if only momentarily, that dogs and people have far more in common than previously thought.
3. These two phrases are brief descriptions of the images or icons that certain freedom-for-animals groups use to elicit sympathy for their cause. One can imagine a photograph of a cute fluffy poodle, for example, portraying either helplessness or agony.
4. An *organism* is a form of life composed of mutually interdependent parts that maintain various vital processes. A *species* is a class of individuals having some common characteristics or qualities. Hearne uses these terms to strengthen in her readers' minds the idea of our common, reciprocal dependence upon one another.

A Nation of Welfare Families
Stephanie Coontz

Teaching Suggestions

Because Stephanie Coontz begins her argument by summarizing the positions of her opposition, one way to approach her essay would be to ask your students how well she captures their own attitudes in her first paragraph. If her formulation is pretty much on the mark, you might point out that such a beginning serves a two-fold purpose. By accurately summarizing positions the reader recognizes as true, she favorably disposes that reader to her own opposite point of view that immediately follows. And, in a reasonable way, she immediately casts doubt on the positions she will argue against.

The structure of her argument is also worth examination. The first three paragraphs she uses as her introduction. In the first, she summarizes the commonly held attitudes toward welfare, from both conservative and liberal points of view. In the second paragraph, she declares the idea of family self-reliance a "myth" and shows why that's so by using examples from her own family history and then from the broader perspective of the country's history. When she declares her thesis in the third paragraph, she is logically concluding her introduction in a kind of mini essay within an essay. She introduces the body of her argument (4–11) by contrasting the common attitude toward government assistance in early America (a positive attitude, since aid reflected a sense of community, an official tie between the individual and the larger community) and the negative contemporary idea that public aid is in some way a diminishment of the individual who receives it (4). She then gives a series of historical examples to demonstrate that state aid is neither recent nor diminishing. She concludes in her final two paragraphs (12–13) with the imperative that we face the fact that it is indeed the very function of government to assist families. The only question is how.

We also encourage you to teach this essay in conjunction with David Kelley's "The End of Welfare as We Know It?" Kelley and Coontz argue from two diametrically opposed points of view about welfare.

Notes

Paragraph 1
Coontz succinctly sums up the positions of both conservatives and liberals on welfare. She will attack in her argument the precise assumption on which the two sides agree, "that American families traditionally achieve success by establishing their independence from the government."

Paragraph 2
After a clear topic sentence, Coontz uses two examples to demonstrate the validity of its assertion. The first she derives from personal history and uses to show how compelling the idea of self-reliance is. The second she takes from the broader history of the country to demonstrate how that idea of self-reliance is simply untrue, a "myth." Her two examples, therefore, create a paragraph structure of comparison/contrast.

Paragraph 3
The entire paragraph serves as the essay's thesis.

Paragraph 4
Coontz contrasts the positive attitude of early Americans to the current negative view.

Paragraphs 5–9
In these middle paragraphs, Coontz cites several specific government programs throughout the country's history that benefited American families.

Paragraphs 7–9
Taking the two examples most often cited as exemplars of family self-reliance, pioneer families (7) and the suburban family of the 1950s (8–9), Coontz demonstrates how the contrary is actually true, that both were largely dependent on government aid.

Paragraph 10
Coontz shows here the negative effects on those who were systematically denied government aid in the 1950s, while those who received aid prospered.

Paragraph 11
Here Coontz attacks the argument that government assistance to families is destructive of the poor by showing how such aid has had precisely the opposite effect on the middle class.

Paragraphs 12–13

In her two paragraph conclusion, Coontz emphasizes how totally wrong the commonly held assumptions about welfare are and challenges the reader to accept the fact "that assisting families is, simply, what government does."

Possible Answers

Meaning and Purpose

1. The entirety of paragraph 3, a single sentence, serves as the essay's thesis. Coontz restates her thesis in slightly different form in the first sentence of paragraph 13. She reasserts her thesis a third time in the essay's final sentence, this final time as an imperative.
2. Both conservatives and liberals, according to Coontz, believe that "dependence on government assistance is a recent and destructive phenomenon" (1). Coontz sets her task to prove that government assistance is neither recent nor destructive.
3. From the country's beginning, American families have depended on government social support systems (3), and, for early Americans, this dependence was regarded as a positive thing, a relationship between the individual and the larger society "that confirmed our social and personal interdependence" (4).
4. Pioneer families were able to move west only because of government financed military excursions against the indigenous Native American and Mexican peoples. The government also financed transportation systems, easing travel west. Further, the Homestead Act of 1862 allowed families to buy land from the government below cost (7). Coontz then outlines the myriad government benefits to middle-class families in the 1950s in paragraphs 8 and 9. The government support to these families was so extensive, in fact, that "the 1950s suburban family was far more dependent on government assistance than any so-called underclass family today" (8).
5. While public money was used to build roads that allowed suburban families to commute, the transportation systems that served the city poor were allowed to decay. And while federal loans were made easy for suburbanites, people who lived in what today is called the inner city were systematically declared ineligible for those same loans (10).
6. People opposed to the idea of welfare have argued that government subsidies demoralize their recipients because they "induce dependence, undermine self-esteem, or break down family ties" (11). Coontz counters that "myth" by claiming that in the 1950s and 1960s "federal subsidies to suburbia encouraged family formation, residential stability, upward occupational mobility, and rising educational aspirations" (11), precisely the opposite results of what welfare opponents claim is the result of aid to the poor.

Strategy

1. In the first paragraph, Coontz claims that the notion that the ideal family is a self-reliant unit is no more than "lore," and in the second she calls family self-reliance a "myth." In context, the words indicate that those ideas are simply untrue.

2. To argue that families don't need some form of public support in the face of the fact that they do is just as wrong-headed as sixteenth-century thinkers insisting that the earth was the center of the universe, against all evidence to the contrary. Both positions resulted in contorted reasoning to justify those mistaken beliefs that, in turn, have resulted in positions and policies based on mere figments.

3. Answers to how convincing Coontz's many examples are will, of course, vary. But the idea that government assistance to U.S. families has been policy since the country's inception, and is not a recent phenomenon, will come as a surprise to many.

Style

1. The words Coontz places in quotation marks do not have their common meanings because they are based on false assumptions.

2. *Myth* can mean a traditional or legendary story, with or without a determinable basis in fact; stories of gods and goddesses meant to explain natural phenomena; or any invented story, idea, or concept. Or, it can mean an unproved or false collective belief that is used to justify a social institution or attitude. Coontz uses the word in this latter sense.

3. *Entrenched*: firmly established; *aggravated*: made worse or more severe; *apparatus*: a combination of things intended for a specific use; *saps*: undermines, weakens, or destroys insidiously; *lore*: the body of knowledge, especially of a traditional, anecdotal, or popular nature, on a particular subject; *spectrum*: a broad range of varied but related ideas that overlap to form a continuous sequence; *mantle*: something that covers; *exacerbated*: increased the severity of; *heritage*: something inherited; *subsidy*: a grant or contribution of money; *allotted*: distributed or parceled out; *domain*: land having absolute ownership; *inception*: beginning; *ludicrous*: causing laughter because of its absurdity; *parochial*: limited or narrow in outlook; *rampant*: raging, unchecked; *abolition*: the act of abolishing; *arbitration*: the hearing and determining of a dispute by a person agreed to by both parties; *compulsory*: mandatory; *legend*: a nonhistorical or unverifiable story handed down by tradition from earlier times and popularly accepted as historical; *clapboards*: long, thin boards used to cover the outer walls of buildings; *prefabricated*: constructed beforehand for quick assembly; *comprised*: constituted; *unprecedented*: unexampled or unparalleled; *recipients*: those who receive; *boon*: something to be thankful for; *pervasive*: spread throughout; *redlining*: to designate for rejection; *beneficiaries*: those who receive benefits; *afflict*: trouble or pain greatly or grievously; *intrinsically*: by the very nature of; *induce*: cause; *intervene*: intercede; *perspective*: being able to see all of the relevant data in a meaningful relationship; *caricatures*: to represent by ludicrously exaggerating the peculiarities of a thing; *contortions*: distortions; *reminiscent*: awakening memories of something similar; *Ptolemaic universe*: a universe elaborated by Ptolemy (C.E. 127–151, Hellenistic mathematician, astronomer, and geographer in Alexandria) and subsequently modified by others, according to which the earth was the fixed center of the universe, with the heavenly bodies moving about it; *postulated*: claimed the truth of; *reconcile*: make compatible or consistent; *convoluted*: complicated or intricately involved; *cumbersome*: unwieldy; *paradigm*: an example serving as a model.

The End of Welfare as We Know It?
David Kelley

Teaching Suggestions

College writing students must learn to gage their audience. Most of their formal writing in college will be for a literate, informed audience, we hope. The question of audience might be a way to first approach "The End of Welfare as We Know It?" The essay is taken from David Kelley's book, *A Life of One's Own: Individual Rights and the Welfare State*, published by the Cato Institute, a libertarian think tank headquartered in Washington, D.C., that promotes individual freedom and the shrinking of government to its least intrusive level. Kelley's book argues that government welfare programs undermine individual freedoms and values, as well as the economic stability of society. His book as a whole, and this essay in particular, is most likely directed to those already committed to libertarian values, or to those emotionally and intellectually inclined in that direction. Kelley appeals to widely held attitudes hostile to the very idea of the welfare state and to welfare recipients, especially the poor. The essay refers to only two instances of middle-class welfare, student grants and loans and Social Security, and never addresses corporate welfare, generous government subsidies, tax breaks, and bailout money to wealthy U.S. corporations, government welfare that far exceeds welfare to the middle class and poor. He is certainly not addressing, therefore, an audience more disposed to the idea that it is indeed the function of government to aid individuals and families in need. Such an audience might question Kelley's oversimplifications and emotion-laden language. But these rhetorical tactics can be quite effective with an audience already predisposed or sympathetic to Kelley's point of view.

We also suggest you teach this essay in conjunction with Stephanie Coontz's *A Nation of Welfare Families*. Not only does she argue a point of view diametrically opposed to that of Kelley, but she addresses a wider audience, as well. So the two essays can be discussed both for the merits of their ideas as well as for how effectively they address their target audiences.

Notes

Paragraph 1
Kelley begins with a list of personal responsibilities that many people think of as self-evident. Many readers, therefore, should immediately feel sympathetic to Kelley's initial assertions and even, perhaps, a bit virtuous that they hold such responsible values.

Paragraph 2
Kelley now presents public welfare policies that contrast with the private values he listed in the previous paragraph. Within the paragraph, Kelley sets up another set of contrasts when he characterizes the welfare state as "the sprawling network of programs for transferring wealth from taxpayers to recipients. . . ." From this point on, the "recipient" half of that equation he always describes in negatively nuanced terms and the "taxpayer" half in positive language.

"Medicaid": A U.S. government program, financed by local, state, and federal funds, of hospitalization and medical insurance for persons of all ages within certain income limits.

"Social Security": Public programs designed to protect individuals and their families from income losses due to unemployment, old age, sickness, or death and to improve their welfare through public services (e.g. medical care) and economic assistance in the task of raising a family. The term may include social insurance programs, health and welfare services, and various income maintenance programs.

"Medicare": A U.S. government program of hospitalization insurance and voluntary medical insurance for persons aged sixty-five and over and for certain disabled persons under sixty-five.

Paragraph 3

A critical reader might find this part of Kelley's argument a bit weak because, in his attempt to emphasize the voluntary nature of individual public help, he ignores the fact that most communities finance such things as ambulance and firefighting services with community tax dollars.

Paragraph 6

"American Enterprise Institute for Public Policy Research": A "Think Tank" promoting such conservative values as private enterprise and strong foreign policies and national defense.

Paragraph 7

"the New Deal": The name given the domestic program of the administration of U.S. President Franklin D. Roosevelt between 1933 and 1939, which took action to bring about immediate economic relief from the Great Depression, as well as reforms in industry, agriculture, finance, waterpower, labor, and housing, vastly increasing the scope of the federal government's activities.

"the Great Society": A political slogan used by U.S. President Lyndon B. Johnson (served 1963–1969) to identify his legislative program of national reform. Johnson declared "war" on poverty, called on medical care for the aged through an expanded social security program, and insisted on legal protections for African–American citizens deprived of the right to vote by certain state registration laws in the South. Congress passed almost all of the president's proposals.

Possible Answers

Meaning and Purpose

1. According to Kelley, as individuals we recognize that we must take responsibility for our own lives, and we "realize the world doesn't owe us a living" (1). In our public lives, on the other hand, "we have accepted an obligation to provide food, shelter, jobs, education, pensions, medical care, child support, and other goods to every member of society" (2). It is this seeming dichotomy that Kelley sees almost as a social schizophrenia: "The concept of a right to the goods and services provided by the welfare state is the chief source of disparity between our private and our public morality" (7).

2. In our personal lives we take responsibility for providing for our own needs. Public policy, in the form of the welfare state, provides many personal needs and thus supersedes personal responsibility. Answers to whether or not Kelley's statement is true will, of course, vary. Some students might detect a logical problem with Kelley's position. That is, even in our personal lives we assume the responsibility for the welfare of others—our wives, husbands, and children, for instance. And if we think of society as a kind of extended family in which we are all interrelated and interdependent one upon the

other, as many people do, then all of our personal responsibilities extend to everyone else in society.

3. Other than aid for the needy, Kelley cites two instances of middle-class welfare: Grants and loans to college students and social security (6). In both cases, he claims an unjustified attitude in the recipients that they have a right to such aid, "a sense that the world does owe us a living" (7).

4. Kelley claims that, like communism, the welfare state's foundation is built on a myth and, therefore, the institution can crumble from its own weight: "The welfare state has . . . been sustained by nothing more than myth, and is . . . vulnerable to collapse" (10).

Strategy

1. Kelley uses comparison/contrast as his primary organizational pattern. He contrasts entire paragraphs when he opposes private lives (1, 3) to public lives (2, 4), for instance. He also employs contrast in internal paragraph structure where he regularly contrasts welfare recipients and taxpayers.

2. Kelley implies that those who receive welfare benefits don't pay taxes, which is not necessarily true. By doing so, he hopes to create the sense that it is unfair to expect taxpayers to provide for someone who "is unable or unwilling to support himself" (2).

3. Kelley appeals to both reason and emotion. He appeals to emotion in several different ways. Primarily, though, he couches the ideas he means to disparage in negative language, while he uses positive language for the ideas he means to promote. For instance, the beneficiaries of welfare programs "make claims on the public purse" while it is the "productive members of society who pay taxes" (4). Or, welfare programs unfairly "empower those who make claims" while it "silence[s] those who do the providing" (7). The essay is replete with other examples. While Kelley appears reasonable when he points out the seeming disparities between our public and private lives, he also presents the reader with some logical problems. In paragraph 3, for instance, he oversimplifies when he says that when we help a stranger hurt in the street, or a neighbor whose house has burned down, we, as individuals, "choose to do so voluntarily. . . ." Maybe so, but as a community, more often than not, we pay for the ambulance and the firefighters with tax dollars because we recognize the community needs to do so in its own self-interest. He oversimplifies, too, when he says in paragraph 2 that "'If someone fails to save for retirement, the Social Security system provides a pension" because he never mentions the fact that most social security beneficiaries have paid social security taxes all their working years.

Style

1. The answer to number 3 in Strategy deals, in part, with the way Kelley employs language to emotionally sway the reader. Students should have no problem in finding other words and phrases that shed positive light on ideas Kelley looks kindly on and negatively colors ideas he looks on with disfavor.

2. On one level, Kelley's analogy seems to work logically. Communism was certainly more powerful than the welfare state, and it collapsed. Therefore, so might the welfare state collapse. Kelley also creates guilt by association. Simply by comparing communism to the welfare state, he transfers much of

the weight of the onerous baggage of the former to the latter. On another level, however, the analogy is a false one. First, it appears unfair to compare a welfare system that in many ways justifiably aids the destitute and handicapped to a totalitarian form of government that destroyed millions. Second, the analogy is a gross oversimplification. The forces leading to the collapse of communism were certainly more vast and complex than a mere myth losing its credibility.

3. *Myth* can be used in a positive way to mean a traditional or legendary story, or stories of gods and goddesses meant to explain natural phenomena, or any invented story, idea, or concept. Negatively, it can mean an unproved or false collective belief used to justify a social institution or attitude. Kelley, like Coontz in *A Nation of Welfare Families,* uses the word in this latter way.

4. *Incapacitating:* making incapable or unfit, disabling; *recipients:* those who receive; *compensation:* something given or received as an equivalent for services, debt, loss, injury, etc.; *entitlements:* the rights to guaranteed benefits under a government program; *elevates:* moves or raises to a higher place; *monumental:* exceptionally great; *presumption:* unwarrantable, unbecoming, or impertinent boldness; *beneficiaries:* those who receive benefits; *precedence:* the right to precede in importance; *obliged:* bound morally or legally, as by a promise or a contract; *fiscal:* of or pertaining to public treasury or revenues; *intractable:* not easily controlled or directed; *intransigence:* being uncompromising or inflexible; *disparity:* lack of similarity or equality; *pathologies:* deviations from healthy or normal conditions; *legitimacy:* the state of being in accordance with established laws, rules, principles, or standards; *coherently:* logically, consistently; *naive:* unsophisticated, ingenuous; *inertia:* sluggishness; *sanctifying:* making holy; *myth:* an unproved or false collective belief used to justify a social institution or attitude; *credibility:* believability; *vulnerable:* susceptible to being hurt.

The Shrieking of the Lambs
Andrew Klavan

Teaching Suggestions

Klavan's opinions on the relationship between fictional and real violence is, to say the least, not in the mainstream at the present moment. Undoubtedly many students will react strongly to the essay, some, we suspect, willing to defend his point of view, while others, the majority we venture to guess, willing to attack him. But we would also guess the majority of those students will not have thought out the reasons for their opinions. If this is true, the situation could lead to a worthwhile discussion of the necessity of credible evidence in developing a believable argument. Is Klavan's evidence credible? Is his logic solid, believable? Does he effectively do away with opposing points of view? What evidence can the students gather to support their own opinions?

Klavan's essay is also full of allusions (see the notes to the essay), and a valuable lesson could be given on how well-thought-out allusions can add depth and meaning to what one writes. Attendant to this, of course, is the lesson that the more one has read, the more meaningful any piece of informed writing will be for the reader.

It would also be valuable to use Klavan's essay in conjunction with Stephen King's "Why We Crave Horror Movies" (Klavan and King are in basic agreement—no surprise for two men who make a living writing horror fiction) and Michael Medved's "Denial Behavior," which takes a diametrically opposite point of view, one that Klavan attacks directly in his essay.

Notes

Paragraph 5

"15 minutes": The allusion is to Andy Warhol (1928?–1987, Pop artist and underground film maker) and his pronouncement that "everyone will be famous for fifteen minutes."

Michael Medved: American film critic. His "Denial Behavior," included in this section, argues that film violence has a definite, deleterious effect on society.

American Psycho: A novel (1991) by American novelist Bret Easton Ellis. The novel's protagonist, Patrick Bateman, works by day on Wall Street making a fortune. At night he tortures and murders women, described graphically by Ellis.

Catharine MacKinnon: Pro-censorship feminist and professor of law. MacKinnon and her colleague, writer Andrea Dworkin, maintain that pornography should not be accorded the same kinds of protection as other forms of speech because it is not speech *per se*. Rather, it is sex discrimination and promotes the subjugation of women.

Paragraph 6

Hannibal Lecter: From *The Silence of the Lambs*.

Ice-T: American rap artist. He is a controversial rap singer and film actor who pioneered "gangsta rap" with works that express the rage and fantasies of inner city street life. He outraged many with his 1991 song "Cop Killer."

"sound bytes": Refers to 10–15 second TV news segments.

Paragraph 9

Just William: The innocent looking, middle class, naughty school boy in a series of stories set in England during the first half of the twentieth century.

"Lords of the Flies": Refers to William Golding's novel *Lord of the Flies* (1954) in which a group of British schoolboys are stranded on a remote island and gradually degenerate into a savage horde. The novel was adapted to film twice, in 1963 and 1990.

"*What rough beast . . . at last*": Lines 20 and 21 of W. B. Yeats's justifiably famous poem, "The Second Coming," in which Yeats expresses his sense of the dissolution of the civilization of his time. Klavan refers to the poem here and other places in the essay. These references are particularly apt considering the subjects of both the poem and essay.

Paragraph 10

Martin Amis: (b. 1949) English novelist and journalist. His novels have won widespread acclaim, *The Rachel Papers* (1974) winning the Somerset Maugham Award.

Paragraph 12

Child's Play 3: The last of three horror films in which a doll named Chucky is really a monster, possessed with the spirit of a dead murderer.

Paragraph 13

In this paragraph Klavan demonstrates by specific examples how the British press and politicians grabbed on to easy but irrelevant solutions to explain the Bulger crime, thus ignoring the real issues he lists in the third sentence.

The Good Son: A terror film (1993) in which Macauley Culkin, an unremorseful, pubescent sociopath, terrorizes his cousin, and many others.

Reservoir Dogs: A sometimes highly praised and often gruesomely violent Quentin Tarantino film (1992) that is a post-mortem dissection of a fatally bungled robbery.

Liberal Democrat MP: A member of the British Parliament in the Liberal Democratic Party, a middle of the road, but minor, party between the conservative to reactionary Tory Party and the liberal to socialist Labor Party.

My Cousin Vinny: A film comedy (1992) about a "lawyer's" attempt to defend his innocent cousin and a friend on a murder charge in the deep south. Klavan makes this statement with tongue in cheek, probably.

Paragraph 14

"passionate intensity": "The best lack all conviction, while the worst/Are full of passionate intensity," lines 7 and 8 of "The Second Coming."

Paragraph 15

This one sentence paragraph is a synecdoche (see *Figures of speech* in the Glossary) in which Klavan has Chucky stand for all fictional violence.

Paragraph 16

Plato: A Greek philosopher (c. 427–348 B.C.). Plato aspired to political activity. Dismayed at the inequities of Athenian tyranny, and later at the execution of his teacher Socrates under democracy, he turned toward philosophy in search of an alternative to the unjust and unstable public life of the time. Klavan quotes from his political treatise, the *Republic*.

"Dionysian": Dionysus, the Greek god (Bacchus in Roman mythology) of wine and fertile crops. He was often honored by orgiastic fertility rites, thus the adjectival form of his name indicating recklessly uninhibited, unrestrained, undisciplined, and yes, orgiastic. He represents man's dark side.

Paragraph 18

Vaclav Havel: (b. 1936) Czech dramatist and poet. Havel became a spokesman for the Czech civil rights movement after the Soviet invasion of Prague in 1968. After Czechoslovakia gained its independence, Havel became its first democratically elected president. He has always been concerned about the relation of language to reality, and many of his works present the crisis of communication as a symptom of deep social malaise.

Paragraph 19

"an unfathomable spirit and an infinite mind": Klavan's rather mystical locution seems to refer to a level of mind well beyond the conscious, and may well allude to Carl Jung's "collective unconscious." Most certainly he alludes to Yeats' *Spiritus Mundi* (1. 13) in "The Second Coming," The Spirit or Soul of the Universe, with which all individual souls are connected through the "Great Memory," which Yeats held to be a universal subconscious in which the human race preserves its past memories. It is thus a source of symbolic images for the writer.

"a shadow of the world": Klavan turns Platonic philosophy upside down here. In the "Allegory of the Cave," Plato claims that those things we normally think of as constituting the real world are merely shadows of the ideal forms that lie behind them and that are the true reality. Here, the imaginative transformation of the real world gives us mere shadows.

Paragraph 21

Death Wish: A 1974 film in which a liberal minded business man's wife and daughter are savagely raped, and his wife dies. This atrocity transforms the previously mild mannered man into a vigilante on the streets of New York.

Red Dragon: A novel (1981) by Thomas Harris in which a former FBI agent is called back into service to capture a serial killer, which he does by using the power of his imagination to think like the killer. The psychopathic genius, Hannibal Lecter, who will become a central figure in the later Harris novel, *The Silence of the Lambs*, is introduced as a minor character in this book. *Red Dragon* was made into the movie *Manhunter* in 1986.

Catcher in the Rye: A novel (1951) by J. D. Salinger. The book presents two days in the life of Holden Caulfield who has run away from his prep school just before the start of Christmas vacation. He wanders around New York getting himself into a number of wryly humorous adventures. He is a sophisticated, articulate, and amusingly unbalanced adolescent who uniquely represents contemporary youth's dissatisfaction with adult society.

Ceausescu's murderous Roumania: Nicolae Ceausescu was president of Roumania from 1967 until the collapse of Communism in Eastern Europe. His authoritarian regime was particularly brutal.

Dracula: The best known novel (1897) by English writer Bram Stoker (1847–1912). The novel is a wild tale of vampires and werewolves. It has been made into several motion pictures and sequels.

Paragraph 22

Psycho: (1960) Alfred Hitchcock's most notorious film is still terrifying after all these years.Its 1999 remake was not very successful.

David Koresh: The head of a religious cult that came into conflict with federal law enforcement. The conflict ended with the horrific conflagration in Waco, Texas, in 1994.

Paragraph 24

"for taking such pleasure in make-believe acts": Here and elsewhere in the essay Klavan attacks the puritanical tendency to deny others the pleasures that one feels personally guilty for. Thus the phenomenon of censorship.

Thelma and Louise: A popular film (1991) in which two women friends leave their responsibilities behind to take a short trip, but an unexpected incident turns them into fugitives.

Paragraph 26

Agatha Christie: (born Agatha Mary Clarissa Miller, 1890–1976) English detective-story writer, the most widely translated author in English. Her detective novels usually featured her idiosyncratic sleuths Hercule Poirot, a vain but clever Belgian, or Miss Jane Marple, a shrewd and elderly spinster with an endless fascination for murder. Christie had a particular interest in abnormal psychology.

Hemingway: Ernest Hemingway (1899–1962), American novelist and short-story writer. Early in his career as a newspaperman and foreign correspondent, Hemingway was already the craftsman whose terse style, with its dramatic understatement and superb dialogue, was to influence several generations of writers.

Faulkner: William Faulkner (1897–1962), American novelist and short-story writer. Faulkner, who was awarded the Nobel Prize in Literature in 1949, is recognized as one of the greatest of American writers.

Paragraph 28

Dickens: Charles Dickens (1812–1870), English novelist, the most popular and considered by many the greatest of England. He became a popular success at the age of twenty-four with the publication of his serialized novel *Pickwick Papers*.

Paragraph 30

"Nietzschean": Reference to Friedrich Nietzsche (1844–1900), German philosopher, classical scholar, and poet. His philosophy emphasized the will to power as the chief motivating force of both the individual and society.

The Robber Baron: We have been unable to track down any film, novel, or story with this precise title. The Brothers Grimm have a folktale entitled "The Robber Bridegroom" in which an old crone hides a young woman in a cellar to have her watch her fiancé and his cutthroat companions dismember another young woman, a fate that would be hers soon. Eudora Welty's first novel (1945) of the same name is based on this tale. The title of Margaret Atwood's *The Robber Bride* is also derived from the Grimm story. There is also a novel by Joyce Brandon titled *The Lady and the Robber Baron*. Which, if any, of these Klavan is referring to, we simply don't know.

Homer: 9th century B.C. Greek epic poet. He is the reputed author of both the *Iliad* and the *Odyssey*. He is traditionally represented as blind, thus "deep-browed."

Paragraph 31

Klavan contrasts the theories of experts in this paragraph with what he considers are the real causes that give fiction life in the next paragraph (32).

Falling Down: A movie (1993) in which a previously retiring nobody loses control one morning, abandons his car on the freeway, and starts wandering L.A. on an increasingly violent odyssey.

Paragraph 32

"*gravitas* . . . catharsis": In his *Poetics*, Aristotle (384–322 B.C.) applies the term *catharsis* (in the original Greek, "purgation," or "purification," or both) to describe that undeniable, if extraordinary, fact that in drama many tragic representations of suffering and defeat leave an audience feeling not depressed, but relieved, or even exalted. This is a literary theory with substance and weight (*gravitas*).

Paragraph 35

Medea: In Greek mythology, a sorceress and priestess of Hectate who was involved in several bloody murders, two of whom were her own children.

Caliban: In Shakespeare's *The Tempest*, the deformed, half-human slave of Prospero. The son of the witch Sycorax and a devil, Caliban symbolizes mankind's primitive urges.

St. Francis of Assisi: (c. 1181–1226) Italian monk, founder of the order of Franciscans. The son of a prosperous merchant, he turned at about age twenty-six to a life of asceticism and mysticism, devoting himself to the care of the poor, the sick, and the leprous, as well as to prayer. His approach to religion was characterized by its joyousness and its love of nature. He called both animate and inanimate creations his brothers and sisters, and his preaching to the birds has become a popular subject of artists.

"take them out for a walk": See Stephen King's "Why We Crave Horror Movies" (pp. 355–358).

Paragraph 37

Dr. Seuss: (pen name of Theodor Seuss Geisel, 1904–1995), American writer and illustrator of scores of immensely popular, humorous children's books, such as *The Cat in the Hat*, *How the Grinch Stole Christmas*, and *Green Eggs and Ham*.

Paragraph 39
Klavan uses an anecdote here to demonstrate how people take a natural delight in fictional gore that is effectively done.

The Exorcist: A film (1973) adapted from the best-selling novel of Peter Blatty. In it a twelve-year-old girl's body is possessed by the Devil, and a troubled priest attempts to confront the demon in her—and in himself.

Paragraph 40
Titus Andronicus: (c. 1590) A tragedy by William Shakespeare (1564–1616). The play is particularly violent, even by Elizabethan standards.

de Sade: Comte Donatien Alphonse Francois de Sade, known as Marquis de Sade (1740–1814), French author. Sadism, a type of sexual perversion in which gratification is found by torturing the object of love, is so called from de Sade whose works first brought such practices to public attention.

Paragraph 41
Time's Arrow: Martin Amis's seventh novel (1992) in which the narrator is a "passenger or parasite" inside the mind of Tod Friendly who experiences Tod's life in strict reverse order. In this inverted world people walk backwards, absorb excrement, and regurgitate food which they assemble and take to the supermarket. From this point of view, all things become strange and comic, including the Holocaust. For this reason the book was condemned by many. After much controversy, the novel was eventually short-listed for the Booker Prize.

Goodfellas: A critically acclaimed 1990 film that presents both the allure and reality of day-to-day life in a Mafia family.

"the Menendez trial": The brothers Menendez, Eric and Lyle, confessed to planning and then carrying out the murders of their parents. In their first trial a hung jury was unable to decide between second degree murder and manslaughter. The jury in their second trial found them guilty of first degree murder. A month later, in April, 1996, they were sentenced to life imprisonment without possibility of parole.

"the Amy Fisher case": As an underage teenager, Amy Fisher had an affair with an older, married man, Joey Buttafuoco, and attempted to murder his wife.

Paragraph 42
"graver purposes": Klavan puns here.

Paragraph 43
"Rome is burning": Alludes to Nero, Emperor of Rome (54–68 A.D.) who was responsible in 64 A.D., according to popular history, for lighting a great fire that destroyed a sizeable portion of Rome in order to see how Troy looked when it was in flames, and then occupied himself musically "while Rome burned." The story is now generally held to be mere legend. But Klavan's allusion adds depth and meaning to the idea that those who see fictional violence as destroying the fabric of society are as apocalyptic and wrong in their vision as those who wrongfully blamed Nero for the destruction of Rome.

Paragraph 44
South Kensington: A section of London.

Paragraph 45
Schindler's List: (1993) The film adaption by Steven Spielberg of Thomas Keneally's best-seller about the real-life Catholic war profiteer who initially flourished by currying favor with the Nazis, but eventually went broke saving the lives of more

than 1,000 Polish Jews by employing them in his factory, manufacturing crockery for the German army.

Mississippi Burning: (1988) A film based on real-life events in which two FBI agents head a government investigation into the disappearance of three civil rights workers in Mississippi during the summer of 1964.

Paragraph 46
Keats: John Keats (1795–1821), English poet.

Paragraph 49
Robert Chambers: Better known as the "preppie murderer," Chambers killed a young woman during what could have been a date rape in New York in 1986.

Lorena Bobbitt: Was found innocent by reason of insanity after admitting cutting off her husband's penis while he slept.

Paragraph 52
Ed Gein: (b. 1906) Wisconsin murderer and necrophile. Gein lived alone on a farm in Plainfield, Wisconsin, after his mother and brother died. He developed a strong interest in the female anatomy and apparently desired to change his sex. Around 1947 he began digging up female corpses from remote graves and bringing them to his farm for experiments. Later he turned to killing women to obtain cadavers. The local sheriff eventually found the skins, heads, hearts, livers, sex organs, etc., of at least fifteen women in Gein's home. He was sent to a state institution for the criminally insane, where he eventually died.

Paragraph 55
"the sleep of reason": An allusion to the Spanish artist Francisco Goya (1746–1828) and his etching in which a man sleeps with his head on a desk, on which there is the inscription, "The sleep of reason brings forth monsters." The figure is surrounded by nocturnal creatures—bats, owls, and cats—which symbolize the dark forces that continually threaten rationality.

Paragraph 56
Carlyle: Thomas Carlyle (1795–1881), Scottish born English prose writer.

"I-and-Thou": Martin Buber (1878–1965), an Austrian Jew, was a philosopher, theologian, and Zionist thinker. His deeply religious world view emphasized the relationship between man and man and between man and God. *I and Thou* (1923), a philosophical treatise that examines these relationships, had a considerable influence on both Christian and Jewish thinkers.

The Piano: A film (1993) about love and sex, told from a woman's point of view, and the complications that result when a woman, her daughter, and her piano arrive on a remote New Zealand island for an arranged marriage with a farmer in the late 19th century.

Possible Answers

Meaning and Purpose

1. Although the idea that fictional violence leads to real violence may be a popular assumption, it has no basis in fact. Michael Medved, says Klavan, may believe it is so, but he has no way of knowing it (40, 46). Klavan, therefore, draws a clean line between belief and knowledge. The judge in the Jamie Bulger murder case makes the same leap of faith as Medved (8–14). And Klavan's Scottish friend who connected the rude and boorish behavior of a

movie audience with the violence on the screen has, again, made that same irrational leap (44–45). It is this false causal relationship that blurs fiction and reality when it is a clear distinction that must be made. The distinction must be made clear because in real life real people really get hurt (49). When we blur the distinction between fiction and reality we begin to apply fictional standards to real life situations with disastrous results (49), and we begin to lose our will to defend the sacredness of human life, or as Martin Amis says, "the gentleness of human flesh" (51).

2. The fictional, scholarly journals in *The Silence of the Lambs* can never call the madman, Dr. Lecter, either evil or crazy because they are uncomfortable with moral absolutes (55), and, ironically, reflect the best of us in real life who "lack all conviction, while the worst are full of passionate intensity" (14).

3. Blaming fictional violence is popular because it's easy. Facing the problems of real life (56) can be daunting, and trying to solve those real problems can be overwhelming.

4. With no evidence whatsoever, the judge in the Bulger case speculated that the brutal murder may have been committed because of the noxious effects a horror movie, *Child's Play 3*, had on the two murderous children. The cause-and-effect relationship he suggested had no basis in fact. He made a leap of faith. And the press immediately picked up on the false connection because it was easy to understand.

5. Klavan agrees with Stephen King that all men are potentially violent (see Stephen King's "Why We Crave Horror Movies," pp. 355–358) and that that violence needs to be repressed, and, in turn, that that repression needs a healthy outlet. But for Klavan, this formulation smacks too much of a guilty defense. The enjoyment of fictional violence delights us because it fulfills a deep-seated need. Therefore there's no reason for guilt or defensiveness. But there's every reason for celebration.

6. Klavan argues that would-be censors feel unconscious guilt for enjoying those acts in fiction that would be reprehensible in real life. This is a peculiarly Puritan attitude that Klavan attacks at various points of his essay.

7. Although fiction can make us more human because it allows us to imaginatively empathize with others, it is not powerful enough to transform people's lives. People with hollow lives who turn to violence, among other things, have been hollowed by real life experiences, not by fiction. To fathom the problems of life, we must face those problems head on rather than debate what kinds of fiction people should be allowed to enjoy. Such debate can't solve real problems; rather, it exacerbates the problems.

Strategy

1. In one sense, Klavan is condescending to those with opposing views. He implies in paragraph 5, for instance, that any attack on fictional violence is insane. He dismisses opposing views as "nonsense" (6). He labels any argument that insists that fiction can actually cause violence as "homeopathic" (16) and "superstitious fallacy" (17). But while he makes fun of "expert" theories of fictional violence, he very carefully explains why he does so (32). And, while initially dismissive of opposing arguments, he always comes back

to admit that his opponents hold on to partial truths, but those truths are indeed just partial explanations of problems and often reductionist (21, 34, 46, 47). In this attitude, he establishes himself as honest, thoughtful, and rational, dispositions not always held by his opponents.

2. Klavan summarizes several opposing arguments in paragraph 5. After calling them "nonsense," he points out some reasons for their popular appeal (6). He then uses the long narrative of the Bulger killing and trial to show that, as in the trial, there is no evidence to show a cause-and-effect relationship between fictional and real violence (8–14). He agrees with his critics that fiction has an effect on real life, but claims that it is far too complex to reduce that relationship to the simplicity of cause and effect. To do so, therefore, is reductionist (21–23). He undermines Michael Medved's argument that the constant barrage of negative images in the media tends to erode values by pointing out that neither he (Klavan) nor Medved actually knows whether or not the connection is true. Using the Bulger case as an example, he questions the validity of that point of view (46). And, finally, he points out that the reasons for the rude behavior of the two audiences viewing *Cliffhanger* reside in their real lives and not in the make-believe on the screen. Besides, he points out, that behavior, though inappropriate and rude, was harmful to no one (47).

3. Fiction, like sex, is profoundly joyful and provides necessary and needed emotional experience (32). Both fulfill deeply personal needs, and, thus, no one has the right to intrude on either (48).

4. All of the paragraphs give the reader visual relief in a longish essay with many fully developed paragraphs. Each summarizes the section of the argument that has immediately preceded it and serves as a transition into the next section.

5. Klavan cites modern authors whose use of violence in their fiction is respectable (26), goes back to Greek myth and drama with Medea (35), and further cites the traditional literature of Shakespeare (*Titus Andronicus*), Stoker (*Dracula*), and de Sade (40).

Style

1. The event is "nonreal" because it exists only in fiction, and it is "nonmeaningful" because it, as fiction, has no relationship to real life.

2. When Klavan talks about the fiction that he means to celebrate in the essay, his language is appropriately casual, sometimes slangy, or imitative of the language of horror fiction. When he seriously pursues his argument his language becomes standard, even formal at times.

3. "Trough," a feeding receptacle for animals, is most often associated with pigs. Thus, would-be censors are at least partially motivated by the desire to feed on fame, however fleeting the feast.

4. *Priapic*: suggestive of or resembling a phallus; *plummets*: plunges; *oblivion*: the state of being completely forgotten or unknown; *squeamish*: sensitive, shrinking from contact with; *goading*: prodding, inciting; *posthumous*: occurring after one's death; *jitterbug*: a strenuously acrobatic dance performed chiefly to boogie-woogie and swing, popular in the early 1940's; *coital*: pertaining to sexual intercourse; *jeopardy*: hazard or risk; *estate*: a period or con-

dition of life; *dusted*: killed (slang); *commode*: toilet; *quash*: to put down or suppress completely; *banal*: devoid of freshness or originality; *urbane*: polished, suave, sophisticated; *emblematic*: symbolic; *pundits*: experts or authorities; *distraught*: deeply agitated; *mutilated*: injured, disfigured; *tenuous*: flimsy, weak; *mea culpa*: [Latin, through my fault]: a formal acknowledgement of personal fault or error; *Draconian*: extremely harsh or cruel; *rampaging*: to rush, act, or move furiously or violently; *verities*: truths; *utopian*: founded upon or involving idealized perfection; *Dionysean*: recklessly, uninhibited; *homeopathic*: the treating of a disease by the administration of minute doses of a remedy that would in healthy persons produce symptoms of the disease treated; *template*: something overlayed; *fallacy*: a false or erroneous idea; *isomorphic*: being of identical or similar form, or shape, or structure; *alchemies*: powers or processes of transforming something common into something precious; *sublimate*: to divert the expression of an instinctual desire or impulse from its primitive form to one that is considered more socially or culturally acceptable; *pith*: importance, significance; *literati*: intelligentsia or, more specifically, men of letters; *unfathomable*: incomprehensible; *palliative*: superficial or temporary relief; *specious*: apparently good or right but lacking in real merit; *screed*: a long discourse or essay, especially a diatribe; *jeremiad*: a prolonged lamentation or complaint; *hallelujah*: a shout of joy, praise, or gratitude; *resonant*: resounding or echoing, as sounds; *stichomythic*: closely connected, as when two actors speak alternate lines (as in classical Greek drama); *sociopaths*: those who exhibit asocial or antisocial behavior; *guise*: assumed appearance; *factotum*: a general servant; *mayhem*: a state of rowdy disorder; *hausfrau*: housewife (German); *risible*: laughable; *peccadilloes*: slight offenses; *gravitas*: substantial, consequential (Latin); *catharsis*: a purification or purgation of the emotions, primarily through art; *palaver*: idle, misleading, or beguiling speech; *expended*: consumed by use; *denounce*: to condemn or censure openly; *expended*: used up; *catharsis*: the purging of emotions or relieving of emotional tensions; *icon*: a sign or representation that stands for its object by virtue of a resemblance or analogy to it; *benevolent*: characterized by or expressing good will or kindly feelings; *nubile*: sexually developed or attractive; *in flagrante*: shortened form of *in flagrante delicto*, in the very act of committing the offense; *goblins*: grotesque sprites or elves that are mischievous or malicious towards people; *menarche*: the first menstrual period of an individual; *evisceration*: the removing of the entrails from, disembowelment; *disembowels*: to remove the entrails from; *geyser*: a hot spring that spews forth hot liquid; *placid*: pleasantly calm or peaceful; *satori*: a sudden enlightenment; *atrocities*: things that are extremely shocking, wicked, cruel, or brutal; *aesthetic*: pertaining to the nature of beauty; *promiscuous*: having sexual relations with a number of people on a casual basis; *mitigated*: lessened in force or intensity; *consigning*: handed over or delivered formally or officially; *corollaries*: immediate consequences or easily drawn conclusions; *ubermensch*: superman (German); *auctorial*: of, by, or pertaining to an author; *atomizing*: to split into many sections, groups, or factions; *humanize*: to make humane, kind, or gentle; *bloke*: man, fellow, guy (informal Britishism); *oubliette*: a secret dungeon, with an opening only in the ceiling, as in certain old castles; *devolve*: to roll down, descend.

Denial Behavior
Michael Medved

Teaching Suggestions

The debate over what, if anything, to do about sex and violence in media takes place at all levels of American society. Most students have already given some thought to it and many have formed strong opinions. Recent legislation mandates the development of a V-chip to be inserted into all new television sets to allow parents to control which programs are available to their children. The film industry is frequently assailed for its lack of restraint in producing ever more dramatic and lurid films. A discussion of the V-chip may be a good starting point. Most people favor such a chip at first glance. Parents have a right to control their children's viewing, and the chip makes it easy and automatic. Since such a chip would control others' viewing, not mine, why not? Some have doubts, though, when they learn that the chip, as presently envisioned, is not programmable at the individual set. When it's turned on, it will block all programs that have been given a certain rating. The ratings will presumably be applied by some government or industry board.

If such a discussion sparks some interest, turn to Medved's provocative essay which takes us to the heart of the matter: Does the content of films, television programs, and popular songs influence our social behavior? Medved says yes, and he offers a telling argument: If brief commercials and fleeting product placements influence us, then the much longer exposure to sex and violence must also.

You will probably want to assign this essay along with Stephen King's "Why We Crave Horror Movies" (pp. 355–358) and/or Andrew Klavan's "The Shrieking of the Lambs" (pp. 602–619).

Notes

Paragraphs 1–5
This section sets up the charge and the denial. Some observers insist that violence in entertainment affects behavior. The industry denies any cause and effect connection between the products of the media and social behavior.

Paragraph 6
American Enterprise Institute: Established in 1943, the American Enterprise Institute in Washington, D.C., sponsors research on government policy, the American economy, and American politics. Its stated purpose is to preserve and to strengthen the foundations of a free society—limited government, competitive private enterprise, vital cultural and political institutions, and vigilant defense.

Jack Valenti (b:. 1921): This former advertising executive became president of the Motion Picture Association of America in 1966 and the same year was one of the writers of a code for classifying movies which was designed to reflect public values rather than dictate them.

Paragraphs 6–12
Medved quotes from four people, giving an overview of the industry's position so he can attack it in his next section.

Paragraphs 13–16
Medved states his personal position: media messages encourage destructive behavior and the accumulated effect of these messages causes problems in our culture.

Paragraphs 17–18
Although Medved says it is a mistake to concentrate on shocking examples of cause-and-effect connections between media and particular acts of violence, he does devote a rather long paragraph to a recital of some of the most dramatic examples.

Paragraphs 19–20
Medved reminds us that his concern is the media's contribution to the general social climate.

Paragraphs 21–23
Here Medved insists that research does show a connection between media and behavior.

Paragraphs 26–27
Medved dismisses industry sponsored studies as biased.

Paragraph 28
He accepts, however, one industry study which supports his views, though he makes no effort to explain why it is valid and the other studies mentioned in paragraph 26 are not.

Paragraphs 30–43
In the last section of the essay, Medved reasons that the success of commercials and product placements in programs and films is itself proof that media messages affect behavior. It is a telling argument, though no hard evidence is amassed to support it. He simply reasons that the commercials and product placements are effective or they wouldn't be used. This section is heavy with emotional language.

Possible Answers

Meaning and Purpose

1. Medved claims that it "exacerbates [social problems] and has become an important contributing factor in many of our current difficulties" (15); that "the most significant problems of the popular culture stem from the pervasive presence of anti-social material" (16); and that it contributes "to a general climate of violence and self-indulgence" (20).

2. Medved does not agree. While he calls such cases "dramatic and disturbing" (19), he recognizes that these incidents usually involve "unbalanced individuals" (17). He says that such attention to dramatic cases only distracts us from the more significant issue: what the pervasiveness of such material does to the rest of us.

3. Yes. He claims that more than three thousand such studies between 1960 and 1992 confirm the connection (22). He cites a report of the Surgeon General of the United States and a 1991 resolution of the American Psychological Association to support his statement (23). He also cites a study commissioned by CBS and conducted by the Survey Research Center of the London School of Economics in which the project supervisor said, "the evidence is very strongly supportive of the hypothesis that long-term exposure to violence increases the degree to which boys engage in violence of a serious kind" (28). He dismisses as biased other studies performed by the entertainment industry itself (26).

4. Medved ridicules the industry's denial, saying that it "contradicts the most basic assumptions of their industry" (30). Product placements and TV commercials are marketed with the assurance that they will influence viewers,

yet the industry denies that the larger content of films and TV programs have any influence on behavior.

He states this contradiction succinctly in paragraph 34: "In short, they have adopted the outrageously illogical assumption that a sixty-second commercial makes a more significant impression than a sixty-minute sitcom."

5. Medved's main point is that we are all affected, in the long-term, by the entertainment industry's "contribution to a general climate of violence and self-indulgence" (20).

Strategy

1. By quoting the president of the Motion Picture Association of America, the chairman of TriStar Pictures, a newspaper columnist, and a popular entertainer, Medved creates for his reader a sense that the entire entertainment industry has a monolithic view. Thus, when he successfully discredits one industry spokesperson, he is successfully discrediting them all.

2. A *straw man* is a weak or imaginary argument that is easy to destroy. In the second section of the essay, Medved claims that the arguments of the four industry spokesmen are really arguments against positions not really taken by those who oppose violence in entertainment. If this is true, the spokesmen's arguments can be dismissed.

   The straw man point is best applied to Teller's statement in paragraph 9. Teller claims that those who oppose the content of popular entertainment think that "if we stop showing rape in movies people will stop committing it in real life" and that "people are not smart enough to tell make-believe from reality." Medved states that none of the critics he knows take these positions. Therefore, Teller is arguing against a straw man in his attempts to ridicule these critics.

3. It's probably his most effective argument because it points out a logical problem in the entertainment industry's defense: How can some images influence people and others have no effect? It also has a quality of newness because it is an argument seldom heard in this debate. Writers often place their most effective argument last.

4. The first sentence of paragraph 5 concisely states the view of the industry, at least as Medved sees it: "popular entertainment is by its very nature inconsequential, and . . . no one is seriously damaged by the fleeting images or subtle themes in a movie."

5. The argument about advertising and product placements is presented through reasoning alone. In the absence of hard evidence, notice the increase in the use of emotional language.

Style

1. Examples of emotional language abound. Here are a few; students will find additional ones.

   The titles of the first and last sections: "A Cultural Nuthouse" and "The Height of Hypocrisy."
   Paragraph 5 "industry apologists"
   Paragraph 21 "rhetorical tricks"; "laughably bald-faced lies"
   Paragraph 24 "stunning display of corporate arrogance"
   Paragraph 26 "research is regularly dusted off and trotted out"
   Paragraph 28 "equally ludicrous"

Paragraph 30 "utterly implausible position"
Paragraph 31 "hired gun experts"
Paragraph 32 "this nonsense"
Paragraph 34 "outrageously illogical assumptions"
Paragraph 35 "bizarre notion"
Paragraph 37 "absurd internal contradiction"
Paragraph 42 "naked, gorgeous bodies in transports of passion"
Paragraph 43 "flagrantly dishonest and lavishly illogical"

2. *Zealots*: fanatics, extremists; *exacerbates*: intensifies, worsens; *pernicious*: hurtful, causing harm; *lurid*: glaringly vivid or sensational, shocking; *conglomerates*: wholes consisting of many semi-independent parts; *moguls*: powerful or influential people; *hypocrisy*: the pretense of having belief, character, or principle that one does not have; *charismatic*: having qualities that give an individual influence over large numbers of people.

—— 12 / The Artful Essay ——

A Modest Proposal
Jonathan Swift

Teaching Suggestions

History pre-1980 is often rather murky for many college students, and English-Irish relations pre-1680 are probably a dark void for most. Yet to understand the true brilliance of Swift's classic and artful essay, students need at least an inkling of that unhappy relationship between the English and Irish that eventually moved Swift to write this scathing satire. Ireland had been reduced to near subjugation after the Norman English conquest (C.E. 1160), and Elizabeth I's armies finished the job in the sixteenth century by ruthlessly suppressing all Irish rebellions. Then the English confiscated the lands of the Irish Catholic nobility and distributed them to English Protestant colonizers. Hearing of atrocities by Irish Catholics against English Protestants in the Rebellion of 1641, Oliver Cromwell led an English army into Ireland, killing thousands of native Irish. By 1653, Cromwell's forces had subjected all of Ireland. By Swift's time, 10 percent of Ireland's population was Protestant, and that 10 percent controlled over 90 percent of the land. This Protestant Ascendancy, as it was called, lasted into the last quarter of the ninteenth century.

Nine years before the publication of "A Modest Proposal" in 1729, the English dropped all pretext of home rule and made the English Parliament Ireland's governing body and the English House of Lords Ireland's Supreme Court. England used Ireland as a source of raw material and discouraged industrial development that could have alleviated some of the abject poverty to which the native Irish had been reduced. Swift wrote "A Modest Proposal" primarily to protest the barbaric conditions imposed on the Irish by the English.

Meaning and Purpose

Inevitably, some students miss the severe irony of Swift's devastating satire because they don't recognize that the narrator of "A Modest Proposal" is a fictional voice used by Swift, and not the voice of Swift himself. Swift uses the persona of a "projector," a person who suggests plans for social and economic change (4). This persona writes as an efficient, rational, and humorless man who sincerely wants to solve the problems of Ireland in a reasonable and humane way. He points out that because the Irish poor are cruelly oppressed by their English landlords and have no reliable source of income, they have no way to escape their poverty. His proposal, he claims, would remedy this social ill. In language most reasoned and measured, he proposes to solve this most vexing social problem by killing one-year-old Irish infants and selling their flesh to the wealthy English for food. It is precisely this vast discrepancy between the madness of the narrator's more than "modest" proposal and the humane reasonableness of his voice that creates the severe irony with which Swift condemns the cruel exploitation and oppression of the Irish by the English. Swift allows his own voice to surface twice, in paragraph 12 and again in paragraphs 29–31. We can tell it's Swift's voice in paragraph 12 because the narrator has no quarrel with landlords and no sympathy with tenants. The pun on "devour" ironically gives away the stratagem because the humorless narrator would never have punned. Swift offers realistic solutions to the Irish problems in paragraph 29 and voices exasperation that these real solutions have never been tried by the English government. Underneath his irony, therefore, Swift pleads for charity and compassion.

Strategy

Swift constructs his essay as a formal argument, or a formal proposal for a change in social policy. His introduction, paragraphs 1–7, sets out the problems Swift's narrator addresses in his proposal, and some of the calculations on which it is based. But slyly, artfully, he vividly depicts poor women and their children in the first paragraph, engaging the readers' sympathies so that they will react with horror to the narrator's proposal. In paragraph 6 he uses process analysis to describe his method of calculation. In the essay's next major segment, paragraphs 8–16, he presents the proposal itself, more calculations to demonstrate its potential, and a few ideas about how it might work. Within this section, paragraphs 10–15 compose a process analysis, the workings of the proposal. Paragraph 10 itself is cause-and-effect analysis. In paragraphs 17 and 18, the narrator presents, then rejects, a possible refinement to the proposal, and in paragraph 19 dispenses with a potential problem. The narrator then describes the proposal's numerous advantages in paragraphs 20–28. In this section, the single sentence paragraph 20 serves as a transition and introduction. The rest of the section (21–28) is cause-and-effect development. The advantages of the proposal, says the narrator, are that it will benefit the poor (24–26) as well as the rich (21–23, 25, 27–28). In paragraph 21, Swift attacks English prejudice against Irish Catholics, as well as the motives of many Protestant dissenters from the Church of England. In his conclusion (29–33), the narrator anticipates objections to his proposal and disposes of them. When Swift allows his own voice to intrude in paragraph 31, he says, in essence, that the English may as well eat Irish children since they have already delighted in eating up the nation. And the final paragraph serves at least two subtle purposes: Swift takes one last poke at those whose motivation is profit, and he aligns himself with the oppressed and dispossessed, the implication being that if the narrator had infants they, too, would be up for sale.

While the narrator's "modest proposal" is patently insane and cruel (but no more so than England's Irish policy), his language is that of a man who is reasonable, ethical, humane, and trustworthy. Continually calling his mad proposal "modest," he repeatedly describes the time and care he spent pondering the problem (4) and uses the first person with verbs of consideration: "I calculate," "I subtract," "I apprehend," and so on (6). He cites authorities and experts, such as the "very knowing American" (9). He puts forth his proposal with modesty and humility (8, 10). His attitude is respectful throughout: "as I must confess" (15); "although I rather recommend" (16); "But with due deference" (17). He piously objects to cruelty (5, 17). He refers repeatedly to the good of the nation (2, 7, 19, 21, 23, 29, 33). He carefully lists the advantages of the proposal (21–28). He fears the flesh would spoil if exported (31). And he ironically professes at the end that he wouldn't make a penny from the proposal. But the narrator's diction also enforces the proposal's barbarity. For instance, when he refers to the Irish poor with language usually reserved for livestock—"breeders" (6) and "fore or hind quarter" (10)—he dehumanizes them, making his proposal more palatable (excuse the pun) to his readers—and Swift's satire more horrifying. These expressions also reflect, and thus satirize, common eighteenth-century English attitudes toward the Irish.

A Hanging
George Orwell

Teaching Suggestions

George Orwell, whose real name was Eric Arthur Blair, was born in India in 1903 and died in England in 1950. In 1922, deciding to follow family tradition, he journeyed to Burma (now Myanmar) to serve in the Indian Imperial Police. He recounted some of his experiences and his reactions to imperial rule in this autobiographical sketch and in another essay titled "Shooting an Elephant," both classics of expository prose. "A Hanging" is a straight chronological narrative that conveys Orwell's deep sympathy for the oppressed in society.

Meaning and Purpose

The simple title, "A Hanging," lends a solemn, matter-of-fact tone and lack of emotion to the descriptions. The title itself implies no judgment, just as Orwell in this essay makes none explicit. However, the reader is left with little choice but to wonder at the shallowness of the people responsible for the hanging. The narrator sees clearly that the prisoner has a life "in full tide" (10) when the prisoner avoids a puddle. The narrator feels, as noted in paragraph 10, that somehow he is connected with all the men there, "together, seeing, hearing, feeling, understanding the same world." But the larger issue, to Orwell, involves the morality of capital punishment and the colonial rule that imposed it, as well as the small value placed on one Indian life.

Strategy

Writing in the first person, Orwell refers to the groups of men he is with as "we." Because he and the others are spectators, the first-person voice creates an objective, detached sound that understates the situation, thus making it all the more stark. Orwell uses chronological order in this essay, beginning with his "waiting outside the condemned cells" (1), moving through the action of the hanging itself (15), and ending with the author's having a drink (24). This strategy lends a ho-hum atmosphere to the hanging, as if it were just a routine event in a routine day. That the dead man's identity and specific crime are not mentioned expresses inferentially Orwell's point about the casual injustice of colonial rule.

Style

The somber tone is solemn to the point of depression. In the opening paragraph, phrases such as "sodden morning of the rains," "sickly light," and "brown, silent men," establish the mood. Later in the essay, "desolately thin" (3) and "The Indians had gone gray like bad coffee" (13) carry this tone through the hanging. Then, beginning in paragraph 17, the words change to describe the men's elation and laughter, yet the somber mood lurking under the gaiety maintains Orwell's emotionless tone.

Once More to the Lake
E. B. White

Teaching Suggestions

Elwyn Brooks White (1899–1985) has often been called the leading American essayist and stylist of his time. In 1959, White revised and published *The Elements of Style*, a manual originally written by William Strunk, Jr., one of White's English professors when White attended Cornell University. With only minor changes, the manual has remained in print ever since. White's three books for children, *Stuart Little* (1945), *Charlotte's Web* (1952), and *The Trumpet of the Swan* (1970), are considered classics. In "Once More to the Lake," first published in *Harper's* (1941) and later collected in *One Man's Meat* (1944), White uses the force of reminiscence to enhance a meticulous description of a recent event. On a fishing trip to a lake in Maine with his young son, as the author recalls his own childhood summers at the same lake, he inevitably begins to see himself in his son and is jolted into awareness of his own mortality. This evocative essay, then, deals with time: its delightful past, its pleasant present, and its tragic future—when the author finally acknowledges its passing.

Meaning and Purpose

The first paragraph sets the scene for White's wanting to return to the lake: He wants to return to fish and to "revisit old haunts." The essay's title itself has a poetic ring that suits White's descriptions of nature. The words *Once More* are not final; instead, they suggest that this might not be White's last visit to the lake. White's first thought when seeing the lake again is that time at the lake has seemingly stood still because so many things are the same as when he was a boy: "The small waves were the same, chucking the rowboat under the chin as we fished at anchor, and the boat was the same boat, the same color green and the ribs broken in the same places . . ." (5). He even confuses his identity with his son's (4). At the same time, White notices changes all around him (e.g., 7), and understands that change is inevitable, which causes him to be confronted suddenly with thoughts of his own death.

White deals strategically with time throughout—he creates the impression of a storm as a natural drama of time played out (12). First it is oppressive, then percussive, then calm, perhaps White's extended metaphor for his own life. White also uses many transitions to avoid confusion about time. In paragraph 2, thinking about returning to the lake with his son, he slips into a memory. In paragraph 5, he describes fishing with his son, saying, "There had been no years between the ducking of this dragonfly and the other one," the other one being a part of his memory. Another shift to memory occurs in paragraph 9, when White discusses "those times and those summers [that] had been . . worth saving." White offers his lake as a symbol of timelessness and goodness and American family values, the necessary retreat from the ills of the city.

Style

The essay, nostalgic and affectionate in tone, is nevertheless a bit sad and peaceful, much like a reverie, as if White somehow needs to reconnect with the lake before it's too late, before he, too, passes on. Some of his descriptive words for the lake, "this holy spot," "cool and motionless," "sweet outdoors," and "the stillness of a cathedral" (2), show that White viewed the lake as a nearly sacred place, undisturbed and natural; he seems to have respected the lake to the point of holding it in awe. In paragraph 3, the phrase "remote and primeval" reinforces this impression, as if to say that the lake is prehistoric, without the imprint of people, a thought that foreshadows the essay's ending with a shock of recognition: "suddenly my groin felt the chill of death."

Letter from Birmingham Jail
Martin Luther King, Jr.

Teaching Suggestions

It is sad that the heroic struggle of African-Americans to gain their civil rights in this country is often as unclear for many American students as the Irish struggles against English colonization addressed by Jonathan Swift in "A Modest Proposal." Most will know that Martin Luther King Day is a national holiday, but few will know that in 1955 Mrs. Rosa Parks, a courageous seventy-two-year-old African-American woman, was arrested for breaking Montgomery, Alabama's segregation laws by refusing to give up her seat on a city bus to a white passenger. Outraged African-Americans organized the Montgomery Improvement Association to boycott the city's public transportation system. Martin Luther King, Jr., pastor of a Montgomery Baptist church, was elected leader of the Association. After a year of difficult struggle, the organization successfully desegregated the city's public transportation. King, greatly influenced by the New Testament teachings of Jesus, by Thoreau's views on civil disobedience and Ghandi's principle of nonviolent civil disobedience, then formed the Southern Christian Leadership Conference, which was committed to using nonviolent resistance to accomplish desegregation.

King put Birmingham, Alabama, the most segregated city in the South, in world news in 1963 when he led a campaign to desegregate the city's lunch counters. King and his forces staged demonstrations and sit-ins. The Birmingham police responded by turning firehoses and dogs on the demonstrators and by arresting King and 2,400 other civil rights workers. Eight local white clergymen issued a public letter agreeing with the aims of the movement but deploring the methods it used. King's "Letter from Birmingham Jail" is a response to theirs. In it, he employs both logical argument and strong emotional appeal to convince his readers that his actions are morally compelling. The letter stands as one of the most eloquent and powerful statements in the English language for racial equality and human justice.

Meaning and Purpose

In his very first statement, King reinforces the fact established in his title that he is writing his response to his clergymen critics while incarcerated in the Birmingham jail. Jail usually silences and intimidates its inmates, rendering them powerless. King, however, is neither silent, nor intimidated, nor powerless as he puts pen to paper in his jail cell, working for racial equality and human justice even while serving jail time for doing exactly that. Incarceration now gives him the time to answer his critics, "men of genuine good will," whose objections to his tactics are sincere, though mistaken (1). After reasonably explaining why he is in Birmingham in the first place, King then outlines the four progressive steps a nonviolent campaign must take to effect social change (6). Negotiation, the second step after determining that a social injustice exists in the first place, has already failed and the third step, "self-purification," has already been accomplished. That leaves, he explains, only the inevitable fourth step: direct action, or demonstrations. History amply demonstrates, he says, that freedom must be demanded because it is never voluntarily given over by an oppressor (13), and he then catalogues segregationist human abuses that legitimate immediate action (14). That action must necessarily involve breaking unjust laws. King then clearly distinguishes just from unjust laws (15–22). An unjust law is "out of harmony with the moral law"; is not rooted in natural law; "degrades human personality" (16); "is inflicted upon a minority that, as a result of being denied the right to vote, had no part in enacting or devising the law" (18). He then presents historical and biblical precedents for breaking unjust laws (21–22).

Finally, in this carefully reasoned progression, he concludes that a person who breaks an unjust law is willing to suffer the consequences for doing so, expresses the highest respect for the law (20). Because King has broken laws he considers unjust, his critics have accused him of being an extremist. But King cleverly turns this criticism to praise by first establishing himself as "in the middle of opposing forces in the Negro community," between the extremes of complacency on one side and bitterness and hatred that could easily lead to violence on the other (27). But, if he must be considered an extremist, he is in the good company of Amos in the Old Testament, of St. Paul, Martin Luther, and John Bunyan, and of Thomas Jefferson, Abraham Lincoln, and Jesus (31).

Strategy

In his introduction (1–4), King explains his presence in Birmingham to protest racial segregation by using a cause/effect development pattern, moving from practical, immediate causes to more philosophical, ultimate causes. The body of his essay (5–31) he structures around his rebuttals to each of the objections directed against him by his clergymen critics. He employs paragraphs 5–9 to dispose of their first objection, their deploring that Birmingham is the site of his demonstrations. Blacks, he explains deductively, had no alternative. He sets his argument up in this section as a syllogism: There must be direct action after three more moderate steps have been taken; those steps have been taken; there must, therefore be direct action. The major premise is stated as a given. The minor premise, that all necessary preliminary steps have already been taken, King fully documents. Paragraphs 12–14 refute the clergymen's second charge, that the demonstrations are untimely, by clearly demonstrating the opposite to be true.

In the next section (15–22), King refutes the clergymen's objection that the civil rights demonstrators are breaking the law by arguing that it is their moral responsibility to break unjust laws. To demonstrate this, King distinguishes between just and unjust laws and offers substantial evidence to support the idea that the laws they have broken are indeed unjust (16–20). In the final portion of this section, King presents several historical examples to justify that the demonstrators have not only the right to break unjust laws, but have the very responsibility to do so (21–22). In a brief digression from his closely reasoned argument (23–24), King criticizes white moderates. The next charge against him, that the demonstrators "precipitate violence," he refutes by citing historical examples that show the objection to be illogical (25). King then answers the final charge, that the demonstrators are extremists, by showing that they are, in fact, taking a middle course that will prevent a "racial nightmare" in the future (27–31).

Style

King appeals to both reason and emotion in his eloquent appeal. In one central section of his essay, he reasons that a law is unjust and democracy thwarted if the minority has no voice in "enacting or devising the law" (18). His language here is entirely rational, not emotional. His logic, typically, is deductive: If democracy means that the people participate in the making of the law, and if a large group of people is denied this right, then the law does not meet democratic standards and is unjust. He appeals to emotion in the sections of the essay that list the horrible injustices suffered by blacks because of unjust and inhumane laws. His language in these sections is laden with emotion.

The brilliance of King's rhetorical skills is amply demonstrated in paragraph 14, a passage capable of moving even the emotionally inert. The periodic sentence that begins "But when you have seen" is masterful. King withholds its full meaning until the last words, keeping the reader in suspense about how the sentence will come out, both structurally and semantically. The 300-word catalogue of some of the cruel human tragedies that have resulted because of segregation he organizes into eleven subordinate clauses, enforcing order and clarity. Repeating "when" connects the clauses and contributes to the drama in the switch to "then" in the short independent clause ending the sentence. And the very length of the sentence emphasizes how incredibly long African-Americans have waited for justice.

On Natural Death
Lewis Thomas

Teaching Suggestions

Lewis Thomas had a long and distinguished career as a practicing physician, researcher, medical administrator, and writer. Most of his early writings were technical papers on pathology, his specialty. He also wrote and published some poetry. But in 1971 he began to write a monthly column for the *New England Journal of Medicine*, titled "Notes of a Biology Watcher," that allowed him to explore the less technical, more humanitarian and philosophical issues science sometimes raises. Like cultural anthropologist Loren Eiseley (1907–1977) and paleontologist Stephen Jay Gould (b. 1941), he was able to write so lucidly about scientific matters that he made often arcane material readily accessible to the lay public. Like them, too, he often wrote poetically about the more mysterious aspects of science. Novelist and critic Joyce Carol Oates wrote that his book *Lives of a Cell* (1975) "anticipates the kind of writing that will appear more and more frequently, as scientists take on the language of poetry in order to communicate human truths too mysterious for old-fashioned common sense." In "On Natural Death," Lewis takes on the ultimate mystery.

Meaning and Purpose

Thomas says at the outset of his essay that some people treat human death as if it were in some significant way different from death in the rest of nature. His essay means to demonstrate that it is not. He does this by demythologizing death by showing objectively how all deaths are natural. Logically enough, he begins with plants, moves to animals, and ends with a firsthand description of, and reflection on, human death. His tone is calm, rational, and contemplative. But he is also concerned, feeling, and humane. He tells us at the beginning of the essay that as a child, he oftentimes witnessed the "dying of a field mouse at the jaws of an amiable household cat" (4). Each time he winced. He came to the conclusion that "Nature was an abomination" (4). By the end of the essay, however, he understands death is such an integral part of the natural process that if he "had to design an ecosystem in which creatures had to live off each other and in which dying was an indispensable part of living, I could not think of a better way to manage" (10). His calm, rational examination of death should have brought the reader to the same conclusion, and, therefore, to the realization that those who treat human death as somehow outside or beyond nature (1–2) are unreasonable, even irrational.

Strategy

Thomas develops his essay primarily by examples, and he arranges those examples inductively. That is, instead of stating his thesis first and then illustrating it by examples (deduction), he instead gives the reader the examples first and only then comments on their meaning. In his first example, Thomas describes the death of a tree and its removal (3). The workers who remove the tree sing after their job is done. This obliviousness to the natural death of a tree will eventually extend, by the essay's logic, to the natural death of a human. Thomas's second example (4) involves the life and death of a mouse and establishes his own humaneness. This example illustrates the observation that no death is trivial and establishes the fact that nature has supplied all animals with the physiological ability to face death calmly and even painlessly (5–7). This idea easily extends, then, to his final example, the death of two soldiers (9). Thomas uses comments from the creator of the personal essay, Michel de Montaigne (1533–1592), to reflect back to his speculation on the painless death of the mouse, and then project forward to the idea that the same speculation applies to the death of the soldiers.

Style

By constructing his essay inductively, moving from specific examples to a general conclusion, Thomas is able to accomplish several things at one time, all of them furthering his purpose. First, the essay's induction approximates the scientific method in general and Thomas's scientific thought in particular. Second, inductive reasoning is a powerful persuader. Thomas cites enough sound, specific evidence first to gently pull the reader to his final general truth. Third, Thomas's reasoning and diction together create a reflective tone that is comforting, and that in itself is a persuasive element of the essay, since his subject of death is so innately uncomfortable for many. Fourth, Thomas asks the reader to consider death from an unusual angle, and his inductive arrangement allows the reader to witness what appears to be his thought process. Finally, his method leads to speculative conclusions rather than certain ones, and this enhances the essay's meditative tone, intimate and objective simultaneously.

On Keeping a Notebook
Joan Didion

Teaching Suggestions

Born in 1934, Joan Didion was at the height of her writing career when she wrote "On Keeping a Notebook," which is part of her collection of essays titled *Slouching Towards Bethlehem* (1968). In "On Keeping a Notebook," Didion reflects upon memories, on how to best preserve them and on how one creates memories, ironically, from memories.

Meaning and Purpose

Didion notes that it is quite important to distinguish between a diary and a notebook, a diary being one's "actual factual record" of what one has been doing, a notebook being one's place to tell "what some would call lies" (7). Therefore, if one already keeps a written record of one's journey through life, with its highs, its lows, and its flat plains and valleys, one should determine early on which record to keep, that of a diary or that of a notebook. Clearly, Didion would recommend the latter because she is talking about the writing process in a special way, intuitively, meaning in her own case that she relies on quick and ready insight, an immediate apprehension without evident rational thought and inference. It is not the ticking of the clock that counts, as in a diary, but the apprehension of the passage of time and of what time does to the passage of the memories of one's life that matters.

Strategy

Didion opens the essay in the middle of things, giving her reader a taste of the immediacy of one's life combined with the relatively calm reflection that one can muster after the fact. She does not provide us with a context for what she is saying until paragraph 4. By then, the reader is already hooked by the details of the little scene in the bar. Didion then backs away from the scene to talk about having written the note, a strategy far more effective than if she had begun the essay with a definition of *notebook*, followed by the merits of keeping one, followed by the merits of using the notebook's entries to remember former events in one's life, and so forth and so on. In other words, Didion is not trying to sell the reader on the idea of keeping a notebook so much as she is showing by the example the strengths of such an enterprise.

Style

Didion's language, informal and conversational, makes it seem as if she is talking aloud while sharing something quite personal in her notebooks. The transition from paragraphs 7 to 8 illustrates this "thinking-aloud" voice. She wonders here about the truth of one of her notes when she suddenly realizes that the note itself is not factually truthful; instead, as she says with sudden realization, the note shows "*How it felt to me*" (8). When Didion in a sense brings the essay full circle by explaining at the end the import of the sauerkraut recipe mentioned earlier, she shows another reason for keeping a notebook—"It all comes back" (17). That is, this stylistic device of circling her topic illustrates what she herself has been saying throughout the essay, that a notebook entry will flood the mind with memories that, after time, add luster and context to the entry, whereas a diary entry is entire unto itself, requiring no additional information, perceptive or otherwise.